FOURTH EDITION

Comparative Health Information Management

Ann H. Peden, PhD, RHIA, CCS

CENGAGE
Learning·

Australia • Brazil • Mexico • Singapore • United Kingdom • United States

Comparative Health Information Management, Fourth Edition
Ann H. Peden

SVP, GM Skills & Global Product Management: Dawn Gerrain

Product Manager: Jadin Babin-Kavanaugh

Senior Director, Development: Marah Bellegarde

Product Development Manager: Juliet Steiner

Senior Content Developer: Elisabeth F. Williams

Product Assistant: Mark Turner

Vice President, Marketing Services: Jennifer Ann Baker

Marketing Coordinator: Courtney Cozzy

Senior Production Director: Wendy Troeger

Production Director: Andrew Crouth

Senior Content Project Manager: James Zayicek

Senior Art Director: Jack Pendleton

Cover image(s):

© Czanner | Dreamstime.com;

© Photopal604 | Dreamstime.com, © iStockPhoto.com | baona;

© iStockPhoto.com | gmutlu, © Dave Bredeson | Dreamstime.com;

© iStockPhoto.com |MivPiv

For product information and technology assistance, contact us at
Cengage Learning Customer & Sales Support, 1-800-354-9706
For permission to use material from this text or product,
submit all requests online at **www.cengage.com/permissions**
Further permissions questions can be e-mailed to
permissionrequest@cengage.com

Library of Congress Control Number: 2015950181

ISBN: 9781285871714

Cengage Learning
20 Channel Center Street
Boston, MA 02210
USA

Cengage Learning is a leading provider of customized learning solutions with office locations around the globe, including Singapore, the United Kingdom, Australia, Mexico, Brazil, and Japan. Locate your local office at: **www.cengage.com/global**

Cengage Learning products are represented in Canada by Nelson Education, Ltd.

To learn more about Cengage Learning, visit **www.cengage.com**

Purchase any of our products at your local college store or at our preferred online store **www.cengagebrain.com**

Notice to the Reader

Printed in Canada
Print Number: 01   Print Year: 2015

To Terry Winkler, who walked into heaven in 2014

CONTENTS

SECTION 1   The Health Care System

1   Introduction to Health Care Systems   1

Mary E. "Lisa" Morton, PhD, RHIA
Dorthy K. Young, PhD, MHSA
Ann H. Peden, PhD, RHIA, CCS

SECTION 2   Acute, Ambulatory, and Managed Care

2   Hospital-Based Care   28

Angela L. Morey, MSM, RHIA, CPHIMS
Leigh T. Williams, MHIIM, RHIA, CPC, CPHIMS
Ann H. Peden, PhD, RHIA, CCS
Sonya D. Beard, MSEd, RHIA

9   Facilities for Individuals with Intellectual Disabilities   316

Nan R. Christian, MEd
Judy S. Westerfield, MEd
Elaine C. Jouette, MA, RHIA

SECTION 4   Post-Acute Care

10   Long-Term Care   353

Barbara A. Gorenflo, RHIA
Kris King, MS, RHIA, CPHQ

11   Rehabilitation   400

Ann H. Peden, PhD, RHIA, CCS
Terry Winkler, MD

12   Home Health Care   446

Pamela R. Dodd, RHIA
Ida Blevins, RHIA
Gwen D. Smith, RHIA
Kim A. Boyles, MS, RHIA

13   Hospice   478

Teresa Sherfy, RHIT
Karen M. Staszel, RHIA

SECTION 5   Other Specialized Care Settings

14   Donal Care Settings   508

Francis G. Serio, DMD, MS, MBA
Denise D. Krause, PhD
Cheryl L. Berthelsen, PhD, RHIA

15   Veterinary Settings   550

Valerie Ball, RHIA, CHIT-IS
Margaret L. Neterer, MM, RHIA

SECTION 6   Other Health Care Related Settings

Health care is provided in a wide variety of settings, with regulatory, reimbursement, and other health information management (HIM) issues that are unique to each. Today's health information managers are building challenging careers in what were once considered nontraditional sites, and they need the most accurate, up-to-date, and relevant information to master their respective positions and maximize their influence and value. *Comparative Health Information Management*, fourth edition, is written by an elite team of expert professionals from both the educational and practice arenas, who were chosen for their particular expertise in the different content areas.

Managing the information flow within and among differing care sites, especially in light of the technologies that make electronic health records possible, is a challenge for today's health information managers. *Comparative Health Information Management*, fourth edition, was developed to assist health information students meet this challenge. This text has 17 chapters, covering diverse settings in which students of health information management may find employment upon graduation, ranging from hospital-based care to veterinary care to consulting. Because many health information management professionals have found careers in cancer registry settings, chapter 17 is new to this fourth edition.

ABOUT THE FOURTH EDITION

The revised fourth edition opens with an introductory chapter that describes the recent history of health care in the United States and the changes taking place in the twenty-first century. Included are topics such as the effect of changes in payment systems on health care; an overview of regulatory and accreditation issues affecting health care, including a section on the Health Insurance Portability and Accountability Act (HIPAA); and the evolution of the electronic health record. This fourth edition includes new federal initiatives and other changes affecting health information services that have been brought about by federal action. Chapter 1 explores how these changes affect the HIM professional and lays a foundation of resources that can assist in meeting the challenges of the twenty-first century.

The remaining setting-based chapters follow a consistent template, facilitating a comparison of the different sites. Each chapter includes discussions of the following: introduction to setting; regulatory issues; documentation; reimbursement and funding; information management, including data flow, coding and classification, electronic information systems, and data sets; quality improvement and utilization management; risk management and legal issues; role of the HIM professional; and trends. Although the chapters refer to and build on one another, they can stand alone and may be used out of sequence or as modules.

Chapter 2 discusses HIM issues unique to hospital-based care and includes both acute and ambulatory care in the hospital setting. Chapter 3 details a wide variety of ambulatory health care settings and their information management issues, including a discussion of meaningful use of electronic health records. Chapter 4 provides fundamental information on the spectrum of managed care models with which health information managers interact today. Chapter 5 discusses both dialysis providers and the regional networks that monitor them. Chapter 6 explains terms and issues related to health care for incarcerated persons. Chapter 7 discusses both community-based and inpatient mental health care issues. Chapter 8 explains health information issues affecting facilities offering treatment and rehabilitation for chemical dependencies. Chapter 9 describes the unique information maintained in facilities offering care and training for individuals with intellectual disabilities. Chapter 10 explains the increasingly sophisticated data management needs of long-term-care settings, including information on quality reporting, as well as changes in federal regulations and an introduction to the "culture change movement" in long-term care. Chapter 11 is devoted to information management issues in programs designed to improve the function of patients who have suffered a debilitating illness or injury. This chapter also provides an introduction to proposals to bundle payments for various types of post-acute care. Chapter 12 discusses home care information management issues, including the home health prospective payment system and provides information on both federal regulations and voluntary accreditation for home health services. Chapter 13 outlines requirements for entities providing health care and support for persons who are terminally ill and their families. This chapter reflects the latest Conditions of Participation for hospice as well as current trends in hospice care. Chapter 14 provides insight into health information needs for maintaining and improving oral health. Dental terminology is provided to help familiarize students with the specialized language of dentistry. Chapter 15 describes the health information services in the veterinary medicine setting. The chapter gives current information on health information management in settings providing care for animals. Chapter 16 provides practical advice to the health information practitioner considering working as a consultant in any health care setting, including information on the impact of recent federal legislation on the consultant's practice. Chapter 17, a new addition to the book, offers an introduction to health information management in cancer registries.

NEW TO THE FOURTH EDITION

- **Coverage of laws and regulations** has been thoroughly updated to reflect changes in regulations and legislation that readers must understand to work effectively in each of the varied care settings.
- **Self Review.** This new feature, sprinkled throughout each chapter, offers self-review questions that engage the student in active learning and self-reflection. Suggested responses can be found in the online Instructor Resource Center.
- **Professional Spotlight.** This new element highlights individuals working in health information management roles in various settings, to provide students with a practical look at what it might be like to work in a given specialty area.

- **MindTap**. MindTap is a fully online, interactive learning platform that combines readings, multimedia activities, and assessments into a singular learning path, elevating learning by providing real-world application to better engage students. MindTap includes an interactive eBook with highlighting and note-taking capability, self-quizzes, and learning exercises such as matching activities, multiple choice questions, flash cards, and more. MindTap can be accessed at http://www.cengagebrain.com.

FEATURES OF THE TEXT

Each chapter of *Comparative Health Information Management*, fourth edition, contains the following learning elements:

- **Learning Objectives.** The learning objectives are outcome-based and identify and organize learning expectations for more effective studying.
- **Introduction to Setting.** This feature opens each chapter and gives learners a quick snapshot of the specific setting under discussion, including common names for the setting, a description, and synonyms.
- **Self-Review.** This feature allows students to pause throughout their reading to check their understanding of concepts presented in each section of the chapter. Suggested responses can be found in the online Instructor Resource Center.
- **Professional Spotlight.** These are accounts from real-life professionals who work in the setting under discussion. The feature will help students envision what it might be like to pursue a career in that specialized area of practice.
- **Summary.** Each chapter includes a brief narrative review of the chapter content, with a focus on key points the learner should retain.
- **Key Terms and Definitions.** Unfamiliar or critical vocabulary words are boldfaced and defined in the margins of each chapter, and also appear in the master glossary at the back of the text.
- **Review Questions.** A series of knowledge-based and critical thinking review questions challenge readers to apply what they have learned. These may be used for self-study or assigned for class discussion. The answers to the review questions appear in the Instructor's Manual.
- **Web Activity.** These internet-based exercises challenge learners to explore information beyond the book for each setting.
- **Case Study.** Real-world case studies present actual situations a learner might encounter in practice, and include a series of questions to guide learners through the problem-solving process. Cases may be used for in-class discussion or assigned for individual practice. Suggested answers to the cases are included in the Instructor's Manual.
- **References and Suggested Readings and Key Resources.** Each chapter includes a list of references for further self-guided exploration, and a separate listing of organizations and associations pertinent to the chapter that will lead the learner to additional information.

LEARNING PACKAGE FOR THE STUDENT

MindTap

MindTap is the first of its kind in an entirely new category: the Personal Learning Experience (PLE). This personalized program of digital products and services uses interactivity and customization to engage students, while offering a range of choice in content, platforms, devices, and learning tools. MindTap is device agnostic, meaning that it will work with any platform or learning management system and will be accessible anytime, anywhere: on desktops, laptops, tablets, mobile phones, and other Internet-enabled devices. *Comparative Health Information Management*, fourth edition, on MindTap includes:

- An interactive eBook with highlighting, note-taking functions, and more
- Drag-and-drop microbiology exercises
- Flashcards for practicing chapter terms
- Computer-graded activities and exercises

TEACHING PACKAGE FOR THE INSTRUCTOR

Instructor Resources

The *Instructor Companion Website to Accompany Comparative Health Information Management*, fourth edition, contains a variety of tools to help instructors successfully prepare lectures and teach within this subject area. This comprehensive package provides something for all instructors, from those teaching health information management for the first time to seasoned instructors who want something new. The following components in the website are free to adopters of the text:

- A downloadable, customizable *Instructor's Manual* containing lecture notes, teaching strategies, class activities, answers to review questions, and more.
- A *Test Bank* with several hundred questions and answers, for use in instructor-created quizzes and tests.
- Chapter slides created in PowerPoint® to use for in-class lecture material and as handouts for students.

MindTap

In the new *Comparative Health Information Management*, fourth edition, on MindTap platform, instructors customize the learning path by selecting Cengage Learning resources and adding their own content via apps that integrate into the MindTap framework seamlessly with many learning management systems. The guided learning path demonstrates the relevance of basic principles in health information management through engagement activities, interactive exercises, and animations, elevating the study by challenging students to apply concepts to practice. To learn more, visit www.cengage.com/mindtap.

ACKNOWLEDGMENTS

This book is the result of the efforts of numerous persons. Shirley Anderson had the vision for Delmar (now Cengage) Learning's HIM (Health Information Management) series and first suggested this text to its editorial staff. In 1994, the publisher assembled a focus group of HIM practitioners and educators to plan the first edition. Accepting the role of editor for this text was much easier given the groundwork that had been laid by the thoughtful contributions of my HIM colleagues.

The author is very grateful for the work of the contributors to previous editions, who created a superb body of work that the current contributors were able to update, revise, and refine. The names of all contributors, both previous and current, are listed following each chapter heading, although some of the earlier contributors were not able to participate in the fourth edition. I would like to give the following individuals special recognition for their groundbreaking work in the development of previous editions of this text: Sonya Beard for the chapter on hospital care, Beth Bowman for the chapter on freestanding ambulatory care, Lynn Kuehn and Cecile Favreau for the chapter on managed care, Nina Dozoretz, Barbara Manny, and Brianna McCloe Rogers for the correctional chapter, Harrell Weathersby for the mental health chapter, Frances Wickham Lee and Kimberly Taylor for the substance abuse chapter, Elaine C. Jouette and Judy S. Westerfield for the chapter on services for individuals with intellectual and developmental disabilities, Ida Blevins, Gwen D. Smith, and Kim Boyles for the home health chapter, Karen Staszel for the hospice chapter, Cheryl Berthelsen for the dental chapter, and Margaret Neterer for the chapter on veterinary health care. I also remember with gratitude two individuals who are no longer physically present in this world, though their contributions are very much alive—Kris King and Terry Winkler, who wrote the original chapters on long-term care and rehabilitation, respectively. I owe a tremendous debt of gratitude to all of these contributors for developing the first three editions, thereby providing an excellent foundation for the current volume.

The reviewers also played a major role in the development and refinement of this book. Their insights kept us focused on the needs of the readers, and their excellent suggestions have helped make the fourth edition "new and improved." The author and publisher would like to thank the following persons for their role in shaping this text by serving as reviewers during the preparation of the manuscript:

Mona Calhoun, MS, RHIA
Chair, Health Information
Management Program
Coppin State University
Baltimore, Maryland

Monica L Carmichael, BS, MHSA,
MHRM, CPC
Allied Health Program Director
Miller-Motte Technical College
Charleston, South Carolina (online
division)

Crystal A. Clack, MS, RHIA, CCS
AHIMA Approved ICD-10-CM/
PCS Trainer
Adjunct Faculty
Lane Community College
Eugene, Oregon

Stephanie A. Donovan, MBA, RHIA
Faculty Chair Health Programs
Peirce College
Philadelphia, Pennsylvania

Melissa H. Edenburn, RHIA
Associate Professor, Health
Information Technology
McLennan Community College
Waco, Texas

Robert Haralson, RHIT, CCS
Instructor
Ozarks Technical Community
College
Springfield, Missouri

Kerry Heinecke, MS, RHIA
Biomedical Informatics Technician
Program Director
Mid-State Technical College
Marshfield, Wisconsin

Lorraine Kane, MS, RHIA
Associate Professor
SUNY Institute of Technology
Utica, New York

The chapter authors also are grateful for expert assistance and advice provided to them by others. For Chapter 5: Brenda Dyson and the staff of Network 8 for sharing their knowledge of the ESRD networks and dialysis facilities (Fresenius). For Chapter 6: *Nina Dozoretz* for reviewing the chapter and suggesting updates. For Chapter 7: Tessie Smith, Ellen Crawford, Ted Lutterman, Barbara Carpenter, and Mary Crossman. For Chapter 11: Mary Montana of Methodist Rehabilitation Center, Jackson, Mississippi, for her careful review and suggestions for updates. For Chapter 15: Various members of the American Veterinary Health Information Management Association (AVHIMA) for providing editorial support, especially Kathleen Ellis, RHIT, RN, BS, and Roberta Schmidt, RHIA, health information management professionals for the colleges of veterinary medicine at the University of Illinois and Ohio State University, respectively.

I would like to thank the editorial staff of Cengage Learning for their work on the project and the many ways that they supported and enhanced my efforts, including thanks to Jadin Babin-Kavanaugh and Beth Williams for their patience and resourcefulness. Finally, I would like to thank my co-author, Jody Smith for stepping in to help wrap-up the project.

I am very grateful for the support and encouragement I have received from my colleagues at the University of Mississippi Medical Center. I want to thank my dean, Dr. Jessica Bailey, for creating an environment conducive to professional growth and the acceptance of professional challenges. I also thank my fellow faculty members for giving their best to our students and for their support and encouragement, including their service as contributors to this edition. I thank the many professionals who have shared their knowledge of health information management in traditional and nontraditional settings with my students and with me. I want to thank Doris Austin for the many ways she helps me to "stay on top of things," especially when faced with time constraints. I also thank Casey Bell and Hope Peden Vandersteen for their assistance with some of the new features of the book.

I thank my family, especially my husband, Sam, my children, Eric, Jericho, and Hope, and their spouses, my mother and father, my mother-in-law, and also my church family for their encouragement and their prayers. And I thank the One who hears and answers prayer, His Son, who "always lives to make intercession," and His Spirit, who "also helps in our weaknesses."

ANN H. PEDEN, PHD, RHIA, CCS, is professor of health informatics and information management in the School of Health Related Professions at the University of Mississippi Medical Center in Jackson, Mississippi. She has her PhD in Clinical Health Sciences from the University of Mississippi and her MBA from Louisiana Tech University, where she also previously taught. Before teaching, she served as director of medical records at St. Francis Medical Center in Monroe, Louisiana. She completed her undergraduate education at the University of Mississippi.

Dr. Peden's awards include the American Health Information Management Association's "Professional Achievement Award" and the Mississippi Health Information Management Association's "Distinguished Member Award" and "Legacy Award." She has been honored as "Teacher of the Year" for the University of Mississippi's School of Health Related Professions and was also named to the university's Nelson Order in recognition of teaching excellence. Her service to the profession of health information management includes serving as a member of the board of directors of the Commission on Accreditation of Health Informatics and Information Management Education and terms as president of the Louisiana Medical Record Association and the Mississippi Health Information Management Association. She has also served as a member of the nominating committee of the American Health Information Management Association (AHIMA), and as the chair of AHIMA's Coding Policy and Strategy Committee.

K. JODY SMITH, PHD, RHIA, FAHIMA, is professor emeritus of health informatics and information management in the Doisy College of Health Sciences at Saint Louis University in St. Louis, Missouri. She has her PhD in Higher Education Administration from Saint Louis University and her MS from Maryville University in St. Louis. Prior to retiring in 2014, Dr. Smith chaired the department of health informatics and informatics at Saint Louis University. Before teaching, she served as director of medical records at Memorial Medical Center in Springfield, Illinois and the University Hospital in St. Louis, Missouri. She completed her undergraduate education at Illinois State University in Normal, Illinois.

Dr. Smith's awards include the Missouri Health Information Management Association's "Distinguished Member Service Award" and "Outstanding Health Information Management Educator". She was named "Distinguished Alumnus" for the College of Applied Science and Technology at Illinois State University. Dr. Smith received the "Faculty Excellent Award" from the Student Government Association at Saint Louis University and the "Faculty Excellence in Advising and Mentoring" awarded by the Doisy College of Health Sciences at Saint Louis

University. Her service to the profession of health information management includes serving as chair of the scholarship committee for the American Health Information Management Association (AHIMA), the editorial review board for *Perspectives in Health Information Management* (AHIMA), and member of the Council on Certification (AHIMA). She served terms as president of the Illinois Medical Record Association and the Missouri Health Information Management Association.

ABOUT THE CONTRIBUTORS

VALERIE E. BALL, RHIA, CHIT-IS, currently serves as the manager for the health information management department at the North Carolina State Veterinary Hospital, Raleigh, NC. She has been employed in this capacity for twenty four (24) years and also served in a similar capacity at the Virginia Tech College of Veterinary Medicine for almost nine (9) years. She graduated from Virginia Commonwealth University-Medical College of Virginia with a Bachelor of Science in Health Information Management. She also completed graduate coursework in educational administration at Viginia Tech and counseling education at North Carolina State University. Throughout her career she has been involved with various professional and community organizations in various leadership capacities. She continues to serve as a preceptor and placement site for several community college HIM programs.

MONA Y. CALHOUN, MS, MED, RHIA, FAHIMA, is the Chairperson for the Health Information Management Baccalaureate Program at Coppin State University in Baltimore, Maryland. She is a graduate of Texas Woman's University in Denton, Texas with a B.S. in Medical Records Administration and M.S. degree in Healthcare Administration. She obtained a second M.S. degree in Rehabilitation Counseling from Coppin State University. Mrs. Calhoun has close to 30 years of extensive professional experience in the Health Information Management profession in a variety of healthcare settings, including behavioral health, rehabilitation and acute care settings. She has also provided consultative services to outpatient clinics and home health care agencies. The last nine years of her career has been in education.

NAN R. CHRISTIAN, MS, LCIDDT, LCMHT, is Director of Education/Quality Service Manager at Hudspeth Regional Center. She is a graduate of the University of Mississippi with a B.A. in Communicative Disorders and received her M.S. degree in Speech and Hearing Services from the University of Southern Mississippi. She obtained post-graduate work from the University of Southern Mississippi in School Supervision and Administration and School Psychometry. Ms. Christian has over 42 years of professional experience in special education, administration, and speech pathology. She has been recognized by Cambridge Who's Who as "Professional of the Year" representing Special education administration for the 2009–2010 year.

PAMELA R. DODD, RHIA, is the Corporate Health Information Manager and Privacy Officer for Alacare Home Health and Hospice located in Birmingham, AL. She holds a BS degree, *cum laude*, in Medical Record Administration from the University of Alabama at Birmingham. She has worked in health care for 24 years with over 18 years in home health care. She has served as preceptor for over 10 years to local community colleges and Universities. She serves as an Advisory Committee member at Wallace State Community College and has received their Outstanding Clinical Education Award. She authored two other publications in 2001. She has presented at annual and local health information management meetings as other long-term care association meetings.

BARBARA A. GORENFLO, RHIA, is the Administrator of Blocher Homes, the Assisted Living Facility of Beechwood Continuing Care in Williamsville, New York. Before her current position, she was the Assistant Administrator of the Skilled Nursing Facility and prior to that the Director of Health Information Management at Beechwood. She has a BS degree in Medical Record Administration from Daemen College, Amherst, New York. She has served as Clinical Instructor for Health Information Technology students at Trocaire and Erie Community Colleges. Mrs. Gorenflo contracts with several long-term care facilities and renal dialysis centers for medical record consulting services. She is a presenter on medical record documentation issues as well as on HIPAA compliance.

DENISE D. KRAUSE, PHD, is an associate professor of preventive medicine at the University of Mississippi Medical Center and associate director of technology and research with the Office of Mississippi Physician Workforce. She is a graduate of the University of Kansas and has Masters' degrees in International Policy and Russian from the Monterey Institute of International Studies in California, and Master's and PhD degrees in Preventive Medicine with a emphasis in epidemiology from the University of Mississippi Medical Center. She has completed extensive professional technical training in networking and other aspects of information technology. Dr. Krause is managing numerous technology projects to support research and education, and to inform policy, especially on topics related to improving access to health care and services.

ANGELA MOREY, MSM, RHIA, is an assistant professor in the Health Informatics and Information Management Department at the University of Mississippi Medical Center. She is a graduate of the Health Information Management program at the Medical College of Georgia and has a Master of Science in Management degree with a concentration in Organizational Behavior and Development from Georgia State University. Ms. Morey has extensive experience in teaching health information practices in acute settings as well as medical terminology, performance improvement, organizational management, healthcare statistics and legal aspects of health information management.

MARY E. "LISA" MORTON, PHD, RHIA, is an associate professor in the Health Informatics and Information Management Department at the University of Mississippi Medical Center. She completed her undergraduate degree at Louisiana Tech University, holds a Master of Library and Information Science from Louisiana State University, and a PhD in Information Science and Technology from Drexel University. Dr. Morton was previously on the faculty at Temple University and served as a department manager in an academic medical center. She received the Mississippi Health Information Management Association's (MSHIMA) Research Award in 2010 and the MSHIMA Educator Award in 2014.

MELISSA NEWELL, MPPA, RHIA, COPM is the Medical Practice Administrator for Otolaryngology Associates, a specialty clinic in Mississippi. She has previous work experience in a community mental health center and an adolescent acute residential setting. She obtained a bachelor's degree in Health Record Administration from the University of Mississippi Medical Center. She obtained her Master's Degree in Public Policy and Administration from Mississippi State University. She has extensive experience in all aspects of health information management in community mental health, including alcohol and drug treatment programs, reimbursement issues, and information systems planning, implementation, and maintenance.

CARISA D. NIXON, RHIA, is an instructor in the health informatics and information management program at the University of Mississippi Medical Center in Jackson, Mississippi. She earned her Baccalaureate degree in the health informatics and information management program at the University of Mississippi Medical Center in 2011. She completed her Baccalaureate in Nursing in 1997 at Union University in Jackson, Tennessee. She has worked in various roles in healthcare for over 15 years. She is currently enrolled in the Doctorate of Nursing Practice program at the University of Mississippi Medical Center.

REBECCA B. REYNOLDS, EDD, RHIA, FAHIMA is Professor and Chair of Health Informatics and Information Management and Privacy Coordinator for the University of Tennessee Health Science Center. She is a fellow of the American Health Information Management Association.

Reynolds has taught HIM students in Healthcare Policy, Health Information Technology and Systems as well as Legal Issues while providing HIPAA training and interprofessional seminars for the medical, pharmacy, nursing and health professions students on the UTHSC campus and the UT Knoxville campus. She has taught HIPAA seminars throughout Tennessee and has spoken at the Tennessee Bar Association's Health Law Forum, the Tennessee Chapter of the American College of Surgeons, and the National Conference for Nurse Practitioners. She is co-editor and chapter author of the AHIMA publication Fundamentals of Law for Health Informatics and Information Management.

Reynolds is active in the American Health Information Management Association (AHIMA) serving as a former Tennessee delegate to the AHIMA House of Delegates, as a member of the AHIMA Nominating Committee and on the AHIMA Foundation Committee on Excellence in Education Committee. She is also past president of the Tennessee Health Information Management Association (THIMA). Reynolds received the Outstanding New Professional Award from THIMA in 1995 and in 2004 received the THIMA Distinguished Member Award. In 2010 she was a co-recipient of the AHIMA Triumph Legacy Award.

DEIRDRE B. ROGERS, MS, CTR, is the Director of the Mississippi Cancer Registry at the University of Mississippi Medical Center. She completed her undergraduate studies in Mathematics at the University of Mississippi and received her M.S. degree in Mathematics/Statistics from the University of Mississippi, as well. She is currently a Ph.D. candidate in Clinical Health Sciences at the University of Mississippi Medical Center. Ms. Rogers has more than 10 years of experience in cancer registration and received her Certified Tumor Registrar certification from the National Cancer Registrars Association in 2007. She has served on numerous committees with the North American Association of Central Cancer Registries including the Institutional Review Board, Change Management Board, and, most recently, as the Chair of the Professional Development Steering Committee.

FRANCIS G. SERIO, DMD, MS, MBA, FICD, FACD, FADI, is currently a staff dentist at the James D. Bernstein Dental Services in Greenville, NC. He is formerly the founding dean at the proposed Bluefield College School of Dental Medicine and Associate Dean for Clinical Affairs and Professor at the East Carolina University School of Dental Medicine. He is also a Diplomate of the American Board of Periodontology. Dr. Serio completed his undergraduate studies at The Johns Hopkins University and received his D.M.D. degree from the University of Pennsylvania. He earned his M.S. and certificate in Periodontics at the University of Maryland and his MBA from Millsaps College. He was inducted into the International College of Dentists in 2003, and the American College of Dentists in 2004. Dr. Serio previously taught at the University of Maryland and was Professor and Chairman of the Department of Periodontics and Preventive Sciences at the University of Mississippi School of Dentistry from 1993–2009. His professional interests include educating predoctoral dental students, the pathogenesis of aggressive periodontitis, periodontal plastic surgery, international volunteer dentistry, and the continuing dental education of general dentists and dental hygienists. He has presented over 160 lectures and continuing education courses in the United States and around the world. He is founder of the Dominican Dental Mission Project, which has received both The President's Volunteer Action Award and The Daily Points of Light Award and is the 2015 recipient of the American Dental Association's Humanitarian Award. He has also been actively involved in Dentistry Overseas, a joint project between the American Dental Association and Health Volunteers Overseas, and many other international volunteer dental activities. Dr. Serio has written or co-authored over 40 scientific articles and four books.

TERESA SHERFY, RHIT, is the Health Information Manager at Hospice of Southern Illinois in Belleville, Illinois. She is a graduate of Southwestern Illinois College with an associate degree in Health Information Technology. Mrs. Sherfy has more than 19 years of experience working in hospice medical records, quality improvement, compliance, and information systems management.

LEIGH WILLIAMS, MHIIM, RHIA, CPC, CPHIMS is director of revenue cycle & health information management at the University of Mississippi Medical Center (UMMC). She serves on both the hospital and physician revenue cycle leaderships teams with direct responsibility for the hospital and professional fee coding, electronic health records, and clinical documentation improvement departments. Leigh has served as the institute's executive director for ICD-10 implementation since 2013 and oversees the institute's clinical documentation excellence program for 6 hospitals and more than 100 clinics. Leigh lectures across the nation on how to engage physicians in change initiatives, EHR work flow optimization, revenue cycle process improvement, and on current issues in health information management. Leigh has partnered with physician leadership at UMMC to develop a business of medicine curriculum for the Systems-Based Practice competency for residents at UMMC and she co-chairs the Mississippi Health Information Management Association's continuing education program. Founder of the Mississippi ICD-10 Collaborative, Leigh also provides ICD-10 transition training as a community service to physicians and their support staff across the state. Leigh is a registered health information administrator (RHIA), a certified professional coder (CPC), a certified professional in healthcare information & management systems (CPHIMS), an AHIMA approved ICD-10-CM/PCS trainer and ambassador, and is certified in Epic EHR Professional Billing. Leigh holds a bachelor's degree from Wellesley College and a master of health informatics and information management from the University of Mississippi Medical Center.

KAREN WRIGHT, MHSA, RHIA, RHIT, has a Master of Health Administration from Ohio University and a bachelor's degree in Health Information Administration from Ohio State University. She has been the coordinator and instructor of Health Information Technology at Hocking College for over 20 years. In addition to being the transcription supervisor and then director of a medical record department in a 365-bed acute care hospital, Karen has been a consultant at acute care hospitals; nursing, chemical dependency, and behavioral health care facilities; as well as for physician's private practices.

SCOTT WRIGHT, MBA, has a Master's of Business Administration from Ohio University and has been the Director of the Athens County Small Business Development Center and Director of the Center for International Business and Education at Ohio University College of Business. He currently is a Senior Lecturer of Finance at Ohio University, where he has taught for over 25 years. Scott also serves as Director of the China Global Consulting Program and Director of Brazilian Executive Education. In addition, he has owned and operated many types of businesses.

DORTHY K. YOUNG, PHD, MHSA, is the Deputy Administrator for Health Services in the Office of the Governor, Division of Medicaid for the State of Mississippi. Dr. Young is a graduate of Furman University in Greenville, South Carolina, and holds a Master of Health Services Administration degree from Mississippi College in Clinton, Mississippi. She earned her PhD in Clinical Health Sciences from the University of Mississippi Medical Center in Jackson, Mississippi. In addition to her role with the Office of the Governor, Dr. Young is a member of the faculty at the School of Health Related Professions at the University of Mississippi Medical Center. She has experience in hospital administration, health information and informatics and life sciences research, and healthcare reimbursement, analytics and policy development.

Introduction to Health Care Systems

Mary E. "Lisa" Morton, PhD, RHIA | Dorthy K. Young, PhD, MHSA | Ann H. Peden, PhD, RHIA, CCS

LEARNING OBJECTIVES

Upon successful completion of this chapter, you should be able to:

- Describe significant changes affecting health care delivery and reimbursement in the United States.
- Explain the impact of health care changes on the health information manager.
- Identify expanding opportunities available to health information managers.

TWENTIETH-CENTURY HEALTH CARE IN AMERICA

Before the twentieth century, hospitals were perceived as places where people went to die. Antibiotics had not yet been developed, and hospitals offered little in the way of technology. No outside regulatory authority offered effective oversight of hospital operations. The twentieth century, however, began a new era for hospitals. For example, in 1910 the **Flexner Report** examined the state of medical education in the United States. The authors of this report, who had been commissioned by the Carnegie Foundation, emphasized the importance of hospital-based training in preparing competent physicians (Litman & Robins, 1991).

Shortly after publication of that report, the **American College of Surgeons (ACS)** was founded and began establishing standards for hospitals as part of its mission to improve the quality of care for surgical patients (ACS, 2010). The Flexner Report and the ACS's hospital standardization program inaugurated needed changes that improved the quality of hospital care and increased the American public's expectations of hospitals.

The first health information managers (or "medical record librarians," as they were called then), played a significant role in efforts to improve patient care in hospitals. The American College of Surgeons' hospital standardization program emphasized the importance of maintaining medical records, and subsequent accrediting agencies, such as The Joint Commission, have continued to emphasize the role of accurate and complete health information in providing high-quality patient care.

In 1946, the **Hill-Burton Act** authorized an investigation to determine the need for more hospitals and provided money for their construction. During the mid-twentieth century, admissions to hospitals increased dramatically, as did hospital costs. This period of hospital expansion resulted in increased opportunities for health information practitioners, because at that time a large majority of health information managers practiced in hospital settings.

The latter part of the twentieth century was marked by continued changes in health care, and the pace of change has increased in the twenty-first. New legislation and payment issues, technological advances, and changes in society are making a significant impact on the delivery of health care in the new millennium.

Payment Issues Affecting Health Care Delivery

Payment issues have had a tremendous impact on health care delivery in the United States during the late twentieth and early twenty-first centuries. With an increasing number of patients insured under federal and state health programs, changes in payment mechanisms for these programs have affected all types of health care settings.

Flexner Report   a document published in 1910 examining the state of medical education in the United States and Canada. The Flexner Report resulted in sweeping changes in the way North American physicians were educated.

American College of Surgeons (ACS) a professional organization founded in 1913 to "improve the quality of care for the surgical patient by setting high standards for surgical education and practice" (ACS, n.d.). In the early twentieth century, the ACS established a hospital standardization program that was the forerunner of today's accreditation organizations.

Hill-Burton Act   the "Hospital Survey and Construction Act" enacted by Congress in 1946. This legislation provided federal money to determine the need for more hospitals and to pay for their construction. (Note: Facilities receiving Hill-Burton funds agreed to provide a reasonable volume of service to patients who are unable to pay, an obligation that is still monitored by the federal government today.)

Overview of Federal and Federal-State Health Programs

In 1965, Congress enacted Title XVIII and Title XIX as amendments to the Social Security Act, commonly known as Medicare and Medicaid. **Medicare** (Title XVIII) provides health benefits for Social Security recipients and other qualified individual. It consists of four parts: Part A, Hospital Insurance; Part B, Medical Insurance; and—more recently—Part C, Medicare Advantage, and Part D, Prescription Drug Coverage. Part A helps to pay for hospital inpatient care, some home health care, skilled nursing care, and hospice care. Part B provides coverage for physician services, hospital outpatient services, some home health care, medical equipment and supplies, and other health services (CMS, 2013a).

Part D, created by the **Medicare Prescription Drug, Improvement, and Modernization Act of 2003 (MMA)**, is optional insurance coverage available to all Medicare beneficiaries that is designed to lower prescription drug costs (Casto & Forrestal, 2013). Medicare beneficiaries pay a monthly premium for the Parts B and D benefits, but not for Part A (CMS, 2013a, 2015a).

Beneficiaries may opt to purchase a managed care plan to provide their health care services and prescription drugs. Under this option, known as Part C, or Medicare Advantage, the beneficiary purchases a health insurance plan offered by one of the private companies approved by Medicare. These plans may offer coverage for services excluded by Parts A and B, but the premiums, out-of-pocket expenses, and rules for coverage vary by plan. Under Part C, beneficiaries pay a monthly premium for the insurance plan, in addition to their Part B premium (How do Medicare Advantage Plans Work? n.d.).

Medicaid (Title XIX) provides medical assistance to lower-income individuals and families. Federal and state governments jointly fund the Medicaid program. Because each state establishes and administers its own program, Medicaid services and eligibility requirements vary from state to state (Klees, Wolfe, & Curtis, 2012). The Patient Protection and Affordable Care Act (or simply the Affordable Care Act), passed in 2010, expanded Medicaid eligibility requirements, provided additional opportunities for coverage through health insurance exchanges, and mandated changes to private insurance (Pub. L. No. 111-148, 2010).

The **Centers for Medicare and Medicaid Services (CMS)** is a federal agency within the Department of Health and Human Services. It was created in 1977 to administer the Medicare and Medicaid programs. CMS, with headquarters in Baltimore, Maryland, has 10 regional offices nationwide. The central office administers the national direction of the Medicare and Medicaid programs, and the regional offices provide CMS with the local presence necessary for quality customer service and oversight.

CMS acts mainly as a purchaser of health care services for Medicare and Medicaid beneficiaries. Four key principles for Medicare/Medicaid standards are:

1. Assuring that Medicare and Medicaid are properly administered by their contractors and state agencies.

Medicare   Title XVIII of the 1965 Amendments to the Social Security Act, providing health benefits for Social Security recipients and other qualified individuals.

Medicare Prescription Drug, Improvement, and Modernization Act of 2003 (MMA)   also known as the Medicare Modernization Act. MMA made significant revisions to the Medicare program by calling for the creation of Part D, e-prescribing for prescription drug plans, revision of claims processing, and a Medicare payment recovery demonstration project that ultimately resulted in the Recovery Audit Contractor (RAC) initiative.

Medicaid   Title XIX of the 1965 Amendments to the Social Security Act. Medicaid is jointly funded by federal and state governments and provides medical assistance to lower-income individuals and families.

Centers for Medicare & Medicaid Services (CMS)   a federal agency within the Department of Health and Human Services with its main focus to administer the Medicare and Medicaid programs. It formerly was known as the Health Care Financing Administration (HCFA).

2. Establishing policies for the reimbursement of health care providers.

3. Conducting research on the effectiveness of various methods of health care management, treatment, and financing.

4. Assessing the quality of health care facilities and services.

Medicare/Medicaid manuals, interim manual instructions, and Medicare transmittals are distributed to **Medicare administrative contractors (MACs)**, CMS regional offices, federal agencies, state agencies, and congressional offices. Medicare providers may obtain copies of Medicare/Medicaid manuals and transmittals from the CMS website.

Congress created the **Children's Health Insurance Program (CHIP)** as part of the Balanced Budget Act of 1997. CHIP (Title XXI) allows states to offer health insurance plans for children to age 19 who are not already insured. CHIP affords families who earn too much to qualify for Medicaid an opportunity to obtain health insurance for their children (CMS, n.d.a). The Affordable Care Act also provided additional federal funding for Medicaid and CHIP. The increase in federal and state health insurance programs has made governmental regulations and payment systems important factors in health care delivery.

Payment Changes Affected Hospitals First

When Medicare was implemented in 1966, it paid for health care benefits under a **fee-for-service** plan, which operated in a way similar to that of most health insurance plans of the day. Health care providers received a fee for each service provided—each office visit, each day in the hospital, each treatment, and so on. As the costs of this program continued to escalate, the federal government began to look at ways to hold down the costs, initially by targeting hospital costs.

In 1982, enactment of the Medicare inpatient **prospective payment system (PPS)** (a system based on payment amounts determined before services are rendered) forced hospitals into a new way of looking at the utilization of their services. This signaled a change in the locations and methods of health care delivery for the future. Medicare payments to hospitals switched from a **per diem** (per day) basis to a per case basis. Before the prospective payment arrangement, hospitals received payment for each day the patient stayed in the hospital (per diem). Prospective payment, however, based any reimbursement primarily on the patient's condition and surgical treatment, regardless of the number of days the patient stayed in the hospital.

Under prospective payment, the hospital's cash flow improved if patients were discharged earlier, because costs for extra days in the hospital could not be recovered adequately from Medicare. Hospitals, particularly those with a high volume of Medicare patients, began to have an incentive to encourage shorter inpatient stays and to treat patients in the least costly setting possible. In some states, payers other than Medicare began to implement prospective payment. Increasingly, hospitals began to emphasize programs that shifted care from inpatient settings to alternative care settings such as outpatient and home care.

Medicare administrative contractors (MACs) a group of organizations or businesses that contract with Medicare to enroll providers, process claims and appeals, and educate providers and beneficiaries. MACs are organized into jurisdictions based upon provider type and geographical location.

Children's Health Insurance Program (CHIP) also known as Title XXI of the Balanced Budget Act of 1997. It allows states to offer health insurance plans for children to age 19 who are not insured already. CHIP affords families who earn too much to qualify for Medicaid an opportunity to obtain health insurance for their children.

fee-for-service a method of payment for health care in which the health care provider charges and is paid for each item of service provided.

prospective payment system (PPS) a method in which payment levels for health care services are determined before the services are rendered. In a prospective payment system, the unit of payment is not based solely on the individual services provided but, rather, on payment units that represent general groupings of patient encounters, hospital stays, or episodes of care.

per diem per day. A per diem payment is a payment rendered to an institution based on the number of days of service provided.

Health information managers are crucial to a hospital's success under prospective payment, because the data provided by health information services are the basis for inpatient reimbursement under Medicare. Just as the American College of Surgeons' hospital standardization program first brought attention to the role of the then medical record librarians in the provision of quality patient care in hospitals, Medicare's prospective payment system highlighted the role of health information managers in the financial health of hospitals. The transformation of data into information by health information services continues to be a factor in numerous decisions that hospitals must make in the twenty-first century, such as decisions regarding contracts with managed care organizations.

During the 1990s, managed care organizations (discussed more fully in Chapter 4) became a force that further lowered hospital utilization rates. The earliest so-called prepaid health care models, such as Kaiser Permanente in the western United States, have existed since the 1930s (Kaiser Permanente, n.d.). In the mid-1970s, the federal government stimulated the development of one type of managed care organization— the health maintenance organization (HMO). The name "health maintenance organization" relates to the financial incentive for the health care provider to keep patients healthy. A common method of paying providers in an HMO is the **capitation** model. Under capitation, providers are paid based on the number of patients they agree to treat, rather than on the number of services they provide. Therefore, it is more profitable to the provider if the patient requires fewer services. These types of plans emphasize disease prevention (health maintenance). When disease does occur, though, treatment is provided in the least costly setting.

Increased Scrutiny of Improper Payments, Fraud, Abuse, and Waste

Federal legislation passed in the early twenty-first century created audit programs and compliance initiatives to prevent improper or fraudulent payments made under federal health programs. CMS's **Recovery Audit Contractor (RAC)** program was designed to recover improper Medicare payments (Dimick, 2010), whereas the **Medicaid Integrity Program (MIP)** focuses upon Medicaid overpayments (CMS, 2013b).

In the **Zone Program Integrity Contractor (ZPIC)** program, the contractors identify and investigate malicious fraud within seven geographic zones (CMS, 2013c). Federally designated **quality improvement organizations (QIOs)** also monitor Medicare services. The QIOs work under contract with CMS to improve the quality of care delivered to Medicare beneficiaries (CMS, 2013d). These responsibilities include conducting focused coding and documentation audits at the direction of CMS (Gentul & Davis, 2011). Using specialized software, QIOs are able to identify hospitals with outliers and

capitation a method of payment for health care in which the health care provider receives a monthly payment based on the number of persons the provider has agreed to treat, regardless of the number of persons actually treated or the amount of service rendered.

Recovery Audit Contractor (RAC) a third-party entity working under the direction of CMS to detect improper Medicare payments by reviewing providers' medical records and Medicare claims data.

Medicaid Integrity Program (MIP) a national strategy created as a result of the Deficit Reduction Act of 2005 (Section 1936 of the Social Security Act) to detect and prevent Medicaid fraud, waste, and abuse. It uses contracted reviewers to audit the accuracy of Medicaid payments made to health care providers.

Zone Program Integrity Contractor (ZPIC) program a program implemented by CMS to identify and investigate malicious fraudulent claims activity within Medicare's seven geographic regions (zones).

quality improvement organizations (QIOs) "group of health quality experts, clinicians, and consumers organized to improve the care delivered to people with Medicare. QIOs work under the direction of the Centers for Medicare & Medicaid Services to assist Medicare providers with quality improvement and to review quality concerns for the protection of beneficiaries and the Medicare Trust Fund" (CMS, 2014c).

clinical documentation improvement (CDI) program   a locally implemented program focused upon improving the quality of clinical documentation to "facilitate an accurate representation of health care services through complete and accurate reporting of diagnoses and procedures" (AHIMA, 2010a.

payment errors (Casto & Forrestal, 2013). In 2014, the QIO program was restructured. Beneficiary and Family-Centered Care (BFCC) QIO contractors to perform the program's case review and monitoring activities separately from the quality improvement activities performed by Quality Innovation Network (QIN)-QIOs. The QIN-QIOs focus on data-driven quality initiatives (CMS, 2014a).

These federal initiatives also have led to increased auditing by private payers (Dimick, 2010). To meet the demands of increasing external scrutiny, many providers have developed **clinical documentation improvement (CDI)** programs to facilitate accurate documentation, coding, and reporting of quality data (AHIMA, 2010a).

PROFESSIONAL SPOTLIGHT   HEALTH CARE CONSULTING FIRM

Who I am: Brenda Ikerd, RHIA

Where I work: Anthelio Healthcare Solutions. Anthelio Healthcare Solutions, Inc. is the largest independent provider of technology and services to hospitals, physician practice groups, and other health care providers. Anthelio provides "end-to-end" services expertise, including information technology (IT), service desk, patient portal, electronic medical record (EMR) implementations, data warehousing, clinical analytics, clinical transformation, coding, ICD-10, transcription and revenue cycle services.

What I do: I'm Senior Director of Health Information Innovations. This position requires me to be passionate about driving growth through the implementation of cutting edge technology and HIM transformation services to the evolving health care market. In this role, I develop and implement service and technology solutions that help meet the continued challenges around cost management, quality improvement, and information use in health care. We like to call ourselves "solutionists."

Why HIM knowledge is important in my role: Throughout my career, I've taken the opportunity to broaden the typical HIM role to meet the challenges of information management and integrity into atypical roles. Some of these include

- working with physician quality data and credentialing,
- establishing a statewide health information exchange, and
- continuing to work with a variety of health care organizations to develop solutions with their business and clinical workflows and information systems.

HIM's knowledge of health care organizations' operations, from the clinical perspective as well as the financial/revenue cycle areas, ensures that we are much more than file supervisors or coders.

In my current position, having the basic HIM knowledge provides opportunities in organizations from single physician practices, to critical access hospitals, to large academic health care settings, to identify solutions to meet their many challenges.

Value-Based Payment Models

A rising emphasis on quality care and cost containment has led to federal health care initiatives and newer payment models. Requirements mandated by the **Affordable Care Act (ACA)**, the American Recovery and Reinvestment Act (ARRA), and the **Health Information Technology for Economic and Clinical Health (HITECH)** Act call for changes in health care delivery and reimbursement methods. These emerging models include **pay-for-performance (P4P)**, **value-based purchasing (VBP)**, shared savings programs through **accountable care organizations (ACOs)**, bundled payments, and incentives for adopting health information technology. ACOs that opt to partner with Medicare through the Medicare Shared Savings Program must meet certain quality metrics in order to receive savings incentive payments. The ACO model encourages participating organizations through tracking of nearly 30 quality metrics and with shared financial risk relationships (CMS, n.d.b).

Pay-for-Performance and Value-Based Purchasing Reimbursement is becoming tied more closely to quality outcomes with the emergence of pay-for-performance (P4P) and value-based purchasing systems. These incentive-based programs reward or penalize providers based upon their ability to meet preestablished targets for delivery of health care services. This emphasizes the quality of care provided rather than the volume of services rendered by an individual provider or a facility. The growth of P4P programs is evident within Medicare and Medicaid, as well as private health insurance and managed care companies (Casto & Forrestal, 2013).

CMS requires hospitals to report quality information for established inpatient quality measures through the **Hospital Inpatient Quality Reporting (IQR)** program. In addition, the **Hospital Outpatient Quality Data Reporting Program (HOP QDRP)** became effective in 2009. Data from IQR and HOP QDRP are made publically available to enable consumers to make more informed decisions about their health care. Hospitals that do not participate receive a reduced annual Medicare payment.

The **Physician Quality Reporting System (PQRS)** is CMS's reporting program for physician providers. Under the PQRS, participants initially received an incentive for reporting quality measures for Medicare beneficiaries. Beginning in 2015, providers who do not report quality measure data to CMS receive decreased Medicare reimbursement. State Medicaid programs can implement P4P programs to target specific providers, beneficiary populations, reimbursement methodologies, and quality measures.(Casto & Forrestal, 2013; CMS QualityNet, n.d.b).

Medicare Hospital Value-Based Purchasing Program The Medicare **Hospital Value-based Purchasing Program (HVBP)** was established by the ACA to improve quality of care for inpatients by reimbursing acute-care hospitals based upon clinical best practices. These value-based incentive payments are tied to

Affordable Care Act of 2010 (ACA) see Patient Protection and Affordable Care Act

Health Information Technology for Economic and Clinical Health Act (HITECH) Enacted as part of the American Recovery and Reinvestment Act of 2009 to promote the adoption and meaningful use of health information technology.

pay-for-performance (P4P) emerging incentive-based reimbursement programs that reward or penalize providers based upon their ability to meet preestablished quality and performance targets for delivery of health care services. Also known as value-based purchasing.

value-based purchasing (VBP) see pay-for-performance (P4P).

accountable care organizations (ACOs) Groups of medical providers or facilities that collaborate to achieve higher quality outcomes, to earn incentive payments, and to share financial risk.

Hospital Inpatient Quality Reporting (IQR) a national quality initiative implemented by CMS as required by the Medicare Prescription Drug, Improvement, and Modernization Act (MMA) of 2003. IQR requires hospitals to submit data for certain quality measures, which are made publically available to consumers via the Hospital Compare website.

Physician Quality Reporting System (PQRS) a system for reporting quality of care metrics to Medicare.

Hospital Outpatient Quality Data Reporting Program (HOP QDRP) a national quality program implemented by CMS that is modeled after the Hospital Inpatient Quality Reporting (IQR) initiative. Hospitals must report data for standardized quality measures for outpatient hospital services, which are made publically available to consumers via the Hospital Compare website.

data reported through the Hospital Inpatient Quality Reporting (IQR) Program and are made through Medicare's Inpatient Prospective Payment System (IPPS) (CMS QualityNet, n.d.a). The HVBP program was intended to provide reimbursement based upon performance and improvement across time, rather than the volume of services a facility renders.

Medicare Shared Savings Program: Accountable Care Organizations   The ACA required CMS to create an Innovation Center in order to pilot-test newer health care delivery and payment models. These emerging models emphasize better coordination of care among providers to enhance treatment outcomes and efficient utilization of resources (CMS, n.d.c., DHHS, 2011). The Innovation Center has several key functions intended to support providers, payers, and patients. A data and reporting component houses data sets and reports that researchers, analysts, and HIM professionals may utilize. The Innovation Center also hosts webinars and forums on interesting and trending health care topics and has an interactive portal for idea submission.

SELF REVIEW 1.1

1. True or False? The Flexner Report authorized an investigation to determine the need for more hospitals and provided money for their construction.
2. True or False? The first health information managers were referred to as "medical record librarians."
3. True or False? Under Medicare Part C, beneficiaries pay a monthly premium for optional prescription drug coverage.
4. True or False? Prospective payment systems are utilized solely by Medicare.
5. True or False? Under the capitation payment model, it is more profitable to the provider if the patient requires fewer services.
6. True or False? Zone Program Integrity Contractors (ZPICs) work under contract with CMS to improve the quality of care delivered to Medicare beneficiaries.
7. True or False? The purpose of a clinical documentation improvement program is to focus on Medicaid overpayments.
8. How are the Hospital Inpatient Quality Reporting (IQR) program, the Hospital Outpatient Quality Data Reporting Program (HOP QDRP), and the Physician Quality Reporting System (PQRS) alike? How are they different?
9. Which of the following emphasizes better coordination of care among providers to enhance treatment outcomes and efficient utilization of resources?
   a. Prospective Payment System
   b. Medicare Integrity Program
   c. Inpatient Quality Reporting
   d. Accountable Care Organizations

Incentive-Based Program for Adoption of Health Information Technology

The **American Recovery and Reinvestment Act (ARRA)**, also known as the Stimulus Act or the Recovery Act, was passed in 2009. The HITECH Act, enacted as Title XIII of ARRA, implemented the Medicare and Medicaid **electronic health record (EHR)** incentive programs to assist providers and organizations in the adoption of electronic health records (Dennis, 2010). Providers failing to demonstrate **meaningful use** of health information technology by 2015 were designated to be financially penalized in the form of "payment adjustments" (CMS, 2014b). ARRA has impacted the health care industry significantly in other areas, discussed further later in this chapter.

Effects of Payment and Financial Changes on Other Settings

Other settings, such as ambulatory care, home-based and community-based services, and long-term care, have been affected both directly and indirectly by payment and other financial changes.

The adoption of payment methodologies such as the hospital inpatient prospective payment system (IPPS) has impacted the delivery of care to patients in an inpatient or an acute care setting. The IPPS, along with a shift toward managed care and outcomes- based payments, has contributed to the increased utilization of ambulatory health care services (services provided in settings where patients typically do not stay overnight). With an increased volume of services rendered in an ambulatory setting, payers began to monitor ambulatory data and reimbursement information more rigorously.

Starting with payments to physicians, Congress enacted a law in 1991 creating a professional fee schedule (PFS), which was implemented in 1992. Before implementation of the fee schedule, Medicare payments to physicians were based on charges. If the physician's charge was in line with what other physicians in the same specialty usually charged for that service, Medicare would pay its share of the charge. When the fee schedule was implemented, it quantified the physician work, practice expense, and malpractice expense of each service to determine what that service was "worth" relative to other services. Implementation of a payment system based on the "relative value" of services removed from participating physicians the ability to establish their own charges for Medicare patients. Payments under the fee schedule are based on codes representing services performed by physicians and other qualified providers (CMS, 2015b). (More information on the relative value system can be found in Chapter 3.)

In 2000, Medicare began paying hospitals for ambulatory care under an outpatient prospective payment system (OPPS), which is based on codes submitted by the hospital. (See Chapter 2.) As with the hospital IPPS, adequate documentation and accurate coding are extremely important, along with an understanding of the complex regulations governing the PPS. For both physicians and hospitals, greater demands are being placed on the health information systems of ambulatory health

American Recovery and Reinvestment Act (ARRA) also known as the "Stimulus Act" or the "Recovery Act." ARRA (Public Law 111-5) was enacted in 2009 with its main purpose to create jobs and stimulate economic growth; however, it contains many provisions for health care, including billions of dollars for health information technology. Title XIII of ARRA was given a subtitle—Health Information Technology for Economic and Clinical Health Act (HITECH)—which addresses many of the health information and technology requirements, including Subpart D–Privacy.

electronic health record (EHR) a system in which a health care provider maintains individual patient health records electronically. Fully developed EHRs include capabilities such as generating clinical alerts and reminders and providing readily available decision support.

meaningful use a concept called for by ARRA. For health care providers to become eligible for reimbursement incentives and avoid financial penalties through Medicare and Medicaid, they must demonstrate meaningful use of certified electronic health record (EHR) technology. The concept refers to a set of criteria and measures, rather than a single definition, and is being implemented in phases though a series of published rules.

care providers. Health information managers must be knowledgeable in coding, billing, clinical documentation, and reporting—all crucial components in the increasingly complex health data environment facing all types of health care providers.

Medicare payment changes also have affected other health care settings. Skilled nursing facilities came under a prospective payment system in 1998. (See Chapter 10.) The home health prospective payment system became effective in the year 2000. (See Chapter 12.) A prospective payment system for inpatient rehabilitation hospital services (Chapter 11) was implemented in January 2002, followed by implementation of a PPS for long-term care hospitals (see Chapter 2) in October of that year. In January 2005, a PPS for inpatient psychiatric facilities (Chapter 7) became effective. A prospective payment system for federally qualified health centers (Chapter 3) was implemented in 2014 (CMS, n.d.d.).

Although the hospital-oriented PPSs are based largely on diagnostic and procedural coding, other PPSs rely on additional types of clinical data that are captured on patient assessment instruments periodically throughout each episode of care. (See Table 1-1 for an overview of Medicare PPSs.) Health information managers with skills in systems analysis can be valuable team members in ensuring a smooth flow of accurate data for any prospective payment system.

TABLE 1-1   Medicare Prospective Payment Systems

Setting	Basis for Payment	Key Data Collection Instrument	Year PPS First Implemented
Hospital Inpatient	Medicare Severity Diagnosis Related Groups (MS-DRGs)	Uniform Bill-04 (UB-04)	1982
Skilled Nursing Facilities	Resource Utilization Groups (RUGs)	Minimum Data Set (MDS)	1998
Hospital Outpatient	Ambulatory Payment Classifications (APCs)	Uniform Bill-04 (UB-04)	2000
Home Health	Home Health Resource Groups (HHRGs)	Outcomes and Assessment Information Set (OASIS)	2000
Inpatient Rehabilitation	Case Mix Groups (CMGs)	Inpatient Rehabilitation Facility Patient Assessment Instrument (IRF-PAI)	2002
Long-term Care Hospitals	Long-term Care Diagnosis Related Groups (MS-LTC-DRGs)	Uniform Bill-04 (UB-04)	2002
Inpatient Psychiatric Facilities	Per diem payment, adjusted for specific DRGs and comorbidities	Uniform Bill-04 (UB-04)	2005
Federally Qualified Health Center (FQHC)	National rate which is adjusted based on the location of where the services are furnished and other factors	CMS-1500	2014

Source: Prospective Payment Systems—General Information, Centers for Medicare and Medicaid Services. http://www.cms.gov/ProspMedicareFeeSvcPmtGen/ (CMS, 2010).

Other Regulatory and Accreditation Issues Affecting Health Care

Although much attention has been focused on health care financing issues in recent years, many other challenges face today's health care organizations. These range from standardization of electronic transactions to implementation of electronic health records (EHRs).

The Health Insurance Portability and Accountability Act of 1996 (HIPAA)

The Health Insurance Portability and Accountability Act of 1996 (HIPAA) was enacted to achieve many purposes. As the name implies, one purpose of this legislation was to address the problem of rising numbers of uninsured and underinsured Americans by making health insurance portable. For example, HIPAA allows a person with a preexisting medical condition to obtain insurance benefits related to that condition when changing jobs. Another aspect of HIPAA addresses problems of health care fraud and abuse. However, the provisions of HIPAA that have had the greatest impact on health care providers have been its administrative simplification provisions. (See Figure 1-1 for an overview of the HIPAA legislation.)

Health Insurance Portability and Accountability Act of 1996 (HIPAA) also known as the Kassebaum-Kennedy Act. Provisions include the portability of health care benefits (for example, upon an individual change of employment), prevention of fraud and abuse in health care, and simplification of the electronic interchange of health care data, while improving the privacy and security of health information.

administrative simplification provisions of the Health Insurance Portability and Accountability Act (HIPAA) that address standardization of electronic data interchange, privacy of health information, and security of health data.

FIGURE 1-1

HIPAA Administrative Simplification Provisions.

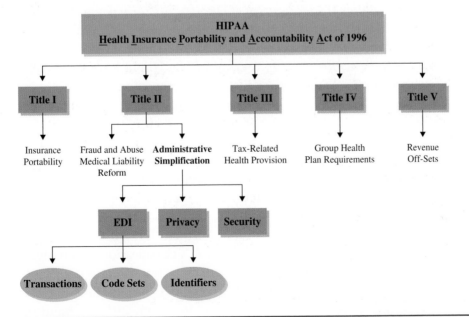

covered entities (CEs) under HIPAA, health plans, health care clearinghouses, or any health care providers that transmit health information in an electronic form.

business associate (BA) a partner or contractor performing a job or service on behalf of a covered entity. To perform the contracted work, the original HIPAA legislation required covered entities to have a business associate agreement with any organization that handled or encountered its PHI. BAs also are accountable for complying with certain provisions in the privacy and security regulations, as required by ARRA.

personal health record (PHR) "an Internet-based set of tools that allows people to access and coordinate their lifelong health information and make appropriate parts of it available to those who need it" (Markle Foundation, 2003, p. 2).

ICD-10-CM the United States' clinical modification of the World Health Organization's diagnostic disease classification (International Classification of Diseases, 10th Revision, Clinical Modification).

ICD-10-PCS the United States' procedural coding system for inpatient, acute care settings (International Classification of Diseases, 10th Revision, Procedural Coding System). ICD-10-PCS is the replacement for ICD-9-CM, volume 3, one of the original code sets required by HIPAA.

To whom do the administrative simplification provisions apply? In the original HIPAA legislation, **covered entities (CEs)** are health plans, health care clearinghouses, and health care providers who transmit health information in electronic form (Standards for Privacy of Individually Identifiable Health Information, 2000; Security and Privacy, 2009). The Health Information Technology for Economic and Clinical Health Act (HITECH) was passed in 2009 as Title XIII of the American Recovery and Reinvestment Act (ARRA). HITECH amended the HIPAA privacy and security rules by introducing additional privacy regulations, breach notification rules, and stiffer penalties for security violations (AHIMA, 2010c; DHHS, 2013). HITECH, along with the Genetic Information Nondiscrimination Act of 2008 (GINA) were intended to clarify the information protected under the HIPAA Privacy Rule and to prohibit most providers and health plans from inappropriately disclosing information for nonmedical purposes (DHHS, 2013).

A **business associate (BA)** (a partner or contractor working for covered entities) also may be held accountable for complying with certain provisions in the privacy and security regulations. These requirements also extend to emerging entities not in existence when the HIPAA rule was released initially, such as health information exchanges, **personal health record (PHR)** operators and e-prescribing gateways (Dennis, 2010; Rhodes & Rode, 2010; DHHS, 2013).

Health information managers play an important role in the implementation and oversight of HIPAA standards. For example, HIPAA's electronic data interchange (EDI) standards include standards for code sets, an arena in which health information managers have expertise. The August 17, 2000, final rule regarding transactions and standardized code sets for EDI included the following code set standards: *International Classification of Diseases, 9th Edition, Clinical Modification (ICD-9-CM), Volumes 1, 2, and 3, National Drug Codes (NDC), Code on Dental Procedures and Nomenclature (CDT),* and the combination of *Health Care Common Procedure Coding System (HCPCS)* and *Current Procedural Terminology© (CPT)* (Standards for Electronic Transactions, 2000).

On January 16, 2009, the U.S. Department of Health and Human Services (HHS) published a Final Rule for adopting **ICD-10-CM** and **ICD-10-PCS** code sets to replace the ICD-9-CM code sets required by HIPAA (DHHS, 2009). The compliance date for adoption subsequently was delayed by later legislation, but at the time of publication was no earlier than October 1, 2015 (DHHS, 2014). Both of these systems offer greater detail and more current terminology than does ICD-9-CM. ICD-10-CM and ICD-10-PCS also provide greater capacity for future expansion. Further, ICD-10-CM is compatible with ICD-10, the World Health Organization's classification system, which is used by most other countries. To accommodate the transition to ICD-10-CM/PCS, DHHS also mandated plans and providers to upgrade transaction standards for processing electronic claims (Moynihan, 2010; Administrative Requirements, 2009).

As longstanding advocates for confidentiality of patient information, health information managers also play a key role in the implementation and enforcement of the HIPAA privacy rule. The privacy rule established regulations for handling **protected health information (PHI)**, which consists of any individually identifiable health information.

The privacy rule is complex, and only a brief overview of HIPAA privacy is provided here. The complete rule and other educational materials are available at the Office of Civil Rights website, http://www.hhs.gov/ocr/privacy/

The privacy rule describes how PHI, whether in paper or in electronic form, may be used or disclosed. In general, an authorization from the patient or a legal representative is required for use or disclosure of PHI. The authorization must contain certain core elements, such as a description of the information to be used or disclosed, who is authorized to make the disclosure, to whom the covered entity may make the requested use or disclosure, the purpose of the requested use or disclosure, an expiration date or event, and the signature of the individual and date. The authorization also must contain certain required statements, such as the individual's right to revoke the authorization in writing. A covered entity, however, is permitted to use or disclose PHI for treatment, payment, or health care operations (TPO), within the definitions of the regulation, without a specific authorization for each use or disclosure.

HIPAA also requires that each covered entity provide its patients with a written notice of privacy practices (NPP) that explains how the covered entity might use or disclose the individual's health information. The NPP also must contain certain required elements and statements. In addition, the privacy rule explains how the individual may restrict uses and disclosures of PHI as well as the individual's right to access or amend PHI.

The HITECH Act extends a consumer's right to restrict disclosures under certain conditions (Rhodes & Rode, 2010; DHHS, 2013). Further, an individual has a right to receive an accounting of disclosures of PHI made by a covered entity in the six years before the date on which the accounting is requested, with exceptions for certain types of disclosures made for TPO (ONC, n.d.). HITECH, however, shortened the disclosure period for routine disclosures made to an entity's business associates to three years (Miaoulis, 2010). In addition, HITECH obligates CEs maintaining EHRs to provide the requesting parties with an electronic copy of their PHI or, at the direction of the requestor, to transmit an electronic copy to a designated party (Dennis, 2010; DHHS, 2013).

Whereas the privacy rule protects PHI in both paper and electronic formats, the purpose of the security rule is to protect PHI that is maintained in electronic form. Each covered entity must analyze its systems for the electronic maintenance and transmission of PHI to identify and correct security risks. Security risks can be anything from unauthorized "hacking" of information systems to damage caused by natural disasters. The security standards have some required elements, but some of the implementation specifications are stated to be "addressable."

protected health information (PHI) individually identifiable health information.

For addressable implementation specifications, the covered entity must describe how it will implement the required standards in a manner that is appropriate for the environment of the facility (Amatayakul, 2013).

To minimize security risks, system users have to be identified and properly authenticated, audit trails and logs should be maintained and reviewed, appropriate backup systems should be in place, members of the workforce should be educated about system security, and so on. The American Health Information Management Association (AHIMA) and the Healthcare Information and Management Systems Society (HIMSS) are good sources of information for health information managers with regard to HIPAA security issues. HITECH also requires business associates and certain noncovered entities to comply with certain administrative, physical, and technical safeguards described in the security regulations (Dennis, 2010).

A helpful source for security and privacy standards for the electronic health records is the *Code of Federal Regulations*, Title 45, Subtitle A, Subchapter C, Part 164, which can be accessed electronically at www.ecfr.gov. This site lists the security and privacy rule, including sections amended by HITECH, such as the breach notification rules, which specify when individual patients, the media, and the Secretary of HHS must be notified of security breaches.

Accreditation Issues Affecting Health Care

licensure a governmental process in which a facility must meet certain regulations, set by the State, to provide care.

Health care organizations generally must be licensed by a designated state agency. Licensure is a governmental process that requires a facility to meet certain regulations set by the state to be able to provide care. Many government and private payers require licensure as a condition of enrollment in their program. Health care organizations also choose to pursue accreditation, which is a voluntary process in which facilities agree to follow a set of standards and receive recognition for having met those standards.

accreditation a voluntary process in which facilities agree to follow a set of standards and receive recognition for having met those standards.

The health care settings described in this book may be accredited by a variety of organizations, whose accreditation standards and processes are updated regularly and may change. Health information managers play an essential role in the accreditation process and should stay up-to-date regarding the latest information from the organizations that accredit their facilities. Table 1-2 provides an overview of the settings covered in this textbook and some of the accrediting organizations for each setting. Contact information for these organizations is listed in the Key Resources section of the appropriate chapters.

Other Regulatory Issues Affecting Health Care

Medicare certification a process in which a state agency determines that a health care organization meets the standards set forth in the relevant Conditions of Participation or Conditions of Coverage and therefore is eligible for participation in the Medicare program.

Many health care settings also are affected by federal regulations known as Conditions of Participation or Conditions for Coverage. Health care organizations that want to participate in federal programs must have Medicare certification, demonstrating that they meet the standards set forth in the relevant Conditions of Participation/Coverage. Routine surveys to determine whether health

TABLE 1-2 Health Care Settings and Examples of Relevant Voluntary Accrediting Organizations

Chapters	Setting	Organizations
2	Hospital-Based Care	American Osteopathic Association DNV Healthcare (National Integrated Accreditation for Healthcare Organizations) The Joint Commission
3	Freestanding Ambulatory Care	Accreditation Association for Ambulatory Health Care Commission for the Accreditation of Birth Centers The Joint Commission American Association for Accreditation of Ambulatory Surgery Facilities
4	Managed Care	Accreditation Association for Ambulatory Health Care The Joint Commission National Committee for Quality Assurance
6	Correctional Facilities	American Correctional Association The Joint Commission National Commission on Correctional Health Care
7 and 8	Mental Health and Substance Abuse	Commission on Accreditation of Rehabilitation Facilities The Joint Commission
9	Facilities for Individuals with Intellectual or Developmental Disabilities	Commission on Accreditation of Rehabilitation Facilities Council on Quality and Leadership The Joint Commission
10	Long-Term Care	The Joint Commission
11	Rehabilitation Facilities	Commission on Accreditation of Rehabilitation Facilities The Joint Commission
12	Home Health Care	Community Health Accreditation Program The Joint Commission Accreditation Commission for Health Care, Inc.
13	Hospice	Community Health Accreditation Program The Joint Commission Accreditation Commission for Health Care, Inc.
15	Veterinary	American Animal Hospital Association

Note: This list is not exhaustive.

care organizations meet these standards are conducted by the designated **state agency** for each state.

In addition to administering the federal requirements for participation in Medicare and Medicaid programs, the state agency ordinarily administers applicable state licensure requirements as well. Because the state agency conducts its surveys in accordance with federal guidelines, CMS publishes detailed instructions for state surveyors in its *State Operations Manual (SOM).* The appendices to the *SOM* contain survey forms and other instructions specific to each setting

state agency the agency of the state government responsible for administering the federal requirements for participation in Medicare and Medicaid programs. The state agency is ordinarily charged also with administering applicable licensure requirements for the state.

TABLE 1-3   Selected Appendices from the *State Operations Manual*

Appendix Letter	Description
A	Hospitals
AA	Psychiatric Hospitals
B	Home Health Agencies
E	Outpatient Physical Therapy or Speech Pathology Services-Interpretive Guidelines
G	Rural Health Clinics (RHCs)
H	End-Stage Renal Disease Facilities
J	Intermediate Care Facilities for Persons With Mental Retardation
K	Comprehensive Outpatient Rehabilitation Facilities
L	Ambulatory Surgical Services Interpretive Guidelines and Survey Procedures
M	Hospice
N	Psychiatric Residential Treatment Facilities (PRTF) Interpretive Guidance
P	Survey Protocol for Long-Term Care Facilities
PP	Interpretive Guidelines for Long-Term Care Facilities
R	Resident Assessment Instrument for Long-Term Care Facilities
W	Critical Access Hospitals (CAHs)

Note: This list of appendices is not all-inclusive, but provides examples of different settings for which CMS provides survey guidance. A complete list of appendices is available at http://www.cms.gov/Regulations -and-Guidance/Guidance/Manuals/Downloads/som107Appendicestoc.pdf

deemed status the recognition of a health care provider that is said to meet federal *Conditions of Participation* by virtue of accreditation by a federally approved voluntary accrediting organization. With deemed status, the health care provider's accreditation satisfies the *Conditions of Participation*; routine surveys by the state agency are unnecessary.

Institute of Medicine health division of the National Academy of Sciences. It is an independent, nonprofit organization that serves as a national advisor on matters related to health improvement.

that health information managers may find helpful. Table 1-3 lists selected appendices to the SOM related to some of the settings discussed in this text.

The federal government has granted "deeming" authority to certain voluntary accrediting organizations for some of their programs. This means that a health care provider who is accredited by such an organization is "deemed" to meet the Conditions of Participation and does not have to undergo a separate survey process by the state agency. This concept is known as **deemed status**. For many of the health care settings described in this book, however, deemed status is not available, meaning that if these facilities choose voluntary accreditation, they still are required to undergo regular surveys by the state agency as well.

The Impact of Quality on Health Care

A series of reports published by the **Institute of Medicine** in the early twenty-first century highlighted the prevalence of medical errors and the importance of improving patient safety (Institute of Medicine, 1999, 2001, 2003, 2011,

2012a, 2012b). This heightened awareness triggered a number of initiatives focused upon improving the quality of care delivered in the United States. In 2002, The Joint Commission created a **National Patient Safety Goals (NPSG)** program to help accredited health care institutions focus on specific patient safety concerns (TJC, 2015). In 2005, Congress enacted the Patient Safety and Quality Improvement Act. The final rule was subsequently passed in 2008 and became effective in January 2009. The Act created a voluntary program to promote the sharing of patient safety event information with **patient safety organizations (PSOs)**. Health and Human Services is aggregating and de-identifying the data in order to uncover trends and patterns in patient safety (Viola, Kallem, & Bronnert, 2009).

The **National Quality Forum (NQF)**, a private, not-for-profit organization focused on improving quality through development and endorsement of performance measurement, collaborated with CMS to develop measures for the initial physician quality reporting system. Through a contract with the U.S. Department of Health and Human Services, NQF continues to provide support for improved quality of health care services (Zeman, 2010).

Several additional pieces of legislation subsequently passed, stressing the urgency to reduce medical errors, as well as improve the efficiency and efficacy of care. The Medicare Prescription Drug, Improvement, and Modernization Act of 2003 (MMA), the American Recovery and Reinvestment Act of 2009 (ARRA), and the **Patient Protection and Affordable Care Act (PPACA)** of 2010 call for increased reporting of quality measures by health care providers. Further, each emphasizes the potential role for health information technology and electronic health records in reducing preventable medical errors.

Technological Changes Affecting Health Care

Fragmented health records can lead to medical errors, duplicate testing, and increased costs. It is estimated that electronic health records (EHRs) can improve patient care, reduce medical errors, and provide simultaneous access to patient data, greater security, improved legibility, better communication, and more complete documentation (Shekelle, Morton, & Keeler, 2006; Institute of Medicine, 1991, 1997). Because patients are treated in a variety of settings, health care professionals have recognized the need for a **longitudinal patient record** to maintain health care information throughout the patient's life. Within a given enterprise (which can range from a single facility to a complex integrated health care delivery system), electronic data can be stored in a clinical data repository (CDR). Access to the data in the CDR can be structured to provide clinicians with a view of the patient's data over time through a single point of entry (Soule, 2001).

Although this technology produces a longitudinal view of data within the enterprise, lack of data from providers outside of the enterprise prevents such a system from maintaining a complete lifetime view of patient data. Groups ranging from the Institute of Medicine to the U.S. General Accounting Office have

National Patient Safety Goals (NPSG) a program created by The Joint Commission in 2002 to help accredited health care institutions focus on specific patient safety concerns. In an effort to focus on the most critical patient safety issues, NPSGs are updated annually based upon review of literature and available databases.

patient safety organizations (PSOs) "organizations that can work with clinicians and health care organizations to identify, analyze, and reduce the risks and hazards associated with patient care" (AHRQ, online).

National Quality Forum (NQF) a private, nonprofit, membership organization focused on improving the quality of care through national goal setting, development and endorsement of performance measurement standards, and educational initiatives.

Patient Protection and Affordable Care Act (PPACA) a federal statute signed into law on March 23, 2010, as Public Law 111-148. PPACA contains a number of health care provisions, most notably an expansion of Medicaid eligibility requirements.

longitudinal patient record documentation of a patient's health status, conditions, and treatments throughout his or her life and across multiple facilities, providers, and health care encounters.

health information
technology (HIT)
electronic health records
and related information
systems to manage health
care processes. The major
focus of the HITECH Act
of 2009 is to promote
adoption of HIT in an
effort to improve the
quality, efficiency, and
safety of health care
delivery while reduc-
ing costs and minimizing
medical errors.

Office of the National
Coordinator for Health
Information Technology
(ONC)   "the principal
Federal entity charged
with coordination of
nationwide efforts to
implement and use the
most advanced health in-
formation technology and
the electronic exchange
of health information.

Nationwide Health
Information Network
(NwHIN)   "is broadly
defined as the set of
standards, specifications
and policies that enable
the secure exchange of
health information over
the Internet. This program
provides a foundation for
the exchange of health
information across diverse
entities, within communi-
ties and across the coun-
try, helping to achieve the
goals of the HITECH Act."
(HealthIT.gov, n.d.)

health information
exchange (HIE)
a process defined as "the
electronic movement of
health-related informa-
tion among organizations
according to nationally
recognized standards"
(NAHIT, 2008, p. 6).

HIE organization   an
entity that "oversees and
governs the exchange of
health-related informa-
tion among organizations
according to nationally
recognized standards"
(NAHIT, 2008, p. 6).

emphasized improvements in the quality of patient care, patient safety, and cost savings that could be achieved through implementation of information technology. The information technology goal for most health care organizations is to achieve an electronic health record (EHR) that goes beyond merely storing and retrieving data in a repository. EHRs that include capabilities such as generating clinical alerts and reminders and furnishing readily available decision support can provide patient care benefits in all health care settings.

The IOM first called for adoption of electronic health records in 1991 in its landmark publication, *The Computer-Based Patient Record: An Essential Technology for Health Care* (Institute of Medicine, 1991). The Institute's subsequent reports (1999, 2001, 2003, 2011, 2012a, 2012b) addressing patient safety concerns prompted the federal government to launch a **health information technology (HIT)** adoption initiative in 2004 that envisioned electronic health records (EHRs) for all Americans by the year 2014.

The **Office of the National Coordinator for Health Information Technology (ONC)** was established in 2005 to promote HIT adoption and guide the development of a **Nationwide Health Information Network (NwHIN)**. Using a shared architecture, the network would facilitate interoperable standards for the health information exchange (HIE) of data and communication among health care providers, payers, government, and consumers (Amatayakul, 2013).

In 2009, the American Recovery and Reinvestment Act (ARRA), was passed, which included numerous programs and incentives promoting HIT adoption. Title XII of ARRA, subtitled Health Information Technology for Economic and Clinical Health Act (HITECH), contains many of the provisions required to advance development of the NwHIN and health information exchange. In addition to the HIT adoption incentive program, ARRA provided billions of dollars to fund health IT, standards development initiatives, training and workforce development, broadband expansion, and additional requirements for health information exchange (Blumenthal, 2010).

Health information exchange (HIE) is a process that has been defined as "the electronic movement of health-related information among organizations according to nationally recognized standards" (NAHIT, 2008, p. 6). An **HIE organization** "oversees and governs the exchange of health-related information among organizations according to nationally recognized standards" (p. 6). This term has been used synonymously with **regional health information organization (RHIO)**, which is a "health information organization that brings together health care stakeholders within a defined geographic area and governs health information exchange among them for the purpose of improving health and care in that community" (p. 6). In recent years, the term "HIE" has come to mean both the process and the organization. Today, most such organizations refer to themselves as HIEs rather than RHIOs.

ARRA allocated $564 million to support state programs in the development of HIE within their geographic regions. Further, ARRA directed the ONC to establish up to 70 Health IT Regional Extension Centers (RECs) to provide technology assistance to health care providers in the adoption and meaningful use of HIT (Blumenthal, 2010; Dennis, 2010).

A key component of the NwHIN is a focus on consumers, as patients today are more empowered and actively involved in their health care than ever before. Personal health records (PHRs) enable consumers to track data related to their own health. According to the Markle Foundation, a personal health record (PHR) is "an Internet-based set of tools that allows people to access and coordinate their lifelong health information and make appropriate parts of it available to those who need it" (Markle Foundation, 2003, pp. 2–3). The Markle Foundation goes on to describe the following attributes of a PHR:

- Each person controls his or her own PHR. Individuals decide which parts of their PHR can be accessed, by whom, and for how long.
- PHRs contain information from one's entire lifetime.
- PHRs contain information from all health care providers.
- PHRs are accessible from any place at any time.
- PHRs are private and secure.
- PHRs are "transparent." Individuals can see who entered each piece of data, where it was transferred from, and who has viewed it.
- PHRs permit easy exchange of information with other health information systems and health professionals.

Is there any relationship between an EHR and a PHR? An EHR can contribute toward a PHR in that some EHRs provide personal health record capabilities that allow patients to view their own information and to communicate with their health care providers (Soule, 2001).

Private companies, such as Apple, Google, and Microsoft, are continuing to actively research PHR technology and introduce health tracking technology and devices to the marketplace. These proprietary devices collect and track an individual's health status information. Integration with EHRs and the NwHIN is actively under development, and collaborations with academic medical centers and payers is forthcoming.

These technological advances offer expanded career opportunities to the health information management professional. Expertise in the areas of privacy, security, health care standards, and management of electronic health information will be required to achieve health information exchange.

Other Issues Affecting the Delivery of Health Care

Social, political, and technological factors have all contributed to changes in health care delivery. For example, another change that is occurring in health care is a shift from independent institutions and practitioners to networks of health care providers. Hospitals, physicians, and other health care providers have joined

regional health information organization (RHIO) a "health information organization that brings together health care stakeholders within a defined geographic area and governs health information exchange among them for the purpose of improving health and care in that community" (NAHIT, 2008, p. 6). See also HIE organization.

Regional Extension Centers (RECs) nonprofit organizations called for by ARRA and initially funded by federal grants to provide health information technology support to providers. RECs offer technical assistance, guidance, and support to help providers become meaningful users of certified electronic health record technology.

together to provide the broad range of services necessary to meet the expectations of the various types of health care plans currently available.

Technological advances in care delivery have also had an important impact on health care services. As technology has improved, it has become possible to provide in other settings treatment that once required days or weeks of hospital inpatient care. Patients undergo procedures in ambulatory surgery centers and go home after a short (4- to 6-hour) waiting period, thus avoiding costs associated with an overnight stay in a hospital. Other treatments once provided only in hospitals are now provided to patients in home and community based settings, bringing health care practitioners and equipment to the patient rather than transporting the patient to a health care facility.

telemedicine   the practice of medicine in which a patient is generally in a remote location and receives medical care in real-time via an audio-visual connection with a provider located off-site and directly by a provider at that location.

With the advent of **telemedicine**, patients and clinicians separated by hundreds of miles can interact with one another by electronic means. In a real-time telemedicine session, the patient is generally in a remote location from the physician and receives medical care remotely via an audio-visual connection with a provider located off-site while also being seen by a clinician (for example, a clinical nurse practitioner or a physician of another specialty) at the patient's location. Store-and-forward telemedicine is another type of telemedicine service in which medical information is captured electronically and transmitted to a remote site for a health care provider to review, analyze, or report at a later time rather than in real-time.

telehealth   "includes such technologies as telephones, facsimile machines, electronic mail systems, and remote patient monitoring devices, which are used to collect and transmit patient data for monitoring and interpretation" (Telemedicine, n.d.).

telesurgery   the use of robotic technology to assist with or perform procedures remotely.

Use of technologies and devices to remotely monitor a patient's condition is referred to as **telehealth** (Telemedicine, n.d.). Other examples of telehealth services are remote physiological monitoring and medication adherence remote monitoring. **Telesurgery** involves use of robotic technology to assist with or perform procedures remotely (Sterbis et al., 2008). The advantages of using these technologies include "reduced costs, increased patient access to providers, improved quality and continuity of care, and more convenience to the patient" (Majerowicz & Tracy, 2010, p. 53). This technology, however, presents new challenges in health information management with regard to confidentiality and security of information, maintenance of appropriate licensure and regulatory requirements, and reimbursement.

patient-centered medical home model   a care model in which the primary care physician acts as a "gatekeeper" to coordinate the patient's care across providers. It addresses preventive, acute, and chronic care needs and also provides patients with access to electronic tools such as provider-patient e-mail, online appointment scheduling applications, and electronic health record data.

The **patient-centered medical home model** was developed in an effort to better coordinate care across the continuum. Under this model, the primary care physician acts as a "gatekeeper" to coordinate the patient's care across providers. It addresses preventive, acute, and chronic care needs (Dimick, 2008). The Patient Protection and Affordable Care Act (PPACA) or the Affordable Care Act (ACA) calls for use of the medical home model and extension of telehealth services to improve health outcomes (Patient Protection and Affordable Care Act, 2010). The Health Reform Act also requires increased quality reporting requirements for health care providers, which impact the health information manager's role.

In addition to technological trends, changes in society are affecting health care providers. The average age of the U.S. population is increasing, and a growing number of Americans are suffering from chronic diseases and illnesses associated with advancing age. Long-term care facilities, home health agencies, hospices, and dialysis facilities care for patients with chronic and sometimes terminal diseases. Elderly and younger patients alike benefit from services provided by rehabilitation facilities and mental health services. Individuals with addictive behaviors can find help in substance abuse treatment facilities. The large prison population in the United States creates a demand for health care services in correctional institutions. Good health information management practices are valuable in the care of all of these special populations.

1. Name the Act that implemented the Medicare and Medicaid incentive program for the electronic health record.

2. True or False? The Medicare Prospective Payment System applies only to the hospital inpatient.

3. True or False? The privacy rule permits an individual to access or amend personal health information.

4. Name three ways in which an organization can minimize security risks to its information system.

5. Which one of the following is required by the State for a health care organization to provide care?
   a. accreditation
   b. licensure

6. Health care organizations that desire to participate in federal programs must be Medicare-certified, which means that they have met the standards set forth in the
   a. Joint Commission Accreditation Standards
   b. Medicare Guidelines
   c. State licensure and certification requirements
   d. Conditions of Participation or Conditions for Coverage

7. Which office in the federal government is charged with promoting the adoption of health information technology and guides the development of a nationwide health information network?
   a. Office of Health Information Technology
   b. Office of the National Coordinator for Health Information Technology
   c. Office of the Coordinator of the Electronic Health Record
   d. National Institute of Medicine and Technology

8. Explain the relationship between an electronic health record and a personal health record.

9. What is the patient-centered medical home model?

10. Name five health care settings, other than hospitals, that can benefit from good health information management practices.

IMPACT ON THE ROLE OF THE HEALTH INFORMATION MANAGER

Regulatory, technological, and social changes have affected the role of the health information manager. Although the profession of **health information management (HIM)** originated in the acute care hospital setting, the shift from inpatient to other care settings has expanded opportunities for health information managers beyond this traditional role. In the acute care setting, the skills of the health information manager are vital, because quality information is more important than ever to the hospital. In today's hospital, health information managers can be found working in the emergency department coordinating the collection of trauma data, in clinical areas developing documentation improvement programs, in administration working with quality reporting systems or overseeing revenue cycle processes, as well as in traditional HIM roles.

Responsibilities in the more traditional roles also are transitioning to management of a "virtual department." The electronic health record has removed the physical boundaries from the HIM department, allowing many employees to work from home or remote sites. Although many acute care facilities have reduced the ranks of middle managers, many excellent opportunities are still available in the acute care setting for those who possess the data analysis and information management skills to help a hospital thrive in this increasingly data-driven health care environment. The greatest growth in employment opportunities for health information managers, however, is occurring outside of the purely acute care setting.

Although HIM professionals always have been valued for their expertise in data analytics, the accelerated adoption of EHRs and other systems that electronically generate data create further opportunities for more in-depth analysis. HIM practitioners continually utilize analytical techniques and visualization tools to enhance executive and clinical decision-making. Government initiatives, contemporary payment models and a growing emphasis on population health will further increase demands for data analytics skills. HIM practitioners must adapt their competencies continually to stay abreast of workforce requirements (Sandefer et al., 2014).

As stated earlier, other issues affecting health care delivery, such as changing patient demographics and societal factors, have increased the number of persons needing certain types of health care services (e.g., long-term care, care in correctional facilities). Health information managers currently are being employed in an ever-widening array of health care facilities. Skills of the health information manager are valuable in ambulatory care facilities, health maintenance organizations, home health care agencies, hospices, dialysis facilities, long-term care facilities, rehabilitation organizations, facilities for persons with intellectual or developmental disabilities, mental health facilities, treatment centers for substance abuse, correctional facilities, dental clinics, veterinary hospitals,

health information management (HIM) "the practice of acquiring, analyzing, and protecting digital and traditional medical information vital to providing quality patient care" (AHIMA, n.d.).

and cancer registries. Health care providers in a wide variety of settings look to health information managers for expertise as employees or as consultants.

Resources for HIM professionals interested in developing and maintaining skills in diverse practice arenas may be found in the Engage online communities sponsored by AHIMA. The online communities provide a forum for information sharing among health information professionals with specialized interests. The communities are dynamic—new communities may be created and inactive communities may be dissolved in response to the needs of the participants. AHIMA members can access the Engage communities at AHIMA's website. The knowledge and talents of health information managers will continue to be needed in the vast assortment of individual provider settings and to the health care system as a whole, in light of the growing need for high-quality patient information that is accessible in a secure and confidential manner within and across settings.

SELF REVIEW 1.3

1. Provide an example of how the role of a health information manager in a traditional hospital setting is changing as the result of technological changes in health care.

2. How have changing patient demographics and societal factors affected employment opportunities for health information managers?

SUMMARY

Health care in the United States, which underwent drastic changes in the twentieth century, has continued its evolution in the new millennium. The hospital industry flourished as medical science and technology made strides in improving patient care. As health care costs increasingly became a public concern, the health care field became more diverse, with a much broader range of care settings available to the patient.

Changes in the health care field have affected the profession of health information management, adding more opportunities for employment and diversifying the field. The health information manager's skills in data collection, retrieval, analysis, and reporting, as well as technical skills in information technology, which have long been appreciated in the inpatient setting, are now needed and valued in other settings as well. Changes in reimbursement methodologies, the regulatory environment, patient care delivery, information technology, relationships among health care providers, and in society in general have affected health care and the role of the health information manager. The result has been that additional employment and consulting opportunities are available to health information managers today that did not exist in the past.

REVIEW QUESTIONS

Knowledge-Based Questions

1. What are some of the changes that have affected hospitals during the twentieth and twenty-first centuries?
2. How have payment issues affected health care delivery?
3. What is fee-for-service payment?
4. What is a per diem payment?
5. What is pay-for-performance?
6. As a general rule, what is the basis for payment in a health maintenance organization?
7. Explain the administrative simplification provisions of HIPAA.
8. What is the patient-centered medical home model?
9. What impact have the changes in health care had on the health information manager?
10. Into what health care settings other than hospitals have health information managers moved?

Critical Thinking Questions

1. How can the health information manager contribute to improved data quality in a variety of settings?
2. What are some common concerns with regard to health information management in health information exchange, telemedicine, and the longitudinal patient record.
3. Select a health care setting other than a hospital. What would you expect the similarities to be between the role of the health information manager in a hospital and in one of the other health care settings? What would you expect the differences to be?

WEB ACTIVITY

Visit The Joint Commission's website at http://www.jointcommission.org

1. Search for a fact sheet on the "tracer methodology" used by surveyors in The Joint Commission site visit process. Describe how the tracer methodology works and what its impact might be on health information management.
2. Search for information on *deemed status*. Give examples of Joint Commission programs that offer federal deemed status options?

CASE STUDY

Kerry Kaiser, RHIA, is Getwell Hospital's HIPAA privacy officer and the chair of its HIPAA Compliance Committee. The committee is concerned with all aspects of HIPAA compliance, including transactions, privacy, and security.

1. What items might the committee's agenda include in each of these three areas?
2. Where might Kerry find resources to assist the committee in carrying out its duties?

REFERENCES AND SUGGESTED READINGS

Administrative Requirements, 45 C.F.R. pt. 162 (2009).

AHRQ Agency for Healthcare Research and Quality. 2010. *Patient Safety and Quality Improvement Act of 2005 (Patient Safety Act): An Overview*. [Online] http://www.pso.ahrq.gov/regulations/regulations .htm [2010, May 31].

Amatayakul, M. K. (2013). *Electronic health records: A practical guide for professionals and organizations* (5th ed.). Chicago: American Health Information Management Association.

ACS (American College of Surgeons). n.d.. About ACS [Online]. https://www.facs.org/about-acs [2015, July 7].

AHIMA (American Health Information Management Association). (1997). (Fletcher, D. M., author). *Issue: Telemedical Records* [practice brief]. [From *Journal of the American Health Information Management Association, 68*(4).]

AHIMA (American Health Information Management Association). (2010a). Practice brief: Guidance for clinical documentation improvement programs. *Journal of AHIMA, 81*(5), 45–50.

AHIMA (American Health Information Management Association). (2010b). Meaningful use: Provider requirements. *Meaningful Use White Paper Series*, http://www.ahima.org/arra/documents/Paperno2-MeaningfulUse-ProviderRequirements.pdf [2010, May 12].

AHIMA (American Health Information Management Association). (2010c). *Health Care Reform and Health IT Stimulus: ARRA and HITECH* [Online]. http://www.ahima.org/arra/ [2010, May 12].

AHIMA (American Health Information Management Association). n.d.. What is Health Information? [Online]. http://www.ahima.org/careers/healthinfo?tabid=what [2015, July 7].

Asmonga, D. (2009). ARRA opportunities and omissions: New legislation seeks to jumpstart health IT, but issues remain. *Journal of the American Health Information Management Association, 80*(5), 16–18.

Blumenthal, D. (2010). Launching HITECH. *New England Journal of Medicine, 362*(5), 382–385.

Casto, A. B., & Forrestal, E. (2013). *Principles of healthcare reimbursement* (4th ed.). Chicago: AHIMA.

CMS (Centers for Medicare & Medicaid Services). (2013a). *Medicare program: General information* [Online]. *http://www.cms.gov/MedicareGenInfo/* [2014, June 4].

CMS (Centers for Medicare & Medicaid Services). (2013b). Medicaid Integrity Program: General information [Online]. *http://www.cms.gov/MedicaidIntegrityProgram/* [2014, June 9].

CMS (Centers for Medicare & Medicaid Services). (2013c). Benefit integrity (Chapter 4). *Medicare Program Integrity Manual.* http://www.cms.gov/Regulations-and-Guidance/Guidance/Manuals/downloads/pim83c04.pdf [2014, June 9].

CMS (Centers for Medicare & Medicaid Services). (2013d). *Quality improvement organizations* [Online]. http://www.cms.gov/QualityImprovementOrgs/ [2014, June 9].

CMS (Centers for Medicare & Medicaid Services). (2014a). CMS launches next phase of new Quality Improvement Program [Online]. http://www.cms.gov/Newsroom/MediaReleaseDatabase/Press-releases/2014-Press-releases-items/2014-07-18.html [2015, July 7].

CMS (Centers for Medicare & Medicaid Services). (2014b). EHR Incentive Programs [Online]. *http://www.cms.gov/Regulations-and-Guidance/Legislation/EHRIncentivePrograms/index.html* [2014, June 10].

CMS (Centers for Medicare & Medicaid Services). (2014c). Quality Improvement Organizations [Online]. *https://www.cms.gov/Medicare/Quality-Initiatives-Patient-Assessment-Instrments/QualityImprovementOrgs/index.html?redirect=/QualityImprovementOrgs/* [2015, July 7].

CMS (Centers for Medicare & Medicaid Services). (2015a). *Medicare and you: 2015* [Online]. http://www.medicare.gov/publications/pubs/pdf/10050.pdf [2015, July 7].

CMS (Centers for Medicare & Medicaid Services). (2015b). *Physician fee schedule.* [Online]. http://www.cms.gov/PhysicianFeeSched/ [2015, July 7].

CMS (Centers for Medicare & Medicaid Services). n.d.a. *Children's Health Insurance Program (CHIP)* [Online]. *http://www.medicaid.gov/CHIP/CHIP-Program-Information.html* [2014, June 9].

CMS (Centers for Medicare & Medicaid Services). n.d.b. *The Affordable Care Act: Helping providers help patients—a menu of options for improving care* [Online]. *http://www.cms.gov/Medicare/Medicare-Fee-for-Service-Payment/ACO/downloads/ACO-Menu-Of-Options.pdf* [2014, November 29].

CMS (Centers for Medicare & Medicaid Services). n.d.c. Innovation Center. http://innovation.cms.gov/About/index.html [2014, June 11].

CMS (Centers for Medicare & Medicaid Services). n.d.d. Prospective Payment Systems – General Information. *http://www.cms.gov/Medicare/Medicare-Fee-for-Service-Payment/ProspMedicareFeeSvcPmtGen/index.html?redirect=/ProspMedicareFeeSvcPmtGen* [2015, July 7]

CMS QualityNet. n.d.a.. Hospital Value-Based Purchasing Overview. [Online]. *http://www.qualitynet.org* [2014, June 11].

CMS QualityNet. n.d.b. Physician Quality Reporting System. [Online]. *http://www.qualitynet.org* [2014, June 4].

Dennis, J. C. (2010). *Privacy: The impact of ARRA, HITECH, and other policy initiatives.* Chicago: AHIMA.

DHHS (U.S. Department of Health and Human Services). *Federal Register.* Vol. 74, No. 11. (January 16, 2009). 45 CFR pt. 162. HIPAA Administrative Simplification: Modifications to Medical Data Code Set Standards to Adopt ICD–10–CM and

ICD–10–PCS Final rule [Online]. http://edocket.access.gpo.gov/2009/pdf/E9-743.pdf [2010, May 12].

DHHS (U.S. Department of Health and Human Services). *Federal Register, 76* (212). (November 2, 2011). 42 CFR pt. 425. Medicare Program; Medicare Shared Savings Program: Accountable Care Organizations Final rule [Online]. http://www.gpo.gov/fdsys/pkg/FR-2011-11-02/pdf/2011-27461.pdf [2014, June 11].

DHHS (U.S. Department of Health and Human Services). *Federal Register, 78*(17). (January 25, 2013). 45 CFR pts. 160 & 164. Modifications to the HIPAA Privacy, Security, Enforcement, and Breach Notification Rules Under the Health Information Technology for Economic and Clinical Health Act and the Genetic Information Nondiscrimination Act; Other Modifications to the HIPAA Rules; Final Rule [Online]. http://www.gpo.gov/fdsys/pkg/FR-2013-01-25/pdf/2013-01073.pdf [2014, November 29].

DHHS (U.S. Department of Health and Human Services). *Federal Register, 79*(149). (August 4, 2014). 45 CFR pt. 162. Administrative Simplification: Change to the Compliance Date for the International Classification of Diseases, 10th Revision (ICD–10–CM and ICD–10–PCS) Medical Data Code Sets; Final Rule [Online]. http://www.gpo.gov/fdsys/pkg/FR-2014-08-04/pdf/2014-18347.pdf [2014, November 29].

Dimick, C. (2008). Home sweet home: Can a new care model save family medicine? *Journal of the American Health Information Management Association, 79*(8), 24–8.

Dimick, C. (2010). The year of the audit. *Journal of the American Health Information Management Association, 81*(3), 22–25, 64.

Gentul, M. K., & Davis, N. A. (2011). Structure and organization of the coding function. In L. A. Schraffenberger & L. Kuehn (Eds.), *Effective management of coding services: The clinical coding manager's handbook* (pp. 3–51). Chicago: AHIMA.

HealthIT.gov. n.d. [Online]. http://www.healthit.gov/ [2014, November 29].

How do Medicare Advantage Plans work? n.d. [Online]. http://www.medicare.gov/sign-up-change-plans/medicare-health-plans/medicare-advantage-plans/how-medicare-advantage-plans-work.html [2014, June 4].

Institute of Medicine. (1991). R. S. Dick & E. B. Steen (Eds.). *The computer-based patient record: An essential technology for health care.* Washington, DC: National Academy Press.

Institute of Medicine. (1997). R. S. Dick, E. B. Steen, & D. E. Detmer (Eds.). *The computer-based patient record: An essential technology for health care* (Rev. ed.). Washington, DC: National Academy Press.

Institute of Medicine. (1999). *To err is human: Building a safer health system.* Washington, DC: National Academy Press.

Institute of Medicine. (2001). *Crossing the quality chasm: A new health system for the 21st century.* Washington, DC: National Academy Press.

Institute of Medicine. (2003). *Patient safety: Achieving a new standard for care.* Washington, DC: National Academies Press.

Institute of Medicine. (2011). *Health IT and patient safety: Building safer systems for better care.* Washington, DC: National Academies Press.

Institute of Medicine. (2012a). *How can health care organizations become more health literate? Workshop summary.* Washington, DC: National Academies Press.

Institute of Medicine. (2012b). *Facilitating state health exchange communication through the use of health literate practices: Workshop summary.* Washington, DC: National Academies Press. Joint Commission. 2015. *2015 National Patient Safety Goals* [Online]. http://www.jointcommission.org/standards_information/npsgs.aspx [2015, July 7].

Kaiser Permanente. n.d.. *Kaiser Permanente: More than 60 years of quality* [Online]. http://xnet.kp.org/newscenter/aboutkp/historyofkp.html [2014, June 9].

Klees, B. S., Wolfe, C. J., & Curtis, C. A. (2012). *Brief summaries of Medicare & Medicaid: Title XVIII and Title XIX of the Social Security Act.* Baltimore: Centers for Medicare & Medicaid Services. [Online]. http://www.cms.gov/Research-Statistics-Data-and-Systems/Statistics-Trends-and-Reports/MedicareProgramRatesStats/downloads/MedicareMedicaidSummaries2012.pdf [2014, June 9].

Litman, T., & Robins, L. (1991). *Health politics and policy* (2nd ed.). Clifton Park, NY: Delmar Cengage Learning.

Majerowicz, A. & Tracy, S. (2010). Telemedicine: Bridging gaps in healthcare delivery. *Journal of the American Health Information Management Association, 81*(5): 52–53, 56.

Markle Foundation. (2003, July 1). *The personal health working group: Final report* [Online]. http://www.connectingforhealth.org/resources/final_phwg_report1.pdf [2010, June 3].

Miaoulis, W. M. (2010). Access, use, and disclosure: HITECH's impact on the HIPAA touchstones. *Journal of AHIMA, 81*(3), 38–39, 64.

Moynihan, J. (2010). Preparing for 5010: Internal testing of HIPAA transaction upgrades recommended by December 31. *Journal of the American Health Information Management Association, 81*(1), 23–26.

NAHIT (National Alliance for Health Information Technology). (2008, April 28). *Report to the Office of the National Coordinator on defining key health information technology terms* [Online]. http://healthit.hhs.gov/portal/server.pt/gateway/PTARGS_0_10741_848133_0_0_18/10_2_hit_terms.pdf [2010, May 14].

ONC. n.d. Office of the National Coordinator for Health Information Technology. *Guide to privacy and security of health information.* Version 1.2 060112 [Online]. http://www.healthit.gov/sites/default/files/pdf/privacy/privacy-and-security-guide-chapter-4.pdf [2014, November 29].

Patient Protection and Affordable Care Act of 2010, Pub. L. No. 111-148 (March 23, 2010).

Rhodes, H., & Rode, D. (2010). ARRA on the job: HIPAA too. *Journal of the American Health Information Management Association, 81*(1), 38–39.

Sandefer, R. H, DeAlmeida, D. R, Dougherty, M., Mancilla, D., & Marc, D. T. (2014). Keeping current in the electronic era: Data age transforming HIM's mandatory workforce competencies. *Journal of AHIMA, 85*(11), 38–44.

Security and Privacy. (2009). 45 C.F.R. pt. 164.

Shekelle, P. G., Morton, S. C., & Keeler, E. B. 2006, April. *Costs and benefits of health information technology* (AHRQ Publication No. 06-E006). Rockville, MD: Agency for Healthcare Research and Quality.

Soule, D. (2001). What's new in clinical data repositories? *Journal of the American Health Information Management Association, 72*(10), 35–39.

Standards for Electronic Transactions. (2000, August 17). *Federal Register*, pp. 50311–50373.

Standards for Privacy of Individually Identifiable Health Information; Final Rule. (2000, December 28). *Federal Register*, pp. 82461–82829.

Sterbis, J. R., Hanly, E. J., Herman, B. C., Marohn, M. R., Broderick, T. J., Shih, S. P., Harnett, B., Doarn, C., & Schenkman, N. S. (2008). Transcontinental telesurgical nephrectomy using the da Vinci Robot in a porcine model. *Urology, 71*(5), 971–973.

Telemedicine. n.d. [Online]. http://www.medicaid.gov/Medicaid-CHIP-Program-Information/By-Topics/Delivery-Systems/Telemedicine.html [2015, July 7]

U.S. Department of Health and Human Services. *See* DHHS.

Viola, A. F., Kallem, C., & Bronnert, J. (2009). A next act for patient safety: Previewing the Patient Safety and Quality Improvement Final Rule. *Journal of the American Health Information Management Association, 80*(4), 30–35.

Zeman, V. L. (2010). Clinical quality management. In K. M. LaTour & S. E. Maki (Eds.), *Health information management: Concepts, principles, and practice* (3rd ed., pp. 517–558). Chicago: AHIMA.

KEY RESOURCES

American College of Surgeons
http://www.facs.org

American Health Information Management Association
http://www.ahima.org

The Carnegie Foundation for the Advancement of Teaching
http://www.carnegiefoundation.org

Centers for Medicare & Medicaid Services (CMS)
http://www.cms.gov
http://www.medicare.gov (for beneficiary questions about Medicare)

Code of Federal Regulations
http://www.ecfr.gov

Commission on Accreditation of Rehabilitation Facilities
http://www.carf.org

DNV Healthcare, Inc.
http://www.dnvaccreditation.com

Federal Register
http://www. ecfr.gov

Healthcare Information and Management Systems Society (HIMSS)
http://www.himss.org

National Quality Forum
http://www.qualityforum.org

Office of the National Coordinator for Health Information Technology (ONC)
http://healthit.gov

The Joint Commission
http://www.jointcommission.org

SECTION 2 Acute, Ambulatory, and Managed Care

CHAPTER 2

Hospital-Based Care

Angela L. Morey, MSM, RHIA, CPHIMS | Leigh T. Williams, MHIIM, RHIA, CPC, CPHIMS | Ann H. Peden, PhD, RHIA, CCS | Sonya D. Beard, MSEd, RHIA

LEARNING OBJECTIVES

Upon successful completion of this chapter, you should be able to:

- Define "hospital" and describe types of hospital settings.
- Describe types of care provided by hospitals.
- Explain regulatory and accreditation standards that apply to hospital-based care.
- Discuss documentation issues in hospital-based care.
- Describe reimbursement methods for hospital-based care.
- Identify coding and classification systems used in hospital-based care.
- Describe data sets utilized for hospital-based care.
- Cite factors in avoiding legal risk in hospital-based care.
- Define roles of the health information management professional in hospital-based care.

Setting	Description	Synonyms
Examples of Hospital Inpatient Settings		
Hospital Inpatient Unit	An organizational unit of a hospital providing room, board, and continuous general nursing service in an area of the hospital where patients generally stay overnight (Glondys, 2000)	Ward; Nursing Unit
Intensive Care Unit	"A hospital patient care unit for patients with life-threatening conditions who require intensive treatment and continuous monitoring" (Slee, Slee, & Schmidt, 2008, p. 305)	ICU
Examples of Hospital Outpatient Settings		
Hospital Outpatient Unit	An organizational unit of a hospital providing health services to patients who are generally ambulatory and who are not currently inpatients (Glondys, 2000)	Outpatient Department
Hospital Outpatient Clinic	A type of hospital outpatient unit generally organized based on the clinical specialty of the care providers or the types of services needed by the patients (Glondys, 2000)	Clinic
Hospital Emergency Unit	An organizational unit providing medical services needed on an urgent or emergency basis (Glondys, 2000)	Emergency Department
Hospital Observation Unit	An organizational unit for monitoring unstable patients and assessing whether or not they require inpatient admission	Observation Services
Hospital Ambulatory Surgery Unit	An organizational unit for performing elective surgical procedures on patients who generally do not stay at the hospital overnight	Ambulatory Surgery Department
Partial Hospitalization Unit	An organizational unit providing services to behavioral health patients who spend part of the day or night in the hospital setting	Partial Hospitalization Services
Hospital-Based Long-Term Acute Care		
Long-Term Acute Care Hospital	A facility providing specialized acute care for patients averaging a length of stay of 25 days or more	Long-Term Care Hospital LTAC, LTCH, or LTACH

INTRODUCTION TO SETTINGS

In the twenty-first century, the role of hospitals has expanded from provision of short-term acute care to include a wide array of services. For example, some hospitals offer ambulatory services in multiple specialty clinics, and others specialize in long-term acute care. Some hospitals provide extensive, high-level trauma services on-site, whereas others offer telemedicine services to connect to distant specialists. To discuss every possible type of hospital care could fill several volumes, so this chapter will focus on three broad categories of care: hospital-based ambulatory care, hospital inpatient care, and long-term acute care.

Types of Settings

A hospital is a "healthcare institution that has an organized professional staff and medical staff, and inpatient facilities, and which provides medical, nursing, and related services" (Slee, Slee, & Schmidt, 2008, p. 270). According to the American Hospital Association (AHA, 2013), a hospital must maintain at least six inpatient beds, and care must be readily available for the patients who stay an average of 24 hours or more per admission. Health care services provided to patients in a hospital can be categorized as either inpatient (acute care) or outpatient (ambulatory care). Inpatient care consists of health care services, room and board, and continuous nursing care provided to a patient in a hospital unit. Outpatient care includes health care services provided in a hospital-based clinic or department that is not dedicated as an acute care unit (Odom-Wesley, 2009). Long-term acute care is provided in a hospital setting where the patient length of stay is 25 days or longer, on average.

Inpatient Short-Term, Acute Care

Inpatient short-term acute care is the type of care generally associated with hospitals. Patients who are in need of around-the-clock acute care are admitted as hospital inpatients upon the order of a physician. Hospitals may be general hospitals or they may be specialty hospitals focusing on certain types of services, illnesses, or specific types of patients (e.g., pediatric hospitals). Hospitals provide a comprehensive range of services to patients who are acutely ill. Patients are discharged when their conditions are stable and further recuperation can continue in a less acute setting. In U.S. hospitals in 2011, the average length of stay was 5.4 days (AHA, 2013).

Hospital-Based Ambulatory Care

ambulatory surgery (also called "same-day" surgery) surgery in which it is planned that the patient will arrive at the facility, have surgery, recover from any anesthesia, and be ready for discharge in a single day, thus avoiding an overnight stay in the health care facility.

Hospital-based **ambulatory surgery** began developing in hospitals during the 1970s and grew rapidly in subsequent years as advances in technology enabled health care providers to perform many types of surgery on an ambulatory basis, which once could be performed only on an inpatient basis. Actually, third-party payers reimburse certain surgical procedures only when performed in the ambulatory setting (unless a patient's condition makes ambulatory surgery unsafe) (Lawrence & Jonas, 1990).

Another type of ambulatory care that hospitals have provided since the late 1800s is the hospital clinic. Early hospital clinics offered care for the poor, which also provided an educational experience for physicians-in-training. With the advent of Medicare and Medicaid, most clinic visits now are reimbursed, but this was not always the case before implementation of these federal programs (Lawrence & Jonas, 1990). Many hospitals still facilitate the teaching function of the clinics by organizing their clinics according to medical specialty.

An additional type of ambulatory service provided by hospitals is emergency care. Most hospitals have an organized emergency department (ED) with a wide range of services. The emergency department may be staffed as a trauma center, the first area in which an acutely ill patient is treated before hospitalization. Many patients, however, use the emergency department as an ambulatory care service.

For example, a physician may see his or her private patients in the emergency department to evaluate an acute condition or a trauma outside of normal office hours. Other patients present themselves in the emergency department for treatment as outpatients when a primary care physician is not available to them (Lawrence & Jonas, 1990). Emergency department visits in the United States account for a substantial source of medical care, with more than 131 million total ED visits occurring in 2011 (HCUPnet, 2011).

One type of outpatient setting that largely resembles the inpatient setting is that of hospital **observation services**. Observation services may be provided in a regular inpatient unit or in a designated observation unit. According to Medicare, observation services are "furnished by a hospital on the hospital's premises, including use of a bed and periodic monitoring by a hospital's nursing or other staff, which are reasonable and necessary to evaluate an outpatient's condition or determine the need for a possible admission to the hospital as an inpatient" (CMS Manual System, 2004, Sept. 10, p. 2).

The physician should determine whether the patient meets criteria for admission as an inpatient within a 24-hour timeframe. Some payers have strict rules limiting observation care to 23 hours and 59 minutes, whereas other payers have no strictly enforced limits on observation care. If an observation patient is not admitted to an inpatient status, arrangements are made for care in another setting, the patient is discharged or transferred, and the stay is counted and billed as an outpatient encounter.

A **partial hospitalization program (PHP)** is another type of hospital outpatient program. Medicare defines partial hospitalization as "a distinct and organized intensive treatment program for patients who would otherwise require inpatient psychiatric care" (CMS Manual System, 2004, May 7, p. 3). In a partial hospitalization program, the patient may receive a variety of services such as individual or group therapy, occupational therapy, diagnostic services, and services of social workers, psychiatric nurses, and other staff, along with other types of services (CMS, 2003a). The patient receives services for a substantial number of hours each day but is not present at the hospital on a 24-hour basis.

Finally, many settings in the hospital that offer services to inpatients also provide services to outpatients. For example, hospital ancillary services, such as the hospital laboratory and the radiology department, may perform tests on hospital outpatients as well as inpatients.

Long-Term Acute Care

Another type of hospital setting is the **long-term care hospital (LTCH)**. A long-term care hospital can be either a freestanding facility or a "hospital within a hospital." In the 1980s, the Medicare program defined the characteristics of LTCH facilities and exempted them from the original hospital inpatient Prospective Payment System (PPS). By the year 1997, there were 195 LTCHs in the United States,

observation services "services furnished by a hospital on the hospital's premises, including use of a bed and periodic monitoring by a hospital's nursing or other staff, which are reasonable and necessary to evaluate an outpatient's condition or determine the need for a possible admission to the hospital as an inpatient" (CMS, 2003a, §230.6A).

partial hospitalization program (PHP) an intensive treatment program in which patients receive services for part of each day. These patients would otherwise require inpatient psychiatric care.

long-term care hospital (LTCH) an acute care hospital in which the average length of stay is 25 days or longer. LTCHs are designed for inpatients who are seriously ill, but may recover with lengthier acute care and treatment.

and by 2007 the number had grown to 396—more than doubling in a 10-year period. Growth in the number of LTCHs has continued, but at a slower rate, with 420 LTCHs reported in 2012. A specialized PPS for LTCHs has been in place since 2002 (MedPAC, 2014). The LTCH PPS will be discussed later in this chapter.

Types of Patients

Hospital patients come from every walk of life and are treated for a wide range of conditions, whether as inpatients, outpatients, or long-term acute care patients.

Hospital Inpatients

hospital inpatient   an individual receiving health care services as well as room and board and continuous nursing care in a hospital unit where patients generally stay overnight.

A hospital inpatient is an acutely ill individual who is treated in an area of the hospital where patients generally stay overnight (Glondys, 2000). A patient may be admitted for a medical condition that can be managed without surgical intervention, or the patient's condition may require surgery. Depending on the size and complexity of the hospital, different types of inpatients may be cared for in designated units (cardiology, orthopedics, and so on.) Critically ill inpatients may be cared for in an intensive care unit.

Hospital Outpatients

hospital outpatient a hospital patient who receives care at the hospital but who is not admitted as an inpatient.

clinic outpatient   an outpatient treated in an organized clinic of the hospital, in which hospital staff evaluate the patient and manage the patient's care.

referred hospital outpatient   an outpatient who is referred to the hospital for specific services, such as laboratory or radiology examinations. The hospital is responsible only for providing the diagnostic or therapeutic services requested, while the referring physician is responsible for evaluating and managing the patient's care.

Both acute and chronic illnesses can be treated on an ambulatory basis. The following classification of patients is based on the types of services the patients receive rather than on characteristics of the patients themselves (Hanken & Waters, 1994). In general, a hospital outpatient is a patient who is evaluated or treated at a hospital facility but is not admitted as an inpatient. Examples of various categories of hospital outpatients are:

- Clinic outpatient: an outpatient treated in an organized clinic of the hospital in which hospital staff members evaluate the patient and manage the patient's care.
- Referred hospital outpatient: an outpatient who is referred to the hospital for specific services, such as laboratory or radiology examinations. The hospital is responsible only for providing the diagnostic or therapeutic services requested, whereas the referring physician is responsible for evaluating and managing the patient's care. A related term is *reference laboratory services*, which is used to describe laboratory services performed for other providers. (Note that the term *referral* carries a different meaning when one physician "refers" a patient to another physician. In a physician-to-physician referral, the responsibility for evaluating and managing the patient's care is often transferred from the referring physician to the receiving physician.)

- **Emergency outpatient:** an outpatient evaluated and treated in the hospital's emergency department.

emergency outpatient an outpatient evaluated and treated in the emergency department of the hospital.

Long-Term Acute Care Hospital Patients

Patients admitted to a long-term care hospital (LTCH) generally are more acutely ill than patients in other long-term care settings. Actually, patients often are admitted to the LTCH directly from a short-stay hospital intensive care unit. Their medical conditions are complex (e.g., respiratory conditions with ventilator dependence), and they require more acute-type services, such as cancer treatment, head trauma treatment, or pain management. Comprehensive rehabilitation also is a common service provided to LTCH patients. As contrasted with that of a short-stay acute care hospital, the average length of stay in an LTCH is 25 days or more (Liu et al., 2001; ALTHA, 2010).

Types of Caregivers

Just as there are many different types of hospital patients, many different types of caregivers participate in hospital care. Physicians from every specialty see hospital patients on both an inpatient and an outpatient basis. Nurses provide nursing care both to inpatients and outpatients. Other health professionals, such as physical therapists, occupational therapists, clinical laboratory scientists, and pharmacists—to name only a few—may provide diagnostic or therapeutic services to hospital patients.

In the typical inpatient acute care area of the hospital, physicians visit their patients daily to manage their care. This daily physician-visit pattern also is generally found in LTCHs. In other areas of the hospital, such as the hospital emergency department, physicians typically are on duty 24 hours a day. Often, specialty certifications are necessary for physicians and other caregivers in specialized hospital areas. For example, caregivers in the emergency department usually have received specialized training and certification in basic and advanced life support.

One type of caregiver unique to the hospital setting is the **hospitalist**, a physician who provides comprehensive care to hospitalized patients but who ordinarily does not see patients outside of the hospital setting. The hospitalist communicates with the patient's primary care physician during the hospital stay and returns the patient to the primary physician's care after the patient is discharged. The advantage to the patient is that the hospitalist is a specialist in dealing with conditions that require hospitalization and is not distracted by the duties of seeing patients in the clinic setting.

hospitalist "a physician who specializes in inpatient medicine" (Slee, Slee, & Schmidt, 2008, 275).

The number of hospitalists in the United States was estimated to be about 1,000 in 1996, but that number had grown to more than 34,000 by 2012. This number is expected to increase as more hospitals continue to add hospitalist programs (Elliott, 2012).

SELF REVIEW 2.1

1. What is the difference between hospital inpatient care and hospital-based ambulatory care?
2. When a patient is admitted for observation services, the physician must determine whether the patient meets inpatient criteria within what timeframe?
3. What does PHP stand for, and how does it differ from inpatient care?
4. Name and discuss three types of patients.
5. What is a hospitalist, and what is the advantage to the patient when a hospital has one?

REGULATORY ISSUES

Licensure

Hospitals must be licensed by the state in which they are located. Licensure requirements vary from state to state. In some states, meeting federal standards or the standards of a voluntary accrediting agency largely fulfills licensing requirements. To obtain the licensure requirements for hospitals in a given state, a health information manager would contact the agency in that state who is responsible for licensure of hospitals. Often, licensure requirements are available at the state agency's website.

Federal Regulations

To be eligible to receive payment from Medicare, hospitals must meet the federal requirements contained in the Conditions of Participation for Hospitals (2010) or be "deemed" to meet these requirements by virtue of voluntary accreditation by an approved agency. Accreditation by The Joint Commission (TJC), the Healthcare Facilities Accreditation Program (HFAP) of the American Osteopathic Association (AOA), or the National Integrated Accreditation of Healthcare Organizations (NIAHO) program of DNV Healthcare, Inc. provides "deemed" status for hospitals with regard to the Conditions of Participation.

To meet federal program requirements, each state's own certifying agency surveys nonaccredited hospitals, comparing their practices to standards in the Conditions of Participation for Hospitals. In addition, both state-surveyed and voluntarily accredited hospitals may be selected randomly for validation surveys conducted by the Centers for Medicare & Medicaid Services (CMS).

Accreditation

Hospitals voluntarily seek accreditation to demonstrate to their patients, to their communities, to insurers, to managed care organizations, and to others that their organizations are providing quality care. As mentioned previously, The Joint

Commission, the AOA's Healthcare Facilities Accreditation Program (HFAP), and DNV Healthcare's NIAHO program offer voluntary accrediting programs whose standards and survey processes are "deemed" to be in compliance with the federal Conditions of Participation. The majority of U.S. hospitals are accredited by The Joint Commission. Of the three accrediting programs with deeming authority (TJC, HFAP, and NIAHO), the most recent addition is the NIAHO, a program of DNV Healthcare, Inc., an international organization originating in Norway. CMS granted DNV deeming authority in 2008 (DNV, 2010). The DNV approach is based on a combination of the ISO 9001 quality management protocols and the Conditions of Participation for Hospitals (Dowling, 2008). The Joint Commission and HFAP both perform on-site surveys every three years, whereas DNV performs an annual on-site survey.

SELF REVIEW 2.2

1. What is the difference between licensure and accreditation?
2. What federal requirements must an organization meet to receive Medicare payments?
3. What three accrediting organizations are "deemed" to be in compliance with the federal Conditions of Participation?

DOCUMENTATION

The fundamentals of good patient documentation are essential in the hospital setting. This is important not only to meet accrediting and regulatory guidelines but also to provide high-quality care and to demonstrate the appropriateness of payments to the hospital. The extent of documentation in a hospital record depends in part on the type of services received. For example, the records of a surgery patient, whether ambulatory surgery or inpatient surgery, typically include:

- A history and physical examination report,
- An operation report,
- Anesthesia records,
- Postoperative recovery notes,
- Pathology reports (when appropriate).

Another example of how the nature of service affects the documentation is the extensive and detailed documentation required for patients who are treated in critical care units. Some hospital records, however, such as those of referred outpatients, contain minimal information that sometimes consists of a set of orders and test results. Because there must be a physician order documented for every test the hospital performs, though, even these records frequently are audited by third-party payers.

An additional documentation element that must be obtained from the physician when a test is ordered is clinical information describing the reason for the test. Without information on the diagnoses or symptoms that prompted the physician to order the test, the hospital lacks the information to demonstrate that the test was medically necessary and thus risks losing reimbursement.

Joint Commission Documentation Requirements

As the body that surveys most hospitals, The Joint Commission's standards regarding documentation merit attention. The Joint Commission has transitioned itself to accommodate the changes in health care that have taken place since the turn of the century. The Information Management (IM) standards for hospitals reflect a health care system in which health care information is managed, stored, and transmitted electronically as well as in non-electronic formats, with attention to the following major areas (TJC, 2015):

- Management of information,
- Continuity of information management processes,
- Privacy of health information,
- Security and integrity of health information,
- Management of the collection of health information (i.e., data sets),
- Retrieval, dissemination, and transmission of health information in usable formats,
- Availability of knowledge-based information resources,
- Maintenance of accurate health information.

Although many of the standards that have a direct impact on health information and health information services are found in the Information Management (IM) section, several other relevant Joint Commission standards are found in the Record of Care, Treatment, and Services (RC) and the Provision of Care, Treatment, and Services (PC) sections.

To outline all of The Joint Commission's documentation standards is beyond the scope of this chapter. Instead, the chapter will demonstrate how a health information manager could review the standards to locate those that are relevant to a specific purpose. For example, standard RC.02.01.03 concerns the use of moderate or deep sedation or anesthesia during operative or other high-risk procedures and would be relevant in assessing documentation for surgical cases. Elements of performance (EPs) for this standard deal with the following issues, to name a few (TJC, 2015):

- Documentation must be provided of a preoperative or provisional diagnosis before surgery by the licensed independent practitioner responsible for the patient.
- Medical history and physical examination must be recorded in the medical record before a procedure is performed.

- Operative reports have to be dictated or written upon completion of the procedure and before the patient is transferred to the next level of care. Operative reports include the name of the practitioner performing the procedure and assistants, name and description of the procedure, findings, estimated blood loss, specimens removed, and the postoperative diagnosis.
- When the operative report is not placed in the medical record immediately after surgery, a progress note is entered before the patient is transferred to the next level of care.

A second example is found in the standards that The Joint Commission has established for documentation in the records of patients receiving "continuing ambulatory care services," such as clinic outpatients. As required by standard RC.02.01.07, "The medical record contains a summary list for each patient who receives continuing ambulatory care services" (TJC, 2015). This summary list must be initiated for the patient by the third visit and should include lists of:

- Significant medical diagnoses and conditions,
- Significant operative and invasive procedures,
- Adverse and allergic drug reactions,
- Current medications, over-the-counter medications, and herbal preparations.

The summary list also should be updated when there are changes in diagnoses, medications, or allergies to medications and whenever a procedure is performed. The summary list must be readily available to other clinicians who provide care, treatment, or other services (TJC, 2015).

Although the description of the summary list brings to mind a form bound in the front of a paper record, this information often is maintained in electronic format. Figure 2-1 depicts how the data required to meet this standard might be collected. Other information also may be collected and displayed with the summary list, such as immunization records for pediatric patients.

A third example of service-specific documentation requirements is found in The Joint Commission standards pertaining to records of emergency patients. Some items that must be documented in the records of patients receiving emergency, urgent, or immediate care are found under standard RC.02.01.01 as follows (TJC, 2015):

- time and means of arrival,
- if a patient left against medical advice,
- conclusions at termination of treatment, including final disposition, condition at discharge, and instructions for follow-up care, treatment, and services, and
- a copy of the information made available to practitioners or organizations providing follow-up care, treatment, or services.

FIGURE 2-1

Sample summary list form for ambulatory care patient records.

YOURTOWN HOSPITAL
YOURTOWN, USA
AMBULATORY SUMMARY LIST

<Patient Identification>

SIGNIFICANT MEDICAL DIAGNOSES AND CONDITIONS   **SIGNIFICANT OPERATIVE/INVASIVE PROCEDURES**

DATE	DIAGNOSES/CONDITIONS	DATE	PROCEDURES

ALLERGIES AND ADVERSE DRUG REACTIONS

DATE	ALLERGY	DATE	ALLERGY	DATE	ALLERGY

MEDICATIONS, INCLUDING OVER-THE-COUNTER AND HERBAL PREPARATIONS

DATE	MEDICATION	DATE	MEDICATION

FIGURE 2-1 (*continued*)

DATE	MEDICATION	DATE	MEDICATION

Other Factors in Hospital Documentation

Documentation in the hospital setting also is important because of its role in determining the level of physician service provided. The level of service determines the appropriate code, which determines the physician's reimbursement. (Reimbursement to the *hospital* is discussed in the Reimbursement section of this chapter.) This issue is particularly important in teaching hospitals in which **residents**, as part of their graduate medical education, participate with teaching physicians in caring for patients. The *Code of Federal Regulations* contains the basic rules that regulate Medicare payments to teaching physicians (Physician Services in Teaching Settings, 2014). How these rules are applied is explained in the *Medicare Claims Processing Manual*, along with specific examples of acceptable and unacceptable documentation (CMS, 2014).

Most teaching hospitals pay residents a salary, to which Medicare contributes through indirect medical education allowances. In such a situation, a professional service performed by a resident is not paid on a fee-for-service basis but, rather, a teaching physician who is present during the service may bill Medicare. For evaluation and management services, the teaching physician's documentation must make it clear that the teaching physician was present during the key portion of the service and that the teaching physician evaluated and participated in

residents primarily, licensed physicians, dentists, or podiatrists who participates in an approved graduate medical education (GME) program. The term *resident* also may be applied to physicians with temporary or restricted licenses, or to unlicensed graduates of foreign medical schools who are authorized to practice only in a hospital (Physician services in teaching settings, 2009).

management of the patient. Merely countersigning the resident's note is insufficient documentation to justify payment (CMS, 2014).

Medicare rules regarding fee payments for services of teaching physicians appear in the *Code of Federal Regulations*, Section 415.172, Physician fee schedule payment for services of teaching physicians (www.gpo.gov). These rules are relevant to a discussion of hospital-based care, because teaching physicians practice in teaching hospitals. The rules apply to documentation in Medicare records in all states, and in some states to Medicaid records as well.

These rules have an "outpatient exception." Not all outpatient care is included under the outpatient exception, though, so the "general" rules will apply in those instances. An example of exceptions can be found in the *Code of Federal Regulations*, Section 415.174, Evaluation and management services furnished in certain centers (www.gpo.gov)

An early audit initiative of the Office of the Inspector General (OIG) of the U.S. Department of Health and Human Services was known as PATH (Physicians at Teaching Hospitals). As a result of the PATH audits, teaching hospitals that lacked documentation to substantiate Medicare payments to faculty physicians who supervised residents repaid millions of dollars to the Medicare program. Although the PATH initiative is no longer part of the OIG work plan, documentation in teaching hospitals is monitored in other ways, including by the hospital's own internal compliance program.

SELF REVIEW 2.3	
	1. True or False? A medical history and physical examination must be recorded in the medical record within 12 hours after a procedure is performed.
	2. True or False? When emergency, urgent, or immediate care is provided, the time and means of arrival also must be documented in the medical record.
	3. True or False? The *Code of Federal Regulations* contains the basic rules that regulate Medicare payments to teaching physicians.

REIMBURSEMENT

Various mechanisms are in place for reimbursing hospital care. Reimbursement concepts related to managed care are discussed in Chapter 4, but other reimbursement mechanisms, including diagnosis related groups (DRGs) and ambulatory payment classifications (APCs), are discussed here.

Hospital Chargemaster or Charge Description Master (CDM)

chargemaster or charge description master (CDM) a computer file that contains a list of the Healthcare Common Procedural Coding System codes and associated charges for services provided to hospital patients.

All billable services in a hospital are cataloged in a computerized data table called the chargemaster or Charge Description Master (CDM). Services include procedures performed by nursing and other professional staff, room and board charges, ancillary services such as laboratory testing and radiological imaging, drugs, medical equipment, and supplies used in the care of the patient. The CDM data table stores elements of each item, including a description of the item used across the hospital services spectrum, a numerical key, a corresponding *Current Procedural Terminology*© (CPT), the number of units or other unit of measure, a location code if the item is specific to a particular area within the hospital system, a revenue code to associate the charge with a service area for revenue generation, and an assigned price.

The CDM serves as a key document in negotiating reimbursement for hospital services during contract negotiations and is the reference point for any reimbursement that is based on a percent of charges. Whereas hospital inpatient services require medical coders to review and code the patient's stay, hospital outpatient services often are coded straight from the CDM by using the CPT code assigned to the item. This automated coding practice is used most frequently for billing ancillary services. Annual maintenance of the CDM is recommended for most facilities to ensure that the table is updated to include all current services and to reflect accurate pricing and CPT coding for each item.

Medicare

Medicare is a federal program that pays for health care for American citizens aged 65 or older or citizens with certain disabilities, end stage renal disease, or amyotrophic lateral sclerosis (ALS or Lou Gehrig's disease). Payments to hospitals fall under Part A of Medicare, whereas payments for physician's services fall under Part B. CMS contracts with private organizations that handle the claims processing and payments for the Medicare program in a given region. In the past, the claims processing organization for Medicare Part A was called the **fiscal intermediary (FI)**, and the organization that processed Medicare Part B claims was known as the **Medicare carrier**.

As a result of the Medicare Prescription Drug, Improvement, and Modernization Act of 2003, however, CMS has replaced these contractors with entities called **Medicare Administrative Contractors (MACs)**. CMS awarded a total of 19 MAC contracts including 15 A/B MACs that covered both Medicare Parts A and B and 4 DME MACs that covered durable medical equipment. In 2010, Medicare announced that the 15 A/B MACs were to be consolidated into 10 A/B MACs over the coming years. The A/B MACs are required to develop payment policies called Local Coverage Determinations (LCDs) or Local Medical Review Policies (LMRPs). These policies educate health care providers on how to submit accurate claims for reimbursement. Although the issues related to documentation by teaching physicians discussed earlier in this chapter are Part B issues, the information provided in this section relates to hospital reimbursement, or Part A of Medicare.

Current Procedural Terminology (CPT)   a coding system developed and maintained by the American Medical Association for use by health care providers in reporting procedures to third-party-payers for reimbursement.

fiscal intermediary (FI)   before the implementation of MACs, an organization with a contract with CMS to process and pay Part A Medicare claims.

Medicare carrier   before the implementation of MACs, an organization having a contract with the CMS to process and pay Part B Medicare claims.

Medicare Administrative Contractor (MAC)   an organization that has contracted with CMS to process Medicare claims. MACs have replaced fiscal intermediaries and Medicare carriers.

The Hospital Inpatient Prospective Payment System (IPPS) and Diagnosis Related Group (DRG) Payment Window

Hospital Inpatient Prospective Payment System (HIPPS or IPPS) Medicare's payment system for hospital inpatient services. The basic unit of payment in the IPPS is the Medicare Severity Diagnosis Related Group (MS-DRG).

diagnosis related group (DRG) groupings of inpatient services (based on the diagnosis, expected resource consumption, and other characteristics) that determine the payment the hospital receives under the Hospital Inpatient Prospective Payment System (HIPPS).

Medicare Severity-Diagnosis Related Groups (MS-DRGs) groupings of inpatient services (based on the diagnosis, expected resource consumption, and other characteristics) that determine the payment the hospital receives under the Hospital Inpatient Prospective Payment System (HIPPS) The Medicare severity system adjusts the original DRG algorithm for severity by classifying some complications and comorbidities as major complications and comorbidities (MCCs), indicating the potential for higher resource consumption when an MCC is present.

Medicare reimburses hospitals for inpatient care under the **Hospital Inpatient Prospective Payment System (IPPS)**, which pays the hospital on a "per case" basis according to the **diagnosis related group (DRG)** assigned to each patient's stay. Prior to 2007, there were 538 DRGs that grouped patients according to diagnosis, expected resource consumption, and other characteristics. In 2007, CMS replaced these DRGs with 745 **Medicare Severity-DRGs (MS-DRGs)**, taking into account various levels of patient illness, using secondary diagnoses. Some secondary diagnoses are classified as complications or comorbidities (CCs), and others represent the highest level of severity for a secondary diagnosis classified as major complications or comorbidities (MCCs), depending on the impact of the condition in combination with the patient's principal diagnosis.

Surgical and certain other procedures also influence the MS-DRG assignment, as do the patient's discharge status and other factors, in some instances. Codes for diagnoses and procedures, along with other data elements, are submitted as part of the bill to the contractor that processes Medicare Part A claims. A software program known as a "grouper" uses these data elements to assign the case to the appropriate DRG. Each DRG is associated with a relative weight that serves as a multiplier to determine the payment to the hospital. The relative weight is multiplied times the hospital's PPS rate or blended rate to arrive at a payment.

For example, if the relative weight of a DRG is 1.5000 and the hospital's PPS rate is $6,500, the payment for that DRG would be calculated as follows: $1.5000 \times 6,500 = \$9,750$. An excerpt from the MS-DRG table for 2014, presented in Figure 2-2, illustrates the impact of MCCs and CCs on the relative weights of the DRGs, and thus on the payments to the hospital. Note the three DRGs for "Tracheostomy for Face, Neck, and Mouth Diagnoses" (011, 012, and 013), and observe the difference in their relative weights, depending on whether the case involved an MCC, CC, or neither.

DRG payments are reduced when the patient's length of stay (LOS) is less than the geometric mean LOS for the DRG and the patient is transferred to another hospital covered by the acute IPPS or, for certain MS-DRGs, discharged to a post-acute setting such as a long-term care hospital, rehabilitation or psychiatric facility, skilled nursing facility, or certain other settings (CMS, 2013). The second and third columns in Figure 2-2 specify whether and how the DRG is subject to the post-acute transfer policy. Payment is reduced even further for qualifying transfers in DRGs that are subject to the "special pay" rule.

When a hospital provides services to a Medicare patient as an outpatient within 72 hours before a related inpatient admission, charges for those outpatient services must not be billed separately; this is commonly referred to as the "72-hour rule." Instead, the outpatient diagnoses and procedures must be coded and submitted with the inpatient bill. Because some hospital admissions occur

FIGURE 2-2

Selected MS-DRGs excerpted from the 2014 MS-DRG Table.

MS-DRG	FY 2014 Final Rule Post-Acute DRG	FY 2014 Final Rule Special Pay DRG	MDC	TYPE	MS-DRG Title	Weights	Geometric Mean LOS	Arithmetic Mean LOS
001	No	No	PRE	SURG	HEART TRANSPLANT OR IMPLANT OF HEART ASSIST SYSTEM W MCC	25.3518	28.3	35.9
002	No	No	PRE	SURG	HEART TRANSPLANT OR IMPLANT OF HEART ASSIST SYSTEM W/O MCC	15.2738	15.9	18.6
011	No	No	PRE	SURG	TRACHEOSTOMY FOR FACE, MOUTH & NECK DIAGNOSES W MCC	4.7246	11.4	14.0
012	No	No	PRE	SURG	TRACHEOSTOMY FOR FACE, MOUTH & NECK DIAGNOSES W CC	3.2291	8.3	9.8
013	No	No	PRE	SURG	TRACHEOSTOMY FOR FACE, MOUTH & NECK DIAGNOSES W/O CC/MCC	2.1647	5.7	6.5
052	No	No	01	MED	SPINAL DISORDERS & INJURIES W CC/MCC	1.4102	4.0	5.3
053	No	No	01	MED	SPINAL DISORDERS & INJURIES W/O CC/MCC	0.8746	2.7	3.3

unexpectedly within 72 hours after outpatient treatment, hospitals inadvertently have submitted both inpatient and outpatient bills to Medicare in these cases, in violation of the 72-hour rule. Medicare requires hospitals to implement systems to avoid submitting separate bills for outpatients admitted to inpatient status within the 72-hour window. Failure to comply with the 72-hour rule may result in financial penalties to the hospital. The Office of the Inspector General's (OIG's) work plan for 2010 included a commitment to review the appropriateness of outpatient payments for patients seen immediately before or after acute care stays (OIG, 2010).

In 2015, the OIG shifted the focus of review for appropriateness of outpatient services billed under the IPPS to a review of the admission status for patients whose admission for acute services spanned less than two days. The "two–midnight policy" emphasizes that patients whose level of acuity requires treatment for less than two days should be billed as outpatients (OIG, 2015). The policy is intended to force physicians to carefully consider the need for an inpatient stay and create a cost savings for Medicare by channeling lower acuity patients to ambulatory care.

Medicare has recognized that the Medicare Severity Diagnosis Related Group (MS-DRG) system was not formulated for billing patients outside the scope of Medicare. During the 1990s, the 3M Clinical and Economic Research Department, the Children's Hospital Association, and several physician groups worked collaboratively to create an All Patient Refined DRG (APR-DRG) Classification System. Whereas the CMS MS-DRGs focus on the Medicare population, the 3M APR-DRGs classify acute care patients and are designed specifically to adjust data for **severity of illness** ("How sick is the patient?") and **risk of mortality** ("How likely is it the patient will die?") in assigning a DRG for reimbursement (3M, 2013).

The APR-DRG methodology is commonly used to bill inpatient stays for Medicaid beneficiaries, who predominantly include pediatric and obstetrical patients. By ranking the patient's severity of illness and risk of mortality on independent 4-point scales, the APR-DRG can indicate the resource needs for the patient while assessing a hospital's ability to provide quality care through an assessment of the outcome of the patient's stay compared to expected outcomes for patients of the same severity of illness and risk of mortality.

The Hospital Outpatient Prospective Payment System (OPPS) and Ambulatory Payment Classifications (APCs)

The basic units of payment in Medicare's **Hospital Outpatient Prospective Payment System (HOPPS or OPPS)** are known as **Ambulatory Payment Classifications (APCs)**. The APC system, implemented in the year 2000, established groups of outpatient procedures and services with similar clinical characteristics and similar costs. One major difference between the APC and the DRG systems is that an outpatient may be assigned more than one APC per encounter, whereas an inpatient is assigned only one DRG per hospital admission.

severity of illness the extent of physical illness or loss of organ function of the patient. Ranked on a scale of 1 to 4, indicating mild (1), moderate (2), major (3), or extreme (4) severity.

risk of mortality the likelihood that the patient will die while in the hospital. Ranked on a scale of 1 to 4, indicating mild (1), moderate (2), major (3), or extreme (4) risk of mortality.

Hospital Outpatient Prospective Payment System (HOPPS or OPPS) Medicare's payment system for hospital outpatient services. The basic unit of payment in the OPPS is the ambulatory payment classification (APC) of each service provided.

Ambulatory Payment Classifications (APCs) groupings of outpatient services (based on the HCPCS code assigned) that determine the payment the hospital receives under the Hospital Outpatient Prospective Payment System (HOPPS).

Consider the case of an emergency department patient whose visit includes evaluation and management, X-rays, and a procedure. In such a case, as many as three APCs may be generated—one APC for the evaluation and management services, a second APC for the X-rays, and a third APC for the procedure. APCs are based on **Healthcare Common Procedural Coding System (HCPCS)** codes assigned by the hospital. The hospital's reimbursement from Medicare is the dollar amount associated with each APC as updated by CMS on an annual basis. See Figure 2-3 for excerpts from the APC table for the calendar year 2014.

Notice that in Figure 2-3 each APC is assigned a **status indicator**, which is an alphabetic character that indicates the APC type and whether or how that APC is paid under the OPPS. The four status indicators that appear in the excerpt in Figure 2-3 are S, T, P, and V. A status indicator of T means that the associated APC represents a significant procedure that is **discounted** (paid at less than the full amount) when other procedures are performed in combination with it. The S status indicator represents a significant service that is *not* discounted when more than one APC is present on a claim. The P status indicator means that the associated APC is a partial hospitalization service. The V status indicator represents a medical visit with its associated evaluation and management services. All four of the status indicators in Figure 2-3 are paid under the OPPS. Status indicators S, T, and V are paid as separate APCs, and status indicator P is paid on a per-diem APC basis. As of 2015, there are 19 different status indicators (Hospital Outpatient Prospective Payment–Proposed Rule, 2015).

Healthcare Common Procedural Coding System (HCPCS) the system required by CMS for coding services provided to Medicare patients.

status indicator an alphabetic character that indicates the type of each APC and whether or how that APC is paid under the Hospital Outpatient Prospective Payment System (OPPS):

discounted reduced payment for additional procedures or ambulatory patient groups. When discounted, these other items are not paid at the full rate, as they would be if they had been the only services performed in a given encounter.

FIGURE 2-3

Selected APCs excerpted from the 2015 Addendum A.

APC	Group Title	SI	Relative Weight	Payment Rate	National Unadjusted Copayment	Minimum Unadjusted Copayment
4	Level I Needle Biopsy/Aspiration Except Bone Marrow	T	6.5703	$487.34		$97.47
5	Level II Needle Biopsy/Aspiration Except Bone Marrow	T	14.1916	$1052.63		$210.53
175	Level I Partial Hospitalization (3 services) for Hospital-based PHPs	P	2.4157	$179.18	.	$35.84
176	Level II Partial Hospitalization (4 or more services)) for Hospital-based PHPs	P	2.6384	$195.70	.	$39.14
177	Level I Echocardiogram with Contrast	S	6.6127	$490.48	$126.79	$98.10
178	Level II Echocardiogram with Contrast	S	9.2840	$688.62	$172.48	$137.73
634	Hospital Clinic Visits	V	1.2977	$96.25	.	$19.25

Medical visits in a hospital clinic or emergency department (ED) are classified and paid according to level of service based on evaluation and management (E&M) coding. In determining the level of service of an encounter, hospitals have developed their own criteria for assigning the E&M codes and have not followed the same guidelines as physicians. Although CMS at one time expressed the intent to develop standard guidelines for hospital evaluation and management services, in 2009 CMS announced that no such guidelines seemed to be necessary. CMS studies have shown that the current system of permitting hospitals to use their own guidelines based on the use of hospital resources has produced acceptable results (CMS, 2009).

In 2008, CMS implemented "Composite APCs" for certain categories of encounter-based hospital outpatient services. These composite APCs allow only a single payment for certain common combination services provided on the same date of service. For example, an emergency department visit followed by observation services would be combined into an "Extended Assessment and Management Composite" APC. Composite APCs are meant to provide incentives to health care providers to efficiently utilize resources while conducting similar services. A list of CMS composite APCs includes:

- APC 8001 LDR Prostate Brachytherapy,
- APC 8002 Level 1 Extended Assessment and Management Composite,
- APC 8003 Level 2 Extended Assessment and Management,
- APC 8004 Ultrasound,
- APC 8005 CT and CTA without Contrast,
- APC 8006 CT and CTA with Contrast,
- APC 8007 MRI and MRA without Contrast,
- APC 8008 MRI and MRA with Contrast,
- APC 0172 Level 1 Partial Hospitalization (3 services),
- APC 0173 Level 2 Partial Hospitalization (4 or more services).

Because of the potential savings to the Medicare program, this trend of bundling services continues with expansion to more APCs.

Another change related to observation services is that CMS no longer requires specific diagnosis criteria (chest pain, asthma, congestive heart failure) that were previously necessary for separate payment of observation. There is a separate code that must be used for billing observation services. All related services provided to the patient, including specified "visit" or evaluation and management codes, should be coded in addition to the observation code. A written order from a physician is required for admission to observation care. (If the physician determines during the observation stay that the patient needs a higher level of care, another order must be written to admit the patient as an inpatient.) The patient must be in observation care for at least 8 hours as documented in the medical record by timed admission notes, progress notes, and discharge instructions (notes) signed by the physician. Medical record documentation also must note that the physician explicitly assessed patient risk to determine that the patient would benefit from observation care (American College of Emergency Physicians, n.d.).

The OPPS allows additional payments to cover the costs of innovative medical devices, drugs, and biologicals. Called "pass-through payments," these categories provide separate payments in addition to regular APC payments. Payments for a given drug, device, or biological can be made on a pass-through basis for 2 to 3 years.

Hospital-based clinics are considered to be "provider-based clinics" under the OPPS. When a Medicare patient is seen in a hospital-based clinic, the clinic receives an APC payment and the physician receives a reduced payment for his or her services (because there is no practice expense—it has been shifted to the hospital). The total of the two payments is greater than the full fee schedule payment that a physician in a freestanding clinic would receive. Further, hospitals with provider-based facilities "may receive higher reimbursement when they include the costs of a provider-based entity on their cost reports. (F)acilities may also benefit from enhanced disproportionate share hospital (DSH) payments, upper payment limit (UPL) payments, or graduate medical education payments for which they would not normally be eligible. In addition, provider-based status for outpatient clinics may increase coinsurance liability for Medicare beneficiaries" (OIG, 2009, p 3). For these reasons, CMS scrutinizes applications for provider-based status from clinics that had not claimed any hospital affiliation before implementation of the OPPS. Also, the provider-based status of existing facilities may be reviewed by the Office of the Inspector General for appropriateness (OIG, 2015).

It is important to remember that details of the OPPS change annually. To obtain the most current information, the health information manager should consult the latest regulations at the CMS or *Federal Register* websites.

Long-Term Care Hospital Prospective Payment System (LTCH PPS)

Since October 1, 2002, Medicare payments to long-term care hospitals have been determined by a diagnosis related group (DRG)–based prospective payment system (PPS). Although the numbers and titles of most of the Medicare severity long-term care diagnosis related groups (MS-LTC-DRGs) are similar to those of inpatient MS-DRGs, the LTC-DRGs differ from inpatient DRGs in relative weights and in their associated lengths of stay. LTC-DRGs also are similar to inpatient DRGs in that they are based on the patient's principal diagnosis, additional diagnoses, and procedures performed during the stay, age, sex, and discharge status. The LTCH PPS calculates a per-discharge payment to the facility, based on the product of the LTC-DRG relative weight multiplied times a federally determined payment rate. For MS-DRGs unlikely to be used in the LTCH setting, the relative weight is zero. A listing of the top 20 MS-LTC-DRGs for 2008 in Table 2-1 provides an overview of the types of cases commonly treated in a long-term acute care hospital.

TABLE 2-1	Top 20 MS-LTC-DRGs in 2011		
MS-LTC-DRG	**Description**	**Discharges**	**Percent**
207	Respiratory system diagnosis with ventilator support 96+ hours	16.101	11.5
189	Pulmonary edema and respiratory failure	13.042	9.3
871	Septicemia or severe sepsis without ventilator support 96+ hours with MCC	8,543	6.0
177	Respiratory infections and inflammations with MCC	4,997	3.6
592	Skin ulcers with MCC	3,425	2.5
208	Respiratory system diagnosis with ventilator support <96 hours	3,029	2.2
949	Aftercare with CC/MCC	3,004	2.1
190	Chronic obstructive pulmonary disease with MCC	2,769	2.0
193	Simple pneumonia and pleurisy with MCC	2,573	1.8
539	Osteomyelitis with MCC	2,541	1.8
573	Skin graft and/or debridement for skin ulcer or cellulitis with MCC	2,101	1.5
314	Other circulatory system diagnosis with MCC	2,039	1.5
919	Complications of treatment with MCC	2,033	1.5
862	Postoperative and post-traumatic infections with MCC	2,008	1.4
166	Other respiratory system OR procedures with MCC	1,988	1.4
682	Renal failure with MCC	1,987	1.4
4	Tracheostomy with ventilator support 96+ hours or primary diagnosis except face, mouth, and neck without major OR	1,887	1.4
559	Aftercare musculoskeletal system and connective tissue with MCC	1,808	1.3
870	Septicemia or severe sepsis with ventilator support 96+ hours	1,774	1.3
291	Heart failure and shock with MCC	1,713	1.2
	Top 20 MS-LTC-DRGs	79,272	56.6
	Total	139,741	100.0

Source: MedPAC, 2013

Medicare has developed specific rules to discourage the transfer of patients between the LTCH and other facilities for financial rather than clinical reasons. Three payment mechanisms address this issue. One is the concept of the "interrupted stay," which applies to transfers to and from an acute care hospital, inpatient rehabilitation facility, or skilled nursing facility. In the case of a patient who is discharged to one of these facilities and is readmitted to the same LTCH within a certain number of days (the number of days varies according to the type of facility), the LTCH episode is considered as one interrupted stay and the LTCH receives only one MS-LTC-DRG payment rather than two.

Another mechanism is the 5% rule, which applies only to transfers to and from a colocated facility, such as a hospital-within-a-hospital or a satellite facility. After 5% of all discharges for the fiscal year are made up of transfers from the LTCH to the colocated facility and back, these cases are paid as one LTCH admission rather than two, regardless of the number of days in the intervening stay.

The third rule applies to the initial admission from any given hospital to the LTCH. This rule allows the LTCH to be paid MS-LTC-DRG rates for patients admitted from a specific acute care hospital until the number of patients admitted from that facility exceeds 25% of the total admissions to the LTCH. After the 25% threshold is reached, the LTCH is paid the lesser of the LTCH PPS rate or the acute hospital PPS rate for admissions from that hospital. There are some exceptions to the 25% rule to accommodate rural LTCHs and those in metropolitan areas with dominant or single acute care hospitals. Other factors beyond the scope of this discussion such as short-stay and high-cost outliers also can affect Medicare payment to the LTCH (MedPAC, 2008).

Other Payers

Other payers may pay for hospital outpatient care under a variety of systems. Traditional indemnity insurance plans pay the usual, customary, and reasonable charges of the hospital. However, fewer patients are enrolled in a pure indemnity type of plan. Generally, patients have incentives to use the services of a provider who has agreed not to exceed certain limits on charges. For more information on the wide range of payment mechanisms for health care, see Chapter 4.

Billing

The Uniform Bill (UB-04 or CMS-1450) is the standard form for submitting information to third-party payers when filing claims for hospital services (see Figure 2-4). In 2007, The National Uniform Billing Committee (NUBC) updated the form to accommodate more diagnosis and procedure codes in anticipation of the implementation of ICD-10-CM and ICD-10-PCS. The Health Insurance Reform: Modifications to the HIPAA Electronic Transaction Standards Final Rule, published on January 16, 2009, implemented the current version 5010 accommodating the longer, alphanumeric ICD-10 codes in preparation for the implementation.

FIGURE 2-4

The UB-04 (CMS-1450) Uniform Bill.

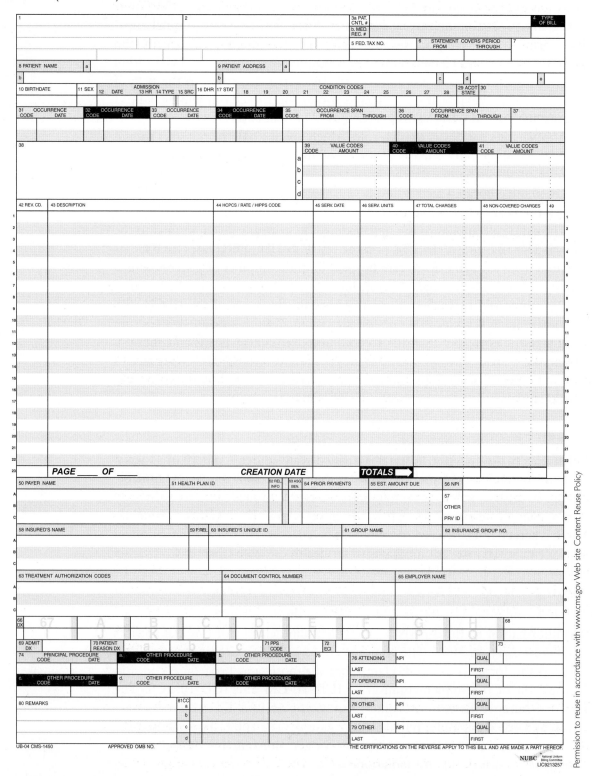

The revised form also meets electronic data standards and allows for Present on Admission indicators as well as National Provider Identifiers. Under HIPAA, physicians use the CMS-1500 (08-05) form for submitting claims. This revised form allows for National Provider Identifier reporting. The use of paper bills and claim forms, however, is diminishing. Electronic transmission of claims is the norm for hospital and physician claim submission alike.

SELF REVIEW 2.4

1. Payment policies developed by A/B MACs help educate health care providers on how to submit accurate claims for reimbursement. These payment policies are called _____.
2. What does MS-DRGs stand for?
3. What is the 72-hour rule?
4. What are pass-through payments?
5. In what ways are LTC-DRGs similar and different from inpatient DRGs?

INFORMATION MANAGEMENT

Coding and Classification

Coding of diseases and procedures serves several purposes in hospital-based care. Hospitals can use coded data to study patterns in the services they render or to assist in evaluating the outcomes of care. Accurate coding is crucial to receiving appropriate reimbursement for hospital-based care.

International Classification of Diseases

The clinical modification of the *International Classification of Diseases*, developed by the National Center for Health Statistics, is the classification system used for coding the patient's condition, diagnosis, or reason for encounter for inpatients and outpatients alike. Federal regulations scheduled *ICD-10-CM* to replace the disease classification of *ICD-9-CM* in 2015. Likewise, *ICD-10-PCS* (the inpatient procedure classification system developed by CMS) was announced as the replacement for the procedure section (Volume 3) of *ICD-9-CM* with the 2015 compliance date. Hospitals are required to use the *ICD* procedure classification for reporting operations and other procedures only for inpatients. Hospital outpatient services use ICD diagnosis codes paired with CPT codes for procedures to describe ambulatory services including evaluation and management services.

Healthcare Common Procedural Coding System (HCPCS)

The Healthcare Common Procedural Coding System (HCPCS) is the system required by CMS for coding services provided to Medicare patients. CMS adopted the American Medical Association's *Current Procedural Terminology*© as the coding system comprising the bulk of HCPCS. The *CPT* codes are designated by

CMS as "Level I" codes. The codes that CMS developed are known as HCPCS "Level II" or national codes. These are alphanumeric codes, consisting of a letter (A–V) and four numerical digits. (Note: HCPCS Level III or local codes were discontinued in 2003.)

Revenue Codes

revenue codes used on the UB-04 to indicate the general nature of the services provided.

Revenue codes are reported on the UB-04 to indicate the general nature of the service provided, such as pharmacy, room and board, or intensive care. To file a valid claim, the revenue code must be appropriate to the HCPCS code listed with it. Therefore, to avoid rejection of claims, the appropriate revenue codes usually are included in the chargemaster file along with the HCPCS code for the service being billed.

Coding Edits

Medicare Administrative Contractors process hospital inpatient bills using the Medicare Code Editor (MCE) and hospital outpatient claims using the Outpatient Code Editor (OCE). These code editors identify coding errors on hospital bills that can cause the claim to be rejected. National Correct Coding Initiative (NCCI, or CCI) edits also apply to the APC system. The purpose of the CCI edits is to prohibit unbundling of procedures, a practice that results in excessive payment to the provider when multiple codes are reported instead of a combination code.

The CCI edits are voluminous and are updated quarterly, making it difficult to keep abreast of them using manual methods. Most hospitals use code-editing software to flag codes that contain possible code editor or CCI errors. Identifying and correcting errors before the bill is submitted results in more efficient claims processing and a better cash flow for the hospital.

Data and Information Flow

Most hospitals begin the patient's record with the registration process. Information necessary to identify the patient is gathered and recorded. Generally, this identifying information is entered into an electronic database, or master patient index (MPI) system, and also may be printed out or manually recorded for immediate reference. Many electronic health records store a local version of the MPI on business continuity devices to ensure that the Index is available during system downtime. As various assessments, diagnostic procedures, and treatments are completed, the results are incorporated into the patient's record, along with diagnostic impressions or conclusions and plans for future care.

The patient's record must be readily available when a patient is seen in any hospital setting. When a hospital uses an electronic health record (EHR), the patient's record can be accessed by diverse providers throughout the hospital as the patient arrives at various departments for different services. A hospital using a paper record or a hybrid (part electronic, part paper) record could achieve this goal by maintaining all components of the paper record together and delivering the record to the hospital locations where the patient is being seen.

When a complete paper record is maintained in one location, it is called a unit record. In this scenario, all records of inpatient, clinic, emergency, or any other type of hospital encounter would be maintained in a single record, centralized in the health information services area of the hospital. However, in a large facility with numerous clinics that may not be physically close to one another, maintaining a single paper record is much more challenging. In this situation, certain clinics may maintain their own records. When a patient has more than one record in various hospital locations, The Joint Commission requires that "the hospital either assemble or make available in a summary in the medical record all information required to provide patient care, treatment, and services" (TJC, 2010, p. 405).

Because of ARRA incentives, more hospitals are adopting electronic health records—meaning that more components of the patient's clinical record are accessible electronically. The move toward EHRs will help solve the problem of making the record quickly available in any setting.

Electronic Health Records and Computer Systems

As with many areas of health care, the first computer applications in hospitals were related to billing functions. The importance of maintaining clinical information electronically began to receive attention in the 1990s, receiving impetus from the Institute of Medicine (IOM) 1991 publication, *The Computer-Based Patient Record: An Essential Technology for Health Care*. Although decades passed after this seminal work was released, hospitals lagged in the adoption of electronic health records.

In 2009, Congress passed the **American Recovery and Reinvestment Act (ARRA)**, which included a Medicare and Medicaid incentive program for health care providers who demonstrate the ability to "meaningfully use" EHRs. To meet the definition of "meaningful use," providers must utilize a certified EHR product in such a way that the electronic exchange of information improves the quality of care provided to patients, including the capability of submitting clinical quality measures data (AHIMA, 2010). Although this program initially encouraged EHR adoption by providing incentive payments to hospitals and clinicians, the law included penalties for Medicare providers who did not meet meaningful use requirements after the conclusion of the program.

American Recovery and Reinvestment Act (ARRA) a federal law that, among other things, created an incentive program for health care providers to utilize EHRs for improved patient care.

The meaningful use requirements were designed to be implemented in three stages with more electronic health record functionality and usage required at each. Stage 1 meaningful use requirements focused on data capture and sharing and were implemented in 2011. Stage 2 expanded the requirements in order to achieve more impact on clinical processes, and the hospitals who had met the Stage 1 requirements in 2011 were in a position to meet the Stage 2 requirements in 2014. The original implementation date for Stage 3 had been 2015, but as the deadline approached, an implementation date of 2016 appeared more likely. Different hospitals have progressed through the various stages of meaningful use at varying rates. Although as of 2015, the meaningful use program was somewhat behind schedule, overall, the program has resulted in a significant increase in the use of electronic health records in hospitals.

The architects of the "meaningful use" regulations intended to benefit the patients and the clinicians who care for them through the implementation of EHRs. Because in a given day a patient may receive evaluation and treatment in several different hospital departments, an EHR that is readily available to all who see the patient can improve patient care. Patient safety can be enhanced through the use of computerized provider order entry (CPOE) by linking to decision support systems that warn of possible drug interactions or wrong dosages and by alerting prescribing clinicians to patient allergies.

An EHR also can generate reminders of services that a patient needs or to alert clinicians to critical lab values or other new information that falls outside established safe values. Using "big data" or "deep machine learning" to perform analysis of patient data captured in the EHR database is underway with plans to begin using predictive analytics for patient risk factors, such as the risk for a heart attack or pressure ulcer given the patient's readily available health data. These are just a few of the ways in which an EHR can benefit patient care in a hospital setting.

Although the initial meaningful use criteria did not specify that all physician documentation be maintained electronically, this is likely to be an ultimate goal in many hospitals. In hospitals with electronic physician documentation systems, the physician may enter progress notes and other health information using a keyboard.

Another method of capturing physician documentation for use in an EHR is already being used in some hospital departments—voice recognition technology. With a voice recognition system, the physician can dictate reports directly to an electronic system. The computer converts the spoken word into a report without the labor of a transcriptionist typing the report, although a transcriptionist or the physician may edit the report for accuracy before it becomes part of the record. The report also can be electronically signed by the physician who generated the report.

Voice recognition systems have been found to be particularly useful in emergency and radiology departments. In many instances, voice recognition systems also include voice commands to control navigation within the EHR, allowing the physician to enter notes into the computer without touching a keyboard.

Data Sets

Standardization Efforts

The two basic data sets that apply to hospital-based care are the **Uniform Hospital Discharge Data Set (UHDDS)** and the **Uniform Ambulatory Care Data Set (UACDS)**. The UHDDS is important for inpatient coding and reporting, as it specifies definitions and rules for selecting the principal diagnosis, other diagnoses, the principal procedure, and several other elements that are critical

Uniform Hospital Discharge Data Set (UHDDS) standard data elements to be collected from individual inpatient records. The UHDDS data definitions are essential for correct reporting of inpatient data, for example on the UB-04.

Uniform Ambulatory Care Data Set (UACDS) a 16-item data set approved by the National Committee on Vital and Health Statistics (NCVHS); one of the first attempts to standardize ambulatory data collection efforts.

in DRG assignment and payment. The UACDS is a 16-item data set that differs from the UHDDS. For example, the UHDDS definition and rules for principal diagnosis do not apply in the outpatient setting. The National Committee on Vital and Health Statistics (NCVHS, 1996) developed a set of 42 core health data elements that could be used in either the inpatient or the outpatient setting, which has been under review but never has been rejected or adopted.

Data Elements for Emergency Department Systems (DEEDS) is a data set specific to the emergency department setting. Version 1.0 of DEEDS included more than 150 data elements in the following eight categories (NCIPC, 1997):

- Patient identification data,
- Facility and practitioner identification data,
- ED payment data,
- ED arrival and first assessment data,
- ED history and physical examination data,
- ED procedure and result data,
- ED medication data,
- ED disposition and diagnosis data.

DEEDS also includes standards for electronic data interchange (EDI) and, therefore, can facilitate the exchange of information with other health care information systems.

The greatest impetus toward collection of standardized data in ambulatory and all other health care settings has been provided by the Health Insurance Portability and Accountability Act (HIPAA). The HIPAA electronic data interchange (EDI) provisions require the adoption of standards for transactions, code sets, and identifiers. The Health Care Financing Administration (HCFA, the predecessor of CMS) delegated development and maintenance of the EDI standards to the following designated standards maintenance organizations (DSMOs):

- Accredited Standards Committee X12,
- Dental Content Committee of the American Dental Association,
- Health Level Seven,
- National Council for Prescription Drug Programs,
- National Uniform Billing Committee,
- National Uniform Claim Committee (HCFA, 2000).

HIPAA Eligibility Transaction System

For Medicare beneficiaries, a file, called the common working file (CWF), formerly was maintained for each beneficiary. Information from both Part A and Part B claims was maintained in these files, which Medicare Administrative Contractors (MACs) use for coordination of benefits, for claims validation, and for tracking utilization patterns.

In 2013, CMS announced a transition from the prior Common Working File (CWF) eligibility functions to the Health Insurance Portability & Accountability Act (HIPAA) Eligibility Transaction System (HETS) to work within the new 5010 transactions standard (CMS, 2014, August). Medicare Part A and Part B beneficiary information is maintained in the HETS system, allowing real-time eligibility requests for coverage using a secure closed private network to communicate with a CMS data center or via the CMS Extranet. This real-time eligibility information exchange is intended to provide hospitals with information about the beneficiary's coverage only at the time of the query; the hospital's MAC may be contacted to discuss coverage issues requiring clarity beyond the scope of the HETS.

SELF REVIEW 2.5

1. True or False? Revenue codes are reported on the UB-04 to indicate the general nature of the service provided, such as pharmacy, room and board, or intensive care.
2. What is the purpose of CCI edits?
3. What piece of legislation included a Medicare and Medicaid incentive program for health care providers who demonstrate the ability to "meaningfully use" EHRs?
4. What are the two basic data sets that apply to hospital-based care?
5. What data set is specific to the emergency department setting?

QUALITY AND UTILIZATION MANAGEMENT

Quality Assessment and Performance Improvement (QAPI)

Hospital accrediting agencies require that accredited hospitals implement hospital-wide performance improvement programs. For example, The Joint Commission's approach to performance improvement emphasizes designing processes, collecting data related to performance, analyzing the data collected (including comparing the hospital's performance to a standard or to that of peer hospitals), establishing priorities for processes to be improved, developing improvements for the priorities identified, and evaluating the extent of improvement achieved and sustained. DNV Healthcare utilizes performance improvement standards from the International Standards Organization's ISO 9001 quality management system requirements.

CMS has implemented both a Hospital Inpatient Quality Reporting (IQR) initiative and a Hospital Outpatient Quality Data Reporting Program (HOP QDRP) to enhance public awareness of quality-of-care issues. The IQR requires participating hospitals to submit patient-level data on discharges involving: (1) Acute Myocardial Infarction (AMI) Care, (2) Heart Failure (HF) Care, (3) Pneumonia (PN) Care, and (4) Surgical Care Infection Prevention (SCIP).

This information is displayed on the Hospital Compare (www.hospitalcompare.hhs.gov) website for public viewing.

For hospitals to receive their full Medicare annual payment update for the IPPS, they must fulfill all requirements for this program. The HOP QDRP includes outpatient department measures that focus on four topic areas: (1) Emergency Department (ED) Acute Myocardial Infarction (AMI) Care, (2) Chest Pain (CP), (3) Surgery, and (4) Imaging Efficiency (CMS, 2010). These results are made available to the public, and fulfilling HOP QDRP requirements also is necessary to receive the full payment update for the OPPS.

Another way in which quality affects reimbursement is the identification of hospital-acquired conditions (HACs) through the Present on Admission (POA) indicator associated with additional diagnoses coded on the hospital bill for inpatient services. Conditions that otherwise might increase reimbursement as CCs or MCCs do not increase reimbursement if they were acquired in the hospital—i.e., they were not present upon admission.

In addition to and in alignment with CMS performance standards, The Joint Commission also reviews (1) Pregnancy and Related Conditions (PR) and (2) Children's Asthma Care (CAC). The results for all of these hospital core quality measures are reported on The Joint Commission's Quality Check (www.qualitycheck.org) website.

Utilization Management (UM)

Utilization management focuses on the appropriateness, efficiency, and cost-effectiveness of health care. In the current climate of managed care and with prospective payment systems for Medicare in place, it is more important than ever for hospitals to be certain that they are rendering services efficiently. In the past, hospitals were reimbursed based on either their costs or their charges. Now both Medicare and private payers limit the charges and costs they will pay. To operate efficiently in such an environment requires a team effort from physicians, hospital staff, and administration.

In many hospitals, the staff members most directly responsible for monitoring utilization management are known as case managers. In earlier days, case managers often focused on working as liaisons between the medical staff and the patient and patient's family to make sure that necessary arrangements were made for a timely discharge. In recent years, however, the case management team responsibilities have expanded to include working with the managed care contracting office, decision support personnel, and health information services, in addition to their traditional role with clinicians, patients, and patients' families. In some instances, the case management team may work with health information services in clinical documentation improvement programs to help assure the presence of all the documentation necessary for correct coding. In some hospitals, health information management professionals have administrative authority over case management services. Many hospitals maintain both Utilization Review and Case Management teams allowing staff to focus on the use of resources and the coordination of care between families and facilities as separate functions. Regardless of reporting relationships, the case management team can be an important ally to health information services.

RISK MANAGEMENT AND LEGAL ISSUES

potentially compensable
events (PCEs) occur-
rences that may result in
litigation against the health
care provider or that may
require the health care
provider to financially
compensate an injured
party.

Many hospitals have risk management departments, whose role is to protect the organization from financial loss that could occur as a result of **potentially compensable events (PCEs)**, which are occurrences that may result in litigation against the health care provider or that may require the health care provider to compensate an injured party. Almost all hospitals have occurrence (or incident) reporting systems that allow risk managers to track PCEs and to identify risk areas within the organization that can be targeted for improvement. Policies and procedures should be instituted to identify errors to be reported. Documentation of errors should be to the point and impartial (Roth, 2009). Some hospitals have moved from paper-based occurrence reporting to electronic systems that allow risk managers to receive, review, and analyze occurrence reports online. The specific challenges for risk management in hospitals are described next.

Providing high-quality documentation of all patient encounters and services is a vital component of any risk management program. Health care providers must understand that only information documented in a manner that can be clearly interpreted will be used to judge whether or not appropriate patient care was given. Therefore, providers must ensure that all documentation is both legible and complete. All record entries should thoroughly describe the given situation and meet all regulatory requirements for content and authentication. Making sure that providers have properly timed/dated/signed an order or entry is an important step in following appropriate documentation guidelines.

Hospital outpatient services present unique challenges for hospital risk managers. Financial incentives to treat patients on an outpatient basis rather than an inpatient basis should be balanced with policies that encourage inpatient admission when appropriate in a given situation. Also, the limited duration of face-to-face contact between caregivers and patients in the outpatient setting requires extra attention to patient relations and documentation (Eubanks, 1990).

Because telephone contact often precedes or follows an outpatient visit, documentation of these calls is necessary. What the patient tells the caregiver and what the caregiver tells the patient both should be recorded. A follow-up telephone call is routine after many ambulatory surgery procedures. Proper documentation verifies that the patient was given the correct instructions and provides evidence of the patient's condition after surgery. A follow-up phone call can be a good public relations tool as well—which is also an important element in risk management (Eubanks, 1990).

Phone calls should be HIPAA-compliant. When the patient is not available, a message containing clinical information (such as test results) should not be delivered by voice mail or to a person other than the patient. A solid policy regarding which provider should contact the patient about an abnormal test result, what timeframe is acceptable for notification of test results, and the preferred mechanism for patient notification is critical to reducing liability. For noncompliant patients or for patients who cannot be reached directly, health care providers should consider sending test results via certified mail so documentation can be maintained indicating attempts at notification.

The emergency department is an area in which the hospital is particularly at legal risk. Patients and family members being treated in the emergency room are often under extreme stress and are sometimes unlikely to be understanding of the stresses that the emergency department staff may be facing. Emergency department staff must be well versed not only in clinical assessment and treatment, but also in customer service and in legal aspects of emergency care.

An example of a law with which the emergency department staff should be familiar is the **Emergency Medical Treatment and Active Labor Act (EMTALA)**, which imposes a legal duty on hospitals to screen and stabilize, if necessary, any patient who arrives in the emergency department (Curran, Hall, Bobinski, & Orentlicher, 1998). The purpose of EMTALA is to prevent the "dumping" of patients who may not be able to pay for emergency department services. Therefore, an appropriate screening cannot be delayed to inquire about insurance status or method of payment. If the patient is found to have an emergency medical condition, the hospital is required to stabilize the patient before attempting to transfer the patient elsewhere. In the case of a woman in active labor, stabilization generally means that delivery is completed before transfer (Special responsibilities of Medicare hospitals in emergency cases, 2009).

> **Emergency Medical Treatment and Active Labor Act (EMTALA)** a federal law that imposes a legal duty on hospitals to screen and stabilize, if necessary, any patient who arrives in the emergency department. The purpose of EMTALA is to prevent the "dumping" of patients who may not be able to pay for emergency department services.

SELF REVIEW 2.6

1. True or False? Fulfilling HOP QDRP requirements is necessary to receive the full payment update for the OPPS.

2. What are HACs, and how are they identified?

3. What is the name for staff members most directly responsible for monitoring utilization management?

4. True or False? When a patient is not available, a message containing clinical information (such as test results) should be left via voicemail or with a close family member/friend so the health care provider can remain HIPAA-compliant.

5. What does EMTALA stand for, and what is its purpose?

ROLE OF THE HEALTH INFORMATION MANAGEMENT PROFESSIONAL

The health information management (HIM) professional can play a variety of roles in hospital-based care. A health information manager may take a traditional role in health information services or may work in one of many other available positions. Most hospitals now have compliance departments, and the skills of health information managers are vital in promoting compliance with billing and HIPAA regulations. Many hospitals also are employing health information managers in positions related to coding, such as chargemaster coordinators. HIM has many other possible roles in performance improvement, cancer registry, trauma registry, information systems, and financial services. The specifics of each of these positions will vary from institution to institution, but a general idea of what could be expected in selected positions is provided in the following sections.

PROFESSIONAL SPOTLIGHT HOSPITAL

Who I am: Danielle Berthelot, MHI, RHIA, CHTS-IM. I have worked in health information management for more than 24 years. During this time I have been an active member, volunteer and advocate of the local, state, and national HIM associations (AHIMA). I served as Louisiana Health Information Management Association president in 2003–2004 and as Advocacy Strategy Manager for many years. I received both my bachelor's and master's degrees from Louisiana Tech University in Ruston, Louisiana.

Where I work: Woman's Hospital in Baton Rouge, Louisiana. Woman's Hospital is the largest, freestanding, nonprofit women's specialty hospital in the United States. More than 8,500 babies are born at Woman's each year, placing it among the 20 largest obstetric services in the United States and the largest in Louisiana. It has been named one of the Top 100 Best Places to Work in Healthcare, is a Breast Imaging Center of Excellence, is recognized by the National Accreditation Program for Breast Centers, and was the first area hospital to achieve the prestigious nursing Magnet® designation. Woman's also manages an outpatient women's clinic with the aim of improving access to medical care for impoverished women, and educating Louisiana's next generation of physicians though the LSU OB/GYN residency program.

What I do: I am the Privacy Officer and Director of Health Information Management, Utilization Management and Cancer Registry at Woman's Hospital. In my role, I serve as an advocate for the privacy and confidentiality of health information. I am responsible for the organization-wide release of health information, as well as ensuring that the organization's information privacy practices are in compliance with state and federal laws. I assist in providing quality data through the planning, development, implementation and monitoring of health information systems. I help to ensure that medically necessary, quality care is provided in the most efficient manner and in the most appropriate setting. I also play a vital role in the revenue cycle through accurate coding and reimbursement.

Why HIM knowledge is important in my role: HIM knowledge provides the foundation needed to meet the challenges presented by the constant changes and advances in health care and health information systems. HIM knowledge affords me the ability to be a resource to others within my organization. HIM knowledge is crucial to the design and implementation of new processes, such as those needed as health care organizations transition to a fully automated and integrated health record. HIM knowledge provides the basis for ensuring compliance with standards and regulations such as The Joint Commission and CMS.

Health Information Services

The health information services department deals with both inpatient and outpatient issues. Those in leadership positions in health information services must be familiar with accrediting and regulatory requirements that affect the patient record and must provide training for others in the department as appropriate.

Coding specialists typically work in health information services, although sometimes they report to patient financial services or the chief financial officer. In some instances, coders may specialize in coding specific types of cases, such as outpatient coding. Because HCPCS/CPT codes are not required on inpatient bills, health information services often assign certain coders to code all outpatient services. This arrangement allows coders to develop a specialization in outpatient coding rules, which are different from inpatient coding rules. Such specialization can lead to greater accuracy in outpatient coding. On the inpatient side, coders may specialize by service line—for example, coding for cardiovascular services.

In hospitals that still deal with paper records, some hospitals may have level positions designated to handle issues arising from the challenges of filing and retrieving a large number of records that may be requested at short intervals. As more hospitals implement electronic health records, positions in health information services will deal less with storage and retrieval of records but still will be vital in assuring the accuracy, completeness, and legal acceptability of the electronic record. Activities such as release of information or data collection and analysis are still within the purview of the health information manager, whether the record is paper or electronic.

Compliance Officer

Most hospitals appoint fulltime compliance officers who manage the compliance program. A health information manager possesses skills ideally suited for this position. In a large hospital or academic medical center, the compliance of many activities may be monitored, and a number of health information professionals may serve on the compliance staff.

In many hospitals the compliance program has developed into a distinct department. Health information managers may lead the compliance department and/or work in specialized compliance areas within the department. For example, some members of the compliance staff may focus on coding and billing issues, which requires expert knowledge of documentation and coding guidelines.

HIPAA compliance is another area in which a health information manager can provide expertise. To meet HIPAA requirements, hospitals should have a privacy officer and a security officer. In some hospitals, these positions are combined, and in others they are separate. In some hospitals, these responsibilities may fall under the compliance department, and in others these duties are delegated to a member of the information systems or health information services staff. A HIPAA compliance officer and his or her staff can provide HIPAA training; develop policies, procedures, and forms; or monitor the hospital's ongoing compliance with the HIPAA privacy, security, and/or EDI regulations.

Auditing is also an essential activity of the compliance program, whether auditing records against codes submitted, auditing release of information for appropriate authorization, or auditing the appropriateness of employee access to electronic health information—to name a few areas that may be addressed in the compliance plan. Whenever an audit identifies a problem area, plans for corrective action are developed in conjunction with the hospital service involved. Because developing an effective compliance program is a team effort involving many departments and health care professionals, good leadership skills are vital.

Revenue Cycle

In a typical business, the revenue cycle involves all of the activities from pricing to selling and then collecting what is owed from the purchaser. In health care in general and in hospitals in particular, the revenue cycle is complex for many reasons, not the least of which is the involvement of third-party payers. To present an extreme oversimplification of a hospital revenue cycle, the revenue cycle begins before any services are rendered, when patient identification and insurance information are collected. Then, as the patient begins to receive services, there are charges to capture and clinician documentation to be recorded in the patient record. At the conclusion of services, information from the record must be abstracted and coded for the bill. Specialized software "scrubs" the bill and errors are corrected before the bill goes to the payer.

Electronic systems usually are used to submit bills to payers, and paper processes are the norm for submitting bills to patients for the amounts that are the patient's responsibility. Accounts receivable are maintained, denials from third parties are investigated, and collection processes are initiated as appropriate until the hospital has determined that it has received the appropriate payment.

Because many of the activities in the revenue cycle involve matters in which the health information manager possesses expertise, an HIM professional can play a variety of roles that in this arena. One obvious role is that of coding specialist, which has been mentioned already. Clinical documentation improvement programs also are important to the revenue cycle, and HIM professionals are knowledgeable about the type of documentation needed for accurate coding. Because much of the coding for an ambulatory patient's bill is generated automatically by the hospital's chargemaster, someone with knowledge of coding has to be involved in chargemaster maintenance. Some hospitals bring in health information managers as consultants to review their chargemasters. Sometimes health information managers are employed fulltime in the patient financial services office and have supervision of the chargemaster among their duties. This is to make sure that HCPCS codes are added, changed, or deleted as appropriate and that they accurately reflect the procedures being performed. Their duties also may involve working with the leaders of various departments to help set appropriate prices for services included in the chargemaster. A health information manager also may work in or with patient financial services to investigate rejected claims.

Another role in the financial area is that of charge capture analyst, whose responsibilities include reviewing outpatient charges to ensure that all charges are accurate and complete. Health information managers have found employment in information systems, too, working with various electronic applications that move the revenue cycle along.

Other Roles

A health information manager can play many other roles in the hospital setting. For example, performance improvement is an area in which the skills of health information managers are well utilized. An HIM professional can serve as a performance improvement specialist, collecting, analyzing, and reporting data. In some hospitals, a health information management professional serves as director of the performance improvement department. Health information professionals sometimes play a role in utilization management, medical staff services, and many other areas of the hospital as well.

SELF REVIEW 2.7

1. Name various areas within a hospital setting that have possible roles for HIM professionals.
2. True or False? To meet HIPAA requirements, hospitals should have a privacy officer and a security officer.
3. What kind of services does a HIPAA compliance officer and his/her staff provide?
4. True or False? Because much of the information for an ambulatory patient's bill is generated automatically by the hospital's chargemaster, it is not necessary for someone with a knowledge of coding to be involved in chargemaster maintenance.

TRENDS

Hospitals continue to merge with other health care facilities and to incorporate a wide variety of ambulatory and other services into their systems, increasing the complexity of hospital-based care. The role of hospitalists in caring for inpatients has expanded greatly since the mid-1990s, and more growth in the number of hospitalists is expected in the future. Although the number of long-term acute care hospitals rose dramatically in the three decades following the 1980s, the growth rate in this sector seems to have stabilized in recent years. Federal regulators and private accrediting organizations have placed a renewed focus on quality improvement initiatives within health care organizations. Reimbursement rates often are tied to these initiatives, and reported data made available to the public via the Internet.

Implementation of electronic health records is accelerating rapidly in light of the incentives and penalties promulgated by ARRA. One trend that cuts across several areas—documentation, coding, reimbursement, and revenue-cycle management—is the increasing scrutiny given to coding and payment issues by auditing initiatives such as those described in Chapter 1. Health information managers will experience increasing opportunities and challenges in addressing the information needs and reimbursement requirements of more complex hospital and health care networks.

SUMMARY

Hospitals offer a broad range of services. These include services performed in acute care units, ambulatory surgery units, hospital clinics, emergency services, observation services, partial hospitalization, and ancillary services.

Many different types of health care professionals participate in hospital patient care. Physicians, nurses, physical therapists, occupational therapists, clinical laboratory scientists, pharmacists, and others may provide diagnostic or therapeutic services to hospital patients. One type of provider unique to hospital care is the hospitalist—a physician who provides comprehensive hospital inpatient care to patients.

Hospital regulations require that all hospitals be licensed by the state in which they are located. Other regulations to which hospital services may be subject are found in the federal Conditions of Participation for Hospitals and in the accreditation standards of voluntary groups such as The Joint Commission, DNV Healthcare, and the American Osteopathic Association's Healthcare Facilities Accreditation Program (HFAP).

Documentation requirements for hospital inpatients and outpatients depend on the type of services received. Requirements for documentation in patient records can be found in the regulations and standards of governmental and voluntary accreditation agencies. Factors other than regulatory and accreditation requirements play a role in hospital documentation. Documentation audits to determine whether services billed are documented appropriately in the patient record are increasingly common. Health care providers lose reimbursement for services that are not documented properly. Rules have been promulgated to clarify what documentation is necessary to justify services billed by teaching physicians.

Reimbursement methodologies for inpatient and outpatient hospital care include managed care contracts, fee schedule payments, and prospective payment systems. A renewed focus on the efficient use of health care resources will be a continuing trend as providers and payers seek ways to improve quality of care while reducing overall costs.

The major coding and classification systems used in the hospital inpatient and outpatient settings are the current modifications of ICD and HCPCS (whose major component is CPT). Medicare requires that diagnoses be reported using the current clinical modification of ICD for inpatients and outpatients alike. Inpatient procedures are coded with the most current version of the ICD procedure classification, whereas outpatient procedures must be reported with HCPCS. Revenue codes are used on both inpatient and outpatient bills to explain the general nature of the service performed.

Data and information flow into the patient record from each significant patient contact with a member of the health care team. The hospital must be able to provide access to all components of the patient's record when a patient is seen in any hospital setting. When using paper records, maintaining a comprehensive, yet readily accessible, record is a challenge. Electronic health record systems can help to solve the challenge of making the record quickly available to any patient unit. An electronic health record can be accessed by diverse providers throughout the hospital as the patient presents to various departments for different services.

HIPAA is one of the driving forces that determine the standards for the data elements that should be maintained for every patient. UHDDS is a data set for hospital inpatients, and UACDS is an outpatient data set. DEEDS is a standard data set for emergency department services. A data set for each Medicare beneficiary is also found in the HETS maintained by Medicare Administrative Contractors.

Measuring and improving the quality of care is vital to providing quality services, meeting accreditation standards, and achieving optimum payment for services. Utilization management programs analyze the appropriateness, efficiency, and cost-effectiveness of patient care. Risk management focuses on improving care, documentation, and patient satisfaction to reduce the possibility of legal liability.

The HIM professional can play a variety of roles in the hospital setting. A health information manager may take a traditional role in health information services or may work in one of many other hospital departments. Health information managers are particularly well suited to the position of compliance officer. Many hospitals also are employing health information managers in various positions to help manage the revenue cycle. Health information managers also work in performance improvement roles and sometimes in other areas, such as utilization management.

REVIEW QUESTIONS

Knowledge-Based Questions

1. What has been the trend in the utilization of hospital-based services? What factors help to account for this trend?
2. List and describe five different types of outpatient services.
3. List and describe three different types of hospital outpatients.
4. What organization accredits the majority of hospitals in the United States? Which accrediting organization most recently received "deeming authority" from CMS for its hospital accreditation program?
5. What key components must both inpatient and outpatient records contain in the documentation of surgery?
6. What are the key issues with regard to documentation of services rendered by teaching physicians?
7. What is the hospital chargemaster or charge description master?
8. What are DRGs? What are APCs? What is their impact on hospital reimbursement?

9. What coding systems are used in hospital-based care?
10. What is EMTALA?
11. What is ARRA?
12. What factors should be considered to avoid legal risk in hospital-based care?
13. Describe various roles of the HIM professional in hospital-based care.

Critical Thinking Questions

1. If The Joint Commission requires that "the hospital initiates and maintains a medical record for every individual assessed or treated," what factors allow a hospital to maintain minimal data, such as test results in the case of some referred outpatients?
2. Select two of the three hospital accrediting organizations mentioned in this chapter, and write a brief essay comparing and contrasting the two organizations that you selected. Use outside resources, if necessary, but remember to think critically and avoid relying heavily on marketing or promotional information.

WEB ACTIVITY

Visit the website of the Healthcare Compliance Association at http://www.hcca-info.org. Locate information about the "CHC" certification offered by this group. Find the Healthcare Compliance Certification Board (HCCB) handbook, and look at the detailed content outline for HCCB's certification examination.

1. In which content areas do you think you could demonstrate skill as a result of your health information management training?
2. Which content areas would require more training on your part?

CASE STUDY

Grace Greene, RHIA, has been offered a leadership position at Greater Good Hospital to assist in improving the hospital's revenues. The hospital recognized that her knowledge and experience in coding and clinical documentation would be valuable in this effort, but these are not the only skills that will be needed to fine-tune the hospital's revenue cycle. Recognizing that many components of the revenue cycle and many hospital departments have a role to play, what are some of the processes that Grace and her team should examine in assessing where the hospital currently stands and in looking for possible areas of improvement?

REFERENCES AND SUGGESTED READINGS

ACEP (American College of Emergency Physicians). n.d. *Costs of Emergency Care.* [Online]. http://www3.acep.org/patients.aspx?id=25902 (2010, May 24)

ACEP (American College of Emergency Physicians). n.d. *Observation Care Payments to Hospitals* FAQ. [Online]. http://www.acep.org/content.aspx?id=30486 (2014, Nov. 28).

AHA (American Hospital Association). (2013). *Hospital statistics.* Chicago: Health Forum LLC.

ALTHA (Acute Long Term Hospital Association). n.d. [Online]. http://www.altha.org (2010, June 3).

Brodnik, M., McCain, M. C., Rinehart-Thompson, L. A., & Reynolds, R. B. 2009. *Fundamentals of Law for Health Informatics and Information Management.* Chicago: American Health Information Management Association.

CMS (Centers for Medicare & Medicaid Services). (2002). Prospective Payment System for Long-Term Care Hospitals: Implementation and FY 2003 Rates. *Federal Register, 67*(169), pp. 55954–56090.

CMS (Centers for Medicare & Medicaid Services. (2009). Medicare Program: Proposed Changes to the Hospital Outpatient Prospective Payment System and CY 2010 Payment Rates; Proposed Changes to the Ambulatory Surgical Center Payment System and CY 2010 Payment Rates; Proposed Rule. [Online]. http://edocket.access.gpo.gov/2009/E9-15882.htm (2010, May 29).

CMS (Centers for Medicare & Medicaid Services). (2010). New health care electronic transactions standards Versions 5010, D.0, and 3.0. *Medicare Learning Network.* [Online]. http://www.cms.gov/Regulations-and-Guidance/HIPAA-Administrative-Simplification/Versions5010andD0/downloads/w5010BasicsFctSht.pdf (2014, Nov. 28).

CMS (Centers for Medicare & Medicaid Services). (2012), May. Chapter II: Coverage of hospital services. *Hospital Manual.* [Online]. http://www.cms.gov/Regulations-and-Guidance/Legislation/CFCsAndCoPs/Hospitals.html (2014, Nov. 28).

CMS (Centers for Medicare & Medicaid Services). (2013), April. Acute care hospital inpatient prospective payment system. *Medicare Learning Network Payment System Fact Sheet Series.* [Online]. http:/www.cms.gov/Outreach-and-Education/Medicare-Learning-Network-MLN/MLNProducts/downloads/AcutePaymtSysfctsht.pdf (2014, Nov. 28).

CMS (Centers for Medicare & Medicaid Services). (2014), July. Section 100—Teacaing physician services. *Medicare Claims Processing Manual, Chapter 12—Physicians/Nonphysician Practitioners.* [Online]. http://www.cms.gov/Regulations-and-Guidance/Guidance/Manuals/downloads/clm104c12.pdf (2014, Nov. 28).

CMS (Centers for Medicare & Medicaid Services). (2014, August). HIPAA Eligibility Transaction System (HETS) Healthcare eligibility benefit inquiry and response (270–271) 5010 companion guide. [Online]. http://www.cms.gov/Research-Statistics-Data-and-Systems/CMS-Information-Technology[HETSHelp/Downloads]HETS270271 CompanionGuide5010.pdf (2014, Nov. 28).

CMS (Centers for Medicare & Medicaid Services). (2015). Hospital outpatient prospective payment—proposed rule. [Online]. http://www.cms.gov[Medicare]Medicare-Fee-for-Service-Payment[HospitalOutpatientPPS[Hospital-Outpatient-Regulations-and-Notices-Items[CMS-1613-P.html (2014, Nov. 28).

CMS Manual System Pub. 100-02 Medicare Benefit Policy. (2004, May 7). Transmittal 10: Partial Hospitalization. [Online]. https://www.cms.gov/Regulations-and-Guidance/Guidance/Transmittals/downloads/R10BP.pdf (2015, July 8).

CMS Manual System Pub. 100-02 Medicare Benefit Policy. (2004, September 10). Transmittal 19: Hospital Services Covered under Part B. [Online]. https://www.cms.gov/Regulations-and-Guidance/Guidance/Transmittals/downloads/R19bp.pdf (2015, July 8).

Conditions of Participation for Hospitals, *Code of Federal Regulations*, Title 42, pt. 482, 2010 ed.

Curran, W. J., Hall, M. A., Bobinski, M. A., & Orentlicher, D. (1998). *Health Care Law and Ethics*. New York: Aspen Law & Business.

DNV. 2010, Jan. 11. DNV Accreditation Program: Frequently asked questions. [Online]. http://www.dnvaccreditation.com (2010, May 26).

Dowling, D. A. 2008. Industry trends. *Journal for Healthcare Quality Web Exclusive, 30*(6), W6–W13. [Online]. www.nahq.org/journal/online (2010, May 26).

Electronic Health Record Incentive Program; Proposed Rule, 75 Fed. Reg. 1844–2011 (2010) (to be codified at 42 C.F.R. pts. 412, et al.).

Elliott, V. 2012, Sept. 3. Evolution of the Hospitalist, *American Medical News*. [Online]. http://www.amednews.com/article/20120903/business/309039970/4 (2014, Nov. 28).

Eubanks, P. (1990). Outpatient care: A nationwide revolution. *Hospitals*, August 5, pp. 28–35.

Glondys, B. (2000). Glossary of healthcare services and statistical terms. In K. G. Youmans, *Basic Healthcare Statistics for Health Information Management Professionals* (pp. 139–175). Chicago: American Health Information Management Association.

Hanken, M. A., & Waters, K. A. (1994). *Glossary of Healthcare Terms*. Chicago: American Health Information Management Association.

HCFA (Healthcare Financing Administration). (2000), Aug. 17. Announcement of Designated Standard Maintenance Organizations. 65 *Federal Register*, 50373.

HCUPnet. (2011) National Statistics, All ED Visits. [Online]. http://hcupnet.ahrq.gov/HCUPnet.jsp (2014, Nov. 28).

Institute of Medicine. (1991). *The Computer-based Patient Record: An Essential Technology for Healthcare*. Washington, DC: National Academy Press.

Lawrence, R. S., & Jonas, S. (1990). Ambulatory care. In A. R. Kovner (Ed.), *Health Care Delivery in the United States* (4th ed., pp. 106–140). New York: Springer Publishing Company.

Liu, K., Baseggio, C., Wissoker, D., Maxwell, S., Haley, J., & Long, S. (2001). Long-term care hospitals under Medicare: Facility-level characteristics. *Health Care Financing Review, 23*(2), 1–18.

MedPAC. (2008), October. Long-term care hospitals payment system. *Payment Basics*. [Online]. http://www.medpac.gov (2010, May 29).

MedPAC. (2014), March. Long-term care hospital services. *Report to the Congress: Medicare Payment Policy*. [Online]. http:/www.medpac.gov (2015, July 22).

NCIPC (National Center for Injury Prevention and Control). (1997). Data elements for emergency department systems, release 1.0. Atlanta, GA: Centers for Disease Control and Prevention. [Online]. http://www.cdc.gov/ncipc/pub-res/pdf/deeds.pdf (2003, Aug. 4).

NCVHS (National Committee on Vital and Health Statistics). (1996). Core health data elements: Report of the National Committee on Vital and Health Statistics. [Online]. http://www.ncvhs.hhs.gov/ncvhsr1.htm#Future (2003, Aug. 4).

Odom-Wesley, B. (2009). *Documentation for Medical Records*. Chicago: American Health Information Management Association.

OIG (Office of the Inspector General, U.S. Department of Health and Human Services). (2009). Centers for Medicare & Medicaid Services work plan for fiscal year 2009. [Online]. https://oig.hhs.gov/publications/docs/workplan/2009/WorkPlanFY2009.pdf (2015, July 24).

OIG (Office of the Inspector General, U.S. Department of Health and Human Services). (2010). Centers for Medicare & Medicaid Services work plan for fiscal year 2010. [Online]. http://oig.hhs.gov/publications/docs/workplan/2010/Work_Plan_FY_2010.pdf (2014, Nov. 28).

OIG (Office of the Inspector General, U.S. Department of Health and Human Services). (2015). Centers for Medicare & Medicaid Services work plan for fiscal year 2015. [Online]. http://oig.hhs.gov/reports-and-publications/archives/workplan/2015/FY15-Work-Plan.pdf (2014, Nov. 28).

Physician Services in Teaching Settings. 42 C.F.R. pt. 415, subpt. D, (2014 ed.) [Online]. http://www.ecfr.gov/cgi-bin/text-idx?tpl=/ecfrbrowse/Title42/42cfr415_main_02.tpl (2014, Nov. 28).

Roth, J. A. (2009). Risk management ad quality improvement. In M. Brodnik, M. C. McCain, L. A. Rinehart-Thompson, & R. B. Reynolds (Eds.), *Fundamentals of Law for Health Informatics and Information Management* (pp. 289–314). Chicago: American Health Information Management Association.

Slee, D. A., Slee, V. N., & Schmidt, H. J. (2008). *Slee's Healthcare Terms* (5th ed.). Sudbury, MA: Jones and Bartlett.

3M Health Information Systems. (2013), July. 3M™ APR DRG Classification System and 3M™ APR DRG Software. [Online]. /http://multimedia.3m.com/mws/media/478415O/fact-sheet-apr-drg-classification-apr-drg-software-07-13.pdf?fn=aprdrg_fs.pdf (2014, Nov. 28).

Special Responsibilities of Medicare Hospitals in Emergency Cases. 42 C.F.R pt. 489, Sect. 24, (2009 ed.)

The Joint Commission. (2015). Comprehensive *Accreditation Manual for Hospitals*. Oak Brook, IL: Author.

KEY RESOURCES

Acute Long Term Hospital Association
http: //www.altha.org

American College of Emergency Physicians
http://www.acep.org

American Health Information Management Association
http://www.ahima.org

American Hospital Association
http://www.aha.org

American Society for Healthcare Risk Management (ASHRM)
http://www.ashrm.org

Association of American Medical Colleges
http://www.aamc.org

Centers for Medicare & Medicaid Services
http://www.cms.gov

Code of Federal Regulations
http://www.gpo.gov

Health Care Compliance Association
http://www.hcca-info.org

Healthcare Facilities Accreditation Program (American Osteopathic Association)
http://www.hfap.org

Healthcare Financial Management Association
http://www.hfma.org

MedPac, The Medicare Payment Advisory Commission
http://www.medpac.gov

National Association of Long Term Hospitals
http://www.nalth.org

National Integrated Accreditation of Healthcare Organizations (NIAHO)
http://www.dnvaccreditation.com
and
http://www.dnv.com

Office of the Inspector General
http://oig.hhs.gov

Society of Hospital Medicine
http://www.hospitalmedicine.org

The Joint Commission
http://www.jointcommission.org

CHAPTER 3

Freestanding Ambulatory Care

Rebecca B. Reynolds, EdD, RHIA, FAHIMA |
Elizabeth D. Bowman, MPA, RHIA, FAHIMA

LEARNING OBJECTIVES

Upon successful completion of this chapter, you should be able to:

- List the types of freestanding ambulatory centers and differentiate among them regarding the kinds of programs and services they offer.
- Define basic terms related to freestanding ambulatory care facilities.
- List the major agencies or organizations that set standards for the facility, and interpret their standards.
- Discuss pertinent record completion, filing, quality assessment, coding, indexing, and computer systems for freestanding ambulatory care facilities.
- Discuss payment systems for freestanding ambulatory care.

Setting	Description	Synonyms/Examples
Public Health Department	Organization that provides services to promote the health of the community as a whole, such as immunizations and disease screenings	Community Health
Community Health Center	Ambulatory setting originating in the 1960s to provide ambulatory care to the indigent of a particular neighborhood; subsequent legislation expanded scope to any medically underserved area or population	Federally Qualified Health Center (FQHC) Neighborhood Health Center
Rural Health Clinic	A health care clinic located in an underserved rural area and offering physician services as well as services of mid-level providers or advanced practice clinicians	RHC
Industrial Health Centers	Ambulatory setting in which care is provided to employees at their place of work or at an employer-contracted site	Industrial Clinic Occupational Health Center
Ambulatory Surgery Centers	Setting provided for surgery on an ambulatory basis	Surgicenter
Urgent Care Centers	Ambulatory care setting in which patients are seen on a walk-in basis without appointments	Minor Emergency Center Walk-in Clinic
Physician Private Practices	Setting in which physicians practice independently rather than being employed by an organization such as an urgent care center or clinic	Doctor's Office Solo Practice Group Practice
University Health Centers	Ambulatory setting in which care is provided to students while they are in college, as well as faculty and staff in some cases	Student Health University Health Employee Health
Birth Centers	Ambulatory setting that provides labor and delivery services for uncomplicated deliveries	Birthing Centers

INTRODUCTION TO SETTING

freestanding ambulatory care outpatient care provided to patients in a non-hospital setting.

Freestanding ambulatory care differs from hospital-based ambulatory care in that freestanding ambulatory care sites are not owned by or operationally integrated with a hospital. The various freestanding settings include public health departments, community health centers, rural health clinics, and urgent care centers. The setting in which most people receive care is the physician's private practice. The type of ambulatory care facility determines the types of patients seen, the types of caregivers, and, therefore, the types of information collected.

physician private practice a setting in which physicians practice in their own business rather than working for an organization such as a clinic or urgent care center owned or operated by others.

A large portion of freestanding ambulatory care is provided by **physician private practices** in an office where physicians see ambulatory patients. Physicians may practice alone, called solo practice, or in a group. A group practice usually involves three or more physicians, either all of the same specialty or of different specialties. Physicians practicing together usually share records, equipment, and offices and have an arrangement to divide the profits of the practice. Historically, these practices have been the most common setting in which ambulatory care is provided.

public health department an organization that provides services to promote the health of the community as a whole, such as immunizations and disease screenings; usually an agency of state or local government.

Other types of ambulatory care have been developed to meet the needs of patients. The **public health department,** for example, provides a variety of services to improve the health of the community as a whole, in addition to health care for individuals. Emphasis is placed on preventive services such as immunizations, screenings, and notifying contacts of patients with infectious conditions such as tuberculosis and syphilis, to prevent further spread of the condition throughout the community.

The **community health center** setting came into being as a result of federal social legislation in the 1960s. The purpose is to meet the medical needs of people who, because of their location and their inability to pay, may not receive the care they need in the traditional physician's office or clinic. These clinics typically serve a defined neighborhood area that typically is an underserved area or population (Geiger, 2005).

In 1989, Congress passed legislation allowing community health centers (and also migrant health centers) to receive enhanced reimbursement for Medicare and Medicaid services as a **federally qualified health center (FQHC)**. FQHC's include organizations receiving grants under Section 300 of the Public Health Service Act. FQHCs are nonprofit or public organizations that provide or arrange for comprehensive health care services to medically underserved areas or population, offer a sliding fee scale, provide comprehensive services, have an ongoing quality assurance program and have a governing board of directors (HRSA, 2006).

The **Rural Health Clinic (RHC)** is a health care clinic that utilizes advanced practice clinicians such as physician assistants and nurse practitioners in addition to physician services and is located in an underserved rural area. RHCs make health care services available to non-urbanized communities as defined by the U.S. Department of Commerce census bureau. RHCs offer services that might not be accessible if the services were reimbursed with traditional payment models—www.raconline.org

The **urgent care center** arose to meet the need for care outside of regular physicians' office hours. Prior to urgent care centers, patients sought care in expensive hospital emergency departments. Urgent care centers usually see patients on a walk-in basis without appointments and provide the same services as physicians' offices. Most urgent care centers are open seven days a week plus holidays to meet the needs of the patients.

The **ambulatory surgery center (ASC)** arose to meet the need for a less expensive setting than the hospital for low-risk surgical procedures. Its growth was fed by the Omnibus Reconciliation Act of 1980, which set up a Medicare payment system specifically for ASCs (ASC, 2010). Although some physicians perform minor surgical procedures in their offices, the main difference in a freestanding ASC is that it usually has at least one full, dedicated operating room; is often licensed by the state; and provides surgical privileges to doctors in the community, not just in one practice.

An **industrial** or **occupational health center** provides care to employees at their place of work or at an employer-contracted site. Services range from providing care for work-related injuries, to new employee evaluations, and return-to-work physicals following an accident. These centers often provide immunization and screenings such as auditory tests for employees at risk for hearing loss or medical surveillance screening for employees with exposure to or who work with identified hazards.

community health center an ambulatory setting developed in the 1960s to provide ambulatory care to indigent people in a specified neighborhood. Subsequent legislation expanded the scope of these health centers to any medically underserved area or population.

federally qualified health center (FQHC) a nonprofit or public organization that provides or arranges for comprehensive health care services to a medically underserved area or population.

rural health clinic (RHC) a health care setting that, in addition to physician services, utilizes advanced practice clinicians such as physician assistants and nurse practitioners, and is located in an underserved rural area.

urgent care center an ambulatory care setting in which patients are seen on a walk-in basis without appointments. These centers provide service for longer hours than most private physician practices.

ambulatory surgery center (ASC) a setting provided for surgery on an ambulatory basis. Centers usually have at least one fulltime operating room and provide surgical privileges to physicians in the community.

industrial or occupational health center an ambulatory setting where care is provided to employees at their place of work.

university health center   an ambulatory setting in which care is provided to the university staff and students.

The **university health center** provides care to students while they are enrolled in college, and in some cases, also to faculty and staff. Some centers provide only minor services, whereas others provide the full scope of care. The extent of their services often depends on the size of the university and the range of services available to students outside of the university community. Services may include immunizations, new employee evaluations, treatment for injuries and exposures, and training and wellness programs.

birth center   an ambulatory setting that provides labor and delivery services in uncomplicated deliveries.

The **birth center** setting arose to counteract what was thought to be rigidity by hospitals in providing birthing options. Birth centers provide a homelike atmosphere for deliveries and provide contraceptive and other family planning services. Hospitals historically would not allow family or other support persons within the labor and delivery suites. Alternative caregivers such as midwives also were not allowed to perform deliveries. Freestanding birth centers and family planning centers were developed to provide the homelike environment requested by patients, along with a variety of caregivers providing support.

family planning center   an ambulatory setting that provides family planning services.

The concept of a **family planning center** was established by the U.S. Department of Health and Human Services' Office of Population Affairs Title X funding. Family planning centers offer various FDA-approved contraceptive methods and counseling, breast and cervical cancer screening, pregnancy testing and counseling, screening for sexually transmitted infections, and patient education (Fowler et al., 2012).

Types of Patients

The first factor to consider in developing health information management services is the type of freestanding ambulatory facility. The second factor is the type of patients seen in the setting. As can be seen from the types of settings providing ambulatory care, these include a variety of patients. Patients seen in the ambulatory setting are not critically ill. Care may be provided to well patients, as in the case of well-baby care and the health screenings provided in occupational health settings. Most of the patients, however, are the ambulatory sick who may have minor acute problems, such as sore throats and earaches, or chronic conditions, such as heart disease and diabetes.

All ages of patients are included. Some facilities see only a certain type of patient. Birth centers, for example, see only pregnant women. Ambulatory surgery centers see patients with surgically treatable diseases. The types of patients seen by a facility affect the information that must be maintained. In a pediatric clinic, for example, information on immunizations, growth, and development is necessary. Birth centers must provide information on labor and delivery.

Types of Caregivers

In planning HIM services, the next consideration involves the types of caregivers who are treating patients in the facility. Different types of caregivers provide different types of documentation, affecting the information available (see Figure 3-1). Because physician practices provide most ambulatory care services, physicians are the main caregivers. They may be in private practice, or they may be employees of settings such as university health or urgent care centers.

Other professionals such as **nurse practitioners (NP)** also provide care in the ambulatory setting. A nurse practitioner is a registered nurse who has had additional training in areas such as family or pediatric care. NPs often are the primary caregivers in settings such as industrial clinics and neighborhood health centers. A **certified nurse midwife (CNM)** often practices in a birth and family planning center. A **physician assistant (PA)** may be seen in a setting similar to settings employing nurse practitioners. PAs are not nurses but have received training to use independent judgment in treating patients. Non-physicians such as NPs, CNMs, and PAs, whose licenses allow them to exercise a degree of independent judgment under the supervision of a physician, are called a **mid-level provider (MLP)** or an **advanced practice clinician**. Other practitioners that may be seen include dentists, nutritionists, and counselors.

nurse practitioner (NP) a registered nurse who has additional training and credentials that allow for limited independent practice.

certified nurse midwife (CNM) a nurse practitioner who handles pregnancy, labor, and delivery.

physician assistant (PA) a professional who is not a nurse but has received training to use independent judgment in treating patients.

mid-level provider (MLP) also called an advanced practice clinician; a health care professional whose license permits a degree of independent judgment in treating patients, generally under the supervision of a physician. Examples of mid-level providers include nurse practitioners, physician assistants, and certified nurse midwives. Scope of practice and requirements for supervision vary by type of provider and by state.

advanced practice clinician also called a mid-level provider; a health care professional whose license permits a degree of independent judgment in treating patients, generally under the supervision of a physician. Examples of advanced practice clinicians include nurse practitioners, physician assistants, and certified nurse midwives. Scope of practice and requirements for supervision vary by type of provider and by state.

FIGURE 3-1

Caregivers in Freestanding Ambulatory Care.

Ambulatory Caregivers	Type of Service Provided
Physician	MD or DO providing complete medical care
Nurse Practitioner (NP)	Advanced practice RN providing care within a certain area of practice such as family care or pediatrics
Certified Nurse Midwife (CNM)	Advanced practice RN providing care during pregnancy, labor, and delivery in uncomplicated cases
Physician Assistant (PA)	Non-RN using independent judgment under the supervision of a physician in providing care
Dentist	DDS or DMD specializing in care of the teeth and gums
Nutritionist	Practitioner providing advice and planning for patients' nutritional needs
Counselor/Therapist	Practitioner providing care for behavioral and mental problems
Psychologist	PhD providing care for behavioral and mental problems
Social Worker	Practitioner assisting patients with social and environmental problems
Chiropractor	Practitioner providing manipulation, usually of the spine, to improve health
Podiatrist	Practitioner providing care of the feet

1. The major difference between freestanding ambulatory care and hospital-based ambulatory care is _____.
   a. services
   b. patients
   c. ownership
   d. providers

2. The setting where care for an urban, underserved population would most likely be provided is _____.
   a. public health department
   b. rural health clinic
   c. urgent care centers
   d. community health centers

3. Which of the following is not considered to be a mid-level provider/advanced practice clinician?
   a. nurse practitioner
   b. dental hygienist
   c. physician assistant
   d. certified nurse midwife

REGULATORY ISSUES

Determining the types of caregivers in a facility identifies both who is entering information into the health information system and the internal users of information. The regulations that a facility must follow determine the external users of information and standards for what information should be maintained. Regulations and standards usually are determined by licensure, accreditation, certification bodies.

Licensure

Licensure is required for a health care facility to operate, and typically is granted, reviewed, and surveyed by the state department of health or other state-level department. Requirements for licensure vary by the type of facility. Because licensure standards are set by the state, often through the state's department of health or board of medical examiners, they are different in every state. Laws governing which facilities must be licensed also differ from state to state. In most states, physician offices do not require licensure; however, the physician office records are governed by rules and regulations governing the practice of medicine in the state. For example, the Tennessee State Board of Medical Examiners (BME), Chapter 0880-2.15 Medical Records state that the purpose of the rules are to give physicians, their professional and non-professional staffs, and the public direction about the content, transfer, retention, and destruction of those records.

A distinction exists between a physician's medical records for a patient receiving services in the physician's office and those records created by the physician for that patient for purposes of services provided in a hospital. State law also dictates the services that other licensed independent practitioners (LIPs) are authorized to perform under the supervision of a licensed physician. Most state laws outline the required statutory oversight of physician assistants, orthopedic physician assistants, and Certified Nurse Practitioners. A licensed independent practitioner may have some practice autonomy and may assess, diagnose, treat, and manage patient health problems and needs. For information related to the health professionals and the health-related professional boards recognized in the state, readers should refer to the specific state statutes.

Ambulatory surgical treatment centers (ASTC) and birth centers, however, usually have to meet licensure standards. Most licensure standards include rules for what information the facility must maintain in its health records. They are, therefore, an excellent source of information on what must be included in the information system.

The content of the medical record for an ASC is similar to the content of the hospital record. There must be a complete history and physical work-up in the chart of every patient prior to surgery, except in emergencies. If the history has been dictated, but not yet recorded in the patient's chart, there must be a statement to that effect and an admission note in the chart by the practitioner who admitted the patient. A properly executed informed consent, advance directive, and organ donation forms must be in the patient's chart before surgery, except in emergencies. An operative report describing techniques, findings, and tissues removed or altered must be written or dictated immediately following surgery and signed by the surgeon.

Adequate provisions for immediate post-operative care have to be included. The operating room register must be complete and up-to-date.

Nursing Service

A licensed registered nurse (R.N.) must be on duty at all times. Additional appropriately trained staff members are to be provided as needed to ensure that the patient's medical needs are fully met.

Pharmaceutical Services

The ASTC is required to provide drugs and biologicals in a safe and effective manner in accordance with accepted standards of practice. These drugs and biologicals must be stored in a separate room or cabinet, which has to be kept locked at all times.

Ancillary and Laboratory Services

All ancillary or supportive health or medical services, including but not limited to, radiological, pharmaceutical, or medical laboratory services have to be provided in accordance with all applicable state and federal laws and regulations. Any patient terminating pregnancy in an ASTC must have an Rh type performed on her blood, documented prior to the procedure. In addition, she has to be given the opportunity to receive Rh immune globulin after an appropriate crossmatch procedure has been performed within a licensed laboratory.

Medical Records/Documentation Requirements

In Tennessee, for example, the ASTC must comply with the Medical Records Act of 1974, T.C.A. § 68-11-301, et seq. A medical record shall be maintained for each person receiving medical care provided by the ASTC and shall include the following:

1. Patient identification
2. Name of nearest relative or other responsible agent
3. Identification of primary source of medical care
4. Dates and times of visits
5. Signed informed consent
6. Pertinent medical history
7. Diagnosis
8. Physician examination report
9. Anesthesia records of pertinent preoperative and postoperative reports including pre-anesthesia evaluation, type of anesthesia, technique, and dosage used
10. Operative report
11. Discharge summary, including instructions for self-care and instructions for obtaining postoperative emergency care
12. Reports of all laboratory and diagnostic procedures along with tests performed and the results authenticated by the appropriate personnel
13. X-ray reports

Medical records shall be current and confidential. Medical records and copies thereof shall be made available when requested by an authorized representative of the board or the department.

Medicare Certification

Certain types of health care facilities must be Medicare-certified according to Medicare Conditions of Participation or Conditions of Coverage before they can participate in the Medicare program. Conditions of Participation/Coverage exist for ambulatory surgical services, for rural health clinics, and for federally qualified health centers. In the case of rural health clinics (RHCs), Medicare certification confers a special status that permits reimbursement from both Medicare and Medicaid.

The goal of the rural health clinic program is to increase access to primary care in medically underserved rural areas by using PAs, NPs, and CNMs in areas of physician shortage (Rural Health Clinics, 2015). Similarly, federally qualified health centers (FQHCs), which may provide health care to any medically underserved area or population, must meet the requirements in the FQHCs Conditions for Coverage to be eligible to receive special Medicare and Medicaid payments (42CFR491.1).

The Conditions of Coverage require ambulatory surgery centers to "maintain a medical record for each patient," including documentation of (42CFR416.47):

1. Patient identification
2. Significant medical history and results of physical examination
3. Preoperative diagnostic studies (entered before surgery), if performed
4. Findings and techniques of the operation, including a pathologist's report on tissue removed during surgery, except those exempted by the governing body
5. Any allergies and abnormal drug reactions
6. Entries related to anesthesia administration
7. Properly executed informed patient consent
8. Discharge diagnosis

Medicare standards for rural health clinics and FQHCs include a requirement that records be maintained for each patient and that a designated professional staff member be assigned the responsibility for maintenance of the records. Included in the requirements for record content are identification and social data, consent forms, pertinent medical history, assessment of the health status and health care needs of the patient, a brief summary of the visit, disposition and instructions to the patient, physical examinations, laboratory and other diagnostic results, consultant's findings, physician's orders, reports of treatment, and medications. In addition, the standards require that medical records be retained for at least six years from the date of the last entry in the record unless a longer retention period is required by state law (42CFR491.10).

Accreditation

Unlike licensure, which must be undertaken if required by the state, accreditation is a voluntary process. There are a variety of organizations that accredit ambulatory care facilities. Some of the organizations, like the Accreditation Association for Ambulatory Health Care Inc. and The Joint Commission accredit a wide variety of ambulatory settings. Other accrediting organizations, like the American Association for Accreditation of Ambulatory Surgery Facilities, Inc., only focus on a narrow segment of ambulatory care. (See Figure 3-2 for the accreditation organizations commonly found in ambulatory care.)

FIGURE 3-2

Accreditation Organizations in Freestanding Ambulatory Care.

Accreditation Organization	*Standards*
The Joint Commission	*Comprehensive Accreditation Manual for Ambulatory Health Care Accreditation Manual for Office-Based Surgery*
Accreditation Association for Ambulatory Health Care Inc.	*Accreditation Handbook for Ambulatory Health Care*
Commission for the Accreditation of Birth Centers	*CABC Birth Center Standards*
American Association for Accreditation of Ambulatory Surgery Facilities, Inc.	*Standards and Checklist Booklet Resource Manual*

The Joint Commission is the best-known health care accreditation agency. It has developed the *Comprehensive Accreditation Manual for Ambulatory Health Care*, which includes standards for freestanding ambulatory care settings. The types of facilities currently accredited by The Joint Commission include ambulatory health care, surgery centers, office-based surgery, imaging centers, sleep centers, and urgent care centers. When freestanding ambulatory facilities are accredited, they typically are accredited by the Accreditation Association for Ambulatory Health Care Inc. Its standards are published in the *Accreditation Handbook for Ambulatory Health Care*.

Other accreditation agencies accredit only a specific type of ambulatory care. An example is the American Association for Accreditation of Ambulatory Surgery Facilities, Inc., which accredits only single or multispecialty surgical facilities owned or operated by surgeons who are members of the American Board of Medical Specialties, as well as surgeons who are members of the American Osteopathic Association Bureau of Osteopathic Specialists. Another specialty accreditation organization is the Commission for the Accreditation of Birth Centers, with its *CABC Birth Center Standards*.

Although many facilities do not choose to be accredited, accreditation standards still can provide health information managers with a set of benchmarks for the information system within their facility. HIM professionals should be aware of accreditation standards in setting up new systems and evaluating existing ones to establish that they are following the best practices.

Other Regulations: Compliance

Office of the Inspector General (OIG)   the office in the Department of Health and Human Services is responsible for monitoring compliance with reimbursement laws and regulations.

The **Office of the Inspector General (OIG)** in the Department of Health and Human Services (HHS) is charged with protecting the integrity of HHS programs such as Medicare by detecting and preventing fraud, waste and abuse.

This office has identified large sums of money that providers received through error or fraud. The Department of Justice has recouped billions of dollars under laws such as the Federal False Claims Act and the Health Insurance Portability and Accountability Act (HIPAA). Every year the OIG publishes a work plan outlining the focus areas for the upcoming year.

To ensure compliance with billing and reimbursement rules and to avoid the potential for penalties, providers are encouraged to develop a compliance plan that ensures conformity with federal requirements. The OIG has published model **compliance plans** to provide guidance for a variety of health settings, including individual and small-group physician practices in developing internal controls. These plans include the following seven components:

> **compliance plan** a method for ensuring that a facility/practice is complying with all laws and regulations, including those pertaining to reimbursement under Medicare and Medicaid.

1. Conducting internal monitoring and auditing
2. Implementing compliance and practice standards
3. Designating a compliance officer or contact
4. Conducting appropriate training and education
5. Responding appropriately to detected offenses and developing corrective action
6. Developing open lines of communication
7. Enforcing disciplinary standards through well-publicized guidelines

When conducting internal monitoring and auditing, practices are urged to audit both standards and procedures as well as claims submission. The claims audit may be retrospective (looking at previous claims) or prospective (looking at claims before submission). When a Medicare overpayment is discovered in a retrospective audit, the health care provider is required to disclose and refund the overpayment. One advantage of conducting a prospective audit is that errors can be caught before claim submission, allowing the practice to avoid the additional paperwork resulting from overpayment refunds. From a baseline audit, problem areas can be identified, and periodic audits must then be carried out at least once a year. Monitoring should be an ongoing process.

Once the risk areas have been identified, practice standards and procedures must be developed to deal with those risks. The OIG has published compliance guidance for different provider types which is available at www.oig.hhs.gov including the following suggestions: "(1) Developing a written standards and procedures manual; and (2) updating clinical forms periodically to make sure they facilitate and encourage clear and complete documentation of patient care" (OIG, 2000, p. 59438). The main risk areas to be addressed include coding, billing, reasonable and necessary services, documentation, improper inducements, kickbacks, and self-referrals.

Ideally, one person should be designated as a compliance officer or contact. This person's role would be to oversee adherence of the practice/facility to the compliance plan that it has developed.

Targeted training and education programs should emphasize the provision of training for staff members most in need of training and for the areas of most risk.

General training, however, should cover all risk areas and include all staff members who could participate in or identify an error or a violation of the compliance program. Training must be ongoing and must address any changes in the laws, regulations, and coding systems that affect compliance.

When offenses are detected, a corrective action plan must be developed. A Provider Self-Disclosure Protocol, developed by the OIG, should be followed in such cases. Open lines of communication are necessary to ensure that everyone is aware of how to report what they believe to be fraudulent or in error. Finally, disciplinary procedures must be in place to deal with violations of the compliance plan.

Another program that targets fraud and abuse is the **Medicaid Integrity Program** (MIP). This is a state and federal government initiative to identify fraud and abuse in the Medicaid program (CMS State Program Integrity, n.d.). Under this program, Medicaid Integrity Contractors (MICs) audit Medicaid providers to identify overpayments and to decrease inappropriate Medicaid claims (CMS, 2012).

Medicaid Integrity Program (MIP) a joint federal and state government initiative to identify fraud and abuse in the Medicaid system.

SELF REVIEW 3.2

1. Health care facilities and providers are required to be _____ to provide health care services.
   a. accredited
   b. licensed
   c. approved
   d. certified

2. In order for health care facilities to participate in the Medicare program the facility must be _____ by CMS.
   a. accredited
   b. licensed
   c. approved
   d. certified

3. Accreditation is a(n) _____ process of review of a provider of health care facility.
   a. state-required
   b. federally-mandated
   c. voluntary
   d. universally compulsory

4. The Joint Commission accredits all of the following health care facilities except _____.
   a. ambulatory surgery centers
   b. office-based surgery centers
   c. sleep centers
   d. dialysis center

5. The Office of Inspector General (OIG) is responsible for protecting the integrity of which of the following?

   a. Medicare programs

   b. Insurance programs

   c. Federal Qualified Health Centers

   d. Community centers

DOCUMENTATION

Documentation involves the process of recording information about the care provided in the ambulatory care center. Among the many factors that influence what must be documented are the type of facility, types of patients, types of caregivers, and internal and external users of information. It is easiest to think about documentation by going through the care process with the patient to see what items of data must be maintained (see Figure 3-3). The documentation may be entered and maintained in a paper or an electronic medical record format.

Registration/Demographic Information

The first contact the patient usually has with any ambulatory care setting is the **registration** process. During this step, demographic information, such as the patient's name and address, and financial information, such as responsible party and insurance coverage, are collected. Often this information is first documented by having the patient complete a form upon arrival at the facility. This information

registration   the process by which basic demographic and financial information is obtained from the patient and entered into the health information system.

FIGURE 3-3

Flow of care and documentation.

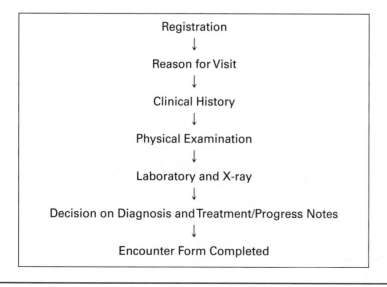

Registration

↓

Reason for Visit

↓

Clinical History

↓

Physical Examination

↓

Laboratory and X-ray

↓

Decision on Diagnosis and Treatment/Progress Notes

↓

Encounter Form Completed

is then entered into the patient's record by clerical personnel either on an information form or in the demographics/finance section of an electronic information system or electronic medical record (see Figure 3-4). Usually the original form completed by the patient does not become a part of the official record.

History and Physical

reason for visit the patient's reason for requesting care.

After the basic information has been received from the patient, the actual care process begins. The first step is to find out why the patient is seeking care, or the **reason for visit**, and obtaining a history of the illness. The medical assistant or nurse often begins this process by asking the patient for the reason for visit and a

FIGURE 3-4

Computer-generated registration form.

ABC Hospital
1000 Inpatient Lane
Hospital City, New York 12345

FACE SHEET

PATIENT RECORD NUMBER: 23345670   TYPE OF ADMISSION: Inpatient   6/08/YYYY   13:40

NAME/ADDRESS: AGE: 085Y   SEX: M   RACE: W
Sam Jones   REL: SRC: 7   ROOM/BED: MD 220 1
123 Wood Street
Endwell, NY 13456   ATTENDING DOCTOR: Best, Sarah
    REFERRING DOCTOR: Great, Beth

NEAREST RELATIVE: EMPLOYER NAME: EMERGENCY CONTACT:
Sandy Jones (daughter)   Retired   Sandy Jones (daughter)
45 Brook Street   45 Brook Street
Liberty, PA 56789   MARITAL STATUS   Liberty, PA 56789
(607) 123-3456   Widowed   (607) 123-3456

GUARANTOR #: 1123   GUARANTOR EMPLOYER: R

ADMITTING DIAGNOSIS: Dyspnea. Dehydration.

INS # 1: Medicare   PLAN: 10
SUBSCRIBER: Sam Jones
ID #: 098586389T

INS # 2: Mutual of Omaha   PLAN: 20
SUBSCRIBER: Sam Jones
ID #: 67890TNH

COMMENTS: POWER OF ATTORNEY: None   ADVANCE DIRECTIVE: On file

CONSULTANT: DISCHARGE: 6/12/YYYY   10:30
Fenton, Sean
    CONDITION AT DISCHARGE: Improved

    Abby Keen   *06/12/YYYY*
ATTENDING PHYSICIAN   _____   _____
Keen, Abby   SIGNATURE   DATE

brief history of the reason for the visit. Sometimes the patient completes a history form, either manually or on the computer.

The comprehensiveness of the history depends on the patient's reason for the visit. A visit for a sore throat, for example, would require only minimal information. A visit for shortness of breath would require a more exhaustive inquiry into the patient's past history and family and social history. The health care provider—the physician, the nurse practitioner, or the physician assistant—then completes the physical examination. Like the history, the physical examination varies in completeness depending on the reason for visit.

Laboratory and Radiograph Reports

The history and the physical examination begin the fact-finding process to gain the information needed to make a diagnosis and to determine a plan of treatment. Sometimes additional information is necessary, such as clinical laboratory tests and radiographs. Simple tests are often provided in the office or clinic, but more complicated procedures may require that the patient be referred elsewhere. In a paper system, results of the tests may be kept in a computer printout or may be recorded on a reporting slip. Providers striving for meaningful use of an electronic health record (EHR) should enter or import clinical lab test results into the EHR as structured data.

Progress Notes

Once all the needed information has been collected, the caregiver usually records diagnoses or major problems in narrative form, along with plans for treatment, such as medications prescribed. In some settings the documentation for the entire encounter may take the format of a long note, which may be handwritten or typed. In electronic health records, structured progress notes that may or may not utilize templates are common.

encounter face-to-face contact between the patient and the provider (Uniform Ambulatory Care Data Set).

Encounter Form

At the end of the visit, an encounter form or superbill usually is generated (Figure 3-5). This form includes information on the patient's diagnoses and treatments, along with disease and procedure codes and charges. Usually completed, at least in part, by the provider, the encounter form may become a part of the patient's record. It may, however, be stored separately, because its main purpose is to provide information for billing and insurance processing rather than documenting the care process.

encounter form a document used for billing purposes that includes the services the patient received, the charges, and the diagnosis and procedure codes.

superbill a form used for billing purposes that includes the services the patient received, the charges, and diagnosis and procedure codes.

Copies of Hospital Records

If the patient has been hospitalized, copies of records from the hospital, such as the operative report and discharge summary, are often sent to the referring provider and typically are included in the patient record. As a health information

FIGURE 3-5

Encounter form.

ENCOUNTER FORM

Tel: (101) 555-1111   Kim Donaldson, M.D.   EIN: 11-9876543
Fax: (101) 555-2222   INTERNAL MEDICINE   NPI: 1234567890
                             101 Main Street, Suite A
                               Alfred NY 14802

OFFICE VISITS	NEW	EST	OFFICE PROCEDURES		INJECTIONS	
☐ Level I	99201	99211	☐ EKG with interpretation	93000	☐ Influenza virus vaccine	90656
☐ Level II	99202	99212	☐ Oximetry with interpretation	94760	☐ Admin of Influenza vaccine	G0008
☐ Level III	99203	99213	**LABORATORY TESTS**		☐ Pneumococcal vaccine	90732
☐ Level IV	99204	99214	☐ Blood, occult (feces)	82270	☐ Admin of pneumococcal vaccine	G0009
☐ Level V	99205	99215	☐ Skin test, Tb, intradermal (PPD)	86580	☐ Hepatitis B vaccine	90746
OFFICE CONSULTS (NEW or EST)			☐		☐ Admin of Hepatitis B vaccine	G0010
☐ Level I	99214		☐		☐ Tetanus toxoid vaccine	90703
☐ Level II	99242		☐		☐ Immunization administration	90471
☐ Level III	99243		☐		☐	
☐ Level IV	99244		☐		☐	
☐ Level V	99245		☐		☐	

DIAGNOSIS

☐ Anemia, iron deficiency	280.9 (D50.9)	☐ Ventricular flutter	427.42 (I49.02)	☐	
☐ Anemia, protein deficiency	281.4 (D53.0)	☐	————	☐	
☐ Anxiety state, unspecified	300.00 (F41.9)	☐	————	☐	
☐ Appendicitis	541 (K37)	☐		☐	
☐ Chest pain	786.50 (R07.9)	☐		☐	
☐ Cholecystitis, acute	575.0 (K81.0)	☐		☐	
☐ Dizziness	780.4 (R42)	☐		☐	
☐ Epistaxis	784.7 (R04.0)	☐		☐	
☐ Fever	780.60 (R50.9)	☐		☐	
☐ Loss of weight	783.21 (R63.4)	☐		☐	
☐ Obsessive-compulsive Disorder	300.3 (F42)	☐		☐	
☐ Palpitations	785.1 (R00.2)	☐		☐	
☐ Peritioneal abscess	567.22 (K65.1)	☐		☐	
☐ Syncope & collapse	780.2 (R55)	☐		☐	
☐ Ventricular fibrillation	427.41 (I49.01)	☐		☐	

PATIENT IDENTIFICATION		FINANCIAL TRANSACTION DATA	
PATIENT NAME:		INVOICE NO.	
PATIENT NUMBER:		ACCOUNT NO.	
DATE OF BIRTH:		TOTAL FOR SERVICE:	$
ENCOUNTER DATE		AMOUNT RECEIVED:	$
DATE OF SERVICE:	/ /	PAID BY:	☐ Cash
RETURN VISIT DATE			☐ Check
			☐ Credit Card
DATE OF RETURN VISIT:	/ /	CASHIER'S INITIALS:	

exchange becomes available in more communities, information can be transmitted electronically between the hospital and the ambulatory setting. Providers who are affiliated with hospital systems may utilize the same patient record system and have access to patient information from the ambulatory and inpatient records via the same system.

Problem List

In facilities that see patients on an ongoing basis, a **problem list** is often used (Figure 3-6). This is a numbered list of the patient's diagnoses or problems, often including allergies and medications. It should appear in a conspicuous place in the record, usually at the front, and must be updated regularly. The problem

problem list   a numbered listing of the patient's issues over time that serves as a table of contents for the problem-oriented medical record.

FIGURE 3-6

Problem list.

PROBLEM LIST (current and chronic problems)

PROBLEM NUMBER	DATE OF VISIT	PROBLEM DESCRIPTION	DATE RESOLVED	COMMENTS

list, therefore, serves as a table of contents for the record by summarizing the patient's care over time. In electronic health record systems, maintaining an up-to-date problem list of current diagnoses as discrete data based on a standard coding system can demonstrate meaningful use (www.cms.gov).

Special Requirements

The process just outlined is universal for most ambulatory care encounters. Some types of facilities or encounters may have more specialized documentation requirements because of the specialized care provided, as shown in Figure 3-7. In designing documentation methods for a facility, the type of facility and the care provided must be considered carefully.

Ambulatory Surgery Centers

Ambulatory surgery centers add surgical documentation to the basic documentation just discussed. Necessary testing often is done before the day of surgery and must be present in the record before the surgery. Another essential item of documentation is the consent for treatment. The surgeon is responsible for explaining the risks and alternatives associated with the surgery and for obtaining the patient's consent to the procedure. This consent process often is documented on a consent for surgery form that includes the name of the surgery, name of the

FIGURE 3-7

Special Documentation Requirements.

Type of Setting	Special Documentation Requirements
Ambulatory Surgery Center	Surgical Consent Operative Report Anesthesia Report Recovery Room Report Pathology Report Discharge instructions
Birth Centers	Prenatal Record Labor and Delivery Record Physical Assessment of Newborn Follow-Up Plan
Pediatric Care	Growth and Development Charts Immunization Record
Industrial Health	New-Hire Physical Return-to-Work Physical Transfer/Promotion and Annual Physical Health Monitoring Auditory and Vision Records

surgeon, alternatives to the surgery, and the risks involved. The record should be checked to see that preoperative documentation is available—such as history and physical and pertinent laboratory findings. Intraoperative documentation includes data about the surgery.

Each caregiver has a role in documenting the care given. The anesthesiologist must document the anesthesia given, any fluids given, and the patient's pulse, respiration, and blood pressure throughout the procedure. The surgeon must document the preoperative and postoperative diagnoses, findings of the surgery, and methods used. When the patient leaves the surgical suite, the care given during the recovery period also must be documented, including vital signs and recovery from general anesthesia. If tissue was removed during the surgery, a pathology report describing the gross and microscopic findings is included as well. Finally, instructions to the patient must be documented to ensure that the patient knows about the postoperative wound care, complications to watch for, and when to return for follow-up, if necessary.

Birth Centers

In birth centers, labor and delivery must be documented. This documentation usually begins with the prenatal record, which starts when the woman comes for initial care during the pregnancy. Because this care usually occurs in the physician's or midwife's office throughout the pregnancy, a copy of the office prenatal record must be sent to the birth center at regular intervals late in the pregnancy so it will be available at the time of the delivery. Prenatal documentation includes prenatal history and physical, weight gain, prenatal testing, gestational stage of the pregnancy, and any pregnancy complications.

Labor and delivery records provide documentation of the labor process, including the onset of labor, length of labor, labor monitoring, pain management during the labor process, and the method of delivery.

Physical assessment of the newborn also is entered in the birthing center record. This includes the Apgar score (a rating based on certain physical functions at one minute and at five minutes after birth), an overall scoring of the physical condition of the newborn, weight, and other physical assessments.

Finally, a follow-up plan must be included, documenting follow-up instructions such as when the mother and baby should return to the caregiver for evaluation.

Pediatric Preventive Health Services

For children, immunizations must be documented on an **immunization record** so the caregiver can tell at a glance whether an immunization is needed on a given visit (see Figure 3-8). A **growth and development chart** also is included, recording height and weight to monitor growth patterns (see Figure 3-9). Electronic plotting and display of growth charts for children ages 2 to 20 years, including body mass index (BMI), is a requirement for meaningful use of an electronic health record.

immunization record a listing of immunizations that a child has received and often indicates when additional immunizations will be required.

growth and development chart a graphic recording of a child's height and weight over time.

FIGURE 3-8

Immunization record.

ALFRED STATE MEDICAL CENTER

PATIENT IMMUNIZATION RECORD

PATIENT LAST NAME _____

PATIENT FIRST NAME _____

PATIENT DATE OF BIRTH _____

PARENT/GUARDIAN _____

VACCINE	ADMINISTRATION DATE	PATIENT AGE (YR, MO)	ADMINISTRATION SITE	VACCINE MANUFACTURER	VACCINE LOT NUMBER	PATIENT EDUCATION	NURSE INITIALS
DTP1							
DTP2							
DTP3							
DTP/DTaP4							
DTP/DTaP5							
DT							
DTP/Hib1							
DTP/Hib2							
DTP/Hib3							
DTP/Hib4							
Td							
OPV/IPV1							
OPV/IPV2							
OPV/IPV3							
OPV/IPV4							
MMR1							
MMR2							
Hib1							
Hib2							
Hib3							
Hib4							
HepB1							
HepB2							
HepB3							

Industrial Health Services/Occupational Medicine

Many different types of documentation are included in industrial health records, depending on the type of service provided. The record frequently includes physical examinations. Examinations may be done after hiring but before placement on the job. They provide a basis for assessing the employee's health at the time of hire versus various times later during the employment period.

A **return-to-work physical** is done for an employee who is injured on the job and must be judged fit to work before returning to the workplace. Transfer or promotion and annual physicals frequently are provided for executive personnel. Health monitoring for exposure to hazardous or toxic substances or other health threats, such as loud noise, is another common part of the industrial record. Vision records may be included for work settings where vision is an important factor in job performance, such as for pilots. Finally, if care is provided in the clinic for treatment of an illness or accident, the usual documentation of the care process must be included.

return-to-work physical a physical done before an employee is able to return to the job after an injury or illness.

FIGURE 3-9A

(a) Length and weight record. (b) Stature and weight record.

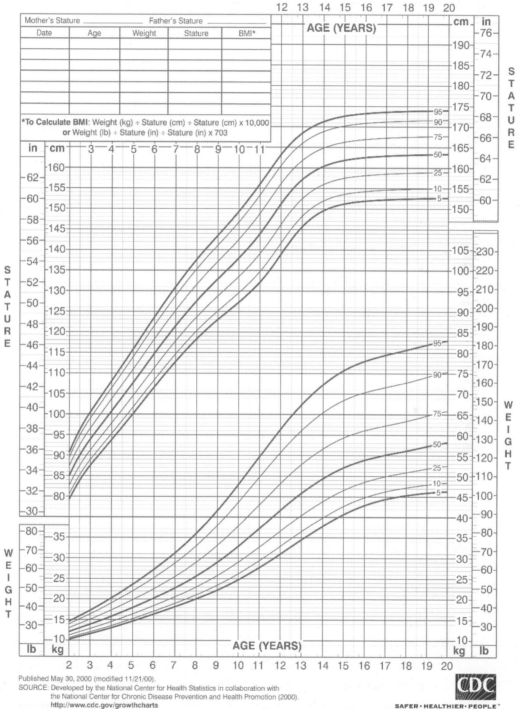

2 to 20 years: Girls
Stature-for-age and Weight-for-age percentiles

FIGURE 3-9B *(continued)*

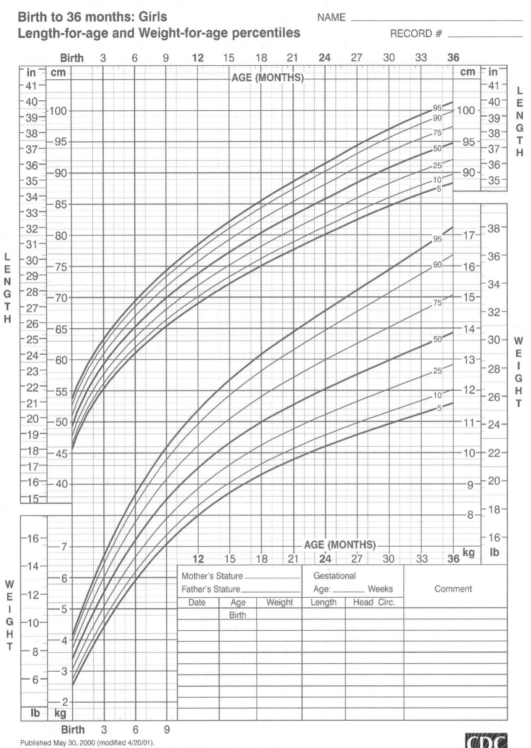

Birth to 36 months: Girls
Length-for-age and Weight-for-age percentiles

NAME _____

RECORD # _____

Published May 30, 2000 (modified 4/20/01).
SOURCE: Developed by the National Center for Health Statistics in collaboration with
the National Center for Chronic Disease Prevention and Health Promotion (2000).
http://www.cdc.gov/growthcharts

SAFER · HEALTHIER · PEOPLE™

When selecting the documentation requirements for a given facility, the HIM professional should begin with the universal components such as history and physical, progress notes, and laboratory and imaging data. Then the particular needs of the site should be determined by looking at the type of care provided, which must be documented. Accreditation and licensure standards for the specific type of facility also help define the content of the documentation.

Record Format

The organization of data and information is defined as the record format (see Figure 3-10). Three common formats for paper records are: source oriented, integrated, and problem oriented. The traditional format is called the source oriented format, in which the information is presented according to its source, such as laboratory, radiology, physician, nursing, and other services. This format has the advantage of being familiar to caregivers, but it increases the difficulty of reading the record and integrating data from the different sources.

In physician offices, the integrated format is used frequently. In this format, all information is entered in chronological order by visit. Other events, such as telephone calls, are listed chronologically between visits. Test results and copies of hospital records are entered as they are received. This method makes it easy to look at each episode of care, but it is more difficult to look at the patient's care across time or, especially, to monitor a specific data element over time. For example, it often is desirable to look for trends in laboratory values. This is more difficult with the integrated format because the laboratory results are scattered throughout the record rather than grouped into one location.

The problem-oriented medical record (POMR) is a third format that is used occasionally. This record was developed by Dr. Lawrence Weed to provide a more systematic method of record keeping. The key component of the POMR is the problem list. As discussed previously, this is a list of the patient's problems and diagnoses and serves as a quick overview of the patient's health. In a true

source-oriented format   a record format in which the information is organized according to the source of the information, such as laboratory, nursing, etc.

integrated format   a record format in which the information is entered in chronological order.

problem-oriented medical record (POMR) format   a record format in which the parts of the record are keyed to the problem number listed on the problem list.

FIGURE 3-10

Record formats.

Format	Characteristics
Source Oriented	Arranged according to source (e.g., laboratory, nursing, etc.)
Integrated	Chronological
Problem Oriented	Problem list Keyed to problem number
Electronic	Electronic format

problem-oriented record, all parts of the record are indexed to the problem list. First, the clinical database, consisting of the history, physical, and laboratory and radiology/imaging findings, is developed. Then a list of problems is developed and numbered. A plan indexed to the problem list then is generated, with a plan for each problem identified by problem number. Each order and progress note also is indexed to the problem number so it can be seen at a glance what problem is being addressed.

Although the POMR is a systematic record-keeping process, it has not gained wide usage in ambulatory care. Generally, it is seen more likely in larger clinics with more caregivers and a greater need for coordination of care.

The choice of record format for paper records depends primarily on the preference of the caregivers. The main principle that must be followed, however, is that all caregivers within a facility must use the same format. Without this uniformity, it is difficult to find data in records documented by different caregivers. When transitioning to an electronic medical record, paper records from previous encounters often are scanned into an electronic imaging system. An effective format is important for efficient retrieval of these archived records. Committees frequently are formed to suggest a format, and should consider the variety of users in making the decision.

The number of ambulatory care providers utilizing electronic record formats is increasing, at least in part because of the incentives in ARRA/HITECH for adopting electronic health record (EHR) systems, and later the penalties for failing to adopt. Information in an EHR can be organized and entered in a variety of ways. The provider should select a certified EHR system with a format that will facilitate meeting the requirements of meaningful use. For example, some ambulatory providers have previously adopted electronic systems that incorporated clinical lab results into their electronic medical record systems as scanned images, which would not meet the meaningful use requirement to incorporate lab test results into the EHR as structured data.

One electronic format that is common in EHR systems is the use of templates for entering data. Some providers find that templates facilitate the record completion process. A number of EHR products include templates for different specialties and also permit customization of the templates by the provider. Figure 3-11 provides an example of a template for collecting information for a patient history.

Patient Identifier/Filing Methods

patient identifier   an item of data that identifies the patient in the health information management system, such as the patient's name or medical record number.

The term **patient identifier** refers to how the patient is identified in a health information system, whether paper-based or electronic, and how information about that patient is located (see Figure 3-12). In small settings, the patient's name may be the primary identifier. If a paper-based filing system is used in such a setting, the records are filed alphabetically by the patient's name. Such a system quickly becomes cumbersome, because patients frequently have the same name. In an electronic system, although the patient's name may be used to access that individual's record, electronic records must utilize a unique identifier for tracking

FIGURE 3-11

An example of a structured template in an electronic health record. In this particular system, when a checkbox in a section of the template is checked, that section expands for additional data entry.

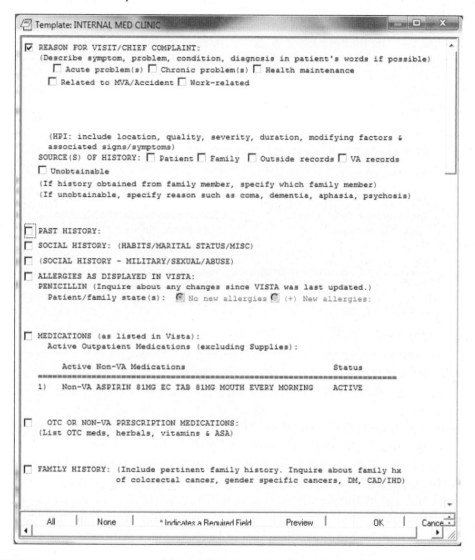

Source: Department of Veterans Affairs, http://www.ehealth.va.gov/CPRS_demo.asp/

the data associated with a given patient. The patient's name is not suitable for use as the patient identifier in an EHR, because names are not unique.

When a system is too large to use an alphabetical system, a number usually is assigned to identify the patient. If a number is used, there must be a master patient index file by patient name to provide the patient's number. In an EHR, the patient's record could be found by searching the database using the patient's name or number. A secondary piece of information frequently must be used to

FIGURE 3-12

Patient identifiers used in ambulatory care.

Patient Identifier	Advantage	Disadvantage
Patient Name	Easily obtained	Misspellings
	No need for master patient index	Many patients with same/similar names
		Need for secondary identifier to verify
		Cumbersome with a large number of records
Patient Number—unit or serial	Unique to each patient	Requires patient index to locate record
	Uniform in length	
	Confidentiality	
Patient Number—Social Security number	Most patients have Social Security number	Some patients do not have Social Security number
		Threat to privacy
Family Numbering	Availability of information for all family members together	Frequent changes in family structure require changes in identification system
	Useful for billing	
	Useful in mailings	

verify that the correct patient has been found. Common secondary identifiers are the Social Security number, birth date, or mother's maiden name.

Various methods are used to assign these identifier numbers. One way is to first decide the number of digits to be used in the number and then to start at zero and assign the numbers. A six-digit number often is used to allow an adequate amount of numbers for the patient population. A decision would have to be made on whether the patient would keep the same number for all visits (a unit system) or would receive a new number for each visit to enable the facility to distinguish among visits by the number (serial system). Most ambulatory care facilities use the unit numbering system.

Some facilities have used the Social Security number to identify patients. Providers have found this method useful because most Americans have a Social Security number. Use of the Social Security number as the primary identifier, however, is no longer considered a good practice for many reasons. Some patients, such as babies, do not have a number, and other patients may be using an incorrect number. If the patient does not have a Social Security number, a pseudo number (false number) must be assigned. Using the Social Security number also raises issues of privacy, because the government maintains information about individuals using the Social Security number as an identifier. The primary reason for discontinuing the Social Security number as the primary identifier, however, is the increased risk of identity theft, which has become a serious problem in the United States.

A **family numbering system** is used in some facilities. With this numbering system, the family is assigned a number. All members of the family use the same number, with a suffix specifying their unique identifier within the family. The family number might be 425687, with the father being 425687-1, the mother 425687-2, and the child 425687-3. This system may be used in settings in which the whole family is treated and when social and medical information about the entire family might be helpful in treating individuals. Family numbering also can be useful for billing purposes and mailings to family members. With the frequent changes in family structure because of divorce and other family breakups, however, keeping up with the family unit and changing the record system to match it is frustrating and not always possible.

In selecting a patient identifier, the needs of the facility must be the primary consideration. In a facility where the patient may be seen once and never again, such as an ambulatory surgery center, utilization of a family numbering system would be impractical. Industrial settings might use the employee number. A small facility using paper records may be well served by an alphabetical system. With an alphabetical system, a separate master patient index to identify the patient's number would not be needed. Again, the facility type, caregivers, and patient type should determine the decision.

family numbering system a method in which the family is given a number and each individual receives that number with a suffix indicating his or her position within the family.

SELF REVIEW 3.3

1. The reason for the patient visit typically is recorded in what part of the health record?
   a. Registration information
   b. History and physical
   c. Laboratory reports
   d. Progress notes

2. A _____ is a list of the patient's diagnoses and problems that is compiled over time.
   a. progress note
   b. problem list
   c. superbill
   d. encounter form

3. Which form typically would be included in a pediatric health record and may not be found in other patient records?
   a. immunization records
   b. growth chart
   c. return-to-work
   d. radiology reports

4. All of the following are examples of typical organizational formats for ambulatory records except?
   a. source oriented
   b. problem oriented
   c. patient oriented
   d. integrated

REIMBURSEMENT

Fee for Service

How is care paid for in freestanding ambulatory care settings? (See Figure 3-13.) The traditional method is called fee for service. In this system, the patient pays according to the type and amount of service provided. Usually, for example, there is a basic fee for the visit. Separate fees are assigned for laboratory tests, radiographs, or other services provided beyond the basic visit.

In some facilities treating low-income patients, the fee for service may be charged based on a sliding scale, with the amount determined by the patient's income. The problem with fee for service has been that payers think it offers an incentive to provide more service. A variety of systems have been devised to change the incentives from providing more service to providing only what is absolutely required by the patient's condition.

Medicare Physician Fee Schedule

For physician reimbursement, Part B of Medicare now pays using the Medicare Physician Fee Schedule (MPFS or PFS), which is based on the resource-based relative value scale (RBRVS). Medicare Part B includes physician payment and payment for services for limited-license practitioners who treat only particular

fee for service a reimbursement system in which the payment is based on the type and amount of service provided.

Medicare Physician Fee Schedule (MPFS or PFS) a list of Medicare-covered services and their payment rates.

resource-based relative value scale (RBRVS) a reimbursement system used by Medicare Part B to reimburse physicians; based on the relative value of the services provided.

FIGURE 3-13

Payment methods in freestanding ambulatory care.

Payment System	Setting
Fee for Service	Any setting
Physician Fee Schedule	Physicians/Medicare Part B
ASC System	Ambulatory surgery/Medicare
Capitation	Any setting

types of problems or parts of the body, such as optometrists, podiatrists, and chiropractors. Other services included are diagnostic tests other than clinical diagnostic lab tests, diagnostic and therapeutic radiology services, and physical and occupational therapy services (independent practice only). Non-physician caregivers such as physician assistants, nurse practitioners, certified registered nurse anesthetists, certified nurse midwives, clinical psychologists, and clinical social workers also are paid at a rate tied to the RBRVS (Medicare Learning Network, 2014).

Services provided to a patient by nurse practitioners or physician assistants when the physician is on site (termed incident to services) are fully reimbursed at the physician's rate provided by the fee schedule. Locum tenens physicians are those who are working temporarily in place of another physician. The regular physician files a claim for the services provided by the locum tenens physician.

The fee schedule is based on the Healthcare Common Procedure Coding System (HCPCS). For each HCPCS code, three main components or relative value units (RVUs) influence payment: an amount for physician work, an amount for overhead expenses, and an amount for malpractice expenses. These three amounts are specific for each HCPCS code.

Each of these RVUs is adjusted by a geographic factor for the area in which the practice is located. The sum of the amounts from the three RVUs adjusted for geographic location then is multiplied by a uniform conversion factor, which is a fixed dollar amount, to determine the fee (Medicare Learning Network, 2014). The fee schedule is revised to include new HCPCS codes and is published annually in the *Federal Register*.

Ambulatory Surgery Center Reimbursement

Freestanding ambulatory surgery centers are paid by Medicare based on a list of HCPCS/CPT codes for covered surgical procedures for Ambulatory Surgery Centers (ASCs), updated annually. Medicare's ASC reimbursement system was revised in 2008 and provides that ASCs receive a percentage of the outpatient prospective payment system rates (CMS, 2009). The CMS website has links to the Medicare Claims Processing Manuals with updates as changes are published in the Federal Register. Chapter 14 of this manual applies to ambulatory surgery centers and may be accessed at http://www.cms.gov.

Capitation

RBRVS and ASC payments were efforts to prospectively set prices and to discourage excessive utilization of services. Capitation is a method of payment that carries this effort even further. Under capitation, caregivers receive a fixed payment per month for everyone under their care enrolled in a given health care plan. For this fixed amount of payment, all necessary health services must be provided. The incentive is, therefore, to provide only care that is absolutely necessary to avoid losing money.

incident to   services provided to patients by mid-level providers or advanced practice clinicians, such as nurse practitioners or physician assistants, when the physician is onsite.

locum tenens   an arrangement by which one physician temporarily works in place of another physician.

ASC reimbursement system   a Medicare plan for ambulatory surgery in which the HCPCS codes are listed (ASC list) and reimbursed according to a percentage of the outpatient prospective payment system rates.

capitation   a method of reimbursement in which the physician or facility receives a fixed amount each month for each patient enrolled in the plan, regardless of the amount of care the patient receives.

Knowing the reimbursement methods affecting the facility is essential for the HIM professional. Documentation of the patient's care must support the level of billing from the facility. For Medicare Physician Fee Schedule and ASC payments based on HCPCS codes, the documentation must support the codes selected. Nowadays, more third-party payers are auditing ambulatory documentation to ensure that reimbursement matches the care documented.

Medicaid—Early and Periodic Screening, Diagnostic, and Treatment (EPSDT) Service

The **Early and Periodic Screening, Diagnostic, and Treatment (EPSDT) Service** is a program of Medicaid for children younger than age 21. It ensures that these services are provided and paid for whether or not they are normally included under the state's Medicaid program. Screening services include history and physical, appropriate immunizations, health education, vision, hearing, and dental services. Problems identified under the screening provisions then must also be fully diagnosed and treated.

Reimbursement Resources

The Centers for Medicare & Medicaid Services (CMS) offer a variety of manuals and materials that provide information about reimbursement under the Medicare and Medicaid programs. **Program manuals** provide the basic instructions for the two programs. **Program transmittals** are issued periodically to provide a revision for a specific manual. These manuals and transmittals must be reviewed to ensure that the facility is following the latest guidance.

Claims for Medicare ambulatory care under Part B are filed with the Medicare administrative contractor (MAC-Part B) in a given state or region. These Part B contractors (previously known as Medicare carriers) publish **Local Coverage Determinations (LCDs)**, which must be consistent with federal guidelines but provide further guidance for providers in the area served by a specific contractor. Most coverage determinations are local. Medicare, however, also has developed **National Coverage Determinations (NCDs)** that apply to all contractors and providers nationwide. LCDs and NCDs are important references for coders, because they list diagnosis codes that indicate the medical necessity of certain procedures and services.

Early and Periodic Screening, Diagnostic, and Treatment (EPSDT) Service a Medicaid program for children younger than age 21 that ensures that these services (screening, diagnostic, and treatment) are provided and paid for whether or not they normally are included under the state's Medicaid program.

program manuals for Medicare and Medicaid basic instructions for the two programs, developed by the Centers for Medicare & Medicaid Services.

program transmittals revisions issued periodically by CMS for a specific program manual.

Local Coverage Determinations (LCDs) guidance documents published by Medicare Administrative Contractors (MACs) that include information on codes that indicate medical necessity of services. These policies apply to services covered under Medicare in the region served by the contractor. Local Coverage Determinations formerly were known as Local Medical Review Policies (LMRPs).

National Coverage Determinations (NCDs) guidance documents published by Medicare that include information about codes that indicate medical necessity of services. These policies apply to services covered under Medicare throughout the nation.

SELF REVIEW 3.4

1. Physician reimbursement is based on _____.
   a. resource-based relative value scale
   b. reference-based relative value scale
   c. encounter form
   d. fee sheet

2. The Early and Periodic Screening, Diagnostic and Treatment service is a Medicaid program for _____.
   a. all Medicaid beneficiaries
   b. all Medicare beneficiaries
   c. children younger than 21
   d. children younger than 18

INFORMATION MANAGEMENT

After the basic facts about the setting have been determined, the health information manager is able to evaluate or develop systems to meet the needs of the facility. All of the pieces of the puzzle come together in the HIM system.

Coding and Classification

Most facilities use some method to code diagnoses and procedures. This process involves assigning a string of characters (a combination of numbers and/or letters) to each of the diagnoses and procedures according to an established classification method (see Figure 3-14). Coding is done in ambulatory care primarily to expedite the reimbursement process. Most third-party payers require codes for the diagnoses and procedures be submitted on claim forms. Electronic systems can more easily process codes rather than written descriptions of the patient's diagnoses and procedures.

The main factor considered in choosing coding systems for ambulatory care, is which systems are required by the third-party payers. Most ambulatory care

FIGURE 3-14

Most common coding systems used in freestanding ambulatory care.

Coding System	Use	Organization Responsible
International Classification of Diseases, Clinical Modification (ICD-10-CM in 2015)	Coding diagnoses	National Center for Health Statistics
Healthcare Common Procedure Coding System (HCPCS)	Coding procedures	
Level I Current Procedural Terminology		American Medical Association
Level II National Codes		Centers for Medicare & Medicaid Services (CMS)

settings do not want to code with one system for reimbursement and another for other classification purposes.

The current clinical modification of the *International Classification of Diseases* is the system used most often for coding diagnoses in ambulatory care. The disease classification for *ICD* is maintained by the National Center for Health Statistics of the U.S. government and is revised semiannually. These updates take effect in April and October of each year and require that ambulatory facilities update their systems to accept codes, especially the preprinted codes included on encounter forms or superbills. The **Healthcare Common Procedural Coding System (HCPCS)** is used to code procedures and evaluation and management services in ambulatory care. Two levels of codes make up the HCPCS system. Level I consists of *Current Procedural Terminology (CPT)* codes developed by the American Medical Association (AMA). Each year the AMA revises this coding system and publishes a new version of the codebook. As with the revised diagnosis codes, changes in the codes must be reflected in encounter and superbill forms.

Level I codes reflect physician services. Level II codes in HCPCS are called national codes and are developed by the Centers for Medicare & Medicaid Services (CMS) of the U.S. government. Level II codes classify nonphysician services such as durable medical equipment and ambulance services. Types of injections also can be specified using Level II codes. Most third-party payers require reporting of diagnoses using the current modification of *ICD*, and reporting of procedures and evaluation and management services using HCPCS.

Other coding systems occasionally are seen in ambulatory settings. The **International Classification of Primary Care (ICPC)**, for example, is a coding system developed by the World Organization of National Colleges, Academies, and Academic Associations of General Practitioners/Family Physicians (WONCA). It includes chapters arranged by body systems, with components that describe the reason why the patient is being seen for care at the primary care level.

Data and Information Flow

Many health information professionals are most familiar with the workflow within the hospital's HIM department. The work begins with the patient's discharge, and staffing requirements often are determined based on the number of discharges to be processed each day. In ambulatory care, in contrast, the visit is the driving force in determining the work flow and staffing requirements (Figure 3-15). The visit creates the need for the patient's record to be available so past care can be reviewed and the current treatment recorded.

The workflow begins when an **appointment** is scheduled for the patient. Standard scheduling and block appointment methods are typical appointment scheduling patterns. In **standard scheduling**, patients are scheduled continuously throughout the day, with appointment times at specific intervals (e.g., every

---

International Classification of Diseases (ICD), a classification system used by ambulatory care facilities for coding diagnoses.

Healthcare Common Procedural Coding System (HCPCS) a method used by ambulatory care facilities to code procedures and services.

Current Procedural Terminology **(CPT)** a coding system for procedures that is used extensively in ambulatory care and that forms a part of HCPCS.

International Classification of Primary Care (ICPC) a coding system developed by the World Organization of National Colleges, Academies, and Academic Associations of General Practitioners/Family Physicians (WONCA). It includes chapters arranged by body systems, with components that describe the reason why the patient is being seen for care at the primary care level.

appointment scheduled time when a patient is to arrive at the health care facility.

standard scheduling a method in which appointments are scheduled continuously throughout the day, with appointment times at specific intervals (e.g., every 15 minutes).

FIGURE 3-15

Work flow in a paper-based system.

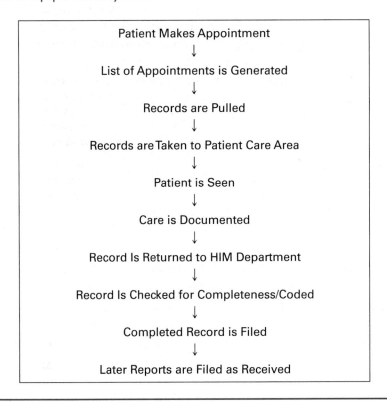

Patient Makes Appointment
↓
List of Appointments is Generated
↓
Records are Pulled
↓
Records are Taken to Patient Care Area
↓
Patient is Seen
↓
Care is Documented
↓
Record Is Returned to HIM Department
↓
Record Is Checked for Completeness/Coded
↓
Completed Record is Filed
↓
Later Reports are Filed as Received

15 minutes). This method sometimes results in wasted physician time when visit lengths are shorter than expected or when patients are "no-shows." Standard scheduling does not eliminate patient waiting time, because some visits run longer than the time allotted, putting all subsequent visits behind schedule.

The **block appointment method** helps to alleviate wasted physician time by scheduling multiple patients for the same time slot. In this method, patients are assigned at the same appointment time (e.g., 9:00 a.m. for all morning appointments), then patients are seen on a first-come, first-served basis. The disadvantage to the block appointment method is that patient satisfaction suffers when some patients have to wait several hours to see the physician.

A modification of the standard and block appointment methods is used sometimes, such as scheduling two patients at the top of each hour and two patients at the half hour, then seeing the patients in the order in which they arrive. The HIM department commonly receives a list of appointments several days before the patient's scheduled appointment.

In a paper-based system, records for established patients are located and made available on the day the patient is to be seen. An electronic health record system provides the patient's information immediately at the time of encounter. For new patients, the record must be initiated at the time of the patient's appointment.

block appointment method an appointment scheduling method that assigns all patients in a large block for the same appointment time (e.g., 9:00 a.m. for all morning appointments), then patients are seen on a first-come, first-served basis.

Usually this process is begun by the receptionist or admissions clerk, who will see that demographic information is recorded, and basic record forms are provided in a new record for a paper-based system. Each encounter must be documented during the patient's visit.

Walk-ins present challenges in the flow of information. Walk-ins are patients who arrive without an appointment or who receive an appointment at the last minute. In paper-based systems, methods must be established for ensuring that medical records are available for these patients. After the visit, the paper-based record must be returned to the HIM department and checked in to assure that it was received. In some facilities, the paper record then is filed. Other facilities, however, review the record to confirm that the documentation has been completed and that the sections of the record are placed in the correct order before the record is filed.

The workflow in a facility with an electronic health record is quite different. The patient makes an appointment, which is entered in the registration/appointment system. When the patient arrives for the appointment, the demographic information is verified. When the care is given, the provider accesses the electronic health record and documents the care. Coding is done from the EHR. Results of diagnostic tests may be fed automatically into the EHR as they are received after the appointment (Figure 3-16).

The patient identifier has an influence on how paper records are filed. When the patient's name is the primary identifier, the records obviously are placed in alphabetical order by the patient's last name. In systems using a number as a primary identifier, the record may be filed in straight numerical order. Large systems, however, often are set up in **terminal digit** order, in which the record is filed first by the last two digits of the number. For example, if the patient's number is 93-02-78, it would first be filed in the 78 section. Then it would be put in order by the middle digits, 02, and finally in numerical order by the first two digits, 93.

walk-ins patients who arrive without an appointment or who receive an appointment at the last minute.

terminal digit a filing system in which records are filed first by the last two digits of their numbers, allowing files to expand evenly.

FIGURE 3-16

Workflow in an Electronic Health Record System.

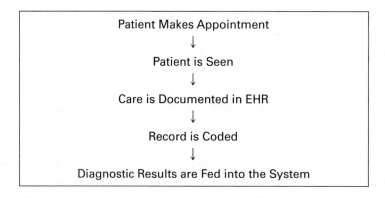

Patient Makes Appointment
↓
Patient is Seen
↓
Care is Documented in EHR
↓
Record is Coded
↓
Diagnostic Results are Fed into the System

This system allows for the files to expand evenly rather than having most of the activity at the end of the numbers to be assigned, as is found in a straight numerical system. If several clerical personnel perform the filing function, terminal digit has the additional advantage of spreading them throughout the filing area. In an electronic record system, patient records may be retrieved using their names, their patient numbers, or other pieces of information. Many ambulatory EHR systems begin the patient search with the patient's birth date and then identify the individual patient from the list generated.

Paper-based records are usually kept in file folders. These may be plain manila filing folders marked with the patient's identifier. Often, however, in either an alphabetical or a numerical system, a method of **color coding** is used on the folder. Each set of numbers or a group of letters is assigned a color on the folder. It then is easy to look at the files and to identify misfiles by the presence of a different color in a block of records of the same color. Paper records may be kept in a variety of equipment. File cabinets with file drawers sometimes are used, although these take up more space. Open-shelf filing also is common. Sometimes motorized filing units are selected to house the records.

color coding a system that helps to prevent the misfiling of records, by assigning colors to numbers or letters and displaying those colors on the record folder so misfiled records are spotted easily by their mismatched color patterns.

The addition of late reports is another function of the HIM department in a paper-based or image-based system. Laboratory and radiology results often are sent to the HIM department after the visit and must be filed in the proper record.

Record Linkage to Other Sites/Facilities

Many freestanding ambulatory care centers have multiple sites and must find a way to provide patient information among the various sites. This task is easiest with an electronic health record that can be accessed from all sites. In such a system, any of the locations can access the patient's information through the system.

In paper-based systems, the record can be in only one site at a time. Facilities use a variety of ways to maintain the location or home base of the record. In some sites the patient designates a home facility where he or she usually is seen, and the record is routinely kept at that location. Other facilities keep the record in the last site where the patient was seen. In either case, if the patient is seen at a site other than the record's home base, a method must be in place to have information available at another site when the patient is seen there.

For scheduled visits, a courier often is used to transport the record to the site of the visit. For unscheduled visits, the pertinent parts of the record may be faxed to the other site from the home base. In either case, policies and procedures must be in place to ensure the safety of the record. If a courier is used, locked courier pouches may be necessary to hold the record during transport and to avoid unauthorized viewing. Facilities that fax information between sites must ensure that the fax is being attended when the material is sent, to avoid unauthorized access to the record. Care also must be taken to dispose of the facsimile copies properly. Electronic health records make access to a record available at any point of care.

Computer Systems

Ambulatory care centers often use computers to assist in the operation of the facility (see Figure 3-17). A **patient registration system** or **appointment system**, for example, is often an important part of such a system for the HIM department. The patient's scheduled visit is entered into the computer, and a list of records needed for a particular day then can be generated automatically from the schedule.

A patient registration or appointment system also is vital for keeping up with basic demographic information about the patient. In such a system, basic information about the patient—name, address, insurance, and responsible party—is collected when the patient is first seen. This information must be updated at each visit to maintain an accurate file. The registration system may provide a master patient index for the HIM department, including the patient's record number, which is needed to enable the department to locate the patient's records in a paper-based system.

A **financial system** maintains information on services billed, determination of insurance coverage, payment received from patients and insurance companies, and collections efforts. Some systems provide for electronic data interchange (EDI) so bills are sent electronically to third-party payers rather than using paper bills. Financial systems often tie in with the encounter form to show the services that the patient received during the visit.

patient registration system a computer system that contains demographic and financial information for every patient.

appointment system a plan by which appointments are scheduled for patients.

financial system a computer system that maintains information on services billed, insurance determination, payment received, and collection efforts.

FIGURE 3-17

Computer applications commonly seen in freestanding ambulatory care.

Computer Applications	Functions
Scheduling or Appointment System	System used to set up patient appointments
Patient Registration System	System used to enter demographic and financial information about the patient
Financial System	System used to maintain information on services billed, insurance coverage, and billing and collections
Electronic Health Record (EHR) System	System in which the patient record is kept in electronic form in a computer-based system
Decision Support System	System that aids the caregiver in making a diagnosis or treatment decision
Reminder System	System that reminds the caregiver of preventive services that should be scheduled on a regular basis, such as annual mammograms

The HIM department may use data from the financial system to retrieve information for activities such as utilization management and quality assessment. The financial system also has information on items billed, such as medications, diagnostic tests, and procedures.

Electronic health records (EHRs) are used in some freestanding ambulatory care settings. Some physicians' offices and other ambulatory care settings are leading the way toward an electronic health record, because the ambulatory record is less complex and easier to maintain electronically than is the hospital record. EHR modules can be integrated with the current practice management system. Other facilities still depend totally on the paper-based record. In most ambulatory care settings, the computer has been used primarily for administrative tasks. In 2013, 78% of office-based physicians used any type of electronic health record (EHR) system—an increase from 18% in 2001 (Hsiao & Hing, 2014).

Some advantages of an electronic health record extend beyond just having the information on the computer where it can be accessed by multiple users across broad geographic areas. One of these functions is decision support. In a decision-support system, information about the patient's signs and symptoms, as well as laboratory and other diagnostic tests, may be used with an artificial intelligence system to help the physician in selecting a diagnosis. Automated online reminders also can be built into the system to remind physicians that patients need certain services such as immunizations for children, yearly mammograms, or routine monitoring.

decision-support system a computerized method that assists physicians in deciding on a diagnosis or treatment.

Because of the potential of the EHR to improve patient safety and the quality of care, the federal government has created incentives for providers to move quickly to an EHR. Under the American Recovery and Reinvestment Act (ARRA), CMS was authorized to offer Medicare and Medicaid incentives to hospitals and providers to become "meaningful users" of electronic health records. Ultimately, Medicare providers are required to be penalized if they do not comply with the meaningful use requirements. Professionals covered by the Act include doctors of medicine or osteopathy, doctors of dental surgery or dental medicine, doctors of optometry, and chiropractors. The EHR technology used by these professionals must meet federal standards or be certified. Adoption of EHRs varies by state, but overall, 69% of physicians intended to participate in the Medicare EHR incentive programs (Hsiao & Hing, 2014).

CMS has offered providers an incentive for adopting e-prescribing, which requires providers to submit electronic prescriptions (eRx) via certified EHR technology. The incentives are being phased out, as eRX is now part of the meaningful use incentives (CMS, 2014).

e-prescribing a method of entering prescriptions into an electronic system that also transmits the prescription to the pharmacy to be filled.

Although e-prescribing is thought to improve the safety of the prescribing process, there had previously been limited adoption by providers. The incentive was intended to accelerate the adoption of this technology. The regulations require that a certain percentage of prescriptions must be submitted through an eprescribing system. Other technologies are affecting ambulatory care, too.

Handheld computers, smart phones, and other mobile devices provide caregivers with a pocket-sized device that can be used to access information about topics, such as drugs. The device also can be connected to the ambulatory care center computer system through a secure wireless network that allows parts of the electronic medical record to be downloaded from or uploaded to the main system. Patients also can use smart phones to monitor and manage their health records.

Many facilities are adopting secure patient portals for patients to access medical records directly from the provider system and to communicate with providers. These often are referred to as personal health records (PHRs), and many health systems including the Veterans Administration (VA) provide patients with electronic access to their health record.

A main issue with smart phones is security, because they are small enough to be lost or easily stolen. Inputting large amounts of data is also difficult. Proper encryption of devices and files is critical to protecting patient information and complying with HIPAA.

Unencrypted e-mail is not secure, so providers should not utilize e-mail for patient queries about problems or ask for refills on medication refills. Once again, security can be an issue, because unauthorized persons may access the e-mail if appropriate safeguards are not in place. Although discouraged from use, any e-mail communications should be entered into the patient's medical record for documentation purposes.

The Internet can be used for remote accessing of information, too. Once again, security is the biggest issue, and means must be included in the system to ensure data security and integrity. Who may access information through the Internet also must be addressed. In some cases, patients wish to access their own records through the Internet, and policies must be devised to define what information they may access.

patient portal a secure method of patient access to his or her own information through a facility's electronic information system.

The **patient portal** is one answer to the confidentiality concerns regarding e-mail and patient access to the health record. A patient portal is a secure online web link that gives patients access to personal health information (HealthIT.gov, n.d). Patients can use secure portals to carry out activities such as scheduling visits, viewing health information such as laboratory reports, and requesting medication refills. Stage 2 meaningful use of an EHR requires that patients have electronic access to their health information. Implementing patient portals is becoming more common.

Data Sets

In many settings, minimum data sets have been developed to provide guidance on the information that should be kept in patient records. A second function of these data sets is to provide standard definitions for the data set items collected. In ambulatory care, the Uniform Ambulatory Care Data Set (UACDS) has been introduced to serve that purpose. This data set includes three main types of data: patient data, provider data, and encounter data. Patient data provides basic identifying information about the patient. Provider data includes information about the provider, such as a unique provider identifier and location.

Encounter data includes the date, reason for encounter, services received, and disposition (Abdelhak et al., 2012). The minimum data set provides an excellent source for the HIM professional to determine the minimum data that must be kept for each encounter. In addition, definitions for terms such as *encounter* can help the HIM professional in developing statistical measures. The statistics must measure the indicated items uniformly.

SELF REVIEW 3.5

1. The main factor usually considered in choosing a coding system for ambulatory care is _____.
    a. what is easiest for the physicians
    b. what is required by third-party payers
    c. what is easiest for the coders
    d. what is required by the state health department
2. Which information is most likely to be included in the appointment system?
    a. physician orders
    b. problem list
    c. demographic data
    d. allergies

QUALITY IMPROVEMENT AND UTILIZATION MANAGEMENT

Quality Assessment and Performance Improvement

A major use of health information in ambulatory care is the assessment of the quality of care provided by the facility. The quality assessment and improvement process in ambulatory care follows the same methods used in other care settings. Problems or processes must be chosen for study, data must be collected to measure these processes, data must be assessed, and a method for improvement must be developed. The major difference in ambulatory care is that many factors affecting the quality of care are not within the sole control of the ambulatory facility. The patient's contact with the facility is usually brief, and the patient's outcome depends in large part on the patient's compliance with the care plan developed (Shalowitz, 2010).

The patient's continuity of care may depend on factors in the patient's, not the facility's, control, such as missed appointments and consistent use of a primary provider to coordinate care. Methods to improve compliance must be included in the quality assessment process, because they affect the patient's outcome. Patient satisfaction is also an important part of the quality assessment process in ambulatory care, because the patient's compliance may be closely tied to satisfaction with the care received. The ability to determine the quality of care within a facility is highly dependent on the quality of data collected within the health record.

The Centers for Medicare & Medicaid Services have established a **physician quality reporting system** (PQRS). PQRS is a reporting program that uses a combination of incentive payments and payment adjustments to promote reporting of quality information by eligible providers (EPs). Under this program, physicians, podiatrists, physician assistants, nurse practitioners, and physical therapists reporting on a list of quality measures defined each year by CMS. The measures to be collected may vary from year to year, and each year's requirements are published in the *Federal Register*. This information is posted on the CMS.gov website as program updates are approved and published. Measures include items such as the percentage of patients who received counseling on diet and exercise as well as a variety of screening tests such as mammograms and colonoscopies.

Utilization Management

Utilization management is the process of determining the appropriateness of services and treatment provided to the patient, based on the patient's needs (Abdelhak et al., 2012). In the hospital setting, this process often focuses on whether the patient requires hospitalization. In ambulatory care, utilization management is more likely to focus on the necessity of a service such as referral to a specialist or the use of an expensive procedure such as a magnetic resonance imaging study or the appropriateness of referrals for hospitalization. Emphasis should be on services that are either high volume or high cost, because not all services can be examined. Standards or criteria that are credible and specific should be established.

Utilization management has two basic approaches. One is **prospective review/precertification**, in which the service is examined before it is provided. Data are collected, usually by a nurse, from the patient and the physician. The facts of the individual case are compared to the appropriateness criteria. If the standards are met, the nurse can usually approve the service. If the standards are not met, a physician advisor may be asked to review the case and make a determination. Types of activities typically undergoing prospective review include authorization for referral, authorization for a procedure, preadmission review before hospitalization, and second surgical opinion.

The second major approach is **retrospective review**. In this methodology, care is looked at after it is given. Usually a sample of cases is selected. Data are collected from medical records, and the information from the record is compared to the appropriateness standards. Feedback then is given to the appropriate caregiver regarding inappropriate care provided.

---

physician quality reporting system a system for physicians to report quality measures to CMS.

prospective review/precertification one of two basic approaches to utilization management, prospective review determines whether services are needed before they are provided.

retrospective review one of two basic approaches to utilization management; examines care after it has been given, to identify inappropriate care and provide feedback to the caregiver.

1. What is the physician quality reporting system (PQRS), and who created it?
2. How does utilization management within the hospital setting differ from utilization management in the ambulatory care setting?
3. Distinguish between the two basic approaches to utilization management: prospective review/precertification and retrospective review.

RISK MANAGEMENT AND LEGAL ISSUES

Many legal and risk management issues that arise in freestanding ambulatory care relate to the reality that much of the care is not provided by the caregiver but instead by the patient and the family (see Figure 3-18). Communication is vital to ensure that the care is given as prescribed. Care recommendations, for example, often are provided through telephone calls. These calls must be documented in the record to authenticate care recommendations. Prescribed medications, especially, must be documented, including name of the medication, dosages and amounts dispensed, dispensing instructions (with signature), prescription dates and discontinued dates, and problem identification numbers for which each medication was prescribed (Odom-Wesley et al., 2009).

Preventing adverse drug events is crucial to physicians and patients alike and makes documentation in the medical record imperative. Failure to document such care can lead to a situation of the caregiver's word versus the patient's word on whether or not needed advice was given and followed.

Documenting missed and canceled appointments also is vital, because patients can incur adverse effects from not keeping an appointment as scheduled. Documenting that the appointment was missed or canceled provides additional information concerning the patient's responsibility in such a situation (Office

FIGURE 3-18

Risk management issues in freestanding ambulatory care.

Risk Management Issues

Documenting Telephone Calls

Documenting Missed and Canceled Appointments

Documenting Written Discharge Instructions

Documenting Informed Consent Process

Documenting Changes since Last Visit

Documenting Noncompliance

Documenting Incidents

Practice, n.d.). Freestanding ambulatory sites, particularly ambulatory surgery centers, often provide written instructions for patients to take home to help patient compliance and understanding (Odom-Wesley et al., 2009). The instruction sheets should be included in the medical record. If they are not, a statement should be included in the record that a specific instruction sheet was given to the patient, and copies of the different instruction sheets should be kept on file in the facility.

Documentation of the physician's discussion regarding informed consent is especially important in ambulatory surgery settings but must be furnished for any invasive procedure, whatever the setting. A consent form signed by the patient should contain the substance of the items discussed, including alternatives to the procedure and any risks involved. Narrative progress notes should include further detail about the discussion regarding the procedure or service to be provided (Brodnik et al., 2012).

Caregivers should be advised to include documentation of any changes after the patient's last visit and any evidence of noncompliance (What should be documented, n.d.). Such facts could be vitally important if a legal case results.

Legibility is another risk management issue. If prescriptions are illegible, for example, the risk is that the medication will be dispensed incorrectly, which potentially can cause harm to the patient. Some organizations have implemented systems in which providers use handheld devices to generate and print prescriptions to address this patient safety concern. An e-prescribing system also eliminates the problem of illegible prescriptions. Illegibility is a problem in the area of compliance. If an auditor cannot read a provider's records, the documentation cannot be used to support the services billed, which could lead to legal issues with the OIG. Electronic health records solve the legibility issue, because all entries are present in an easily readable, digital format.

It is essential that abnormal test results be reviewed by the ordering physician. Each facility should develop a procedure to ensure that the physician sees the results and documents any actions taken on the basis of the results. For example, in a paper record, physicians may be asked to initial the laboratory report and document in the progress notes section of the record that the patient was contacted and advised of what to do about abnormal results. An electronic health record system could place the laboratory result in the physician's queue for review and could prompt the physician for documentation on actions taken. Laboratory results that reveal a serious problem can send an automatic alert to the physician (Ferris et. al., 2009).

Many facilities use an **incident report** or **occurrence report** as internal documentation of unusual events such as falls, incorrect medications given or taken, or other untoward occurrences. The purpose of the incident or occurrence report is to provide documentation of events so facilities can take steps to avoid such events in the future. The report usually goes to the facility's attorney and thus is protected by attorney–client privilege. A copy of the incident report should not be placed in the record, but details about the event should be recorded there (Odom-Wesley et al., 2009).

incident report internal documentation of an unusual event such as a fall, incorrect medications given or taken, or some other untoward occurrence. (See also occurrence report).

occurrence report internal documentation of an unusual event such as a fall, incorrect medications given or taken, or some other untoward occurrence. (See also incident report).

SELF REVIEW 3.7

1. True or False? Many risk management issues that arise in freestanding ambulatory care relate to the fact that much of the care is not provided by the caregiver but, rather, by the patient and the family.
2. A(n) _____ system eliminates the problem of illegible prescriptions by using handheld devices to generate and print prescriptions.
3. What is an incident/occurrence report, and what is its purpose?
4. True or False? A copy of the incident report should not be placed in the record, but details about the event should be recorded there.

ROLE OF THE HEALTH INFORMATION MANAGEMENT PROFESSIONAL

The role of the HIM professional in freestanding ambulatory care often includes providing expertise in the areas of information management, regulatory compliance, electronic information systems, and administrative functions. In a paper-based ambulatory care setting, the primary role of the HIM department is chart location and control, making information management and supervision of personnel the main functions of the HIM professional in this scenario.

Information must be organized and stored in a way that makes it easy to retrieve, either through computerized or paper-based storage. With a paper-based system, personnel are needed to file and retrieve records and to make sure that loose sheets such as laboratory reports are placed in the correct record. These employees must be trained in filing methods and in confidentiality and security so information is not released improperly. This training function may include instruction of employees and caregivers outside of the HIM department in proper documentation, use of the record, and confidentiality.

The role of the health information manager has been affected by the move to the EHR in freestanding ambulatory care. As facilities decide to implement EHRs, health information managers are involved in implementing these new systems and may serve as project managers. HIM professionals also can play a role in helping physicians and other caregivers successfully make workflow changes to utilize the functions of the EHR more effectively (When the Doctor Calls, 2005).

Implementation of an electronic record system changes the role of the HIM professional from one of managing the filing and retrieval of the paper record to one of managing the data contained in the record and the electronic record process. HIPAA also adds new roles for the HIM professional who may serve as the privacy and/or security officer for the facility.

In smaller ambulatory care settings, HIM professionals often undertake roles outside of those usually identified with health information management. In some settings, for example, HIM professionals have duties in areas such as purchasing or patient registration. Some HIM professionals have expanded their knowledge of the ambulatory setting and now utilize their management and administrative skills to become medical group managers.

Because the HIM field has not been as well known in ambulatory care as it has been in the hospital industry, HIM professionals in these settings also serve as marketers for their skills and demonstrate flexibility to assume a variety of responsibilities. This is illustrated in the Professional Spotlight.

PROFESSIONAL SPOTLIGHT   NOT-FOR-PROFIT, AMBULATORY OPTOMETRIC TEACHING FACILITY

Who I am: Kim Branscomb, RHIA

Where I work: The Southern College of Optometry (SCO), an institution of optometric education located in Memphis, Tennessee. SCO offers clinical services as part of its mission, including the following programs:

- The Eye Center is the primary clinical facility, providing care to more than 60,000 individuals per year. As both a clinical and a teaching facility, services are provided to approximately 350 patients daily by 35 optometric physicians, 106 interns, and 45 other staff members.
- Community Vision Health Services (CVHS) includes the Nursing Home/ Assisted Living Program, the Community Outreach Program, and the School Screening Program. Through these programs, students and interns are exposed to the provision of eye care in non-office settings.
- The External Clinics (EC) of SCO allow staff doctors, residents and interns to provide care to special populations through clinical sites in the Students & Advocates for Vision in Education (S.A.V.E.) Program, Diocese of Memphis Angel Program, the Star Center for Rehabilitation, and through inpatient services in the Baptist Rehabilitation Hospital. SCO has opened a fully independent external clinic, University Eye Care of SCO, on the campus of the

University of Memphis. Approximately 10,000 individuals are served annually in these external clinic settings

What I do: I am the Compliance Officer. I oversee all aspects of HIPAA and other State and Federally mandated laws for the Eye Center. I oversee all release of information (ROI) activities. In addition, I also manage credentialing processes for all the doctors' privileges. I have a variety of other responsibilities. For example, I am the coordinator for preventive health, and "Special Projects" are also incorporated into my title. With regard to the implementation of electronic health records, I am the project manager for Meaningful Use.

Why HIM knowledge is important in my role: HIM knowledge was the single most important aspect to the evolution and advancement of my career. I was hired as a case manager, managing external patient referrals. I began at the advent of HIPAA which gave me an edge to introduce my knowledge of HIPAA and what would be needed to begin implementation. I was then promoted to Privacy Officer. I created all the policies and procedures needed for the implementation. Within that next year, SCO was up for accreditation with the Accreditation Council on Optometric Education (ACOE). Documentation required for accreditation included the Eye Center's (TEC) quality manual, which did not exist. The Chief of Staff came to me, knowing that I could quickly create this, as we only had a few months. In the development of this manual, I relied heavily on

AHIMA resources and HIM text books from school. I had to create new processes within TEC to support the policies. One example was a new process of peer review for the doctors. I developed the policies, procedures, data capturing tools, and the peer review committee format that still exists today.

I also have redeveloped many of the policies and procedures to make them more legally sound, e.g., the privileging of the doctors, terminating physician-patient relationships, responding to subpoenas, and all new federally mandated laws (Red Flag Rules, Elder Abuse, ROI, HITECH Act, etc.).

HIM knowledge also kept me informed of all the new EHR incentive programs, which has allowed us to receive incentive payments from Meaningful Use and Direct Messaging.

My HIM background has helped me to serve the Southern College of Optometry in many important ways. I was honored to receive the President's Special Recognition Award in 2011.

Other information: My duties at SCO include the following committee service:

- Clinic Council
- Chair of the Credentialing and Privileging Committee
- EHR Committee
- Performance Improvement Committee
- Process Improvement Committee

SELF REVIEW 3.8

1. List four areas of expertise through which the HIM professional can contribute to freestanding ambulatory care.

2. True or False? The HIM field has not been as well known in ambulatory care as it has been in the hospital area.

3. Using the Professional Spotlight as an example, what are some of the varied roles that an HIM professional may play in ambulatory care?

TRENDS

Several trends are evident in freestanding ambulatory care. The first is the continuing shift of care to the ambulatory setting. As government programs such as diagnosis related groups (DRGs) have attempted to hold down hospital costs, a shift has taken place to the less-expensive ambulatory setting. This movement will continue, and the role of ambulatory care settings in the health care arena will be enhanced.

Another trend is more integration of freestanding ambulatory care sites with other health care facilities. Health care is increasingly provided by networks, including all facets of health care from primary care to specialized hospital care. Ambulatory care settings find themselves part of this continuum of care and, therefore, part of larger health care corporations or networks. This shift provides more support for individual ambulatory care settings but also will be expected to provide increased regulation and standardization of the health care process. An emphasis on holding down health care costs is resulting in additional scrutiny of ambulatory care documentation to determine whether it supports the reimbursement requested.

medical home a method of providing care in which the primary care provider works with a team of health care professionals to provide care to patients using a whole-person concept.

The **medical home** provides innovations in health care that impact the HIM professional. In the medical home concept, the primary care provider works with a team of health care professionals to provide care to patients using a whole-person concept. The primary care professional either provides all of the care to the patient or arranges for other care, regardless of the site of care or the patient's stage of life (Rosenthal, 2008). Without an EHR, the concept of a medical home for each patient would be difficult to carry out. The HIM professional will be involved in ensuring that the necessary health information is available at any point of care where the patient may be seen.

There is greater use of electronic health records in ambulatory care. Financial incentives provided through ARRA to move to the EHR have increased the momentum for adopting electronic health information systems. The expertise of the HIM professional in this area provides excellent opportunities to participate in this trend.

SELF REVIEW 3.9

1. List two trends that are evident in freestanding ambulatory care.
2. Explain the concept of the medical home.

SUMMARY

Before providing information management services, the HIM professional must be aware of many factors about a facility. The type of facility determines the types of caregivers and the types of patients seen, thus defining the documentation that must be provided. Accreditation and licensing standards, as well as the reimbursement systems applicable to the setting, also serve as benchmarks for documentation and storage and retrieval methods. HIM professionals looking at quality of care and utilization must be aware of the patient's role in following the plan of care and, thus, in the outcome achieved. Patients' participation in their care, or their lack of such participation, is also a risk management factor that affects documentation requirements. Knowledge of all of these elements provides the HIM practitioner with the tools necessary to offer exceptional service to meet the needs of the ambulatory facility.

REVIEW QUESTIONS

Knowledge-Based Questions

1. List and describe three types of freestanding ambulatory care settings.

2. Define the following terms used in ambulatory care: encounter, nurse practitioner, reason for visit, superbill.

3. Name the two main organizations that accredit ambulatory care.
4. List the major types of documentation that are basic to all ambulatory care encounters and settings.
5. What types of patient identifiers are used in ambulatory care?
6. What types of data are included in the uniform ambulatory care data set, and how do these affect the content of the ambulatory record?
7. What is the ASC reimbursement system, and how is it used in Medicare reimbursement?

Critical Thinking Questions

1. Compare and contrast the fee-for-service and PFS/RBRVS reimbursement systems.
2. How does documentation in an industrial health center differ from that in a physician's practice and why?
3. How is quality assessment in ambulatory care similar to and different from quality assessment in the acute inpatient setting?

WEB ACTIVITY

LCDs and NCDs can be reviewed at the Medicare Coverage Database at the CMS website. To begin, go to http://www.cms.gov. Then select "Medicare," then under "Coverage" select "Medicare Coverage Determination Process." Review the information in the "Overview," then select "Coverage Center" under "Related Links inside CMS." At the Medicare Coverage Center, review the available resources. Select "Medicare Coverage Database," then locate and review the LCD or NCD of your choice. What type of information does the LCD/NCD document contain? How might this information be useful to a freestanding ambulatory care provider?

CASE STUDY

Judy Jordan has just begun working as the health information manager in a large physicians' group practice. The patient's name is the primary patient identifier, and the records are filed alphabetically. Misfiles are a frequent problem, and in the large practice, patients sometimes have similar names. The records are not kept in a uniform format. Many of the doctors use an integrated format, but three of the physicians use the POMR. The practice wants to transition to an electronic health record. In reviewing the encounter forms, Judy finds codes that are no longer valid. She questions the staff and finds that no one can remember when the encounter form was updated. Bills frequently are returned for invalid codes. Electronic systems for patient registration and appointments have been implemented, but the staff also keeps a manual appointment log.

A computer-generated list of appointments is given to the HIM clerk on the day prior to the appointments so the records can be pulled and available when the patients arrive. Many appointments that are entered in the manual log are not also entered into the electronic appointment system. The HIM clerk, therefore, spends extensive time each day pulling records for those appointments that are not on the computer-generated list. Judy has been asked to make suggestions for making the office run more smoothly.

1. What main problems should she identify?
2. Develop a plan to solve each of the problems identified above.

REFERENCES AND SUGGESTED READINGS

Abdelhak, M., Grostick, S., Hanken, M.A., Jacobs, E.B. (2012). *Health information: Management of a strategic resource* (4th ed.). Philadelphia: Saunders Publishing.

AHIMA (American Health Information Management Association). (2003). E-mail as a provider-patient communication medium and its impact on the electronic health record: Practice brief. [Online]. http://library.ahima.org [2010, May 3].

ASC (Ambulatory Surgery Centers). (2010, April 30). *Encyclopedia of surgery.* [Online]. www.surgeryencyclopedia.com/A-Ce/Ambulatory-Surgery-Centers.html [2015, October 6].

Boland, P. (2007). The emerging role of cell phone technology in ambulatory care. *Journal of Ambulatory Care Management, 30*(2), 126–133.

Brodnik, M. S., McCain, M. C., Rinehart-Thompson, L. A., & Reynolds, R. (2012). *Fundamentals of law for health informatics and information management*. Chicago: American Health Information Management Association.

CMS (Centers for Medicare & Medicaid Services). (2009). Chapter 14, Ambulatory surgery centers, in *Medicare Claims Processing Manual*. [Online]. http://www.cms.gov/Regulations-and-Guidance/Guidance/Manuals/Downloads/clm104c14.pdf [2015, October 6].

CMS (Centers for Medicare & Medicaid Services). (2010). Physician quality reporting initiative. [Online]. http://www.cms.gov/PQRI/ [2010, May 3].

CMS (Centers for Medicare & Medicaid Services). (2012). Medicaid integrity provider audits. [Online]. http://www.cms.gov/medicare-medicaid-coordination/fraud-prevention/provider-audits/downloads/mip-audit-fact-sheet.pdf [2014, November 28].

CMS (Centers for Medicare & Medicaid Services). (2014, January 31). Electronic prescribing (eRx) incentive program. [Online]. http://www.cms.gov/Medicare/Quality-Initiatives-Patient-Assessment-Instruments/ERxIncentive [2015, October 6].

CMS (Centers for Medicare & Medicaid Services). (2014, May). Eligible professional meaningful use core measures. [Online]. http://www.cms.gov/Regulations-and-Guidance/Legislation/EHRIncentivePrograms/downloads/3_Maintain_Problem_ListEP.pdf [2015, October 6].

CMS (Centers for Medicare & Medicaid Services). (n.d.). Overview, state program integrity support and assistance. [Online]. http://www.cms.gov/FraudAbuseforProfs/ [2010, May 3].

Ferris, T. G., Johnson, S. A., Co, J. P. T., Backus, M., Perrin, J., Bates, D. W., & Poon, E. G. (2009). Electronic results management in pediatric ambulatory care: Qualitative assessment, *Pediatrics, 123*(Suppl. 2), S85–S91.

Fowler, C., Lloyd, S., Gale, J., Wang, J., & McClure, E. (2012), November. *Family Planning Annual Report: 2011 National Summary*. Research Triangle Park, NC: RTI International.

Geiger, H. Jack. (2005). The first community health centers: A model of enduring value. *Journal of Ambulatory Care Management, 28*(4), 313–320.

HealthIT.gov. (2014). What is a patient portal? [Online]. http://www.healthit.gov/providers-professionals/faqs/what-patient-portal [2015, October 6].

HRSA (Health Resources and Services Administration). (2006, June). *Federally Qualified Health Centers.* [Online]. http://www.raconline.org/topics/federally-qualified-health-centers [2014, Feb 13].

Hsiao, C., & Hing, E. (2014). Use and characteristics of Electronic Health Record Systems among office-based physician practices: United States, 200–2013. NCHS Data Brief, Centers for Disease Control and Prevention, number 143, January. [Online]. http://www.cdc.gov/nchs/data/databriefs/db143.htm [2015, October 6].

Medicare Learning Network. (2014, November). *Medicare Physician Guide: A Resource for Residents, Practicing Physicians, and Other Healthcare Professionals.* [Online]. http://gi.org/wp-content/uploads/2011/07/physicianguide.pdf [2015, October 6].

Odom-Wesley, B., Brown, D., & Meyers, C. (2009). *Documentation for Medical Records.* Chicago: American Health Information Management Association.

Office practice: What works—Missed and cancelled appointments. (n.d.). CRICO/RMF. [Online]. http://www.rmf.harvard.edu/patient-safety-strategies/office-practices/main/index2.aspx?id=14 [2010, May 3].

OIG Compliance Program for individual and small group physician practices. (2000). *Federal Register, 65*(194), 59434–59452.

Rosenthal, T. C. (2008). The medical home: Growing evidence to support a new approach to primary care. *Journal of the American Board of Family Medicine, 21*(5), 427–440.

Shalowitz, Joel. (2010). Implementing successful quality outcome programs in ambulatory care: Key questions and recommendations. *Journal of Ambulatory Care Management, 33*(2), 117–125.

Walters, B., Barnard, D., & Paris, S. (2006). "Patient portals" and "e-visits." *Journal of Ambulatory Care Management, 29*(3), 222–224.

What should be documented. (n.d.). CRICO/ RMF. [Online]. http:// www.rmf.harvard.edu/patient-safety-strategies/documentation/articles/index.aspx. [2010, May 3].

When the doctor calls: Opportunities in ambulatory care. (2005, August). *AHIMA Advantage, 9*(5).

KEY RESOURCES

Accreditation Association for Ambulatory Health Care, Inc. (AAAHC)
   http://www.aaahc.org

Ambulatory Surgery Center Association
   http://www.ascassociation.org

American Association for Accreditation of Ambulatory Surgery Facilities, Inc.
   http://www.aaaasf.org

American Health Information Management Association
   http://www.ahima.org

Commission for the Accreditation of Birth Centers
   http://www.birthcenteraccreditation.org

Department of Health and Human Services
Office of Inspector General
Fraud Prevention and Detection
   http://oig.hhs.gov

Medical Group Management Association (MGMA)
   http://www.mgma.com

National Association of Community Health Centers
   www.nachc.com

Professional Association of Health Care Office Management
   http://www.pahcom.com

Rural Assistance Center
   http://www.raconline.org

The Joint Commission
   http://www.jointcommission.org

CHAPTER 4

Managed Care

Dorthy K. Young, PHD, MHSA | Cecile Favreau, MBA, CPC |
Lynn Kuehn, MS, RHIA, CCS-P, FAHIMA

LEARNING OBJECTIVES

Upon successful completion of this chapter, you should be able to:

- Identify the various forms of managed care organizations and compare how they are structured and operate.
- Explain why the term "member" is used to refer to individuals in this setting.
- Identify the accreditation organization and regulations that impact the various forms of managed care organizations.
- Explain how managed care organizations generate revenue.
- Describe the types of reimbursement that a managed care organization receives and the various methods of reimbursing providers of care.
- Describe the concept of coordination of benefits, and explain why it is important to a managed care organization.
- Explain why the structure of the managed care organization affects the way health care documentation is managed.
- Identify the basic requirements for electronic information systems in managed care.
- Explain why the Healthcare Effectiveness Data and Information Set (HEDIS) is helping to improve the quality of health care delivery in managed care.
- Identify the types of consumer-directed health plans and their characteristics.
- List and define the utilization management activities of a managed care organization.

Setting/Plan	Description	Synonyms/Examples
Health Maintenance Organization (HMO)	An insurance entity that provides or arranges for health services for a covered population after prepayment of a fixed premium.	Staff Model HMO Group Model HMO Network Model HMO IPA Model HMO Mixed Model HMO
Preferred Provider Organization (PPO)	An insurance entity that contracts with providers to create a preferred network. The insured population is allowed to use any provider, but using network providers results in a lesser cost to the patient.	Preferred Provider Network Preferred Provider Option
Point of Service (POS) Plan	An insurance plan that combines the health maintenance and preferred provider concepts, creating several levels of out-of-pocket cost options for the insured. The insured makes the choice at the time of service.	Point of Sale Plan Open-Ended HMO Open-Access HMO
Managed Indemnity Plan	An insurance plan that reimburses the insured for expenses incurred but incorporates some managed care principles to help control costs.	Modified Indemnity Insurance
Consumer-Directed Health Plans	Insurance plans that provide incentives to control costs of health benefits and health care. Individuals have greater freedom in health care spending up to a specific dollar amount and receive full coverage for in-network preventive care. Members incur higher out-of-pocket costs in the form of coinsurance and deductibles.	Customized Sub-Capitation Plan (CSCP) Flexible Spending Accounts (FSA) Health Savings Account (HSA) Health Savings Security Account (HSSA) Health Reimbursement Arrangement (HRA)
Integrated Delivery System (IDS)	A group of facilities contracted together to provide the comprehensive set of services that any patient may need. They are owned, leased, or grouped together by long-term contracts and are recognized by the public as a combined operating entity.	Integrated Delivery Network (IDN)

INTRODUCTION TO SETTINGS AND PLANS

Patient Protection and Affordable Care Act landmark federal legislation enacted in 2010 that changed coverage requirements for all insurers and employers, established health insurance exchanges, and impacted eligibility for Medicaid and claims and benefit processing for all insurers.

A health care professional must continually adapt to ever changing advances in technology, new regulations such as those found in the 2010 Patient Protection and Affordable Care Act (ACA), and improvements in care delivery methods. The managed care industry is not immune to these changes and must evolve to meet the needs of the health care environment.

Managed care is the provision of comprehensive health care services coordinated by a third party with the goal of improving an individual's access to quality medical services and preventive care while increasing efficiency and cost effectiveness. Based on a preventive model, managed care aims to ensure reduced utilization of costly tertiary health care services through effective coordination of care for individuals who are enrolled in the program. This is accomplished by promoting preventive services and medication compliance and incorporating predictive data algorithms to identify at-risk patients prior to the occurrence of an acute health crisis or event. This coordinated effort to reduce emergency service utilization and decrease poor patient outcomes ultimately results in more efficient use of health care provider resources and reduced costs.

Managed care began as an alternative delivery system in the mid-1970s and has been transformed over the last few decades into an industry standard for private, employer self-funded, and government health care plans. As employers, government entities, and other purchasers of health care continue to seek means of providing higher-quality care at a lower costs, managed models are likely to expand in prevalence.

The major types of **managed care organizations (MCOs)** are health maintenance organizations (HMOs), preferred provider organizations or networks (PPOs), point of service organizations (POSs), and indemnity insurance plans that have incorporated some managed care features. Each of these organizations is unique, and this dynamic industry also contains hybrid combinations of all of the major types of MCOs.

The terms *managed care* and *health maintenance organization* are not synonymous, although they often are misused interchangeably. HMOs use managed care techniques and, therefore, are, MCOs. Not all managed care organizations are HMOs, though—for example, PPOs and managed indemnity plans. The definitions, structure, operation, and information technology needs of the various types of organizations are the subject of this chapter.

Types of Managed Care Organizations

The types of managed care organizations found in the industry today are health maintenance organizations, preferred provider organizations, point of service plans, and managed indemnity plans.

Health Maintenance Organizations

The **health maintenance organization (HMO)** is a business entity that either arranges for or provides health services to an enrolled population. Individuals enroll in the plan and are obligated to pay a fixed sum of money, called a premium, on a monthly or annual basis. Theoretically, prepayment of a premium serves as an incentive for the individual member to participate in preventive care services and to seek treatment before a condition is exacerbated. It also serves as an incentive for the caregiver to provide care with the greatest efficiency and the best possible outcome, because the amount of reimbursement for services rendered is fixed. Thus, the care provider is incentivized to diagnose illness at an early stage when treatment and management are less costly.

HMOs are found in a variety of different forms, each named by its organizational structure. Regardless of the structure, "the entity must have three characteristics to call itself an HMO:

1. An organized system for providing health care or otherwise assuring health care delivery in a geographic area

managed care organizations (MCOs) entities that provide comprehensive health services in a coordinated manner in an effort to improve patient outcomes and reduce costs through efficient health care delivery.

health maintenance organization (HMO) a business entity that either provides or arranges for health services for a covered population after prepayment of a fixed premium.

2. An agreed-upon set of basic and supplemental health maintenance and treatment services

3. A voluntarily enrolled group of people."

(United HealthCare Corporation, 1994)

Staff Model   The staff model HMO is the most tightly organized HMO structure. The HMO entity owns the facilities and employs the health care providers to which the covered individual has access. Health care providers employed by the HMO are paid fixed salaries and are obligated contractually not to treat patients outside of the HMO network. Because profits earned through this model go directly to the HMO rather than to the individual health care providers, physicians have no financial incentive to perform unnecessary diagnostic tests or procedures.

Some staff model HMOs own only the ambulatory clinic facilities and contract with local providers for the remainder of the services, such as inpatient hospital and ambulatory surgery services. Other staff model HMOs own a comprehensive group of facilities that provide all of the services under the same ownership. The staff model is the only model in which the HMO actually owns the facilities where care is provided. An example of a staff model HMO is the Harvard Pilgrim Health Plan, which operates in Massachusetts, Maine, and New Hampshire. The staff model HMOs structure fell out of favor in the 1990s, and most plans have since evolved into another model.

staff model HMO the most tightly organized HMO structure. The HMO entity owns the facilities and arranges for health care through employed physicians, who are allowed to see only the specified HMO's patients.

Group Model   The group model HMO, unlike the staff model, operates on a contractual basis with health care provider medical groups and facilities that provide services to members. The HMO has an exclusive contract with a multispecialty medical group that provides all physician services and separate contracts with the other facilities necessary to provide comprehensive care.

The contract with the multispecialty group may contain a year-end reconciliation clause, in which the multispecialty group may receive a percentage of any unused premiums at year-end. This provides a significant incentive for efficient patient care and financial management. The health care providers are employed by the group practice rather than the HMO. A few group model HMOs are still active, including the well-known Kaiser Foundation Health Plan, in which the Permanente Medical Group employs nearly 175,000 individuals who provide medical services for an estimated 9.1 million members (see Web Activity for Kaiser Permanente).

group model HMO a model in which the HMO has an exclusive contract with a multispecialty medical group that provides all physician services and contracts with other facilities as necessary to provide comprehensive services.

Network Model   The network model HMO is a more expansive model than the group model and contracts with more than one physician group, hospital, and other facilities to provide a comprehensive health care package. The health care providers may share in some of the profit or loss of the HMO according to contract terms but are not required to provide care only to the patients of a certain HMO. The HMO portion of their business may vary from low to high

network model HMO an HMO that contracts with multiple physician groups, hospitals, and other facilities to provide a comprehensive health care package.

participation. This model is often popular for plans that cover an expansive geographic area or serve rural populations.

Independent Practice Association Model   The **independent practice association (IPA) model** was developed primarily as a way for the solo practice physician to participate in the managed care market. This model has two varieties: the physician initiated and the insurance entity initiated. In the model initiated by physicians, the HMO is formed by the physicians who are placing their own resources as the start-up funds. The HMO contracts with each physician and the other facilities necessary to make up the HMO. In this variety of IPA, the physicians are at high risk for the resources they use to back the HMO. They also may purchase large amounts of reinsurance, or stop-loss insurance, to provide insurance after expenses of a given amount have been paid per enrollee—such as after $50,000 or $100,000 per enrollee has been paid per year.

Insurance entities also develop IPA model HMOs because of their ease of development. A comprehensive group of providers and facilities plus financial resources are the only ingredients necessary to develop an IPA model—readily available through most insurers. Either of these IPA models provides a wide choice of physicians from which enrollees may choose. Financial viability has been difficult to achieve, however, as the independent physicians have little incentive to change their practice patterns, which are necessary to maintain profitability.

Mixed Model   The **mixed model HMO** operates within two or more different types of organizational structures to provide flexibility to members, diversity of income to the HMO, and attractive pricing to the employers. Each HMO organization evolved over time in an effort to increase profitability and maintain compliance with regulatory legislation. Through these changes, along with mergers and acquisitions, the mixed model became more prevalent.

Preferred Provider Organizations

Any aspect of a managed care program that is left to the member to decide can be difficult to predict or control. Managed care entities have a vested interest in having participants receive care from providers who can perform a procedure or provide a service in the most cost effective manner. In an effort to guide enrollees to more cost-effective providers, the insurance industry developed the **preferred provider organization (PPO)**. Providers that participate in the PPO agree to provide services to PPO patients at a discounted rate in return for the promise of a higher volume of patients. Therefore, while the profit margin for each individual patient may be less for the provider, the increased volume of patients creates an environment for overall profitability. Members of PPO networks pay little or no out-of-pocket expenses when they obtain care from specified providers, whereas members who use other providers pay significantly higher portions of the providers' charges.

---

independent practice association (IPA) model an HMO model that was developed primarily as a way for the solo health practitioners to participate in the managed care market.

mixed model HMO an HMO that operates within two or more different types of organizational structures to provide flexibility to members.

preferred provider organization (PPO) an insurance entity that contracts with providers to create a preferred network. The insured population is allowed to use any provider, but using network providers results in lesser cost to the patient.

Although the patient is not limited to a certain list of providers, there is a strong financial incentive to choose providers that are included in the PPO. The success of a PPO depends on the organization's ability to maintain an extensive provider network. An example of a PPO model that exists in many states is the Blue Cross Blue Shield plan.

Point of Service Plans

A point of service plan (POS) is a hybrid of the HMO and PPO models. An individual enrolled in the PPO plan pays a premium, and the care is managed by a primary care provider, similar to an HMO. Unlike an HMO, however, the member still can obtain care from a provider outside of the preferred network. The coverage for services rendered by an out-of-network provider is reimbursed at a lesser rate in keeping with the PPO model. The remaining charges and increased copays resulting from receiving services from a provider outside of the preferred group are the responsibility of the insured. By enrolling in a point of service plan, members choose the type of provider to use and how much out-of-pocket expense they are willing to pay in return for that ability to choose. (United HealthCare Corporation, 1994).

As an example, a member experiences flu-like symptoms and wants to see a physician. The member can choose to see an in-network physician employed by the POS plan with no out-of-pocket cost (similar to the HMO model), a PPO in-network provider at a 10% coinsurance cost, or a PPO out-of-network provider at a 20% coinsurance cost. The provider closest to the patient's home is out-of-network, but is open early and can see the member within the hour. The member may decide it is worth the price of paying 20% of coinsurance to be seen quickly for the flu-like symptoms. Many patients find POS plans appealing, as they have more freedom of choice in determining who will deliver their health care.

As with all of the managed care plan options, there are advantages and disadvantages to providers and patients alike. The greater the freedom to choose a provider, the higher is the out-of-pocket expense to the patient. The more heavily the POS plan is modeled after HMO control over practice patterns, the less at risk the provider income becomes. The individual patients and providers choose the amount of freedom or control with which they are willing to live and work. Examples of POS model insurance plans can be found in every state offered by companies such as United Health Care, Aetna, and many others.

Managed Indemnity Plans

The industry term for traditional health insurance is indemnity insurance, in which the insured patient is reimbursed for expenses after receiving the care. This traditional insurance often has deductible and coinsurance responsibilities for the insured. A deductible is the amount that the member must pay out of pocket each year before the insurance plan will make payments to providers.

point of service plan (POS) a type of managed care health plan that permits members who are willing to pay larger coinsurance costs to seek treatment at non-network providers. Specialty referrals may still be coordinated through a primary care physician.

indemnity insurance traditional health insurance in which the insured is reimbursed for expenses after care is provided.

deductible the amount of expense that the insureds must pay each year from their own pockets before the plan will reimburse them.

coinsurance the amount of expense that is the responsibility of the insured under an indemnity insurance policy, often 20% of the charges billed.

Coinsurance is the portion of the cost for which the member has financial responsibility, usually based on a fixed percentage. This coinsurance becomes effective for expenses above the deductible amount. For example, a patient who received care for a broken leg will be responsible for paying the $1,000 deductible. After the initial $1,000 is paid to the health care provider, the insurance plan will pay 80% of the provider's charges and the patient will pay 20% of the provider's charges.

Although traditional indemnity insurance places financial responsibility on the members, it also gives them total freedom to use any provider of care they wish, at whatever price. It is in the patient's best financial interest to avoid costly medical bills for acute or emergent care by obtaining preventive care and wellness screenings. The health care provider, however, is not incentivized to provide only medically necessary or cost-effective care, as the insurance plan and the member will be responsible for any costs incurred. Insurance companies theorized that these deductible and coinsurance features would encourage members to consume and purchase health care wisely. In reality, these features have had little effect on purchasing decisions while the costs of health care and health care premiums continued to rise out of control. The increase in costs impacted the profitability of insurance providers negatively.

managed indemnity plans indemnity insurance options that do not limit the insured's choice of health care providers but do include cost-control measures such as preauthorization of expensive tests, surgical procedures, and inpatient hospitalization.

Managed indemnity plans were created to provide members with the freedom to choose their health care provider and also to control premium levels while reducing health care costs for the insurance company. The managed indemnity plans operate in a manner similar to traditional insurance plans, with the addition of cost-control measures. The most common cost-control measures included in these plans are preauthorization of expensive tests, surgical procedures, inpatient hospitalizations, and elective procedures, with the assumption that many of these may be medically unnecessary.

Critics say that managed indemnity plans are just an indemnity insurance company disguised as managed care. The biggest difference between this type of plan and a true managed care organization is the direct involvement of the insurance plan in delivery of care. Determining medical necessity through preauthorization only determines whether or not the insurance company will reimburse a provider for services rendered, whereas a managed care organization that employs providers or has contractual oversight over providers or facilities can influence health care the member receives.

Consumer-Directed Health Plans

Consumer-directed health plans arose out of an employer's need to curtail the double-digit premium increases they were experiencing every year. Another contributing factor to the increased interest in these types of plans is the frustration of physicians and consumers concerning the restrictions and complexity of managed care. These plans are appealing because consumers have flexibility in managing their own care.

Of course, a price is associated with the flexibility—increased out-of-pocket costs. These types of plans are not managed care plans, because they contain no provisions to manage the patient's care. Rather, they give consumers control of routine health decisions and provide them with an additional method of reimbursing their health care expenses.

A **Flexible Spending Account (FSA)** is a plan set up by the employee through the employer to cover health care costs. The employee cannot withdraw money from this account for anything other than health care. The amount deposited into the account is predetermined by the employee on a pay period basis, is pre-tax, and any amount left in the account at the end of the benefit year is retained by the employer, creating a "use it or lose it" incentive. This type of plan is used to supplement generous benefit plans by paying low copayments and deductibles.

The **Health Reimbursement Arrangement (HRA)** is a mechanism by which an employer funds an account for its employees to pay for otherwise unreimbursed health care expenses. The employer makes tax-deductible contributions into the account. Funds withdrawn by the employee to pay for health care are also tax-exempt for the employee. Employees cannot cash out the balance of the account when they leave employment, but some employers may allow them to roll over the amount into retirement.

The **Health Savings Account (HSA)**, created as part of the Medicare Modernization Act, permits individuals and families who purchase high-deductible health insurance coverage to contribute to the account. These contributions then can be used to pay for costs associated with health care, including those that are applied to their deductible. Consumers who have coverage through an HSA cannot purchase supplemental insurance to cover costs incurred until the deductible is reached.

Just as with the HRAs, contributions to this account are not taxed, and any withdrawals to pay for health care also are tax exempt. Withdrawals for nonmedical expenses can be made; however, the withdrawal will be subject to income taxation and an early withdrawal penalty of 10% for individuals under the age of 65. Balances roll over from year to year, and the employee retains any balance in the account if changing jobs (CBO, 2006).

Types of Patients

Patients within a managed care organization are referred to as **members**. They have chosen a particular health plan, usually for a period of one year, and become members of the organization for that period of time. Some plans also refer to members as **subscribers** if they are the primary recipients of the insurance benefit, and as **dependents** if they are a spouse or a child of the primary recipient. Families, or *insured units*, also are referred to as *contracts*, because the primary recipient makes the insurance decision for the entire family. If the subscriber of the insurance makes the decision to change managed care plans, the contract is lost to another managed

---

Flexible Spending Account (FSA) pre-tax income that an employee sets aside from his or her salary to use during a specified period for health care expenses; funds left in the account at the end of the benefit year are forfeited by the employee.

Health Reimbursement Arrangement (HRA) a mechanism by which an employer funds an account for its employees to pay for otherwise unreimbursed health care expenses.

Health Savings Account (HSA) an account set up by an employee with pretax income that also is not taxed when the employee withdraws from the account for medical expenses. Amounts left in the account at the end of the benefit year roll over to the next year. Withdrawals for nonmedical expenses are subject to income tax and a 10% penalty.

members individuals who are enrolled in a managed care organization.

subscribers primary recipients of the insurance benefit.

dependent the spouse or child of the primary insurance recipient.

care organization. Managed care organizations also refer to the number of individuals holding coverage with their company as the number of "covered lives."

All people eligible to receive care within the MCO are still referred to as "patients" while they are accessing the health care system. Because managed care organizations arrange for or provide care using a network of facilities, the patients are the same types of patients as seen in the individual facilities.

Types of Caregivers

The caregivers encountered in managed care are the traditional caregivers mentioned throughout this text. These caregivers provide illness-related care. In addition, managed care uses health educators to educate patients in preventive measures that can help them retain good health and case managers to administer disease management and chronic illness programs.

Illness

The primary care component of managed care uses physician extenders or midlevel providers to provide illness-related care more than do most other settings. Physician assistants (PAs) and nurse practitioners (NPs) both assist primary care physicians by performing preventive services such as patient teaching and routine physical examinations, and by performing assessments of acute but non-life-threatening conditions for the physician. PAs and NPs are trained to perform tasks that otherwise might be completed by a physician but do not require the same level of education.

PAs must practice under the direction of a physician and have their documentation reviewed and countersigned by the physician. NPs are licensed registered nurses who have received master's-level training in areas of specialty such as adult, family, or pediatric practice. NPs can work independent of a physician but most frequently work as part of a team of primary care practitioners.

Wellness

Preventive care and wellness are a central focus of a health maintenance organization and most managed care organizations. Wellness coordinators or health educators are used in health plans to assist primary care providers in this portion of the mission.

No formal educational preparation is specifically required for the role of health educator. Other health professionals who enjoy the teaching portion of health care fill this role. Nurses and dietitians function in a preventive role in managed care. Some organizations also may employ an exercise physiologist or physical therapist for cardiopulmonary rehabilitation and strengthening of members. A frequent role of the health educator is to teach chronic disease management for conditions such as asthma and diabetes. Specialized nurse educators extend the care provided by primary providers when they teach prenatal classes or write educational material for the members.

1. Name and describe the types of managed care organizations.
2. What are the major differences between HMO staff, group, and network models?
3. Compare and contrast the HMO, PPO/ and POS models.
4. What are the major types of consumer directed health plans?
5. What role does a case manager play in an MCO?

REGULATORY ISSUES

Managed care is concerned with two types of regulatory organizations: governmental agencies and voluntary accrediting associations.

Governmental Regulation

Governmental regulation takes place at the federal and state levels. Federal regulation is concerned with care provided to enrollees of government programs, and state regulation is concerned with the managed care organization's insurance license.

The Centers for Medicare & Medicaid Services (CMS)

Medicare entered the managed care arena as a direct purchaser through the Balanced Budget Act of 1997, with a plan called Medicare+Choice (M+C), or Medicare Part C. The Medicare Modernization Act of 2003 increased payments to this program and renamed it **Medicare Advantage**. A beneficiary who enrolls in a Medicare Advantage plan is responsible for both the Medicare Part B premium, which is retained by the Medicare program, and any additional premium collected by the Medicare Advantage plan. Medicare Advantage plans may offer additional benefits, such as prescription drugs, eye exams, hearing aids, or routine physical exams, but at a minimum must provide the coverage that Medicare would provide.

Enrollment in M+C plans in 2002 was estimated at 5.6 million beneficiaries, or 11% of the Medicare population, but enrollment had started to decline. In 2004, after CMS implemented Medicare Advantage and increased payments to participating health plans, enrollment in the program began to rebound. In 2014, Medicare Advantage enrolled over 15.8 million beneficiaries, about 30% of the Medicare population.

The *Medicare Managed Care Manual* (found at http://www.cms.gov) provides information on participation, including information on the Quality Assessment and Performance Improvement requirements for Medicare managed care plans.

Clinical Laboratory Improvement Amendments of 1988

The **Clinical Laboratory Improvement Amendments of 1988 (CLIA)** originally were developed in response to concerns about potentially preventable

Medicare Advantage a program by which eligible Medicare beneficiaries may choose to receive their health care through a qualified managed care plan, which in turn receives capitation payments from Medicare for each enrollee.

Clinical Laboratory Improvement Amendments of 1988 (CLIA) federal legislation that provides for regulation of all clinical laboratories, including those operated by HMOs and physician practices within managed care networks.

deaths caused by poor Pap smear testing. This law, which became effective on September 1, 1992, refers to all laboratories, including those operated in HMOs and physician practices within managed care networks.

The basic items that CLIA addresses are testing complexity, personnel standards, proficiency testing requirements, quality-control standards, patient test management, cytology testing, inspections, and fees. The CLIA regulations require that every laboratory possess a certificate to operate, and that sanctions are imposed on a laboratory that fails to meet the operational standards or proficiency testing guidelines. MCOs require proof of CLIA compliance during the laboratory contracting process. (Requirements are found online at http://www.cms.gov)

State Regulation

Although many MCOs providing services to Medicare and Medicaid beneficiaries are regulated by CMS, many MCOs are not. MCOs with only commercial enrollees are regulated solely by their individual state insurance laws. These laws vary throughout the United States and are administered by the insurance commissioner's office or HMO regulatory agency in each state to ensure that the MCO is financially able to operate as an insurance company.

Voluntary Accreditation

Managed care has several voluntary accreditation options. For example, the MCO could decide on any of these approaches:

- National Committee for Quality Assurance (NCQA) accreditation
- The Joint Commission (TJC) accreditation or Accreditation Association for Ambulatory Health Care (AAAHC) accreditation
- Both NCQA and TJC or AAAHC accreditation

An MCO could also select specific accrediting organizations for specific types of facilities within its network. For example, the MCO could choose among TJC, HFAP, or DNV (discussed in Chapter 2) for accreditation of its hospitals.

National Committee for Quality Assurance

National Committee for Quality Assurance (NCQA)   an accreditation association that accredits managed care organizations and related services. Its accreditation programs include health plan accreditation, wellness and health promotion, managed behavioral health care organizations, new health plans, and disease management.

The National Committee for Quality Assurance (NCQA, pronounced NIK-QWA) was formed in 1979 by the managed care industry. The Washington, DC-based organization originally did governmental reviews for federally qualified HMO status in the 1980s. In 1990, NCQA became an independent nonprofit organization, receiving a grant from the Robert Wood Johnson Foundation to develop a new set of standards separate from those of trade associations. In 2010, NCQA offered accreditation programs for health plan accreditation, wellness and health promotion, managed behavioral health care organizations, new health plans, and disease management.

The NCQA health plan accreditation standards include the following sections: quality management and improvement, utilization management, credentialing and recredentialing, members' rights and responsibilities, standards for member connections, and performance measures (NCQA, 2010). Other NCQA accreditation standards are organized differently. For example, the disease management accreditation program standards have seven sections: evidence-based programs, patient services, practitioner services, care coordination, measurement and quality improvement, program operations, and performance measurement. The accreditation process involves a two- to four-day site visit by three members of a survey team. Accreditation is granted for a provisional one-year or a full three-year status, with any accreditation status being difficult to obtain. Although the survey is all-encompassing, the central focus is on the insurance aspects of the MCO.

NCQA manages the Healthcare Effectiveness Data and Information Set (HEDIS), the performance measurement tool used by more than 90% of the nation's health plans. (For additional information, see Data Sets later in this chapter.) HEDIS performance measurement data are the basis for NCQA's Health Plan Report Card, a tool designed to help consumers learn more about their health plan options and the quality of care that the health plans provide. The Health Plan Report Card is available on the NCQA Web site and reports quality based on a star system, from one to four stars being assigned in five categories: Access and Service, Qualified Providers, Staying Healthy, Getting Better, and Living with Illness. Accredited HMOs and PPOs are rated against regional and national averages and benchmarks. Viewing this report card data allows consumers to make health plan enrollment choices based on both quality and cost.

The Joint Commission

The Joint Commission (TJC), formerly known as The Joint Commission on Accreditation of Healthcare Organizations (JCAHO), performs accreditation surveys for many types of facilities that are included in managed care networks, using the appropriate accreditation manual for each type of facility.

Accreditation Association for Ambulatory Health Care

The Accreditation Association for Ambulatory Health Care (AAAHC) accredits the health care delivery portion of staff model, group model, and network model HMOs. AAAHC uses the Accreditation Handbook for Ambulatory Health Care to survey the physician office and clinic portions of these HMOs. The survey consists of an on-site visit by at least two surveyors for a minimum of two days and is aimed at the health care delivery aspect rather than the insurance aspect of the HMO or MCO.

TABLE 4-1	Voluntary Accreditation Associations
Accreditation Association	**Applicability**
National Committee for Quality Assurance (NCQA)	All HMO, PPO, and POS plans
Accreditation Association for Ambulatory Health Care (AAAHC)	Staff model HMOs at each clinic site, but not as an HMO; group model HMOs at the physician group, but not as an HMO; network model HMOs at the clinic site, but not as an HMO
The Joint Commission (TJC)	Each part of the entity may be individually accredited by the Joint Commission or another organization
URAC	Health Plan accreditation standards for HMOs and other integrated health plans; health network accreditation for PPOs

URAC

URAC   an independent, nonprofit organization offering accreditation, education, and measurement programs. URAC's Health Plan standards are appropriate for HMOs and other integrated health plans. Its Health Network accreditation does not include utilization management and is better suited for PPO accreditation.

URAC (formerly the Utilization Review Accreditation Commission) began accrediting health plans and preferred provider organizations in 1996. URAC publishes both health plan and health network standards. On the one hand, the Health Plan accreditation program provides a comprehensive review of health plan operations in five areas: network management, quality improvement, credentialing, and member protection and utilization management. The Health Plan standards are appropriate for HMOs and other integrated health plans. On the other hand, Health Network accreditation does not include utilization management and is better suited for PPO accreditation. Table 4-1 provides examples of voluntary accreditation associations and the organizations they accredit.

SELF REVIEW 4.2

1. What is the role of managed care in relation to Medicare and Medicaid?
2. Compare and contrast the various organizations that can provide an MCO with accreditation.

REVENUE GENERATION

The MCO produces its revenue by selling an insurance product, which enables it to provide quality health care to the member. In turn, the MCO must pay or reimburse the providers of care for the services they provide to the members on behalf of the MCO.

Managed Care Organization Revenue

Premium payments are received from multiple sources in MCOs. Employers pay the premiums for a large percentage of members, but some members pay their own premiums because of changes in employment or self-employment. Some MCOs also contract with the government to ensure Medicare and Medicaid patients, and the MCO receives the premium directly from CMS or the individual states on behalf of these members.

The amount of premium payment can be determined in several ways:

- Community rating is a method of determining premiums that is based on actual or anticipated costs for members in a specific geographic location (city, metropolitan area, or state).
- Age/sex rating is a method of structuring premiums based on enrollee/membership statistics of age and sex.
- Composite rating is a method of determining premiums in which one uniform premium applies to all subscribers regardless of the number of claimed dependents.
- Experience rating determines premiums based on the actual utilization of individual subscriber groups. This method is not acceptable in a federally qualified HMO, but is the most frequently used method in traditional indemnity insurance.

Patient conditions as identified by coded diagnoses also can be a factor in risk adjustment of premiums. (See the Coding and Classification section of this chapter for more information on diagnosis-based risk adjustment.)

Any premium rate can be structured to a lower amount by requiring a copayment from the member at the time of care. A copayment usually is a flat amount, such as $10 per visit.

copayment a flat-rate payment, such as $10 per visit, made by the covered individual for a specific service, paid at the time of the service.

Reimbursement to the Provider of Care

Salary

In a staff model HMO, providers of care are actual employees of the HMO. Providers work under contract but receive a monthly or bimonthly salary payment, regardless of whether their patient panel is full. A provider's panel is the group of patients who have chosen the provider as their primary care provider. The size of the panel is HMO-specific, either by raw numbers of members, such as 1,600 members, or stratified by age group, such as 400 children, 1,000 adults, and 200 seniors.

panel the group of patients who have chosen a specific provider as their primary care provider.

Capitation (Per Member Per Month)

Capitation is the payment of a fixed dollar amount for each covered person, for providing a predetermined set of health services for a specific period of time. Providers are responsible for providing all of the care needed to each of the patients for whom they receive capitation. With this capitation arrangement, the provider assumes the risk for the cost and the frequency of the services provided.

capitation payment of a fixed dollar amount to a provider or a facility for an individual patient, regardless of the amount of care the patient receives.

As an example, the provider may receive $40 per month for each patient assigned to him or her, whether or not the patient receives care or makes multiple visits. This capitation payment usually is made monthly, based on the monthly patient panel, or assigned group of patients. This rate is known as "per member per month," or PMPM. Out of this capitation payment, providers must pay the support staff and office expenses. Claims are sent to the MCO for information purposes only and not for payment processing. Under this arrangement, providers who practice effectively can make money, whereas those who do not manage their resources well are financially at risk.

Per Diem

per diem a reimbursement methodology in which a set payment is reimbursed to a health care provider or facility based on the number of days of care provided to a patient.

Per diem means "paid by the day or at a daily rate." These rates are negotiated with centers such as hospitals and skilled nursing facilities (SNFs). The per diem covers the nursing care plus room and board charges. Special procedures or surgical services are charged separately. This amount is the only payment the facility receives for the care.

Fee Schedule, Negotiated

The MCO and the provider can negotiate a fee schedule for a flat rate per procedure, visit, or service. This allows any provider willing to negotiate to be part of the MCO network, even those for which no historical data are available on use and cost. This method is normally used when services are needed less frequently, but the cost varies widely from case to case. Negotiating a fee schedule allows more consistent budgeting of payment dollars by the MCO.

Fee Schedule, Resource-Based Relative Value Scale

Another way to negotiate a fee schedule is to use the resource-based relative value scale (RBRVS) unit value as the base and negotiate the conversion factor (the dollar amount per unit) that provides appropriate reimbursement. As an example, if the RBRVS unit value for a procedure is 2.5 and the negotiated conversion factor is $45 for all procedures, the fee paid to the provider in this case would be $112.50.

Fee Schedule, Percentage of Medicare Physician Fee Schedule

In addition, some payers create their fee schedules based on a percentage of the Medicare fee schedule (e.g., 135% of Medicare Physician Fee Schedule). For example, if the Medicare allowable for a service is $85.60, the payer allowable would be $115.56.

Diagnosis Related Groups

Diagnosis Related Groups (DRGs) the basis for the inpatient prospective payment system used by Medicare and some state Medicaid programs to reimburse acute care facilities; also used in some MCO contracts.

Diagnosis Related Groups (DRGs) form the basis of the inpatient prospective payment system (IPPS) used by Medicare, some other payers, and some managed care organizations to reimburse acute care facilities. This payment system is a prospective payment system, meaning that the rates are established before care is provided. Each patient's discharge is categorized into a DRG based on the principal and secondary diagnoses including comorbidities and complications. Each DRG is assigned a payment weight based on the average resources to treat patients with that DRG. The goal of this payment system is to encourage facilities to manage their operations more efficiently by finding ways to deliver more cost-effective patient care without sacrificing the quality of the care.

Discounted Charges

In the discounted charges method, the provider agrees to see MCO patients and charge the MCO the regular fee-for-service rate. The MCO discounts the rate by a certain amount, usually a percentage, before the payment is made. Negotiating this payment method is the easiest to accomplish, offers the greatest financial risk to the MCO, and gives little financial incentive to the provider to practice more cost-effectively. The total charge may be limited by a maximum allowable threshold for a given service.

Depending on the type of provider and the contract with the MCO, the provider receives payment from the MCO by means of one or more of these reimbursement mechanisms. Except when copayments are required as a provision of the health plan contract, any remaining balance cannot be billed to the member. Those balances become the "cost of doing business" for the provider and cannot be billed to any other party. Table 4-2 summarizes the advantages and disadvantages of the various reimbursement methods.

Coordination of Benefits

Coordination of benefits (COB) means determining the primary insurance payer and ensuring that no more than 100% of the charges are paid to the provider and/or reimbursed to the patient.

coordination of benefits (COB) determining which insurance is the primary payer and ensuring that no more than 100% of the charges are paid to a provider and/or reimbursed to a patient.

Dual Insurance Coverage

Some patients have two insurers because both spouses receive coverage through their employer or because they have purchased an HMO policy to supplement the deficiencies of a basic policy such as Medicare. It is in the best interest of an MCO to determine and record the primary insurance carrier for each member so the coordination of benefits rules can be applied correctly. In some cases, the MCO may be a secondary payer.

The method of determining the primary payer in dual-coverage cases is different from state to state. The most popular method used in determining the primary payer when both spouses carry insurance for the family is the

TABLE 4-2	Reimbursement to Providers of Care		
Method	**Provider**	**Advantage**	**Disadvantage**
Salary	Physicians	Predictable revenue for the provider, regardless of number of patients in panel	Efficient providers cannot ask for a payment larger than the maximum panel size, limiting their total salary.
Capitation	Primarily physician services	Predictable expenses for the MCO and predictable revenue for providers	Works only when some patients do not seek care and a significant portion are not "sicker" than average.
Per Diem	Primarily inpatient facilities	Flat rate regardless of type of care given	Good historical data is required to negotiate an appropriate rate.
Fee Schedule, Negotiated	Any non-inpatient facility or physicians	Allows per-unit billing, but at a controlled and predetermined cost per unit	Can be negotiated without good historical data or for less frequently used providers.
Fee Schedule, RBRVS Based	Physician services	As above, but can be related to Medicare reimbursement	Not all procedures have an RBRVS value assigned to them.
Fee Schedule, Percentage of Medicare Physician Fee Schedule	Physician services	As above, and completely dependent on Medicare fee schedule	If the percentage is not significantly higher that Medicare, poor reimbursement is the result.
Diagnosis Related Groups (DRGs)	Acute inpatient facilities	Improved patient record documentation; incentive to improve quality of care	The hospital receives a flat amount regardless of the extent of care provided or the length of stay.
Discounted Charges	All providers	Easiest to establish, but provides no incentive for cost-effectiveness by providers	Provides the greatest flexibility of charges for the provider and the greatest financial risk for the MCO.

"birthday rule." The spouse with the birthday earliest in the calendar year is the primary insurer for the children, with each spouse's insurance being primary for them.

Determining whose insurance is primary for the family is important to the MCO, because, for a dual-covered family, the MCO may be the primary carrier for the subscriber only and not for the other family members. If the subscriber's spouse carries the primary insurance for the family, the MCO is responsible for the full benefit level for the subscriber and only the unpaid balance—usually 20% or less—on the other family members. HMOs must follow the rules for determining when Medicare is the secondary payer.

The MCO that owns health care facilities can bill other primary payers for the care provided in its facilities or by its salaried or capitated providers, thus offsetting the expense of care. When paying claims, the MCO can direct claims to other payers if it is not the primary payer.

Workers' Compensation, Motor Vehicle Accidents, and Personal Injury Cases

If an MCO member is injured at work, in a motor vehicle accident, or by another individual, the member may prefer to receive care from the PCP. Actually, it may be better for the patient's overall health and wellness to see the PCP, who knows his or her medical history. In these situations, the MCO can submit a claim to the workers' compensation, motor vehicle, or personal injury carrier and receive reimbursement for the care provided. This diverts the expense to the appropriate insurance carrier while the MCO's overhead and/or capitation remains the same.

SELF REVIEW 4.3

1. What are the various mechanisms by which an MCO can generate revenue?
2. Compare and contrast capitation payment, per diem payment, and fee schedules.
3. What is a prospective payment system?
4. Why is coordination of benefits important to an MCO?

INFORMATION MANAGEMENT

The information management system in a managed care organization is determined by the structure of the organization. If the managed care organization owns facilities that are part of the organization, the health information management system would be similar to the systems described in other chapters of this book. The information gathered and maintained in the insurance portion of the organization is managed using procedures and systems similar to those used in the medical insurance industry.

Coding and Classification Systems

The two basic coding and classification systems used to collect and manage data in managed care are the *ICD* diagnosis system and the HCPCS procedure system. The following systems may be used as the individual needs of an organization dictate.

International Classification of Disease, Clinical Modification

The *International Classification of Disease, Clinical Modification* (initially *ICD-9-CM* and later *ICD-10-CM*) is the classification system for diagnoses required by CMS on all health care claims received. This coding system is the only one used throughout the health care industry to describe diagnoses, and these codes are collected on all claims for all services in managed care.

HCPCS Codes and CPT Procedure Codes

Current Procedural Terminology (CPT), also known as Level 1 of the HCPCS coding system, is an American Medical Association (AMA) publication that describes physician diagnostic and therapeutic procedures and their codes. CMS incorporated the *CPT* codes into its Healthcare Common Procedural Coding System (HCPCS), used to describe physician services for reimbursement. *CPT* and the full HCPCS coding systems form the basis for the resource-based relative value scale (RBRVS) system. *CPT* codes are collected routinely on all claims except facility charge claims for inpatients. Using *CPT* and HCPCS codes allows the MCO to compare services used and costs across delivery sites.

ICD-9-CM Volume 3 and ICD-10-PCS Procedure Codes

The Centers for Medicare & Medicaid Services (CMS) developed separate codes to describe medical procedures. *ICD-10-PCS* procedure codes were developed to replace *ICD-9-CM* Volume 3 procedure codes. These codes best describe procedures from a facility perspective and are used mainly to describe hospital inpatient services. MCOs collect these codes on UB-04 claims, the standard facility charge claim form.

Special Uses of Coded Data

Managed care diagnosis codes have an additional use in Medicare Advantage plans—as a component of a system for adjusting premiums paid to health plans based on the patient's health status. Traditionally, Medicare adjusted its payments to health plans based on geographic and demographic factors associated with each enrollee (e.g., age, gender, Medicaid eligibility, and institutional status) (Tully & Rulon, 2000). Adding a diagnosis-based risk adjustment factor had the effect of increasing payments to a health plan for enrollees with conditions representing higher risk for more costly services.

In 2000, the **Principal In-Patient Diagnostic Cost Group (PIP-DCG)** model was phased in as an initial mechanism for adjusting payments to Medicare managed care organizations based on patient diagnoses. When an enrollee was hospitalized, the principal diagnosis code determined the PIP-DCG, which in a limited way identified a certain amount of added risk based on the enrollee's health status.

In 2004, CMS implemented a more comprehensive model that considered all sites of service, not just inpatient hospitalization, as well as other traditional risk adjustment factors such as sex and age. The new model uses selected diagnosis codes to place patients into groups known as **Hierarchical Condition Categories (HCCs)**. The numerical risk factor associated with each HCC is a component in determining the amount by which payment to the MCO is increased.

Principal In-Patient Diagnostic Cost Group (PIP-DCG)   the first risk adjustment model that Medicare used to adjust capitation payments made to Part C plans, based largely on the principal diagnoses of hospitalized enrollees. PIP-DCGs were replaced by HCCs in 2004.

Hierarchical Condition Categories (HCCs)   disease groupings based on *ICD* codes from both inpatient admissions and outpatient visits in Medicare Advantage organizations. HCCs are used to risk-adjust Medicare payments to MCOs.

Depending on the specific HCCs involved, if an enrollee falls into more than one HCC, additional risk may be calculated and the payment to the organization increased further. The risk adjustment factors are different for beneficiaries residing in the community and those in a long-term care institution. (See Table 4-3 for an excerpt from the Medicare Advantage Ratebook, listing some of the HCCs and their risk adjustment factors.) In addition to the CMS-HCCs for Medicare Advantage health plans, there also are RxHCCs for adjusting Part D payments for beneficiaries enrolled in prescription drug plans. For both types of HCCs, diagnoses from one year are used to predict costs for the following year.

Diagnosis Related Groups   Diagnosis related groups (DRGs) were implemented in the early 1980s for use in describing inpatient services. The classification system groups inpatients who are medically related by diagnosis, treatment, and length of stay. Patients are grouped into major diagnostic categories (MDCs) and further subgrouped into a specific DRG. Only one DRG is assigned per stay.

Many MCOs collect the DRG number or determine the number by entering the diagnosis and procedure codes into a computer program called a "grouper." Generally, Medicare pays a flat rate per inpatient stay, based on the DRG for that stay. This allows Medicare to predict the expenses for the insured population more accurately and forces the inpatient facility to share

TABLE 4-3   Excerpt from Medicare Advantage HCC Coefficients Table

Variable	Disease Group	2014 Community Factors	2014 Institutional Factors
HCC1	HIV/AIDS	0.470	1.904
HCC2	Septicemia, Sepsis, Systemic Inflammatory Response Syndrome/Shock	0.535	0.575
HCC5-6	Opportunistic Infections	0.440	0.344
HCC7-8	Metastatic Cancer and Acute Leukemia	2.484	1.203
HCC9	Lung, and Other Severe Cancers	0.973	0.674
HCC10	Lymphoma and Other Cancers	0.672	0.412
HCC11	Colorectal, Bladder and Other Cancers	0.317	0.296
HCC12	Breast, Prostate, and Other Cancers and Tumors	0.154	0.198
HCC17	Diabetes with Acute Complications	0.368	0.474
HCC18	Diabetes with Chronic Complications	0.368	0.474
HCC19	Diabetes without Complication	0.118	0.182
HCC21	Protein-Calorie Malnutrition	0.713	0.399
HCC22	Morbid Obesity	0.365	0.579

a large portion of the risk. The hospital receives a set payment, regardless of how many days the patient stays and how large the bill actually might be. This payment method also is used by some MCOs to pay inpatient claims, for similar reasons.

UB-04 Revenue Codes   Revenue codes are collected on all claims submitted on a UB-04 claim form. Normally these forms contain facility and service charges from hospitals, skilled nursing facilities, and home care agencies. Revenue codes define a specific type of accommodation, ancillary service, or billing calculation. They are four-digit numbers grouped into categories of numbers having similar meaning.

Data and Information Flow

Data Collection and Transfer

Data are collected differently depending on the structure of the MCO. Staff model and group model HMOs are able to collect encounter data on the patients they see in their clinics. All types of HMOs are able to collect referral data after a referral has been issued, and all types of MCOs are able to collect claims data from providers requesting payment.

encounter   contact between a patient and a health care provider who is responsible for the assessment and evaluation of the patient at a specific contact, exercising independent judgment.

Encounter Data   An **encounter** is "a professional contact between a patient and a provider during which services are delivered" (Abdelhak et al., 2007, p. 133). Encounter data are collected at the time of the service and reported in raw form, rather than in the form of claims (billing) data.

referral   an authorization to receive a specific health service from a specialized provider that will be paid for by the HMO.

Referral Data   A **referral** is an authorization to receive a specific health service from a specific health provider that will be paid for by the HMO. HMOs issue referrals before specialty care can be given. PPOs and managed indemnity plans do not issue referrals, because patients are allowed to see other providers if they are willing to pay the additional cost. Referral data are collected at the time the referral is given by all organizations that issue referrals.

Most MCOs process referrals by online request systems or telephone voice and data recognition systems to speed the processing. Authorization for care ahead of time in the form of a referral allows the MCO to direct patients to appropriate providers in the network and to record the estimated future expense that will be incurred for the care.

Claims Data   Claims data are collected as a byproduct of the claims payment process. IPA model HMOs, PPOs, and managed indemnity plans can access service data in the form of claims data. For facilities such as hospitals, the data available are from the UB-04 claim form. Data for physicians and similar providers are from their billing form, the CMS 1500.

Statistical Data

All available data, including encounter, referral, and claims data, are combined and organized to provide useful management statistics. The two major ways by which statistics are divided in MCOs are by member and by contract. HMOs frequently work with statistical data by member, and PPOs and managed indemnity plans work with their data by contracts, although MCOs may use both methods.

- Per Member Per Month (PMPM): Frequency of service utilization and the cost of procedures are evaluated and displayed by employer purchasing group, by provider or facility site, and by provider panel, based on the number of members in the MCO for that month.
- Per Contract Per Month (PCPM): Frequency and cost are evaluated and displayed in the same way, based on the number of total contracts the MCO has for the month.

Electronic Information Systems

An electronic information system that is able to perform the functions necessary for managed care is vital to the profitability of the MCO. Some information system requirements for an MCO are much different than for either a hospital or a physician office practice, even though MCOs may include these facilities in their networks. Many information system functions are designed to assist care providers and staff to appropriately utilize resources.

Basic System Requirements

Eligibility/Enrollment

Enrollment is the process of placing a person into the database of covered individuals of the MCO. Eligibility refers to whether the person is allowed to receive care under the MCO contract and the dates of coverage. The enrollment database is similar to the master patient index found in health care facilities and includes dates of enrollment and disenrollment, demographic information, and the party responsible for paying the premium.

eligibility determination of whether a person is able to receive benefits under an insurance policy.

Benefit Levels The benefit level may not be the same for all members of an MCO. Most managed care organizations sell a variety of insurance packages, some that allow more services than others or that allow certain benefits at a higher payment level than others. Benefit levels must be tracked for each individual member, because many members have dual insurance coverage or different benefit packages, even within the same family or contract. A system that tracks this information only for the subscriber may miss the detail necessary to divert claims to another, more appropriate payer.

Patient Registration and Scheduling   Hospitals within an MCO require a patient registration system, and all service providers require some form of scheduling software to manage their health care environment.

Authorization and Referral Management   Managed care organizations provide preauthorization for admissions and procedures and issue referrals for care that cannot be provided by the PCP. This information must be maintained in the computer system and must be accessible to the PCP. The best systems include practice guidelines that are accessible and allow the PCP to review and document clinical decisions in real time within the information system.

Utilization Management/Case Management   Computer software should identify cases that are appropriate for case management through evaluation of encounter data, referral data, or claims data. This allows the utilization management staff to assist the PCP in managing the multiple resources needed to care for complicated cases properly. The best systems provide accessible information about clinical practice guidelines for both inpatient and outpatient management.

Billing/Claims Production   Staff model and group model HMOs require software to create claims for another primary insurer for patients with dual insurance coverage. In addition, this software should have the ability to post payments to these charges and maintain accounts receivable information for tracking purposes.

Payment/Claims Processing   The claims processing software allows the MCO to pay claims for authorized services and should verify the eligibility/enrollment files, benefit levels, and referral data before the payment is processed. Capitated visits should be recorded in the claims database even though no actual payment is processed. Without this capitated data, there is no information to manage the financial aspects of the MCO that are covered under capitation.

Cost Accounting   The cost accounting module of the information system should tie together the accounts payable portion of the business and the accounts receivable portion from premiums. In staff model HMOs, coordination of benefits (COB) income also must be tracked. COB income is received when the staff model HMO bills another primary insurer for services it provided in its clinics.

Advanced System Requirements

Electronic Health Record (EHR)   The answer to collecting patient health information and having it available throughout the network of facilities is ultimately the electronic health record. Without the EHR, the MCO is still a combination of different facilities that try their best to achieve effective communication in real time.

The HITECH Act, a component of the American Recovery and Reinvestment Act of 2009, was signed into law to provide incentives to physician practices and other health care organizations for the implementation of EHR systems. This law provided incentive payments to physicians and hospitals that demonstrate "meaningful use" of a "qualified EHR." The law also provided an additional $20,000 to physicians who utilize an electronic prescribing system and the Physician Quality Reporting Index (PQRI).

The HITECH Act also specified that providers who had not adopted an EHR by the conclusion of the program would experience a decrease in Medicare reimbursement. The purpose of this legislation was to encourage providers to shift their medical documentation to an EHR to provide accurate, timely, and legible patient information and better continuity of patient care (CMS, 2009).

Executive Decision Making   Data from any or all of the information systems may be needed to determine where and when decisions are needed and to help in the decision-making process.

Data Sets

Healthcare Effectiveness Data and Information Set

The **Healthcare Effectiveness Data and Information Set (HEDIS)** is a core set of performance measures for managed care plans. HEDIS was designed in 1991 by NCQA to help employers compare health plans, understand the value of what their health care premium is purchasing, and hold the health plan accountable for performance against these measures. HEDIS provides a consistent measure of key performance areas, such as "Effectiveness of Care," "Access/Availability of Care," "Satisfaction with the Experience of Care," "Use of Services," "Cost of Care," and "Health Plan Stability." HEDIS contains more than 70 measures, such as the number of pregnant enrollees receiving prenatal care within the first trimester and childhood immunization status. Information about HEDIS measures is available at the NCQA website.

> **Healthcare Effectiveness Data and Information Set (HEDIS)** a core set of standard performance measures for managed care in the areas of effectiveness of care, access/availability of care, satisfaction with the experience of care, use of services, cost of care, health plan descriptive information, health plan stability, and informed health care choices.

Employer-Specific Data Sets

Some national employers, such as IBM and Xerox, request data specifically about their enrollees, either using HEDIS indicators or by identifying their own issues for tracking. This information helps them determine whether the health plans they are contracted with are providing cost-effective, quality service to their employees and their families.

SELF REVIEW 4.4

1. What various systems are used for classifying diagnoses and procedures?
2. Explain the concept of a diagnosis grouper.
3. What are the three major types of data collected by an MCO?
4. What types of statistics are utilized by an MCO?
5. Explain the use of performance measures, such as HEDIS, by an MCO.

QUALITY IMPROVEMENT AND UTILIZATION MANAGEMENT

The accreditation associations, CMS, and many employer purchasing groups require an active quality improvement program within managed care organizations to ensure that care is delivered in a cost-effective manner, with consistently appropriate outcomes.

Quality Improvement

The components of a quality improvement program for a managed care organization are detailed as follows. These include an oversight committee that uses a comprehensive plan and the use of quality indicators to identify trends.

Oversight Committee Using a Comprehensive Plan

To ensure that quality improvement is a continuous process, MCOs utilize an oversight committee that is guided by a comprehensive quality plan. The quality plan is developed by the senior staff and approved by the board of directors at least annually. The oversight committee receives and reviews reports and project requests from subcommittees within the organization. The committee structure is designed to provide a place for each area of the business to report its quality issues and findings.

Quality Indicators

Quality indicators are a quantitative measuring tool for monitoring and evaluating performance. These indicators are important to an MCO, because it is difficult to manage what has not been measured. Quality in an MCO depends on operational indicators, medical indicators, and financial indicators.

Operational Indicators   The operational effectiveness indicators measure how well the MCO is performing in comparison to preset goals. These also can include patient satisfaction goals about how well the "customer" or patient thinks the MCO is performing. Examples include:

Telephone call turnaround time

Percentage of telephone calls answered in less than 30 seconds

Appointment availability—all service areas

Percentage of rescheduled appointments—administrative reasons

Pharmacy refill turnaround time

Lobby wait times

Claims processing turnaround time.

Medical Indicators   Medical indicators also are referred to as "outcome measures," because they express the MCO's ability to obtain a successful outcome from the care that is delivered. Some examples are:

Percentage of members receiving prenatal care in the first trimester

Percentage of babies born at or above an appropriate birth weight

Percentage of operative patients without wound infection

Unanticipated emergency room visits within 24 hours after surgery

Unplanned emergency department visits after primary care visit on same day

Rates of mammograms, Pap smears, immunizations, or physicals.

Financial Indicators   Financial stability can be measured using the following indicators:

Days in Claims Payable (calculated as the reverse of Days in Accounts Receivable) or claims payable at the end of the period divided by the average claims per day during the period.

Hospital bed days per 1,000 members

Number of avoidable hospital days.

A hospital **bed day** is equivalent to the inpatient statistic known as inpatient service day. The measurement of bed days per 1,000 members is a standard MCO measurement that can be compared among MCOs nationwide. "Avoidable hospital days" is defined through the utilization management program and includes items such as performing an ambulatory diagnostic work-up as an inpatient; delay in obtaining or failure to use home care services appropriately; and delay in receiving consultation, testing, or procedures. These types of indicators measure the MCO's overall ability to act as a unit for successful patient care and financial outcomes.

bed day   an inpatient service received by one member for one 24-hour period.

Tools from the Agency for Healthcare Research and Quality

The Agency for Healthcare Research and Quality (AHRQ) of the U.S. Department of Health and Human Services has developed several tools that can be of benefit to managed care organizations as well as other health care organizations (Stanton, 2003). A few of these tools include the following:

- National Guideline Clearinghouse™ (NGC)—a database of evidence-based clinical practice guidelines
- National Quality Measures Clearinghouse™ (NQMC)—a repository for evidence-based quality measures and measure sets

- Consumer Assessment of Healthcare Providers and Systems (CAHPS)—includes standardized survey instruments for assessing patients' experiences with ambulatory and facility care; also provides access to comparative data through its benchmarking database

Utilization Management

Utilization management is part of the quality improvement function of an MCO, as well as a method of cost control through prospective and retrospective review of services. These activities consist of:

preadmission certification review and approval of the medical necessity of inpatient care prior to the patient's admission.

preauthorization review and prior approval for payment of a health care service.

concurrent review verification of the medical necessity of tests and procedures ordered during an inpatient hospitalization.

discharge planning arranging post-discharge services for patients prior to discharge to provide continuity of care, to aid in recuperation, and to reduce unnecessary readmissions or emergency department visits.

- **Preadmission certification**, which involves reviewing the necessity of an admission prior to its occurrence
- **Preauthorization**, a review of elective procedures requiring prior approval for reimbursement
- **Concurrent review**, reviewing services ordered for medical necessity during an inpatient hospitalization before they are provided
- **Discharge planning**, arranging services that patients may require upon discharge

Preauthorization and/or Concurrent Review

Using clinical practice guidelines on potentially expensive or difficult cases can provide consistent quality of care and can save money for the MCO by assuring provision of the correct test or procedure at the correct time in the treatment plan. Preauthorization of expensive procedures also can perform the same function and can assist the MCO in locating the best-possible facility for performing the procedure.

Written Utilization Protocols and Coordination of Care

Written utilization protocols help providers deal with basically uncomplicated but common cases, and can help to avoid unnecessary hospitalizations and provide quicker recovery for the patient. Coordination of care staff helps to ensure that the patient receives care at the correct point from the correct providers. In addition, coordination of care staff helps the PCP to manage chronic disease patients more effectively. Discharge planning is one form of coordination of care that helps inpatients by arranging a smooth transition to post-acute care.

SELF REVIEW 4.5

1. What type of quality indicators do MCOs utilize for quality purposes?
2. What is the purpose of utilization management?
3. What is the difference between prior authorization and concurrent review?

RISK MANAGEMENT AND LEGAL ISSUES

Risk management in managed care is more comprehensive because of the wide variety of services provided under the managed care concept. Each of the facilities included in the managed care organization, both owned and contracted, monitors for potential risks that are unique to its own settings.

Documentation of care coordination between these settings is essential in managed care, because patients believe that "managed care" means that care happens, or should happen, seamlessly across many facilities. If this does not happen, patients may see their care as less than optimal and consider litigation.

Identifying Unusual Events

Unusual events are reported and tracked within the MCO. Unusual events represent a primary source of litigation for MCOs, similar to other health care providers. Unusual events can be the delay or denial of services that are later determined to have been necessary or emergent, failure to direct a patient to the proper source of care, or any medical incident that normally is tracked elsewhere, such as incorrect administration of medication.

Informed Consent for Procedures

Providers within the MCO use the same procedures as other providers when they obtain informed consent from patients or their legal representatives before performing procedures. In addition to individual liability on the part of the physician or facility, the MCO is at risk for being a party to a malpractice suit.

Credentialing

Credentialing is "a process of review to approve a provider who applies to participate in a health plan. Specific criteria and prerequisites are applied in determining initial and ongoing participation in the health plan" (United HealthCare Corporation, 1994). The MCO performs its own investigation or contracts with an independent **credentials verification organization (CVO)** to conduct credentialing reviews. NCQA offers a certification program for credentials verification organizations. A CVO that achieves certification provides assurance to MCO clients that the CVO is qualified and competent to conduct credentialing activities. The prerequisites that are evaluated include the credentialing elements verified traditionally by hospitals. These include:

1. Current competence in the field
2. Work history
3. Physical and mental health status
4. Challenges to licensure and registrations
5. Limitation or termination of clinical privileges
6. Pending professional liability actions

credentialing   a process of review to approve a provider who applies to participate in a health plan.

credentials verification organization (CVO)   a third party organization that contracts with a managed care organization or other health care organization to provide credential verification services for health care providers seeking clinical privileges or inclusion in an insurance network.

7. Felony convictions
8. Federal Drug Enforcement Administration registration
9. National Practitioner Data Bank information

Provider's Office Evaluation

In addition to personal credentialing of the provider, the provider's office is evaluated to assess whether the office is organized and managed appropriately for inclusion in the MCO network.

Review of Structural Components   Before the signing of a contract, the provider's office is evaluated for items such as acceptable facilities, available staff, accessibility of care, and systems for medical management including electronic information systems appropriate for the office or facility.

Record Review   A health record review is completed to determine if the records are accessible, standardized in format, and whether paper records are legible, secured to the folder properly, signed and dated, and contain the patient's name on each page. Other items may be evaluated based on the applicability of various accreditation standards, such as those of the Accreditation Association for Ambulatory Health Care (AAAHC), The Joint Commission (TJC), or the National Committee for Quality Assurance (NCQA).

Economic Credentialing

Economic credentialing is performed to ensure that the provider is not under-utilizing services and compromising the health of the member or overutilizing services and creating unnecessary expense. The MCO uses statistical data such as the number of inpatient admissions per 1,000 members and charges per HCPCS code or DRG to evaluate financial performance. Economic credentialing results in the exclusion of a provider only in the rarest of situations and primarily for severe underutilization of services.

Recredentialing

Providers are recredentialed every two years to be sure that no new information is ignored. A tickler system is used to help reevaluate providers on time, checking items such as medical quality indicator results, malpractice claims experience, overall patient satisfaction rating, and the number of member complaints.

Contract Management

The MCO is built on contracted relationships. An index of contracts, including expiration dates and any proposed contract changes, is maintained to be sure that all contracts remain valid and at an optimal level of reimbursement.

1. What is credentialing?
2. Why is credentialing vital to the success of an MCO?

ROLE OF THE HEALTH INFORMATION MANAGEMENT PROFESSIONAL

PROFESSIONAL SPOTLIGHT **MANAGED CARE**

Who I am: Sherell B. Singleton, RHIA

Where I Work: eQHealth Solutions, Inc.

What I Do: My job title is Corporate Project Director. In this position I report directly to eQHealth's Chief Operations Officer, and I perform the following duties:

- Provide internal consultancy services to Senior and Middle Management. Topic areas typically involve utilization review, quality of care review and DRG (or APR-DRG) validation review, present on admission, ICD-10-CM/PCS requirements, etc.
- Lead or participate in implementation of new business lines and/or refine existing programs to promote operational efficiencies. These programs may involve utilization review, quality of care review and DRG (or APR-DRG) validation review and may include other types of new business.
- Tasks include development of workflows, associated policy, and procedures, and review of result notification letters.
- Identify, recruit, and direct, as needed, employees throughout the organization who possess skill sets that are needed for new initiatives or projects.
- Work with information services to identify data fields, business rules and report and report contents required to support and monitor the new program process and outcomes.
- Collaborate with analytical team to clarify review data definitions and business rules, increase understanding of billing rules and claims data, and to define monitoring and performance measures. Participate in development of focused studies or special projects involving topics such as utilization of services, atypical patterns of billing, including but not limited to short-stay, DRGs, etc.
- Use cross-organizational knowledge of workflows and processes to facilitate the use of best practices and standardization where appropriate and applicable through the various business unit and service settings in the organization. This work results in increased efficiency in operations and improved performance.
- Develop, implement, and maintain training programs for staff as needed.
- Participate in responding to request for proposals (as a writer or a reviewer).
- Research state or federal laws, regulations or administrative codes to support decisions and/or program designs.

Why HIM knowledge is important in my role: Health Information management

(continued)

knowledge is important in my role because it provides me with the foundation upon which I rely when performing all of my job functions. Much of my work involves using information and technology to develop or improve processes. I use a combination of HIM knowledge, project and people management skills, technology, coding, analytical approaches and skills, and privacy and security of health care data and records. Working with and educating others regarding HIM practices may impact decisions that do not seem to be affected by HIM practices.

The training and exposure I received (and continue to receive through continued education) provides an understanding of the health care delivery system from a variety of aspects and, therefore, the real and potential impact that eQHealth's medical management and quality improvement organization programs may have on those systems, the providers, and ultimately the patients.

Developing and Implementing Information Plan Based on Organizational Needs

The health information management (HIM) professional in managed care is found mainly in the staff model, group model, and network model HMO, performing the traditional role of health information manager. These HMO settings require the HIM professional to maintain security and confidentiality of records. In addition, the HIM professional performs data collection and coding of encounter data. The HIM professional is concerned with information storage and retrieval, appropriate information technology within the facilities, and personnel management. As in other facilities, this person normally participates extensively in, or leads, the preparation for an accreditation survey visit.

Specialized Functions

The HIM professional receives a unique mix of education and training that allows the individual to perform other functions that are less traditional within an MCO.

Enrollment Management

The enrollment database in an MCO is a highly detailed version of a master patient index, an index traditionally maintained by the HIM professional. The HIM professional's knowledge of data management and patient identification systems provides some of the best foundation possible for performing or supervising the enrollment management function.

Claims Processing/Management

One of the largest databases maintained in most MCOs is the claims database. In addition to managing the claims database, the claims processing supervisor helps to determine whether claims are coded properly and are acceptable for payment. The HIM professional's medical knowledge, combined with financial experience or ability, can prepare him or her well for the role of claims processing supervisor.

Quality Management/Performance Improvement

Specialization in quality management/performance improvement by the HIM professional is likely in a managed care organization. Knowledge of all areas of health care provides an excellent foundation for a leadership role in performance improvement.

Risk Management and Credentialing

HIM professionals frequently fill the role of risk manager. The HIM professional's study of medicine, management, and the legal system provides an excellent background for performing the duties of risk manager, which include looking for ways to minimize the potential for injuries, responding promptly and appropriately when injuries occur, and planning for potential liability resulting from injuries (Abdelhak, 2007).

A related function is that of a credentialing specialist. An HIM professional may perform this function for the MCO directly or for a credentials verification organization (CVO). Some HIM professionals serve as chief executive officers or in other management positions in CVOs.

Chief Information Officer

The information technology expertise of the HIM professional can easily be used to perform the role of chief information officer (CIO) for a managed care organization.

1. What are some of the traditional roles of an HIM professional in an MCO?
2. What is risk management, and how does it impact an MCO?

SELF REVIEW 4.7

TRENDS
Integrated Delivery Systems/Networks

Integrated delivery systems/networks (IDS/Ns) are groupings of facilities contracted together to provide the comprehensive set of services that a patient may need. These facilities and services are owned, leased, or grouped together through long-term contracts and are recognized by the public as being a combined operating entity.

Integrated delivery systems are not the same as managed care organizations, because they do not always contain an insurance provision. Because an MCO requires a full network of providers, however, the IDS/N is a natural place to look when contemplating an MCO contract.

integrated delivery systems/network (IDS/N) a group of facilities contracted together to provide the comprehensive set of services that any patient may need. These are owned, leased, or grouped together by long-term contracts and are recognized by the public as a combined operating entity.

The Changing Role of the PCP

gatekeeper the primary care provider who coordinates all of the patient's health care and decides what, if any, additional care is required.

In many MCOs, the primary care provider is playing less of a role in gatekeeping than ever before. Although most Medicare and Medicaid HMOs still retain the PCP gatekeeper function, other HMOs are abandoning the concept and reallocating the funds into stronger disease management and chronic care management programs. Evidence points toward this trend continuing as resources are funneled to the proper management of the sickest patients in the HMO. In addition, the population will continue to transition to less restrictive MCO models, PPOs, and POS products without the gatekeeper function, if premiums remain comparable.

Federal Programs

In 2009, the Medicare Payment Advisory Commission (MedPAC) noted that Medicare Advantage (MA) programs cost the Medicare program 14% more than traditional Medicare, on average. The Commission recommended changes that would bring the costs of this program in line with the Medicare fee-for-service (FFS) program and also made recommendations to address the uneven quality of care across Medicare Advantage plans, including a mechanism to compare quality between MA plans and FFS providers. Changes implemented since that time have reduced the cost difference between MA and FFS programs.

Accountable Care Organizations (ACOs)

Accountable Care Organization (ACO) "a local entity and a related set of providers, including at least primary care physicians, specialists, and hospitals, that can be held accountable for the cost and quality of care delivered to a defined subset of traditional Medicare program beneficiaries or other defined populations, such as commercial health plan subscribers. The primary ways the entity would be held accountable for its performance are through changes in traditional Medicare provider payment featuring financial rewards for good performance based on comprehensive quality and spending measurement and monitoring" (Devers & Berenson, 2009, pp. 1–2).

The Affordable Care Act established Accountable Care Organizations (ACOs) as one of the new pilot payment models for Medicare. Devers and Berenson (2009) provide the following description of ACOs:

> ACOs can generally be defined as a local entity and a related set of providers, including at least primary care physicians, specialists, and hospitals, that can be held accountable for the cost and quality of care delivered to a defined subset of traditional Medicare program beneficiaries or other defined populations, such as commercial health plan subscribers. The primary ways the entity would be held accountable for its performance are through changes in traditional Medicare provider payment featuring financial rewards for good performance based on comprehensive quality and spending measurement and monitoring. Public reporting of cost and quality information to affect public perception of an ACO's worth is another way of holding the ACO accountable for its performance. Proponents generally view three ACO characteristics as essential. These characteristics include: (1) the ability to provide, and manage with patients, the continuum of care across different institutional settings, including at least ambulatory and inpatient hospital care and possibly post acute care; (2) the capability of prospectively planning budgets and resource needs; and, (3) sufficient size to support comprehensive, valid, and reliable performance measurement." (pp. 1–2)

The way in which ACOs combine payment mechanisms and care delivery is similar to the premise of an HMO (Cohen, 2010). Several different organizational models, however, can utilize the ACO concept. The ACO model is one of several health care reform models with which health information managers may be involved in the twenty-first century.

SELF REVIEW 4.8

1. Explain the basic concepts of an ACO.
2. Accountable Care Organizations were established as a result of the _____.

SUMMARY

The structure of MCOs continues to change to meet market demand, with more MCOs changing to open network styles. Two key areas within the managed care environment are quality improvement and data management. These and many other areas hold excellent employment opportunities for HIM professionals. The managed care field will continue to change and grow, to meet the needs of purchasers and in an attempt to control health care expenses.

REVIEW QUESTIONS

Knowledge-Based Questions

1. What coding systems would be used to code a hospital claim submitted to an MCO for payment? What systems would be used for a physician claim?
2. What three characteristics are required for an organization to qualify as an HMO?
3. How does an MCO perform coordination of benefits?
4. What does the abbreviation PMPM mean, and why is it important in managed care?
5. What two benefits will the MCO realize from using online referral processing?
6. Explain the difference between coinsurance and copayment.
7. What contributed to the introduction of consumer-directed health plans?
8. Identify the types of consumer-directed health plans and their characteristics.
9. Describe the key pieces of recent legislation that impact an MCO.

Critical Thinking Questions

1. Why wouldn't a managed indemnity plan collect referral data?
2. Why could the discounted charges reimbursement mechanism seem attractive to both the physician and the MCO?
3. Why would an MCO want to reimburse hospitals by a DRG payment?
4. An HMO with 50,000 members had 13,024 inpatient service days for the last month. What formula would you use to determine bed days per 1,000, and what was this HMO's rate for last month?
5. Why is it crucial for an MCO to conduct utilization management activities?
6. What are the benefits of an EHR to an MCO, a physician practice, and its patients?
7. How will ACO models potentially impact MCOs in the future?

WEB ACTIVITY

Visit the NCQA website at http://www.ncqa.org and locate the information on HEDIS measures. If you were a health information manager in a pediatric clinic and were planning to present HEDIS results to your medical staff, which of the measures listed would you select for your report?

CASE STUDY

The senior management team of Efficient Network HMO is evaluating the year-end data related to emergency room (ER) expenses. One physician group within the network had ER expenses that were three times the rate of any other group within the network. Senior management has studied group operations and theorizes that three factors are influencing the high rate of expense. The group does not utilize triage nurses, does not have after-hours urgent care services, and has limited office hours from 8:30 to 11:30 a.m. and 1:30 to 5:00 p.m. An answering service, not staffed by nurses, relays calls during the remainder of the hours.

The physician group is willing to work on the problem but is asking for detailed, comparative information from the HMO's senior management team before it implements any changes. How would you, as the clinical data specialist for the HMO, answer the following questions:

1. What information would be useful to the senior management of the HMO and the physician practice in evaluating the ER expenses?
2. What data sources would you use to obtain data?
3. How could the reports be structured to provide meaningful information?

REFERENCES AND SUGGESTED READINGS

Abdelhak, M., Hanken, M. A., Grostick, S., & Jacobs, E. (Eds.). (2007). *Health Information: Management of a Strategic Resource* (3rd ed.). St. Louis, MO: Saunders/Elsevier.

CBO (Congressional Budget Office). (2006, December). *CBO Study: Consumer-Directed Health Plans: Potential Effects on Health Care Spending and Potential Outcomes.* Congress of the United States, Congressional Budget Office. [Online]. http://www.cbo.gov/ftpdocs/77xx/doc7700/12-21-HealtPlans.pdf

CMS (Centers for Medicare & Medicaid Services). (2009, December 30). CMS proposes requirements for the electronic health records (EHR) Medicare incentive. [Online]. http://www.cms.hhs.gov/apps/media/press/factsheet.asp?Counter=3563

Cohen, J. T. (2010, March 11). A guide to accountable care organizations, and their role in the Senate's health reform bill. *Health Reform Watch.* [Online]. http://www.healthreformwatch.com/2010/03/11/a-guide-to-accountable-care-organizations-and-their-role-in-the-senates-health-reform-bill/ [2010, November 2].

Devers, K., & Berenson, R. (2009, October). Can accountable care organizations improve the value of health care by solving the cost and quality quandaries? *Robert Wood Johnson Foundation: Timely Analysis of Immediate Health Policy Issues.* [Online]. http://www.rwjf.org/files/research/acobrieffinal.pdf [2010, November 2].

NCQA (National Committee for Quality Assurance). (2010). *2010 NCQA Health Plan Accreditation Requirements.* [Online]. http://www.ncqa.org [2010, July 4].

Stanton, M. W. (2003). AHRQ tools for managed care. *Research in Action 11.* AHRQ Pub. No. 03-0016. Rockville. MD: Agency for Healthcare Research and Quality.

Tully, L., & Rulon, V. (2000). Evolution of the uses of ICD-9-CM coding: Medicare risk adjustment methodology for managed care plans. *Topics in Health Information Management, 21*(2), 62–67.

United HealthCare Corporation. (1994). *A Glossary of Terms: The Language of Managed Care and Organized Health Care Systems* (rev. ed.). Minnetonka, MN: author.

KEY RESOURCES

Accreditation Association for Ambulatory Health Care, Inc. (AAAHC)
http://www.aaahc.org

American Health Information Management Association (AHIMA)
http://www.ahima.org

Clinical Laboratory Improvement Amendments of 1988
http://www.cms.gov/clia

Kaiser Permanente
share.kaiserpermanente.org

Medicare Managed Care Manual Publication #100-16
http://www.cms.gov/Manuals/IOM

National Committee for Quality Assurance (NCQA)
http://www.ncqa.org

The Joint Commission (TJC)
www.jointcommission.org

URAC
http://www.urac.org

CHAPTER 5

Dialysis

Ann H. Peden, PhD, RHIA, CCS

LEARNING OBJECTIVES

Upon successful completion of this chapter, you should be able to:

- Explain the various terms and synonyms referring to kidney disease.
- Outline the kidney disease stages.
- Name the organizations that serve patients with kidney disease.
- Describe the types of care givers to patients with end-stage renal disease (ESRD).
- Describe how and by whom dialysis facilities are surveyed for compliance with various regulations and standards.
- List key documentation requirements for dialysis patient records.
- State the source of payment for most dialysis treatment in the United States.
- Explain the role of the ESRD networks in the collection and aggregation of data on dialysis patients.
- Describe quality improvement activities in ESRD organizations.
- Describe the role of the health information management professional in organizations dealing with ESRD.

Setting	Description	Synonyms
Dialysis Facility	A facility where patients receive dialysis treatments, or home dialysis training and support services, or both.	End-stage renal disease ESRD facility Dialysis unit Dialysis center Dialysis clinic Limited care unit
ESRD Network	An organization that contracts with the Centers for Medicare & Medicaid Services (CMS), to assess the quality of care rendered to ESRD patients and to collect and analyze ESRD data	Network

INTRODUCTION TO SETTING

This chapter discusses dialysis, a procedure that is necessary to maintain the life of a person whose kidneys have failed. Chronic kidney disease (CKD) is a gradual loss of kidney function classified into five stages, from mild loss of kidney function in the early stages to severe or total loss in the later stages. In the final stage (Stage 5), the kidneys are no longer able to excrete the body's wastes or promote homeostasis. At Stage 5 CKD, the patient requires some type of renal replacement therapy (RRT) (e.g., dialysis or a kidney transplant) to survive. The final stage of chronic kidney disease also has been known as end-stage renal disease (ESRD). Although the term *chronic kidney disease* is preferred over the term *ESRD* in clinical usage, ESRD is still the term by which the U.S. national health insurance program for people with irreversible chronic kidney failure is known.

Numerous organizations are involved in caring for dialysis patients and in monitoring the quality of care rendered to dialysis patients. The two settings discussed in this chapter are ESRD facilities and ESRD networks. Of these two general types of settings, only the ESRD facilities actually provide patient care. The ESRD networks process and analyze data provided by the ESRD facilities and provide other types of services, such as patient education.

Facilities providing services to dialysis patients have several synonyms. The federal government uses the terms *ESRD facility* and *dialysis facility* for a facility offering dialysis services. The Joint Commission uses the terms *dialysis center* and *dialysis unit* for this type of facility. None of these terms is universally preferred over the others. This chapter uses the terms interchangeably.

According to the Conditions for Coverage for End-Stage Renal Disease Facilities (2008), a dialysis facility is "an entity that provides (1) outpatient maintenance dialysis services; or (2) home dialysis training and support services; or (3) both. A dialysis facility may be an independent or hospital-based unit or a self-care dialysis unit that furnishes only self-dialysis services." (20476)

dialysis "the process of artificially removing metabolic end products and water across a semiperme-able membrane by diffusion" (McAfee, 1987). The two most common types of dialysis are hemodialysis and peritoneal dialysis.

chronic kidney disease (CKD) a gradual loss of kidney function classified into five stages, ranging from mild loss of kidney function to severe or total loss.

renal replacement therapy (RRT) a treatment that replaces kidney function. For chronic renal failure, the treatment typically is some type of dialysis, or it may be kidney transplantation.

end-stage renal disease (ESRD) stage 5 of chronic kidney disease, the extreme at which the patient has irreversible renal failure with little or no kidney function. When a patient is in end-stage renal disease, he or she requires either dialysis or a kidney transplant to maintain life.

ESRD networks organizations that have contracted with the Centers for Medicare & Medicaid Services (CMS) to assess the quality of care rendered to ESRD patients and to collect and analyze ESRD data.

Types of Patients

Patients requiring treatment in a dialysis unit generally are persons with stage 5 chronic kidney disease who have not yet undergone a kidney transplant or who for some reason are not candidates for a transplant. Because the kidneys of these patients are unable to filter out wastes, the end products of metabolism must be removed from their bodies by artificial means. Dialysis is a means of removing these wastes and maintaining the body's proper fluid, electrolyte, and acid-base balance by the processes of osmosis and diffusion.

The two types of dialysis are hemodialysis and peritoneal dialysis. In **hemodialysis (HD)**, the patient's blood circulates outside the body (extracorporeally) through an artificial kidney (dialyzer) that removes metabolic wastes and helps to maintain homeostasis. When a patient is expected to be on long-term hemodialysis, surgery usually is performed to create an easy means of vascular access, such as the creation of an arteriovenous fistula. To keep the body free of excessive waste products, the patient typically dialyzes three times per week for 3 to 5 hours per session. Patients may obtain hemodialysis treatment in freestanding dialysis facilities, in the dialysis unit of a hospital, or in their own homes. In 2011, more than 90% of dialysis patients in the United States received hemodialysis on-site in an ESRD facility (USRDS, 2013).

The most common type of dialysis facility is the freestanding dialysis facility. As noted, the ESRD facility provides dialysis care on-site for most of its patients. About 9% of dialysis patients perform some type of dialysis at locations other than a dialysis center (USRDS, 2013). After training, some patients are able to perform their own hemodialysis at home with the aid of a friend or relative. These home hemodialysis patients and the peritoneal dialysis patients described as follows, however, still present themselves at least monthly for evaluation. This evaluation may take place in a variety of ways—at the dialysis facility, at the physician's office, or even electronically.

Peritoneal dialysis (PD) uses the patient's own abdominal cavity to filter out wastes. A tube is inserted through an incision into the patient's abdomen, and the dialysis solution, termed **dialysate**, is introduced into the peritoneal space. The dialysate draws the urea and other toxins out of the blood across the peritoneal membrane. Other products from the dialysate diffuse across the membrane into the blood.

In **continuous ambulatory peritoneal dialysis (CAPD)**, the patient is able to perform his or her own dialysis throughout the day, because little special equipment is required. The CAPD patient completes an exchange of fluid three or four times a day, at home or at work.

Continuous cycling peritoneal dialysis (CCPD) utilizes a machine to perform peritoneal dialysis once each day while the patient sleeps, rather than three or four times throughout the day as in CAPD. Like the CAPD patients, CCPD patients generally come to the ESRD facility only for training and for monthly evaluations or when a complication arises.

---

dialysis facility "an entity that provides (1) outpatient maintenance dialysis services; or (2) home dialysis training and support services; or (3) both.

hemodialysis (HD) cleansing of the blood as it circulates through an artificial kidney machine outside of the patient's body.

peritoneal dialysis (PD) filling the patient's abdominal cavity with a solution (dialysate). The semipermeable membrane across which the products diffuse is the patient's own peritoneal membrane. The fluid containing the wastes is withdrawn later from the peritoneal cavity.

dialysate a solution used to filter products across a semipermeable membrane by the process of diffusion. Waste products filter into the dialysate from the blood, whereas certain other products, such as bicarbonates, filter into the blood from the dialysate.

continuous ambulatory peritoneal dialysis (CAPD) a form of peritoneal dialysis in which the patient is able to dialyze himself or herself three or four times a day without special assistance and with a minimum amount of equipment.

continuous cycling peritoneal dialysis (CCPD) a form of peritoneal dialysis in which the patient uses a cycler machine to dialyze once a day for 9 or 10 hours, usually while sleeping.

TABLE 5-1	U.S. Prevalence of Various Dialysis Modalities, December 31, 2012	
Modality	**Count**	**Percentage**
Center hemodialysis	400,713	88.9
Center self-hemodialysis	75	<0.1
Home hemodialysis	7,923	1.8
CAPD	9,400	2.1
CCPD	31,231	6.9
Other PD	97	<0.1
Uncertain dialysis	1,163	0.3

Source: United States Renal Data System, 2014 annual data report: An overview of the epidemiology of kidney disease in the United States. National Institutes of Health, National Insti-tute of Diabetes and Digestive and Kidney Diseases, Bethesda, MD, 2014.

The type of dialysis treatment used is largely the patient's choice. CAPD patients tend to choose this method because they can incorporate it into their routine and do not have to rely on others to assist with their dialysis. CCPD is a popular choice for children and working adults because they can continue their daily routine and dialyze at night while sleeping. The disadvantage of both forms of peritoneal dialysis is the increased risk of infection. The most common dialysis-related infection for patients on peritoneal dialysis is peritonitis (Mayo Clinic, 2013). Any type of self-administered dialysis requires a patient who is motivated and capable of practicing good hygiene and performing and documenting self-care. (See Table 5-1 for a summary of the prevalence of each modality.)

Types of Caregivers

A multidisciplinary team cares for patients in a dialysis unit. The caregivers who have the most contact with the patient on each visit are registered nurses and licensed practical nurses who are assisted by certified dialysis technicians. Nurses and technicians are employees of the dialysis facility and are present with the dialysis center patients on a daily basis.

Other professionals maintain a regular schedule of visits to the dialysis unit, although they ordinarily do not practice at the dialysis center daily. In a moderately large freestanding dialysis unit, these professionals are on-site to see patients several times a month. For example, physicians see patients on a regular basis and have a primary role in determining the patient's treatment regimen. Dietitians educate patients about the importance of following the prescribed diet and also monitor nutritional status. Social workers discuss psychosocial issues with patients and address concerns that relate to family support, transportation, and other environmental factors that could affect the patient's compliance with the program of treatment. These other professionals usually see individual patients monthly, and often more frequently.

ESRD personnel evaluate home hemodialysis and peritoneal dialysis patients' conditions on a regular basis, usually monthly. As part of the evaluation visit, a nurse may examine the dialysis log sheets kept by the patient, containing information about each dialysis session. Health care workers check the patient's blood pressure, weight, and medications, and also review the results of monthly lab tests. A nurse checks the patient's dialysis access sites for signs of infection. In addition, these monthly evaluations include visits with the social worker, dietitian, and physician.

One other caregiver, the transplantation surgeon, may see the dialysis patient infrequently. The transplantation surgeon periodically evaluates dialysis patients to determine whether they are eligible for a transplant. Usually, one transplantation surgeon sees many dialysis patients from numerous dialysis facilities in a given geographic area. With regard to eligibility for transplant, criteria for a kidney transplant vary from one transplant center to another. In general, to be eligible for transplant, a patient in an advanced stage of chronic kidney disease must be healthy enough to undergo this type of surgery. Serious medical problems, current substance abuse, or noncompliance with medical treatment may prevent a patient from receiving a kidney transplant (UNC Kidney Center, n.d.).

SELF REVIEW 5.1

1. Provide two examples of renal replacement therapy.
2. Distinguish between an ESRD facility and an ESRD network.
3. Distinguish between hemodialysis and peritoneal dialysis.
4. In the dialysis setting, which health care professionals would carry out the following tasks? They
   a. … have primary responsibility for determining the patient's treatment regimen.
   b. … educate patients on the importance of following the prescribed diet and monitor nutritional status.
   c. … discuss psychosocial issues with patients and address problems relating to family support, transportation, and other environmental factors that could affect the patient's compliance with the program of treatment.
   d. … have the most contact with patients on each visit.

REGULATORY ISSUES

The most significant regulations for dialysis providers are the federal regulations for ESRD facilities. Because almost all dialysis facilities offer dialysis services to Medicare patients, nearly all dialysis facilities are subject to federal regulations. This is true whether the facility is freestanding or is affiliated with a hospital or other organization.

A dialysis unit in a hospital accredited by The Joint Commission or another voluntary accrediting organization, such as NIAHO, also is subject to that organization's standards in addition to the federal standards. The federal regulations, however, usually are more detailed with regard to dialysis operations than are voluntary standards, so a hospital dialysis facility that meets federal standards should have no problems meeting voluntary standards such as those of The Joint Commission.

Individual states also may have their own regulations for dialysis facilities. These usually are modeled on federal standards, so, again, the predominant regulatory issues in most states are found in the federal guidelines.

Surveys

Dialysis units are surveyed by each state's own surveying agency to determine if the dialysis unit is in compliance with both state and federal guidelines. For example, a survey team from the state department of health visits a dialysis facility to compare the facility's performance to federal regulations (and any state regulations that may apply). Each state reviews data from dialysis facilities and targets lower performing facilities to survey. These surveys usually are unannounced, so the facility must be ready for a survey at any time.

In addition, federal surveyors from the CMS regional offices may conduct an unexpected **validation survey** to determine whether the state agencies to whom the regular surveys have been delegated are evaluating facilities appropriately according to federal regulations. Even though the primary purpose of the validation survey is to serve as a check on the state surveying agency, any deficiencies noted in the validation survey still must be corrected by the dialysis facility.

validation survey a survey conducted by a regional office of the CMS to determine whether the surveys being conducted by state agencies (or other groups) are assessing the facility's operations appropriately.

Federal Regulations

Federal regulations affecting ESRD facilities are found in the Conditions for Coverage for End-Stage Renal Disease Facilities (42 C.F.R. Part 405 Subpart U, 2008). These regulations are comprehensive and apply to every facet of the facility's operation. Relevant information from federal regulations is interspersed throughout this chapter, under topics such as "Documentation" and "Data and Information Flow."

The Conditions for Coverage, inaugurated in 1972, were revised extensively in 2008. Prior to the 2008 revision, dialysis facilities were required to obtain the services of a "medical record practitioner," such as a registered health information administrator (RHIA) or a registered health information technician (RHIT). The 2008 revisions dropped this requirement and also deleted the requirement that a member of the facility's staff must be designated to serve as supervisor of medical records. Although there is no longer a federal requirement to do so, it is still good practice to designate an employee of the facility to monitor whether medical records are properly documented, completed, and preserved. In addition to designating an employee to oversee health record functions, many dialysis centers still contract with an RHIA or RHIT on a consulting basis to review their documentation systems.

ESRD Networks

ESRD networks were established by federal law to monitor quality and appropriateness of care provided to ESRD patients. The Omnibus Reconciliation Act (OBRA) of 1986 reorganized the ESRD program and set up 18 network areas across the United States to assess the quality of care given to ESRD patients. The network map can be accessed at www.esrdnetworks.org

These ESRD networks perform their work under contract with the Centers for Medicare & Medicaid Services (CMS). In addition to their quality assessment activities, the networks collect and analyze data on ESRD patients in their regions. The networks monitor patient status changes and handle patient grievances. They also publish an annual report of these and other activities. Some of these roles of the ESRD networks are discussed later in the chapter.

SELF REVIEW 5.2

1. Which regulations do almost all dialysis providers in the United States follow?
2. True or False? Survey visit dates are announced to dialysis facilities three months prior to the survey. *False*
3. The federal regulations for ESRD facilities are called the _conditions for coverage for end stage renal disease facility_
4. How many networks were set up in the United States in 1986 to monitor quality and appropriateness of care provided to ESRD patients? *18*

DOCUMENTATION

Dialysis facility records can be voluminous, because a patient can remain in dialysis treatment for decades and also because the treatments and evaluations are so frequent. Maintaining portions of the record electronically is a common practice in ESRD facilities because of the detailed information that must be documented about the patient's condition, status, and treatment. Many dialysis facilities utilize hybrid records, maintaining a portion of the record electronically and the remainder of the record in paper format. Regardless of the method of maintaining patient records, the facility must be careful to document all required items.

According to the Conditions for Coverage, §494.170, the dialysis facility "must maintain complete, accurate, and accessible records on all patients, including home patients...."

Patient Assessment and Plan of Care

Two important documentation requirements in the dialysis patient record are the patient assessment and the patient plan of care. The patient assessment is developed by an interdisciplinary team consisting of at least the following participants: the patient or the patient's designee, a registered nurse, a physician treating the patient for ESRD, a social worker, and a dietitian. According to federal regulations (42 C.F.R. 494.80), the comprehensive assessment must include evaluation in each of the thirteen areas below:

1. Current health status and medical condition, including comorbid conditions
2. Appropriateness of the dialysis prescription, blood pressure, and fluid management needs
3. Laboratory profile, immunization history, and medication history
4. Factors associated with anemia, such as hematocrit, hemoglobin, iron stores, and potential treatment plans for anemia, including administration of erythropoiesis-stimulating agent(s)
5. Factors associated with **renal bone disease**
6. Nutritional status (evaluated by a dietitian)
7. Psychosocial needs (evaluated by a social worker)
8. Dialysis access type and maintenance (for example, arteriovenous fistulas, arteriovenous grafts, and peritoneal catheters)
9. The patient's abilities, interests, preferences, and goals, including the desired level of participation in the dialysis care process; the preferred modality (hemodialysis or peritoneal dialysis) and setting (for example, home dialysis); and the patient's expectations for care outcomes
10. Suitability for a transplantation referral, based on criteria developed by the prospective transplantation center and its surgeon(s). If the patient is not suitable for transplantation referral, the basis for nonreferral must be documented in the patient's medical record
11. Family and other support systems
12. Current patient physical activity level
13. Evaluation for referral to vocational and physical rehabilitation services

renal bone disease   also known as renal osteodystrophy, a disorder that results from an imbalance in calcium, parathyroid hormone (PTH), phosphorus, and activated vitamin D, which can occur in chronic kidney disease. It can result in weakened bones that break easily, and also hardening of soft tissues of the body including the heart. Disorders of mineral metabolism are associated with a higher death rate in people with end-stage renal disease (ESRD).

The following excerpt from the federal regulations (42 C.F.R. 494.80, p. 20479) outlines the required schedule for various assessment activities:

b) Standard: Frequency of assessment for patients admitted to the dialysis facility.
   1. An initial comprehensive assessment must be conducted on all new patients (that is, all admissions to a dialysis facility), within the latter of 30 calendar days or 13 outpatient hemodialysis sessions beginning with the first outpatient dialysis session.
   2. A follow up comprehensive reassessment must occur within 3 months after the completion of the initial assessment to provide information to adjust the patient's plan of care specified in § 494.90.

c) Standard: Assessment of treatment prescription. The adequacy of dialysis as described in § 494.90(a)(1), must be assessed on an ongoing basis as follows:
   1. Hemodialysis patients. At least monthly by calculating delivered Kt/V or an equivalent measure.
   2. Peritoneal dialysis patients. At least every 4 months by calculating delivered weekly Kt/V or an equivalent measure.

d) Standard: Patient reassessment...(A) comprehensive reassessment of each patient and a revision of the plan of care must be conducted—
   1. At least annually for stable patients; and
   2. At least monthly for unstable patients including, but not limited to, patients with the following:
      (i) Extended or frequent hospitalizations;
      (ii) Marked deterioration in health status;
      (iii) Significant change in psychosocial needs; or
      (iv) Concurrent poor nutritional status, unmanaged anemia, and inadequate dialysis.

Federal regulations (42 C.F.R. 494.90) require the development of "a written, individualized comprehensive plan of care that specifies the services necessary to address the patient's needs, as identified by the comprehensive assessment and changes in the patient's condition," (Conditions for Coverage, 2008, p. 20479). Key elements of the plan of care are excerpted below (Conditions for Coverage, pp. 20479–20480):

(a) Standard: Development of patient plan of care. The interdisciplinary team must develop a plan of care for each patient. The plan of care must address, but not be limited to, the following:
   1. Dose of dialysis. The interdisciplinary team must provide the necessary care and services to manage the patient's volume status; and achieve and sustain the prescribed dose of dialysis to meet a hemodialysis Kt/V of at least 1.2 and a peritoneal dialysis weekly Kt/V of at least 1.7 or meet an alternative equivalent professionally-accepted clinical practice standard for adequacy of dialysis.
   2. Nutritional status. The interdisciplinary team must provide the necessary care and counseling services to achieve and sustain an effective nutritional status. A patient's albumin level and body weight must be measured at least monthly. Additional evidence-based professionally accepted clinical nutrition indicators may be monitored, as appropriate.
   3. Mineral metabolism. Provide the necessary care to manage mineral metabolism and prevent or treat renal bone disease.
   4. Anemia. The interdisciplinary team must provide the necessary care and services to achieve and sustain the clinically appropriate hemoglobin/hematocrit level. The patient's hemoglobin/hematocrit must be measured at least monthly. The

adequacy of dialysis a determination of whether the patient's dialysis treatment is removing sufficient waste and excess fluid from the body. To be adequate, the patient must dialyze long enough and often enough to achieve the goals of treatment. Adequate dialysis is essential to patient survival.

Kt/V a means of measuring the adequacy of dialysis (i.e., a way to determine whether the patient is dialyzing long enough or often enough to remove sufficient waste and excess fluid from the body). Target Kt/V values in the *Conditions for Coverage* are 1.2 for hemodialysis and a weekly Kt/V of at least 1.7 for peritoneal dialysis.

dialysis facility must conduct an evaluation of the patient's anemia management needs. For a home dialysis patient, the facility must evaluate whether the patient can safely, aseptically, and effectively administer erythropoiesis-stimulating agents and store this medication under refrigeration if necessary. The patient's response to erythropoiesis-stimulating agent(s), including blood pressure levels and utilization of iron stores, must be monitored on a routine basis.

5. Vascular access. The interdisciplinary team must provide **vascular access monitoring** and appropriate, timely referrals to achieve and sustain vascular access. The hemodialysis patient must be evaluated for the appropriate vascular access type, taking into consideration co-morbid conditions, other risk factors, and whether the patient is a potential candidate for arteriovenous fistula placement. The patient's vascular access must be monitored to prevent access failure, including monitoring of arteriovenous grafts and fistulae for symptoms of stenosis.

6. Psychosocial status. The interdisciplinary team must provide the necessary monitoring and social work interventions. These include counseling services and referrals for other social services, to assist the patient in achieving and sustaining an appropriate psychosocial status as measured by a standardized mental and physical assessment tool chosen by the social worker, at regular intervals, or more frequently on an as-needed basis.

7. Modality.
   (i) Home dialysis. The interdisciplinary team must identify a plan for the patient's home dialysis or explain why the patient is not a candidate for home dialysis.
   (ii) Transplantation status. When the patient is a transplant referral candidate, the interdisciplinary team must develop plans for pursuing transplantation. The patient's plan of care must include documentation of the
      (A) Plan for transplantation, if the patient accepts the transplantation referral;
      (B) Patient's decision, if the patient is a transplantation referral candidate but declines the transplantation referral; or
      (C) Reason(s) for the patient's nonreferral as a transplantation candidate as documented in accordance with § 494.80(a)(10).

8. Rehabilitation status. The interdisciplinary team must assist the patient in achieving and sustaining an appropriate level of productive activity, as desired by the patient, including the educational needs of pediatric patients (patients under the age of 18 years), and make rehabilitation and vocational rehabilitation referrals as appropriate.

(b) Standard: Implementation of the patient plan of care.
   1. The patient's plan of care must—
      (i) Be completed by the interdisciplinary team, including the patient if the patient desires; and
      (ii) Be signed by team members, including the patient or the patient's designee; or, if the patient chooses not to sign the plan of care, this choice must be documented on the plan of care, along with the reason the signature was not provided.
   2. Implementation of the initial plan of care must begin within the latter of 30 calendar days after admission to the dialysis facility or 13 outpatient hemodialysis sessions beginning with the first outpatient dialysis session. Implementation of monthly or annual updates of the plan of care must be performed within 15 days of the completion of the additional patient assessments specified in § 494.80(d).
   3. If the expected outcome is not achieved, the interdisciplinary team must adjust the patient's plan of care to achieve the specified goals. When a patient is unable to achieve the desired outcomes, the team must—
      (i) Adjust the plan of care to reflect the patient's current condition;
      (ii) Document in the record the reasons why the patient was unable to achieve the goals; and

vascular access monitoring physical examination of the dialysis access site to detect possible access complications. Types of monitoring include visual examination of the access site to detect changes, palpation (examination by touching), and auscultation (listening with a stethoscope).

  (iii) Implement plan of care changes to address the issues identified in paragraph (b)(3)(ii) of this section.

 4. The dialysis facility must ensure that all dialysis patients are seen by a physician, nurse practitioner, clinical nurse specialist, or physician's assistant providing ESRD care at least monthly, as evidenced by a monthly progress note placed in the medical record, and periodically while the hemodialysis patient is receiving in-facility dialysis.

(c) Standard: Transplantation referral tracking. The interdisciplinary team must—
1. Track the results of each kidney transplant center referral;
2. Monitor the status of any facility patients who are on the transplant wait list; and
3. Communicate with the transplant center regarding patient transplant status at least annually, and when there is a change in transplant candidate status.

(d) Standard: Patient education and training. The patient care plan must include, as applicable, education and training for patients and family members or caregivers or both, in aspects of the dialysis experience, dialysis management, infection prevention and personal care, home dialysis and self-care, quality of life, rehabilitation, transplantation, and the benefits and risks of various vascular access types.

The *ESRD Program Interpretive Guidance* document is used by site surveyors when surveying a program under the Conditions for Coverage and provides more details about what type of documentation is needed to demonstrate that a dialysis facility meets federal standards. For example, Figure 5-1 provides an excerpt from the Measures Assessment Tool (MAT) found in the *Interpretive Guidance* document, which highlights documentation that should be present in the record to evaluate elements related to the required patient assessment.

The Forum of ESRD Networks' Quality Assurance Committee also has described a document titled the Medical Record Model to improve the quality of the dialysis medical record. Improving the quality of the medical record improves the team's ability to provide care and encourages a consistent approach. The Medical Record Model presents a format for medical records that should contain the information necessary for continuity of patient care and qualitative review. Although the 2008 revisions to the Conditions for Coverage are more stringent in some regards than the 2001 version of the Medical Record Model, this record model still provides additional guidance for facilities seeking to improve their documentation. For example, the Medical Record Model provides recommendations regarding the contents of progress notes, as outlined in the following excerpt.

"Progress notes should provide an accurate picture of the progress of the patient, which reflects changes in patient status, plans and results of changes in treatment regimen, diagnostic testing, consultations, unusual events, etc. Either single discipline or integrated multidisciplinary progress notes may be utilized. The following are minimal entries:

• Each discipline, physician(s), nurse(s), social worker(s) and dietitian(s) should record the progress of the patient at regular intervals...

• Patient condition and response to treatment noted on daily treatment record

FIGURE 5-1

Excerpt from the Measures Assessment Tool (MAT) found in the ESRD Program Interpretive Guidance.

494.80 Patient assessment: The interdisciplinary team (IDT), patient/designee, RN, MSW, RD, physician must provide each patient with an individualized & comprehensive assessment of needs.

Condition/Standard	Measure
- Health status/comorbidities	- Medical/nursing history, physical exam findings
- Dialysis prescription	- Evaluate: HD every mo; PD first mo & q4 mo
- BP & fluid management	- Interdialytic BP & wt gain, target wt, symptoms
- Lab profile	- Monitor labs monthly & as needed
- Immunization & meds history	- Pneumococcal, hepatitis, influenza; med allergies
- Anemia (Hgb, Hct, iron stores, ESA need)	- Volume, bleeding, infection, ESA hypo-response
- Renal bone disease	- Calcium, phosphorus, PTH & medications
- Nutritional status	- Multiple elements listed
- Psychosocial needs	- Multiple elements listed
- Dialysis access type & maintenance	- Access efficacy, fistula candidacy
- Abilities, interests, preferences, goals, desired level of participation in care, preferred modality & setting, outcomes expectations	- Reason why patient does not participate in care, reason why patient is not a home dialysis candidate
- Suitability for transplant referral	- Reason why patient is not a transplant candidate
- Family & other support systems	- Composition, history, availability, level of support
- Current physical activity level & referral to voc & physical rehab	- Abilities & barriers to independent living; achieving educational & work goals

Permission to reuse in accordance with http://www.cms.gov Content Reuse and Linking Policy.

- Regular review of abnormal labs/clinical findings and any action taken
- Monthly review of laboratory results (including adequacy) & hepatitis status
- Vascular Access Assessment" (Forum of ESRD Networks, 2001, p. 4)

SELF REVIEW 5.3

1. Why are dialysis records frequently so voluminous? *Pt seen @ freq̲u̲e̲n̲t̲ ̲i̲n̲t̲e̲r̲v̲a̲l̲s̲ ̲o̲v̲e̲r̲ ̲a̲n̲ ̲e̲x̲t̲ ̲p̲e̲r̲i̲o̲d̲ ̲o̲f̲ ̲t̲i̲m̲e̲.*

2. At a minimum, the interdisciplinary team that develops the patient assessment must be composed of what five categories of individuals?

3. How soon after admission to a dialysis facility must an initial comprehensive assessment be conducted on a new patient? *— Reqd all new pt w/30 days or 13 outpatient dialysis sessions.*

patient, RN, physician treating patient for ESRD, social worker Dietician

4. At a minimum, how often should stable patients be reassessed and the plan of care revised? *Stable pt - annually, non-stable pt monthly*

5. According to the Conditions for Coverage, how often must dialysis patients be seen by a physician, nurse practitioner, clinical nurse specialist, or physician's assistant providing ESRD care, as documented by a progress note placed in the medical record? *At least monthly*

6. What document used by site surveyors provides more details about the type of documentation needed to demonstrate that a dialysis facility meets the Conditions for Coverage? *ESRD Pgm interpretive guidance*

7. What other optional guidance is available for monitoring the quality of documentation in a dialysis facility, in addition to the Conditions for Coverage?

Form ESRD Networks Quality assurance committees medical record module

REIMBURSEMENT

A person with ESRD is generally eligible for Medicare coverage on the basis of the ESRD diagnosis if the individual meets any one of these requirements:

- Has worked the required amount of time under Social Security, the Railroad Retirement Board (RRB), or as a government employee
- Is receiving or is eligible for Social Security or Railroad Retirement benefits
- Is the spouse or dependent child of a person who has worked the required amount of time to be eligible for Medicare, or who is getting Social Security or Railroad Retirement benefits (How to Sign up for Medicare, n.d.)

To receive maximum coverage for ESRD services, an eligible patient should sign up for both Medicare Part A (covering treatment in a hospital or skilled nursing facility) and Medicare Part B (covering outpatient treatment). Medicare coverage ordinarily starts the first day of the fourth month after regular dialysis treatments begin, although in some circumstances coverage can begin in the first month if the patient takes part in a home dialysis training program.

At present, most dialysis patients receive benefits through Medicare's ESRD program. For patients with existing group health insurance, however, Medicare is the secondary payer during the first 30 months of ESRD-based eligibility (DHHS, 2012). Even after Medicare has become the primary payer, many patients receive some benefits from other insurance programs, too, such as an employer's group insurance policy. Because of this type of dual coverage, dialysis facilities frequently deal with third-party payers other than Medicare.

Facility Reimbursement

Prior to changes brought about by the Medicare Improvements for Patients and Providers Act of 2008 (MIPPA), Medicare paid the dialysis facility a composite rate per treatment for three treatments per week for each patient on chronic dialysis, with no payment for patients who miss treatments (no-shows). This composite rate included payment for some of the other services the patient received, such as some of the routine laboratory tests. Certain types of tests and treatments, such as administration of **erythropoieis stimulating agents (ESAs)**, however, were separately billable and accounted for about 40% of Medicare's costs for the ESRD program. MIPPA required the development of a prospective payment system for ESRD services that utilized a single payment for dialysis services, to be phased in beginning January 1, 2011, and fully implemented by January 1, 2014 (CMS, 2010). MIPPA also required that payments be adjusted according to performance measures, described more fully in the quality improvement discussion in this chapter.

The prospective payment system for ESRD facilities combines payments for the composite rate and certain services that previously were billable separately into a single base rate. The base rate then is adjusted using patient-specific case-mix adjustment factors, including age, body surface area (BSA), low body mass index (BMI), the onset of renal dialysis (new patient), and six comorbidity categories: bacterial pneumonia, gastrointestinal bleeding, hereditary hemolytic and sickle cell anemia, monoclonal gammopathy, myelodysplastic syndrome, and pericarditis (End-Stage Renal Disease Prospective Payment System Final Rule and Proposed Rule, 2010).

Comorbidities are classified as either chronic or acute. Payment adjustments for chronic comorbidities are paid for as long as the condition is reported on the claim. Payment adjustments for acute comorbidities continue for a maximum of four consecutive months (unless there is a reoccurrence of the condition). (ESRD Co-morbidity Conditions, 2012).

A **value-based purchasing (VBP)** or "pay-for-performance" program went into effect for ESRD facilities in 2012. A VBP program is one that can increase the payment to a health care provider or not based on whether the provider meets or doesn't meet specified performance standards. The VBP program for ESRD facilities is called the ESRD Quality Incentive Program (QIP), which can reduce the payment to a facility when the facility doesn't meet certain clinical performance and reporting standards. When a facility doesn't meet performance standards, the payment to the facility can be reduced by up to, but not more than, 2 percent.

Physician Reimbursement

In general, a physician receives a monthly payment from Medicare Part B based on the number of visits for each patient. Physicians may receive additional payments for other services, such as evaluation and management services rendered to inpatients.

---

erythropoiesis stimulating agents (ESAs) agents that stimulate the bone marrow to make red blood cells and are used to treat and prevent anemia, a common complication of chronic kidney disease in patients on dialysis.

value-based purchasing (VBP) a "pay-for-performance" program that can either increase the payment to a health care provider based on whether the provider meets or doesn't meet specified performance standards. The VBP program for ESRD facilities is called the ESRD Quality Incentive Program (QIP), which can reduce the payment to a facility when the facility doesn't meet certain clinical performance and reporting standards.

1. List one of the three requirements that a person with ESRD must meet to be eligible for Medicare coverage. Worked w/ Req amount of time

   under Soci &

2. True or False? To receive maximum coverage for ESRD services, an eligible patient should sign up for both Medicare Part A and Medicare Part B.

3. For what time period of ESRD-based eligibility do dialysis patients with existing group health insurance have Medicare as the secondary payer?

4. What legislation required the development of a prospective payment system for ESRD services utilizing a single payment for dialysis services?

5. True or False? Medicare Part A pays physicians monthly based on the minutes spent with each patient.

INFORMATION MANAGEMENT

Coding and Classification

The ESRD facility codes diagnoses using the current version of the *International Classification of Diseases* approved for use in the United States. Coding in an ESRD facility is necessary for reimbursement. For Medicare, the code submitted to the ESRD network, and ultimately to CMS when dialysis is first initiated, must be a code that CMS recognizes as end-stage renal disease. The ESRD prospective payment system (PPS) also utilizes diagnostic codes submitted on claim forms to identify comorbidities. If a patient has more than one comorbidity, only the comorbidity with the highest adjustment factor affects the payment. Table 5-2 lists the ESRD PPS comorbidity categories as either chronic or acute.

As explained in the reimbursement discussion in this chapter, chronic comorbidities and acute comorbidities affect the facility's payment in different ways.

TABLE 5-2 ESRD Prospective Payment System Co-Morbidity Categories Eligible for Co-Morbidity Adjustment

Chronic Comorbidity Categories	
	Hereditary hemolytic or sickle cell anemia
	Myelodysplastic syndromes
	Monoclonal gammopathy
Acute Comorbidity Categories	
	Bacterial pneumonias
	Gastrointestinal tract bleeding with hemorrhage
	Pericarditis

All of the patient's comorbid conditions, not just those in the six categories that affect reimbursement, should be reported on the claim form.

For reimbursement, physicians who see ESRD patients also must code their encounters with the patient. For physician reimbursement, diagnoses are coded with the current version of *ICD*, and the services performed by the physician are coded with the Healthcare Common Procedural Coding System (HCPCS).

At the national level, CMS maintains coded data submitted by dialysis providers that can be used for purposes other than reimbursement, including research.

Data and Information Flow

Data and information flow can be viewed at the level of the individual patient and at the aggregate level of many patients in a given area.

Individual Patient Data

At the level of the individual patient, the initial information for a dialysis patient is gathered when the patient is admitted to the dialysis facility. Information flows into the patient record from many sources. The caregivers document their interactions with, and assessments of, the patient. The patient contributes to portions of the record, such as the plan of care. The facility also receives copies of portions of the patient's hospital record whenever the patient is admitted to the hospital. Information from reference laboratories and other facilities that have treated or tested the patient also are included in the patient's record.

When a dialysis patient is transferred to another facility, the information must be transferred between the two facilities. Federal regulation 42 C.F.R. 494.170 requires that all requested medical record information be transmitted to the receiving facility within one working day. A transfer agreement between the dialysis facility and a local hospital can facilitate the transfer of information when a dialysis patient is admitted to or discharged from one location and transferred to another.

Because hemodialysis patients should dialyze at least three times per week, the ESRD facility has to be involved when the patient is planning a vacation or an extended trip out of town. In that case, the local dialysis facility must contact another facility in the location to which the patient is traveling. The distant facility must agree to treat the patient while the patient is there. The transfer of referral information back and forth between the local and the distant facility is important in providing quality patient care.

Aggregate Data

As mentioned previously, the ESRD networks are responsible for collecting and analyzing data on ESRD patients in their areas. The facilities that treat patients are responsible for submitting information on each patient and on the facility itself to the appropriate network. In 2010, electronic submission of information through

Consolidated Renal Operations in a Web-enabled Network (CROWNWeb) CMS internet-based software application, the required method by which dialysis facilities submit data about patients and facility operations.

a system named Consolidated Renal Operations in a Web-enabled Network (CROWNWeb) began to be phased in (CMS, 2008). The network processes the data, which also are transmitted electronically to CMS, where they are aggregated on a national scale. CMS created CROWNWeb to collect data from patient records, clinical performance measures, and information about each dialysis facility.

Using these data and other beneficiary-specific data, CMS has developed a comprehensive database called the End-Stage Renal Disease (ESRD) Program Management and Medical Information System (PMMIS). The ESRD PMMIS includes medical and demographic information for the Medicare ESRD population. CMS uses the data for program analysis, policy development, and epidemiologic research. The Renal Management Information System (REMIS) determines Medicare coverage periods for ESRD patients and serves as the chief means for storing and accessing information in the ESRD PMMIS Database. REMIS tracks both Medicare and non-Medicare ESRD patients. It also includes interfaces with the Medicare Beneficiary Database and with the ESRD Network Organizations' Standard Information Management System (SIMS) (CMS, 2009).

Renal Management Information System (REMIS) a protocol that determines Medicare coverage periods for ESRD patients and serves as the primary mechanism to store and access information in the ESRD Program Management and Medical Information System (PMMIS) Database. REMIS tracks the ESRD patient population for both Medicare and non-Medicare patients.

Electronic Health Record (EHR) and Information Systems

To plan a successful dialysis treatment program, the physicians and nurses require data on the patient's condition and response to treatment. Because of the large amount of clinical information collected on dialysis patients, dialysis facilities were among the first health care providers to adopt electronic health records.

EHR applications in the dialysis setting may include the ability to track patient data from each treatment session, electronic charting at the patient chairside, electronic patient flow sheets, tracking of prescriptions, progress notes for various disciplines, reports, graphing capability, calculations to measure the adequacy of dialysis, and, in some instances, the ability to collect data through an interface with dialyzer equipment. Some EHR systems also facilitate CROWNWeb reporting.

By maintaining medication records and data from each dialysis session electronically, clinicians can track the patient's response to treatment. The EHR system can generate reports showing the patient's weight, blood pressure, and so forth, before and after each treatment, and can compute monthly averages for various clinical data elements. These simple reports can be used to educate the patient and to encourage compliance with the prescribed diet and medication regimen. The caregivers also learn more about each patient from studying the accumulated data available in EHR-generated reports.

Even though this essential clinical information often is stored in an electronic system, most dialysis facilities find it necessary to maintain a portion of the patient's record on paper. A hybrid record may be needed to maintain consents, referral information, and so forth, which frequently are maintained in paper format. As in most health care facilities, electronic systems also are used for billing and accounting purposes.

Data Sets

Examples of data sets used by dialysis facilities include the CMS 2728, "End-Stage Renal Disease Medical Evidence Report Medicare Entitlement and/or Patient Registration," and the CMS 2746, "ESRD Death Notification." These forms previously were submitted on paper, but now are generated electronically through the electronic reporting process. The "End-Stage Renal Disease Medical Evidence Report: Medicare Entitlement and/or Patient Registration" (CMS 2728) is generated from data that are submitted by the dialysis facility for each new dialysis patient. The "ESRD Death Notification" form (CMS 2746) is generated from data submitted for each ESRD patient who expires. The data included in both of these data sets are transmitted electronically through CROWNWeb to the networks and ultimately to CMS. CROWNWeb also provides the capability of printing these data sets as CMS 2728 and CMS 2746 forms. (See Figure 5-2 and Figure 5-3.)

In addition to patient record information, clinical performance measures, and facility data, CROWNWeb includes a listing of all ESRD facilities within each network. It also includes a list of employees and patients within each facility.

The ESRD networks also collect census data from each dialysis facility. In addition, they maintain records on the status of each patient, including information on patient follow-up and transplants. Maintenance of patient-specific records requires that the networks maintain an accurate master patient index.

Data on kidney transplants are available from the United Network for Organ Sharing (UNOS). Under a contract with the Health Resources and Services Administration of the U.S. Department of Health and Human Services, UNOS manages the Organ Procurement and Transplantation Network (OPTN). One of the most important functions of OPTN is to facilitate the matching of donor organs and transplant recipients. This is accomplished by means of a computer system and an Organ Center that operates 24 hours a day. OPTN, however, also collects and manages data about organ donation and transplantation for kidney, pancreas, liver, intestine, heart, and lung procedures. Most candidates on the UNOS waiting list for organs are waiting for kidney donations (UNOS, 2010; OPTN, 2010).

SELF REVIEW 5.5

1. Coding in an ESRD facility is important for _____.
2. True or False? According to the ESRD prospective payment system, if a patient has more than one comorbidity, the comorbidity with the lowest adjustment factor affects the payment.
3. How do physicians use ICD codes? How do they use HCPCS?
4. Who created CROWNWeb, and what is its purpose?
5. _____ determines Medicare coverage periods for ESRD patients and serves as the chief means for storing and accessing information in the ESRD PMMIS database.
6. Name two examples of data sets used by dialysis facilities.
7. What network aids in the matching of donor organs and transplant recipients?

FIGURE 5-2

CMS Form 2728.

DEPARTMENT OF HEALTH AND HUMAN SERVICES
CENTERS FOR MEDICARE & MEDICAID SERVICES

Form Approved
OMB No. 0938-0046

END STAGE RENAL DISEASE MEDICAL EVIDENCE REPORT
MEDICARE ENTITLEMENT AND/OR PATIENT REGISTRATION

A. COMPLETE FOR ALL ESRD PATIENTS   *Check one:* ☐ Initial   ☐ Re-entitlement   ☐ Supplemental

1. Name *(Last, First, Middle Initial)*

2. Medicare Claim Number	3. Social Security Number	4. Date of Birth
		___/___/___ MM DD YYYY

5. Patient Mailing Address *(Include City, State and Zip)*	6. Phone Number ( )

7. Sex	8. Ethnicity	9. Country/Area of Origin or Ancestry
☐ Male ☐ Female	☐ Not Hispanic or Latino ☐ Hispanic or Latino (Complete Item 9)	

10. Race *(Check all that apply)*
☐ White
☐ Black or African American
☐ American Indian/Alaska Native
Print Name of Enrolled/Principal Tribe _____
☐ Asian
☐ Native Hawaiian or Other Pacific Islander*
*complete Item 9

11. Is patient applying for ESRD Medicare coverage?
☐ Yes ☐ No

12. Current Medical Coverage *(Check all that apply)*
☐ Medicaid ☐ Medicare ☐ Employer Group Health Insurance
☐ DVA ☐ Medicare Advantage ☐ Other ☐ None

13. Height
INCHES _____ OR
CENTIMETERS _____

14. Dry Weight
POUNDS _____ OR
KILOGRAMS _____

15. Primary Cause of Renal Failure *(Use code from back of form)*

16. Employment Status *(6 mos prior and current status)*

Prior Current
☐ ☐ Unemployed
☐ ☐ Employed Full Time
☐ ☐ Employed Part Time
☐ ☐ Homemaker
☐ ☐ Retired due to Age/Preference
☐ ☐ Retired (Disability)
☐ ☐ Medical Leave of Absence
☐ ☐ Student

17. Co-Morbid Conditions *(Check all that apply currently and/or during last 10 years)* *See instructions
a. ☐ Congestive heart failure
b. ☐ Atherosclerotic heart disease ASHD
c. ☐ Other cardiac disease
d. ☐ Cerebrovascular disease, CVA, TIA*
e. ☐ Peripheral vascular disease*
f. ☐ History of hypertension
g. ☐ Amputation
h. ☐ Diabetes, currently on insulin
i. ☐ Diabetes, on oral medications
j. ☐ Diabetes, without medications
k. ☐ Diabetic retinopathy
l. ☐ Chronic obstructive pulmonary disease
m. ☐ Tobacco use (current smoker)
n. ☐ Malignant neoplasm, Cancer
o. ☐ Toxic nephropathy
p. ☐ Alcohol dependence
q. ☐ Drug dependence*
r. ☐ Inability to ambulate
s. ☐ Inability to transfer
t. ☐ Needs assistance with daily activities
u. ☐ Institutionalized
☐ 1. Assisted Living
☐ 2. Nursing Home
☐ 3. Other Institution
v. ☐ Non-renal congenital abnormality
w. ☐ None

18. Prior to ESRD therapy:

	Yes	No	Unknown	If Yes, answer:	6-12 months	>12 months
a. Did patient receive exogenous erythropoetin or equivalent?	☐ Yes	☐ No	☐ Unknown	If Yes, answer:	☐ 6-12 months	☐ >12 months
b. Was patient under care of a nephrologist?	☐ Yes	☐ No	☐ Unknown	If Yes, answer:	☐ 6-12 months	☐ >12 months
c. Was patient under care of kidney dietitian?	☐ Yes	☐ No	☐ Unknown	If Yes, answer:	☐ 6-12 months	☐ >12 months
d. What access was used on first outpatient dialysis:	☐ AVF	☐ Graft ☐ Catheter	☐ Other			
If not AVF, then: Is maturing AVF present?	☐ Yes	☐ No				
Is maturing graft present?	☐ Yes	☐ No				

19. Laboratory Values Within 45 Days Prior to the Most Recent ESRD Episode. (Lipid Profile within 1 Year of Most Recent ESRD Episode).

LABORATORY TEST	VALUE	DATE	LABORATORY TEST	VALUE	DATE
a.1. Serum Albumin (g/dl)	___ . ___		d. HbA1c	___ ___ . ___ %	
a.2. Serum Albumin Lower Limit	___ . ___		e. Lipid Profile TC	___ ___ ___	
a.3. Lab Method Used (BCG or BCP)			LDL	___ ___ ___	
b. Serum Creatinine (mg/dl)	___ ___ . ___		HDL	___ ___ ___	
c. Hemoglobin (g/dl)	___ ___ . ___		TG	___ ___ ___	

B. COMPLETE FOR ALL ESRD PATIENTS IN DIALYSIS TREATMENT

20. Name of Dialysis Facility	21. Medicare Provider Number *(for item 20)*

22. Primary Dialysis Setting
☐ Home ☐ Dialysis Facility/Center ☐ SNF/Long Term Care Facility
☐ CAPD ☐ CCPD ☐ Other

23. Primary Type of Dialysis
☐ Hemodialysis (Sessions per week____/hours per session____)

24. Date Regular Chronic Dialysis Began Dialysis at Current Facility
___/___/___ MM   DD   YYYY

25. Date Patient Started Chronic
___/___/___ MM   DD   YYYY

26. Has patient been informed of kidney transplant options?
☐ Yes ☐ No

27. If patient NOT informed of transplant options, please check all that apply:
☐ Medically unfit
☐ Unsuitable due to age
☐ Psychologically unfit
☐ Patient declines information
☐ Patient has not been assessed
☐ Other

FIGURE 5-2   *(continued)*

C. COMPLETE FOR ALL KIDNEY TRANSPLANT PATIENTS

28. Date of Transplant MM DD YYYY	29. Name of Transplant Hospital	30. Medicare Provider Number for Item 29

Date patient was admitted as an inpatient to a hospital in preparation for, or anticipation of, a kidney transplant prior to the date of actual transplantation.

31. Enter Date MM DD YYYY	32. Name of Preparation Hospital	33. Medicare Provider number for Item 32

34. Current Status of Transplant *(if functioning, skip items 36 and 37)* ☐ Functioning ☐ Non-Functioning	35. Type of Donor: ☐ Deceased ☐ Living Related ☐ Living Unrelated
36. If Non-Functioning, Date of Return to Regular Dialysis MM DD YYYY	37. Current Dialysis Treatment Site ☐ Home ☐ Dialysis Facility/Center ☐ SNF/Long Term Care Facility

D. COMPLETE FOR ALL ESRD SELF-DIALYSIS TRAINING PATIENTS (MEDICARE APPLICANTS ONLY)

38. Name of Training Provider	39. Medicare Provider Number of Training Provider (for Item 38)
40. Date Training Began MM DD YYYY	41. Type of Training ☐ Hemodialysis a. ☐ Home b. ☐ In Center ☐ CAPD ☐ CCPD ☐ Other
42. This Patient is Expected to Complete *(or has completed)* Training and will Self-dialyze on a Regular Basis. ☐ Yes ☐ No	43. Date When Patient Completed, or is Expected to Complete, Training MM DD YYYY

I certify that the above self-dialysis training information is correct and is based on consideration of all pertinent medical, psychological, and sociological factors as reflected in records kept by this training facility.

44. Printed Name and Signature of Physician personally familiar with the patient's training a.) Printed Name b.) Signature c.) Date MM DD YYYY	45. UPIN of Physician in Item 44

E. PHYSICIAN IDENTIFICATION

46. Attending Physician *(Print)*	47. Physician's Phone No. ( )	48. UPIN of Physician in Item 46

PHYSICIAN ATTESTATION

I certify, under penalty of perjury, that the information on this form is correct to the best of my knowledge and belief. Based on diagnostic tests and laboratory findings, I further certify that this patient has reached the stage of renal impairment that appears irreversible and permanent and requires a regular course of dialysis or kidney transplant to maintain life. I understand that this information is intended for use in establishing the patient's entitlement to Medicare benefits and that any falsification, misrepresentation, or concealment of essential information may subject me to fine, imprisonment, civil penalty, or other civil sanctions under applicable Federal laws.

49. Attending Physician's Signature of Attestation *(Same as Item 46)*	50. Date MM DD YYYY
51. Physician Recertification Signature	52. Date MM DD YYYY
53. Remarks	

F. OBTAIN SIGNATURE FROM PATIENT

I hereby authorize any physician, hospital, agency, or other organization to disclose any medical records or other information about my medical condition to the Department of Health and Human Services for purposes of reviewing my application for Medicare entitlement under the Social Security Act and/or for scientific research.

54. Signature of Patient *(Signature by mark must be witnessed.)*	55. Date MM DD YYYY

G. PRIVACY STATEMENT

The collection of this information is authorized by Section 226A of the Social Security Act. The information provided will be used to determine if an individual is entitled to Medicare under the End Stage Renal Disease provisions of the law. The information will be maintained in system No. 09-70-0520, "End Stage Renal Disease Program Management and Medical Information System (ESRD PMMIS)", published in the Federal Register, Vol. 67, No. 116, June 17, 2002, pages 41244-41250 or as updated and republished. Collection of your Social Security number is authorized by Executive Order 9397. Furnishing the information on this form is voluntary, but failure to do so may result in denial of Medicare benefits. Information from the ESRD PMMIS may be given to a congressional office in response to an inquiry from the congressional office made at the request of the individual; an individual or organization for research, demonstration, evaluation, or epidemiologic project related to the prevention of disease or disability, or the restoration or maintenance of health. Additional disclosures may be found in the *Federal Register* notice cited above. You should be aware that P.L.100-503, the Computer Matching and Privacy Protection Act of 1988, permits the government to verify information by way of computer matches.

FORM CMS-2728-U3 (06/04)   2

FIGURE 5-3

CMS Form 2746.

DEPARTMENT OF HEALTH AND HUMAN SERVICES
CENTERS FOR MEDICARE & MEDICAID SERVICES

Form Approved
OMB No. 0938-0448

ESRD DEATH NOTIFICATION
END STAGE RENAL DISEASE MEDICAL INFORMATION SYSTEM

1. Patient's Last Name | First | MI | 2. Medicare Claim Number

3. Patient's Sex
   a. ☐ Male   b. ☐ Female

4. Date of Birth
   ___ / ___ / ___ ___
   Month   Day   Year

5. Social Security Number

6. Patient's State of Residence

7. Place of Death
   a. ☐ Hospital   c. ☐ Home   e. ☐ Other
   b. ☐ Dialysis Unit d. ☐ Nursing Home

8. Date of Death
   ___ ___ / ___ ___ / ___ ___ ___ ___
   Month   Day   Year

9. Modality at Time of Death
   a. ☐ Incenter Hemodialysis   b. ☐ Home Hemodialysis   c. ☐ CAPD   d. ☐ CCPD   e. ☐ Transplant   f. ☐ Other

10. Provider Name and Address (Street)

11. Provider Number

Provider Address (City/State)

12. Causes of Death (enter codes from list on back of form)

   a. Primary Cause ___ ___ ___

   b. Were there secondary causes?

      ☐ No

      ☐ Yes, specify: ___ ___ ___   ___ ___ ___   ___ ___ ___   ___ ___ ___

   C. If cause is other (98) please specify:_____

13. Renal replacement therapy discontinued prior to death: ☐ Yes ☐ No

   If yes, check one of the following:
   a. ☐ Following HD and/or PD access failure
   b. ☐ Following transplant failure
   c. ☐ Following chronic failure to thrive
   d. ☐ Following acute medical complication
   e. ☐ Other
   f. Date of last dialysis treatment ___ ___ / ___ ___ / ___ ___ ___ ___
      Month   Day   Year

14. Was discontinuation of renal replacement therapy after patient/family request to stop dialysis?

   ☐ Yes   ☐ No

   ☐ Unknown   ☐ Not Applicable

15. If deceased ever received a transplant:
   a. Date of most recent transplant ___ ___ / ___ ___ / ___ ___ ___ ___   ☐ Unknown
      Month   Day   Year
   b. Type of transplant received
      ☐ Living Related   ☐ Living Unrelated   ☐ Deceased   ☐ Unknown
   c. Was graft functioning (patient not on dialysis) at time of death?
      ☐ Yes   ☐ No   ☐ Unknown
   d. Did transplant patient resume chronic maintenance dialysis prior to death?
      ☐ Yes   ☐ No   ☐ Unknown

16. Was patient receiving Hospice care prior to death?

   ☐ Yes   ☐ No

   ☐ Unknown

17. Name of Physician (Please print complete name) | 18. Signature of Person Completing This Form | Date

This report is required by law (42, U.S.C. 426; 20 CFR 405, Section 2133). Individually identifiable patient information will not be disclosed except as provided for in the Privacy Act of 1974 (5 U.S.C. 5520; 45 CFR Part 5a).

Form CMS-2746-U2 (08/06) EF 08/2006

Permission to reuse in accordance with http://www.cms.gov Content Reuse and Linking Policy.

QUALITY ASSESSMENT, PERFORMANCE IMPROVEMENT, AND UTILIZATION MANAGEMENT

Individual dialysis facilities must engage in quality assessment, performance improvement, and utilization management. These are also major responsibilities of the ESRD networks. Federal regulation 42 C.F.R. 405.2112 charges the ESRD networks with:

(a) Developing network goals for placing patients in settings for self-care and transplantation.

(b) Encouraging the use of medically appropriate treatment settings most compatible with patient rehabilitation and the participation of patients, providers of services, and renal disease facilities in vocational rehabilitation programs.

(c) Developing criteria and standards relating to the quality and appropriateness of patient care and, with respect to working with patients, facilities, and providers of services, for encouraging participation in vocational rehabilitation programs.

(d) Evaluating the procedures used by facilities in the network in assessing patients for placement in appropriate treatment modalities.

....

(g) Evaluating and resolving patient grievances.

(h) Appointing a network council and a medical review board (each including at least one patient representative)...

(i) Conducting on-site reviews of facilities and providers as necessary, as determined by the medical review board or CMS...

(j) Collecting, validating, and analyzing data...

(ESRD Network Organizations, 2009, pp. 258–259)

Quality Improvement

The Conditions for Coverage require each dialysis facility to conduct its own internal **quality assessment and performance improvement (QAPI)** program. The following excerpt from the Conditions for Coverage, § 494.110 provides details regarding the QAPI program:

> The dialysis facility must develop, implement, maintain, and evaluate an effective, data-driven, quality assessment and performance improvement program with participation by the professional members of the interdisciplinary team. The program must reflect the complexity of the dialysis facility's organization and services (including those services provided under arrangement), and must focus on indicators related to improved health outcomes and the prevention and reduction of medical errors. The dialysis facility must maintain and demonstrate evidence of its quality improvement and performance improvement program for review by CMS.
>
> (a) Standard: Program scope.
>
>   1. The program must include, but not be limited to, an ongoing program that achieves measurable improvement in health outcomes and reduction of medical

quality assessment and performance improvement (QAPI) the *Conditions for Coverage* require each dialysis facility to adopt a data-driven performance improvement program that utilizes indicators or performance measures associated with improved health outcomes and with the identification and reduction of medical errors.

errors by using indicators or performance measures associated with improved health outcomes and with the identification and reduction of medical errors.

2. The dialysis facility must measure, analyze, and track quality indicators or other aspects of performance that the facility adopts or develops that reflect processes of care and facility operations. These performance components must influence or relate to the desired outcomes or be the outcomes themselves. The program must include, but not be limited to, the following:
    (i) Adequacy of dialysis.
    (ii) Nutritional status.
    (iii) Mineral metabolism and renal bone disease.
    (iv) Anemia management.
    (v) Vascular access.
    (vi) Medical injuries and medical errors identification.
    (vii) Hemodialyzer reuse program, if the facility reuses hemodialyzers.
    (viii) Patient satisfaction and grievances.
    (ix) Infection control. . . .

MIPPA also required the establishment of quality incentives in the ESRD program. Provider payment rates are affected by specific performance-based measures that assess iron management (avoiding anemia), adequacy of dialysis, mortality, albumin levels, bone mineral metabolism (e.g., calcium and phosphorus control), and vascular access, including maximizing the placement of arterial venous fistulas. Providers not meeting performance standards will experience a payment reduction of up to 2 percent. (Gadzik & Raney 2010).

The ESRD networks also perform quality improvement activities for their regions. For example, the ESRD **Clinical Performance Measures (CPM) Project** collects clinical data on ESRD patients and other performance data related to dialysis facilities and clinicians (CMS, 2009, December 24). According to the *Medicare ESRD Network Organizations Manual*, the networks are responsible for developing and conducting quality improvement projects based on the CPMs for "adequacy of dialysis, anemia management, and vascular access, or other CPMs developed or adopted by CMS" (CMS, 2003, p. 2).

The CPM project has resulted in significant quality improvement over the years. For example, in 2003, 87% of patients received adequate hemodialysis, compared to only 43% in 1994. Also in 2003, 80% of patients had a mean hemoglobin greater than 11, compared to only 46% in 1994 (CMS, 2006).

As part of the value-based purchasing program discussed in the "Reimbursement" section of this chapter, CMS implemented the ESRD Quality Incentive Program (QIP). The measures used in this program are reviewed regularly, and typically are refined and changed annually. An overall total performance score (TPS) is calculated for each facility based on the QIP measures. For example, the final rule for 2016 established clinical measures and reporting measures that make up the total performance score, with 75% of the score determined by clinical measures and 25% determined by reporting measures. The total performance score for each facility is reported at the Dialysis Facility Compare website, to allow patients and others to compare the performance scores of different facilities. Figure 5-4 lists the measures for payment year (PY) 2016.

Clinical Performance Measures (CPM) Project an ongoing project of CMS, implemented through the ESRD networks, to measure and report the quality of renal dialysis services provided under the Medicare program.

FIGURE 5-4

ESRD QIP measures for Performance Year (PY) 2016

PY 2016 Measures: Overview

Clinical Measures – 75% of Total Performance Score (TPS)

1. Anemia Management – Hgb >12 g/dL
2. Kt/V Dialysis Adequacy Measure Topic – Adult Hemodialysis
3. Kt/V Dialysis Adequacy Measure Topic – Adult Peritoneal Dialysis
4. Kt/V Dialysis Adequacy Measure Topic – Pediatric Hemodialysis
5. Vascular Access Type Measure Topic – Arteriovenous Fistula (AVF)
6. Vascular Access Type Measure Topic – Catheter ≥90 days
☆ 7. National Healthcare Safety Network (NHSN) Bloodstream Infection in Hemodialysis Outpatients
☆ 8. Hypercalcemia

Reporting Measures – 25% of TPS

1. In-Center Hemodialysis Consumer
   Assessment of Healthcare Providers and Systems
   (ICH CAHPS) Patient Satisfaction Survey (expanded)
2. Mineral Metabolism – Serum Phosphorus
3. Anemia Management

☆ **New measure for PY 2016**

Permission to reuse in accordance with http://www.cms.gov Content Reuse and Linking Policy.

In the past, CPM data were collected on a statistically significant sample of patients, but the implementation of CROWNWeb allows data needed for performance measures to be submitted electronically to the networks and to CMS for all patients.

Other projects have included the Elab project to collect results from lab tests for performance-improvement purposes, and the Fistula First breakthrough initiative to increase the number of hemodialysis patients using arteriovenous fistulas for dialysis access.

Clinical practice guidelines represent another quality improvement mechanism. The National Kidney Foundation (NKF) has developed evidence-based guidelines as a component of a project called the Kidney Disease Outcomes Quality Initiative (KDOQI). KDOQI has published four sets of clinical practice guidelines for dialysis care: for hemodialysis adequacy, for peritoneal dialysis adequacy, for vascular access, and for cardiovascular disease in dialysis patients.

In addition, KDOQI has issued several sets of guidelines for care of patients with chronic kidney disease (CKD), including treatment of anemia in chronic kidney disease, bone metabolism and disease in chronic kidney disease, among others. KDOQI has an established process for maintenance and revision of guidelines, as well as principles for determining when new guideline topics are needed (NKF, 2010). CMS has incorporated outcome measures from the KDOQI guidelines into its clinical performance measures.

Utilization Management (UM)

In each dialysis facility, an interdisciplinary team assesses and develops a plan of care for each dialysis patient. As a part of this process, the team must consider the suitability of the patient for a transplant referral. Patients who have kidney transplants generally have higher survival rates, a better quality of life, and lower overall medical costs than do patients on dialysis. Therefore, one aspect of utilization management in a dialysis program involves making it possible for patients to leave dialysis by referring them for transplant when appropriate.

When making recommendations for transplant referral, the interdisciplinary team must consider the criteria developed by the prospective transplantation center. The patient is a vital member of the interdisciplinary team as well, and the patient's desire regarding transplantation is an important consideration. It is still incumbent upon the clinicians on the team, though, to educate the patient about the advantages and disadvantages of various modalities of renal replacement therapy. The patient's nephrologist, a registered dietitian, a qualified social worker, and a registered nurse participate with the patient in determining the type of treatment that would be best for him or her.

Data submitted to the ESRD networks also are used by the networks and CMS to study overall utilization patterns. For example, the networks may examine laboratory values submitted through CROWNWeb to evaluate trends in their regions regarding the appropriateness of initiation of dialysis.

SELF REVIEW 5.6

1. What are three responsibilities of the ESRD networks according to federal regulation 42 C.F.R. 405.2112?

2. True or False? MIPPA required the establishment of quality incentives in the ESRD program.

3. What are the four sets of clinical practice guidelines for dialysis care established by the Kidney Disease Outcomes Quality Initiative?

4. In each dialysis facility an interdisciplinary team develops a plan of care for each patient. Who are the members that make up this team?

5. True or False? Patients who have kidney transplants generally have lower survival rates and higher overall medical costs than do patients on dialysis.

6. True or False? The networks and CMS use data submitted by the ESRD to study overall utilization patterns.

7. The total performance score for each facility is reported at the _____ website, to allow patients and others to compare the performance scores of different facilities.

RISK MANAGEMENT, LEGAL, AND ETHICAL ISSUES

Many of the legal issues in a dialysis facility are the same as in any other health care facility. The patient must give consent to treatment, must authorize the release of medical information, and has the right to expect that the confidentiality of clinical information will be protected. Records also must be protected against loss, destruction, or unauthorized use (42 C.F.R. 494.170). Because dialysis facilities are "covered entities" under the Health Insurance Portability and Accountability Act of 1996 (HIPAA), they must comply with all of HIPAA's privacy, security, and transactions standards. Dialysis treatment facilities may release protected health information to the ESRD networks as public policy disclosures required by law for health oversight. The facilities must be able to provide an accounting of disclosures to its patients as mandated by HIPAA and the HITECH Act (see Chapter 1), so facilities should maintain records of their disclosures to the ESRD networks and other regulatory authorities, and facilities with an EHR should develop systems to provide the necessary accounting for all disclosures.

The retention period for clinical information on dialysis patients, according to federal statute, is 6 years after the patient's discharge, transfer, or death. Of course, when the requirements of state law are more stringent than the federal regulations, the state retention statutes must be followed.

Because the success of dialysis treatment depends largely on patient compliance, clinical professionals must document patient education. They also should record action taken when the patient is not complying with the treatment regimen.

As a long-term life-sustaining treatment, renal replacement therapy has been a focal point for numerous ethical issues. For example, a disruptive, abusive patient can create unsafe conditions for other patients in a dialysis facility. An ethical and legal dilemma in this situation arises in determining whether or how the health care provider may transfer or discharge such a patient, given that the patient's life depends on continued dialysis.

Kidney transplant is also a type of renal replacement therapy and, unlike many other types of transplants, a kidney may be obtained from a living donor. This brings its own unique set of ethical issues, ranging from the competency of the prospective donor to the suitability of the prospective recipient (Friedman, 2000). As with other life-saving measures, additional ethical issues surround the initiation of and withdrawal from dialysis. The Renal Physicians Association and the American Society of Nephrology have addressed this subject through the development of a comprehensive clinical practice guideline and tool kit entitled *Shared Decision-Making in the Appropriate Initiation of and Withdrawal from Dialysis* (RPA/ASN, 2000).

1. True or False? Dialysis facilities are not considered to be covered entities under HIPAA and, therefore, do not have to comply with all of HIPAA's privacy, security, and transactions standards.
2. What is the retention period for clinical information on dialysis patients?
3. True or False? Patient compliance plays a role in the success of dialysis treatment, so documentation of patient information is important.

ROLE OF THE HEALTH INFORMATION MANAGEMENT PROFESSIONAL

PROFESSIONAL SPOTLIGHT   QUALITY IMPROVEMENT ANALYST

Who I am: My name is Kristi Durham, and I have a bachelor's degree in health information administration.

Where I work: Network 8, Inc., in Ridgeland, Mississippi

What I do: I oversee the Healthcare Associated Infection Learning and Action Network (HAI LAN) for Network 8, an End-Stage Renal Disease Network serving the three-state area of Tennessee, Alabama, and Mississippi. The HAI-LAN is tasked with promoting the CDC's infection prevention tools to dialysis facilities in our coverage area. We also conduct quality improvement activities that monitor specific measures and give the facilities data about their performance on these measures. I also coordinate the HAI LAN workgroup that meets to develop activities that will take place throughout the contract year. The other members of the workgroup include dialysis facility managers, regional managers for dialysis providers, representatives from the Quality Improvement Organization in our area, and the Mississippi and Tennessee Departments of Health.

A recent initiative in which I am involved is the National Healthcare Safety Network (NHSN). The NHSN is a new electronic system into which providers enter dialysis event information. I oversee that process for our network, educating facilities on the enrollment process and monitoring data quality. The facilities confer viewing rights to us so we can see dialysis event data. I monitor the system and do monthly data checks to assure that the data are entered correctly. The reports include IV anti-microbial starts, positive blood cultures, and signs of infection at the vascular access site, which enables the system to generate measures for bloodstream infections, local access site infections, and so on.

I analyze the data to make sure that the reports make sense, to determine whether facilities are overreporting, underreporting, and similar checks. As the system matures, the findings will be studied and reported to CMS, and feedback provided by CMS will be taken back to the facilities. I also take patient grievance calls, working as a mediator between the patient and the facility to help resolve the situation.

I'm really enjoying this contact with patients and helping to solve problems, which can range from something as simple as the temperature in the facility to a serious concern about quality of care issues.

Why HIM knowledge is important in my role: To be able to conduct quality-of-care reviews, knowledge of the patient record and understanding how to review documentation are essential in this role. I also use the training that I received in statistical methods more in this job than in any previous position. Database management is a big part of what I do, and I have used those skills in every job that I have had.

Other information: Earlier in my career, I was a medical record manager for a behavioral health care clinic and also worked as a government contractor. Before moving into my present position, I was employed in the performance improvement department at a large academic medical center. In that position, I worked with Surgical Care Improvement Project (SCIP) measures, root cause analyses, and Plan-Do-Study-Act (PDSA) cycles with various departments. This provided a good background when I joined Network 8, because of an annual quality improvement activity involving 20% of the facilities in our region for which we provide data and assistance to the facilities in analyzing processes that may have to be revised.

Health information management (HIM) professionals practice in a variety of roles in ERSD health care. A health information manager may work fulltime for an organization providing dialysis services or as a consultant. In this role, the HIM professional is concerned with procedures related to the documentation, storage, retrieval, and security of individual patient records. The consultant provides advice on the development of systems to provide timely, appropriately accessible patient information to caregivers and administrators. A consultant visits the dialysis unit periodically to review a sample of records and to discuss procedures for record maintenance with facility staff. Often, several dialysis units are owned by a single entity, such as a corporation. In this type of arrangement, the company headquarters may employ an HIM professional fulltime to assist all of the units with HIM issues.

The ESRD networks also employ health information professionals. A health information manager may work as a data coordinator, a quality improvement coordinator, a quality manager, or even as an executive director in an ESRD network.

SELF REVIEW 5.7

1. What are two tasks for which the Healthcare Associated Infection Learning and Action Network (HAI-LAN) is responsible?

2. According to Kristi Durham, knowledge of the patient record and understanding how to review documentation is a vital part of her role. What other skills does she use in her daily role?

3. Give four examples of roles that a Health Information Professional may have when employed by an ESRD network.

4. Briefly describe a Health Information Professional's role as a consultant within an ESRD health care organization.

SUMMARY

Dialysis facilities treat patients who are experiencing renal failure as a result of Stage 5 chronic kidney disease—also known as end-stage renal disease, ESRD. The two types of dialysis are hemodialysis and peritoneal dialysis. Hemodialysis usually is administered by nurses and technicians in a dialysis facility, but it may also be self-administered by the patient at home. Peritoneal dialysis is a portable process that can be self-administered by the patient at home or in a variety of locations.

Interdisciplinary teams of registered and licensed nurses, technicians, physicians, dietitians, and social workers, along with the patient, plan and administer the dialysis treatment regimen. Health information management professionals can assist in ensuring that the patient records are documented and preserved properly.

Most freestanding dialysis units must meet the federal guidelines for ESRD facilities, because Medicare is the chief funding source for these facilities. Therefore, the federal documentation requirements in the Conditions for Coverage represent the minimum guidelines for quantity and quality of documentation for dialysis patient records. Other federal regulations include the ESRD prospective payment system, which bundles services into a single per-treatment rate and standardized data set reporting, which is accomplished electronically through CROWNWeb.

Information management for dialysis facilities requires the implementation of systems to meet a variety of needs. Not only must information be coded and transmitted for reimbursement purposes, but data must be submitted to the ESRD networks for quality improvement and utilization management. Dialysis facilities also conduct their own quality assessment and performance improvement (QAPI) programs. Medicare's quality incentive program affects reimbursement through payment reductions to facilities that do not meet standards. Electronic health record systems are commonly used for information management in the dialysis facility setting.

A health information manager can play several roles in the dialysis health care system. HIM professionals provide services both in treatment settings (ESRD dialysis units) and in regulatory settings (ESRD networks). HIM professionals work in positions extending from medical record supervisor to executive director.

REVIEW QUESTIONS

Knowledge-Based Questions

1. Explain the following types of care given to end-stage renal disease patients: hemodialysis, CAPD, and CCPD.
2. Who performs regular surveys of dialysis facilities? Who performs validation surveys of dialysis facilities?
3. What items of information should be documented for each dialysis patient?
4. What is the source of payment for most patients who have been on dialysis for more than 30 months?
5. What role do the ESRD networks play in the collection and aggregation of data on dialysis patients?

6. What types of QAPI activities take place in dialysis facilities?
7. What are possible roles for the health information manager in organizations dealing with end-stage renal disease?

Critical Thinking Questions

1. Compare and contrast ESRD networks with quality improvement organizations.
2. What resources would a health information consultant find helpful in consulting for ESRD facilities?

WEB ACTIVITY

Visit the website http://www.medicare.gov

1. Scroll down and select "Find Dialysis Facilities." This will take you to the "Dialysis Facility Compare" website.
2. Explore the Dialysis Facility Compare website to find and compare information on dialysis facilities:
   a. Find three dialysis facilities near your location by entering your zip code to see a list of dialysis facilities in your area.
   b. Compare the three facilities by reviewing information at the links to "General information," "Best treatment practices," and "Hospitalizations & deaths."
   c. Based on the comparison you just made, which of the three facilities do you think you would prefer if you were a dialysis patient, or do you think the differences are negligible?
3. Now go back to the Dialysis Facility Compare homepage to look at the Quality Incentive Program (QIP) data.
   a. Select the link for the Quality Incentive Program.

   b. Select links to each of the performance measures that are in effect for the current year and for each measure select a specific facility to review by clicking on the menu symbol to the left of the facility's name; then click the pop up menu to "View Single Row Data."
   c. Compare the facility's performance on each measure to the national average. (You may have to scroll down to see the data.)
   d. After looking at the individual measures, click the link to the Total Performance Scores.
   e. Select a facility and click the menu symbol to "Select Single Row Data."
   f. Scroll down if necessary, and compare your selected facility's Total Performance Score to the National Average. Is your facility's score higher or lower than the national average? How would you interpret this score? If you were selecting a dialysis facility for yourself or a family member, would you consider this facility? Which factors would influence your decision most?

CASE STUDY

Kay Carnes has begun consulting for a dialysis facility that began using an electronic health record system approximately six months ago. On her first consultation visit, she examined both the electronic and paper portions of the patient record. She found that certain portions of the record, which were not included in the electronic health record, were maintained in sturdy three-ring binders. These binders were labeled on the spine with the patient's name and the patient's treatment schedule (e.g., John Doe, M-W-F, or Mary Smith, T-T-S).

The paper-based portion of the record included signed consent forms, assessment forms, outside lab reports, history and physical examination reports from the patient's physician or last hospital visit, identification data, CMS data collection forms, and patient plans of care. The electronic portion of the record included data from each dialysis treatment and progress notes from the nurses, the dietitian, and the social worker.

On some of the older records in which all of the progress notes were handwritten, Kay noticed that the physicians had recorded monthly progress notes, but there were no progress notes from the physicians in the electronic portion of the record that covered the past six months. Kay asked the unit director, a registered nurse, about this. The director replied that all of the other disciplines were entering their own progress notes into the electronic health record during or after each patient contact. The physicians were accustomed to handwriting their progress notes and, therefore, did not use the computer. The physicians had continued to see each patient monthly, but the chart had little documentation to indicate this after the electronic health record had been implemented.

1. What issues should Kay address in her consultation report to this facility?
2. What recommendations would you make if you were in her place?

REFERENCES AND SUGGESTED READINGS

CMS (Centers for Medicare & Medicaid Services). (2003). Chapter 5—Quality improvement. *Medicare ESRD Network Organizations Manual.* [Online]. http://www.cms.gov/ manuals/downloads/eno114c5.pdf [2010, July 5].

CMS (Centers for Medicare & Medicaid Services). (2006, January 27). *Summary of the ESRD Network Program.* [Online]. http://www.cms.gov/ESRDNetworOrganizations/Downloads/ESRDNetworkProgramBackgroundpublic.pdf [2010, May 8].

CMS (Centers for Medicare & Medicaid Services). (2008, April 15). 42 C.F.R. pts. 405, 410, 413, 414, 488, & 494. Medicare and Medicaid programs; Conditions for coverage for end-stage renal disease facilities; Final rule. [Online]. http://www.cms.hhs.gov/CFCsAndCoPs/downloads/ESRDfinalrule0415.pdf [2015, October 6].

CMS (Centers for Medicare & Medicaid Services, Office of Public Affairs). (2009, September 15). Press Release: CMS proposes new prospective payment system for renal dialysis facilities. [Online]. https://www.cms.gov/Newsroom/MediaReleaseDatabase/Press-releases/2009-Press-releases-items/2009-09-15.html [2015, October 6].

CMS (Centers for Medicare & Medicaid Services). (2009, December 24). Clinical Performance Measures (CPM) Project. [Online]. http://www.cms.gov/CPMProject [2015, October 6].

CMS (Centers for Medicare & Medicaid Services). (2010). End-stage renal disease (ESRD) payment. [Online]. https://www.cms.gov/Center/Special-Topic/End-Stage-Renal-Disease-ESRD-Center.html [2015, October 6].

Conditions for Coverage for end-stage renal disease facilities. (2008). Final Rule, 73 Fed. Reg. 20370-20484 (to be codified at 42 C.F.R. pt. 494.)

DHHS (Department of Health and Human Services). (2012). Medicare coverage of kidney dialysis & kidney transplant services. [Online]. http://www.medicare.gov/Pubs/pdf/10128.pdf [2015, October 6].

End-stage renal disease prospective payment system, final rule and proposed rule, 75 Fed. Reg. 49030-49214 (August 12, 2010).

ESRD Comorbidity conditions. (2012, February 28). ESRD Payment. [Online]. http://www.cms.gov/Medicare/Medicare-Fee-for-Service-Payment/ESRDpayment/Comorbidity_Conditions.html [2015, October 6].

ESRD network organizations. (2009 ed.). *Code of Federal Regulations*, Title 42, Part 405, Section 405.2112.

Forum of ESRD Networks. (2001). Medical record model. [Online]. http://esrdnetworks.org/resources/medicalrecordsmodel.pdf [2015, October 6].

Friedman, E. A. (2000). *Legal and Ethical Concerns in Treating Kidney Failure: Case Study Workbook.* Dordrecht, The Netherlands: Kluwer Academic Publishers.

Gadzik, D., & Raney, D. A. (2010, March 25). Procedural coding for dialysis services. Chicago: AHIMA Audio Seminar.

How to sign up for Medicare if you have end-stage renal disease (ESRD). (n.d.). [Online]. http://www.medicare.gov/people-like-me/esrd/getting-medicare-with-esrd.html [2015, October 6].

Mayo Clinic. (2013, May 21). *Peritoneal dialysis: Risks.* [Online]. http://www.mayoclinic.org/tests-procedures/peritoneal-dialysis/basics/risks/prc-20013164 [2015, October 6].

McAfee, L. (1987). A consultant's guide to renal dialysis units. *Journal of the American Medical Record Association, 58*(7), 44–46.

National Kidney and Urologic Diseases Clearinghouse. (2009, April). *Financial Help for Treatment of Kidney Failure.* [Online]. http://kidney.niddk.nih.gov/kudiseases/pubs/financialhelp/#medicare [2010, May 24].

NKF (National Kidney Foundation). (2010). *The National Kidney Foundation Kidney Disease Outcomes Quality Initiative (NKF KDOQI ™).* [Online].

http://www.kidney.org/professionals/KDOQI/ [2010, July 6].

OPTN (Organ Procurement and Transplantation Network). (2010). *About OPTN.* [Online]. http://optn.transplant.hrsa.gov [2010, May 8].

RPA/ASN (Renal Physicians Association & American Society of Nephrology). (2000). *Shared Decision-Making in the Appropriate Initiation of and Withdrawal from Dialysis* (Clinical Practice Guideline No. 2). Washington, DC: Authors.

UNC Kidney Center. (n.d.). *Kidney transplant.* [Online]. http://www.unckidneycenter.org /kidneyhealthlibrary/kidneytransplant.pdf [2015, October 6].

UNOS (United Network for Organ Sharing). (2010). *Data.* [Online]. http://www.unos.org/data/ [2010, May 8].

USRDS (U.S. Renal Data System). (2013). Treatment modalities. *2013 USRDS Annual Data Report,* Table D. [Online]. http://www.usrds.org/reference .aspx [2015, October 6].

KEY RESOURCES

American Association of Kidney Patients
http://www.aakp.org

American Nephrology Nurses Association
http:// www.annanurse.org

American Society of Nephrology
http://www.asn-online.org

American Society of Transplantation
http://www.a-s-t.org

American Society of Transplant Surgeons
http://www.asts.org

Association of Organ Procurement Organizations
http://www.aopo.org

Forum of End-Stage Renal Disease Networks
http://www.esrdnetworks.org

National Association for Nephrology Technicians/ Technologists
http://www.dialysistech.net

National Renal Administrators Association
http://www.nraa.org

Project CROWNWeb
http://www.projectcrownweb.org

Renal Physicians Association
http://www.renalmd.org

United Network for Organ Sharing
http://www.unos.org

CHAPTER 6

Correctional Facilities

Carisa Nixon, RHIA | Nina Dozoretz, MA, RHIA, CCHP |
Barbara Manny, MS, RHIA | Brianna McCloe Rogers, RHIA

LEARNING OBJECTIVES

Upon successful completion of this chapter, you should be able to:

- Identify the types of correctional facilities and the responsible authority for each.
- Identify the various health care delivery models that exist in correctional institutions.
- Distinguish among the various types of licensure and certification available for correctional professionals.
- Recognize the different accrediting organizations for correctional health care and the strengths and weaknesses of each.
- Identify the role of HIPAA in correctional facilities.
- Describe situations in which the application of technology can help to reduce costs and increase access to health care.

Setting	Description	Synonyms/Examples
Prisons	Individual facilities operated by a unit of a state or the federal government for the confinement of adults 18 years or older convicted of a felony, whose sentence exceeds one year (Anno, 1992).	The three classifications for prisons are: maximum, medium, and minimum security.
Jails	Institutions intended for adults, usually administered by local units of government (i.e., cities or counties) with the authority to detain for a period of 48 hours or longer (ACA, 1985). Some adult facilities hold juveniles for less than one year or hold them pending trial, awaiting sentencing, or awaiting transfer to other facilities after a conviction (BJS, 2009).	In various locations these facilities may be known as detention centers, county prisons, or workhouses.
Juvenile Detention Facilities	Facilities operated by a unit of government for the confinement of individuals younger than 18 years of age.	
Bureau of Immigration and Customs Enforcement (ICE)	ICE-owned, -operated, or -contracted detention centers are used to hold individuals placed into administrative detention during periods of investigation into their legal status or resolution of a removal order.	
Correctional facilities operated by the Army, Navy, Air Force, or Marines	All branches of the U.S. military operate their own correctional facilities in the United States and overseas.	
Shelters or Halfway Houses	Incarcerated individuals may be released to community residential facilities as a means of completing their sentences or making the transition back to society by receiving substance abuse, rehabilitative, and/or vocational services.	

INTRODUCTION TO SETTING

Over the past century, the correctional industry in the United States underwent dramatic changes as crime rates increased and the **inmate** population grew dramatically. The greatest increase occurred between 1980 and 1990, when the total prison population increased more than 200% (ACA, 1993). The Bureau of Justice Statistics reported that 1,574,700 prisoners were held in prisons and jails nationwide as of December 31, 2009 (BJS, 2013).

inmate a person who is confined to a correctional institution such as a prison.

U.S. correctional institutions are complex organizations. Their purpose is to enhance public safety by separating persons who are deemed a threat to other individuals or their property from the larger population. Each level of government—federal, state, county, and city—is responsible for the operation of some type of correctional facility. The various levels of government operate independently of each other, and even the operation of correctional facilities within the same system varies. This chapter provides health information managers with a general understanding of the nature of correctional institutions and the role of health information management in delivering health care in correctional settings.

Delivering health care to inmates was not of great concern until the early 1970s, when civil rights advocates and health professionals began to take a serious look at the lack of health care services available to inmates. At that time, the conditions under which inmates lived became widely known.

Before 1970, few efforts were made to identify and change the status of health care delivery in correctional facilities. A common misconception was that **prisons** provided better health care than **jails** did. Jails typically lacked the funds necessary to maintain an infirmary, so treatment often was provided by the emergency departments of community hospitals. Prison inmates rarely were sent outside of the system for care, because prisons were more likely to have some type of medical care available on-site. Prison health care staffs usually were not as well trained as their peers working in the private or public sector. The health care staff practicing in correctional institutions often consisted of physicians with restricted licenses or unlicensed foreign medical graduates. The support staff often included unlicensed former medical corpsmen and untrained inmate "nurses" (Anno, 1992). Today, health services in prisons are typically provided by practitioners who are licensed, certified, or registered to practice, in the same manner as required in the community (Anno, 2004).

prisons facilities operated by a unit of the state or federal government for the confinement of adults convicted of a felony whose sentence exceeds one year.

jails institutions administered by local units of government (i.e., cities or counties) with the authority to detain adults for a period of 48 hours or longer and to confine adults convicted of misdemeanors whose sentence does not exceed one year.

Federal and state laws alike affect prisoners' rights. In general, prisoners lose some of their civil rights, such as the right to vote, when they are incarcerated. The Eighth Amendment to the U.S. Constitution, however, prohibits cruel and unusual punishment—which means that prisons must provide a minimum standard of living for prisoners. Also, the Fourteenth Amendment's Equal Protection Clause protects prisoners against unequal treatment on the basis of race, sex, and creed. Prisoners also have limited rights to speech and religion. Other constitutional rights that apply to prisoners include due process in the right to administrative appeals and a right of access to the parole process (Legal Information Institute, n.d.).

In 1976, the landmark case *Estelle v. Gamble* created a "right" to health care for inmates. The case applied a two-prong test to determine the extent of the medical care duty owed to inmates. Correctional institutions would be in violation of inmates' constitutional rights if (1) correctional officials showed a "deliberate indifference" to inmates' medical needs and (2) the inmates' needs were "serious." The vagueness of language used in the court's ruling and the creation of a "right" to health care has created enormous difficulties for correctional institutions, including a continuous rise in inmate petitions claiming violations of their "right" to health care (Posner, 1992).

Today, inmates receive treatment for AIDS (acquired immune deficiency syndrome), cardiovascular disease, and even rehabilitation services. The physical settings have changed substantially and can range from small infirmaries to large medical facilities with specialty clinics. The typical prison clinic today looks much like an ambulatory health facility outside of the prison. It usually has a trauma room, exam rooms, laboratory, radiological suite, pharmacy or medication room, and dental operatories—all of which are reasonably supplied and equipped (Anno, 2004). Advocates for correctional health care seek the availability of even more extensive and expensive treatment and facilities.

Organizational structure and methods of administration vary depending on the level of government operating a facility, corresponding laws and court orders, and characteristics of the incarcerated populations. Health information management professionals should fully understand the structure of the correctional facility and government with which they intend to work.

There is still little empirical data available about the correctional health care delivery systems in operation around the United States. Several organizations have conducted studies and continue to examine the state of correctional health care delivery systems, but large-scale research efforts are needed to provide current, accurate information about the state of correctional health care.

State Departments of Correction

The traditional organizational model places responsibility for health services with wardens. In this model, health professionals must report directly to the warden, which does not promote consistency in the policies and procedures used to operate a health care delivery system. It also can be a source of conflict and ethical concern for health care professionals if the warden is not sympathetic to the health care needs of inmates.

Placing a health services program within a state **department of corrections (DOC)** may be an indication of the perceived importance of health services (Anno, 2001). Such placement provides centralized fiscal management, standardized operations, and reduces potential for conflict between health professionals and prison administration.

department of corrections (DOC) a division of state government responsible for the operation of prisons.

The use of a statewide **health services director (HSD)** is common. An HSD is responsible for overseeing the health care delivery system, developing statewide policies and procedures, and approving the health services budget. An ideal arrangement would have an HSD as head of a separate division, with direct access to the head of the DOC. To be hired, an HSD must have had clinical and administrative experience (Anno, 1992).

health services director (HSD) an individual responsible for the administration and operation of health services within a prison system or DOC.

In the late 1980s, several state DOCs still used the traditional organizational model—meaning that they had no one at the central office with full-time responsibility for overseeing health services, and the health professionals reported to the warden. Historically, an individual might have been responsible for "programs," which could include anything from food service to mental and medical health care. Health professionals may experience difficulties reporting to wardens, because wardens are nonmedical personnel. If the wardens are not progressive correctional administrators, the focus of the health staff could be shifted away from providing adequate care (Anno, 1992).

National Commission on Correctional Health Care (NCCHC)   a national association that offers voluntary accreditation of the health services in correctional facilities.

A survey conducted in 1999 by the National Commission on Correctional Health Care (NCCHC) (Anno, 2001) received responses from 28 (54% percent) of the 52 prison systems surveyed. Because of the low response rate, no definitive conclusions can be drawn about the extent to which states have abandoned the traditional model. All but one of the 28 prison systems, however, had at least one fulltime person operating a central health office for the DOC, and some systems had more than 75 persons employed in the DOC central health office. Of the 28 systems, 21 operated health services with contracted staff instead of or in addition to DOC employees. Only seven prison systems operated their DOC health services solely with their own employees (Anno, 2001).

Operation by State versus Contracted Firms

Correctional facilities have used contracted services for many years, mainly for ancillary services. The first such contract occurred in 1978 at a state correctional facility. The health services contracted out include: mental health, dental services, and clinical services. Supporters of contract firms cite cost reductions to the state and improvements in the efficiency and quality of care as justifications for contracting services. Critics claim that state-operated services can be cost-effective and that savings realized by firms are accomplished at the expense of inmates (Anno, 2001).

Critics also argue that for-profit correctional facilities have no incentive to spend money on adequate health services or appropriate facilities and that the government alone is responsible for punishing criminals. Supporters of private enterprise cite profit as their motive for providing inmates with adequately equipped facilities and appropriate medical care, thereby reducing their risk of litigation. Profit also is an incentive for using proactive policies and programs to hold down costs—something government bureaucracies have been reluctant and unable to do.

Prisons

A prison confines, houses, feeds, clothes, educates, and polices its population. Responsibility for the operation of most prisons falls under the authority of a state DOC. Within a state system, wardens or superintendents run individual prisons. Wardens have more or less complete control over the operation of their prison, so administrative policies and procedures may differ greatly from facility to facility.

Prisons are classified by their level of security, as follows.

- *Maximum security prisons* have heavily armed guards and high fences and walls, as well as extremely restrictive rules for controlling the movement of inmates. These facilities house the inmates who have the longest sentences.

- *Medium security prisons* have slightly less restrictive rules and facilities. Individuals convicted of misdemeanors—offenses less serious than felonies—are kept in medium security prisons.

- *Minimum security prisons* offer the least restrictive rules and facilities. They house individuals convicted of nonviolent crimes such as forgery and obstruction of justice.

The physical structure of prisons is determined in part by the population of prisoners and the security measures required for their confinement. Common configurations include structures that resemble a wheel hub and spokes. The hub usually houses a main security center, and the spokes contain the cells. Other common designs resemble a long pole with intersecting shorter poles with cells, or a campus resembling small groups of apartment buildings (*World Book Encyclopedia*, 1996).

The **Federal Bureau of Prisons (FBP)**, established in 1930 by an act of Congress, is under the direction of the U.S. Department of Justice. The FBP operates more than 100 federal facilities, including penitentiaries, prison camps, and metropolitan correctional/detention centers. The FBP encourages inmates to participate in a range of programs that will help them live crime-free upon their release (USDOJ, n.d.). Federal prisons house individuals charged and convicted of crimes against the United States, such as kidnapping. The FBP is headquartered in Washington, DC, but the administration of facilities is divided into six regions across the country (ACA, 1996).

Federal Bureau of Prisons (FBP) a division of the U.S. Department of Justice, responsible for the administration and operation of federal correctional facilities, including penitentiaries, prison camps, and metropolitan correctional centers.

An individual awaiting trial in federal courts may be free on bond or may be detained by the U.S. Marshals Service. A person who has not been sentenced but is incarcerated while awaiting trial is a **detainee**, whereas a *prisoner* has been tried and sentenced to a period of incarceration. The U.S. Marshals Service must place detainees in custody in an appropriate facility but cannot place detainees in a federal prison. The U.S. Marshals Service ordinarily contracts with local jails, which must meet certain criteria, to house detainees.

detainee a person held in custody awaiting trial or disposition.

Initial health screenings of inmates are carried out within 24 hours of admission to correctional facilities. The screening begins the inmate's health record. Treatment available to inmates during their confinement varies greatly by the type and location of the facility. Variations in levels of care result from financial considerations, characteristics of the inmate population, or availability of resources. Some correctional institutions have little more than an examination room and a visiting physician, whereas others have on-site hospitals with mental health, rehabilitation, and substance abuse services.

Jails

Jails are generally the responsibility of local governments. Sheriffs who are elected officials administer most jails. Reporting to the sheriff is a county administrator or a board of county commissioners. A police chief reports to the administrator or board and oversees law enforcement, and a corrections director oversees administration of the jails. In some areas, a DOC may have been developed to administer county and/or municipal jails. The FBP has its own jails in several cities, which hold individuals awaiting trial in federal courts. Some areas of the

United States have federal courts but no federal detention facility. In these areas, the FBP contracts with the local jail to house the federal pretrial prisoners.

The three primary purposes for jails are (1) to detain those awaiting trial after arrest; (2) to hold those being transferred to a state or federal prison or mental facility; and (3) to incarcerate those serving a sentence of less than a year for a minor crime (misdemeanor).

The three types of jails are: detention, sentenced, and detention sentenced. A *detention jail* is solely for the confinement of those awaiting trial. *Sentenced jails* are for those serving misdemeanor sentences, and *detention-sentenced jails* house both detainees and individuals who have been sentenced (Miller, 1978).

Occasionally, jails are used to house inmates in an effort to alleviate overcrowding in prisons. Typically, a prison has a contractual agreement with a jail for a specific number of beds. As soon as space becomes available at the prison, the inmates are transferred out of the jail. Housing prisoners in jails is only a temporary solution to the problem of overcrowding in prisons.

The provision of health services in jails is the responsibility of the sheriff. Some jurisdictions require screening (upon intake) for communicable diseases such as tuberculosis and venereal diseases, but all jails perform medical examinations after booking procedures have been completed. Some courts have required the screening of intoxicated persons and continuous monitoring throughout the detoxification period. This is a necessary precaution, because intoxication often masks symptoms of fractures, diabetes, and illnesses that could be mistaken for drunkenness.

Most jails do not have on-site medical facilities. The jails that do usually have only an examination room and an office. Most large urban jails have a separate infirmary with beds for inmates who are too ill to remain in their cells but not ill enough to be transferred to a hospital. Inmates can be isolated in an infirmary bed to prevent the spread of communicable diseases and sometimes when their treatment includes devices that could be used as weapons, such as crutches.

Juvenile Facilities

juvenile detention facility a facility operated by a unit of government for the confinement of individuals under 18 years of age.

Before the nineteenth century, juveniles were confined along with adults, and in some jails this still occurs. Today, there are two main types of **juvenile detention facility**: short-term and long-term. Responsibility for juvenile facilities belongs either to the state department of corrections or to the local county.

Short-term facilities include detention centers, shelters, and reception and diagnostic centers. *Detention centers* are similar to county jails in appearance and function. These centers are used to hold juveniles awaiting jurisdictional or dispositional hearings. *Shelters* are used for dependent and neglected juveniles and usually are not secure buildings. Public shelters typically house only children awaiting a court order or those confined by a public welfare agency. *Reception* and *diagnostic centers* are basically way stations for juveniles moving from short-term to long-term facilities. The juveniles received are screened, diagnosed, and sent to an appropriate facility based on the diagnosis. Short-term facilities often are part of state-operated juvenile systems (Klempner, 1981).

Long-term facilities include training schools, ranches, group homes, and halfway houses. *Training schools* typically are located in rural areas. The primary purpose of training schools is the reeducation and development of juvenile offenders. Juveniles learn vocational skills and can complete their high school equivalency examination (GED). *Ranches, camps,* and *farms* also are found in rural settings, and they tend to offer fewer academic and vocational programs. *Group homes* generally are found in urban environments and house approximately 15 to 30 juveniles each. These facilities are not secure, and residents usually attend school or have jobs. *Halfway homes* are similar to group homes. They are generally used for first-time offenders, those almost ready for release, and sometimes for juveniles with no other available living arrangements (Klempner, 1981).

Responsibility for health services at juvenile facilities rests with the authority responsible for their operation. Some juvenile facilities are within the jurisdiction of the state DOC, and others are run by a county authority. Health care services in juvenile facilities are similar to those found in other types of correctional institutions. Depending on the size of the facility, characteristics of the inmate population, and budgetary resources, the health care services may be extensive or almost nonexistent. Accredited facilities often have disease prevention and health promotion programs that address issues such as sexually transmitted and blood-borne diseases, as well as the use of tobacco products and family planning services. Advocates of the juvenile justice system consider counseling and mental health services to be essential.

On-Site versus Off-Site

A great deal of effort and research must go into the decision to provide health services on-site or off-site, and the type of services that must be available at the facility. Planning is the critical first step in designing a health care delivery system. Experts suggest creating a planning committee with a project director and representatives from the medical, custody, budgeting, information systems, and administrative divisions. The committee must have current, accurate data to determine to what extent health services are to be provided.

This setup involves many variables, not the least of which is a health profile of the facility's current and expected population. Examples of information in a health profile include the expected inmate volume, health needs of the population, resources of the correctional system, resources available from other public agencies, staffing needs, and costs of transportation services, to name only a few.

Types of Patients

Inmates as patients present challenges for health care professionals. The goal of medicine to diagnose and cure and the goal of corrections to punish are sometimes in conflict. Security and personal safety are always the priority, yet health care professionals must face serious and legitimate challenges when treating inmates. Legislation that emphases more stringent sentencing restrictions ensures that inmates will stay in the correctional system longer. This and other factors directly impact the types of services and staffing required.

The inmate population overall is not well educated and enters the correctional system already in poor health. Inmates may attempt to manipulate the health staff, creating a difficult and potentially dangerous work environment. Inmates represent all age groups and a growing population of females. Age, gender, and offense all can have an effect on the delivery of health services in correctional settings.

Age

The age of the inmate population affects the type of health care, professionals, and staffing required. Although younger populations usually are healthier and should require less staff, more juvenile offenders are entering correctional institutions in need of psychiatric and drug treatments. Older populations often have chronic conditions that require certain types of care. Inmates older than age 40 comprise a growing segment of the population. In 2005, one in every 23 inmates in prison was age 55 or older (Sentencing Project, 2006).

Geriatric issues may be faced earlier than expected in correctional settings because of the related stress of incarceration and the generally poor health of inmates. Older inmates also are more likely to suffer from chronic illnesses such as hypertension, asthma, and diabetes. Conditions that accompany the aging process, such as hearing and vision loss and mental confusion, also must be addressed. Thus, correctional facilities will have to be modified or built to accommodate inmates who have disabilities and are elderly.

Palliative care and hospice programs are becoming more common in prison systems, but there are institutional obstacles to their effective implementation. These include institutional policies that often limit prescribing narcotics to prisoners, specify limits on family visitation, prohibit visits from other inmates when a patient is in the infirmary, and prohibit inmates from serving as volunteers or workers in any "care giving" capacity (Anno, 2004). Terminally ill inmates have been treated in a number of ways. Some DOCs house terminally ill inmates in separate units; others offer hospice care (Bauersmith & Gent, 2002). Some facilities also allow for compassionate release or medical furlough programs when inmates are known to be terminally ill (Anno, 2001).

Gender

Gender also affects the type of health care services and professionals that must be available. Women will require access to gynecological services and obstetric and prenatal care if they are pregnant. The intake history for female inmates should include questions about menstrual cycles, pregnancy history, and gynecological problems. Female inmates need access to personal sanitary supplies, education on breast self-examinations, and annual Pap smears. Where state law allows, pregnant inmates retain the right to choose abortion services.

Pregnant inmates pose a special concern for correctional facilities, and they should be housed together with other pregnant inmates. Their work assignments must be limited to protect their condition, and special attention should be given to their diet.

Offense

The type of offense that an inmate has committed may affect the treatment received if the inmate poses a threat to security or the safety of the staff. In correctional facilities, custody and security are the primary concerns, and health care is provided in a manner that does not compromise those primary concerns. Inmates are classified and confined based on the type of offense they committed, and although the offense cannot be used as a reason for refusing inmates treatment, it may affect decisions to transfer inmates off-site for treatment. During periods of heightened security such as lock-downs, health staff members treat inmates in their cells.

Nature of Illness

The health status of incarcerated populations reflects and magnifies the worst trends in public health today—namely, the dramatic rise in previously controlled diseases such as tuberculosis, as well as in sexually transmitted diseases, especially AIDS. Here, we will briefly examine some of the trends health that professionals working in correctional settings face today, and the corresponding administrative difficulties.

After intake examinations, many inmates are found to be in the acute stages of respiratory ailments and sexually transmitted diseases. Acute conditions also may include traumas. Although prison violence usually is well controlled by correctional officers and facility rules, some inmates still come in with stab wounds, blunt trauma, and other acute or urgent conditions.

Chronic conditions are on the rise in correctional institutions for several reasons, including the rise in incarceration of individuals older than age 40. From 1995 to 2005, there was an 85% increase in the inmate population older than age 55 in both state and federal facilities (Sentencing Project, 2006). Cardiovascular diseases, end-stage renal disease, and complications from AIDS are not uncommon in correctional facilities.

Communicable diseases are common in inmate populations—most notably tuberculosis and sexually transmitted diseases. The lifestyle that many inmates choose before their incarceration includes heavy drug and alcohol use and indiscriminate sexual behavior, including prostitution. Smoking cigarettes and maintaining poor nutritional habits worsen their health. The treatment of chronic conditions is complicated by incarceration.

Trips to on-site or off-site appointments require correctional officers for escort and the use of transportation in the case of treatment provided outside of the facility. Basic medical information must accompany each prisoner treated. Health professionals for prisoners who are treated off-site or transferred must complete a health transfer summary form. The specific content requirements of the transfer form are unique to each state. The following list is an example of information documented on a health summary transfer form:

- Transfer date
- Name, address, and phone number of the transferring facility and receiving facility
- Inmate's name, identification number, date of birth
- Date of last physical
- Known allergies
- Date of last tuberculin test and results
- Behavioral or mental health conditions, suicide attempt or gesture during current or prior incarceration
- Medical conditions
- Current medications-medication name, dose, frequency
- Restrictions (if any) on activities, diet, housing, other
- Adaptive devices
- HIV status
- Current dental problems
- Follow-up appointments
- Signature of individual preparing the health summary transfer form and the signature of the person receiving the health transfer information

For examples of health summary transfer forms, visit www.ncc.nebraska.gov or www.cor.mt.gov

Types of Caregivers and Services

A variety of health care professionals can be found working in a wide range of correctional settings. The extent to which services, and therefore professionals, will be available at a facility is a constant challenge for correctional administrators.

Clinical Professionals

A well-structured, adequately funded health care delivery system can employ any number of professionals. Professionals include psychiatrists, physicians, nurses (RNs and LPNs), physician assistants, dentists, and optometrists. Other professionals encountered may have nonclinical roles, such as those of social workers and counselors. Sophisticated delivery systems provide case management and other support services.

Previous shortages of physicians often reflected shortages existing in the surrounding communities. Correctional facilities often were built in rural areas, and many had insufficient funds to attract qualified professionals. Still other facilities refused to hire women, thus eliminating a potential source of applicants, and sometimes the working conditions discouraged clinicians from seeking employment in correctional health care (Anno, 1992). Today, however, health services in prisons typically are given by providers who are licensed, certified, or registered to practice—the same as required in the community (Anno, 2004).

Physicians perform the physical examinations and order medications and referrals to specialists. Some of the physician's time is spent attending to administrative tasks. Nurses, and sometimes physician assistants, are responsible for triaging patients, recording health histories and vital signs, and taking samples for laboratory analysis. Dental services also must be included in basic health services, and optometry services should be provided as well.

Ancillary Services

Pharmacy, radiology, laboratory, and dietetics are considered to be ancillary services. Laboratory and radiology services may or may not be performed on-site. Medications must be administered to inmates, if prescribed, at least twice a day, 365 days a year, and some antibiotics require more frequent administration. Some correctional facilities have been successful with "keep-on-person" medication programs that allow some inmates to maintain their own small supply of medications. Facilities commonly have a central area where inmates go to receive their daily medications (Anno, 1992).

Emergency Services

The availability of emergency services is subject to the same variables as other health services. At a minimum, however, correctional facilities must have a plan for handling medical emergencies. Facilities must designate one or more hospital emergency departments to which inmates will be transported in case of medical emergencies. The plan also must specify arrangements, including security, for emergency evacuation and identify modes of transportation to be used. Because of the remote location of many facilities, transportation can be one of the biggest problems. Some state DOCs have their own emergency medical technicians (EMTs) and/or ambulances (Anno, 2001).

Specialty Services

Depending upon a facility's population, specialty health care services may include mental health, speech and rehabilitative therapies, and more extensive dental services. Some prisons must include provisions for inmates who have physical handicaps and those who are have vision or hearing impairments. To avoid victimizing these inmates, some prisons provide separate housing (Anno, 2001).

Mental health services available at correctional facilities often come under attack for their inadequacies. Mental health screening should be part of the intake process to identify inmates who have immediate mental health needs. Aggressive mentally ill and self-mutilating inmates require careful handling and can cause extreme management problems. Many prison and jail systems now have special programs to manage aggressive mentally ill inmates (Anno, 2001).

Mentally ill offenders also receive short shrift regarding treatment for their serious health needs in a number of prison systems. One study indicated that the self-reported prevalence rate for serious mental illness among state prison inmates was 16% (Ditton, 1999). Although the aggressive mentally ill offenders usually are identified and treated, those who may be quietly mentally ill often are not (Anno, 2004). Notably, the accrediting agency, CARF International, publishes specific standards in its Behavioral Health program for "Criminal Justice" and "Juvenile Justice" (CARF, 2010).

Licensure

State licensing boards establish standards that control the number of professionals practicing in a state and determine minimum standards of competence. The licensing boards also define what activities may be legally performed under each type of license. Although licensing standards do not set staffing ratios, their requirements have staffing implications for health care facilities. Licensed independent practitioners employed by the federal government who provide services at federally designated locations need only be licensed in any state. This allows federal agencies the staffing flexibility to meet patient care demands and changes to facility organizational needs. It also represents a valuable recruitment tool to attract physicians and other professional health care practitioners.

SELF REVIEW 6.1

1. What are the three levels of security in prisons? Explain the differences between the different security levels.
2. The Federal Bureau of Prisons was established in
   a. 1945.
   b. 1996.
   c. 1930.
   d. 1952.
3. What are the three primary purposes of jails?
4. Who has the responsibility for providing health care services in a jail? What are some of the screenings that may be included in a jail after booking procedures are completed?

5. Which of the following is not one of the three types of jails?
   a. detention jail
   b. sentenced jails
   c. detention-sentenced jails
   d. DRCT jails
6. Describe the differences between the types of long-term care juvenile facilities.
7. What are some gender issues that may affect the type of health care services and health care professionals that a correctional institution must have available?

REGULATORY ISSUES

Regulations for correctional facilities come in many forms. Those dealing with health care services and professionals are found most often in professional licensing statutes and court orders. Correctional facilities that have hospitals, satellite facilities, mental health programs, and so on must follow established legal and professional standards. Regulation of health services usually is the responsibility of the state department of health, and applicable rules can be found in state statutes.

Accreditation programs provide an opportunity for correctional institutions to evaluate their operations against national standards, identify and correct problems, and continually improve the quality of living conditions and services. Benefits that are recognized most often include improved management, additional defense against lawsuits, enhanced credibility, a safer environment for inmates and staff, and the establishment of objective, measurable criteria for improving the quality of programs, staff, and the physical structure of correctional facilities.

The accreditation process is initiated by completing an application with basic information about the facility. Facilities usually are encouraged to complete a self-assessment before the on-site survey. At the conclusion of the on-site survey, members of the survey team review their findings and submit a report to an accreditation committee within the accrediting organization, which makes the final accreditation decision. (Anno, 1992).

The evolution of correctional standards is significant in that they enable evaluation of correctional facilities based on compliance with objective, measurable standards. Currently, the **National Commission on Correctional Health Care (NCCHC)**, the **American Correctional Association (ACA)**, and the **American Public Health Association (APHA)** publish health care standards for correctional institutions. Except for the APHA, these associations offer voluntary accreditation for the administration of health care services in correctional institutions.

American Correctional Association   a professional association of correctional administrators, wardens, superintendents, and other individuals and institutions, promoting improved correctional standards and studying causes of crime and juvenile delinquency as well as methods of crime control and prevention, offering voluntary accreditation for all components of adult and juvenile corrections.

American Public Health Association (APHA)   a professional group of health care workers, administrators, epidemiologists, planners, community and mental health specialists, and interested individuals who seek to protect and promote personal, mental, and environmental health by promulgating standards, establishing uniform practices and procedures, and conducting research.

National Commission on Correctional Health Care (NCCHC)

The National Commission on Correctional Health Care (NCCHC) standards were developed by a wide range of professional health care associations, including the American Health Information Management Association (AHIMA). The NCCHC used correctional health care standards developed by the American Medical Association (AMA) in the 1970s as a template and developed separate standards for jails, prisons, and juvenile detention facilities.

The NCCHC standards are the most comprehensive health standards of accrediting organizations, are more measurable, and provide the most comprehensive guidance for implementation, because they take into account the size and complexity of facilities and are complemented by an accreditation process. The major disadvantage to NCCHC standards is the lack of comprehensive standards addressing environmental and occupational health issues (Anno, 2001).

American Correctional Association (ACA)

The American Correctional Association was founded in 1870 as the National Prison Association. In 1954, its name was changed to the American Correctional Association. The ACA standards are advantageous in that they were developed and promoted by the nation's leading professional correctional association. The ACA is a private, nonprofit organization and the only organization that provides accreditation for all components of adult and juvenile correctional facilities, whereas the NCCHC standards' primary focus is health services.

The Joint Commission

Of the various standards available from The Joint Commission, its ambulatory care standards are the most applicable to health services provided in correctional facilities. An advantage of these standards is that they reflect community standards and emphasize quality improvement. The greatest disadvantages are that the standards are not specific to corrections and do not address significant concerns of the health staff. The standards also do not cover dental health services (Anno, 2001).

American Public Health Association

The American Public Health Association (APHA) is not listed as an accrediting agency along with the other associations that publish health care standards because it has no corresponding accreditation program for its standards. The absence of an accreditation component makes compliance with the standards difficult to verify. The APHA standards were developed by health care professionals, and they are comprehensive, specific to corrections, and provide some guidance for implementation. A significant disadvantage of the APHA standards is the attempt to apply to large and small institutions simultaneously, even when this is unwarranted or impractical (Anno, 2001).

1. What type of clinical professionals may be found in a well-structured correctional facility?

2. What benefits are gained by correctional facilities that obtain accreditation?

3. Which of the following statements is not true regarding the American Correctional Association (ACA)?

    a. It is not listed as an accrediting agency along with the other associations that publish health care standards because it has no corresponding accreditation program for its standards.

    b. It was founded in 1870 as the National Prison Association.

    c. The ACA standards are advantageous in that they were developed and promoted by the nation's leading professional correctional association.

    d. The ACA is a private, nonprofit organization, and the only organization that provides accreditation for all components of adult and juvenile correctional facilities, whereas the NCCHC standards' primary focus is health services.

4. The evolution of correctional standards is significant in that they enable evaluation of correctional facilities based on compliance with objective, measurable standards. Currently, which of the following organizations publish health care standards for correctional institutions?

    a. National Commission on Correctional Health Care (NCCHC)

    b. American Correctional Association (ACA)

    c. American Public Health Association (APHA)

    d. All of the above

DOCUMENTATION

Published standards recognize the importance of documentation in correctional institutions, whether for health care or for administrative purposes. Reality, however, is sometimes very different. Documentation of factual information is essential for successful management of any organization, and is particularly important in the correctional setting. Inmates comprise a litigious group, and clear, precise, factual documentation is critical to a correctional facility's defense.

The Correctional Health Record

Managing correctional health information will challenge the best health information management (HIM) professional. The test of a truly successful and effective information system is its ability to adapt to the ever-changing needs of a growing inmate population.

The APHA standards require that health records be kept as a unit record. Some mental health and other allied health professionals resist this method of organization. When psychiatric and medical services operate separately, copies of psychiatric consultations and treatment reports should be provided to the health services department and kept in an envelope in the health record. This enables the physician to have access to essential information but restricts the HIM professionals from releasing the reports. The original documentation is physically maintained at another site by the counselor or psychiatrist, and any requests for copies of the information must be directed to him or her.

The primary purpose of the health record, regardless of the setting, is to enhance communication among health professionals who provide care to patients and to document the course of a patient's treatment and outcome. The secondary purpose of the health record is to serve as a legal document to protect both the facility and the patient. It also serves as an educational tool and is the basis for most quality assurance and utilization management activities (Gannon, 1988).

Format

If facility or systemwide procedures are lacking, it is recommended that the health staff assist in establishing a standardized format for the health record. The format chosen should be based on the unique needs of the facility. HIM professionals can play a helpful role in educating other staff members about the advantages and disadvantages of the source-oriented, problem-oriented, and integrated record formats. HIM professionals are reminded to remain flexible and open to new ideas, as must the health staffs who use the record. The format also should facilitate retrieving information from the record. Abstracting is still a widely used method of accessing the wealth of information contained in health records. Neglecting to consider retrieval of information when designing the health record format and forms may hinder future efforts for automation or research.

Numbering and Filing

Inmates in state and federal prisons are assigned identification numbers upon admission to some facilities. Some large jails or detention facilities also may use ID numbers. Most state DOCs have a central office and a computer system that assigns numbers. Other methods of assigning numbers are manual and require the use of ledgers, files, and logs. Some facilities give inmates a new number if they leave and reenter the correctional system, but most facilities assign a number that is retained for all subsequent admissions to the correctional system.

The federal system also assigns inmates a computer-generated number that the inmate keeps throughout his or her confinement, even if transferred to a federal facility in another state (Gannon, 1988). In small rural facilities, HIM professionals may be more likely to find alphabetic filing systems, whereas terminal digit filing may be used in more populated urban facilities.

Retention and Destruction

Retention and storage requirements for inactive health records usually are found in law and jurisdictional policies. To retain the records for the required length of time, some state prisons place records on microfilm or use imaging technology, whereas others store older paper records off-site in a central storage facility. In the federal system, inactive records remain in the facility for one year after an inmate's release. Then the records are sent to a central storage facility, where they are maintained for 30 years and then destroyed. Methods of destruction vary by facility. When contracting with a vendor, the responsibilities of all parties must be defined clearly. Accurate accounts of records sent for destruction must be kept to ensure that the destruction is carried out according to the terms of the agreement.

Written policies governing retention and destruction are essential. HIM professionals must ensure that retention and destruction policies follow state laws and guidelines. The state department of archives or similar authority should be knowledgeable about the applicable regulations for retention and destruction of correctional and health-related records. Careful thought also should be given to disaster policies, such as what should be done to protect records from or restore those that have fire and water damage. Some companies specialize in helping facilities recover records after disasters that cause such damage. Consideration also should be given to the potential for the different types of natural disasters, such as tornadoes and floods.

Health records in corrections present an interesting opportunity for the energetic HIM professional. There is a great need for data analysis in the evolving field of correctional health care, and HIM professionals should lead the way in abstracting and using the information from these records.

Transfer

Transferring inmates is a regular occurrence in correctional settings and often necessitates the transfer of health records. In some systems, a copy of pertinent information is sent with the inmate. Other facilities complete a separate health summary form that may include lab results, medications, allergies, scheduled appointments, and major medical conditions such as seizure disorders. Still other facilities send the entire original record. Typically, the health record will follow the inmate. The health record must be protected from physical damage, and the confidentiality of the information must be protected as well. Frequently, copies of inmate medical records are placed in secure bags or envelopes to ensure their security during the inmate's transfer.

Detailed logs should be kept for tracking records that have been transferred and for copies that have been released. The records should be securely sealed by the transferring facility. The receiving facility should document the condition of the seal and record upon arrival to verify that no tampering has occurred. Correctional officers must not have access to inmates' health information, but they should be informed of a physical condition if the situation warrants.

Confidentiality

It is imperative that HIM professionals stay current regarding changes affecting the confidentiality of inmate health information. Current political trends often have a direct impact on the protection and release of inmates' health information. Diseases such as AIDS and the mental health status of inmates may further complicate already difficult situations. HIM professionals must know under what conditions an inmate's record may be released and what constitutes a valid authorization. HIM professionals can face hostile attorneys, inmates, and other parties that may or may not be legally entitled to know the content of health records. The HIM professional, therefore, must have clear, precise policies, written with strict adherence to current law.

Privacy provisions of the Health Insurance Portability and Accountability Act (HIPAA) apply to correctional facilities that are deemed to be covered entities. HIPAA, however, has some special provisions for correctional institutions. (See the discussion of HIPAA in correctional health care later in this chapter.)

Correctional officers and administrative personnel sometimes pose a special problem. Health and legal professionals agree that inmate health records must be maintained separately from any confinement records kept by the facility. For the protection of the inmates and the institution, correctional personnel should be prohibited from accessing the records. Statutory directives require reporting medical conditions to designated authorities and agencies, and these directives must be followed.

Using inmates to supplement staffing in the health services area may create additional threats to confidentiality and the safety of some inmates. Correctional organizations have standards that detail when inmates may be used as employees. The NCCHC, ACA, and AHPA standards all prohibit inmates from providing or assisting in direct patient care, determining access of other inmates to health services, and handling medical records (Anno, 2001).

Careful, thorough research has no substitute. Policies and procedures must be unambiguous and current. Consents and authorizations make up a large part of the inmate health record. HIM professionals must be well versed in informed consent statutes and current case law, which differ from state to state and between jurisdictions.

Issues surrounding inmates' right to refuse treatment and consents by juveniles arise frequently. Forms must adhere strictly to legal requirements and should not be used without approval by an attorney. Correctional settings face additional problems of handling inmates with substance abuse problems and mentally incompetent inmates. HIM professionals must know the legal ramifications of such conditions on individuals' ability to give consent.

Administrative Information

During litigation, considerable weight is given to the administration's ability to demonstrate compliance with institutional policies and procedures and monitor staff compliance. Well-written policies and procedures imply a thoughtful, well-documented organizational philosophy. For any facility, well-written policies and procedures can reduce training time for new employees and can reduce potential conflicts resulting from a lack of clear direction.

The first step toward achieving a complete set of policies is to evaluate what is available currently. The policies should be read thoroughly. Busy staff members can easily neglect updating procedures when a modification is necessary. It is even easier to ignore badly written procedures. The administration must be confident that the institution's policies are consistent with current practices.

Financial Data

Accurate financial data are essential in managing correctional institutions successfully. Because of the current method of funding (i.e., taxation), correctional facilities have difficulty receiving adequate resources to meet escalating demands for health services. Careful, accurate documentation of costs and expenditures is crucial. Once allocated, funds should be tracked and reported regularly (Anno, 2001).

Statistical Reports

Health administrators require statistical information concerning health care activities for budgeting, planning, and operating correctional health services. Reports should regularly reflect the number of patients served each month by each of the primary programs and information on ancillary and support services. A detailed breakdown of specific activities enhances the utility of statistical data. Statistics for off-site contracted services should be reported and monitored regularly.

Logs, Checklists, and Inspection Forms

Developing tools to monitor and measure compliance is a helpful contribution of HIM professionals. Checklists may be designed to verify compliance with other policies such as routine equipment checks. Daily operation requires tracking of patients scheduled for sick call, chronic clinics, and appointments outside of the correctional facility. Logs are necessary for documenting supply use and release-of-information requests for health records.

SELF REVIEW 6.3

1. The primary purpose of a health care record in any setting is to:
   a. enhance communication among health professionals who provide care to patients and to document the course of a patient's treatment and outcome.
   b. serve as an educational tool.
   c. serve as the basis for most quality assurance and utilization management activities.
   d. serve as a data analysis tool.

2. Are there any requirements for the retention and destruction of inactive health care records? If so, what guidelines must be followed?

3. True or false? Correctional officers who are transferring a prisoner are allowed to have access to all of the prisoner's health care information.

4. Correctional organizations have standards that detail when inmates may be used as employees. The NCCHC, ACA, and AHPA standards all prohibit inmates from providing or assisting in which of the following duties?

    a. direct patient care

    b. determining access of other inmates to health services

    c. handling medical records

    d. all of the above

REIMBURSEMENT AND FUNDING

The reimbursement arrangements of other health care settings have no counterpart in corrections. Funding for all corrections-related activities comes from taxes appropriated by federal and state legislatures.

Managing health care costs is often more difficult for correctional institutions than for other health care facilities. Needs frequently exceed resources. This can be true even during initial stages of budget planning if the legislature rejects the budget and allocates less funding. Budget shortfalls also can crop up at any time of the year because of incorrect original estimates or conditions changing unexpectedly.

Financing correctional health services has limited options Potential sources of funding include federal government sources, private sources, payments from prisoners for care, and appropriations from state legislatures. Of these, the latter is the only funding source of any substance. Medicaid and Medicare payments generally are not available to state prisoners, and few of them carry private health insurance (Anno, 2004).

The vast majority (if not all) of the operating funds used to pay for inmates' health care comes from appropriations from state legislatures. In 2005, health care expenditures for state prison inmates represented an average of 13.3% of DOC total costs (ranging from 21% in Kansas to 6% in Maine) (ACA, 2006). Correctional institutions are increasingly turning to managed care arrangements as a method of paying for care received by inmates. Decision-makers view managed care systems as a way to meet inmates' increasing health care needs while containing costs. Many states have contracted with private managed care organizations (MCOs) to provide health care for incarcerated individuals. An MCO that agrees to capitation payments based on the number of inmates in the system will have more incentive to deliver care efficiently than will a health care organization that is paid on a fee-for-service basis.

Charging inmates for health care has been debated hotly over the years. Those arguing for collecting fees from inmates cite the astronomical cost of correctional health care as a burden to citizens that rightfully should belong to inmates. They also cite overutilization of health services and malingering as incentives for instituting a fee or copayment structure. Charging fees or copayments based on the facility's economy is thought to control abuse of health services. Supporters also argue that paying for their health care forces inmates to become responsible for their health and money. Inmates who spend their money to buy cigarettes rather than save it in case they become ill will continue to make the same irrational choices after they are released.

Critics of this issue argue that if health care is a right, all inmates should have access to services at the continued expense of taxpayers. Another argument is that basing copayments on a facility's economy will not even begin to cover the cost of health services. Payments may constitute a high fee for some inmates, while clearly not compensating the facility for the cost of care. Critics claim that copayments or fees would create a tiered system favoring "wealthy" inmates (NCCHC, 1996). Opponents of fee-for-service correctional health care argue that the use of a clinically trained "gatekeeper" would help to prevent abuse of the health system by malingerers without impeding access to inmates who need health care services (Anno, 2001).

The trends in **inmate self-pay** or **copayment** are illustrated by survey data collected over an 11-year period. At the end of 1994, the NCCHC conducted a survey of 206 jail jurisdictions. Of the 117 systems that responded, 35% charged inmates for health care and 15% were exploring it as an option. The majority of the programs required fixed payments between $2 and $10, and every jail system made provisions for emergency services (Legal issues in correctional health care, 1995). A National Institute of Corrections Survey in 1997 found that 33 state legislatures (almost two-thirds) had authorized imposition of fees on inmates for health services (Anno, 2001). By 2005, 90% of states responding to an American Correctional Association survey indicated that their departments of correction were charging inmates some sort of copay for specified health care services (ACA, 2006).

inmate self-pay or copayment   the practice of requiring inmates to pay a (small) fee for predetermined, nonemergency medical treatments.

copayment   See inmate self-pay

| SELF REVIEW 6.4 |

1. Funding for all corrections-related activity comes from:
   a. taxes appropriated by federal and state legislatures
   b. National Prisoner's Fund
   c. Medicare
   d. none of the above
2. Medicare and Medicaid are normally available for all prisoners.
   a. True
   b. False
3. What do critics of charging inmates for health care state as reasons for not charging inmates a fee for health care services rendered?

INFORMATION MANAGEMENT

Careful information management is essential to providing health professionals with necessary information on which to base their treatment decisions. In principle, health information management in correctional facilities is similar to that of other health care settings.

Data and Information Flow

External data are provided to correctional facilities from local governments, government agencies such as the Federal Bureau of Investigation (FBI) and the Centers for Disease Control and Prevention (CDC), and from health care facilities such as hospitals and community health clinics. Internally, data are collected by various departments during the performance of daily activities, special projects, internal audits, and so forth. Most data specific to health services come from sick call slips completed by inmates and from treatment reports provided by health staff.

A significant barrier to providing inmates with adequate health care comes from a lack of access to inmate health information from hospitals and clinics. Uninformed or misinformed staffs may refuse to release inmate health records to correctional facilities for their continued treatment.

In most states, release of health information is allowed only with the patient's prior written consent. Information, however, may be released without prior consent to a health professional who is directly involved in the care and treatment of the inmate in an emergency situation or when the inmate is unable to sign. Health information management professionals must know under what conditions inmate health information can and cannot be released. HIM professionals working in corrections should develop relationships with other professionals working in facilities with which the correctional system might contract for services. Fostering good relations will facilitate the release of information.

Coding and Classification

Coding of diseases and procedures is not done routinely in DOCs, jails, or juvenile detention centers, but the FBP does utilize the current modification of *ICD* for tracking morbidity and mortality. Classification in correctional facilities relates to the categorization of offenders according to established criteria for making housing and job assignments, as well as determining security status and developing educational or rehabilitation programs. Typically, the criteria include age, gender, legal status (e.g., pretrial, detention, sentenced), and inmates' physical and mental health status (Miller, 1978).

Electronic Information Systems

A fundamental challenge to corrections is the integration of twenty-first-century information technology into nineteenth-century organizational structures.

The primary purpose of current organizational structures is to maintain the integrity and hierarchy of legitimate authority positions that give bureaucratic organizations their strength. These same directives, however, tend to inhibit the flow of information within the organization (Archambeault, 1987).

The number of prisons and jails adopting electronic health record (EHR) systems is growing, although paper systems are still quite common. Even if an EHR is not in use, correctional facilities often use an electronic systems for specific functions, such as various types of logs for tracking (Paris, 2009). Although some of the incentives to convert to an EHR system do not apply to correctional health care, many of the benefits of EHR systems can be reaped in correctional health care when appropriate systems are well implemented.

HIPAA

When the privacy provisions of HIPAA were being implemented in 2003, many correctional institutions still were unsure of their status under HIPAA. A correctional facility that provides health care services and transmits health information electronically in connection with a standard transaction would be considered a HIPAA-covered entity. Because many correctional institutions provide self-funded health care, however, they do not transmit health information in electronic form and, therefore, would not be considered covered entities.

When a correctional facility is considered to be a covered entity, it may designate itself as a **hybrid covered entity**, which is an organization whose activities include both covered and noncovered functions. Any correctional institution that is deemed to be a covered entity would have to appoint a privacy officer, to promulgate policies and procedures protecting the privacy of inmate health information, and to allow inmates access to their health records as a general rule (Orr & Hellerstein, 2002). Correctional institutions are granted an exception to the access rule when such access would "jeopardize the health, safety, security, custody, or rehabilitation of the individual or of other inmates, or the safety of any officer, employee, or other person at the correctional institution or responsible for transporting of the inmate" (DHHS, 2000, p. 82823).

Figure 6-1 provides excerpts from the HIPAA privacy rule that pertain to correctional institutions, inmates, and health care providers that work with them. For example, a health care provider may release an inmate's health information to a correctional institution without the inmate's authorization under certain circumstances. When an inmate is released from custody, however, he or she regains all privacy rights (DHHS, 2000; DHHS, 2002). With regard to providing inmates with a "notice of privacy practices," correctional institutions are exempt from this HIPAA requirement. They should, however, make a good-faith effort to provide such a notice to former inmates who have been paroled (Orr & Hellerstein, 2002).

> **hybrid covered entity** an organization whose activities include both covered and noncovered functions under HIPAA.

Health care providers who do not have an EHR do not have to account for disclosures to correctional institutions as they do for other disclosures. (See Chapter 1 for the impact of the HITECH Act on accounting of disclosures when the covered entity has an EHR.) HIM professionals can play an active role in implementation and maintenance of HIPAA standards by providing expertise and guidance relating to the privacy, security, and transactions rules and regulations.

FIGURE 6-1

Excerpts from HIPAA privacy regulations concerning correctional institutions and inmates. (DHHS, 2000; DHHS, 2002)

---

§ 164.512 Uses and disclosures for which an authorization or opportunity to agree or object is not required....

(j) *Standard: Uses and disclosures* to *avert a serious threat to health or safety.*

(1) *Permitted disclosures.* A covered entity may, consistent with applicable law and standards of ethical conduct, use or disclose protected health information, if the covered entity, in good faith, believes the use or disclosure....

(ii) Is necessary for law enforcement authorities to identify or apprehend an individual....

(B) Where it appears from all the circumstances that the individual has escaped from a correctional institution or from lawful custody, as those terms are defined in §164.501....

(k) *Standard: Uses and disclosures for specialized government functions....*

(5) *Correctional institutions and other law enforcement custodial situations.*

(i) *Permitted disclosures.* A covered entity may disclose to a correctional institution or a law enforcement official having lawful custody of an inmate or other individual protected health information about such inmate or individual, if the correctional institution or such law enforcement official represents that such protected health information is necessary for:

(A) The provision of health care to such individuals;

(B) The health and safety of such individual or other inmates;

(C) The health and safety of the officers or employees of or others at the correctional institution;

(D) The health and safety of such individuals and officers or other persons responsible for the transporting of inmates or their transfer from one institution, facility, or setting to another;

(E) Law enforcement on the premises of the correctional institution; and

(F) The administration and maintenance of the safety, security, and good order of the correctional institution....

FIGURE 6-1   (*continued*)

(iii) No *application after release*. For the purposes of this provision, an individual is no longer an inmate when released on parole, probation, supervised release, or otherwise is no longer in lawful custody.

§ 164.520 Notice of privacy practices for protected health information.

(a) *Standard: notice of privacy practices....*

(3) *Exception for inmates.* An inmate does not have a right to notice under this section, and the requirements of this section do not apply to a correctional institution that is a covered entity....

§ 164.524 Access of individuals to protected health information....

(2) *Unreviewable grounds for denial.* A covered entity may deny an individual access without providing the individual an opportunity for review, in the following circumstances....

(ii) A covered entity that is a correctional institution or a covered health care provider acting under the direction of the correctional institution may deny, in whole or in part, an inmate's request to obtain a copy of protected health information, if obtaining such copy would jeopardize the health, safety, security, custody, or rehabilitation of the individual or of other inmates, or the safety of any officer, employee, or other person at the correctional institution or responsible for the transporting of the inmate....

§ 164.528 Accounting of disclosures of protected health information.

(a) *Standard: Right to an accounting of disclosures of protected health information.*

(1) An individual has a right to receive an accounting of disclosures of protected health information made by a covered entity in the six years prior to the date on which the accounting is requested, except for disclosures....

(vii) To correctional institutions or law enforcement officials as provided in § 164.512(k)(5) (DHHS, 2000; DHHS, 2002)

From www.ecfr.gov

SELF REVIEW 6.5

1. What is a significant barrier to providing inmates with adequate health care?

2. True or false? Information may be released without prior consent to a health professional who is directly involved in the care and treatment of the inmate in an emergency situation or when the inmate is unable to sign.

3. What is the primary purpose of using the current modification of *ICD* in correctional facilities?

4. If a correctional facility is deemed to be a covered entity under HIPAA, what type of officer would have to be appointed? What would be some of the duties of this appointed officer?

QUALITY MANAGEMENT, PERFORMANCE IMPROVEMENT, AND UTILIZATION MANAGEMENT

Over time, different terms have been used to describe the processes of quality management, performance improvement (PI), and utilization management (UM), but the basic purposes of these processes have remained the same. The goal always has been to constantly improve the quality of health care services and the control of costs. Today, the functions of PI and UM overlap considerably and are most effective when they are coordinated with one another and with risk management programs.

Quality Management and Performance Improvement

Quality management (QM) and performance improvement (PI) involve a process of ongoing monitoring and evaluation to assess the adequacy and appropriateness of care provided and to offer a means of initiating effective corrective action when needed.

The infrastructure of correctional facilities in large part determines health professionals' ability to deliver quality care. HIM professionals can play an important role in monitoring and improving the systems that support the efforts of health professionals by assisting with the development of the QM/PI program and objectives, defining the scope and process. Critical to the success of the QM/PI program is the ability to monitor and measure the program's effectiveness and gain the support of administrators. One program that can assist in this task is the Correctional Health Outcomes and Resource Data Set (CHORDS), offered by the NCCHC. Performance measurement and benchmarking opportunities are available through CHORDS to participating facilities.

Services that are provided for the correctional system by contracted professionals, organizations, and other health care facilities also should be monitored. Maintenance of statistical and other data should be forwarded to the medical director and other appropriate authorities to determine whether the terms of the agreement are being met.

Accreditation is a preferred method of external review, because it provides comprehensive, objective analysis of the facility's operations, with a comparison to the facility's policies and procedures. The three accrediting agencies previously cited offer self-assessment and pre-survey consultation services.

Utilization Management

Utilization management (UM) focuses on controlling the use of resources by reviewing a facility's efficiency in providing health care services. The objective of UM is to maintain quality while ensuring appropriate utilization of services.

The UM program should be a component of the organization-wide QM/PI effort. Accurate data are crucial for a successful UM program. A facility must be able to accurately determine the costs of providing care and assess current levels of utilization. Careful monitoring of staff time and supply and equipment costs must be done initially to establish a baseline figure for health service costs. HIM professionals should be instrumental in developing an effective UM program.

SELF REVIEW 6.6

1. True or false? The goal of utilization management and performance improvement always has been to constantly improve the quality of health care services and the control of costs.
2. Why is accreditation the preferred method of external review?
3. What is the overall objective of a UM program, and what are some components that are necessary to the success of a UM program in a correctional facility?

RISK MANAGEMENT AND LEGAL ISSUES

Risk management (RM) and QM share similar beginnings. Both existed in other industries before emerging in health care. RM used to be distinguished from QM by its involvement with financial issues, protection of assets, and limiting professional and general liability. The legal issues faced by correctional facilities necessitate the application of RM principles and techniques.

Risk Management

The primary purpose of RM is to protect the resources of the facility and its staff. The strategies of RM and QM may sometimes overlap. Generally, QM/PI focuses on aggregate data to identify patterns and improve care; risk management focuses on individual events that may involve patients, employees, or visitors. Correctional institutions are charged with the enormous responsibilities of providing a secure environment for inmates and protecting the public, both of which expose them to substantial liability that must be managed.

When the Supreme Court required correctional facilities to provide health care to inmates, the facilities immediately were exposed to additional risk. One risk management tool that correctional facilities have used is the inmate **grievance process**. Grievances identify and document areas of potential risk exposure and allow corrective action to be taken to improve operations and reduce the incidence of litigation. The major objectives of a grievance process are to (1) improve institutional management and problem identification, (2) reduce inmate frustration and the potential for violence, (3) increase prospects for inmate

grievance process a formal administrative process whereby inmates may file complaints against a correctional facility for review by a panel. Institutional policies, and sometimes state statutes, determine timeframes for the review process, decisions, and appeals.

rehabilitation, (4) hold down the volume of litigation, and (5) promote justice in institutional procedures (Brakel, 1983).

Common Legal Issues

There is no limit to the number and types of lawsuits that correctional facilities may be required to address. In the realm of correctional health care, these issues also raise significant ethical questions.

Inmate lawsuits take up a considerable amount of time and money. Even with grievance procedures, the number of inmate lawsuits continues to rise. Lawsuits brought by inmates claiming "deliberate indifference" to their needs are common in all correctional facilities. Defining deliberate indifference is a hotly debated legal issue. Some professional organizations argue for a broader definition, and others for a more specific and limited definition.

Forced medication is another frequent topic of ethical debate in corrections. In some instances of general psychiatric emergencies, state laws allow the use of psychotropic medications without the patient's consent. Accrediting agencies have specific guidelines for the use of such medications and clearly defined rules under which they may be used. Inmates' refusal of treatment is another topic of concern for many professionals working in correction facilities.

Perhaps the ultimate ethical issue for physicians is in their judging inmates' competency for execution. Physicians vow to "do no harm," but some insist that this places them in direct conflict with that oath. The remedy offered by accreditation agencies is to use an independent expert and not a health care professional employed or under contract with the correctional facility.

Other Areas of Risk

Correctional health care delivery systems are at risk in other ways, too. Care delivered by contracted firms must be constantly overseen and reviewed for adequacy by the correctional facility. Reporting to the National Practitioner Data Bank and monitoring credentialing are additional issues that correctional facilities must address.

SELF REVIEW 6.7

1. Which one of the following statements is not a major objectives of a grievance process?
   a. Improve institutional management and problem identification.
   b. Hold down the volume of litigation.
   c. Reduce inmate frustration and potential for violence.
   d. Promote inmate copayments to reduce costs of healthcare in correctional facilities.

2. Describe a circumstance in which utilizing forced medication would be permissible in a correctional facility?

ROLE OF THE HEALTH INFORMATION MANAGEMENT PROFESSIONAL

HIM professionals will find their role in correctional settings clearly defined in some ways and continually evolving in others. They will be expected to manage the inmate health records as they would manage health records in any other setting.

Correctional facilities generate and receive enormous amounts of data, but relatively little data are being converted into useful information. Even less data are shared through electronic networks and databases. Statistical information is requested routinely and is used by a variety of organizations and government agencies, but in too many cases the collection and retrieval of basic data must be done manually. Correctional facilities that are interested in surviving despite dwindling financial resources must look to technology and the effective use of information.

Existing databases that collect correctional information usually reside in well-funded federal agencies such as the National Institute of Corrections and the U.S. Bureau of Justice Statistics. HIM professionals can find the greatest opportunities for improving the management of correctional data at the regional, local, and facility levels.

In 1990, the NCCHC established the **Certified Correctional Health Professional (CCHP) Program** to elevate the level of professionalism in the field of correctional health care. After an individual submits an application, the candidate participates in a proctored, written examination composed of 80 to 100 multiple-choice questions. An advanced certification, CCHP-A, is available to individuals who achieve the CCHP. Many HIM professionals have attained the CCHP credential. AHIMA continues to provide a representative to participate on NCCHC's board of directors. In 2009, the NCCHC Board voted AHIMA's representative as its chairman for 2009–2010—the first time in the history of NCCHC that an RHIA was elected to chair the board.

Another group that offers professional development and support for correctional health care professionals is the **American Correctional Health Services Association (ACHSA)**. ACHSA provides "education, skill development and support for personnel, organizations and decision makers involved in correctional health services...." (ACHSA, 2015).

The American Correctional Association (ACA) also offers certification to health service personnel through its **Correctional Certification Program (CCP)**, but its programs are limited to nurses and individuals who serve in a management capacity. The ACA launched the Healthcare Professional Interest Section, as well as the Correctional Certification Program, in 2007 (ACA, n.d.).

Every setting that provides health services, without exception, can benefit from the expertise of HIM professionals. Working in correctional settings demands the consistent application of all the principles of health information management. The politically charged atmosphere magnifies ethical issues. A successful HIM professional must stay current on a wide variety of legal issues and must be able to support decisions with documentation from any number of

Certified Correctional Health Professional Program (CCHP) a certification program for health care professionals working in corrections; administered by the National Commission on Correctional Health Care.

American Correctional Health Services Association (ACHSA) a professional group of health care providers, individuals, and organizations interested in improving the quality of correctional health services.

Correctional Certification Program (CCP) a program offered by the American Correctional Association to certify correctional officers, correctional staff, staff nurses, and nurse managers working in corrections.

sources, including state and federal laws, court rulings, and guidelines published by professional associations.

Opportunities for careers in corrections will continue to grow along with the industry. Mandatory sentencing, truth in sentencing, and restrictive drug laws have increased the number of inmates housed in correctional facilities. Excellent opportunities are available in corrections for HIM professionals who exhibit a high degree of excellence and maintain their professional and ethical standards. Once employed, HIM professionals should make every effort to foster relationships with educational programs and publish their experiences in professional journals.

Research is another area in which HIM professionals can excel by taking an aggressive leadership role in the proper collection and use of correctional information. It should be noted that prisoners themselves are considered a "protected class" and rarely can participate as research subjects (National Commission for the Protection of Human Subjects, 1979). Many health information managers are trained in research methods, and this knowledge is beneficial to their institutions in planning and implementing research projects appropriate to the correctional setting.

SELF REVIEW 6.8

1. In 1990, the NCCHC established the Certified Correctional Health Professional (CCHP) Program to elevate the level of professionalism in the field of correctional health care. Is the following statement true or false?
   a. True
   b. False

2. Is the CCP available to all health service personnel? What year was this program launched?

3. Which of the following are reasons for an increase in the number of inmates in correctional facilities?
   a. Mandatory sentencing
   b. Truth in sentencing
   c. Restrictive drug laws
   d. All of the above

4. Which of the following programs was created by the NCCHC?
   a. CCP
   b. CCHP
   c. APC-S
   d. CCS

TRENDS

As the correctional industry continues to grow, various professions will continue to define their roles within the industry. Substantial improvements have been made in prison health care delivery systems over the past 30 years, resulting in better treatment for those incarcerated (Anno, 2004).

Technology improves the quality of life and allows health care professionals to be more productive by eliminating redundant tasks. Each new application of a technology creates opportunities for new professional fields. As new technologies prove to be beneficial, increased use will lower costs. Some states have implemented the electronic health record (EHR), which automates the operations of health information management in twenty-first-century correctional facilities. Because there is no formal process for sharing health information from community providers, to jail health staff, to prison health staff, and back to community providers, millions of health dollars are wasted each year repeating the same tests, exams, and information-gathering processes on the same people (Anno, 2004). Electronic health information exchange could help to avoid some of these costs.

Correctional health care has seen the introduction of technology in recent years that, as proven in private industry, has become more affordable and accessible. One technology in particular—telemedicine—is bringing the benefits of improved access to health services and cost savings to corrections. An independent experiment and evaluation of telemedicine conducted in 1999 by the U.S. Department of Justice's National Institute of Justice (NIJ), through the cooperation of the Federal Bureau of Prisons and the U.S. Department of Defense, determined that providing long-distance health care to inmates was feasible. Several federal prisons with different missions and security levels were connected via a telemedicine network. One of the federal prisons was a medical center. A Veterans' Administration hospital in Lexington, Kentucky, was also part of the network (NIJ, 2002).

In the twenty-first century, **telemedicine** or **telehealth** is widely used to provide specialist consultations and digital radiology services to inmates housed in rural to urban correctional and detention facilities—for example, in Texas, Arizona, and Wisconsin. Teleradiology is used at the majority of the DIHS clinic locations located across the country. The Federal Bureau of Prisons uses telepsychiatry at many of their prison facilities. The University of Texas Medical Branch has an extensive telemedicine program that supports its correctional health care programs. Primary care physicians are on-site to treat most medical problems, but specialists are sometimes needed to treat more complicated conditions. By using satellite links and computer networks, specialists are able to provide consultations, examinations, and evaluations to inmates while reducing the tremendous cost and risks associated with transporting inmates to off-site health care facilities. The technology also allows remote areas to have more consistent access to specialists and supplements staffing where health care personnel shortages exist. Telemedicine will not eliminate the need for inpatient care, and there is a distinct disadvantage to the specialist in not being able to touch the patient, but the programs currently in operation are viewed as highly successful.

HIM professionals can make a tremendous contribution to the application of technology in correctional health care. HIM professionals can have a huge impact on the way technology is introduced and applied in correctional settings.

telemedicine or telehealth the application of technology in which a video camera, a high-speed line, and monitoring and imaging equipment are installed at both a correctional facility and a medical facility. The telehealth equipment is linked either by high-speed communication lines, computer networks, or satellite hookups, thus allowing videoconferencing and digital images to be transmitted and received by either site.

SELF REVIEW 6.9

1. Identify some effects that advancements in technology may have on health care in correctional facilities.
2. True or False? Telemedicine or Telehealth is widely used to provide specialist consultations and digital radiology services to inmates who are housed in the range of rural to urban correctional and detention facilities.
3. True or False? Telemedicine will eliminate the need for inpatient.

SUMMARY

The corrections industry is growing rapidly, and correctional health care is growing along with it. Working in a correctional setting creates exciting and challenging opportunities for HIM professionals. Correctional health care has a long and challenging history, with continually increasing emphasis on providing accessible health services of high quality. In this evolving field, the roles and responsibilities for managing correctional health information are still being defined. Bright, articulate, energetic HIM professionals can achieve any measure of success they desire, while creating additional opportunities for themselves and their peers as the true leaders in health information management.

REVIEW QUESTIONS

Knowledge-Based Questions

1. List the different types of correctional facilities.
2. What is the significance of *Estelle v. Gamble* to correctional health care?
3. What are the advantages of placing the health services program within the state department of corrections under a health services director (HSD) as opposed to placement under individual wardens?
4. Briefly describe the accreditation process. Explain options for accreditation of correctional health care programs.
5. What certifications can health professionals working in corrections receive, and through which organizations are the programs administered?

Critical Thinking Questions

1. Explain the different arguments for and against the use of contracted health services and privately operated correctional facilities.
2. What factors will determine the type of health services that correctional facilities may need over the next 10 years?
3. How are correctional institutions affected by the Health Insurance Portability and Accountability Act of 1996 (HIPAA)? In what ways do HIPAA rules apply differently to the correctional setting?

WEB ACTIVITY

Visit the website of the National Commission on Correctional Health Care (NCCHC) at http://www.ncchc .org and click on the "Accreditation" link.

1. What information about the accreditation program is located here?

2. Click on the "CCHP Certification" link.
3. What benefits are listed for a person who obtains the Certified Correctional Health Professional (CCHP) credential?

CASE STUDY

It is your first week as the health information supervisor of a reception facility in a prison system. During your initial interviews with the staff, you hear complaints of staffing shortages and poor relationships with other facilities in the system. There are so few trained medical staff that guards and some record technicians have taken on the responsibility for documenting inmate histories. Members of the medical staff know they are performing duplicate lab tests, but the medical records are not available to verify previous tests and corroborate inmate complaints.

You also learn that several inmates are filing lawsuits claiming deliberate indifference because a tuberculosis test was not performed on another inmate who infected his cellmates after being transferred from your facility. Because the medical records are stored by the discharging facility, they are not available to the reception center. You know that, by law, the staff must complete a health status within 24 hours and a physical exam within 7 days, but most inmates are transferred after 4 days, which does not provide enough time to transfer records. A cursory examination of the electronic information system indicates that it lacks relevant data on prescription drugs, dates of tests, HIV (human immunodeficiency virus) status, and allergies and, therefore, cannot compensate for a lack of medical records. The staff turnover rate at the facility averages 40%.

1. How will you prioritize the issues you identify?
2. What recommendations would you make?

REFERENCES AND SUGGESTED READINGS

ACA (American Correctional Association). (2006). Inmate health care and communicable diseases. *Corrections Compendium.* [Online]. http://www.aca.org /hpis/pdf/Survey%20Summary_Tables.pdf [2010, July 16].

ACA (American Correctional Association). n.d. [Online]. http://aca.org [2010, July 16]

(American Correctional Health Services Association). [Online]. http://www.achsa.org

Anno, B. J. (1992). *Prison Health Care: Guidelines for the Management of an Adequate Delivery System.* Chicago: NCCHC.

Anno, B. J. (2001). *Correctional Health Care: Guidelines for the Management of an Adequate Delivery System.* Chicago: NCCHC.

Anno, B. J. (2004). Prison health services: An overview. *Journal of Correctional Health Care, 10*(3): 287–301.

Archambeault, W. (1987). Emerging issues in the use of microcomputers as management tools in criminal justice administration. In *Microcomputers in Criminal Justice: Current Issues and Applications.* Cincinnati, OH: Anderson Publishing Co.

Bauersmith, J., & Gent, R. (2002). The Broward County Jails hospice program: Hospice in the jail. *Journal of Palliative Medicine, 5*(5), 667–670.

BJS (Bureau of Justice Statistics). (2013). *Statistics of December, 2009.* [Online]. http://bjs.ojp.usdoj.gov / [2010, July 17].

Brakel, S. (1983). Ruling on prisoners' grievances. *American Bar Foundation Research Journal, 2,* 393–422.

CARF International. (2010). *Behavioral Health Program Descriptions.* [Online]. http://www.carf.org /Programs/ProgramDescriptions/

DHHS (Department of Health and Human Services). (2000, December 28). Standards for privacy of individually identifiable health information. *Federal Register, 65*(250), 82461–82829.

DHHS (Department of Health and Human Services). (2002, August 14). Standards for privacy of individually identifiable health information. *Federal Register, 67*(157), 53181–53273.

Ditton, P. (1999). Mental Health and Treatment of Inmates and Probationers. *U.S. Department of Justice, Bureau of Justice Statistics Special Report,* [Online]. https://www.prisonlegalnews.org. [1999, July, NCJ 174453].

Gannon, C. (1988). *Health Records in Correctional Health Care: A Reference Manual.* Chicago: NCCHC.

Klempner, J. (1981). *Juvenile Delinquency and Juvenile Justice.* New York: F. Watts.

Legal Information Institute. (n.d.). Prisoners' rights. [Online]. http://topics.law.cornell.edu/wex/prisoners _rights [2010, March 3].

Miller, E. E. (1978). *Jail Management Problems, Programs, and Perspectives.* Lexington, MA: D. C. Heath & Co.

National Commission for the Protection of Human Subjects of Biomedical and Behavioral Research. (1979, April 18). *The Belmont Report: Ethical Principles and Guidelines for the Protection of Human Subjects of Research.* [Online]. http://ohsr.od.nih.gov /guidelines/belmont.html [2010, July 10].

NCCHC (National Commission on Correctional Health Care. (1996). *Position Statement: Charging Inmates a Fee for Health Care Services.* Chicago: NCCHC.

NIJ (National Institute of Justice). (2002). *Implementing Telemedicine in Correctional Facilities.* [Online]. http://www.ojp.usdoj.gov/nij/pubs-sum/190310 .htm [2010, July 17].

Orr, D., & Hellerstein, D. (2002). Controversy, confusion herald HIPAA. *CorrectCare, 16*(4), 1, 22. [Online]. http://www.ncchc.org/pubs/CC/hipaastudy .html [2010, March 3].

Paris, J. E. (2009). The litmus test of electronic health record performance. *CorrectCare.* [Online]. http://www.ncchc.org/pubs/CC/EHR_litmus .html [2010, July 16]

Posner, M. (1992). The Estelle medical professional judgement standard: The right of those in state custody to receive high-cost medical treatment. *American Journal of Law and Medicine, 18*(4), 347–368.

Sentencing Project. (2006 December). *New Incarceration Figures: Growth in Population Continues.* http://www.sentencingproject.org/doc/publications /inc_newfigures.pdf [Online July 16, 2010].

USCIS (U.S. Bureau of Citizenship and Immigration Services. (2006). *Naturalization Eligibility Worksheet* (M-480 form). [Online]. http://www.uscis.gov /files/nativedocuments/M-480.pdf [2010, July 17].

USDOJ (U.S. Department of Justice, Federal Bureau of Prisons). (n.d.). *About the Bureau of Prisons.* [Online]. http://www.bop.gov/about/index.jsp [2010, March 3].

World Book Encyclopedia. 1996. Chicago: World Book, Inc.

KEY RESOURCES

American College of Correctional Physicians
http://societyofcorrectionalphysicians.org

American Correctional Association (ACA)
http://www.aca.org

American Correctional Health Services Association (ACHSA)
http://www.achsa.org

American Health Information Management Association
http://www.ahima.org

American Medical Association
http://www.ama-assn.org

American Public Health Association
http://www. apha.org

Bureau of Justice Statistics
http://www.bjs.gov

Centers for Disease Control and Prevention
http://www.cdc.gov

Division of Immigration Health Services
http://www.ice.gov/ice-health-service-corps

Federal Bureau of Prisons
http://www.bop.gov

National Commission on Correctional Health Care
http://www.ncchc.org

National Criminal Justice Association
http://www.ncja.org

National Institute of Corrections (NIC), U.S. Department of Justice
http://www.nicic.org

Mental Health: Long-Term and Acute Services

Mona Y. Calhoun, MS, MEd, RHIA, FAHIMA | C. Harrell Weathersby, PhD, MSW

LEARNING OBJECTIVES

Upon successful completion of this chapter, you should be able to:

- Describe the various settings and caregivers commonly associated with provision of mental health services.
- Evaluate the impact of state and federal laws and regulations on the treatment of persons with mental illness.
- Describe the components of a "typical" mental health treatment record, both inpatient and outpatient.
- Discuss current reimbursement issues related to mental health treatment.
- Discuss quality improvement and utilization management within mental health facilities.
- Discuss the role of the health information manager in a mental health facility.
- Discuss the current state and use of electronic information systems in managing mental health treatment information.
- Identify the specific legal and ethical considerations associated with the confidentiality of mental health treatment records.

Setting	Description	Synonym/Examples
Outpatient Mental Health Facility	A facility where clients receive regularly scheduled outpatient mental health treatment	Community Mental Health Center
Group Home	Residential facility providing 24-hour supervision and daily living skills training on a time-limited basis to prepare clients for a less restrictive environment	Halfway House
Personal Care Home	A permanent living facility offering some supervision and meals, but no training, for persons who are too severely impaired to live completely independently	
Psychiatric Crisis Facility	A facility for short-term treatment of psychotic symptoms in an early stage	Acute Care
Inpatient Psychiatric Hospital	A facility providing long-term inpatient treatment for persons whose symptoms do not respond sufficiently to medication to allow them to live successfully in a less restrictive environment	Institution

INTRODUCTION TO SETTING

community mental health centers (CMHC) a network of publicly funded mental health organizations established in communities throughout the United States by the Mental Health Act of 1965.

psychotropic medications a variety of medications designed to reduce psychotic symptoms by altering the chemical processes within the brain. Also sometimes referred to as "neuroleptics."

psychosis a state of extreme disordered thinking in which the person demonstrates symptoms of serious mental illness such as hallucinations and delusions. (See also *hallucination* and *delusions*)

outpatient commitment judicial diversion, of a person to outpatient psychiatric care.

The **community mental health center (CMHC)** is the principal setting for treating serious mental illness in the United States. CMHCs are publicly funded entities established by the Mental Health Act of 1965. This congressional legislation provided the initial funding for CMHCs on a gradually decreasing scale over a period of years, with increased funding from county and state monies intended to replace the majority of the federal grants eventually. The community mental health system was conceived as the conduit for affordable mental health services, to be provided to the public in much the same way as the state departments of health were established earlier to provide a broadly based health care system to all segments of the population.

Over time, this service system became increasingly focused on the more chronic segment of the mentally ill population of adults and children. The increased need for a large-scale effort to provide supportive services for this population grew out of the discovery of **psychotropic medications** in the late 1960s, to reduce the symptoms of **psychosis** and disordered thinking. Although the medications were not universally successful, the majority of individuals who previously had been destined to spend their lives in mental institutions were rendered capable of living in community settings.

The 1970s and 1980s saw a major push to restore to the community those patients who responded well to the new medications. The process of **outpatient commitment** became feasible, allowing courts to place persons in need of psychiatric care in outpatient programs, with stipulations regarding taking medications and maintaining scheduled psychiatric appointments.

This mass deinstitutionalization movement resulted in the downsizing of most large mental hospitals where people had been confined. Figure 7-1 from the National Association of State Mental Health Program Directors (NASMHPD)

FIGURE 7-1

State mental health agency-controlled expenditures for state psychiatric hospital inpatient and community-based services as a percent of total expenditures: 1981 to 2009.

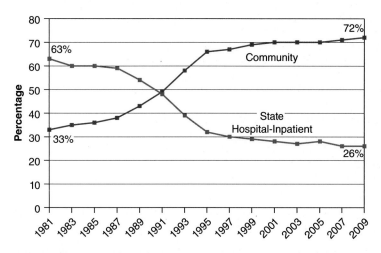

Source: NASMHPD Research Institute, Inc., under contract to SAMHSA, http://www.samhsa.gov.

Research Institute, illustrates this trend, demonstrating how the percentage of State Mental Health Authority expenditures for inpatient care has decreased while the percentage of expenditures for community-based services has increased since 1981. To a limited extent, some private psychiatric hospitals also provide outpatient services, but seldom on the scale and of the variety that are offered by CMHCs.

The enthusiasm with which this medical breakthrough was hailed was shown to be somewhat premature. The medications often had rather unpleasant, and in some cases dangerous, side-effects, and they did not always work as precisely as had been hoped. In addition, many of the persons discharged into the community had lived most of their adult lives in the structured environment of the hospital. They had little idea of how to carry on daily life within society at large. Consequently, many of them experienced extremes of stress that necessitated their return to the hospital. Or worse, they skirted the mental health system and became part of the growing homeless population that burgeoned in the 1980s and has persisted to a lesser degree ever since that time.

Although accurate statistics are elusive because of the hidden nature of homeless persons, it is thought that approximately 20% to 25% of the homeless population is seriously mentally ill (National Institute of Mental Health, 2009). This group consists largely of persons who are unwilling to receive treatment principally because of the unpleasant side-effects of psychotropic medications, or who are incapable of accessing the mental health system because of their disordered thinking.

A second site for provision of mental health services is the acute care inpatient hospital. The two types of acute facilities are (1) short-term psychiatric crisis facilities and (2) traditional inpatient psychiatric hospitals where patients who do not respond to medication can be treated for a lengthier period of time.

As the effectiveness of medication continues to improve in recent years, it has become less necessary for persons with mental illness to undergo long periods of hospitalization. Often during a period of florid psychosis, they are able to access short-term acute psychiatric care that lasts 3 to 4 weeks on average. Admittance to facilities providing this care is either voluntary or involuntary, depending on the ability of the potential patient to recognize the need for treatment. **Involuntary commitment** is a legal process whereby individuals may be admitted to an inpatient facility even though they refuse or cannot consent to the treatment if they are legally adjudicated to be a "danger to self or others."

Inpatient facilities operate in many ways that are similar to long-term psychiatric hospitals. Most offer the same highly structured environment, with emphasis on group therapy and recreational activities, provided in the more traditional long-term facilities. As in the case of long-term psychiatric hospitals, these facilities usually maintain the capacity for restraint and isolation in case of violent behaviors that pose a threat to the patient or to others. The chief distinction is in the brevity of treatment. Patients who do not respond to this type of therapy fairly quickly are usually transferred to long-term hospitals for involuntary treatment through the usual legal commitment procedures.

involuntary commitment a legal process by which individuals who are deemed to be a danger to themselves or to others may be admitted to an inpatient facility even though they refuse or cannot consent to the treatment.

Types of Clients

Although services for adults and services designed for children and adolescents have some similarities, there also are some differences. As might be expected, the differing stages in the life cycle of these two groups necessitate some fundamental differences in status, both legal and educational, and in life tasks. In some cases, the illness also manifests itself differently within these two groups.

Adults

The two types of mental or emotional illness that adults are likely to experience are *temporary* emotional crisis related to traumatic event(s) or *chronic*, long-term mental illness. Temporary mental problems result from some traumatic event or series of events in a person's life, such as loss of a loved one, divorce, or bankruptcy. These emotional upheavals are manifested most often in the form of extreme depression and/or suicidal tendencies. In these cases, mental anguish and sad feelings can be clearly traced to a causal factor that triggered the crisis and that usually can be dealt with through counseling, or at times with a mood-altering medication that can aid in lifting depression.

Long-term mental illness, in contrast, cannot be traced so easily in a causal fashion. Its onset is a result of chemical changes in the brain, with which the mental health profession is becoming increasingly skilled—with rapidly advancing technology—at observing and describing. As yet, we are unable to say in general what causes these changes. This type of mental illness is chronic in nature, in that it often can be controlled with medication, but it cannot be cured. It receives the heaviest funding and greatest research support within the public sector, based on the concept that persons with serious, persistent mental illness are those "most in need" of the insufficient resources available for mental health treatment.

Because of the many myths surrounding this type of mental illness, persons who are afflicted prefer the use of terms in describing the illness that are free of the traditional connotations that arouse pity, fear, or rejection. For this reason, they particularly dislike the use of *chronic* as a descriptive term. They prefer either *long-term, severe*, or *serious* as descriptors of the illness, and persons with **serious mental illness (SMI)** currently being the most preferred epithet. They also favor what is known as "person first" language—such as, "a person with schizophrenia" rather than "a schizophrenic," and "persons with **manic depression**" rather than "manic-depressives."

This group also has a preference in terms describing their status as service recipients. Since the 1970s there has been a movement toward political and social empowerment of persons with mental illness as part of the campaign against public stigmatization. Most service recipients prefer to be known as "mental health service consumers" (usually shortened to "consumers" after the context has been established) or "users of mental health services." Some persons also have chosen to be recognized as "psychiatric survivors," so the term "consumer/survivor" has come into use recently. As a group, they prefer this terminology over the more traditional "client" or "patient" (except in an inpatient situation or medical relationship, as with a doctor or nurse). They believe that these latter terms connote a "one-down" relationship and imply a dependency and inability to participate in treatment planning, as opposed to the implication of a customer relationship suggested by the terms "consumer" and "service user."

The most common forms of serious mental illness are schizophrenia, clinical depression, and bipolar disorder, the latter of which has become the favored term for what has been known more widely as manic depression. Another large category encompasses persons with **dual diagnoses** (two diagnoses). These persons may be diagnosed either as mentally ill with intellectual/developmental disability (mental retardation) or as mentally ill with alcohol and/or chemical addiction.

Schizophrenia is a type of psychosis, a state of extremely disordered thinking, manifesting as a break with reality. Persons with schizophrenia are unable to differentiate reality from **hallucinations** or **delusions** within their own minds. Hallucinations are false perceptions of the five senses (e.g., seeing images that are not present, hearing internal voices, feeling skin sensations that are not the result of external stimuli, tasting or smelling things that are not real). Delusions are false ideas that have no basis in fact (e.g., a belief that the FBI is pursuing a

serious mental illness (SMI) a condition in which a person has a diagnosable mental, behavioral, or emotional disorder resulting in functional impairment that substantially interferes with or limits one or more major life activities.

manic depression see *bipolar disorder.*

dual diagnoses two concurrent diagnoses. Most commonly refers to diagnoses in persons with mental illness and chemical or alcohol addiction, but may also refer to persons who are diagnosed as having a developmental disability and are seriously mentally ill.

schizophrenia a psychosis characterized by a state of extremely disordered thinking, manifesting as a break with reality.

hallucination a form of disordered thinking in which a person reports sensory experience that is not valid, such as seeing, hearing, smelling, or feeling things that are not real. See also *psychosis.*

delusions a form of disordered thinking characterized by unrealistic beliefs (e.g., that someone with this condition is receiving communications from aliens in outer space or that food is being poisoned). See also psychosis.

person, that food is being poisoned, that the person has been chosen by a supreme being as the recipient of a divine message for the world). The root causes of the chemical changes in the brain that result in schizophrenic psychoses are not yet known.

Clinical depression appears as a deep feeling of melancholy and futility that is not situational in nature. It, too, results from chemical imbalances in the brain that are stress-induced, but the reason for this reaction to stress in some persons and not in others remains unknown.

Bipolar disorder presents a spiral of behavior that typically begins with an episode of extreme euphoria, which in its early stages may even be highly creative, but that degenerates into hallucination and/or delusional thinking. This phase usually is followed by deep depression, often reaching suicidal proportions, from which only medication can lift a person.

As indicated previously, there are two types of dually diagnosed persons within the mentally ill population. Persons with developmental disabilities may become mentally ill also, in which case they will carry a diagnosis of mental illness with mental retardation/intellectual disability. The treatment modes for this group are largely behavior-shaping techniques. The chief intervention is the administration of psychotropic medication. Because of the low functioning abilities that result from retardation, persons with this dual diagnosis often have to be followed carefully to ensure that the medication is actually being taken and in the correct dosage.

The other type of dual diagnosis occurs in persons with mental illness and an alcohol/chemical addiction. Treatment programs for these individuals are often referred to as **MICA (mental illness with chemical addiction)** services. This type of dual diagnosis is on the rise within the mental health system. Because of the wide availability of illegal recreational drugs, many young persons in particular begin to experiment, sometimes as a way to cope with the onset of the symptoms of the mental illness. Traditionally, a battle has been waged between substance-abuse service providers and mental health professionals as to who should serve this group. Consequently, members of this group have been shuttled back and forth between the two providers, depending on which illness was most evident at a given time, and ill-served by both. Also, the treatment philosophy between the two providers is fundamentally different, further reducing the likelihood of successful outcomes.

Substance abuse service providers typically take a confrontational approach to the addiction, believing that the client must face up to the addiction before help can begin. This approach often produces negative results in dually diagnosed persons because of the low self-esteem and inability to handle the stress that typically accompany the mental illness. Mental health professionals, however, have tended to ignore the substance abuse altogether, which is equally counterproductive to a successful treatment outcome. Thus, this group often has a high incidence of repeated hospitalizations: People in this group travel the cycle from achieving

clinical depression a serious mental illness appearing as a deep feeling of melancholy and futility that is not situational in nature.

bipolar disorder a form of serious mental illness in which a person alternates between states of ecstatic mania and severe depression. Also known as *manic depression*.

MICA (mental illness with chemical addiction) a program for persons who are dually diagnosed with mental illness and chemical/alcohol addiction. Sometimes written as MIDA or MICAA. This terminology is not considered correct to refer to individuals or to indicate a population.

sobriety in the hospital, to resuming drug usage in the community, to repeating a psychotic episode that returns them to inpatient care—beginning the cycle all over again.

In the past several years there has been a growing trend toward melding elements of both substance abuse and mental health treatment modes designed specifically for this population. Along with the cross-training, an educational model seems to be emerging. This model eschews confrontation in favor of an openness to discussion of the nature of mental illness and symptom management that incorporates knowledge about the detrimental effects of substance abuse on the efficacy of psychotropic medications. Concomitantly, the persons with mental illness are repeatedly presented with nonconfrontational invitations, in both individual and group counseling sessions, to examine the detrimental effects of the addiction in their lives.

The major symptoms for these types of serious mental illness, as well as less common ones, are described in the American Psychiatric Association's *Diagnostic and Statistical Manual of Mental Disorders,* **Fifth Edition, text revision (DSM-5)** (American Psychiatric Association, 2013).

In the 1970s, mental health professionals and politicians began to realize that deinstitutionalization would not work without **continuity of care**, with particular emphasis on providing a smooth transition from inpatient to outpatient services. What was needed was a service system designed to maintain mentally ill persons outside of the hospital. This led to the Community Support Program (CSP) at the federal level, an initiative originating within the National Institute of Mental Health (NIMH), the federal center at that time for research concerning mental health issues. This branch of the institute undertook studies of what services were needed to adequately support mentally ill persons who were attempting to live independently and how those services could best be delivered. Concurrently, the federal funding streams for mental health were diverted to this population as the group "most in need."

Now, disability benefits are provided in the form of **Supplemental Security Income (SSI)** for those who have not been able to establish a work history, and as **Social Security Disability Income (SSDI)** for those with sufficient investiture in the Social Security system to be eligible. In addition, Medicaid benefits are tied to SSI eligibility, and Medicare benefits also are available based on age or SSDI eligibility. Because these benefits are linked to diagnosis, documentation in this area becomes an extremely important part of the person's medical history. In addition to the medical diagnoses determined through use of the *Diagnostic and Statistical Manual (DSM)*, federal guidelines have been set up based on criteria of physical and psychological functioning. According to these criteria:

> "Adults with a serious mental illness are persons age 18 and over, who currently or at any time during the past year have had a diagnosable mental, behavioral, or emotional disorder of sufficient duration to meet diagnostic criteria specified within DSM-III-R [DSM-IV or 5] that has resulted in functional impairment which substantially

Diagnostic and Statistical Manual of Mental Disorders, fifth edition, text revision (DSM-5) a nomenclature, classification and coding system of mental disorders developed by the American Psychiatric Association (APA) that provides clear descriptions of diagnostic categories.

continuity of care a concept that refers to creation of a comprehensive system of care for persons with serious mental illness, with particular emphasis on a smooth transition from inpatient services to outpatient services.

Supplemental Security Income (SSI) federal benefits paid to persons with disability who have not worked a sufficient length of time to qualify for Social Security benefits. A common, and often only, source of income for persons with serious mental illness who are unable to work.

Social Security Disability Income (SSDI) federal benefits paid to persons with disability who have worked a sufficient length of time to qualify to receive Social Security benefits; a frequent source of income for persons with serious mental illness who are not able to work.

interferes with or limits one or more major life activities." (*Federal Register*, May 20, 1993)

CSP efforts to determine the best-practice treatment methods to maintain mentally ill persons outside of the hospital gave rise to some changes in the traditional methods of aftercare following discharge from the hospital. The older concepts centered on partial hospitalization, which provided a setting in which former patients could continue during the day with nonstressful activities similar to those provided during hospitalization, such as handicrafts, group therapy, and recreational activities.

Over time, this emphasis on maintenance gradually changed to a focus on rehabilitation, the concept of moving the mental health consumer to a routine more nearly in keeping with that of a person without the illness, whose day is devoted primarily to meaningful activity. Wherever possible, the goal here is to provide actual employment, even if just part-time, because work provides to the general population one of the most powerful of all psychological connections to the society as a whole. As such, it is a major source of self-esteem. More recently, the term *recovery* has become preferred over *rehabilitation* as a descriptor for the periods of time that persons with mental illness experience when the illness is brought under control. This concept, borrowed from the treatment language for persons with drug or alcohol addictions, suggests a greater potential for long periods of enfolding into routine community life similar to that experienced by addicts during successful attainment of sobriety.

This change in vision also resulted in part from a growing demand by the consumers to have an active voice in the design and purpose of mental health programming. In time, the concept of **psychosocial rehabilitation** arose. This treatment modality consists of an array of support services designed to meet the changing needs of consumers based on the degree of moribundity or floridity of their symptoms at any given point in time. Because the course of the illness and the medication side-effects cannot always be predicted with precision, it is essential to be able to individualize treatment plans with a great deal of flexibility. The system must be designed to meet the service needs of each person as his or her needs change with regard to more structure in times of increased psychosis or sensitivity to medication and less structure as he or she becomes more stable.

The variety of services outside of the mental health system per se indicates the necessity for a holistic approach to service provision to maximize the time period that a person may remain in the community without rehospitalization. Within the mental health setting, some consider the following options to be core services that the majority of seriously mentally ill persons are likely to need at some point in the course of their treatment (Stroul & Friedman, 1994):

- *Diagnostic evaluation and psychiatric medication management.* These services are provided by a psychiatrist, nurse practitioner, and/or nurse. If medical conditions unrelated to mental illness are present, the person

psychosocial rehabilitation   a mode of treatment for serious mental illness that focuses on providing an array of community support services (e.g., development of job skills, if needed) for persons with mental illness, sufficient to allow them to live in the least restrictive environment possible outside of an institution.

typically is referred to appropriate medical personnel within the community for treatment.

- *Case management.* This service area provides linkage and brokerage to other services. Its primary function is to obtain access for the consumer to services both within and outside of the mental health setting. Thus, it is the "glue" that provides coordination of support across the continuum and mitigates fragmentation of the service delivery system.

- *Day programming.* This area varies somewhat from system to system. The goal is to provide an opportunity for consumers to interact with peers as well as professional staff. Some programs offer the more traditional partial hospitalization activities described previously. Others take a more rehabilitative approach, actively preparing and encouraging the consumer to move toward employment in the job market or volunteer work in the community and more independent functioning outside the mental health system.

- *Residential living.* This alternative is offered to consumers whose level of functioning has been impaired to the extent that, upon remediation of their psychotic symptoms, they are not able to maintain themselves initially in an independent setting. They are placed in group home settings (sometimes referred to as halfway houses), where they typically stay for 6 months to a year and practice necessary daily living skills such as cooking, money management, and personal hygiene. Acquiring these skills will allow them to function successfully in more independent settings such as personal care homes, where they will receive some assistance with meals and medication monitoring, or in apartments or houses of their own.

- *Screening and evaluation.* The CMHC professional staff typically determines the need for short-term acute psychiatric care and/or recommendations to the courts for involuntary hospitalization.

- *After-hours crisis services.* Emergency services for psychiatric crises generally are provided on a 24-hour basis through a system of on-call personnel. When necessary, screening and evaluation for involuntary hospitalization also can be provided in this way.

Adolescents and Children

Approximately 9% to 13% of children ages 9 to 17 have a **serious emotional disturbance (SED)** with considerable functional impairment, and 5% to 9% have a serious emotional disturbance with extreme functional impairment (Friedman et al., 1996). As with adults having mental illness, a federal definition for younger population was developed :

> Children with a serious emotional disturbance are persons from birth to 18 who currently or at any time during the past year have had a diagnosable mental, behavioral, or emotional disorder of sufficient duration to meet diagnostic-criteria specified within DSM-III-R [DSM-IV or 5] that resulted in functional impairment which substantially

serious emotional disturbance (SED) a condition in which a young person (from birth to age 18) has a diagnosable mental, behavioral, or emotional disorder resulting in functional impairment that substantially interferes with or limits his or her role or functioning in family, school, or community activities.

interferes with or limits the child's role or functioning in family, school, or community activities. (*Federal Register*, 1993)

The first initiative to examine the extent of need for mental health services for this population was The Joint Commission on the Mental Health of Children in 1969 (Stroul & Friedman, 1994). As further studies were conducted and advocacy groups formed, Congress funded a federal initiative to address the gap in services. The National Institute of Mental Health (NIMH) established the **Child and Adolescent Service System Program (CASSP)** in 1984.

As a result of the dispersion of NIMH programs in the late 1980s, this program, currently known as **system of care** grants, is now under the auspices of the **Center for Mental Health Services (CMHS)** of the **Substance Abuse and Mental Health Services Administration (SAMHSA)**, U.S. Department of Health and Human Services. The goal of this program is to assist states in creating systems of care for children and youth who have severe emotional disturbances. According to CMHS, a "system of care" is:

> "an organizational philosophy and framework that involves collaboration across agencies, families, and youth for the purpose of improving access and expanding the array of coordinated community-based, culturally and linguistically competent services and supports for children and youth with a serious emotional disturbance and their families. Research has demonstrated that systems of care have a positive effect on the structure, organization, and availability of services for children and youth with serious mental health needs." (CMHS, 2009, para 2)

Core services needed within the mental health system itself initially were identified as follows (Stroul & Friedman, 1994). (Although *children* is used to describe the clientele, it should be understood to include adolescents unless otherwise specified.)

- *Early identification and intervention.* This effort necessarily crosses several service systems (e.g., health, education), but mental health has a role to play. The earlier the problem is identified, the better is the chance for successful treatment. Sometimes, however, the problems or their seriousness may not become manifested clearly until latency age or adolescence. Identification of multiproblem families who seek mental health services, regardless of the age of the child, may be a first step.

- *Diagnosis and evaluation.* Again, this area may include several systems. It usually includes assessments of physical health, intelligence level, and academic achievement or potential; social and behavioral functioning; family dynamics; and environmental factors, such as extent of poverty and type of housing.

- *Outpatient treatment.* This intervention usually entails regularly scheduled appointments for individual, group, and/or family therapy, with a frequency based on need. Although there is some question as to the effectiveness of this type of treatment, some studies have indicated that it can be helpful (Sowder, 1979; Casey & Burman, 1985).

Child and Adolescent Service System Program (CASSP) a program that created a comprehensive network of services for children and adolescents with emotional disturbance through a series of demonstration grants.

system of care "an organizational philosophy and framework that involves collaboration across agencies, families, and youth for the purpose of improving access and expanding the array of coordinated community-based, culturally and linguistically competent services and supports for children and youth with a serious emotional disturbance and their families" (CMHS, 2009, para 2).

Center for Mental Health Services (CMHS) the federal agency within the Substance Abuse and Mental Health Services Administration (SAMHSA) that oversees administration of demonstration and research grants and other initiatives at the federal level related to mental health issues.

Substance Abuse and Mental Health Services Administration (SAMHSA) an agency created in 1992 under the umbrella of the U.S. Department of Health and Human Services. Its purpose is to "reduce the impact of substance abuse and mental illness on America's communities."

- *Day treatment.* This service involves an integration of educational and mental health services, whether established formally between agencies or not. Intensive treatment includes carefully integrated components of education, counseling, and family therapy and typically is provided during school hours. Services may be provided in a variety of settings, from regular schools, to special schools, to the mental health center. This service is much like the partial hospitalization program for adults, except for the inclusion and emphasis on the educational component.

- *Emergency services.* Crisis response is similar to that for adults, although it is somewhat more rare for children (Stroul & Friedman, 1994). The services for children also may include runaway shelters and home-based services that are unique to this population.

- *Home-based services.* Other terms for this type of intervention are: in-home services, family-centered services, intensive family services, and family preservation services. This category encompasses a rather wide range of services. The commonality among all of them is that they are family- rather than individual-centered (Hutchinson et al., 1983), and, as the term implies, most of the services are delivered in the home. Most of these programs have the following goals in common: "preserving the integrity of the family and preventing unnecessary out-of-home placement; linking the child and family with appropriate community agencies and individuals to create an ongoing community support system; and strengthening the family's coping skills and capacity to function effectively in the community" (Stroul & Friedman, 1994).

- *Therapeutic foster care.* This service "provides treatment for troubled children within the private homes of trained families" (Stroul & Friedman, 1994). It provides a homelike atmosphere in which to apply treatment interventions. It seems similar to traditional foster care, but the families receive special training in how to cope with the extreme emotional disturbance that led to removal of the child from the family. This setting is considered to be the least restrictive in the continuum of alternative placements because of its capacity to duplicate a home environment most closely.

- *Therapeutic group home.* This type of residential setting involves congregate care somewhat similar to that of the adult group home. Some group homes exist primarily to serve less severely disturbed children who need care of a protective nature because of abuse or neglect. These children typically need a mental health treatment component as well as the highly structured environment typical of these programs. A therapeutic group home has been defined as "a single home, located in the general community, that serves no more than eight children" (Stroul & Friedman, 1994). These entities can vary greatly in staff-to-child ratio, depending on severity of psychological impairment and intensity of treatment. Two distinct models of care are used: (1) The teaching family model employs a married couple who live with the children in family-like arrangements, with relief help to provide time off; (2) the other model employs shifts of workers who rotate to provide 24-hour care and supervision. Although the treatment approaches vary, they generally include individual and group counseling along with a behavior modification program.

- *Inpatient hospitalization.* This setting is utilized in extreme situations. Children who demonstrate signs that they might seriously harm themselves or others are referred for hospitalization. With increasing frequency, as the home-based services become more generally available, such hospital stays are of short duration, usually a matter of days, or a few weeks at most. Occasionally, however, a child's difficulties are so severe that long-term hospitalization becomes the only option. This setting also is used for conducting comprehensive evaluations, particularly if the possible presence of neurological or other physiological complications may require extensive testing and observation over time.

wrap-around services the predominant method of mental health service delivery to children and adolescents with emotional disturbance and their families, consisting of a comprehensive array of professional services that may include home and/or school settings tailored to meet the specific needs of the child and his or her family.

As the core services came into being, a more recent concept, known as **wrap-around services**, has become the predominant method of service delivery for children and adolescents with emotional disturbance. These community-based services attempt to prevent the necessity for more restrictive levels of care. As the term *wrap-around* suggests, this is a comprehensive array of professional services that includes the child's home and/or school setting. The essential features entail individualization of services to fit the specific needs of each child and family, maximization of the family's strengths and natural support systems as resources, and attention to the cultural values of the child's family and community in the way that services are developed and delivered (Furman, 1997).

As an almost necessary adjunct to wrap-around services, the notion of flexible funding has come into use. This concept allows for funding to be used for development of nontraditional services such as respite care, which allows for brief "cooling off" periods during times of high emotional crisis when the child can be cared for temporarily outside the home. As another example of highly successful nontraditional services, mentoring programs encourage successful members of the community to volunteer as companions for troubled youths of similar culture and background, to provide guidance and stability.

Types of Caregivers

There are many professional and educational backgrounds and requirements for caregivers within the mental health system. With only a few exceptions, the types of workers who provide both adults' and children's services tend to be the same. Likewise, the types of staff found in both the inpatient and outpatient settings tend to be similar, although their actual daily duties and responsibilities may differ in the extent of structure and control provided.

Medical Personnel

Because psychotropic medication usually is considered to be essential to maintaining stability in serious mental illness, the psychiatrist plays a central treatment role in performing diagnosis and evaluation and providing medication management. Many of the medications prescribed for the illness can have severe and, in some cases, fatal consequences if the levels are not monitored carefully at regular intervals. Dosages also may have to be adjusted from time to time because of increases or decreases in the amount of stress a person is experiencing or because of metabolic changes in the body over time.

The physician's role is to oversee these matters. In most settings, a nurse assists the physician, providing follow-up care as prescribed. The duties typically include monitoring of blood work and medication levels, providing injections if the psychotropic medication is prescribed in this form, and assisting with minor side-effects of the medication. Although found somewhat less frequently at present in the mental health field, a growing number of nurse practitioners, under the supervision of a physician, can perform some of the physician's functions, including prescription of medication.

Therapists

The therapist category includes a wide diversity of workers, encompassing psychologists, master's-level and bachelor's-level social workers, and community counselors. Each of these disciplines has a certification mechanism at the national level, and most states also require a state license to practice. Persons at the master's level or higher in social work and psychology usually are allowed to perform diagnostic and evaluation screening for mental illness. In some cases, this function is provided under supervision of a psychiatrist. In some states, psychologists have gained the authority to prescribe some drugs on a limited basis and with a physician's oversight.

Where short-term, situational emotional disturbance exists, the therapist—either bachelor's-level or master's level—performs a counseling function. It generally is thought that persons with serious mental illness who are in a stable mental state do not benefit greatly from traditional talk therapy, and that it actually may produce negative effects sometimes by increasing stress when the discussion turns to unhappy events.

One symptom of mental illness that is not always as readily apparent as the psychoses, however, is called "poverty of thought." This symptom is characterized by an inability to generate alternative solutions to a problem. Therefore, it sometimes is useful to have available a person who can counsel the consumer who is experiencing a current life crisis and cannot seem to find a viable solution. In some settings, the therapist also will conduct group therapy, especially if the traditional partial hospitalization model is used as a daycare program. In the inpatient setting, group therapy is a standard form of treatment and typically is conducted by a therapist.

Case Managers

The case manager's credentials vary widely from state to state. Most have a bachelor's degree, but there usually is great latitude as to the field of study. The chief responsibility of the case manager is to provide the consumer in the community with access to services across the spectrum of support services, as indicated. Thus the chief functions of this position are referral to needed services, coordination among service providers, and monitoring for escalation of psychotic symptoms.

In general, case managers are prohibited from offering counseling and therapy because of licensure and Medicaid restrictions. In rare cases, appropriately licensed persons are used in intensive case-management programs that include a counseling component for which the target population is a small caseload of consumers (usually no more than 10) who tend to be high users of inpatient hospitalization. Persons providing the intensive home-based services to families of children with emotional disturbance children also would perform many of the same functions as case managers for adults.

Aides/Direct Care Workers

This group of workers goes by different appellations within the various settings where they work: direct care workers (DCWs), residential living technicians, or certified nursing aides (CNAs). Their primary duties revolve around providing assistance with daily living skills to persons in the inpatient setting or in community group homes. In each of these settings, 24-hour care and supervision typically are provided. Although levels of certification vary, a high school diploma or a general equivalency diploma (GED) usually is required.

Recreation Therapists

Recreation therapists are found more often in the inpatient setting than in the community mental health setting, unless the program is conducting a partial hospitalization component. These therapists usually are employed in the structured setting to provide an antidote for the lassitude that often accompanies the illness, especially in its acute state, and to provide activity and distraction, which generally ameliorate psychotic symptoms.

Occupational Therapists

Occupational therapists typically work in the inpatient setting. They assess patients' functioning abilities and prescribe programs designed to restore patients' capacities to work, when feasible, and they teach daily living skills that will increase the likelihood of the patients' successful transitions to community living. They also are found occasionally in rehabilitative roles within the community setting where the outpatient day program has an emphasis in this direction.

1. What role have psychotropic medications played in the rise of in expenditures for community-based services over the years?

2. A(n) _____ is a legal process whereby individuals may be admitted to an inpatient facility even though they refuse or cannot consent to the treatment if they are legally adjudicated to be a "danger to self or others."

3. Why do persons with long-term mental illnesses prefer "person first" language in describing the illness, and also subscribe to terms such as "consumer," "service user," and "survivors" to describe their status as service recipients?

4. True or False? The *Diagnostic and Statistical Manual of Mental Disorders* is in its fourth edition.

5. Name the core services needed by the majority of seriously mentally ill persons.

6. What is the significance of the system of care grants?

REGULATORY ISSUES

Mental health centers typically receive certification from a designated state regulatory agency—usually a department or office of mental health. These agencies establish licensure standards and perform monitoring functions accordingly. As mental health consumers and their family members have become increasingly politicized in recent years, the agencies have engaged in a steady effort to make the regulations for licensure more outcome-based. The thrust is more toward measuring quality of services than quantity or frequency of delivery.

Another regulatory mechanism exists at the state level for both inpatient and outpatient facilities that wish to receive Medicaid. They must comply with the Medicaid guidelines set and monitored by the state agency designated as the regulatory body for this funding. Similarly, facilities that receive Medicare reimbursement must comply with the applicable Conditions of Participation. The Conditions of Participation for hospitals include special provisions applying to psychiatric hospitals in sections 482.60–482.62, including special medical record requirements for psychiatric hospitals.

The "Interpretive Guidelines and Survey Procedures" for psychiatric hospitals are found in Appendix AA of the *State Operations Manual* (CMS, 2014). These guidelines provide state surveyors with detailed explanations for interpreting and applying the Conditions of Participation during the survey of a psychiatric hospital. Medicare and Medicaid coverage is tied to diagnosis and to a physician's prescription for the entire array of services to be provided as "medically necessary." Thus, accuracy of documentation in this area is crucial.

Several other regulatory entities set standards for mental health service delivery by virtue of their accrediting processes. A mental health service provider may seek accreditation by one or more of the following groups: The Joint Commission (TJC), CARF International (formerly the Commission on Accreditation of Rehabilitation Facilities), the National Committee for Quality Assurance (NCQA), or URAC (formerly the Utilization Review Accreditation Commission).

The Joint Commission provides accreditation for inpatient and outpatient mental health facilities. A facility licensed as a hospital is surveyed under the *Comprehensive Accreditation Manual for Hospitals* (CAMH). If the hospital offers residential treatment, partial hospitalization, or supervised living programs, The Joint Commission conducts a tailored survey using selected standards from the *Comprehensive Accreditation Manual for Behavioral Health Care* (CAMBHC) in addition to the standards in the *CAMH*. Other mental health service providers that are freestanding (i.e., not affiliated with a hospital) are surveyed by The Joint Commission under the *CAMBHC* only. Beginning in 2014, e-editions were available for download at http://www.jointcommission.org/standards _information/edition.aspx

CARF provides an accrediting process for mental health and psychosocial rehabilitation programs. Programs that can be accredited include case management, crisis intervention, outpatient treatment, partial hospitalization, residential treatment, community housing, inpatient treatment, assertive community treatment, and many other services. A mental health facility seeking accreditation from CARF would be surveyed under its *Behavioral Health Standards Manual* (CARF, n.d.).

NCQA offers an accreditation program to managed behavioral health care organizations (MBHOs). An MBHO may be a managed behavioral health care company or a behavioral health program or department within a managed care organization (MCO). At the request of an MCO or MBHO, NCQA surveys mental health services under the *MBHO Standards and Guidelines* (National Committee for Quality Assurance, n.d.).

Clinical services of MBHOs, too, are often accredited by URAC. URAC also accredits case management services.

DOCUMENTATION

Mental health case records are considerably similar, whether inpatient or outpatient, as are other medically oriented records. Although content and arrangement vary, certain information is basic to all treatment of individuals with mental illness and appears in some form in the mental health record. This includes assessment, treatment plan, progress notes, and discharge summary with plans for aftercare (Conditions of Participation, 2014).

Assessment

At the first contact between a consumer/patient and a mental health facility, an initial assessment is performed. This could occur in a telephone contact or in an emergency encounter. The initial assessment focuses on the patient's apparent needs and whether the facility can address those needs appropriately. In some instances, the result of the initial assessment is to refer the patient elsewhere for further services. If it is determined that the patient should be admitted to the original facility, the initial assessment serves as a basis for determining which services of the facility are most appropriate.

The assessment process continues with completion of the intake or general assessment. The mental health professional who performs the intake gathers any remaining demographic information that has not been collected yet. A history of previous hospitalizations or other medical difficulties is elicited. If the consumer or patient is in a psychotic state that renders him or her unreliable, the professional seeks this information from collateral contacts where possible.

Regardless of the patient's mental status, some time should be spent gaining the consumer's perception of why he or she is present for the interview. If possible, the professional should determine the presenting problem from the point of view of the consumer/patient. The assessment has to be holistic in nature so if possible physically based problems can be ruled out as contributory or ancillary to the interviewee's mental problems. For instance, diabetes can cause mania-like symptoms similar to those of bipolar disorder when insulin dosages are not accurate.

A complete assessment may include any or all of the following: physical, emotional, behavioral, social, recreational, legal, vocational, and/or nutritional components (Huffman, 1994). It should be noted that assessment is an ongoing process. Several interviews may be required for the consumer/patient to gain sufficient trust to fully state the nature of his or her problem(s). Also, these concerns may change over time as some problems reach resolution or, in some cases, unfortunately prove to be unsolvable. Certain events or circumstances—such as the use of restraints or seclusion, a recommendation for electroconvulsive therapy, or a recommendation for a therapeutic pass—may trigger a new assessment. Most facilities have policies stating how often the assessments will be repeated routinely. Comments from patients or significant others may trigger a new assessment at a date earlier than scheduled.

The federal Conditions of Participation outline specific medical record requirements for psychiatric hospitals. One of these standards requires that each inpatient receive a psychiatric evaluation. The psychiatric evaluation must be completed within 60 hours of admission and must cover specific content areas such as medical history, mental status, onset of illness, attitudes and behavior, intellectual and memory functioning, orientation, and an inventory of the patient's assets. For other federal requirements specific to psychiatric hospital records, see Figure 7-2 (Conditions of Participation, 2014).

FIGURE 7-2

Excerpt from the Federal Conditions of Participation (2014) outlining special medical record requirements for psychiatric hospitals.

---

§ 482.61 Condition of participation: Special medical record requirements for psychiatric hospitals

The medical records maintained by a psychiatric hospital must permit determination of the degree and intensity of the treatment provided to individuals who are furnished services in the institution.

(a) *Standard: Development of assessment/diagnostic data.* Medical records must stress the psychiatric components of the record, including history of findings and treatment provided for the psychiatric condition for which the patient is hospitalized.

   (1) The identification data must include the patient's legal status.

   (2) A provisional or admitting diagnosis must be made on every patient at the time of admission, and must include the diagnoses of intercurrent diseases as well as the psychiatric diagnoses.

   (3) The reasons for admission must be clearly documented as stated by the patient and/or others significantly involved.

   (4) The social service records, including reports of interviews with patients, family members, and others, must provide an assessment of home plans and family attitudes, and community resource contacts as well as a social history.

   (5) When indicated, a complete neurological examination must be recorded at the time of the admission physical examination.

(b) *Standard: Psychiatric evaluation. Each patient must receive a psychiatric evaluation that must—*

   (1) Be completed within 60 hours of admission;

   (2) Include a medical history;

   (3) Contain a record of mental status;

   (4) Note the onset of illness and the circumstances leading to admission;

   (5) Describe attitudes and behavior;

   (6) Estimate intellectual functioning, memory functioning, and orientation; and

   (7) Include an inventory of the patient's assets in descriptive, not interpretative, fashion.

(c) *Standard: Treatment plan.*

   (1) Each patient must have an individual comprehensive treatment plan that must be based on an inventory of the patient's strengths and disabilities. The written plan must include—

      (i) A substantiated diagnosis;

      (ii) Short-term and long-range goals;

      (iii) The specific treatment modalities utilized;

      (iv) The responsibilities of each member of the treatment team; and

      (v) Adequate documentation to justify the diagnosis and the treatment and rehabilitation activities carried out.

FIGURE 7-2 *(continued)*

---

(2) The treatment received by the patient must be documented in such a way to assure that all active therapeutic efforts are included.

(d) Standard: Recording progress. Progress notes must be recorded by the doctor of medicine or osteopathy responsible for the care of the patient as specified in § 482.12(c), nurse, social worker and, when appropriate, others significantly involved in active treatment modalities. The frequency of progress notes is determined by the condition of the patient but must be recorded at least weekly for the first 2 months and at least once a month thereafter and must contain recommendations for revisions in the treatment plan as indicated as well as precise assessment of the patient's progress in accordance with the original or revised treatment plan.

(e) Standard: Discharge planning and discharge summary. The record of each patient who has been discharged must have a discharge summary that includes a recapitulation of the patient's hospitalization and recommendations from appropriate services concerning follow-up or aftercare as well as a brief summary of the patient's condition on discharge.

(72 FR 60788, Oct. 26, 2007)

From: http://www.ecfr.gov/cgi-bin/text-idx?SID=ab0b9e8d819d696ff81cca54df4bf391&node=42:5.0.1.1.1.5.4.2&rgn=div8

Treatment Plan

Traditionally, the assessment process has been a procedure by which the interviewer or team evaluates the consumer/patient's level of functioning. The problems have thus been defined essentially as deficits in functioning that should be addressed in the treatment plan, with steps to mitigate or eliminate the problem outlined. As consumers have embraced the notion of empowerment, however, they have become more insistent on participating in the treatment planning process. Particularly in the outpatient setting, consumers have complained that the established method placed them in a position of inferiority in relationship to the interviewer and often resulted in a treatment plan in which they had little interest and no investiture.

To expedite and encourage the consumer's participation, a strengths model of treatment planning has emerged in the community mental health sector. Using this approach, the interviewer determines from the consumer what goals he or she is interested in pursuing. The interviewer and the consumer then work out a mutual plan to achieve that goal. If the goal is a result of unrealistic thinking, the interviewer typically does not discourage the goal but, rather, creatively attempts to find some facet of the goal that may be achievable. For instance, if a consumer sets as a goal the fulfillment of a lifelong dream to be a concert pianist but never has had a piano lesson, the interviewer may suggest as a first step that the consumer attend a music appreciation class.

In most instances, the consumer will recognize an unattainable goal, and the goal then can be relinquished in favor of a more realistic goal. At the same time, the professional's acquiescence to and participation in goals of interest to the consumer may open up him or her to eventually consider goals that the professional may believe they need to work on together. If the consumer enjoys the music appreciation class, he or she may be more willing to stay on a medication to avoid relapse and, thus, possibly give up attending the class. This model, and the underlying concept of client empowerment, is increasingly becoming the preferred treatment mode nationwide. A sample treatment plan form for case management using the strengths model is shown in Figure 7-3.

This model poses something of a challenge for health information managers, however, because it is not as easy to document progress using this model as it has been with the functional assessment approach. In using the older model, the professional typically identifies a deficit; prescribes a treatment solution and a timeframe for success; and documents either a successful outcome, in which case the goal is eliminated, or a failure, in which case the goal is either dropped as unattainable or a different intervention strategy is proposed.

Although attempts are increasing to involve the patient within an institution in treatment planning, the extent of the illness makes continued use of the functional assessment methodology necessary to a large extent. The chief goal within the inpatient setting is virtually always stabilization to the point that the patient can be discharged into the community. Accomplishing this aim often requires a highly structured approach to changing behaviors that do not contribute to that end. Therefore, the strengths model must be utilized in a somewhat modified form.

Progress Notes

Progress notes mark the achievement, or lack thereof, in attempts of the consumer or patient to reach the goals stated in the treatment plan. Accreditation surveyors often check to see that every goal in a treatment plan has corresponding progress notes. Although some general progress notes do not relate to a specific treatment plan goal, most progress notes are tied directly to the treatment plan.

Progress notes are essential as documentation that a service was performed as a basis for reimbursement from Medicaid, Medicare, or client insurance ("If it isn't written, it didn't happen."). As a basis for reimbursement, the timeliness of the note also becomes a central issue, because most regulatory agencies place considerable emphasis on regular intervals of review and updates of the treatment plan, which also are usually recorded in a progress note.

One of the advantages of an electronic mental health record is that documentation of progress notes can be monitored electronically. Some systems prompt the clinician with treatment plan goals when the clinician is writing progress notes. Some organizations prepare automated reports that indicate treatment plan goals for which progress notes have not yet been written. The same type of report also can indicate services billed that lack progress notes, or the reverse—progress notes for services performed but not billed.

FIGURE 7-3

Sample assessment form for case management using the strengths model.

LIFE DOMAINS ASSESSMENT

Consumer Name: _____ Case # _____ Dx Code _____ Date _____

Admitted to Case Management: _____Yes _____ No

Frequency of Contact: _____ High _____ Moderate _____ Low _____ Follow Along

_____   _____
        Consumer Signature   Staff Signature

LIFE DOMAINS	CURRENT STATUS (Include Strengths and Barriers)	PERSONAL COAL (What do I want?)
LIVING ARRANGEMENTS		
Location		
Safety		
Adequacy		
LIFE SKILLS		
Home Management/Bill Paying		
ADL's		
Transportation		
Utilization of Resources		
SOCIAL SUPPORTS		
Family/Friends/Spiritual Interpersonal Relationships		
VOC/ED		
Education/Employment		
Skills		
FINANCIAL/LEGAL		
Monthly Income		
Money Management/Debts		
HEALTH/MENTAL HEALTH		
Physical Symptoms/Needs		
Psychological Symptoms/Needs		
Medication/Tx. Compliance		
Substance Abuse		
Physical/Emotional Abuse		
LEISURE/RECREATIONAL		
Exercise		
Recreation/Socialization		
CONSUMER STRENGTHS SUMMARY:		

Source: Case Record Guide produced by the Mississippi Department of Mental Health.

For psychiatric hospitals, the Conditions of Participation specify that physicians, nurses, social workers, and others involved in active treatment of the patient must record progress notes. These standards require progress notes at least weekly for the first 2 months and at least once a month thereafter (see Figure 7-2) (Conditions of Participation, 2014). Because of the importance of progress notes to the care of the patient, accreditation, and reimbursement, there is great incentive in a psychiatric hospital to properly document progress notes.

Special Procedures

Some procedures may be necessary in the mental health setting that may not be used in the treatment of other types of disorders. For example, a patient who is threatening injury to self or to others may be placed in restraints or in seclusion. Examples of other types of special procedures include psychosurgery and electroconvulsive therapy. When special procedures are used, proper documentation of their use is essential (Huffman, 1994).

Documentation regarding the use of seclusion or restraints serves as an example of the extensive documentation necessary when special procedures are used. Following a public advocacy campaign for stricter oversight of policies and procedures with regard to use of restraints and seclusion, Congress initiated an investigation into the use of these emergency safety interventions. The findings indicated an unacceptably high rate of death and injury to both staff members and patients as a result of improper use of or poorly planned procedures for implementing these interventions. Accordingly, Congress called for stricter regulations governing the use of restraints and seclusion for children and adults in facilities that receive Medicaid or Medicare funding.

As a result, the Centers for Medicare & Medicaid Services (CMS) proposed rules in 1999 that granted protection to patients from inappropriate restraint or seclusion. The latest version of these rules was promulgated in the Final Rule, Hospital Conditions of Participation of Patients' Rights, which became effective in January, 2007. These guidelines strengthened the rules for conditions under which these interventions could be used, the procedures to be followed prior to and during use, and the training required for personnel qualified to administer them (*Federal Register*, 2006). Accordingly, documentation must begin upon the patient's entry to the facility with "notification of the right to be free from the inappropriate use of restraint and seclusion with requirements that protect the patient when use of either intervention is necessary" (p. 71378), and continue surrounding the entire event in the case of utilization of such emergency safety interventions—from the decision-making process through implementation of the procedure and including follow-up evaluative measures.

Restraints are defined as being of two types: physical and chemical. **Physical restraint** is described as:

> …mechanical or personal restriction that immobilizes or reduces the ability of an individual to move his or her arms, legs, or head freely, not including devices . . . for

physical restraint "mechanical or personal restriction that immobilizes or reduces the ability of an individual to move his or her arms, legs, or head freely, not including devices ... for the purpose of conducting routine physical examinations or tests or to protect the resident from falling out of bed or to permit the resident to participate in activities without the risk of physical harm to the resident...." (P.L. 106-310, 2000, pp. 1195–1196).

the purpose of conducting routine physical examinations or tests or to protect the resident from falling out of bed or to permit the resident to participate in activities without the risk of physical harm to the resident. ... (P.L. 106-310, 2000, pp. 1195–1196).

In the Children Health Act of 2000 (P.L. 106-310), **chemical restraint** is defined as the use of a drug or medication not part of a person's usual medical regimen that is administered to control behavior or restrict freedom of movement.

The rules for applying restraint or seclusion require an order from a board-certified psychiatrist or a physician with specialized training and experience in diagnosis and treatment of **mental disorders**. Assessing the need for such procedures must include consideration of all possible alternatives and a rationale for the chosen intervention. At its core, the issue must be the safety of the patient. Such intervention also must be the least restrictive possible to achieve the desired outcome. Within one hour of initiation of such an emergency safety intervention, there must be a face-to-face assessment of the psychological and physical well-being of the patient conducted by a physician, registered nurse, or other professionals qualified by special training in the use of emergency safety interventions (*Federal Register*, 2008).

The regulations emphasize in particular the issue of training for all staff members who are involved in any way in the emergency safety intervention process. The training must be conducted upon hire and updated semiannually. Documentation of the type of training developed and staff in attendance at each session is required. Time limits for the procedure also have been changed: The physician's order may not exceed four hours for patients ages 18 to 21, two hours for patients ages 9 to 17, and one hour for residents under age 9. The Final Rule also expands the category of practitioners who may carry out patient evaluation during the first hour of implementation: In addition to physicians, a trained registered nurse (RN) or physician assistant (PA) may conduct the face-to-face observation but must consult with the physician as soon as possible thereafter.

Distinction also is made between time-out, which by definition implies that the patient is not physically restrained from leaving the area, and the more restrictive nature of emergency safety interventions, although staff is also required to monitor persons placed in time-out. In the case of minors, parents or guardians must be notified of the intervention as soon as possible, and notification must be documented.

During restraint, trained staff must be physically present and continually monitor the physical and psychological well-being of the patient and safety of the restraining device. Use of seclusion requires trained staff to be either physically present or just outside the seclusion room, continually monitoring and assessing the patient's physical and psychological well-being. The staff administering the procedure must document its use in the patient's record by the end of the shift in which the intervention has taken place. A physician or appropriately trained registered nurse must conduct an evaluation of the patient's well-being immediately after cessation of restraint or seclusion.

chemical restraint the use of a drug or medication that is not part of a person's usual medical regimen that is administered to control behavior or restrict freedom of movement (P.L. 106–310, 2000).

mental disorder a syndrome characterized by clinically significant disturbance in an individual's cognition, emotion regulation, or behavior that reflects a dysfunction in the psychological, biological, or developmental processes underlying mental functioning.

Within 24 hours after the use of an emergency safety intervention, involved staff and the patient must have a face-to-face discussion. Within the same time-frame, a second debriefing is to occur with all involved staff and appropriate supervisory and administrative staff. A chief topic in both meetings is to see how such an intervention might be avoided in the future. The staff must document both of these meetings. If a patient is seriously injured or dies during or possibly because of restraint or seclusion, the facility must report the incident to both the state Medicaid agency and the state-designated protection and advocacy agency by no later than the close of business the next business day (*Federal Register*, 2001).

In addition, Congress enacted the Children's Health Act of 2000. This legislation applied specific restrictions to emergency safety interventions with children and youth, particularly those residing in nonmedical community-based residential facilities receiving Medicaid. Most notably, the use of mechanical restraints with children was prohibited altogether in these facilities.

Also defined is the concept of "physical escort," as contrasted with "physical restraint." Whereas *physical restraint* is defined as a restriction that immobilizes an individual or severely limits his or her ability to move arms, legs, or head freely (as defined previously), *physical escort* is defined otherwise and is permitted. The latter is "temporary touching or holding of the hand, wrist, arm, shoulder, or back for the purpose of inducing a resident who is acting out to walk to a safe location" (P.L. 106-310, 2000, p. 1196). Distinction also is made between time-out and restraint. Time-out is described as a separation of a resident from his or her peers for the purpose of calming; most important, the separation has to be within an unlocked setting and no physical limitation is imposed. A two-sided form, such as the one depicted in Figure 7-4, may be used to help to meet the special documentation requirements of emergency safety interventions.

Discharge Summary and Aftercare Plans

The discharge summary contains the reason for discharge, noting whether the person left in a timely manner or against program advice, and if the person is living in the community. Hospital discharge in the case of an involuntary commitment has to include the doctor's orders certifying that the person is no longer a danger to self or others and, therefore, is ready for discharge. Although some hospitals have begun to determine that readiness for discharge is a decision of an interdisciplinary team, the treating physician has ultimate responsibility for discharge.

Documentation related to discharge summarizes the goals of the treatment plan and the progress that has been made. It includes linkages with other programs, including mental health, to which the person has been referred, any appointments that have been made, and a prognosis statement as to future expectations for the person's physical and mental health. Other details documented in the discharge summary in a psychiatric hospital include the final diagnoses,

FIGURE 7-4

Seclusion/Restraint/Protective Device Observation Report.

MISSISSIPPI STATE HOSPITAL
SECLUSION/RESTRAINT/PROTECTIVE
DEVICE OBSERVATION REPORT

Addresssograph

DATE:	TIME STARTED:	BUILDING:	Explanation of initiation and goal for discontinuation of seclusion/restraint given to patient/significant other: Time: _____ Nurse's Signature: _____

TYPE OF BEHAVIOR WARRANTING SECLUSION/RESTRAINT/PROTECTIVE DEVICE:
☐ Agitated/Combative   ☐ Self Destructive   ☐ Invasion of Other's Personal Space   other:
☐ Confusion   ☐ Threatening

CRITERIA FOR DISCONTINUATION: ☐ Maintains relaxed, non threatening posture   ☐ Cease verbal threats
☐ Can discuss alternative behavior   ☐ Agrees to follow plan for safety (Contracts)   ☐ Other:

PRIOR INTERVENTION:
☐ Time Out   ☐ Visual Contact   ☐ I:I Observation   ☐ Behavior Management   ☐ Medication
☐ Limit Setting   ☐ Family Participation   ☐ Supervised Physical Activity   ☐ Reduced Stimulation   ☐ Redirection
☐ Frequent Reorientation   ☐ Peer Isolation   ☐ Other:

TYPE OF INTERVENTION   **TYPE OF DEVICE**
☐ Seclusion   ☐ Restraint Bed   ☐ Helmet   ☐ Sleeved Jacket/Vest
☐ Restraint   ☐ Wrist Restraint   ☐ Mittens   ☐ Papoose Board
☐ Protection Device   ☐ Ankle Restraint   ☐ Pelvic Holder   ☐ Restraint Chair
☐ Behavior Management Program   ☐ Lap Belt   ☐ Jump Suit   ☐ Other:

CODE - OBSERVATION (More than one may be used)

1. Yelling or Screaming	8. Restless
2. Attempting Self Harm	9. Requesting Release
3. Kicking	10. Sleeping
4. Threatening Violence	11. Quiet/Calm/Resting
5. Mumbling Incoherently	12. Attempting Removal of Restraint
6. Talking Coherently	13. Other _____
7. Biting	14. Other _____

CODE - INTERVENTIONS (More than one may be used)

A. Offered Fluids (q 1 hour)	H. Released from Restraints
B. Offered Bathroom (q 2 hours)	I. Released from Protective Device
C. Circulation/Skin Check (q 2 hours)	J. Restraints Reapplied
D. "A,B,C"	K. Did not meet criteria for d/c, renew restraints up to 4 hrs.
E. Refused Fluids	
F. Refused Bathroom	L. Other: _____
G. Released from Seclusion	M. Other: _____

BEHAVIORAL CARE ONLY: Observation documentation required Q 15 minutes..... Reassessment for release/renew documentation Q 4 hours

Initials	O	I		Initials	O	I		Initials	O	I
12:00 am				8:00 am				4:00 pm		
12:15 am				8:15 am				4:15 pm		
12:30 am				8:30 am				4:30 pm		
12:45 am				8:45 am				4:45 pm		
1:00 am				9:00 am				5:00 pm		
1:15 am				9:15 am				5:15 pm		
1:30 am				9:30 am				5:30 pm		
1:45 am				9:45 am				5:45 pm		
2:00 am				10:00 am				6:00 pm		
2:15 am				10:15 am				6:15 pm		
2:30 am				10:30 am				6:30 pm		
2:45 am				10:45 am				6:45 pm		
3:00 am				11:00 am				7:00 pm		
3:15 am				11:15 am				7:15 pm		
3:30 am				11:30 am				7:30 pm		
3:45 am				11:45 am				7:45 pm		
4:00 am				12:00 pm				8:00 pm		
4:15 am				12:15 pm				8:15 pm		
4:30 am				12:30 pm				8:30 pm		
4:45 am				12:45 pm				8:45 pm		
5:00 am				1:00 pm				9:00 pm		
5:15 am				1:15 pm				9:15 pm		
5:30 am				1:30 pm				9:30 pm		
5:45 am				1:45 pm				9:45 pm		
6:00 am				2:00 pm				10:00 pm		
6:15 am				2:15 pm				10:15 pm		
6:30 am				2:30 pm				10:30 pm		
6:45 am				2:45 pm				10:45 pm		
7:00 am				3:00 pm				11:00 pm		
7:15 am				3:15 pm				11:15 pm		
7:30 am				3:30 pm				11:30 pm		
7:45 am				3:45 pm				11:45 pm		

MSH 31B (04/05)

(continues)

FIGURE 7-4   *(continued)*

Pre-Seclusion/Restraint Search and Removal Of Items

Items Removed	Description	Disposition	Initials
☐ Clothes	_____	_____	_____
☐ Belt	_____	_____	_____
☐ Shoes	_____	_____	_____
☐ Smoking Materials	_____	_____	_____
☐ Money	_____	_____	_____
☐ Other	_____	_____	_____

☐ **Patient Wishes Family/Correspondent to be Notified**
☐ **Patient Does Not Want Family Notified**
☐ **Family Does Not Want to be Notified**

Date/Time of Notification, if Applicable:

Notified By: _____ _____ at _____ AM/PM
            Signature/Title   Date   Time

Date/Time Released:

Date: _____   Time: _____ AM/PM

Trauma Experienced?

☐ Yes   Explain: _____
☐ No

Patient Debriefing: (To be Completed within 24 Hours After Episode

What could you have done differently to have prevented/avoided seclusion/restraint?

_____

Do you feel like hurting yourself?
☐ Yes   Explain: _____
☐ No

Do you feel like hurting anyone else?
☐ Yes   Explain: _____
☐ No

Debriefed By: _____ _____ at _____ AM/PM
             Signature/Title   Date   Time

Staff Debriefing:

Can staff identify factors that may reduce the risk of future episodes?
☐ Yes   Explain: _____
☐ No

Debriefed By: _____ _____ at _____ AM/PM
             Signature/Title   Date   Time

Treatment Plan Modification Needed and documentation of need placed on Accountability?
☐ Yes   Explain: _____
☐ No

First Name	Last Name	Title	Initials	First Name	Last Name	Title	Initials

---

Courtesy of Mississippi State Hospital, Whitfield, MS. Used with permission.

medications and instructions, disabilities (if any), dietary instructions, and with whom the patient was discharged.

Although discharge summary documentation is necessary in both institutional and community settings, it is particularly important, in a timely manner, in the inpatient setting. Community programs often have policies that prohibit recently discharged patients from participating in their programming until they have received the hospital's discharge summary. There are several reasons for this policy. First, it is more difficult to assist with a treatment plan if the worker does not know where the potential candidate for the program fits on the scale of recovery. Also, the program workers should be aware of any special conditions or needs that were discovered in the hospital, particularly related to physical health needs. And it is vital to identify linkages for funding, such as Supplemental Security Income (SSI) or food stamp eligibility, or for entering the community mental health system via an appointment set up before discharge.

These continuity of care issues are vital in preventing immediate relapse and return to the hospital. How quickly and how well the former patient is reoriented to community living is a key factor in successful transitioning from the institution. The discharge summary, with its delineation of aftercare plans, provides community mental health professionals with invaluable information with which to assist in that process.

SELF REVIEW 7.2

1. A mental health service provider may seek accreditation by one or more of the following groups:
   a. TJC
   b. CARF
   c. NCQA
   d. URAC
   e. all of the above

2. True or False? The psychiatric evaluation for a patient receiving inpatient psychiatric care must be completed within 24 hours after admission.

3. What is an advantage of using a strengths model of treatment planning? What is a disadvantage?

4. What is an advantage of an electronic mental health record?

5. Which agencies are facilities that are required to report an incident of serious injury or death during, or possibly caused by, restraint or seclusion and within what timeframe?

REIMBURSEMENT AND FUNDING

The principal sources of funding for CMHCs are client fees, Medicaid, Medicare, and block grant funding for special projects. Client fees are calculated on a sliding scale based on income, and they account for a small percentage of the overall budget. The majority of the income for community mental health comes from Medicaid and Medicare reimbursement. Some funding comes from federal block grants, typically distributed through the state mental health agency to support special initiatives. CMHCs also receive a prescribed millage (local property tax) from the counties they serve. The great variety of funding streams makes for a complex billing and accounting system that could well become a specialized area into which health information managers might wish to venture.

The larger inpatient institutions have traditionally been supported for the most part by state funds, with a small percentage coming from patient fees. The trend in recent years, however, has been toward becoming accredited, leading to eligibility for the institutions to receive payment through Medicaid funding.

In 2003, CMS published a proposed rule to create an **inpatient psychiatric facility prospective payment system (IPF PPS)** for Medicare payments both to freestanding psychiatric hospitals and to psychiatric units in acute care hospitals. The final rule was issued in 2004, and the new payment system took effect January 1, 2005. Under the IPF PPS, inpatient psychiatric facilities (IPFs) receive per diem payments that are adjusted up or down by four patient-level factors, as follows:

- The patient's age (increasingly higher rates for patients age 45 and older through age 80 and above)
- Variable per diem adjustments (higher per diem payments for the first days of the patient's stay, gradually decreasing through the 22nd day of hospitalization, with no further decrease beyond that point)
- The Medicare Severity diagnosis related group (MS-DRG) for the stay
- Certain comorbidities (Only one comorbidity adjustment is made for each comorbidity category, but adjustments for more than one comorbidity category are possible.)

Because coded data are used to determine the MS-DRG as well as the additional comorbidity factors, the health information department plays a significant role in providing accurate and complete coding for the IPF PPS.

The proposed rule issued in 2003 also included a Case Mix Assessment Tool (CMAT), a data collection instrument designed to capture additional information about the patient's psychiatric symptoms, level of cognitive functioning, and ability to perform activities of daily living, along with limited information about services or treatments provided and diagnostic studies performed. As of 2015, the CMAT had not been implemented in the IPF PPS, but CMS has continued research in this area, and some type of assessment instrument eventually may help to determine Medicare payment amounts for inpatient psychiatric facilities.

Managed care is becoming more prevalent as a payer. States have begun to contract with MCOs to provide mental health services for their Medicaid programs. The program may be capitated, meaning that payment is made based on the number of program participants in the service area. In other types of managed care arrangements, the MCO may authorize the number of services that will be paid during a certain period. This period could be 6 months or a year, or it could be defined as an **episode of care**. An episode of care involves a variety of services (inpatient and/or outpatient) provided by an organization to an individual during a given episode of illness.

---

inpatient psychiatric facility prospective payment system (IPF PPS) Medicare's method of payment both for freestanding psychiatric hospitals and for psychiatric units in acute care hospitals. Under the IPF PPS rule, inpatient psychiatric facilities (IPFs) receive per diem payments that are adjusted up or down by patient-level factors such as age, the MS-DRG, and certain comorbidities, with earlier days of the stay paid at higher rates than later days.

episode of care   a period during which a variety of services (inpatient and/or outpatient) are provided to an individual for a given episode of illness.

The growing concern of politicians and the public regarding health care costs has motivated some states to move mental health services to a system of managed care, which is driven more by economic concerns than by quality assurance issues. The focus within a managed care system becomes the number of services and the length of time that services are performed. This approach has been controversial when applied to the seriously mentally ill population because of the erratic and unpredictable nature of the psychosis. The uncertainty of prognosis renders difficult any reliable prediction as to the number and types of services that a person may need over extended periods of time. Nevertheless, states have begun programs of managed care within mental health, with mixed results.

Of particular concern to mental health consumers and their advocates is the tendency of managed care organizations to define narrowly the range of services that are seen as "medically necessary." This concept allows selective provision, usually limited to medication management during stable periods and hospitalization during psychotic episodes, rather than the full range of treatments and services such as case management and vocational rehabilitation options that are necessary for most persons with mental illness to maintain themselves in a community setting.

SELF REVIEW 7.3

1. Federal block grants are distributed through the _____.
2. What has driven the move toward the use of managed care organizations?
3. True or False? The patient's age affects the per diem payment received by the inpatient psychiatric facility.

INFORMATION MANAGEMENT

Beginning in 1975, there was a movement toward creating a uniform, integrated statistical reporting system for mental health at the national level. In 1975, the Division of Biometry and Epidemiology (DBE) proposed an undertaking to create such a system (Patton & Leginski, 1983). As a result, the **Mental Health Statistics Improvement Program (MHSIP)** became an early initiative within the National Institute of Mental Health (NIMH) to create a uniform data system nationwide for reporting mental health statistics. MHSIP suggested that the State Mental Health Authorities work cooperatively with NIMH to create a broad-based data collection spearheaded by state efforts. The goals were to be as follows:

(a) Enhance state, local, and national mental health agencies' capacity to respond to local, state, and national needs for mental health program management data;
(b) train sufficient systems and statistical personnel to collect, process, and analyze the data generated by these systems;
(c) provide an ongoing cost sharing mechanism for the production of data required by the federal system. (Patton & Leginski, 1983)

Mental Health Statistics Improvement Program (MHSIP) an early initiative begun by the National Institute of Mental Health and continued by the Substance Abuse and Mental Health Services Administration to create a uniform data system nationwide for reporting mental health statistics. MHSIP's work was done largely by a voluntary ad hoc group made up of local, state, and federal personnel.

An ad hoc advisory group consisting of personnel from local, state, and federal programs undertook the early work of establishing data sets that were widely accepted as appropriate and useful. Following the reorganization of NIMH, this initiative was placed with the Center for Mental Health Services (CMHS) branch of the Substance Abuse and Mental Health Services Administration (SAMHSA).

In 1984, the initiative received a second strong impetus with a mandate from Congress to create a system for data collection regarding mental health and substance abuse. Unlike the substance abuse system, in which the move toward uniformity was translated into a set of federally mandated standards for data collection, the mental health system chose to promote guidelines rather than specific standards. Thus, participation in the initiative continued to be voluntary.

Data Standards for Mental Health Decision Support Systems ("FN-10") an early reference source for creation of a national mental health services database.

The congressional directive led NIMH to publish, in the next year, the *Data Standards for Mental Health Decision Support Systems* ("FN-10"). This manual became the basis for all subsequent work in the effort to create a compatible data-reporting system. It had a significant impact on the direction and scope of current thinking about mental health data, as it made a strong case for including more than just client service data. The case was made for expanding the data collection into areas such as finances and human resources as "auxiliaries" to the direct service arena (Leginski et al., 1989).

The MHSIP/FN-10 initiative later entered a second phase, termed Decision Support 2000+, to include incorporation of the HIPAA regulations regarding confidentiality as well as other recent developments in the field. The move toward data standards has continued with submission by State Mental Health Authorities of aggregate information to SAMHSA through the **Uniform Reporting System (URS)**, and also through the reporting of client-level data by the states.

Uniform Reporting System (URS) an organized method by which each State Mental Health Authority (SMHA) reports aggregate data to SAMHSA.

For example, in 2001 the first Data Infrastructure Grants (DIGs) were awarded noncompetitively. The goal of this initiative was to have all State Mental Health Authorities enabled to report performance measures in their Community Mental Health Services Block Grant (CMHSBG) applications. The emphasis on performance measures accompanied new terminology for the block grants, which were to transition to "Performance Partnership Grants" (PPGs). The guiding intention was that state mental health agencies and SAMHSA would collaborate on setting goals and reporting data. The following excerpt from a National Association of State Mental Health Program Directors (NASMHPD) Research Institute report provides information on the evolution of this system:

> "As part of the federal government's effort to change federal block grants into performance-based systems, P.L. 106-310 (2000) required the U.S. Department of Health and Human Services Secretary to submit a Report to Congress on the legislative and other steps required to implement a performance partnership model. This plan would have grown out of the Mental Health Statistics Improvement Program (MHSIP) and data infrastructure grant projects, and would have specified what performance measures would be imposed under a performance partnership. Instead, SAMHSA has required core data elements as part of its annual instructions which phased in de facto uniform performance criteria." (NASMHPD Research Institute, 2007, p. 3)

Several additional factors have affected the move toward a uniform data system. In recent years, the cry for increased democratization of the mental health service delivery system has broadened to include the ways in which those services are measured and quantified. This movement has occurred within the societal context of the growing popularity of consumer service orientation in management. Such an information system would arise from a paradigm entirely different from the traditional collection and analysis of data, shifting the focus "from persons *served within* individual specialty mental health *organizations* toward *persons with significant needs* for mental health services and supports, *regardless of* the number or type of *organizations* that may or may not serve them" (Campbell & Frey, 1993). The emphasis would become one of identifying need across systems and organizations in a much broader context than just that of the mental health system.

Obviously, such a system, in which highly individualized data are being sought and shared in a variety of settings, raises special concerns around issues of confidentiality. (See the discussion of confidentiality, later in this chapter.) Yet, it can be done. South Carolina is one state that has achieved an information system for mental health consumers that reaches across agencies in this way.

With regard to sharing data for the purpose of treatment, several states have laws that make it difficult to include mental health information in broad-based health information exchanges (HIEs). Also, mental health facilities were not included in the original ARRA bill as among those eligible for incentives for meaningful use of EHR technology and the accompanying goal of being able to participate in health information exchanges. (Note that psychiatrists, as physicians, are considered to be eligible providers for the ARRA incentives.) As individual states began setting up their statewide health information exchanges, the idea of including mental health in HIE began to be discussed, as well as how it could be accomplished while still protecting the privacy and rights of the consumers and patients being served.

With regard to the protection of confidentiality in data collection for planning purposes, CMHS implemented a successful pilot project in which client-level data from nine states were submitted in a fashion that did not compromise confidentiality. This was accomplished by submitting the data without the use of identifiers that would allow the data to be associated with an individual. For example, age was submitted instead of date of birth. Also, specific dates for admission and discharge were not used, but timeframes were provided to indicate the duration of service and also to capture changes in the client's status over time. De-identifying the data in this manner protects the patient's confidentiality, and also provides more useful data for analysis than does the submission of aggregate data. As of 2015, most states report mental health client-level data (MH-CLD) for five specific outcome measures.

The other, and quite antithetical, influence on current discussions of data standards and information systems development springs from the managed care system. Here, of course, the driving force is the economic consideration.

Emphases on fiscal responsibility and cost/benefit considerations of this model of service delivery place paramount value on the very type of data supporting organizational accountability that the proponents of "person-centered" information systems find unsatisfactory.

The debate within the managed care camp has focused on using outcome measures versus performance indicators. Outcome measures are more suitable to situations in which an illness has a usual duration and most often ends in a cure. Obviously, these cases have a measurable outcome. Because of the chronic nature of mental illness, though, it is difficult to measure outcome with accuracy. So many factors enter into the possibility of relapse that mental health professionals are hard-pressed to say what specific factors prevent or produce recidivism. Nor can they always predict the duration of a psychotic episode and its aftermath, much less the long-term prognosis of the illness.

For these reasons, mental health professionals strongly believe that a much more accurate way to measure success is through performance indicators. These indicators focus on consumer satisfaction with services delivered rather than on treatment outcomes. To some extent, this approach also bows in the direction of consumer empowerment, as it provides a vehicle by which the consumer can register his or her satisfaction or unhappiness with the mental health system. The MHSIP Consumer Survey is one such vehicle.

Players within the mental health system have taken divergent routes in incorporating newer and more efficient technologies for their data collection, many of which include categories and methods of reporting that are not compatible with SAMHSA's ongoing developments for a uniform reporting system. Nevertheless, uniform reporting is moving forward, notwithstanding the fact that the process of deliberation and experimentation has taken so long.

Data and Information Flow

Intake procedures vary within the community mental health system. Because of staff constraints, few CMHCs are able to take walk-ins except those in emergency situations—usually defined as persons in need of inpatient commitment because they are deemed to be dangerous to self or others. Typically, applications are received and screened as to the seriousness of the case, and appointments are established, including an appointment with a psychiatrist if it is clear from the application that an appointment is needed for medication issues. Priority is given most often to persons who have been discharged from inpatient care; these appointments typically are set up by the social worker at the institution before the person's discharge.

A file for recording service delivery, billing data, and other pertinent information usually is established just before the intake interview. Intake provides an opportunity to gather additional demographic information that is not included or is unclear on the application form. Assessment is conducted, and an initial plan of treatment is agreed upon by the consumer and therapist, with the understanding that it can be modified as needed as the treatment progresses. If necessary, an appointment is made to see a psychiatrist for possible medication.

If appropriate, other services are offered, such as participation in the case management program; attendance at a day program; either psychosocial rehabilitation aimed at vocational opportunity or partial hospitalization; and/or placement in a group home designed to increase daily living skills for a more independent living arrangement in the future. In most cases, these services will be paid for by Medicaid and/or Medicare, so the psychiatrist will have to certify under signature that these are "needed services." From this point, the course of treatment becomes individualized, based on the consumer's needs and preferences as to the services available.

There is no universal standard for content or order of arrangement of information in the consumer's file. Figure 7-5 gives sample items from a large psychiatric hospital. If the services are offered in a satellite office, the essential, most up-to-date information will, quite naturally, be contained in the record at that site. Some CMHCs have a central file for all clients in their main office, with copies of material sent periodically from the satellite file for inclusion in the central record. Others have only the one record at the satellite office. Billing information, in particular, reporting of units of service (15-minute increments in the case of Medicaid) provided, is contained in the record. Surveyors and auditors thus are able to match billing information with documentation of service delivery in the Progress Notes section of the record.

Voluntary admission to a hospital would follow much the same process as that for admission for treatment in the community. The documentation process for involuntary admission to an inpatient facility begins, of course, with the information assembled during the commitment proceedings, from screening and evaluation through the legal order of commitment. This documentation usually arrives with the patient. The institutional social worker typically is responsible for assembling and augmenting the information received, by performing a social history, including contact with family members whenever possible.

In most inpatient settings, the patient's treatment plan is developed by an interdisciplinary team that usually includes at least a psychiatrist, a nurse, a psychologist, and a social worker. The patient is encouraged to participate in the planning to whatever extent possible. An attempt is made to provide a highly structured atmosphere, as activity often alleviates the psychotic symptoms and the debilitating side-effects of some of the medications. Progress notes are entered into the case file by the various disciplines in the same way as is done for persons who are followed in the outpatient setting.

The team meets periodically and decides whether the patient's condition indicates long-term hospitalization or whether progress is being made toward release. The social worker usually begins to develop a tentative discharge plan early in treatment so the necessary steps are in place when the time comes to put

FIGURE 7-5

Examples of items that may be found in the records of a large psychiatric hospital.

Identification and Personal Data
    Demographic Data
    Legal Status (commitment vs. voluntary
        admission)

Physician's Orders

Treatment Plan and Behavioral Documentation
    Treatment Plan
    Treatment Plan Update/Review Note
    Anger Management Assessment
    Psychiatric Intervention History
    Patient/Family Education Record
    Individual Patient Schedule
    Behavior Modification Plan

Progress Notes, including...
    Initial Integrated Summary
    Admission Note
    Transfer Notes
    Elopement Notes
    Diagnostic Summary or Addendum to
        Diagnostic Summary
    Audiology Alert Sheet
    Discharge Summary

Nurses' Notes, including...
    Nursing Assessment
    Child/Adolescent Addendum
    Abnormal Involuntary Movements
    Fall Assessment
    Nursing Discharge Summary

Medication Records
    Monthly Medication Administration
        Records (MARs)
    Monthly PRN medications
    Medication Information Documentation Form
    Specialized Medication Records (for example,
        for patients with diabetes mellitus)

Other Health Records
    Vital Signs Record
    Menstrual Record
    Intake/Output
    Fluid Accountability Record
    Seizure Record
    Immunization and TB Record
    Summary of Ambulatory Visits
    Outpatient Procedure Report

Ancillary Services
    Lab Reports
    X-ray Reports
    EKG

Consultations
    Medical
    CT Scans
    EEC
    Outpatient Unscheduled Visit

Physical Exam

Alcohol and Drug Abuse Needs
    Assessment/Aftercare Plan

Psychology
    Psychology General Assessment
    Psychology Progress Notes
    Psychological Evaluation

Social Service
    Social Service Assessment/Plan
    Social Service Clinical Progress Notes
    Spiritual Assessment
    Social History

Dietary
    Nutritional Assessment
    Dietary Clinical Progress Notes

Pharmacy Medication Review

Activities
    Therapeutic Recreation Assessment
    Rehab Clinical Progress Notes
    Leisure Assessment

Rehabilitation
    Rehabilitation Services Screening
        Assessment
    Rehabilitation Clinical Progress Notes
    Restorative Therapy Note
    Physical Therapy Evaluation Report
    Kinesiotherapy Evaluation Report
    Occupational Therapy Evaluation
    Feeding Evaluation
    Upper Extremity Evaluation
    Splint Information
    Speech, Language, Pathology Assessment
    Dysphagia Assessment

FIGURE 7-5 *(continued)*

Education
    Education Clinical Progress Notes
    Patient Education Progress Report
    Psychosocial Education Program
    Functional Needs Assessment
    Psychosocial Education Program
    Art Assessment
    Music Evaluation
    Hearing and Vision Screening Results

Dental
    Dental Record
    Dental Treatment Plan

Residential Living
    Patient Care Flow Sheet
    Patient Observation Reports

Legal
    Advance Directives
    Admission Checklist
    Patient's Rights Statement
    Smoking Policy
    Ethics Fact Sheet
    Notice of Privacy Practices
    Consent Forms
    Contraband Search, Seizure, Disposition

Legal (continued)
    Admission Papers (Commitment orders)
    Legal Guardianship
    Legal Correspondence

Miscellaneous
    Visitors' Permits
    Patient Transfer Form
    Transfer and Referral Form
    Patient's Valuable Form
    Missing Patient Reports
    Hearing Reports
    Patient's Pass/Discharge Record
    Pass Evaluation Checklist
    Vocational Rehab
    Sheltered Workshop forms
    Work Opportunity forms
    Transitional Living Forms and Progress
       Reports

Electroconvulsive Therapy (ECT)
    ECT Checklist
    Progress Report
    Anesthesia Record
    Electroconvulsive Nursing Care Plans
    Consent for ECT
    Referral for ECT

Excerpted and adapted from procedures of Mississippi State Hospital, Whitfield, Massachusetts. Used with permission.

them into action. As the actual time of discharge nears, the social worker takes steps to ensure continuity of care beyond the hospital. At a minimum, these steps include assurance of housing, establishment of monetary benefits if the patient is eligible, and contact with the community mental health system to set up an initial appointment.

Coding and Classification

Behavioral health organizations use a variety of coding systems. The system used will depend on the purpose of coding and other factors. Prior to 2013, psychiatric diagnoses were coded using the *Diagnostic and Statistical Manual of Mental Disorders*, fourth edition, text revision (*DSM-IV-TR*), published by the American Psychiatric Association. In 2013, the system was updated to *DSM-5*, the current system. This publication provides not only a classification system but also diagnostic criteria to assist clinicians in making psychiatric diagnoses. More information on the structure and utilization of this classification system may be found in Chapter 8.

For billing purposes, behavioral health organizations submitting electronic bills must use the HIPAA standard code sets, which do not include *DSM-5*. Therefore, the current clinical modification of *ICD* and *CPT/HCPCS* codes are used as appropriate.

Data Sets

The key data sets in mental health are found in the reporting requirements that the State Mental Health Authorities must follow in the annual grant application and funding process. The Data Infrastructure Grants support these efforts. In the following excerpt from the 2010 Request for Applications (RFA) for the State Mental Health Data Infrastructure Grants for Quality Improvement (State DIGs), CMHS explained its data collection efforts as follows:

> Building on the results of the CMHS Client Level Data Pilot, CMHS will work with the States through the Data Infrastructure Grants (DIGs) to enable collection and reporting of client level data for five Mental Health Block Grant National Outcome Measures (NOMS) over the next three years. These NOMS are Employment/School Attendance, Stability in Housing, Criminal Justice Involvement, Readmission to State Hospital, and Access/Capacity: Number of Persons Served with Demographic Characteristics. The additional NOMS and Uniform Reporting System (URS) Tables, which do not require direct State or client level data, will continue to be reported, and will add value in decision support at the national and State levels. The population of focus will include mental health consumers served within the purview of the State Mental Health Authorities (SMHAs), as defined in the URS Tables. The project supports the reporting requirements for the National CMHS Mental Health Block Grant Program.
>
> The purpose of the State Mental Health Data Infrastructure Grants for Quality Improvement (DIGs) is to support client level data reporting by the States by 2012 for 5 NOMS. Building upon the Federal/State partnership established through the development of the URS…, this mechanism will be used for collecting client level data for more than 6 million mental health consumers. In addition, by receiving SAMHSA/CMHS funds through the DIGs over the grant period, States will engage in T1 and T2 (to include Admission and Discharge) client level data collection and reporting.
>
> The project supports State Mental Health Authorities (SMHAs) in their continuing implementation and strengthening of the annual collection of URS data through focus on selected NOMS for client level reporting. Historically, great strides have been made in data infrastructure development in the States for reporting the URS and NOMS at the national level. Over a period of years in the DIG grant effort, the States have achieved uniform URS reporting so that by 2008, eight of the 10 NOMS were being reported by 85% of grantees (48 States). The effort has additionally strengthened State and local data infrastructure for reporting and decision support. The future of the SAMHSA/CMHS mental health data reporting program continues to evolve in refining the reporting of NOMS, using the framework of the CMHS Client Level Pilot in which 9 States piloted the feasibility of implementing client level NOMS reporting in the States through FY 2009. In the new grant cycle, the effort will be made to strengthen quality of reporting and performance accountability for selected NOMS, including developing capability to report assessment of service provision and improvement of individual clients from Time 1 to Time 2 (including admission and discharge). (SAMHSA, 2010, para. 1–3)

TERMINOLOGY RELATED TO MENTAL HEALTH DATA SETS

Mental Health Client-Level Data (MH-CLD)   Data reported to SAMHSA at the level of the individual client rather than in aggregate as in the URS tables

Data Infrastructure Grants (DIGs)   Federal grants to assist states in developing infrastructure for reporting performance measures for mental health

National Outcome Measures (NOMS)   Mental health outcome measures collected nationally. Examples of NOMS for which CMHS is seeking to collect client-level data include:

- Employment/School Attendance
- Stability in Housing
- Criminal Justice Involvement
- Readmission to State Hospital
- Access/Capacity: Number of Persons Served with Demographic Characteristics

Uniform Reporting System (URS) Tables   A set of tables by which each State Mental Health Authority (SMHA) reports aggregate data to SAMHSA

State Mental Health Authorities (SMHAs)   The agency in each state that is responsible for oversight of mental health programs in that state.

Time 1 to Time 2 (T1 to T2)   Two points in time for which data are reported, allowing comparison of progress or outcomes over the time period, as well as duration of the time period, without reporting the exact dates, thus avoiding the submission of protected health information (PHI) such as dates of admission and discharge

Historically, the reluctance to mandate uniformity has stemmed from the enormous impact of the consumer empowerment movement, which changed not only the programming for service delivery but also the perception of what constitutes success in rendering those services. Implementation of client-level data reporting brings about a measure of uniformity in data collection for the targeted outcomes measures. Currently, most states use the Mental Health Client-Level Data (MH-CLD) system to report client-level data and the Uniform Reporting System (URS) tables to report aggregate data to SAMHSA.

SELF REVIEW 7.4

1. What are the goals of the Mental Health Statistics Improvement Program (MHSIP)?

2. True or False? Client-level data for mental health are not appropriate for reporting to federal agencies such as SAMSHA.

3. List some initiatives that have been implemented to move toward a uniform data system.

4. True or False? Mental Health facilities were not included in the original American Recovery and Reinvestment Act of 2009 (ARRA).

5. True or False? The Conditions of Participation requires a universal standard for the order of documentation in a consumer's record.
6. What is the process for voluntary admission to a CMHC?
7. Define Time 1 to Time 2 (T1 to T2) client levels.

QUALITY IMPROVEMENT AND UTILIZATION MANAGEMENT

The mental health field has been at least as susceptible as other segments of our society to the current focus on total quality management (TQM), or its more recent manifestation as **continuous quality improvement (CQI)**. The focus of both of these management techniques on customer satisfaction and sharing of decision-making power between administrative and line staff is a natural fit with the mental health consumer movement toward empowerment. These concepts have been, for the most part, well accepted by now and, in general, incorporated into both the outpatient and the inpatient systems of care.

Client-centered approaches permeate the mental health system, affecting all aspects of service delivery, from programming that encourages self-determination, emphasizing consumer strengths rather than functional deficits, to data collection that focuses on client satisfaction and feedback mechanisms. Performance improvement is an important component in The Joint Commission accreditation of inpatient facilities. Because this accreditation is generally accepted by major funding sources such as Medicare and Medicaid, it frequently is sought after by inpatient facilities.

Over the years, utilization management has led to the downsizing of large public mental institutions. The move to deinstitutionalization, while resulting in part from the improvement in stabilization through medication, also has been driven in part by economic considerations. It has proved to be much less expensive, generally speaking, to maintain consumers in the community with a variety of support services than to keep them in the hospital, with its more costly medical orientation. Because the funding from the hospitals did not always follow the consumer to the community, however, some would argue that the consumers have received uneven and often inadequate support outside the hospital. Thus, the lowered cost of community services may in part reflect the inadequate funding that could deprive its customers of a decent quality of life, and may in this sense be somewhat deceptive as to what the actual costs ought to be.

In the outpatient and inpatient settings alike, steps have been taken to further reduce costs. Many CMHCs have created a staff position that serves as the "single point of entry" (SPOE) for emergency hospitalization in either the acute care psychiatric units or the long-term institution. Data sometimes are gathered regarding high users of inpatient services, with an eye to providing more or different supports to those in this category.

continuous quality improvement (CQI) a management concept that focuses on customer involvement in planning services and obtaining feedback about satisfaction with service delivery. This concept has been a feature of the mental health consumer empowerment movement. Also known as total quality management (TQM).

Bed allocation is a further device, particularly within institutions, to encourage utilization of community resources to the fullest extent before resorting to hospitalization. This method assigns beds on a regional basis, using formulas that take into account factors such as total population and past usage of the facility. Then a certain amount of "borrowing" of beds among regions is allowed to take care of emergencies.

SELF REVIEW 7.5

1. _____ is a management concept focusing on customer involvement in planning services and obtaining feedback as to satisfaction with service delivery; also known as total quality improvement (TQM)

2. Why would some argue that the lower costs of caring for consumers in the community may be somewhat deceptive as to what the actual costs ought to be?

RISK MANAGEMENT AND LEGAL ISSUES

Risk management as an organized program exists more frequently in the inpatient treatment sector than in the outpatient treatment sector. The function of this program is to predict, and thereby reduce or eliminate, sources of likely injury and accident or of other potential financial loss to the institution. Such responsibility obviously includes avoiding litigation, which leads to involvement in treatment issues that carry a high risk of violating patients' rights, such as the use of restraints, informed consent regarding administration of medications, and timely discharge when stabilization has occurred.

In addition, protection of confidentiality is of particular importance, especially implementation of the Health Insurance Portability and Accountability Act (HIPAA) regulations. (See Chapter 1, for details regarding HIPAA.) This concern has a direct impact on the duties of the health information manager, who has ultimate responsibility for protection of such information.

Confidentiality

Patient information in mental health settings has always been highly confidential. It was more restricted than other types of medical information until passage of HIPAA, which tightened restrictions on all types of medical information and brought confidentiality more in line with practices already largely in place within mental health. For example, before HIPAA, in settings outside mental health, information such as patient name and dates of service was considered nonconfidential and could be disclosed in the absence of a specific request by the patient to prohibit disclosure (Huffman, 1994).

In mental health facilities, however, this information traditionally has been legally protected. Even acknowledging that a patient was treated at a facility has been considered a breach of confidentiality. Mental health facilities always have placed great emphasis on strict confidentiality, and long before HIPAA, generally required all employees and vendors to sign confidentiality agreements prohibiting staff and vendors alike from disclosing any information regarding patients who had been treated at the facility.

HIPAA provides more protection to psychotherapy notes than to other types of protected health information. The use or disclosure of psychotherapy notes requires valid authorization even for treatment, payment, or health care operations, with the following exceptions: (1) The originator of the notes may use them for continuing treatment; (2) students, trainees, or practitioners may use psychotherapy notes in supervised mental health training programs; (3) the covered entity may use the notes when necessary to defend itself in a legal action brought by the individual; and (4) notes may be used as needed for health oversight activities or other activities as required by law (Standards for privacy of individually identifiable health information, 2002).

As a general rule, the mental health consumer's right to strictest confidentiality regarding matters of illness and treatment is carefully guarded. Legal protections of this right have been enacted legislatively in every state, as well as at the federal level. Traditionally, the relationship of mental health professionals to the consumer/patient has been considered privileged in the same way as that of lawyer to client, or priest to confessing parishioner. The only way in which this information can be released is through a formal, documented procedure whereby the consumer, patient, or patient's guardian provides written consent. The consent form should state the specific type of information to be released, state the exact recipient of the information, and specify the time period for which the consent is valid.

Although these strictures continue to hold true in general, certain court decisions have somewhat eroded the concept of nearly absolute confidentiality. Perhaps the most profound impact on the traditional notion of the inviolability of the therapist–client relationship has been the emergence of the concept of **duty to warn**. This idea stems from a 1976 court decision (*Tarasoff v. Regents of the University of California*), which held that a therapist has an obligation to warn persons against whom their clients make threatening statements, regardless of the fact that such threats are made within a privileged context. The theory behind the decision seems to be that safety from violent assault outweighs the breach of confidentiality and the risk of erroneous warnings. After this court decision, there has been a trend to legislate "duty to warn" clauses into the states' laws regarding confidentiality.

Case information may be required in other instances, too, such as in determining client eligibility for benefits, but these requirements vary somewhat from state to state. Frequently, the courts accept release of a summary of the case record along with specific sections pertaining directly to the legal questions of the case. In cases in which the court does not provide specific designation of information to be released, the responsibility for summaries and/or selections of pertinent material most often falls to the information manager, with possible collaboration with risk management and/or legal counsel staff.

Technological advances also have complicated the maintenance of confidentiality. Organizations must take an aggressive approach to security to protect information stored on computer networks from mischievous or malicious "hackers."

duty to warn a legal concept holding that mental health professionals have an obligation to issue a forewarning about a person whom a client with mental illness has threatened to harm, despite the usual protections of confidentiality in the client–professional relationship.

Widespread use of fax machines likewise has created a potential source of information leakage, through the human error of misdialing the correct fax machine number or through machine malfunction—in either case resulting in transmission of confidential information to unintended recipients.

Public concern about these issues was a major factor in the passage of HIPAA legislation, which now mandates many of the policies and procedures that previously were left to the discretion of the mental health system. These concerns are even more critical in an era of health information exchange as providers, consumers, and the public endeavor to determine the extent to which mental health can be included in health information exchange and still ensure the patient's or consumer's right to confidentiality.

Court-Ordered Treatment

One of the most tragic aspects of serious mental illness is that persons who are in the grips of psychosis are victims of disordered thinking, which prevents their recognizing that they are indeed ill. They often are unable to make decisions in their best interest, such as recognizing their need for psychotropic medication, and may be led by their delusions to acts that are dangerous to themselves or to others. In these cases, the mentally ill persons may be in need of court-ordered treatment.

Treatment under court order generally is predicated by a procedure that is similar throughout the nation, with slight variations from state to state, and in some states even from county to county. Usually, there is an examination of the person deemed in need of treatment by a physician and/or a mental health professional (at least a master's-level psychologist or a social worker). The usual criterion for court-ordered commitment to an inpatient institution is the professional's certification that the person is "a danger to self and/or others."

In recent years there has been an effort to broaden the rationale for commitment to include "person in need of care." This concept provides greater latitude for the court's decision as to whether institutionalization would be a means of improving a person's quality of life even if that person does not pose a direct threat to anyone. It takes into account the ill person's quality of life concerning issues such as homelessness resulting from the inability to access resources because of disordered thinking, or the extent of mental misery inflicted by paranoia and delusional thinking that medication might remediate.

Although family members and the general public support this concept, especially as a means of dealing with the homeless population, some consumer groups are opposed. They fear that such latitude can be misused and would return us to the era of widespread abuse of the commitment laws as a means of removing undesirables from the community who were not actually mentally ill, resulting in the "snake pit" conditions of mental institutions widely publicized by the media in the 1930s and 1940s.

Another solution to the dilemma of recognizing persons who are in need of supervision but who do not pose a threat to anyone is the outpatient commitment, which consists of a court order that outlines guidelines for behavior (e.g., regularly taking prescribed medication, refraining from abusing nonprescribed drugs or alcohol, reporting for mental health appointments) and may include commitment to a specific residence in the community (e.g., a group home, a family residence). Failing to abide by the prescribed conditions may result in a new court appearance and the likelihood of inpatient commitment if the person's condition has deteriorated.

SELF REVIEW 7.6

1. What is the function of the risk management program?

2. True or False? The accessibility of confidential patient information in mental health services has always been more restrictive than in other health care settings.

3. In settings outside of mental health, HIPAA allows the disclosure of confidential information for treatment, payment, or operations (TPO). In which cases does this also apply to psychotherapy notes?

4. The idea of broadening the concept of the rationale for involuntary commitment (court-ordered) from _____ to _____ is to provide more latitude for the court's decision as to whether institutionalization would be a means of improving a person's quality of life even if that person does not pose a direct threat to anyone.

ROLE OF THE HEALTH INFORMATION MANAGEMENT PROFESSIONAL

Increased interest in technological advances in data management is expanding the potential role of health information managers in the field of mental health as in other areas of health care. The traditional role of the profession has been in the institutional sector of mental health services, where the chief responsibilities have been the recording, storing, and monitoring of patient information. Frequently, however, community mental health centers are finding that decision-making in management information systems is becoming increasingly complex and requires an expertise of its own. This area would seem to be a logical extension of the domain of the health information manager in the era of electronic information systems.

Outside the domain of client data collection, another major potential for expanding the traditional role of the health information manager within CMHCs is in the area of reimbursement and the revenue cycle. Because of the multiple and disparate nature of the sources of funding for community mental health services, this is a complex arena for information storage and management (refer back to Reimbursement and Funding for further details).

Health information managers also may assume roles in quality improvement and risk management, or they may work as consultants to mental health facilities. A health information management (HIM) consultant could advise a mental health facility about issues related to accreditation, information management, or automation of patient information. A consultant assisting with the automation of patient information might have responsibilities ranging from helping to write requests for proposals for new information systems to assisting with the actual implementation of a new system.

A health information manager who chooses a career in mental health can find opportunities for advancement within the field. Some have moved into positions of increased responsibility such as oversight of all information systems. With additional education (e.g., attaining an appropriate graduate degree), HIM professionals with experience in the financial and administrative aspects of the mental health system have moved into other managerial positions, such as director of a community mental health center.

SELF REVIEW 7.7

1. List the factors that are expanding the traditional role of HIM professionals.
2. What are the opportunities for advancement as a result of this expansion?

TRENDS

A continuing major effort in the area of mental health information management is the attempt to create nationally standardized data sets along with a universal system of data collection. Several mutually antagonistic factors have impeded this movement somewhat, although there has been more progress in recent years. The thrust toward managed care has created interest in data that in essence justifies an organization's decision-making in service delivery based on cost/benefit issues. The interest in "client-centered" information systems focusing largely on client satisfaction rather than on treatment efficacy per se, however, predicates moving in another direction in the development of data collection and analysis.

Thus, the emphasis at the national level previously had been more on the quality of the standards for data management than on uniformity. Continuation of the State Data Infrastructure Grants and the move to client-level reporting points toward the possibility of more robust data for planning, decision support, and research in mental health.

The movement toward electronic information systems has increased tremendously over the past decades, particularly in the community mental health sector. The level of sophistication of the technology, however, varies widely from locale to locale, as does the capacity for linkages, whether interagency or to statewide systems.

Adoption of electronic health records (EHRs) is increasing in mental health settings even though behavioral health facilities initially were not included in the EHR incentive program of the American Recovery and Reinvestment Act. Because of the need to coordinate mental health care among various providers, advocates have pushed to make mental health facilities eligible for the incentive program, which already includes psychiatrists, who are eligible for the program as physicians.

Regardless of federal incentives, the almost universal dependence on electronic information technology has implications for health information managers.

As the level of complexity of these systems continues to climb, there will be a call for increased sophistication and specialization in their utilization as a tool for data collection. Decisions about a multitude of data-related questions will have to be addressed, from which information system best suits the needs of the specific agency to which programs will best capture the information needed by a given service provider. Questions such as these clearly are within the purview of the HIM profession.

In terms of treatment innovations, recent years also have seen several developments. More emphasis is being placed on client strengths rather than on functional deficits. This change in focus has resulted in a shift in the type of data collected, with increasing emphasis on satisfaction with services rather than specific goals accomplished or failed. As a part of this trend, the concept of "recovery" has been borrowed from substance abuse to contrast with the older mental health concept of "stabilization," which means a reduction of symptomology but does not imply a return to the level of functioning before the illness. To capture progress in this type of program emphasis is difficult and calls for creative and innovative approaches to data collection and analysis.

Telepsychiatry and tele-mental health offer opportunities to bring mental health services to individuals who otherwise may have difficulty accessing services because of a remote or rural location or for some other reason. Videoconferencing is often the only technology needed for the use of telemedicine in mental health, so there have been few barriers to its implementation. Tele-mental health may not be appropriate in every situation, but in some circumstances it has proven to be valuable in overcoming a lack of access to mental health services. In some instances, the consumer may present for an encounter in a specific location staffed by nurses or other care providers for a videoconference with a psychiatrist at a distant site (Tschirch, Walker, & Calvacca, 2006). In other instances, a consumer may use his or her own personal computer with a web camera and high-speed internet connection, providing the opportunity to receive mental health services in the privacy of the consumer's home (Ikelheimer, 2008). Security of transmission is crucial, but tele-mental health services can be delivered in several ways that have proven to be successful under appropriate circumstances.

These are some of the challenges facing health information managers in developing client data systems. Other areas also are opening up for exploration in the profession. Collecting types of data in addition to client service information is a possible area of expansion for the profession. As mentioned earlier, the billing process in outpatient facilities is a complicated weave of funding sources that also requires knowledge of electronic information storage and retrieval.

In addition, there is the possibility of entrepreneurial enterprise in developing and marketing software designed to meet the growing and changing data-collection needs of the mental health system. Consultation on developing data systems targeted at specific program needs is a possible avenue for the skills of health information managers.

1. Describe one of the factors that hindered progress toward national data sets for mental health records.

2. True or False? Adoption of EHR systems in mental health systems is decreasing.

3. Why is there a movement toward using the concept of "recovery" versus "stabilization?"

4. What methods can be used to bring treatment to clients in rural areas or who otherwise have difficulty in accessing services?

SUMMARY

As in other areas of health care, treatment of mental health service consumers has shifted from the inpatient setting to the outpatient setting as a result of advances in treatment methodologies and other factors. Mental health services consumers also may be called clients or patients. Among adults, the most common forms of serious mental illness are schizophrenia, clinical depression, and bipolar disorder. Adolescents and children also may have mental disorders, and specific services have been identified to benefit these categories of mental health services consumers. A variety of caregivers, including medical personnel, therapists, case managers, aides, recreation therapists, and occupational therapists, provide services to clients.

Mental health service providers are licensed by the state. Voluntary accreditation is available from The Joint Commission for inpatient and outpatient providers alike. CARF offers accreditation for programs that offer rehabilitation services. Managed behavioral health care organizations may seek NCQA or URAC accreditation for some services. Medicare and Medicaid guidelines apply to facilities that receive payment from these sources.

Documentation is essential in mental health services. Various assessments help to determine the patient's treatment plan. To demonstrate that every goal in the treatment plan is being addressed, there must be progress notes documenting services provided and the patient's progress toward achieving the treatment goals. Discharge summaries and aftercare plans also are necessary in the continuing care of the patient.

Several forces have helped mental health service providers improve the quality of data and information. The Center for Mental Health Services has worked with state agencies to improve, broaden, and standardize data collection activities. The increase in managed care in the mental health arena also has caused providers to pursue high-quality data and information. High-quality information in the individual patient's record is also important to the patient and the provider. Mental health information is extremely confidential, and the health information manager must ensure that appropriate HIPAA-compliant policies and procedures are in place as safeguards.

The health information manager can find opportunities in mental health hospitals and community mental health centers in a traditional information management role or in risk management, quality assurance, reimbursement, or information services. The increasing use of client-level and aggregate data for mental health services also presents opportunities for health information managers as data analysts in a variety of agencies.

REVIEW QUESTIONS

Knowledge-Based Questions

1. Explain the difference between serious emotional disturbance and serious mental illness.
2. Name the three most prevalent types of serious mental illness.
3. What are two categories of dual diagnoses?
4. Give a term by which persons with mental illness who are living in the community prefer to be called.
5. Define "outpatient commitment."
6. What are the main components of the mental health consumer case record?
7. What is the basis for payment in the inpatient psychiatric facility prospective payment system (IPF PPS)?
8. What is the relationship between the treatment plan and progress notes, and why is it important?
9. How did the "duty to warn" originate, and how does it affect confidentiality of mental health information?
10. What are the URS tables?
11. Provide examples of the national outcome measures (NOMs) for which client-level data are reported.

Critical Thinking Questions

1. Discuss how the mental health consumer empowerment movement may have affected development of mental health data collection systems.
2. Discuss some of the areas in mental health services into which health information managers may expand their roles.

WEB ACTIVITY

Visit the Substance Abuse and Mental Health Services Administration (SAMHSA) National Mental Health Information Center website at http://www.samhsa.gov

1. Select "Data, then under "State and Metro Reports," select "View by State," then select your state."
2. Select the "Uniform Reporting System (URS) Output Tables."
3. Select the latest year for which data are available.
4. Select a report for your state and review the information it contains. Can you find consumer survey results within the report? How does your state compare to the U.S. national average on various measures surveyed?
5. Select a report for another state and compare the two state reports. To what extent do they report the same categories of information? Is some optional information reported by one state and not by the other?

CASE STUDY

You are the director of health information services for a community mental health center that is planning to expand its use of electronic information systems. You have been asked to serve on the steering committee that will be guiding this initiative.

1. What types of electronic systems might the committee investigate?
2. What special considerations might there be for a community mental health center embarking on this project?

REFERENCES AND SUGGESTED READINGS

American Psychiatric Association (APA). (2000). *Diagnostic and statistical manual of mental disorders*, fourth edition (text revision). Washington, DC: Author.

American Psychiatric Association (APA). (2010). *DSM-5 overview: The future manual*. [Online]. http://www.dsm5.org/about/Pages/DSMVOverview.aspx [2010, July 24].

American Psychiatric Association (APA). (2013). *Diagnostic and Statistical Manual of Mental Disorders, Fifth Edition*. Arlington, VA, American Psychiatric Association.

Campbell, J., & Frey, E. (1993). Humanizing decision support systems. Unpublished position paper.

CARF. (n.d.). Behavioral health publications. [Online]. http://www.carf.org. [2010, July 17].

Casey, R., & Berman, J. (1985). The outcome of psychotherapy with children. *Psychological Bulletin, 98*, 388–400.

CMHS Center for Mental Health Services. (2009). *Request for Applications (RFA): Cooperative Agreements for Comprehensive Community Mental Health Services for Children and Their Families Program.* [Online]. http://www.samhsa.gov/Grants/2010/SM-10-005.aspx [2011, February 27].

CMS (Centers for Medicare & Medicaid Services. (2014, February 14). Appendix AA: Psychiatric hospitals—Interpretive guidelines and survey procedures. *State Operations Manual* [Online]. http://www.cms.gov/Regulations-and-Guidance/Guidance/Manuals/downloads/som107ap_aa_psyc_hospitals.pdf

Conditions of participation for hospitals. (2014). *Code of Federal Regulations*, Title 42, Pt. 482, Subpart E—Requirements for Specialty Hospitals, Section 61 Condition of participation: Special medical record requirements for psychiatric hospitals.

Federal Register. (1993, May 20). Definitions of adults with a serious mental illness and children with a serious emotional disturbance, pp. 29422–29425.

Federal Register. (2001, January 22). Psychiatric residential treatment facilities providing psychiatric services to individuals under age 21; Use of restraint and seclusion, pp. 7147–7164.

Federal Register. (2006, December 8). Medicare and Medicaid programs; Hospital conditions of participation; Patients' rights, pp. 71378–71380.

Friedman, R., Katz-Leary, J., Manderscheid, R., & Sondheimer, D. (1996). Prevalence of serious emotional disturbance in children and adolescents. In R. Manderscheid & M. Sonnenschein (Eds.), *Mental Health: United States* (pp. 71–98).

Washington, DC: U.S. Government Printing Office. (HHS Publication Number (SMA) 96-3098).

Furman, R. (1997). Wrap-around services: A comprehensive approach to adolescent mental health services. *Advocates Forum, 4*(1), 8–9.

Huffman, E. (1994). *Health Information Management* (10th ed.). Berwyn, IL: Physicians' Record Company.

Hutchinson, J., Lloyd, J., Landsman, M., Nelson, K., & Bryce, M. (1983). *Family-centered social services: A Model for Child Welfare Agencies.* Iowa City, IA: University of Iowa School of Social Work, National Resource Center on Family Based Services.

Ikelheimer, D. M. (2008). Treatment of opioid dependence via home-based telepsychiatry. *Psychiatric Services, 59*, 1218–1219.

Leginski, W., Croze, C., Driggers, J., Dumpman, S., Geertsen, D., Kamis-Gould, E., Namerow, M., Patton, R., Wilson, N., & Wurster, C. (1989). *Data Standards for Mental Health Decision Support Systems. Series FN No. 10.* Rockville, MD: U.S. Department of Health and Human Services.

NASMHPD Research Institute, Inc. (2007, December 3). Task 25a report: Identifying, collecting and comparing each state's expenditures for use of mental health block grant allocations. *How State Mental Health Agencies Use the Community Mental Health Services Block Grant to Improve Care and Transform Systems: 2007.* [Online]. http://download.ncadi.samhsa.gov/ken/pdf/MHBGReportSection 508-5-6-08.pdf [2010, July 19].

NASMHPD Research Institute, Inc. (2011, August 22). 2012 Profiles Focus Group Meeting. State Mental Health Agency Revenues and Expenditures for Mental Health Services. [Online]. http://www.nri-inc.org/projects/Profiles/RevExp2009/FY09Presentation.pdf

National Committee for Quality Assurance. (2010). NCQA MBHO Accreditation Requirements Link. [Online].http://www.ncqa.org [2010, July 17].

National Institute of Mental Health. (2009, March). Statistics. Available at http://www.nimh.nih.gov

Parrish, J. (1987). *Ideal Community-Based Mental Health Service System for Adults with Long-Term, Disabling Mental Illness.* Washington DC: Substance Abuse and Mental Health Services Administration.

Patton, R., & Leginski, W. (1983). *The Design and Content of a National Mental Health Statistics System. DHHS Publication (ADM) 83-1095.* Rockville,

MD: U.S. Department of Health and Human Services.

P.L. 106-310. (2000). Children's Health Act of (2000).

SAMHSA (Substance Abuse & Mental Health Services Administration). (2010). *Request for Applications (RFA): State Mental Health Data Infrastructure Grants for Quality Improvement.* [Online]. http://www.samhsa.gov/Grants/2010/SM-10-009.aspx [2010, July 24].

Sowder, B. (1979). *Issues Related to Psychiatric Services for Children and Youth: A Review of Selected Literature from 1970–1979.* Bethesda, MD: Burt Associates.

Standards for privacy of individually identifiable health information; Final rule. (2002, August 14). *Federal Register,* pp. 53181–53273.

Stroul, B., & Friedman, R. (1994). *A System of Care for Children and Youth with Severe Emotional Disturbances.* Washington, DC: Georgetown University Child Development Center.

Tarasoff v. Regents of the University of California, 17 Cal 3d 425, 131 Cal Rptr 14, 551 P 2d 334 (1976).

Tschirch, P., Walker, G., & Calvacca, L. T. (2006). Nursing in tele-mental health. *Journal of Psychosocial Nursing & Mental Health Services, 44*(5), 20–27.

KEY RESOURCES

Center for Mental Health Services
http://www.samhsa.gov/about-us/who-we-are/offices-centers/cmhs

CARF International
http://www.carf.org

National Alliance for the Mentally Ill
http://www.nami.org

National Association of State Mental Health Program Directors (NASMHPD)
www.nasmhpd.org

National Committee for Quality Assurance (NCQA)
http://www.ncqa.org

National Institute of Mental Health (NIMH)
http://www.nimh.nih.gov

The Joint Commission
http://www.jointcommission.org

URAC
http://www.urac.org

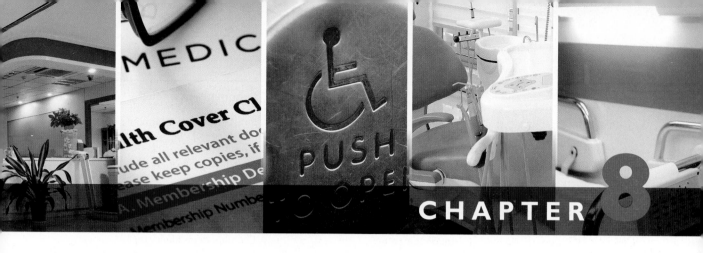

CHAPTER 8

Substance Abuse

Melissa Newell, MPPA, RHIA, COPM | Frances Wickham Lee, DBA, RHIA |
Kimberly D. Taylor, RHIA

LEARNING OBJECTIVES

Upon successful completion of this chapter, you should be able to:

- Describe the various settings and caregivers commonly associated with substance abuse treatment.
- Evaluate the impact of state and federal laws and regulations on the treatment of substance abuse clients.
- Describe the role of the Commission on Accreditation of Rehabilitation Facilities (CARF International) and The Joint Commission (TJC) in setting substance abuse treatment standards.
- Describe the components of a "typical" substance abuse client record, both inpatient and outpatient.
- Discuss current reimbursement issues related to substance abuse treatment.
- Compare *DSM* and the current version of *ICD* as they relate to coding substance abuse client records.
- Discuss quality improvement and utilization management within substance abuse facilities.
- Discuss the role of the health information manager in a substance abuse facility.
- Discuss the use of electronic information system technology in managing substance abuse client information.
- Identify the specific legal and ethical considerations associated with the confidentiality of substance abuse client records.

Setting	Description	Synonyms/Examples
Outpatient Substance Abuse Facility	A facility where clients receive regularly scheduled outpatient substance abuse treatment	Substance abuse treatment program or center
Intensive Outpatient Substance Abuse Facility	A facility where clients spend at least nine hours per week in substance abuse treatment but do not stay overnight	Partial hospitalization Day treatment IOP (Intensive Outpatient Program)
Residential Inpatient Substance Abuse Treatment Setting	A setting where clients are treated for substance abuse in a nonmedical residential setting	Rehabilitation 28-day program Residential treatment program Chemical dependency unit
Medically Managed Intensive Inpatient Substance Abuse Treatment Setting	A setting where clients are treated for substance abuse under the direction of a physician, which includes all services of an acute care hospital	Acute inpatient treatment Inpatient detoxification
Substance Abuse Education and Prevention Program	A program designed to prevent substance abuse problems in individuals or families	Early intervention School intervention programs Children of addicted families programs Alcohol and other drug prevention programs
Self-Help Recovery Groups	Support groups established to assist individuals in maintaining sobriety and a drug-free lifestyle	Alcoholics Anonymous Narcotics Anonymous 12-step programs and other recovery support groups
Aftercare	Usually follows intensive in/outpatient treatment; weekly individual and group sessions; lasts up to two years	Continuing Care Program Relapse Prevention Program

INTRODUCTION TO SETTING

The *Diagnostic and Statistical Manual of Mental Disorders, fifth edition (DSM-5)*, published by the American Psychiatric Association, includes a substance use category. This category is divided by the substance used and the severity of the condition. General synonyms for substance abuse include *alcohol and other drug abuse or dependence* and *psychoactive substance abuse or dependence, drug addiction, alcoholism,* or *chemical dependency*. Where appropriate, these terms may be substituted for *substance use* throughout the various care settings discussed in this chapter. It also is noteworthy that individuals seen in substance abuse treatment settings are often referred to as clients, consumers, or individuals receiving services (IRS), rather than as patients, because the term *patient* implies a more medically oriented model of care.

Substance abuse is a major health problem in the United States. Many different types of treatment settings are available to substance abuse clients seeking assistance, including public and private facilities that provide a full range of services, from educational programs to medically managed intensive inpatient care. In 2012, 23.1 million people aged 12 or older required substance abuse treatment. Of those, 2.5 million received treatment in a specialized facility for substance abuse issues (SAMHSA, 2012). The National Center on Addiction and Substance Abuse (CASA) at Columbia University found federal, state, and local government spending as a result of substance abuse and addiction to be $467.7 billion or more in 2005 (CASA, 2009).

The public sector traditionally has assumed a major responsibility for the operation of substance abuse treatment centers, particularly outpatient treatment centers. According to the *National Survey of Substance Abuse Treatment Services (N-SSATS): 2012*, 52% of all clients in treatment were in private nonprofit facilities. Private for-profit facilities accounted for the treatment of 34% of substance abuse clients (SAMHSA, 2012). Publicly owned treatment centers usually receive their funds from state, city, and county governments; federal grants and contracts; and some client fees and third-party reimbursement. Private substance abuse treatment facilities, in contrast, rely primarily on direct client payments and third-party reimbursement for their funds. Figure 8-1 shows the distribution of substance abuse clients by facility ownership and primary focus of facility.

The evolution of modern substance abuse treatment in the United States began in the 1950s with the development of freestanding residential programs for the treatment of alcohol dependency and with the continued growth and recognition of **Alcoholics Anonymous (AA)** and its 12-step recovery philosophy. The medical community formerly did not consider alcohol treatment programs to be truly a part of the health care system, and these programs often were staffed and run by nonprofessionals, some of whom were recovering alcoholics themselves. Treatment for drug addiction was even more removed from mainstream health care, and the criminal justice system typically referred clients to drug treatment centers.

Although the American Medical Association classified alcoholism as a disease in 1956, not until the 1970s did the public begin to recognize alcoholism as a disease and third-party payers began to offer some reimbursement for inpatient treatment. Outpatient treatment became more prevalent in the 1980s and 1990s when providers and third-party payers realized that substance abuse clients needed a full range of treatment options. According to statistics gathered for the period 2008 to 2012, outpatient rehabilitation was the most widely available type of care, with around 80% of facilities offering this service. Residential rehabilitation was offered by 25% of all facilities, and hospital inpatient rehabilitation was offered by 5% to 6% of facilities. The numbers changed very little between 2008 and 2012 (SAMHSA, 2012).

Alcoholics Anonymous (AA) a worldwide organization of self-help recovery groups that support individuals in maintaining sobriety. AA is based on a 12-step recovery process; other programs that follow the 12-step recovery process sometimes are referred to as 12-step programs.

Care Settings

The following are some of the more common settings for substance abuse treatment and services; however, this is not an exhaustive list. For simplicity, the programs discussed in this chapter have been grouped by care setting under the following general headings:

1. Outpatient treatment
2. Intensive outpatient or partial hospitalization treatment

FIGURE 8-1

Substance abuse treatment clients by facility ownership and by primary focus of facility.

Facility Operation			Clients in Treatment on March 30,2012			
	Facilities		All Clients		Clients Under Age 18	
	No.	%	No.	%	No.	%
Private non-profit	10,816	56	649,431	52	56,519	63
Private for-profit	5,989	31	424,628	34	19,037	22
Local government	967	5	74,934	6	5,653	8
State government	579	3	37,467	3	4,813	6
Federal government	579	3	37,467	3	571	.5
Tribal government	386	2	24,978	2	571	.5
Total	**19,316**	**100.0**	**1,248,905**	**100.0**	**89,521**	**100**

Primary Focus of Facility			Clients in Treatment on March 30,2012			
	Facilities		All Clients		Clients Under Age 18	
	No.	%	No.	%	No.	%
Substance abuse treatment services	10,625	55	761,832	61	39,972	44
Mental health services	1,352	7	62,445	5	6,674	8
Mix of mental health & substance abuse treatment services	6,374	33	374,672	30	40,653	45
General health care	386	2	24,978	2	673	1
Other/unknown	579	3	24,978	2	1,594	2
Total	**19316**	**100.0**	**1,182,077**	**100.0**	**84,326**	**100.0**

Source: Office of Applied Studies, Substance Abuse and Mental Health Services Administration, National Survey of Substance Abuse Treatment Services (N-SSATS), 201209.

3. Residential/inpatient treatment

4. Aftercare/continuing care

5. Educational/prevention programs

6. Self-help recovery groups

Within the substance abuse treatment community, similar programs sometimes are found in an inpatient, outpatient, or community setting. For example, the Alcoholics Anonymous (AA) 12-step philosophy and program originated as part of a self-help recovery network, but over the years this philosophy also has been incorporated into programs at both inpatient and outpatient treatment facilities.

As a general rule, clients should be treated at the lowest or least intensive level of care that will accomplish their treatment goals. The levels are discussed in this chapter as discrete entities, but in reality they represent the continuum of substance abuse treatment services available to clients in most areas of the country.

Outpatient Treatment

Outpatient treatment consists of regularly scheduled sessions with a mental health professional. These sessions can include individual therapy, group therapy, or family therapy. The sessions address current issues and also educate the clients about relapse prevention.

Outpatient providers, such as mental health centers, hospital-based outpatient centers, and freestanding drug and alcohol treatment centers, currently treat substance abuse clients through a variety of treatment modalities, including individual, group, and family therapy. Individual therapy currently is the most common form of outpatient treatment, accounting for 76% of all treatment sessions (SAMHSA, 2012).

Specialized outpatient programs also are found throughout the substance abuse treatment system. Outpatient therapy typically is a long-term commitment for a client, lasting up to a year or more. Some examples of specialized outpatient treatment programs are methadone maintenance programs for heroin addicts, organized school intervention programs for adolescents, court-related programs for individuals convicted of substance abuse–related offenses, and employee assistance programs that contract with companies within the community to provide care to their employees. The discussion of types of clients in this chapter provides more information on these and other specific client populations.

> **outpatient treatment** regularly scheduled sessions with a mental health professional; can include individual therapy, group therapy or family therapy. The sessions address current issues and also educate the clients about relapse prevention.

Intensive Outpatient or Partial Hospitalization Treatment

Intensive outpatient or partial hospitalization is a more structured, rigid form of treatment than is regular outpatient treatment. Intensive outpatient treatment requires a minimum of 9 hours of weekly attendance, usually in increments of 3 to 8 hours a day for 5 to 7 days a week. This treatment often is recommended for patients in the early stages of treatment and for those transitioning from residential or hospital settings. This environment is suitable for patients who do not require full-time supervision and have some available supports but do need more structure than is typical of less intensive outpatient settings.

This treatment option encompasses day treatment or group programs that may offer a full range of services, including outpatient detoxification at times.

> **intensive outpatient or partial hospitalization treatment** a required minimum of 9 hours of weekly attendance, usually in increments of 3 to 8 hours a day for 5 to 7 days a week; often recommended for patients in the early stages of treatment or those transitioning from residential or hospital settings.

The frequency and length of session usually are tapered as patients demonstrate progress, less risk of relapse, and stronger reliance on drug-free community supports. An evening program can provide clients with an alternative to inpatient treatment, thereby avoiding an extended leave from home, work, or school.

Intensive outpatient treatment programs allow adult clients to continue working and adolescent clients to continue schooling while providing a structured treatment environment. Partial hospitalization programs typically are day treatment programs that provide more treatment hours for clients with more severe levels of illness. Clients can spend all day in the treatment program but return home each evening (APA, 2006).

Residential/Inpatient Treatment   Residential/inpatient treatment is directed at clients with sub-acute medical, behavioral, or emotional problems. Residential treatment provides a live-in facility with 24-hour supervision. This type of treatment is better than outpatient treatment for consumers with an overwhelming substance abuse problem, who typically are without the motivation or social supports to abstain from abusing. The length of stay in these facilities ranges from short-term to long-term. Some programs offer less restrictive types of treatment, such as halfway and quarter-way houses, to help the consumer's transition back into the community (APA, 2006).

Educational/Prevention Programs/Early Intervention

Society places significant emphasis on awareness and prevention of substance abuse problems. Substance abuse facilities, particularly those in the public sector, frequently are involved in providing structured prevention, education, and awareness programs. The clients served by these programs differ from those who receive substance abuse treatment; these clients do not necessarily have substance abuse or dependence diagnoses but are considered to be at risk for problems in the future. Many participants in educational programs are children or adolescents who have been identified by the schools, social service agencies, or legal system as having the potential to develop substance abuse problems or who have family members with existing substance abuse problems. A program that targets children of addicted families is an example of a service that a substance treatment facility might offer to help children who are affected by substance abuse within their families.

SAMHSA's **Center for Substance Abuse Prevention (CSAP)** administers a number of grant programs aimed at reducing the incidence of substance abuse. Recognizing the cost-effectiveness of prevention programs, CSAP provides national leadership for community-based prevention programs. Research has demonstrated the effectiveness of various interventions for substance abuse prevention. More than 60 prevention interventions are listed at the National Registry of Evidence-based Programs and Practices (NREPP—discussed later) that meet evidence-based practice criteria for effectiveness.

residential/inpatient treatment   a program directed at clients with sub-acute medical, behavioral, or emotional problems; provides a live-in facility with 24-hour supervision.

Center for Substance Abuse Prevention (CSAP) an agency of SAMHSA that provides national leadership for community-based substance abuse prevention programs. Among other activities, CSAP administers a number of grant programs aimed at reducing the incidence of substance abuse.

Self-Help Recovery Groups

Arguably, including self-help recovery groups in a list of substance abuse care settings is not appropriate, because they are designed to be voluntary and to provide support rather than treatment for recovering addicts. These groups, however, provide lifelong assistance to many individuals with substance abuse problems and are considered to be a significant factor in many successful recoveries.

The most widely recognized self-help organization is Alcoholics Anonymous, a program in which members follow a 12-step program that leads to recovery. AA was founded in 1935 and had reached national prominence by the 1950s (Alcoholics Anonymous World Services, Inc., 1957). Since that time, AA has spawned other self-help groups, such as Narcotics Anonymous (NA), that adhere to a similar 12-step philosophy. No records are kept by 12-step support groups, because anonymity is a key element in the recovery programs. Nevertheless, 12-step programs have reached such prominence in the substance abuse treatment community that many providers actually integrate the philosophy into their treatment services, and this is reflected in client records.

Even though AA is the most widely accepted network of substance abuse self-help groups, other approaches are available as well. For example, some programs offer support groups based on various adaptations of cognitive behavioral therapy as a means to recovery. Client participation in a support group, regardless of the group's philosophy, improves the chances that the client will stay sober. Clients are more likely to participate in groups when they feel a connection to the group's general beliefs. Because various support groups have differing philosophical underpinnings, it is helpful for the treatment professional to assist the client in finding a group that is a good fit for him or her (Atkins & Hawdon, 2007).

Types of Clients

Within the various types of substance abuse settings and programs, the clients served range in age from infants to the elderly and come from all socioeconomic backgrounds. In addition to identifying broad categories of clients, such as inpatients and outpatients, facilities often further identify segments of their client populations by factors such as age, sex, type of referral, or legal status. This categorization facilitates program planning and administration.

In many cases, educational and treatment programs can be tailored to meet the needs of specific client groups. Some examples of client groups served by specific programs or protocols because of their special needs are adolescents, women, clients referred to employee assistance programs, clients who have been dually diagnosed with a mental disorder and a substance abuse disorder, and clients who have been court-referred. A recent trend is to provide group sessions to individuals who are incarcerated. The sessions are provided to the individuals while they are in a jail or other correctional setting. Many other special programs are offered in substance abuse treatment centers throughout the United States, but examining this sample will provide an overview of the scope of clients served.

Adolescents

In addition to potentially causing problems with family, friends, and schoolwork, use of alcohol and other drugs by adolescents can lead to dangerous patterns of lifelong abuse. The 2011 national Youth Risk Behavior Survey indicated that around 71 percent of high school students had tried alcohol. This is a reduction from 75 percent in 2007 (CDC, n.d.). Health care providers, teachers, and parents now recognize that an adolescent can develop serious abuse and addiction problems as a result of this early experimentation. In 2011, the National Survey on Drug Use and Health reported that an estimated 12.9 million adolescents between the ages of 12 and 17 used alcohol and 8.5% reported binge drinking. This does not include the number that sought treatment for drug issues (SAMHSA, 2012).

Most of these clients are treated in a clinical setting that is structured specifically for treating adolescents. Treating an adolescent substance abuse problem is quite different from treating an adult problem. The youthful client's unique emotional, social, and educational needs must be addressed in his or her treatment plan. To highlight the need to use care in selecting a treatment program for adolescents, the American Academy of Pediatrics (AAP) developed a list of program selection criteria that addresses, among other concerns, issues such as (Levy & Kokotailo, 2011):

- Parent and family involvement in treatment
- Low staff-to-patient ratio
- Separation of the adolescent clients based on the developmental level of the adolescents
- Professional staff leading the group sessions
- Treatment facility located close to the client's home

Treatment settings for adolescents span all levels of care and include in-school intervention programs, outpatient therapy, intensive outpatient programs, short-stay residential inpatient treatment, and extended-stay inpatient treatment.

Women

Awareness is growing within the substance abuse treatment community that women, particularly pregnant women and women who are parents of young children, have special care and support needs, as do their children. In 2011–2012, 8.5% of women were pregnant when they were admitted to alcohol abuse treatment (SAMHSA, 2012). Treatment of pregnant women should be a priority because the welfare of both the mother and the unborn baby are at stake. Fetal alcohol syndrome and cocaine addiction in newborns can lead to serious health and developmental problems for children. Pregnant women with substance abuse problems need prenatal care along with substance abuse treatment, and their children need monitoring for potential medical and emotional problems.

Programs developed for pregnant women might include child care incorporating therapeutic activities to assist the children in learning to deal with issues related to living with an addicted parent and easy access to intensive prenatal care and case management services. The levels of service provided in women's substance abuse programs include outpatient, intensive outpatient, and inpatient treatment, depending on the severity of the substance abuse and the individual's treatment plan.

EAP Clients

Many substance abuse agencies and treatment facilities have established **employee assistance programs (EAPs)** to serve working adults and their employers. Businesses contract with local substance abuse organizations to provide services to their employees. Employers have come to recognize that substance abuse problems will have a negative impact on job performance, and that it is in their best interest and that of their employees to encourage treatment of these problems. The actual scope of the substance abuse services provided by the EAP is specified in a contract negotiated between the business and the provider. The contract typically includes at least an assessment, at little or no out-of-pocket cost for the employee and, if needed, referral to one of the education or treatment options available through the provider's existing programs.

Employees can be referred to the EAP by their employers, or in some cases the employees will seek out the EAP services for themselves. As in other substance abuse treatment programs, strict confidentiality of EAP client information is maintained, regardless of the referral source.

> **employee assistance programs (EAPs)** substance abuse assessment and treatment programs established through a contractual arrangement between an organization and a substance abuse treatment facility to serve the employees within the organization.

Dually Diagnosed Clients

A growing portion of the substance abuse client population is **dually diagnosed** with both a substance abuse or dependency disorder and a chronic mental illness. These clients typically have difficulty succeeding in traditional alcohol and drug treatment programs and self-help groups, which has led to the development of programs designed to meet their special care needs. By using assessment tools specifically designed to identify dually diagnosed individuals, treatment facilities can better plan the course of treatment for clients.

In most states, and in most private facilities, substance abuse services and mental health services are offered in the same location or by a single organizational unit, allowing dually diagnosed clients access to treatment for both their substance abuse and their mental health disorders. Over the past few years, treatment facilities have started to identify dually diagnosed clients. Several assessment tools are available to screen for these diagnoses (NAMI, 2014). According

> **dually diagnosed** refers to clients who have both a substance abuse disorder and a chronic mental illness; these clients typically have special treatment needs.

to SAMHSA, 46% of clients treated for substance abuse were dually diagnosed (SAMHSA, 2012).

Court-Referred Clients

Individuals who are arrested and convicted of alcohol- and other drug-related offenses frequently are referred to substance abuse treatment programs for drug and alcohol awareness education, a substance abuse assessment, or substance abuse treatment. For additional information on court-ordered treatment, refer to the later discussion of Risk Management and Legal Issues.

When an individual is convicted of driving while intoxicated (DWI) or driving under the influence (DUI) of alcohol or drugs, the court may order, for example, that the individual has to enroll in an awareness program and to obtain a substance abuse assessment to determine whether treatment will be required. In some states, the assessment or education program actually may be required by law, creating a situation in which law enforcement, the court system, and the substance abuse treatment center must work closely together. DUI clients are not the only court-related clients seen by substance abuse facilities; persons arrested and convicted of other alcohol- or drug-related offenses also may be referred or ordered to obtain assessment and treatment.

Types of Caregivers

The types of caregivers who work with substance abuse clients vary widely. They include individuals who possess a wide range of educational and professional backgrounds, from residential aides to psychiatrists and other physicians. Each of these caregivers is an important member of the substance abuse treatment team, bringing unique experience and expertise to the overall treatment process.

The following discussion includes a representation of direct caregivers who work with substance abuse clients; however, several other caregivers may be involved in the clients' care. Clients treated in an acute inpatient setting are cared for by the various ancillary departments and other medical and allied health specialists found in the hospital. And it is not unusual to see professionals such as occupational therapists, recreation therapists, and dietitians working in substance abuse programs.

Physicians

Some physicians specialize in the treatment of chemically dependent patients. Also, psychiatrists, family practitioners, or other physicians with a general practice orientation can be involved in substance abuse treatment. Any treatment plan that requires a medical intervention, such as prescription medications or detoxification services, is monitored, if not managed, by a physician. Medical services may be provided by full-time staff physicians or by part-time contract physicians, depending on the level of care and the treatment setting—for example, public or private, inpatient or outpatient.

Physician Assistants and Nurse Practitioners

As in other segments of health care, the role of advanced practice clinicians or mid-level providers—physician assistants (PAs) and nurse practitioners (NPs)—varies from state to state and from facility to facility. As a general rule, these professionals treat clients under the supervision of a physician; however, some states allow more independent practice.

Nurses

In addition to medical care and substance abuse treatment, clients in inpatient substance abuse facilities require nursing care. The extent of nursing service in a facility depends on the level of care it offers. An acute care hospital setting provides 24-hour nursing care to its substance abuse patients, just as it does to other patients.

Counselors

Substance abuse counselors are professionals such as social workers and psychologists, with special training and experience in treating clients with substance abuse problems and mental health issues. The educational background of these individuals varies and may depend in part on the state's facility licensure, practitioner licensure, and Medicaid regulations. The counselor provides individual, group, and/or family therapy to the client and the client's family according to the treatment plan. Frequently, the counselor is recognized as the client's primary therapist, particularly in an outpatient setting. The primary therapist is the caregiver responsible for coordinating the client's treatment, including an assurance that all documentation requirements are met.

Case Managers

As with substance abuse counselors, substance abuse case managers come from a variety of professional and educational backgrounds. They may be nurses, social workers, or educational specialists. The case manager's role in substance abuse treatment depends on the level of care and the specific care setting. In an inpatient setting, the case manager may focus primarily on reimbursement issues and organizing follow-up care. The case manager in an outpatient setting assists the client with these and other non-treatment activities, such as obtaining adequate housing, securing financial assistance, keeping medical and counseling appointments, and so on. A case manager differs from a counselor in his or her relationship with the client; the case manager provides assistance with obtaining and coordinating services for clients rather than actual therapy.

Recreational Therapists

Long-term inpatient and other residential treatment programs often employ recreational therapists to work with clients. Recreational therapists design therapeutic recreational activities for residents while they are undergoing treatment. For example, a residential treatment program for adolescents might incorporate a challenge course or other outdoor activities designed to build trust and self-esteem. Adult clients may utilize exercise equipment or engage in basketball games.

SELF REVIEW 8.1

1. True or False? In 2008–2012, hospital inpatient rehabilitation was the most widely available rehabilitation offered.

2. Alcoholics Anonymous is an example of a/n _____.

3. Programs providing 24-hour supervision that help consumer's transition back into the community are called _____.

4. The American Academy of Pediatrics developed criteria to assisting families in selecting substance abuse programs for adolescents. List five of the criteria.

5. True or False? A dually diagnosed client is one who has been diagnosed for substance abuse or dependency in more than one facility.

REGULATORY ISSUES

Confidentiality of Drug and Alcohol Abuse Records, 42 C.F.R. Part 2 federal regulations that mandate strict confidentiality of drug and alcohol patient information in federally assisted substance abuse treatment programs.

Several public and private agencies regulate or set standards for substance abuse treatment facilities and programs. One set of federal regulations, **Confidentiality of Drug and Alcohol Abuse Records, 42 C.F.R. Part 2,** mandates that any federally assisted substance abuse treatment program must adhere to strict confidentiality guidelines and legal procedures. Substance abuse treatment records historically have been the only category of health-related record—except those created in government-operated health care facilities such as Veterans Affairs and Indian Health Service hospitals—whose security and confidentiality are specifically protected by a comprehensive federal law. A discussion of 42 C.F.R. Part 2 is detailed in the Risk Management and Legal Issues section of this chapter.

As discussed earlier in this book, HIPAA also provides guidelines for confidentiality of protected health information (PHI). The federal law that protects substance abuse programs and their information is more comprehensive than the HIPAA requirements in many ways. Therefore, substance abuse programs have not fundamentally changed their approach to maintaining confidentiality.

The other regulatory agencies discussed here set standards for substance abuse treatment facilities, along with other health care facilities, with the intent of promoting high-quality care. Two major private, not-for-profit, voluntary accrediting agencies that set standards for substance abuse facilities are: The Joint Commission (TJC) and CARF International (Commission on Accreditation of Rehabilitation Facilities). The government standards that are applied most frequently to substance abuse treatment programs are state Medicaid guidelines. Facilities treating Medicare clients also have to comply with the applicable Conditions of Participation.

As the best-known voluntary health care accreditation agency in the United States, The Joint Commission's original focus was on improving the quality of hospital-based patient care. Over the years, however, The Joint Commission has developed distinct accreditation programs for nonhospital settings, such as outpatient mental health and substance abuse treatment, ambulatory care, long-term care, and others.

Although Joint Commission accreditation is voluntary, in some states substance abuse treatment facilities, particularly inpatient facilities and hospital-based programs that are accredited do not have to undergo additional surveys for licensure and certification. Inpatient substance abuse facilities, as well as hospital-based ambulatory, residential, or partial hospitalization substance abuse programs, follow the standards outlined in The Joint Commission's *Comprehensive Accreditation Manual for Hospitals* (CAMH). This is the same manual that acute-care hospitals use, but specific standards within CAMH address services to behavioral health patients, including substance abuse clients.

Community-based outpatient substance abuse programs follow the standards outlined in a separate Joint Commission accreditation program manual, the *Comprehensive Accreditation Manual for Behavioral Health Care (CAMBHC)*. This manual and its corresponding accreditation program are designed to meet the needs of nonhospital programs serving mental health, substance abuse, and developmentally delayed clients. Hospital-based and inpatient substance abuse programs are more likely to seek Joint Commission accreditation, often as a part of an organization-wide effort, than are community outpatient programs. Although there are definite advantages for substance abuse treatment programs in seeking Joint Commission accreditation, it can be a costly process, and many publicly funded outpatient programs often choose not to participate.

The mission of **CARF International (Commission on Accreditation of Rehabilitation Facilities)** is "to promote the quality, value, and optimal outcomes of services through a consultative accreditation process that centers on enhancing the lives of the persons served" (CARF, 1994). CARF's core values emphasize the rights of the individuals served by rehabilitation facilities. These values address the importance of treating individuals with respect and empowering them to make their own informed choices. Substance abuse programs can be accredited under several of CARF's core programs, including detoxification, drug court treatment, employee assistance, outpatient treatment, partial hospitalization, prevention, or residential treatment, to name a few. Two CARF standards manuals are relevant to substance abuse programs: the *Behavioral Health Standards Manual, Child & Youth Services Standard Manual* and the *Opioid Treatment Program Standards Manual* (CARF, 1994).

CARF International (Commission on Accreditation of Rehabilitation Facilities) a voluntary accreditation agency that sets standards that promote "the delivery of quality services to people with disabilities" (CARF, 1994). CARF standards include a section devoted to alcohol and other drug treatment programs.

Another major category of regulators of substance abuse treatment consists of the various state agencies responsible for state Medicaid programs. Medicaid is a federally mandated program that provides medical assistance to low-income individuals, as authorized by Title XIX of the Social Security Act of 1965. The actual Medicaid costs, however, are shared by the federal government and the states. The percentages for this cost-sharing and the actual dollar amount spent for Medicaid vary significantly from state to state. State Medicaid agencies are granted a fair amount of independence in determining the levels of coverage and the payment mechanisms they will employ, provided that the basic services as required by the federal regulations are covered. Consequently, most of the standards governing Medicaid providers are developed at the state level and also vary from one state to another.

One basic tenet of Medicaid is that it provides for reimbursement of care that is "medically necessary." For substance abuse treatment programs, this translates into the need for physician involvement and clear documentation of the medical necessity of the prescribed substance abuse treatment for Medicaid clients. Figure 8-2 details the number and percentage of substance abuse facilities licensed, approved, certified, or accredited by various agencies.

FIGURE 8-2

Types of licensing, approval, certification, or accreditation held by substance abuse facilities.

Facility Licensing, Approval, Certification, or Accreditation		
	Facilities[1]	
	No.	**%**
Any listed agency/organization	14,311	95.0
State substance abuse agency	11,593	81
State mental health department	5,348	38
State department of health	6,153	43
Hospital licensing authority	1,002	7
The Joint Commission	2,719	19
CARF[2]	3,291	23
NCQA[3]	429	3
COA[4]	716	5
Other state/local agency/org	1,002	7

[1]Facilities may be licensed by more than one agency/organization.
[2]Commission on Accreditation of Rehabilitation Facilities
[3]National Committee for Quality Assurance
[4]Council for Accreditation

Source: Office of Applied Studies, Substance Abuse and Mental Health Services Administration, National Survey of Substance Abuse Treatment Services (N-SSATS), 201209.

SELF REVIEW 8.2

1. Name the two major accrediting agencies for substance abuse facilities.
2. Facilities treating Medicare clients must comply with the _____.

DOCUMENTATION

As in other health care settings, substance abuse facilities require clear and consistent documentation. Good-quality documentation of care, whether done manually or electronically, is essential. The primary purpose for maintaining client records is to support client treatment. Other purposes for the records include: to improve communication among care providers, to serve as legal records of care provided, to support reimbursement claims, to monitor the quality of care, and to provide data for research and education.

Records are increasingly important for documenting evidence-based practices and outcome measures. Facilities have to demonstrate that a client's treatment was successful. Documentation can help to support this by indicating an increase in an the patient's level of functioning or by documenting recidivism rates.

Although the federal government mandates that a standard set of information be submitted for each client who is treated, the types of documents, computer systems, files, and forms vary considerably from organization to organization. Each facility, however, should develop and maintain standards, policies, and procedures governing its specific documentation requirements (Ohio Administrative Code, 2005). The following lists, adapted from South Carolina Department of Alcohol and Other Drug Abuse Services' *Uniform Clinical Records*, represent typical information that might be found within the record of a substance abuse client, divided into two general groups: legal/administrative documentation and clinical documentation.

Legal/Administrative Documentation

The legal/administrative portion of the client record typically includes essential nonclinical information such as demographic and identifying information, along with any required legal documentation. Examples include:

- Admission information
- Commitment papers
- Fee agreement and financial assessment
- Insurance authorization
- Special-program enrollment forms
- Program or agency rules
- Consents to treatment
- Consents to release of information

- Client rights information
- Notice of privacy practice

Clinical Documentation

The clinical portion of the client's record documents the direct care provided and might include such items as:

- Clinical assessments
- Medical assessment, if necessary
- Individualized treatment plan
- Clinical service notes or progress notes (may be daily or weekly summary notes, depending on the type of program and applicable standards)
- Discharge summary/aftercare plan
- Follow-up information
- List of medications/allergies

clinical assessment
a procedure conducted by a clinician for every client who enters a substance abuse treatment program; used as a basis for the client's diagnosis and individualized treatment plan.

individualized treatment plan (ITP)   a written plan developed by the client's treatment team to identify the type and frequency of services the client needs; includes measurable goals and objectives that address the problems identified in the clinical assessment and should be updated periodically (usually every 6 months) as the client's treatment needs change.

Two key documents in the substance abuse record are the **clinical assessment** and the **individualized treatment plan**. (See Figure 8-3 and Figure 8-4.) Each client should receive a thorough clinical assessment before the development of his or her individualized treatment plan. This assessment typically includes documentation of:

- Identifying information
- Presenting problem
- Health, medical, and/or developmental history
- Family and social history
- History of psychoactive substance use
- History of psychological factors impacting the client's condition
- Educational/vocational history
- Client abilities, strengths, needs, and preferences
- Preliminary diagnoses
- Admission-to-program information, including specific reasons when admission is denied
- Initial problem list
- Clinical assessment summary

Because the severity and unique treatment considerations of substance abuse problems vary significantly from one client to another, an individualized plan of treatment must be established for every case, even if the clients' diagnoses are the same. For example, one client with a diagnosis of cocaine abuse might require both an inpatient stay and outpatient therapy, whereas another client might need only outpatient therapy. The individualized treatment plan (ITP) is

FIGURE 8-3

Sample clinical assessment forms.

Clinical Assessment Outline (sample 1)

Client Name (Last, First, MI)	ID#

Presenting Problem: Include reason for entry, source of referral, legal Involvement, self-identified problems and recent stressors.

_____

_____

_____

_____

_____

_____

Health/Medical History: Describe general health, nutrition, medical problems, medications, hospitallzations, disabilities, tuberculosis screening and HIV-risk behaviors.

_____

_____

_____

_____

_____

_____

_____

(continues)

FIGURE 8-3   (*continued*)

Family/Social Interaction: In chronological order, describe family of origin and present family, including relationships with all family members. Include family history of substance use/abuse and current family use. Describe other intimate and social relationships. Include peer group functioning. Include cultural, ethnic and spiritual factors and expectations. Include any physical and/or sexual abuse history.

_____

_____

_____

_____

_____

_____

_____

_____

_____

_____

_____

_____

_____

FIGURE 8-3   *(continued)*

Client Name (Last, First, MI)	ID#

Drug	Age at First Use	Frequency (last 6 months)	Quantity (specify time frame)	Last Use	How Used
Alcohol					
Amphetamine					
Caffeine					
Cannabis					
Cocaine					
Hallucinogen					
Inhalant					
Nicotine					
Opioid					
PCP					
Sedative Hypnotic					

Psychoactive Substance Use: Include other relevant substance use factors such as loss of control, tolerance, treatment history, patterns of use and problems related to use. Include data to differentiate between use, abuse and dependence.

_____

_____

_____

_____

_____

_____

(continues)

FIGURE 8-3 *(continued)*

Psychological: Include mental status, activities of daily living, communication skills/abilities, present emotional state, management of emotions, violence, suicide attempts/thoughts and psychiatric history (to include history of eating disorder behaviors).

_____

_____

_____

_____

_____

Educational/Vocational: Include years of education, military service, job history, financial status and leisure activities.

_____

_____

_____

Strengths and Needs: Describe client and clinician perceptions and unique factors affecting the course of treatment.

_____

_____

_____

Sources of Information other than client:

Name _____   Relationship _____

Name _____   Relationship _____

Assessment Interview Information		
Assessment Date	Client Time	Clinician Signature and Title
_____	_____	_____
_____	_____	_____
_____	_____	_____

FIGURE 8-3 *(continued)*

Clinical Assessment Outline (sample 2)

Client Name (Last, First, MI)	ID#

Identifying Information

DOB _____   Age _____   Sex _____   Ethnic Group _____

Marital Status _____   Occupation _____   Education _____

Multiaxial Diagnosis

	Code #	Description
Axis 1:	_____	_____
Axis II:	_____	_____
Axis III:	_____	_____
Axis IV:	Psychosocial Stressors:	_____
	Severity:	_____
Axis V:	Global Assessment of Functioning (GAF):	_____(current)

Master Problem List: In concise statements, list the most immediate problems the client is presenting. Indicate whether each problem will be addressed on the Treatment Plan (T); whether it will be referred (R) for services elsewhere; or whether it will be monitored (M). Place the letter that corresponds to the appropriate disposition in the space provided to the left of each problem statemen

_____   1) _____

_____   2) _____

_____   3) _____

_____   4) _____

_____   5) _____

_____   6) _____

_____   7) _____

_____   8) _____

Admitted to services _____ yes   _____ no   Reason for non-admission _____

_____

(continues)

FIGURE 8-3   *(continued)*

Interpretive Summary: Include an integration and interpretation of all pertinent assessment information; the client's perception of his/her needs, strengths, limitations or problems; clinical judgments regarding the course of treatment; recommended treatments; and anticipated level and length of care.

_____

_____

_____

_____

_____

_____

_____

_____

_____

_____

_____

_____

_____

Clinician Signature and Title	**Date**

FIGURE 8-4

Sample individualized treatment plan forms.

Six Month Individualized Treatment Plan

1. Client Name (Last, First, MI)			ID#		
2. Diagnosis and Justification for Treatment or Continuation of Treatment					
3. Proposed Treatment Process					
a. Date Service Ordered	b. Type Service	c. Estimated Frequency	d. Goals		e. Expected Achievement Date
4. Client Signature			Date		
5. Clinician Signature and Title			Date		

(continues)

FIGURE 8-4 (*continued*)

6. Summary of FIRST 90 Day Progress	
(Address progress on goals, appropriateness of service being provided, and need for continued treatment.)	
7. Clinician Signature and Title	Date
8. Summary of SECOND 90 Day Progress	
(Address progress on goals, appropriateness of service being provided, and need for continued treatment.)	
9. Clinician Signature and Title	Date

the document in the client's record that is intended to guide the clinician and the client through the treatment process; therefore, the ITP must be based on the client's comprehensive clinical assessment. An ITP typically includes:

- Identifying information
- *DSM-5* diagnoses
- Strengths of the individual
- Justification or reason for treatment, including duration and frequency of the problem
- Proposed treatment process, including type of service and frequency
- Treatment goals and objectives that are measurable, with target achievement dates

The ITP is updated periodically to reflect changes in the client's condition and revised treatment goals. The ITP should be a flexible document designed to meet the treatment needs of the individual client. Both CARF and TJC have developed standards for the ITP.

1. Admission information, commitment papers, consent to treatment and notice of privacy practice are examples of _____ documentation.

2. An individual treatment plan, list of medications, and aftercare plan would be found in the _____ section of the client's medical record.

3. DSM-5 diagnoses, presenting problem, initial problem list, developmental history, family history, client's abilities, treatment goals and objectives would be documented in the _____.

REIMBURSEMENT AND FUNDING

Reimbursement issues facing inpatient substance abuse facilities are essentially the same as those for other types of inpatient mental health services. The funding stream for outpatient substance abuse treatment is complex, however, involving several government agencies at the state and federal levels, as well as private insurance companies and client fees.

In a community (outpatient or residential) substance abuse treatment center, for example, revenues may come from any combination of the following sources:

- *Client fees.* In the public sector, client fees do not account for a major portion of revenue, but they are collected, generally on a sliding-scale basis (i.e., clients' out-of-pocket fees are set according to their ability to pay). Family size and income both are taken into consideration in determining the clients' copayments.

- *Private insurance.* Individual insurance policies may cover substance abuse services at the inpatient or the outpatient level. In public facilities, the insurance company usually is billed first, before any federal insurance is billed or any applicable sliding-scale copayment is determined.

- *Medicaid.* Medicaid program costs are shared by the federal and state governments. Therefore, eligibility, reimbursement rates and payment mechanisms (fee-for-service, capitation, etc.) for substance abuse treatment vary from state to state. Most publicly supported substance abuse facilities rely heavily on Medicaid as a source of revenue.

- *Medicare.* Medicare covers a limited amount of substance abuse treatment for eligible clients. Services such as inpatient treatment, outpatient treatment, and detoxification are covered for a preset number of days or visits.

- *Other government funding sources.* Several federal agencies administer a variety of block grants and contracts to support substance abuse treatment or prevention. The agency that administers the federal substance abuse prevention and treatment (SAPT) grants is the Substance Abuse and Mental Health Services Administration (SAMHSA). These grants, and others, usually are awarded to individual states, which in turn distribute the money to eligible community agencies. In some of these agencies, federal funding may account for up to 75% or more of total revenue. Certain community-based treatment programs, such as school-based intervention programs, actually may be funded up to 100% by specific grants or contracts—for example, from SAMHSA's Center for Substance Abuse Prevention (CSAP) or Center for Substance Abuse Treatment (CSAT).

SELF REVIEW 8.4	

1. A patient receiving treatment in a public community outpatient substance abuse treatment center has private insurance and Medicare. Which funding source would be billed first?

2. True or False? Substance abuse treatment centers rely heavily on client fees for a major portion of their revenue.

3. Name the agency that administers government funding sources to support substance abuse treatment or prevention.

INFORMATION MANAGEMENT

Other types of health care settings share many of the information management issues faced by substance abuse facilities. This makes sense, because the purpose of maintaining client information in substance abuse facilities is basically the same as in other facilities: to facilitate the documentation of care and services provided; to support quality review activities; to ensure appropriate financial reimbursement; to meet all legal requirements; and to meet a variety of administrative, research, and educational needs. Nevertheless, a few issues are either unique to substance abuse or are found more commonly in this setting. The following discussion describes some of these issues related to the areas of data and information flow, coding and classification, data sets for substance abuse, and computerization of client information.

Data and Information Flow

Each substance abuse facility has its own distinct flow of client information, from the time of admission through discharge and follow-up care. This information flow may or may not include computer-based information, but it should reflect the course of treatment provided to the clients. Figure 8-5 represents a typical flow of information in an outpatient substance abuse center. After a client enters the system, whether as a court-ordered admission or as a voluntary admission, the intake process is the first step in collecting client information and determining the appropriate treatment. During intake, clerical personnel gather all necessary demographic and financial information, as well as the necessary consent to treatment, notice of privacy practice, and release-of-information forms.

FIGURE 8-5

Flow of information within a client's record.

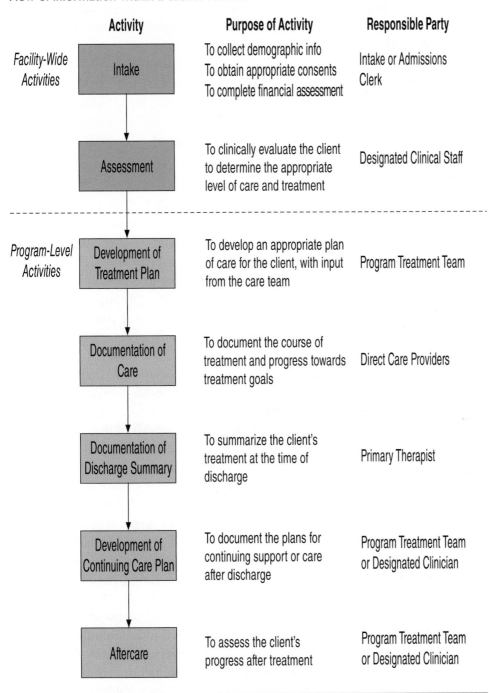

	Activity	Purpose of Activity	Responsible Party
Facility-Wide Activities	Intake	To collect demographic info To obtain appropriate consents To complete financial assessment	Intake or Admissions Clerk
	Assessment	To clinically evaluate the client to determine the appropriate level of care and treatment	Designated Clinical Staff
Program-Level Activities	Development of Treatment Plan	To develop an appropriate plan of care for the client, with input from the care team	Program Treatment Team
	Documentation of Care	To document the course of treatment and progress towards treatment goals	Direct Care Providers
	Documentation of Discharge Summary	To summarize the client's treatment at the time of discharge	Primary Therapist
	Development of Continuing Care Plan	To document the plans for continuing support or care after discharge	Program Treatment Team or Designated Clinician
	Aftercare	To assess the client's progress after treatment	Program Treatment Team or Designated Clinician

After the intake, designated clinical staff members conduct a complete substance abuse assessment to determine the level of care and program most appropriate for the client. His or her treatment team then develops the client's program-specific, individualized treatment plan. This treatment plan lists, among other things, the client's individualized treatment goals and objectives and serves as a "blueprint" to his or her care. While the client is involved in active treatment, all other documentation is tied to the treatment plan and should reflect progress toward the treatment goals. Most substance abuse programs have aftercare staff members who follow up on their discharged clients to evaluate their continued progress after active treatment has been completed.

Coding and Classification

Selecting a coding or classification system for a substance abuse treatment facility depends on the level of care provided by that facility and the type of funding used to support its programs. In general, when *ICD* and *CPT* codes are required for reimbursement purposes, the codes are assigned following the same guidelines and conventions that apply to other inpatient and outpatient settings. The one significant difference in substance abuse coding is the availability of the *Diagnostic and Statistical Manual of Mental Disorders*, **Fifth Edition (DSM-5).** *DSM-5* is a classification and diagnostic tool for mental disorders that was developed by the American Psychiatric Association (APA). This is the classification system developed for use by all mental health providers and is applicable for use in most clinical settings. The term *mental disorders* in *DSM-5* includes conditions related to substance use. *DSM-5* consists of three major components: (1) diagnostic classification, (2) diagnostic criteria, and (3) descriptive text (APA, n.d.).

The diagnostic classification is a list of mental health disorders from which the clinician can choose. These are broad categories derived from the ICD coding system. The diagnostic criteria help the clinician arrive at a diagnosis by identifying duration of the problem, symptoms, and in some situations, a lack of symptoms. The descriptive text provides additional information about each disorder in 12 different categories such as diagnostic features, prevalence, development and course, and so on.

Although DSM-IV and earlier editions used five different axes to report different types of conditions, problems, and levels of functioning, DSM-5 no longer uses this multi-axial approach. However, payers have been accustomed to using Axis V (the Global Assessment of Functioning) in earlier versions of DSM to make determinations of medical necessity, so it is likely that a transitional period will remain for a time in which some elements of DSM-IV will continue to be used for administrative purposes. The advantage of using *DSM-5* in a substance abuse treatment setting is that it represents the latest research findings and acceptable diagnostic terms associated with mental health

Diagnostic and Statistical Manual of Mental Disorders, Fifth Edition (DSM-5)   a classification system and nomenclature of mental disorders developed by the American Psychiatric Association; the standard classification system for all mental health providers, to provide for accurate collecting and reporting of data.

and substance abuse disorders. A disadvantage is that most third-party payers do not accept *DSM-5* codes requiring facilities to use ICD codes. To overcome this barrier, most treatment facilities, use a crosswalk tool to convert *DSM-5* codes to ICD codes.

Data Sets

In 1988, Congress passed Public Law 100-690, which required collection of data on the national incidence and prevalence of mental illness and substance abuse. The message that Congress sent by passing this law was that states had to be able to substantiate the need for federal block grant money. The National Institute of Drug Abuse (NIDA) and the National Institute of Alcohol Abuse and Alcoholism (NIAAA) were the federal agencies charged at that time with administering a national database of substance abuse client information to meet the substance abuse reporting component of the law.

In 1995, this function was taken over by the Substance Abuse and Mental Health Services Administration (SAMHSA), which has developed the **Drug and Alcohol Services Information System (DASIS)**, an evolution of the earlier reporting systems. The goal of DASIS is to provide one data system that provides national- and state-level data on substance abuse clients and on the facilities that receive federal grants or contracts to provide substance abuse treatment. DASIS includes three components: (1) the **Treatment Episode Data Set (TEDS)**, (2) the **National Survey of Substance Abuse Treatment Services (N-SSATS)**, and (3) the **Inventory of Substance Abuse Treatment Services (I-SATS)**.

I-SATS (formerly the National Master Facility Inventory) is a listing of all known public and private substance abuse treatment facilities in the United States and its territories. TEDS, which previously was called the Client Data System, collects uniform data from states that are client-specific but not client-identifiable, including demographic and substance abuse characteristics. Facility-specific information is collected through N-SSATS, an annual survey of all substance abuse treatment facilities known to SAMHSA (i.e., in I-SATS). N-SSATS, formerly known as the Uniform Facility Data Set (UFDS), collects information on location, characteristics, services offered, and utilization for each facility. Information from the N-SSATS is used to maintain the National Directory of Drug and Alcohol Abuse Treatment Programs and the Substance Abuse Treatment Facility Locator.

Electronic Information Systems

Generalizing about electronic information systems within the substance abuse treatment community today is difficult, because these systems vary greatly from facility to facility. Some treatment programs in the United States have sophisticated

Drug and Alcohol Services Information System (DASIS) a data system managed by SAMHSA that provides national and state-level data on substance abuse clients and on the facilities that receive federal grants or contracts to provide substance abuse treatment. The three components are: Treatment Episode Data Set (TEDS), National Survey of Substance Abuse Treatment Services (N-SSATS), and Inventory of Substance Abuse Treatment Services (I-SATS).

Treatment Episode Data Set (TEDS) one of the components of DASIS; collects from states uniform data that are client-specific but not client identifiable, including demographic and substance abuse characteristics.

National Survey of Substance Abuse Treatment Services (N-SSATS) an annual survey of all substance abuse treatment facilities known to SAMHSA; collects facility-specific information on location, characteristics, services offered, and utilization.

Inventory of Substance Abuse Treatment Services (I-SATS) a listing of all known public and private substance abuse treatment facilities in the United States and its territories.

electronic client information systems, and other programs have limited electronic applications. This variability sometimes comes from the differences in levels of care and funding sources. On the one hand, a substance abuse treatment unit within a progressive acute care hospital will benefit from the hospital-wide information systems that are in place. On the other hand, a public community treatment program with limited funds may not have much in the way of computer development.

One generalization that can be made is that as the health care industry moves toward more integrated delivery systems and electronic health records, client information systems within the substance abuse treatment community will take on new importance. Substance abuse treatment facilities will be competing with other health care entities for scarce health care dollars, and the government and other payers are demanding outcomes-oriented data to support continued direct funding or reimbursement. This need for more timely, accurate data should lead to increased development of electronic substance abuse client information systems.

Public community treatment programs are working together to develop a standardized electronic record. This will allow the agencies to pool their resources and create a set of electronic forms that are standardized throughout the state. With the greater use of electronic records, the intake process for clients has become more efficient. Also, the flow of information throughout the course of treatment is more effective.

SELF REVIEW 8.5

1. Name the three major components of *DSM-5*.
2. True or False? Third-party payers accept *DSM-5* on claims submitted for patients with a mental disorder.
3. Explain the rationale for Congress passing Public Law 100-690 in 1988.
4. The purpose of the Drug and Alcohol Services Information System (DASIS) is to:
5. DASIS includes three components: TEDS, NSSATS, and I-SATS. Match the component to what the component collects.

   TEDS:

   NSSATS:

   I-SATS:

   a. a listing of all substance abuse treatment facilities in the United States
   b. client-specific demographic and substance abuse characteristics
   c. location, characteristics, services offered, utilization for each facility; the info is used to maintain the National Directory of Drug and Alcohol Abuse Treatment Programs and Substance Abuse Treatment Facility Locator.

QUALITY IMPROVEMENT AND UTILIZATION MANAGEMENT

Two additional areas within substance abuse facilities are quality improvement (QI) and utilization management (UM). Even though substance abuse treatment organizations do include the QI and UM functions, the level of sophistication of the QI and UM processes depends on the level of care provided by that facility, its primary funding source, and its accrediting organization.

Quality Assessment and Improvement

Providers of substance abuse treatment must ensure that they offer quality care and service. The quality assessment and improvement activities within substance abuse treatment facilities often are related to the level of care provided and whether the facility seeks Joint Commission or CARF accreditation. In some states, specific Medicaid standards also address the need for an organized quality assessment and improvement process. A substance abuse treatment unit in a Joint Commission-accredited hospital would participate in the hospital-wide performance improvement program.

Regardless of the setting, a substance abuse treatment program seeking processes for improvement may consider consensus-based and evidence-based treatment guidelines available at SAMHSA's **Center for Substance Abuse Treatment (CSAT)** as a means to identify effective treatment practices to which its own processes can be compared. Another source for evidence-based interventions for both substance abuse and mental health is SAMHSA's **National Registry of Evidence-based Programs and Practices (NREPP)**, an online searchable database of interventions and treatments that have been demonstrated to be effective. SAMSHA offers the **National Outcome Measures (NOMS)** as a reporting system to create a source for reviewing outcomes measures on a national level (SAMSHA, 2014).

Utilization Management

Providers of substance abuse treatment, just as other health care providers, must demonstrate fiscal responsibility and solid clinical decision-making based on the client's individual need. Facilities must ensure that each client receives the level of care appropriate to his or her severity of illness. As a general rule, clients should be served at the least intensive level that will meet their treatment objectives, such as outpatient therapy, and should move on to a more intensive level, such as residential treatment, only when it is justified by their specific treatment needs.

Severity indexes and other treatment review instruments also have been developed for evaluating treatment and utilizing services within the substance abuse treatment community. The American Society of Addiction Medicine (ASAM)

Center for Substance Abuse Treatment (CSAT) an agency of SAMHSA that "promotes the quality and availability of community-based substance abuse treatment services for individuals and families…[working] with States and community-based groups to improve and expand existing substance abuse treatment services under the Substance Abuse Prevention and Treatment Block Grant Program" (CSAT, n.d., para. 1).

National Registry of Evidence-based Programs and Practices (NREPP) sponsored by SAMHSA, an online searchable database of treatments and interventions that have been demonstrated to be effective for substance abuse and mental health treatment and prevention programs.

National Outcome Measures (NOMS) a reporting system developed by SAMHSA to collect and distribute outcome measures from substance abuse and mental health services.

Addiction Severity Index (ASI)   a rating scale developed for clinicians to measure the severity of a client's substance abuse problems. The ASI measures seven substance abuse–related problem areas: medical condition, drug use, alcohol use, employment, illegal activity, social relations, and psychological findings.

publishes a placement criteria manual that defines levels of care and the specific criteria that should be used in placing adolescent and adult clients in the appropriate treatment setting. The Care Settings section of this chapter describes these levels of care. Managed care organizations have endeavored to use these or similar levels of care to place patients in the most cost-effective settings, yet still achieve the desired treatment results (Kosanke et al., 2002).

Another instrument that is used in utilization management and to facilitate client care is the **Addiction Severity Index (ASI)**, which was developed in 1979. ASI was designed to be administered through an interview process by a trained technician to measure seven substance abuse-related problem areas: medical status, drug use, alcohol use, employment and support, legal status, family/social status, and psychosocial status. Data from the client interview are tabulated and result in a severity "score" for the client. The score can be stated as a 10-point severity rating for clinical use or as a mathematically weighted score for use as an outcomes measure in research studies (McLellan et al, 2002).

SELF REVIEW 8.6	
	1. The level of sophistication of the quality improvement and utilization management processes in substance abuse facilities is influenced by three factors. Name these factors.
	2. SAMHSA offers three resources to substance abuse treatment programs: the Center for Substance Abuse Treatment, the National Registry of Evidence-based Programs and Practices, and the National Outcome Measures. Would these resources be part of the quality improvement or the utilization management process for the facility?
	3. Explain how the Addiction Severity Index is used to measure outcomes for the client.
	4. List four of the seven substance abuse-related problem areas included in the Addiction Severity Index.

RISK MANAGEMENT AND LEGAL ISSUES

Risk management is defined as "a four step process designed to identify, evaluate and resolve the actual and possible sources of loss. The four steps are risk identification, risk evaluation, risk handling, and risk monitoring" (Roach et al., 2006, p. 556). Formal risk management programs are found in inpatient substance abuse treatment settings more often than they are found in outpatient settings. Still, many other relevant legal issues—such as confidentiality and release of information, court-ordered treatment, and commitments—are commonly associated with all levels of substance abuse treatment.

Confidentiality and Release of Information

Confidentiality of client information is vital in substance abuse treatment facilities. Clients who seek alcohol and drug abuse prevention and treatment services must be assured of the greatest possible privacy because of the stigma attached to the labels "alcoholic" and "addict," and because the use of illicit drugs and underage minors' use of alcohol constitute crimes. Clients must believe that they will not be subject to a law enforcement investigation if they seek treatment.

In the early 1970s, the federal government enacted two laws that were written to guarantee this strict level of confidentiality: the Comprehensive Alcohol Abuse and Alcohol Prevention, Treatment and Rehabilitation Act of 1970 and the Drug Abuse and Treatment Act of 1972 (Legal Action Center, 1991). The federal regulations—known as 42 C.F.R. (*Code of Federal Regulations*) Part 2, Confidentiality of Alcohol and Drug Abuse Patient Records—that implemented these confidentiality statutes were issued in 1975 and were revised in 1987 and 1995.

The regulations in 42 C.F.R. Part 2 are more restrictive than the privacy provisions of the Health Insurance Portability and Accountability Act (HIPAA). Except under certain specified conditions, disclosure of information concerning any client who is seen in a federally assisted alcohol or drug abuse program is strictly prohibited. A program is defined as "any person or organization that, in whole or in part, provides alcohol or drug abuse diagnosis, treatment or referral for treatment" (42 C.F.R. pt. 2). This general prohibition has a few exceptions, written into the regulations. Disclosure can be made:

- With the written consent of the patient
- For internal communications on a need-to-know basis
- When there is no patient-identifying information
- In a bona fide medical emergency
- With a court order (with special procedures)
- When a crime is committed at the treatment program or against program personnel
- For research and audits
- In child and vulnerable adult abuse reporting, under the provisions of the applicable state law
- Under the provisions of a **qualified service organization agreement (QSOA)**, through which an organization, such as a commercial laboratory or a private occupational therapy group, has a written agreement to provide services to the substance abuse program. (A qualified service organization also can provide services such as data processing, bill collecting, dosage preparation, legal, medical, accounting, and other professional services.) In these situations, there should be a Business Associate's Agreement signed by the facility and the business partner.

qualified service organization agreement (QSOA) an exception to the 42 C.F.R. Part 2 *Confidentiality of Alcohol and Drug Abuse Patient Records, which* permits disclosure of patient record information to an organization providing services to the substance abuse program, such as laboratory, data processing, bill collecting, dosage preparation, legal, medical, or accounting services. The qualified service organization (QSO) has a written agreement to provide professional services to the substance abuse program, and that agreement requires the QSO to follow the 42 C.F.R. regulations.

No information about a substance abuse client should be disclosed unless the facility can state how these exceptions permit disclosure. When information is released using a patient authorization, the authorization must contain specific items to be considered valid. Figure 8-6 outlines the required elements for an authorization to release drug and alcohol treatment information. Other elements, such as the signature of a witness, may be added to the authorization form at the discretion of the facility. When the information is released, it must be accompanied by a written statement notifying the recipient that the information is "protected by federal confidentiality rules" and that the recipient may not re-disclose the records to a third party (42 C.F.R. pt. 2).

Court-Ordered Treatment

A portion of the substance abuse client population enters treatment as a result of a court order. The court order may come from a conviction for driving under the influence of alcohol or drugs (DUI). In some states, substance abuse assessment is mandated by law for all persons with a DUI conviction, and if the assessment indicates that the individual needs further treatment, this treatment also is mandated. Typically, if the DUI client fails to fulfill an established court-ordered assessment and treatment protocol, he or she will not be reissued a driver's license.

Thus, it is necessary to establish a good working relationship between the substance abuse treatment centers and the legal system. One common practice, for example, is the development of an active partnership with the municipal court

FIGURE 8-6

Required elements for an authorization to release information from an alcohol or drug program, from 42 C.F.R. Part 2, Confidentiality of Alcohol and Drug Abuse Patient Records.

- The name or general designation of the program(s) making the disclosure
- The name of the individual or organization that will receive the disclosure
- The name of the patient who is the subject of the disclosure
- The purpose or need for the disclosure
- How much and what kind of information will be disclosed
- A statement that the patient may revoke the consent at any time, except to the extent that the program has already acted in reliance on it
- The date, event, or condition upon which the consent expires if not previously revoked
- The signature of the patient (and/or other authorized person)
- The date on which the authorization is signed

From Code of Federal Regulations, 42 CFR Part 2, Confidentiality of Alcohol and Drug Abuse Patient Records.

system. A treatment center employee may be assigned to be present in court during the DUI hearings to facilitate the enrollment of court-ordered clients. All necessary consents and authorizations to release information back to the court can be signed and appropriate fees collected before the client leaves the courthouse.

DUI convictions are not the only court procedures that lead to court-ordered substance abuse treatment. Examples of situations that might result in a court order for treatment are child abuse, possession of illegal drugs, sexual assault, underage alcohol consumption, burglary, or assault, when the court deems that the perpetrator's substance abuse was a factor. Typically, the judge will order the client to seek substance abuse treatment as a stipulation in a suspended or reduced sentence or probation. On occasion, the court actually might order an incarcerated individual to obtain appropriate substance abuse treatment, if it is available through the correctional facility.

Involuntary Commitments

Involuntary commitment is a legal process by which individuals who are deemed to be a danger to themselves or to others may be admitted to a treatment program even though they refuse or cannot consent to the treatment. Involuntary commitment is governed by state statutes, and the criteria and procedures vary from state to state. All states require that the person being committed have a mental illness or mental disorder; however, many states do not define the terms *mental illness* or *mental condition*, or they define them broadly. Several states, such as North Carolina, Louisiana, and Hawaii, specifically cite substance abuse as a mental disorder or as a potential cause for involuntary commitment (Bazelon Center for Mental Health Law, 2004).

In states where involuntary commitment for substance abuse treatment is permitted, the actual procedure varies depending on the state laws, but the following steps represent a typical series of events in the overall process (Beis, 1984):

1. A petitioner, law enforcement officer, or other responsible person files a petition stating that the client meets the criteria for involuntary admission (i.e., he or she is a danger to himself or herself or to others).
2. The client is detained for an evaluation by a physician or other qualified clinician for a period of time that may vary from state to state.
3. The clinician certifies that the client meets the standard for involuntary commitment.
4. The petition and the certificate are filed with the court, and a hearing date is set.
5. The court determines whether or not the client meets the standard for involuntary admission.

> **involuntary commitment** a legal process by which individuals who are deemed to be a danger to themselves or to others may be admitted to a substance abuse (or mental health) treatment program even though they refuse or cannot consent to the treatment.

6. The court will require that the client be admitted if the client meets the standard (this admission may be to an inpatient or outpatient program, depending on the needs of the client and the state guidelines).

Figure 8-7 provides an example of a form used to evaluate individuals in a commitment recommendation screening process.

SELF REVIEW 8.7

1. Name the two laws that guarantee the strict level of confidentiality of client information when seeking treatment for substance abuse.

2. True or False? Privacy provisions of HIPAA are more restrictive than those specified in 42 C.F.R. Part 2, Confidentiality of Alcohol and Drug Abuse Patient Records.

3. Explain the purpose of a qualified service organization agreement/Business Associate's Agreement.

4. True or False? A third party, such as an insurance company, may re-disclose the client's medical information to another third party.

5. What document is needed for a judge to require a client to seek substance abuse treatment?

6. Involuntary commitment is governed by which_____ statutes.

ROLE OF THE HEALTH INFORMATION MANAGEMENT PROFESSIONAL

The role of the health information manager is becoming increasingly important in substance abuse treatment settings. The changing health care environment requires that substance abuse facilities collect, analyze, and maintain timely and reliable client information. Managed care organizations and other payers, including the federal government, want "proof" that their enrollees are receiving quality services at the lowest possible cost.

Opportunities for the health information manager within substance abuse facilities are found in the areas of traditional client record management, risk management, utilization management, quality improvement, release-of-information services, client rights coordination, and especially in electronic client records systems. Even though electronic health records first appeared in 1960, they are still underutilized in many treatment facilities (Asp & Peterson, 2003).

As the need to be more efficient in providing treatment—and the need to be more cost-effective with the funding that is utilized by a facility—becomes more apparent, the need for adequate electronic records also will become more

FIGURE 8-7

Pre-commitment evaluation screening form.

```
DEPARTMENT OF MENTAL HEALTH          Name:_____
   Community Counseling Services
      Pre-evaluation Screening Form    Case #:_____
DMH/013                      5/02
```

IN THE_____COURT OF _____COUNTY   RE:_____
        (Type of Court)   *(Name of County)*

CASE NO. _____ SERVICE CODE _____ UNITS OF SERVICE _____ DATE_____

Respondent having been evaluated and pre-screened for commitment pursuant to M.C.A. Section 41-21-67, Region_____
Mental Health Center Offers the following:

Legal Charges Pending: Yes ☐   No ☐

PERSONAL DATA INFORMATION

NAME: _____ SOCIAL SECURITY NO: _____ DOB: _____

RACE: _____ MARITAL STATUS: ☐Single ☐Married ☐Divorced ☐ Widowed   SEX: ☐Male   ☐Female

ADDRESS: _____

            _____

            _____

NAME OF SPOUSE/NEXT OF KIN: _____ COUNTY OF RESIDENCE: _____

MEDICAID # _____   MEDICARE # _____

EDUCATION *(Circle Highest Grade Completed)*1 2 3 4 5 6 7 8 9 10 11 12 13 14 15 16 17 18 GED

OCCUPATION: _____   PRESENTLY EMPLOYED: ☐ Yes   ☐ No

EMPLOYER: _____   LENGTH OF EMPLOYMENT: _____years ____ months

HOUSEHOLD COMPOSITION *(Mark All That Apply)*

☐ Lives Alone   ☐ With Siblings   ☐ With Parents   ☐ With One Parent   ☐ With Children
☐ With Spouse   ☐ With Relatives   ☐ With Legal Guardian ☐ With Others   ☐ Others

NUMBER OF DEPENDENT(S): _____

NAME OF AFFIANT (Person Filing Papers)

Name: _____ Relationship: _____ Phone: (H) _____ (W) _____

Address: _____ City _____ State _____ Zip Code _____

FAMILY CONTACT

Name: _____ Relationship: _____ Phone: (H) _____ (W) _____

Address: _____ City _____ State _____ Zip Code _____

PERSON WITH <u>LEGAL CUSTODY</u>, GUARDIANSHIP, and /or Conservatorship

Name: _____ Relationship: _____ Phone: (H) _____ (W) _____

Address: _____ City _____ State _____ Zip Code _____

(continues)

FIGURE 8-7 *(continued)*

MEDICAL HISTORY INFORMATION

PREVIOUS MENTAL HEALTH HOSPITALIZATION, SERVICE, A&D TREATMENT *(List Where & When)*_____

_____

_____

_____

_____

CURRENT MEDICATIONS *(List Names and Dosage)*

Name	*Dosage*
_____	_____
_____	_____
_____	_____
_____	_____
_____	_____
_____	_____

COMPLAINT WITH MEDICATIONS: ❏ Yes   ❏ No   ❏ Unknown

ALLERGIES: ❏ Yes   ❏ No   If Yes, Explain _____

PREVIOUS SURGERY: ❏ Yes   ❏ No   If Yes, Explain _____

CONCURRENT PHYSICAL CONDITIONS *(Mark all that apply)*

❏ Diabetes   ❏ Emphysema/Cold   ❏ Heart Condition   ❏ Seizures
❏ Hypertension   ❏ S.T.D.   ❏ TB   ❏ Cancer
❏ Contagious Disease ❏ Other Chronic Illness ❏ (Please State) _____
❏ Hepatitis
Elaborate on acute medical conditions of conditions marked (if needed) _____

FAMILY PHYSICIAN: _____

BEHAVIORS EXHIBITED BY RESPONDENT
Also consider information from affiant and/or affidavit.
(Mark appropriate answer and/or write in additional pertinent descriptions.)

History or Present Danger to Self   ❏ Yes   ❏ No   *(If Yes, Mark Appropriate Statements Below)*

❏ Thoughts of suicide   ❏ Threats of suicide   ❏ Plan for suicide   ❏ Preoccupation with death
❏ Suicide gesture   ❏ Suicide attempts   ❏ Family history of suicide ❏ Self-mutilation
❏ Inability to care for self ❏ High risk behavior   ❏ Provoking harm to self from others
❏ Other _____

Describe: _____

History or Present Danger to Others   ❏ Yes   ❏ No   *(If Yes, Mark Appropriate Statements Below)*

❏ Thoughts to harm others   ❏ Threats to harm others   ❏ Plans to harm others
❏ Attempts to harm others   ❏ Stalking   ❏ Has harmed others
❏ Felt like killing someone   ❏ Inability or unwillingness to care for dependents
❏ Other _____

Describe: _____

FIGURE 8-7 *(continued)*

Pre-evaluation Screening Form *(page three)*   Name:_____   Case#:_____

Failure to Care for Self	❏ Yes	❏ No	(If Yes, Mark Appropriate Statements Below)

Failure or inability to provide necessary: ❏ Food   ❏ Clothing   ❏ Shelter   ❏ Safety   ❏ Medical care for self

❏ Other _____

Antisocial/Criminal Behavior   ❏ Yes   ❏No   *(If Yes, Mark Appropriate Statement Below)*

❏ Frequent lying   ❏ Stealing   ❏ Running away from home   ❏ Excessive fighting
❏ Destroys property   ❏ Fire setting   ❏ Cruelty to other   ❏ Cruelty to animals
❏ Arrests   ❏ Gang membership   ❏ Brandishing weapons   ❏ Convictions
❏ Imprisoned   ❏ Promiscuity   ❏ Exhibitionism   ❏ Family desertion
❏ Uses assumed name   ❏ Identify any legal charges which may be pending

❏ Other _____

Describe: _____

Drug Use/Abuse   ❏ Yes   ❏No   *(If Yes, Mark Appropriate Statement Below)*

❏ Has abused   ❏ Is abusing   ❏ Narcotics   ❏ Amphetamines ❏ Barbiturates   ❏ Hallucinogens
❏ Cocaine   ❏ Marijuana   ❏ Absenteeism ❏ Job loss   ❏ Arrests
❏ Has required hospitalization   ❏ Family problems due to drug use   ❏ Currently under the influence of drugs

❏ Other _____

Describe: _____

Alcohol Use/Abuse   ❏ Yes   ❏No   *(If Yes, Mark Appropriate Statement Below)*

❏ Drinking problem suspected   ❏ Intoxicated Now   ❏ Has required hospitalization
❏ D.T. s   ❏ Black-outs   ❏ Absenteeism
❏ Job loss   ❏ Arrests/DUI   ❏ Family problems due to drinking
❏ Currently under the influence of alcohol (BAL, if available)
❏ High-risk behavior occurs primarily when under the influence of alcoholic beverages, including beer.

❏ Other _____

Describe: _____

Depressive-Like Behaviors   ❏ Yes   ❏No   *(If Yes, Mark Appropriate Statement Below)*

❏ Sadness   ❏ Fatigue   ❏ Low Energy   ❏ Loss of interest   ❏ Extreme Withdrawal
❏ Crying   ❏ Poor Concentration ❏ Weight loss or gain   ❏ Guilt feelings
❏ Feelings of worthlessness   ❏ Hopelessness about the future   ❏ Hypoactive
❏ Thoughts/threats of suicide   ❏ Sudden drop in grades or change in friends (especially in adolescents)

❏Other _____   _____

Describe: _____

Manic-Like Behavior   ❏ Yes   ❏No   *(If Yes, Mark Appropriate Statement Below)*

❏ Euphoria   ❏ Hyperactivity   ❏ Grandiosity   ❏ Over-talkativeness and/or pressured speech
❏ Irritability   ❏ Sexual promiscuity ❏ Sleep disturbance ❏ Extravagance with money

❏ Other _____

Describe: _____

Dementia-Like Characteristics   ❏ Yes   ❏No   *(If Yes, Mark Appropriate Statement Below)*

❏ Confusion   ❏ Wanders off   ❏ Disorientation   ❏ Impaired judgement
❏ Absent-mindedness ❏Getting lost   ❏ Confusion   ❏ Significant short- and/or long-term memory
❏ Decline in activities of daily living *(Consider age of respondent)*   ❏Impaired Abstract Thinking

❏ Other _____

Describe: _____

(continues)

FIGURE 8-7   *(continued)*

Psychotic-Like Behavior	❏ Yes	❏ No	*(If Yes, Mark Appropriate Statement Below)*

❏ Poor personal hygiene ❏ Loose Association ❏ Suspiciousness ❏ Bizarre or obscene acts
❏ Withdrawn ❏ Incoherence ❏ Unmanageable ❏ Flat or inappropriate affect
❏ Talks often ❏ Wanders off ❏ Illusions ❏ Disorientation (time, place, people)
❏ Delusions ❏ Confusion ❏ Forgetfulness ❏ Poor judgment
❏ Doesn t make sense ❏ Irritability ❏ Hallucinations
❏ Emotional turmoil ❏ Disorganized speech or behavior

❏ Other _____

Describe: _____

ADDITIONAL INFORMATION

Child/Adolescent Conduct Disturbance   ❏ Yes   ❏ No   *(If Yes, Mark Appropriate Statement Below)*
(Current Behavior or During Childhood)

❏ Theft   ❏ Firesetting   ❏ Cruelty to people   ❏ Cruelty to animals   ❏ Destruction of property
❏ Aggression   ❏ Arrest/detainment   ❏ Sexual misconduct   ❏ Combativeness/aggression
❏ Refusal to attend school   ❏ Running away   ❏ Defiance of authority and rules
❏ Possession/Use of weapons
❏ Other _____

Mental Retardation   ❏ Yes   ❏ No   *(If Yes, Mark Appropriate Statement Below)*

❏ History of special education placement   ❏ Documented IQ below a70
❏ Inability to care for self or activities of daily living   ❏ Significantly sub-average intellectual functioning before age 18
❏ Substantial limitations in adaptive skills (*communication, self-care, home living, social skills, community use, self-direction, health and safety, leisure and work*)
❏ Other _____

Other   ❏ Yes   ❏ No   *(If Yes, Mark Appropriate Statement Below)*

❏ Anxiety   ❏ Panic   ❏ Eating disorders   ❏ Sexual disorders   ❏ Impulsive disorders
❏ Obsessive disorders   ❏ Other _____

RECOMMENDATIONS

Examination for Commitment: ❏ Yes   ❏ No

If yes, is outpatient commitment currently an option for the respondent?   ❏ Yes   ❏ No   Explain:

_____

_____

_____

If no, explain why outpatient commitment is not an option for the respondent:_____

_____

_____

_____

SPECIFIC RECOMMENDATIONS
(Include Treatment Options)

_____

_____

_____

_____

Screener/Credentials	Date	Print Name

Courtesy of Community Counseling Services, Starkville, Mississippi.

important. In addition to adequate record keeping, health information professionals must play a role in collecting and reporting data for statistical purposes and for reimbursement purposes, such as outcome measures. Also, Medicare has offered incentives for providers that utilize electronic health records. The health information manager has an important role in planning, developing, and implementing electronic health records.

Another challenging role for the health information manager working in substance abuse treatment is to be an advocate for client confidentiality. Most health information managers in substance abuse facilities are confidentiality "experts" and must be thoroughly familiar with the federal regulations governing alcohol and drug abuse treatment records. Health information managers can assist in developing policies to meet the requirements of existing and newly developed regulations.

---

1. Implementation of an electronic health record in substance abuse facilities has been slower than in other types of treatment facilities. Still, substance abuse facilities have been motivated to adopt an electronic record system for three reasons. What are they?

2. True or False? Health information managers in substance abuse facilities serve as advocates for client confidentiality.

TRENDS

The trends in substance abuse treatment can be divided into treatment trends and economic or funding trends. The current trends in treatment include many innovative approaches, some of which are discussed in this chapter. Examples of current treatment trends include the growth of programs for women, adolescent prevention programs, and treatment for the dually diagnosed. Substance abuse treatment centers are involved with an increasing number of Employee Assistance Programs (EAPs) and also are becoming more active in identifying the needs of inmates in city or local jails. The economic trends are related to the changing health care environment and to the government's continuing struggle to spend taxpayers' dollars wisely.

Because government support is an essential source of revenue to many substance abuse treatment facilities, the changing political and economic climate will affect the future of the delivery of substance abuse services. Substance abuse education, prevention, and treatment have been significant social issues in the United States for several decades. Congress, in partnership with state governments, has directed a substantial amount of government funds toward increasing awareness of substance abuse issues, as well as toward increasing the availability of treatment services across the socioeconomic spectrum. The national political and economic climate, however, has changed considerably since the 1970s, as taxpayers are asking for validation that their tax dollars are spent appropriately and are questioning the high cost of health care.

One of the most significant trends affecting health information management within the substance abuse treatment community is the government's increased emphasis on the need for data to substantiate the effectiveness of government-funded programs. Programs are being held accountable for the government dollars they are awarded, and this accountability requires the provision of supporting data to the funding agency. In many cases, the information systems within substance abuse facilities are inadequate to provide this type of outcome-oriented data in a timely and accurate manner. To thrive in the current and future climate, substance abuse facilities will have to improve their information systems.

Another political and economic factor that is impacting substance abuse treatment services, along with the other segments of the health care delivery system, is the increased role of managed care organizations (MCOs). Not only are private MCOs expanding their services across the United States, but many states are opting to develop managed care models for Medicaid. Dealing with MCOs will necessitate significant changes in the way that substance abuse facilities traditionally have operated. The need for more sophisticated information systems that can provide financial and client outcomes data will be integral to this change.

Along with changes in government funding procedures and the increase in the number of MCOs, substance abuse facilities will be affected by the trend of multiple health care organizations' building alliances and partnerships to develop integrated health delivery systems and health information exchanges. It is hoped that substance abuse treatment will be valued as a necessary component of any comprehensive health delivery system. Still, this raises issues related to integrated client information systems, access to this information, and client confidentiality, which will have to be addressed.

To this end, SAMHSA (2010) released a "Frequently Asked Questions" document, *Applying the Substance Abuse Confidentiality Regulations to Health Information Exchange* (HIE), explaining under what circumstances substance abuse treatment facilities could participate in a health information exchange without violating the confidentiality provisions of 42 C.F.R. Part 2 or HIPAA. Among other considerations, one required component would be that the HIE would have to be a qualified service organization (QSO) with a written agreement requiring the HIE to follow the 42 C.F.R. regulations.

This is an era of significant change in health care delivery systems, of which substance abuse treatment services are an important element. Substance abuse clients must be afforded the benefits of these changes without compromising their rights to confidentiality.

SELF REVIEW 8.9

1. A current trend in substance abuse treatment is increased involvement by the government. Explain why the government is becoming more involved.
2. Summarize the effect of managed care organizations on the way substance abuse facilities have traditionally operated.

SUMMARY

Modern substance abuse treatment emerged in the 1950s as residential facilities for treating alcohol dependency began to develop across the United States. Since that time, the number of different treatment settings for clients with alcohol and other drug problems has grown to include outpatient treatment, intensive outpatient and partial hospitalization treatment, residential/inpatient treatment, and medically managed intensive inpatient treatment settings. The number of programs within the treatment settings also has expanded to include special programs for women, adolescents, court-referred clients, children of addicted families, and many others.

Substance abuse treatment settings can be either publicly funded or privately funded. For several decades, the government has granted to states significant amounts of money specifically targeted for substance abuse treatment and prevention programs. Public substance abuse treatment settings traditionally have assumed a major responsibility for providing substance abuse treatment services to communities, which receive the majority of their funds from the federal and state governments. Reimbursement from private insurance companies and client fees also account for a portion of their revenue.

Health information managers working in substance abuse treatment facilities not only provide the traditional services associated with health information management, but they must gain expertise in several other areas as well. For example, substance abuse treatment is regulated by federal and state governments and by voluntary accreditation organizations such as TJC and CARF. Many state regulations, and the CARF and Joint Commission standards, address quality-of-care and information management issues. Health information managers working in substance abuse treatment facilities have to be aware of all relevant regulations and standards, as they often are seen as the information management and quality assurance experts within the facilities.

Another aspect of managing substance abuse client information is the necessity of maintaining strict client confidentiality. The federal regulations 42 C.F.R. Part 2, *Confidentiality of Alcohol and Drug Abuse Records*, mandate that all federally assisted substance abuse programs follow certain procedures before releasing client information. The health information manager often oversees compliance with 42 C.F.R. Part 2.

National trends in health care—such as cutting government spending on health care, the growth of managed care, collecting outcome measures, and the development of integrated delivery systems—have had an impact on substance abuse treatment facilities. Centers that had few financial worries when government substance abuse grants were plentiful now face, along with other segments of the health delivery system, the competition for scarce dollars. One potentially positive development to result from this changing environment may well be the growth in use of computer technology to develop and maintain integrated client information systems that provide timely, accurate, complete, legible, and accessible data.

REVIEW QUESTIONS

Knowledge-Based Questions

1. Describe three different settings in which substance abuse treatment can take place.
2. Define the role of a case manager versus the role of a counselor in substance abuse treatment settings.
3. What is Alcoholics Anonymous? How does it relate to substance abuse treatment?
4. List the key elements that should be included in an individualized treatment plan.
5. Name two voluntary accreditation organizations that set standards for substance abuse treatment facilities. What standards are used for outpatient centers? Inpatient programs?
6. Define involuntary commitment. What are the basic steps to obtain an involuntary commitment?

Critical Thinking Questions

1. Why does a health information manager need to be familiar with the ASAM *Patient Placement Criteria Manual*? What is the purpose of this manual?
2. The role of the health information manager in a substance abuse treatment facility often involves serving as the confidentiality expert. Why is confidentiality of special concern in a substance abuse treatment program?
3. What are some current trends in the overall health care delivery system that you believe will impact substance abuse treatment services?

WEB ACTIVITY

Go to the U.S. Government Printing Office's Federal Digital System Web page at http://www.gpo.gov/fdsys to search the *Code of Federal Regulations* for a sample consent form in 42 C.F.R. Part 2, "Confidentiality of Alcohol and Drug Abuse Patient Records."

1. Upon arriving at the site, locate the hyperlink for the Code of Federal Regulations.
2. At the next page, choose a year (the previous year is recommended).
3. When the Titles for the year selected appear, scroll down to Title 42—Public Health, then select "Download" and choose a file type (e.g., "PDF") to download Volume 1.
4. After downloading Volume 1, locate Part 2, then Subpart C.
5. Find the sample consent form in Subpart C, and use it to begin developing a consent form for the

fictitious facility Seven Acres Substance Abuse Treatment Services.
6. Find the notice of prohibition of re-disclosure in the same subpart, and use it in developing a form to accompany information released from the Seven Acres facility.
7. Visit the website of the Legal Action Center at http://www.lac.org to view the resources available there. Under "Resources," select the "Substance Use" hyperlink, which opens a new set of hyperlinks.
8. From these links, select "Confidentiality."
9. Explore the Legal Action Center's resources related to confidentiality of substance use records and select items that would be helpful to you in developing policies and procedures at Seven Acres Substance Abuse Treatment Services.

CASE STUDY

Sarah Johnson is the health information manager for the Columbus County Alcohol and Drug Treatment Center, a CARF-accredited, publicly funded treatment facility. As a member of the quality improvement (QI) committee, Sarah has been reviewing client records, focusing on written clinical assessments and treatment plans. The QI committee is interested in evaluating how consistently the clinicians document appropriate treatment goals based on the information found in the clinical assessment.

One of the records that Sarah reviewed is an outpatient record for Ann Wilson, a 24-year-old female client enrolled in the center's women's program. Based on the following summaries of Ms. Wilson's clinical assessment and treatment plan, what specific feedback should Sarah give to the committee? Do the treatment goals and objectives relate to the person's goals? Are they written in measurable terms? Do they specify treatment interventions and their frequency?

Clinical Assessment

Presenting Problem: The 24-year-old, white female with a history of alcohol and cannabis abuse was referred by the county inpatient alcohol and drug treatment program. She is in need of continuing treatment for her longstanding problem with alcohol and drugs.

Health/Medical History: No current health problems. The client has two children, aged 2 years and 4 years. Other than childbirth and her recent substance abuse treatment, this client has not had any previous hospitalizations.

Family/Social Interaction: The client was raised in a physically abusive environment by her mother and alcoholic stepfather. The natural father was killed in a nightclub when the client was 10 years old. The client indicates that her natural father was also an alcoholic. She currently is living in public housing with her two children. She has little family or other emotional support. Her boyfriend of several years (father of her 2-year-old child) recently moved in with another woman.

Psychoactive Substance Use History

Drug	Age at First Use	Frequency (last 6 mo.)	Quantity	Last Use	How Used
Alcohol	11	Daily	Pint of bourbon per day	One month ago	Oral
Cocaine	18	Once in the last year	Unknown	6 months ago	Smoked
Cannabis	15	Weekly	Two per week	One month ago	Smoked

DSM-5 Diagnoses

Alcohol Use
Cannabis Use
Cocaine Use

Clinical Impression: This client recently completed a 28-day inpatient rehabilitation program. She realizes that she has a problem and is ready to seek treatment on a voluntary basis. She thinks relapse risks are high because of her lack of support. She will be admitted to the women's program so her children can benefit from the daycare services, and she can benefit from the support network. Anticipated level of care consists of weekly individual counseling sessions, as well as participating in group therapy twice a week.

Individualized Treatment Plan

Justification for Treatment: Referred by inpatient program.

Goals: Date Service Ordered: 8/20/XX Expected Achievement Date: 2/22/XX

1. Client will improve her knowledge of addiction by:

    a. reading chapters 2 and 3 from the book on addiction behavior and listing 10 addictive behaviors.

    b. remembering that a drug is a drug.

    c. acknowledging the problems related to alcohol use.

2. The client will improve her self-esteem by

    a. reporting three personal strengths about herself.

    b. using at least three "I statements" per day.

REFERENCES AND SUGGESTED READINGS

Alcoholics Anonymous World Services, Inc. (1957). *Alcoholics Anonymous Comes of Age: A Brief History of A.A.* New York: Author.

APA (American Psychiatric Association). (2006). Practice guidelines for the treatment of patients with substance use disorders (2nd ed.), *DSM.* [Online]. http://www.psychiatryonline.com/pracGuide/loadGuidelinePdf.aspx?file=SUD2ePG_04-28-06

APA (American Psychiatric Association). (2014). *DSM.* [Online]. http://www.psychiatry.org/practice/dsm.

Asp, L., & Petersen, J. (2003). A conceptual model for documentation for clinical information in the EHR. *International Clinical Documentation Models.* Denmark: National Board of Health.

Atkins, R. G., Jr., & Hawdon, J. E. (2007). Religiosity and participation in mutual-aid support groups for addiction. *Journal of Substance Abuse Treatment, 33,* 321–331.

Bazelon Center for Mental Health Law. (2004, June). Summary of state statutes on involuntary outpatient commitment. [Online]. http://www.bazelon.org/issues/commitment/ioc/iocchart.html

Beis, E. B. (1984). *Mental health and the law.* Rockville, MD: Aspen.

CARF. (Commission on Accreditation of Rehabilitation Facilities). *Behavioral Health Standards Manual, Child & Youth Services Standard Manual; Opioid Treatment Program Standards Manual.*

CASA. (National Center on Addiction and Substance Abuse at Columbia University) (2009, May). *Shoveling Up II: The Impact of Substance Abuse on Federal, State and Local Budgets.* [Online]. http://www.casacolumbia.org/addiction-research/reports/shoveling-ii-impact-substance-abuse-federal-state-and-local-budgets

CDC (Centers for Disease Control and Prevention). (n.d.). Trends in the prevalence of alcohol use. National YRBS: 1991–2007. [Online]. http://www.cdc.gov/HealthyYouth/yrbs/pdf/yrbs07_us_alcohol_use_trend.pdf

Confidentiality of alcohol and drug abuse patient records, 42 C.F.R. Part 2. 2009 ed. *Code of Federal Regulations,* Title 42, pt. 2.

Kosanke, N., Magura, S., Staines, G., Foote, J., & DeLuca, A. (2002). Feasibility of matching alcohol patients to ASAM levels of care. *American Journal on Addictions, 11,* 124–134.

Levy, S.J.L., & Kokotailo, P.K. (2011). Substance Use Screening, Brief Intervention, and Referral to Treatment for Pediatricians. *Pediatrics, 128,* 1330–1340.

McLellan, A.T., Kushner, H., Metzger, D., Peters, R., et al. (2002). ASI v.5 Addiction Severity Index. National Institute on Drug Abuse: 2014. [Online]. https://www.assessments.com/catalog/ASI_v5.htm

NAMI (National Alliance on Mental Illness). (2014). *Integrated Treatment and Blended Funding for Co-Occurring Mental and Addictive Disorders.* [Online]. http://www.nami.org

Ohio Administrative Code. (2005, November 17). 3793:2 Program Standards. Chapter 3793:2-1 Alcohol and Drug Addiction Programs 3793:2-1-06 Client records. [Online]. http://codes.ohio.gov/oac/3793:2-1-06

Roach, W. H., Hoban, R.G., Broccolo, B. M., Roth, A. B., & Blanchard, T. P. (2006). *Medical records and the law* (4th ed.). Sudbury, MA: Jones and Bartlett.

SAMHSA (Substance Abuse and Mental Health Services Administration). (2010). *Frequently Asked Questions: Applying the substance abuse confidentiality regulations to Health Information Exchange (HIE)*. [Online]. http://www.samhsa.gov /HealthPrivacy/docs/EHR-FAQs.pdf [2010, July 28].

SAMHSA (Substance Abuse and Mental Health Services Administration). (2012). Results from the 2012 National Survey on Drug Use and Health: National Findings. [Online]. http://www.samhsa.gov/data /NSDUH/2012SummNatFindDetTables/Index .aspx

SAMHSA (Substance Abuse and Mental Health Services Administration, Office of Applied Studies). (2012). *2008-2012 State Profile—United States: National Survey of Substance Abuse Treatment Services (N-SSATS)*. [Online]. http://www.samhsa.gov/data /DASIS/2k11nssats/NSSATS2011TOC.htm

The National Center on Addiction and Substance Abuse at Columbia University (CASA). (2009). *Shoveling Up II: The Impact of Substance Abuse on Federal State and Local Budgets*. [Online]. http://www .casacolumbia.org/addiction-research/reports /shoveling-ii-impact-substance-abuse-federal-state -and-local-budgets [2009, May].

KEY RESOURCES

Alcoholics Anonymous
http://www.aa.org

American Psychiatric Association
http://www.psych.org

American Society of Addiction Medicine
http://www.asam.org

CARF International (Commission on Accreditation of Rehabilitation Facilities)
http://www.carf.org

Center for Substance Abuse Prevention (CSAP)
http://www.samhsa.gov/about-us/who-we-are /offices-centers/csap

Center for Substance Abuse Treatment (CSAT)
http://www.samhsa.gov/about-us/who-we-are /offices-centers/csat

Drug Enforcement Administration
http://www.dea.gov

Legal Action Center
http://www.lac.org

Narcotics Anonymous
http://www.na.org

National Institute on Alcohol Abuse and Alcoholism (NIAAA)
http://www.niaaa.nih.gov

National Institute on Drug Abuse
http://www.drugabuse.gov

National Clearinghouse for Alcohol and Drug Information
http://preventionhub.org/en/who-is-who /ncadi-samhsa-s-national-clearinghouse-alcohol -and-drug-information

Substance Abuse & Mental Health Services Administration, general information
http://www.samhsa.gov

The Joint Commission
http://www.jointcommission.org

CHAPTER 9

Facilities for Individuals with Intellectual Disabilities

Nan R. Christian, MEd | Judy S. Westerfield, MEd | Elaine C. Jouette, MA, RHIA

LEARNING OBJECTIVES

Upon successful completion of this chapter, you should be able to:

- Identify the major differences in services provided to an individual living in an ICF/IID compared to other settings.
- Explain various methods of record keeping and the natural separation of information into sections or divisions for individuals in an ICF/IID setting.
- Explain the need for utilizing various coding systems for capturing and classifying data from the records of individuals with intellectual disabilities.
- Discuss the process involved in risk management in tracking accident/incident reports.
- Discuss technical aspects of health information management in an ICF/IID.

Setting	Description	Synonyms/Examples
ICF/IID	Intermediate care facilities for individuals with intellectual disabilities May be operated as private, religious, or governmental	Services for persons classified with autism spectrum disorders, cerebral palsy, dual diagnoses, and intellectual; parameters set for services based on age, functioning level, and condition Special education

INTRODUCTION TO SETTING

Federal regulations classify an organization that provides specialized services for persons with intellectual disabilities as a **intermediate care facility for individuals with intellectual disabilities (ICF/IID)**. In addition to routine medical and nursing care, this type of facility must be responsive to the unique needs of its population and provide individualized training in areas such as sensorimotor, cognitive, emotional, communicative, vocational, and social development. Organizations licensed as ICF/IIDs are eligible to receive payment for their services from Medicaid (Title XIX). These facilities may be called schools, training centers, development centers, or other similar name.

Individuals who live on the premises of an ICF/IID may have a wide range of needs, so a given ICF/IID may provide a wide range of living arrangements. A typical center has a campus with several homes or dormitories in which persons live. It may provide one building that resembles a small nursing home, with 24-hour nursing care for individuals with severe physical and mental disabilities. The same center may house persons with less severe disabilities in a group home setting in which direct-care staff members with no nursing background provide supervision. Federal regulations encourage the grouping of individuals by age and developmental level but prohibit segregating them solely on the basis of physical disability. For example, persons who are deaf or blind must be integrated with others of comparable social and intellectual development (Conditions of Participation, 2009).

Most often, each building or home houses a small number of individuals—in the range of 3 to 24. Six persons is a typical number of residents, although the total number served can be larger, with a range from fewer than 100 to more than 1,000. Even though this chapter deals largely with the ICF/IID facility, many ICF/IID organizations also offer community-based services for individuals who do not reside in the facility. In some states almost all services are community-based.

The ICFs/IIDs differ from other settings in that individuals are on a 24-hour training schedule. Tasks that can be easily accomplished by the "normal" population, such as tying one's shoes, may take months and even years for these special needs individuals to master, and the ICF/IID is required to include a **training objective** (measurable outcome expected to be achieved by the individual within

intermediate care facility for individuals with intellectual disabilities (ICF/IID) a facility that provides care and training for persons with intellectual disabilities, to increase their adaptive skills—self-care skills, language skills, social skills, vocational skills, and so on.

training objective a single outcome expected to be achieved by the individual within one year as a result of training; measurable outcome, criteria for measuring progress, and projected completion date should be specified relative to strengths, needs, and established goals.

one year) in its plans for each person. ICFs/IIDs are committed to helping individuals reach their greatest potential. These facilities strive for the best quality of life for persons by providing care, treatment, training, and a safe environment for those for whom they are responsible.

Types of Individuals Served

Persons receiving services from an ICF/IID are affected by an **intellectual disability** or intellectual developmental disorder (formerly known as mental retardation), which is "a disability characterized by significant limitations both in intellectual functioning and in adaptive behavior as expressed in conceptual, social, and practical adaptive skills. This disability originates before age 18" (AAIDD, 2010). The term **developmental disability** is used almost interchangeably with the term *intellectual disability*.

The admission of persons with this type of disability may be voluntary, court-ordered, or the result of an emergency situation. The parent/family, the state, and/or regional departments usually make the referrals of the individual to the ICF/IID facility.

The facility conducts a preliminary examination (preadmission screening) of the referred individual. This evaluation can be conducted by an admission committee and focuses on two major areas: (1) Do the facility's services meet the needs of the individual? and (2) Is this the least restrictive environment for the individual?

Individuals admitted to an ICF/IID facility must be in need of receiving **active treatment** services. Therefore, the facility's primary responsibility is to provide health care, training, and habilitative services for individuals who have intellectual or developmental disabilities, under the supervision of qualified professionals.

Over the years, these individuals have been referred to as patients, students, residents, clients, individuals, or customers. The synonyms have changed over time, as there has been a move away from the medical model toward the person-centered approach. The medical model leans toward the goals and accompanying terminology of institutions, patients, basic needs, clinicians, and restoration to health, with the emphasis on good care. The developmental model emphasizes deinstitutionalization. In this model, the generally preferred terms are *individual* or *person*.

Services are offered to promote skill development or behavior change using the interdisciplinary team approach in the active treatment process. The individual supports model is more community-based, with the individual/consumer obtaining support services based on self-determination that is outcome-oriented. Also, facilities may be under different departments and services, and the synonyms tend to favor the service the department renders. For instance, individuals with cerebral palsy may be under the Department of Special Education; therefore, *students* may be the preferred term. However, coauthors Hewitt and O'Nell

intellectual disability significant limitations in both intellectual functioning and adaptive behavior expressed in conceptual, social, and practical adaptive skills, and having an onset before the age of 18.

developmental disability a disability "attributable to a mental or physical impairment that begins before age 18 and is likely to continue indefinitely, and that results in substantial functional limitation in three or more areas of major life activity" (AAI, 2010).

active treatment a continuous program for each recipient, which includes aggressive, consistent implementation of specialized and generic training, treatment, health services, and related services.

(1998), in addressing labels for persons with developmental disabilities, remind us that "it's the person, not the service, that matters. It's a sign of respect" (p. 5).

Types of Caregivers

Personnel vary from facility to facility, depending on the size and scope of the services the facility provides. All ICFs, however, must focus on activities that build or strengthen the person's skills (Janicki, 1992). To this end, an **interdisciplinary (ID) team** identifies and addresses each person's needs. The members of an individual's interdisciplinary team should represent the professions, disciplines, or service areas that are relevant to the person's needs (Conditions of Participation, 2009). Any of the following may serve on an interdisciplinary team: physician, psychologist, social worker, registered nurse, pharmacist, dietitian, physical therapist, occupational therapist, speech-language pathologist, audiologist, dentist, recreational staff member, vocational staff member, education staff member, or resident services staff member. The individual also participates as a member of the team, as well as family members and friends or advocates invited by the individual.

> **interdisciplinary (ID) team** a group that develops an integrated habilitation or program plan that provides individualized services to the individual.

In the traditional planning approach established in the Conditions of Participation, the interdisciplinary team reviews and discusses the individual's past progress and current status. From this review, a program is developed exclusively for the individual, based on the individual **assessment** and identification of needs by the interdisciplinary team. A summary of essential assessment information is developed, which facilitates the identification of needs and provides necessary information to staff members who are responsible for working with the person, along with the goals, objectives, and a service plan for meeting the individual's prioritized needs. This document becomes the product of the interdisciplinary team process, which is a review and revision of services provided.

> **assessment** the process of identifying an individual's functional level, strengths, needs, causes of disabilities, and conditions that hinder development.

Although federal regulations governing this process have not changed, the expectation for including the expressed needs and desires of the individual receiving services is crucial. Several self-advocacy models can be incorporated into the team process that allow persons and their families to make choices and have a major role in developing the program plan. This shift in the planning process toward more personal choice is based on the belief that every person has the right to plan a life that is meaningful and satisfying, known as **person-centered planning**. The set of values, skills, and tools used in person-centered planning is called **person-centered thinking**.

> **person-centered planning** a process that focuses on the preferences of the individual who is receiving services in planning the type of future life the individual wishes to live.

> **person-centered thinking** a set of values, skills, and tools used in person-centered planning.

A **qualified developmental disability professional (QDDP)** is responsible for coordinating and monitoring each person's active treatment program. A QDDP must have at least one year of experience working directly with individuals who have intellectual or developmental disabilities, and is a physician, a registered nurse, or a person with a bachelor's degree in a relevant profession (Conditions of Participation, 2009).

> **qualified developmental disability professional (QDDP)** a person assigned to monitor and coordinate all activities related to the development and implementation of the individual program plan.

Health Care Staff

Members of the health care staff are responsible for providing and administering proper health care to maintain the physical and mental well-being of the person receiving services. These caregivers include, but are not limited to, the following:

- Physicians
- Dentists
- Podiatrists
- Nursing service staff
- Health information staff
- Laboratory technicians
- X-ray technicians
- Respiratory therapists
- EEG technicians
- EKG technicians
- Occupational therapists
- Physical therapists
- Dietary staff
- Pharmacists
- Central supply staff

Habilitative Staff

habilitation   the process by which a person is assisted to acquire and maintain life skills that enable the person to cope more effectively with personal and environmental demands and to raise the level of his or her physical, mental, and social efficiency. Habilitation includes, but is not limited to, programs of structured education and training.

An ICF/IDD provides habilitation, a process by which a person is assisted to acquire and maintain life skills that enable him or her to cope more effectively with personal and environmental demands and to raise the level of physical, mental, and social efficiency. Habilitation includes, but is not limited to, programs of structured education and training. The operative force in the habilitation process often is accomplished by the "person-first" philosophy. Employees are involved in creating an environment for individuals that encourages continuous improvement.

The person-centered approach has been instrumental in improving the services rendered and identifying the least restrictive program alternative. This means that the program is the least confining for the person's condition, service, and treatment, and also is provided in the least intrusive manner that is reasonably and humanely appropriate to the individual's needs and preferences. The habilitative staff members include, but are not limited to, the following:

- Qualified developmental disability professional (QDDP)
- Social service workers
- Psychologists

- Speech-language pathologists
- Audiologists
- Special education staff
- Vocational/life skills coaches
- Recreational therapists
- Music therapists
- Direct care staff

Administrative Staff

Members of the administrative staff work within the guidelines of the ICF/IID federal regulations to produce positive outcomes for individuals who receive services. They manage funds to provide quality care. They are responsible for smooth operation of the facility that will maintain the health, safety, and quality of life for the individuals being served. Administrative staff members include, but are not limited to, the following:

- Administrator
- Finance officer
- Human resources staff
- Health information services staff
- Home life directors/managers/supervisors
- Housekeeping staff

Types of Settings

Facilities for individuals with intellectual or developmental disabilities may be operated by a variety of groups, such as the government, religious groups, private interests, and everything in between. Also, the facilities may be designated by the type of services rendered. Some facilities provide services to individuals based on an age range, such as from ages 3 to 22. Some provide services only to individuals with a specific diagnosis, such as those with cerebral palsy, autism spectrum disorders, and dual diagnoses.

In general, no admission should be considered permanent. The facility provides the individual with the training and guidance necessary to develop and acquire the skills needed to function in a less restrictive setting. This normalization training model has been a major force for individuals with intellectual and developmental disabilities.

Once these goals have been reached, the discharge planning objectives are obtained by referring the person to the appropriate setting, such as a group home, supervised living, or supported living (where the person chooses where and with whom he or she will live, with assistance as needed).

1. What does ICR/IID stand for, and what categories of individuals does it serve?
2. What does QDDP stand for, and what is this individual's role in the program?
3. What does habilitation mean, and what does it include?
4. What is person-centered planning, and why is it a preferable planning method for individuals with ID?
5. Name five habilitative staff members.

REGULATORY ISSUES

Most ICF/IID facilities are funded by Title XIX (Medicaid) and, therefore, must meet the standards of the Conditions of Participation for Intermediate Care Facilities for Individuals with Intellectual Disabilities. As in other settings, a state agency surveys facilities to determine whether they meet federal and any applicable state standards. This annual survey may be conducted by the state department of health, mental health, or hospital licensing division. Because funding is tied to the survey process, the goal of all facilities is to meet regulatory requirements the first time around. If deficiencies are noted that may endanger the safety of the client, however, the facility can be fined several hundreds to thousands of dollars per day, depending on the infraction, until the deficiency has been rectified.

Voluntary accreditation also is available to facilities serving persons with intellectual or developmental disabilities. The Joint Commission offers accreditation for these organizations through its behavioral health care division. The standards to survey these organizations are found in the *Comprehensive Accreditation Manual for Behavioral Health Care.*

Another accrediting body, the Council on Quality and Leadership (CQL), formerly the Accreditation Council on Services for People with Developmental Disabilities, also has set standards for facilities serving persons with intellectual or developmental disabilities. Currently, the CQL has accredited more than 200 organizations. The Council is sponsored by the following organizations and service providers: American Association on Intellectual and Developmental Disabilities, American Network of Community Options and Resources, The Arc (formerly Association for Retarded Citizens of the United States), Autism Society of America, Mosaic, National Association of QDDPs, Self Advocates Becoming Empowered, and United Cerebral Palsy Associations, Inc. The accreditation standards of the Council on Quality and Leadership (2005) are found in its *Personal Outcome Measures.*

In general, voluntary accreditation surveys performed by the Council or The Joint Commission are more stringent than the states' ICF/IID surveying processes. Usually when accreditation is obtained, the facility is considered to be performing above and beyond the state licensing requirements. Although the majority of ICFs/IIDs may not undergo voluntary accreditation by the Council or The Joint Commission, they sometimes use the publications of these organizations to improve the quality of the services they offer.

1. What is the name of the standards that are used to survey most ICF/IID organizations?
2. True or False? Accreditation by The Joint Commission is required for ICF/IID facilities?
3. The Council on Quality and Leadership is sponsored by several organizations. Name three.

DOCUMENTATION

Individual records are the official files on each person at an ICF/IID facility. Although in theory they should consist of only one chart, these records often are divided into administrative, health, and habilitation/training sections. When not in use, all sections must be kept confidential in secure areas.

A number of documentation requirements are found in the Conditions of Participation. For example, the standards for admissions, transfers, and discharge include the following requirements in 42 C.F.R. § 483.440 under Standard (b):

(2) Admission decisions must be based on a preliminary evaluation of the client that is conducted or updated by the facility or by outside sources.

(3) A preliminary evaluation must contain background information as well as currently valid assessments of functional developmental, behavioral, social, health and nutritional status to determine if the facility can provide for the client's needs and if the client is likely to benefit from placement in the facility.

(4) If a client is to be either transferred or discharged, the facility must—
   (i) Have documentation in the client's record that the client was transferred or discharged for good cause; and
   (ii) Provide a reasonable time to prepare the client and his or her parents or guardian for the transfer or discharge (except in emergencies).

(5) At the time of the discharge, the facility must—
   (i) Develop a final summary of the client's developmental, behavioral, social, health and nutritional status and, with the consent of the client, parents (if the client is a minor) or legal guardian, provide a copy to authorized persons and agencies; and
   (ii) Provide a post-discharge plan of care that will assist the client to adjust to the new living environment.

One important documentation requirement in the ICF/IID setting is the **individual program plan (IPP)**. Standards for this document also are detailed at C.F.R. § 483.440, as follows:

(c) Standard: Individual program plan.

   (1) Each client must have an individual program plan developed by an interdisciplinary team that represents the professions, disciplines or service areas that are relevant to—
      (i) Identifying the client's needs, as described by the comprehensive functional assessments required in paragraph (c)(3) of this section; and
      (ii) Designing programs that meet the client's needs.

individual program plan (IPP) a comprehensive written document that states the specific objectives necessary to meet the individual's needs, as identified by a comprehensive individualized assessment. The IPP is the major tool in planning and implementing the care and services rendered to the individual.

(2) Appropriate facility staff must participate in interdisciplinary team meetings. Participation by other agencies serving the client is encouraged. Participation by the client, his or her parent (if the client is a minor), or the client's legal guardian is required unless that participation is unobtainable or inappropriate.

(3) Within 30 days after admission, the interdisciplinary team must perform accurate assessments or reassessments as needed to supplement the preliminary evaluation conducted prior to admission. The comprehensive functional assessment must take into consideration the client's age (for example, child, young adult, elderly person) and the implications for active treatment at each stage, as applicable, and must—
   (i) Identify the presenting problems and disabilities and where possible, their causes;
   (ii) Identify the client's specific developmental strengths;
   (iii) Identify the client's specific developmental and behavioral management needs;
   (iv) Identify the client's need for services without regard to the actual availability of the services needed; and
   (v) Include physical development and health, nutritional status, sensorimotor development, affective development, speech and language development and auditory functioning, cognitive development, social development, adaptive behaviors or independent living skills necessary for the client to be able to function in the community, and as applicable, vocational skills.

(4) Within 30 days after admission, the interdisciplinary team must prepare for each client an individual program plan that states the specific objectives necessary to meet the client's needs, as identified by the comprehensive assessment required by paragraph (c)(3) of this section, and the planned sequence for dealing with those objectives. These objectives must—
   (i) Be stated separately, in terms of a single behavioral outcome;
   (ii) Be assigned projected completion dates;
   (iii) Be expressed in behavioral terms that provide measurable indices of performance;
   (iv) Be organized to reflect a developmental progression appropriate to the individual; and
   (v) Be assigned priorities.

(5) Each written training program designed to implement the objectives in the individual program plan must specify:
   (i) The methods to be used;
   (ii) The schedule for use of the method;
   (iii) The person responsible for the program;
   (iv) The type of data and frequency of data collection necessary to be able to assess progress toward the desired objectives;
   (v) The inappropriate client behavior(s), if applicable; and
   (vi) Provision for the appropriate expression of behavior and the replacement of inappropriate behavior, if applicable, with behavior that is adaptive or appropriate.

(6) The individual program plan must also:
   (i) Describe relevant interventions to support the individual toward independence.
   (ii) Identify the location where program strategy information (which must be accessible to any person responsible for implementation) can be found.

    (iii) Include, for those clients who lack them, training in personal skills essential for privacy and independence (including, but not limited to, toilet training, personal hygiene, dental hygiene, self-feeding, bathing, dressing, grooming, and communication of basic needs), until it has been demonstrated that the client is developmentally incapable of acquiring them.

    (iv) Identify mechanical supports, if needed, to achieve proper body position, balance, or alignment. The plan must specify the reason for each support, the situations in which each is to be applied, and a schedule for the use of each support.

    (v) Provide that clients who have multiple disabling conditions spend a major portion of each waking day out of bed and outside the bedroom area, moving about by various methods and devices whenever possible.

    (vi) Include opportunities for client choice and self-management.

  (7) A copy of each client's individual program plan must be made available to all relevant staff, including staff of other agencies who work with the client, and to the client, parents (if the client is a minor) or legal guardian.

(d) Standard: Program implementation.

  (1) As soon as the interdisciplinary team has formulated a client's individual program plan, each client must receive a continuous active treatment program consisting of needed interventions and services in sufficient number and frequency to support the achievement of the objectives identified in the individual program plan.

  (2) The facility must develop an active treatment schedule that outlines the current active treatment program and that is readily available for review by relevant staff.

  (3) Except for those facets of the individual program plan that must be implemented only by licensed personnel, each client's individual program plan must be implemented by all staff who work with the client, including professional, paraprofessional and nonprofessional staff.

(e) Standard: Program documentation.

  (1) Data relative to accomplishment of the criteria specified in client individual program plan objectives must be documented in measureable terms.

  (2) The facility must document significant events that are related to the client's individual program plan and assessments and that contribute to an overall understanding of the client's ongoing level and quality of functioning.

(f) Standard: Program monitoring and change.

  (1) The individual program plan must be reviewed at least by the qualified developmental disability professional and revised as necessary, including, but not limited to situations in which the client—

    (i) Has successfully completed an objective or objectives identified in the individual program plan;

    (ii) Is regressing or losing skills already gained;

    (iii) Is failing to progress toward identified objectives after reasonable efforts have been made; or

    (iv) Is being considered for training towards new objectives.

  (2) At least annually, the comprehensive functional assessment of each client must be reviewed by the interdisciplinary team for relevancy and updated as needed, and the individual program plan must be revised, as appropriate, repeating the process set forth in paragraph (c) of this section.

The major difference between individual records in an ICF/IID and other long-term settings relates to the fact that some type of training is occurring on a 24-hour basis. For example, persons may practice toileting or grooming skills in their living areas. Thus, the records have to be housed in the living units or homes. This also makes the records more accessible for the authorized chart handlers who follow the 24-hour schedules for daily observation and documentation of training factors for their monthly statistics. The statistics are gathered for annual meetings of the interdisciplinary team, sometimes informally called an **annual staffing**. These staffings are needed to demonstrate the accomplishment or failure of goals set forth for each individual.

Likewise, the health section of the record documents the health/medical needs of the person, the content of which meets the standards of practice for the caregivers. Table 9-1 is a generic listing of data that may be maintained for an individual in an ICF/IID facility. The tabular arrangement is based on the needs of the facility and the user of the various sections of the document. Often, forms are designed to meet several types of charting needs, such as two-sided copies for efficiency, multipart forms for distribution purposes, and forms that can meet the requirements of two or more departments/services. For example, a weight chart could meet both dietary and nursing requirements. Forms should be designed to keep the bulk of the chart as brief as possible while meeting the appropriate documentation standards.

annual staffing an informal term for the annual meeting of the interdisciplinary team during which the individual program plan is reviewed and revised for the coming year; not to exceed 365 days from the previous annual or initial staffing.

TABLE 9-1	Generic Listing of Individual Data in an ICF/IID Facility

Administrative Data

Personal Account	Consents for Off-Campus Visits/Activities with Authorized Individuals
Personal Funds Ledger	
Savings Accounts	Consent for Seizure Medications
Long-Term Care Certification	Consent to Photograph or Record
Medicare/Medicaid	Consent for Behavior Program Using Restricted Procedures
Insurance	Consent for Psychotropic Medications and Treatment Plan
Funeral Home Preference/Verification	Consent for Religious Activities
Financial Agreements	Consent for Off-Campus Activities
Admission Agreements	Correspondence
Legal Data	Letters, Memos, Forms
Guardianships	Resident's Rights
Interdictions	Bill of Rights
Court Commissions	Explanation of Rights of Individuals Served
Authorizations	Review/Approval by Behavior Management Committee
Authorizations for Release of Information	Human Rights Committee Review or Approval Data
Authorizations for Administration of Long-Term Estrogen Substances	Abridgement of Rights
	Office of Family Services Notifications
Consents	Pre-Admission Data
Consents for Disclosure of Information	Birth Certificate
Consent to Medical Treatment/ Therapy/Surgery Procedures	Discharge and Follow-up
	Discharge Summary
Consent Regarding Emergency Medical Treatment	

TABLE 9-1	(continued)

Training Data

Individual Habilitative Program (IHP) Addenda	Training Assessments
Psychological (Comprehensive/Annual) Behavior	Core Team Notes
Treatment Plans	QDDP Monthly Reviews
Individual Education Plan (IEP)	Monthly Core Team Progress Notes
Special Education Assessments	Social Service Assessments
Education Correspondence	Vocational (Life Skills) Assessment/Evaluations
Activity Schedule (24 hours)	Speech and Language Updates
	Comprehensive Evaluations
Audiology Evaluations and Screenings	Physical Therapy Evaluations and Updates
Occupational Therapy Evaluations and Updates	Recreation Therapy Evaluations and Updates
Wheelchair Evaluations	Music Therapy Evaluations and Updates
Adaptive Equipment Evaluations	

Health Care Data (Medical and Nursing)

Medical	*Nursing*
Major and Minor Problem Lists	Height/Weight/Head Circumference
Physician Orders	Nursing Assessments
Health Care Progress Notes	Quarterly
Consultations	Initial
Neurology/EEGs	Medication Administration Records
Occupational	Medication History
Ophthalmology	Pharmacy Medication/Drug Reviews
Orthopedic	Medication Destruction Records
Physical Therapy	Medication on Leave of Absence Form (Visits)
Psychiatry	Seizure Records
Physical Exams	Restraint Checklist
Referrals	Accident/Incident Report Forms
Off-Campus Clinics/Health Care Facilities	Graphic Data
Laboratory	Female Health Care Records (Copies of Consents for Oral
Hematology	Contraceptives and Estrogen Usage)
Chemistry	Diabetic Record
Medication Levels	Immunization Record
Urinalysis	Dietary Data
Microbiology	Nutritional Evaluations
Serology	Dietary Notes
Parasitology	Tube Feedings
Miscellaneous	Growth Graph (under 18 years of age)
Radiology	Death Certificate
X-rays	Autopsy Reports
EKGs	Death Summary
Dental	
Progress and Treatment Received	

SELF REVIEW 9.3

1. Documentation requirements for the patient's medical record can be found in the _____.

2. Within _____ days after admission, the interdisciplinary team must prepare an individual program plan for each patient.

3. True or False? In addition to staff and agencies that work with the patient, a copy of the individual program plan is provided to the parents (if the patient is a minor) or the legal guardian.

4. The patient's program plan must be reviewed by the _____ professional, who will revise the plan as necessary.

5. True or False? The comprehensive functional assessment of each patient must be reviewed by the interdisciplinary team for relevancy at least every 18 months.

REIMBURSEMENT AND FUNDING

Medicaid is the primary source of funding for most ICFs/IID. A facility that meets the requirements of the federal Conditions of Participation is certified to receive payment from Medicaid for persons who have been determined to need its services. A state's mental health or intellectual disability authority determines whether a given individual needs the type of specialized services provided by an ICF/IID (Preadmission Screening and Annual Review of Mentally Ill and Mentally Retarded Individuals, 2009).

When the person has been determined to need active treatment in a facility setting, the ICF/IID receives a per diem payment for each day of care provided to that individual. Other sources of funding include state offices of family services, Veterans Affairs, railroad retirement funds, and so on. Some persons qualify for services covered by Medicare as well.

In some states, the level of care that each person needs is what determines the amount of per diem payment the facility receives. Individuals with more medical complications, behavior problems, and disabilities are funded at higher levels, because they need more specialized treatment and service modalities provided by a variety of professionals and caregivers. Different states use various methods for determining the level of care needed.

Standardized assessment tools that can be used for diagnostic and planning purposes also can be used to determine the level of services needed. Some states have begun using these assessment instruments to establish case-mix reimbursement systems. Under such a system, the provider typically receives a case-mix-adjusted per diem payment for each individual receiving services. The **Inventory for Client and Agency Planning (ICAP)** is an example of an assessment instrument that some states use to provide service scores to adjust payments to providers.

Managed care proposals have been offered as a mechanism for paying for services for persons with intellectual disabilities. Managed care proposals should consider some of the differences between care for the subject population and the other

Inventory for Client and Agency Planning (ICAP) a standardized assessment instrument that can be used for program planning and also is used in several states as a data collection tool for case-mix reimbursement to ICF/IID organizations.

types of care that usually are provided in a managed care program. For example, unlike the typical managed care population, people with intellectual disabilities need more than just health care. They also need training and other types of supports. Because of these differences, states that are considering managed care proposals may find it difficult to determine an appropriate capitation rate. Advocates for persons with intellectual disabilities are urging attention to the special needs of these individuals in any managed care programs developed for them (Goel & Keefe, 2003).

1. To receive payment from Medicaid, the facility must meet the requirements of the _____.

2. True or False? Services provided by an ICF/IID are reimbursed on a fee for services basis.

3. True or False? Level of service or care needed by the patient determines the amount of reimbursement to the facility in some states.

4. An example of an assessment instrument used by some states to provide service scores that can be used to adjust payments to the providers is the _____.

5. What type of information has to be provided in a managed care proposal for persons with intellectual disabilities that differs from a managed care proposal for persons without an intellectual disability?

INFORMATION MANAGEMENT

Data and Information Flow

Chronologically, data tend to flow as shown in Figure 9-1.

FIGURE 9-1

Chronological flow of data.

Admission of the Individual
↓
Comprehensive Diagnostics
↓
Interdisciplinary Team Assessments/Updates
↓
Receipt of Treatment/Services
Documentation of these in the individual record
↓
Discharge/Death of the Individual
↓
Follow-up Documentation

FIGURE 9-2

Relationship between centralized and decentralized record storage.

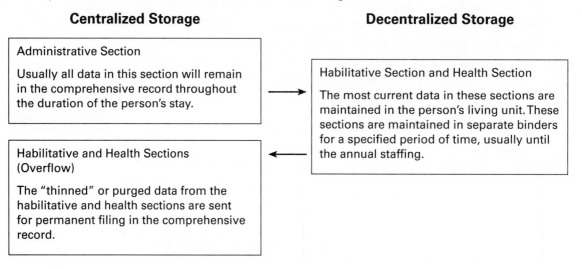

The physical flow of the record varies from facility to facility. Figure 9-2 is a typical flow of information in a paper-based system from decentralized storage in the person's living unit to centralized storage in the health information department. In a paper-based system, information is filed in the centralized comprehensive record as it is received from the living units and other sources. For ease of reference, the centralized record usually is maintained in sections, such as the administrative section, the habilitative or training section, and the health section.

Because the active records can be voluminous, some facilities use imaging technology to store portions of the paper record while the individual is still being served by the facility. Some facilities have a hybrid system in which an electronic record system is used for a portion or all of the active record.

Upon the individual's death or discharge, the active record is closed and retained for the duration of the statute of limitations. If a facility utilizes an imaging program for active records, the remaining portions of the closed records often are imaged at the death or discharge of the person. Some facilities, however, prefer to avoid the additional cost of imaging the entire record and may image only selected portions for research or administrative purposes. The remainder of the paper record in these facilities is destroyed upon reaching the statute of limitations or other legal retention period.

Coding and Classification

In ICF/IID facilities, employees may have to become familiar with three types of coding systems, depending on established policies and procedures. Various coding systems serve different purposes that are helpful in the care of the individual and in research into the causes of intellectual disabilities.

ICD-9-CM and ICD-10-CM

The *International Classification of Diseases* are assigned on an accumulative basis or based on individual "infirmary," "sick call," or "acute care" stays or visits. Coded data may be useful when a survey is in process so individual records containing specific diagnoses or conditions can be obtained for tracking during the survey.

Traditionally, ICD codes appear in the summary sheet, which encompasses infirmary screenings, sick call, or acute care stays whenever these services are rendered in the ICF/IID facility. Facilities often prefer to use an accumulative type of diagnoses/procedures sheet that is chronological in nature and is an inclusive listing of the individual's conditions and procedures, coded for reference purposes. Diagnoses and procedures, however, also may be required on identification sheets for quick reference, and may be used as well on the order sheets because the condition for which the medication is being ordered is also required. Whatever format is utilized, it should be developed in conjunction with facility services and with reference needs in mind. One format, which could be used in the infirmary section, is as shown in the accompanying box. Additional diagnoses and conditions then could be listed.

> Intellectual Disability [mild, moderate, severe, profound]
>
> Etiology: Due to _____

DSM-5

The Diagnostic and Statistical Manual of Mental Disorders, fifth edition, is used by psychologists and psychiatrists in their evaluations and consultations. (For more information on *DSM-5*, see Chapter 8.) Intellectual Disability is classified as a neurodevelopmental disorder in *DSM-5*, which recognizes four degrees of severity of intellectual disability: mild, moderate, severe, and profound. Assessments of adaptive functioning are used to determine the extent of severity (American Psychiatric Association, 2013). This information may be recorded on the consultation, evaluation, or data sheet for retrieval purposes and/or stored electronically for access by authorized individuals through the facility network.

Manual on Terminology and Classification in Mental Retardation, 1983 Edition

The *Manual on Terminology and Classification in Mental Retardation* was published in 1983 by the American Association on Mental Retardation, now the American Association on Intellectual and Developmental Disabilities, and still is cited as the source of definitions of intellectual disability in the *Code of*

Federal Regulations (Applicability and definitions, 2011). The AAIDD (2010) replaced this reference with a publication titled *Intellectual Disability: Definition, Classification, and Systems of Supports*, 11th edition. Some ICFs/IID, however, still use the older publication for classification purposes.

Classifications provide a systematic arrangement of individuals, units, or events into groups with one or more common denominators. They may be useful for administrative purposes and for preliminary planning for groups identified by the system. Classifications can assist with the allocation of funds and personnel to provide special services. Once an individual is classified as intellectually disabled, it is imperative to periodically reassess the diagnosis, classification, and service needs.

The manual includes ten major categories and seven secondary categories, both with sublistings, as well as tertiary categories. Coding usually is done at the time of admission to encompass the necessary information for establishing the comprehensive plan of care required of the facility. An example of this type of coding would be as follows:

Primary

Secondary

Tertiary

    Genetic
    Cranial anomaly
    Sensory impairment
    Perception
    Convulsive disorder
    Psychological impairment

The major and minor categories of this classification system include a variety of helpful levels in both the behavioral and the medical classifications to standardize the data needed for statistical reporting.

Intellectual Disability: Definition, Classification, and Systems of Supports, Eleventh Edition

The Manual on Terminology and Classification in Mental Retardation has continued to evolve over time and now is known as *Intellectual Disability: Definition, Classification, and Systems of Supports*, 11th edition (AAIDD, 2010). The 11th edition of the AAIDD Definition Manual contains current and authoritative information about defining, classifying, and diagnosing intellectual disability and planning lifelong supports for individuals with this condition. The manual includes discussion of 10 dimensions of support areas; a five-step process for assessing, planning, and delivering supports to a person with intellectual disability; and various approaches to individualized service planning.

Electronic Information Systems

Electronic information systems vary from facility to facility and/or within the facility. Acute health care settings are, in general, more advanced than ICF/IID facilities, but, with additional requirements of various licensing and accreditation agencies, electronic information systems are becoming more prevalent. Although some ICF/IID facilities use off-the-shelf programs, the majority of facilities have customized programs to meet the needs and types of persons served.

Private ICF/IID facilities are considered to be businesses. Electronic systems with various functions and features that are needed to accomplish the business aspects of the overall facility operation are seen as vital to the business's survival. The need to control the "paper tiger" has grown to encompass a variety of other areas including, but not limited to, the individual record.

Benefits of electronic systems range from financial reports to program planning, or from timekeeping to rapidly producing all information requested during a survey. The first priority in many facilities is to begin to integrate the various systems that have been developed over time to address specific needs. As various departmental systems begin to interface with each other or with a central system, a partially electronic, or hybrid, record can be achieved. Attempting to go to a completely paperless record probably would not be cost-effective in most facilities at present. More benefits are likely to be achieved by developing databases to help manage individual data and information. A completely electronic record is not possible until computers or workstations are available in all units and in all services.

For facilities that pursue an imaging system, the health information directors must become active participants in establishing standardized forms and reports. With the ease of formatting and designing forms using readily available software, every department or service is likely to develop its own forms or records. In any case, some type of facility-wide forms control is vital to the success of an imaging program.

Data Sets

Data collection varies from state to state, with certain standard items required by the Conditions of Participation. For discussion and illustration purposes, a conservative selection of forms and specific features of typical data sets is included in this chapter, to share some of the information tools that are beneficial to the operation of a 24-hour ICF/IID.

The listing that follows is not exhaustive. Many variables can affect the choice of forms and the management of their use, such as variations in state laws, survey requirements, types of facilities, and even the choice of computer hardware and software. The selected forms serve a twofold purpose. One purpose is to meet requirements, and these forms have a filing designation to ensure that they are filed in the correct sequence and under the correct tab heading. Other selected forms are simply tools that may not become part of the permanent file and can be shredded after they have met their service needs.

Assessment Data

In most states, assessment of the individual is a requirement to determine eligibility for services. Assessment processes vary from state to state and may include psychological, psychiatric, and medical evaluations. To assist in determining the services that the individual may need, many states use standardized assessment instruments. For example, adaptive and maladaptive behavior can be assessed using a variety of instruments, such as the Scales of Independent Behavior–Revised (SIB-R), the Vineland Adaptive Behavior Scales, Second Edition, the AAIDD Diagnostic Adaptive Behavior Scale (DABS), and the Inventory for Client and Agency Planning (ICAP). The use of instruments like these can assist with both diagnosis and program planning. Some states use this type of instrument to provide data for case-mix reimbursement systems as well.

Annual Assessments   When the full interdisciplinary team conducts its annual assessments, forms for categories such as nutritional assessment, recreational assessment, and vocational assessment are used to summarize and address the services rendered by these specialty areas.

Administrative Data

Authorizations/Consent Forms   A variety of consent and authorization forms—such as those for psychotropic drug use and birth control pills—can be generated for each individual, using data from the facility's electronic information system.

Individual Information Release   A record is maintained for the control and authorized release of requested information in the individual records, providing an audit tool of this task area.

Ongoing Inventory of Individual Belongings   This inventory is one of the most useful computer-generated forms, making it easy to update inventories by the touch of a key to add, delete, and/or change the information. Manual labor still is involved in the inventory process, of course, because just keeping up with each person's clothes is a monumental task in itself. Clothing is listed by long sleeves, short sleeves, and a variety of identifying features that can be noted in a specific area of the form.

Identification Data   Identification sheets illustrate a variety of features vital to the care and management of the individual's records. The design of the form provides for a view of the individual's information at a glance. This form usually is reviewed and updated as required—at least yearly at the annual staffing.

A second form is a baseline information sheet applicable at the time of admission, which maintains the same information throughout the person's stay. It is essential for completing vital records such as death certificates.

A third form is used at the time of death/discharge and provides necessary information for tracking and follow-up and is basically used to officially close out the individual's record.

Individual Program Plan (IPP) and Related Training Data

This section of the individual record is unique to an ICF/IID. The following specific forms are examples of training data forms.

Individual Program Plan   As described previously, the individual program plan (IPP) is a composite summary of the goals and the objectives for the individual. The staff uses the IPP to help the individual attain these goals and objectives during the coming year. This individualized program plan is used in the overall care of the person and outlines how the program will guide the individual toward achieving the set goals. The program includes brief summaries of all services rendered during the past year and goals established for the coming year.

The Updating Worksheet   This worksheet is an electronic application used by the interdisciplinary team at the full team meetings for updating the person's record in specific service areas. This tool not only captures the services rendered and the staff member responsible for providing each service, but also provides the capability of immediately making these changes in the person's individual program plan.

The Draft Referral to Staffing   This form is used throughout the year to provide updates to the current individual program plan. It eventually becomes a part of the permanent record as an addendum to the current staffing, which illustrates that program updates have been initiated and approved by appropriate staff members.

Core Team Summary Sheet   The core team summary sheet (Figure 9-3) is a tracking form used to implement the individual program plan. As the staff identifies needs, they are added to the sheet. Because this is a working tool used by the staff, there is no problem with "write-overs" and strikeouts to indicate when goals have been met or when new information is added. A new summary sheet for review purposes is printed at or before a 90-day -interval, with the recommended revisions. Because care is rendered on a 24-hour basis, the summary sheets also are used in developing the 24-hour active treatment schedules, described as follows.

The 24-Hour Active Treatment Schedule   This schedule works in conjunction with the individualized program plan and the summaries (see Figure 9-4). It specifically sets into timeframes the who, what, why, when, and where of the

FIGURE 9-3

Core team summary sheets (excerpt).

CORE TEAM REVIEW SUMMARY FOR X

(Based Upon Client & Staff Interviews and 20–25% Random Sampling of Daily Documentation)

COVERING THE REVIEW PERIOD 02/02/YY THROUGH 04/19/YY

RTA
MEMO:
SEIZURES: Monitor closely and report to Nursing. Wash hair every Wednesday. Apply activator daily. Encourage her to carry purse.

1. Praise good behavior and give extra attention when good. Give attention to dress and appearance.
2. Offer (when patting stomach) to take X to bathroom often (each half hour).
3. Direct her to bathroom and offer shower when highly upset.
4. Remove from loud areas when upset.
5. When agitated and aggressive, contact supervisor.
6. Call for help as needed.
7. Do not "back off" from X; this increases problems.
8. Monitor closely when around Y (may bite when upset).

Time:	Location:	Code:	Current Training Objective:		Flags:	Recommendations:
08:15 AM	DAYROOM/GYM	BC61L -005AAAD	**BASIC COMMANDS**/Also scheduled: 04:45 PM			
			Will remain dressed in same outfit for half			
			hour (RTA to reward with edible)			
			does this on verbal command 1 out of 3 trials			
			to be completed by 08/30/YY			DATE

PERIOD ENDING:	09/01/XX	11/17/YY	02/02/YY	04/19/YY
PROGRESS:	82.30 %	79.76 %	80.00 %	78.90 %	DECLINE
OBJECTIVE:	BC53G	BC53G	BC53G	BC53G
LEVEL:	005 D	005 D	004 D	004 D

08:30 AM BEDROOM HK125N-005 D

HOUSEKEEPING/Also scheduled: 04:30 PM

Will carry two items of dirty clothing
to dirty clothes bucket in bathroom
does this on verbal command
to be completed by 09/30/YY

PERIOD ENDING:	09/01/YY	11/17/YY	02/02/YY	04/19/YY	
PROGRESS:	0.00 %	0.00 %	85.19 %	86.14 %	
OBJECTIVE:			HK79B	HK79C	RECENT OBJECTIVE CHANGE
LEVEL:			011AAAD	011D	RECENT LEVEL CHANGE

08:30 AM BATHROOM [At Workshop]
BATHROOM TO 15F-005AMAS

TOILETING/Also scheduled: 10:00 AM 12:15 PM

Will wash hands after toileting for
30 seconds (RTA to monitor closely)
does this on verbal command to be trained throughout day
to be completed by 10/31/YY

PERIOD ENDING:	09/01/YY	11/17/YY	02/02/YY	04/19/YY	
PROGRESS	81.15 %	94.23 %	83.03 %	76.67 %	DECLINE
OBJECTIVE:	TO19G	TO19G	TO3B	TO3B	
LEVEL:	011 D	011 D	005AMAD	005AMAS	RECENT LEVEL

..

FIGURE 9-4

24-hour schedule—weekday. (The weekend schedule is separate.)

	Weekday Client Active Treatment Schedule	
	12:00 A.M.—11:45 P.M.	
TIME:	*LOCATION:*	*SCHEDULED TRAINING:*
06:00 AM	BEDROOM/BR	Rise; Personal Hygiene Care
06:15 AM	BEDROOM/GYM	TOILETING SKILL Formal Training
07:00 AM	BEDROOM	GROOMING Formal Training
07:30 AM	DINING ROOM	Scheduled Mealtime
08:15 AM	BATHROOM	ORAL HYGIENE Formal Training
08:30 AM	BEDROOM/GYM	TOILETING SKILL Formal Training
09:00 AM	GYM/CR 7	STIMULATION Formal Training
09:15 AM	GYM/CR 7	READING Formal Training
09:30 AM	CLASSROOM 6	KITCHEN MANAGEMENT Formal Training
09:45 AM	BEDROOM/GYM	TOILETING SKILL Formal Training
10:00 AM	CANTEEN	Snack/allowance on Thursdays
10:15 AM	GYM/CR 7	DISCRIMINATION Formal Training
10:30 AM	GYM/CR 7	TIME KNOWLEDGE Formal Training
10:45 AM	BATHROOM	BATHING Formal Training
11:00 AM	BEDROOM	Leisure time until 11:30 AM
11:30 AM	BEDROOM	PERSONAL INFORMATION Formal Training
12:00 PM	BEDROOM/GYM	TOILETING SKILLS Formal Training
12:15 PM	BATHROOM	GROOMING Formal Training
12:30 PM	DINING ROOM	Scheduled Mealtime
01:15 PM	BATHROOM	ORAL HYGIENE Formal Training
	A.M. Medication Times: None	
	P.M. Medication Times: None	
PGTC #		CLIENT:

individual's treatment program. The IPP and the 24-hour schedules are developed for a period of one year, but periodic revisions/summaries/assessments are done at a minimum of 90-day intervals, and more frequently if warranted by the service and treatment modalities of the IPP and schedule changes.

Often, surveyors use this form to ensure that a service or activity is being followed by the **direct care staff**, personnel whose daily responsibility is to manage, supervise, and provide direct care to individuals in the residential living units. If the facility is not adhering to the individualized program based on the timeframe set forth, it can be cited for a deficiency in that specific area of care or service.

direct care staff
personnel whose daily responsibility is to manage, supervise, and provide direct care to individuals in their residential living unit.

Physician Data

Standing orders are individualized forms listing medications, contraindications, allergies, and so forth (see Figure 9-5). Order sheets list every medication that the person is taking, along with a corresponding diagnosis. For example, if the person has diabetes, there must be supporting documentation for the diagnosis so medication will be provided for controlling this condition.

Physician progress notes may be handwritten or may be generated electronically.

Because most ICF/IID facilities do not maintain fulltime medical staff members but, instead, must utilize available community medical services, using the transfer and referral record is vital not only for the individual's care but for communicating the care rendered. This is especially true in emergency transfer situations. The front of the form deals with information that the facility furnishes when the person is transferred, and the reverse side provides for communication of the treatment, evaluation, and consultation rendered.

Specialty services such as x-rays and laboratory work often are provided by outside sources. When they are requested and the facility's documentation of the service rendered is recorded on this form, it also is used for accounting purposes.

The transportation request form is used when the individual must obtain health care services in the community. This is not only a request but actually is required for accounting purposes.

The physical exam form is used at the time of the annual staffing. As noted, the primary and additional diagnoses, as well as personal information, are furnished to the physician, enabling him or her to screen more methodically. For example, if the individual has a heart problem, it would be recorded in the diagnosis section, and the physician could address the status of the heart with a cardiovascular entry.

Nursing assessments are performed throughout the year and, along with the physical exam, provide the data needed to summarize the overall medical and nursing care rendered annually.

Nursing Data

The chronological drug regimen review is a form that is used monthly by the consultant pharmacist, who conducts a review not only of the medication and

FIGURE 9-5

Physician's standing orders.

HUDSPETH REGIONAL CENTER
PHYSICIAN'S STANDING ORDERS

1. PASSES: To include therapeutic leaves: Individualized activities, school and programing; off-campus consultations, appointments and follow-up visits with physicians in clinic, and other diagnostic studies done off campus and other purposes

2. ROUTINE TREATMENT FOR WOUND CARE AND INJURIES:
    1. Superficial wounds: clean with saline twice a day and apply antibiotic ointment (Neosporin or Bacitracin) until healed.
    2. Ice pack as needed.
    3. For sutures: clean with saline twice a day and apply antibiotic ointment and remove sutures in 7 days, unless otherwise ordered.

3. FEVER/PAIN:

    For fever greater than 100.5° F rectally (99.5° oral, 98.5° axillary) and/or for Pain give:
    1. Tylenol 10 mg. per kg up to 650 mg. q. 4 hours as needed or
    2. Tylenol suppository 325 mg. per rectum for clients weighing less than 45 pounds and 650 mg. per rectum for clients weighing more than 45 pounds q. 4 hours as needed.

    For fever not relieved by Tylenol within t hour:

    May give Ibuprofen 10 mg. per kg up to 800 mg. q. 6 hrs. PRN.

    For temperature of 103° rectally (102° oral, 101° axillary) or above:
    3. Use a cooling blanket.
    4. Give tepid sponge bath and Tylenol/Ibuprofen as noted above.
    5. CBC with differential on A shift closest to occurrence of fever
    6. Check complete set of vital signs and Notify MD.

4. HYPOTHERMIA: (temp less than 96° rectal, 95° oral, 94° axillary)
    1. Put socks and cap on client.
    2. Wrap client up with a regular blanket.
    3. If temperature does not respond, put on heating blanket.

5. NAUSEA AND VOMITING: (New Onset)
    1. Check for fecal impaction.
    2. If positive, follow orders for impaction. If negative, and after vomiting 2 times, give Phenergan suppository 2.5 mg., 1 whole one for clients over 45 pounds, ½ for clients under 45 pounds.

NAME: _____   CASE NUMBER: _____

6. DIARRHEA: (New Onset)
    1. Hold any laxatives or prune juice for 48 hrs.
    2. Immodium 2 mg. P.O. after 3rd loose stool. May repeat once within an hour.

FIGURE 9-5 (*continued*)

7. SEIZURES:

After 2nd Grand Mal seizure:

1. Check for impaction.
2. Give Ativan 2 mg. IM for clients weighing greater than 50 pounds or 1 mg. IM for clients weighing less than 50 pounds.
3. Check complete set of vitals and notify MD if seizures not resolved.
4. If impaction was positive, follow orders for impaction.

8. IMPACTION:

1. Give one Dulcolax or Bisacodyl Suppository per rectum.
2. May manually disimpact as needed.

9. CONSTIPATION:

1. Give MOM 30 cc by mouth or PEG.

10. MOUTH INJURIES:

1. Glyoxide application 3 times a day for 5 days.
2. Refer to the physician or dentist as needed.

11. RUNNY NOSE:

Nalex-A:

1. Age greater than 12, give 1 tablet or 2 teaspoons 3 times a day 5 days, or
2. Age less than 12, give 1 teaspoon or ½ tablet 3 times a day 5 days with first and last dose being at least 12 hours apart and middle dose being at least 4 hours from first and last. (Ex. 7am, 4pm, 8pm, or 8am, 12am, 8pm)

OR

Rondec:

1. Age greater that 6, give 1 tablet or 1 tsp. three times a day 5 days, or
2. Age less that 6, give ½ tsp. of the liquid three times a day 5 days with first and last dose being at least 12 hours apart and middle dose being at least 4 hours from first and last. (Ex. 7am, 4pm, 8pm, or 8am, 12am, 8pm)

NAME: _____   CASE NUMBER: _____

12. FOR RED EYES WITH DRAINAGE/CONJUNCTIVITIS: Bacitracin or Neosporin Ophthalmologic Ointment 3 times a day for 5 days with first and last dose being at least 12 hours apart.

13. DIAPER RASH: A & D Ointment as needed and with every diaper change.

14. PURULENT EAR DRAINAGE: Cortisporin Otic Suspension or Cortaine-B, 4 drops in affected ear 4 times a day for 7 days. Do not use if there is a known tympanic membrane perforation or PE Tubes.

15 COUGH:

1. For clients 12 and above, give Robitussin DM 3 teaspoons 4 times a day for 7 days.
2. For clients 12 and under, give 2 teaspoons of Robitussin DM 4 times a day for 7 days.

(*continues*)

FIGURE 9-5   (*continued*)

---

16. EAR WAX (REMOVAL: (Do not use if there is a known tympanic membrane perforation or PE Tubes.)

   1. Cerumenex 3 or 4 drops in affected ear at 8 PM and repeat again at 8 AM the next morning. OR

   2. For more stubborn cerumen: Cerumenex 3 to 4 drops in affected ear 3 times a day for 5 days

   3. Then irrigate with warm water after the Cerumenex treatment.

17. FINGER STICK GLUCOSE: Do a finger stick glucose for signs and symptoms of hypoglycemia or hyperglycemia (nausea, diaphoresis, shakiness, decreased level of consciousness).

   1. If glucose is less than 70, give juice and sugar or Instaglucose and reiheck in 15 minutes. If still less than 70, continue with juice and sugar and/or Instaglucose, check complete set of vitals and notify MD.

   2. If glucose is greater than 400, check complete set of vitals and notify MD.

18. ROUTINE MEDICATION ORDERS THAN RUN OUT ON THE WEEKENDS OR HOLIDAYS: Continue same medications and dosages until the next working day.

19. For any acute illness or change in status, check a complete set of vitals (Blood Pressure, Temperature, Pulse, Respirations) and notify MD.

DO NOT GIVE ANY OF THE ABOVE MEDICATIONS IF ALLERGIC. ANY SPECIFIC ORDERS ON ANY CLIENT SUPERCEDES THESE STANDING ORDERS.

Physician	Date	Nurse	Date

NAME: _____   CASE NUMBER: _____

Courtesy Hudspeth Regional center, Whitfield, MS. Used with permission.

administration of drugs but also of specific protocols that staff members are required to follow in using the medications prescribed for the individual.

The medication administration record (MAR) is a tool used by nursing staffs to initial for the medication administered during their shift. The reverse side of the form is used to explain why medications were not administered—for example, the person was out on pass, NPO (nothing by mouth) prior to surgery, or the person refused medication. The director of nursing and the pharmacist use this form in their medication reviews, to check for problem areas, for incidents in medication administration, and in guidelines when inservice training or other corrective measures are required.

The individual medication and chart audit review summary is used on a monthly basis to audit services provided to the person, such as medications and behavior monitoring activities. This form is used primarily by the director of nursing in medication reviews for checking problem areas, such as incidents in medication administration and in guidelines when inservice training or more severe corrective measures/actions are required. The information could be noted on the medication administration record or on the individual medication and chart audit review summary. Some facilities and nursing staffs elect to conduct their medication review and chart audit on separate forms.

The medication worksheet is a computerized summary used by the nursing staff to assist in the review and audit of medication administration and may be used in conjunction with the process covered in this section. A self-administration of medication progress form is valuable for recording an individual's skill in self-medication administration.

The medication destruction record is used when the medication becomes outdated or unused quantities of medications must be destroyed.

The discharge from facility release of responsibility and medication form is vital when individuals leave the facility and medication is being administered. Often, medication issues can be addressed and the staff alerted to possible medication problems through use of this form. The medication count can reveal if the individual was overdosed, underdosed, or the medication was not given correctly.

The seizure chart provides documentation on individuals with convulsive disorders. This form allows recording of the frequency, time of day, and kinds of seizures, and can assist the staff in adjusting medication for the control of seizures.

Behavior modification is often a major concern in an ICF/IID. To meet the legal and medical needs set forth, forms such as restraint documentation are required in the tracking of restraint use and become valuable in addressing such issues on a timely basis, such as in quarterly summary reviews.

Graphic records, such as weight, are helpful to various services. For example, the dietary department must provide menus based on individuals' diagnoses and nutritional needs. Nursing may have to check the weight records for administration of medications, especially for children. Monitoring of vital signs and menstrual information also is tracked.

The influenza vaccine authorization and administration record serves a dual purpose. The form is sent to the family to obtain permission or refusal for giving the person the flu vaccine. If the response is affirmative, the second portion of the form is used to document administration of the vaccine.

SELF REVIEW 9.5

1. The length of time a deceased patient's medical record is retained is determined by the state's _____.

2. What coding system is used by psychiatrists and psychologists to assign codes to their evaluations and consultations?

3. The *Code of Federal Regulations* cites this publication as its source of definitions for intellectual disability: _____.

4. Which one of the following would be included in the Administrative Data?

   a. Medication Inventory

   b. Physician's Orders

   c. Behavior Modifications

   d. Ongoing Inventory of Individual Belongings

5. The goals and objectives that the staff will assist the individual to attain during the coming year are documented in the _____.

6. True or False? When documenting on the core team summary sheet, it is permissible for the staff to draw a line through it to indicate that a goal has been met.

QUALITY IMPROVEMENT AND UTILIZATION MANAGEMENT

To continue providing excellent care and supports to individuals, every area of a facility must be involved in continuous quality improvement. To make sure that individuals are in the proper setting, utilization management is essential.

Quality Improvement

The purpose of the quality improvement (QI) function is to ensure that each department and service accomplishes its mission completely. This task ultimately is a facility-wide endeavor. Quality must be incorporated into all of the services provided and measured according to acceptable standards. These standards usually are developed as guidelines in meeting licensing and accrediting requirements.

QI can involve a wide range of activities: studies conducted by the Infection Control Committee; comparisons of the frequency of accidents/incidents, medication errors, or seizure frequency; and review of yearly required training in universal precautions and cardiopulmonary resuscitation. Review of the various drills for fire, weather conditions, and toxic spills can be included in the QI function. Other examples of QI in action are audits of documentation requirements on a monthly, quarterly, and yearly basis.

Utilization Management

Utilization management (UM) relates to caring for each individual in the most appropriate setting and also relates to the efficient use of resources. The interdisciplinary team reviews the person's progress at regular intervals and places the individual in the most appropriate care setting. UM also is part of the work of various standing committees. For example, the formulary committee attempts to obtain the medications recommended by the medical and dental staff at the most reasonable price. Department heads and supervisors, too, can practice UM techniques in their daily activities as they strive to provide efficient, quality services.

SELF REVIEW 9.6

1. Quality improvement standards usually are developed to meet _____ and _____ requirements.

2. Provide an example of a quality improvement activity.

3. Differentiate quality improvement and utilization management,

RISK MANAGEMENT AND LEGAL ISSUES

Risk management includes, but is not limited to, reviewing deaths, studying incidents and accidents, correcting errors, changing records properly, and using new technology correctly. Legal issues that must be considered are confidentiality, production of records, policies and procedures for health information, and record retention.

Risk Management

Depending on the organization of the ICF/IID, the governing body, along with its legal counsel, oversees the legal issues and sets the parameters under which the facility must operate. The records maintained by the facility can be risk management's best friend or worst enemy, depending on the documentation contained within the record. Following are some of the areas in which risk management may be involved in the ICF/IID.

Deaths

Usually, every death is automatically reviewed in depth, no matter if the death occurred in-house or in another health care facility. The risk management committee leaves no stone unturned in verifying that all necessary steps were taken to prevent the death from occurring. This investigation is particularly important in deaths that have occurred unexpectedly or without a previous disease process.

Incidents and Accidents

Risk management is responsible for studying every incident and accident report to see if the situation possibly could have been avoided. Often, computer programs are designed to study the incident/accident and the time of day (by shift and hour), place, cause of incident, most effective intervention, and the injury sustained. This information is placed on a grid. From the computer printout, the staff may ascertain something as simple as a hole in a shower curtain allowing puddles of water to accumulate. With this sort of information, the staff can correct the situation and prevent individuals from being placed in an unsafe environment.

Method of Correcting Errors

To eliminate any suspicion of fraudulent documentation, the staff must use the proper method to correct documentation errors. The correct method for changing an entry in a paper record is to draw a single line through an incorrect entry without completely obliterating it. The person making the correction also should date and initial the correction.

Editing Documentation in Records

An addendum should be used when information in a person's record is incorrect. By retaining the original form and including an addendum, legal questions about a change can be reduced. The addendum should include date, time, reason for the change, and signature of the person entering the addendum, followed by professional credentials, such as MD, RN, or other.

Use of Technology

The risk management staff should stay abreast of the possible legal issues involved in the use of technology ranging from electronic signatures to faxing of information. The facility's policies and procedures should address the potential risks of using different types of information technology. A major function of risk management is to watch for changes in laws, regulations, and best practices regarding privacy and security of electronic information.

Legal Issues

Confidentiality

Confidentiality issues are a major concern in an ICF/IID. During their formal educational programs, medical professionals and other professional staff members generally receive training in how to safeguard confidential information. As records become more user-friendly and are placed in the areas where individuals live, direct-care workers must be provided with in-depth inservice training in protecting confidential information. All chart handlers should sign statements agreeing to protect the confidentiality of individual information, and a breach of this responsibility would make the employee subject to disciplinary action, up to and including dismissal.

The confidentiality statement should be obtained from all authorized record handlers before their first handling of any records. All data contained within the record may not be discussed with anyone who has not obtained the appropriate clearance for use of the record. As a rule, no person should be allowed to review an individual's record unless he or she has a job-related need to do so.

With the easy availability of copiers and printers, unnecessary copies of records sometimes are made. All data produced by the facility (originals) should become a part of the person's permanent record. Copies of information from other health services and copies of data retained for reference and/or proof of work completed should be stamped with a "copy" indicator, which would signal to the staff that this information is to be retained as a permanent record. All unnecessary data should be destroyed by shredding.

HIPAA Health Insurance Portability and Accountability Act, which protects the privacy of individually identifiable health information.

HIPAA (Health Insurance Portability and Accountability Act) and related legislation such as the HITECH Act intensified the need for scrutiny in maintaining the confidentiality of protected information in ICF/IID facilities. Facilities have taken steps to ensure compliance with both the privacy standards and the security standards of HIPAA. In taking the protection of confidentiality to a higher level, facilities typically have appointed privacy and security officers and enhanced staff training programs. Policies involving actions such as release of records to third parties, use of photos on bulletin boards, persistence in obtaining parental permissions, and labeling personal articles have been reviewed and brought into compliance. Training procedures have been put into place for business associate activities that require identification of individuals. Maintaining these higher standards will require that compliance with the federal law is everyone's responsibility through continued staff training and advocacy for individual rights. Health information managers have a vital role in this process.

Protection of Records

Individual records are the property of the facility and, as such, should be protected from loss, damage, tampering, or use by unauthorized individuals. Records may be removed from the facility's jurisdiction and safekeeping only in accordance with court order, subpoena, or statute.

Written Policies and Procedures

Written policies and procedures must be in place governing access to, publication of, and dissemination of information from individuals' records. Some points to consider in the management of information are as follows.

Policies should be inclusive and applicable on a facility-wide basis. Inservice training sessions should be implemented for new employees and also serve as a reminder and reference for tenured employees. Procedures can be department/service-specific and are not necessarily applicable on a facility-wide level.

In the ICF/IID setting, policies and procedures may vary depending on the type of facility and the services rendered, but they all must have established guidelines. Some infractions in the day-to-day handling (mishandling) of an individual's records could lead not only to dismissal of the employee for not performing his or her job according to policy/procedure but also fines, imprisonment, and even the loss of license, certification, or accreditation, depending on the severity of the offense.

Record Retention

Laws vary from state to state. Therefore, the retention schedule should be consistent with the state's statute of limitations.

For historical and research purposes, it is recommended that if the individual's records are not retained in their entire original format after the retention period, at least a "skeleton" of the most vital data be considered for retention, for archival purposes.

Health information managers should work with administration, legal staff, or state research centers (e.g., genetic research) to determine the most useful information to retain to enhance specialty study areas and general population data requirements.

The "overretention" of beneficial information in essence becomes a judgment call. The cost of maintaining the data in the original, imaged, or electronic format is a decision factor that must be weighed carefully against the need to retrieve useful information from closed records in the future.

1. List four examples of what is included in risk management.
2. Confidentiality, policies, procedures, and record retention would be considered _____ issues.
3. True or False? To correct a documentation error in a paper medical record, the person who made the error should erase the entry or use "white-out" or correcting tape to cover up the error.
4. True or False? ICF/IID facilities have hired or appointed privacy and security officers to meet the high privacy and security standards of the facility.

ROLE OF THE HEALTH INFORMATION MANAGEMENT PROFESSIONAL

The role of the HIM professional may be either as a regular employee or as a consultant to the facility. The health information manager serving as a regular employee performs duties and responsibilities that are relevant to all levels of management. When issues and problems in the management of the records arise, the expertise of this professional is sought facility-wide. This is doubly true because the most active portion of the individual's record is not housed in the HIM department but, rather, in the living unit. Development of policies and procedures in the handling of records must consider activities more far-reaching than the processes that take place in the centralized department of health information services.

Major duties and responsibilities fall into the following categories:

- Management
- Risk management/legal aspects
- Supervision
- Implementation and maintenance of health information systems
- Designing health care records to address the health needs of the facility and the individuals it serves
- Retrieval and storage of health information
- Maintenance of statistical data
- Coding and indexing of records
- Quality improvement

- Completion of all phases of the record including:
  - active records
  - overflow
  - closed records
  - maintenance and storage of imaged records
- Data analysis

The health information manager consultant assists the administration in establishing policies and procedures to address the maintenance, preservation, completion, and confidentiality of records and the release of information. To accomplish facility objectives for this service, the consultant trains personnel assigned to record-keeping services, using methods that include on-the-job training and in-service education.

The major function of the consultant involves quality management in the review and auditing of the facility records. This task encompasses all facility-wide records—administrative, habilitative, and health records.

---

1. Describe the role of a health information manager consultant in an ICF/IID facility. 2. List five major duties and responsibilities performed by a fulltime health information manager in an ICF/IID facility.	**SELF REVIEW 9.8**

TRENDS

Providing services for individuals with intellectual disabilities is undergoing constant change. As mentioned in the introduction of this chapter, the number of persons receiving services in large public or private facilities is decreasing. As noted by Braddock et al. (2002), "Since the 1970s, many states have vigorously reduced their reliance on institutional facilities and developed community residential settings including group homes, foster care, and supported living options" (p. 1). This trend has continued in the twenty-first century. The number of individuals living in an ICF/IID setting decreased by 25% between 1998 and 2008, while the number of individuals receiving home and community based services increased by 118.5% over the same time period (Lakin et al., 2010).

Reasons for the expansion of community services are varied. The number of persons needing services is increasing partly because of the aging of our society and the increased longevity of persons with developmental disabilities. Many individuals and their families are becoming vocal in expressing their needs and desires and want more choices in the types of supports available.

The **Home and Community Based Services (HCBS) Waiver** became available in 1981, enabling states to expand support for community-based services

Home and Community Based Services (HCBS) Waiver   a federal program that allows states to use Medicaid funding to serve persons in their own homes and communities, not just in institutional settings.

through Medicaid funding. By 2008, HCBS had 525,119 HCBS recipients nationwide. Between 1998 and 2008, Medicaid HCBS program expenditures for persons with intellectual and developmental disabilities increased from $7.133 to $22.310 billion—a 213% increase (Lakin et al., 2010). Services provided by the waiver—such as respite care, home health aides, supported employment, transportation, and various health therapies—can postpone or avoid placement in a facility.

Litigation is another factor influencing the growth of community-based programs: In a landmark case decided in 1999, *Olmstead v. Lois Curtis and Elaine Wilson*, the United States Supreme Court ruled that requiring individuals with disabilities to reside in institutions to be able to receive support services may constitute discrimination based on disability. The court determined that the Americans with Disabilities Act called for states to provide community-based services for individuals with disabilities when such services were more appropriate than institutional placements (National Disability Rights Network, 2009).

Lawsuits based on *Olmstead* and other class action suits have been filed to force states to expand services to persons on waiting lists and to those who have been found eligible for Medicaid services but who did not receive them (Braddock et al., 2002). As states often struggle with a weak economy and limited funds to initiate new services, progress toward implementing the provisions of *Olmstead* have not occurred as rapidly as some would like. Care in an institutional setting is one option that may be appropriate for certain individuals with intellectual or developmental disabilities; however, future growth is most likely to occur in the provision of supports that enable individuals to remain in their home communities.

| SELF REVIEW 9.9 | 1. Identify three trends affecting the needs for services in ICF/IID facilities. |
| | 2. How has the HCBS Waiver program enabled states to expand support for community-based services? |

SUMMARY

The ICF/IID setting serves individuals with intellectual disabilities. This chapter has reviewed the technical aspects of ICF/IID services and how they apply to the practical daily work environment. With the guidelines, suggestions, and recommendations discussed here, health information managers have at their fingertips the basic information as a quick reference in the management of individual records.

In the ICF/IID, health care, habilitative, and administrative staffs work with or on behalf of individuals to help them achieve their goals. The ICF/IID must meet federal standards and may choose to meet voluntary accreditation standards. Providing community-based services is the trend for individuals with intellectual disabilities. This chapter provides health information managers, as members of an interdisciplinary team, with a solid foundation from which to build their skills, talents, and knowledge to best meet the needs, objectives, and goals of individuals receiving services in an ICF/IID.

REVIEW QUESTIONS

Knowledge-Based Questions

1. What types of coding may be utilized in an ICF/IID?
2. What are the sections into which the individuals' charts may be divided?
3. Is an admission to an ICF/IID facility permanent? Why or why not?
4. Who performs regular surveys of an ICF/IID facility?
5. How did the U.S. Supreme Court's *Olmstead* decision affect provision of services in an ICF/IID?

Critical Thinking Questions

1. What would you consider to be one of the major issues in an ICF/IID facility? Why?
2. The HIM professional employed on a regular basis and the HIM consultant have different job roles. How do their jobs differ?
3. How do the services rendered to an individual in an ICF/IID differ from those in other health care settings?
4. Why is it so important to study accident and incident situations?

WEB ACTIVITY

Make the following selections at the CMS website, http://www.cms.gov

1. Select "Regulations & Guidance."
2. Under "Legislation," select "Conditions for Coverage (CfCs) & Conditions of Participation (CoPs)."
3. Select "Intermediate Care Facilities for Individuals with Intellectual Disabilities (ICF/IID)."

4. Select the "Related Link" "CONDITIONS OF PARTICIPATION: ICF/MR (483.400-480)."
5. Select Subchapter G, then Part 483, then Subpart I , then either the PDF or XML version of section 483.440.

What information management issues can you identify in Section 483.440 regarding "Active treatment services?"

CASE STUDY

The interdisciplinary team in the XYZ facility was experiencing problems with the habilitative portion of the individuals' records in that the direct care staff was not addressing changes in the program. Recommendations were being made on the quarterly team reviews but were not getting into the program records to be instituted by the direct care staff as required for the continuity of care.

Jean Deaux, a health information management professional, was contacted about this discrepancy in the program. She noted the recommended program changes and that the revised program was not being carried out, along with the lack of some type of documentation to tie these two together.

After studying the problem and the frequency with which it was occurring, she made the following recommendation: The suggested changes were to be covered in an addendum format so that at any time throughout the year when a major change in the individual's

program was instituted, the change would be reflected in the 24-hour schedule, thus alerting the direct care staff of the addition, deletion, and/or change in the program.

To better track the documentation requirements, Ms. Deaux elected to monitor, in her monthly audit of the records, whether program changes were being documented appropriately and to submit any variance in the program to the assigned QDDP.

1. Who is the "assigned QDDP?" Why do you think Ms. Deaux elected to report variances to the QDDP?
2. How could electronic health records or electronic information systems have made a difference in this situation?
3. Would you have done anything different or additional had you been in Ms. Deaux's place? If so, what would it be?

REFERENCES AND SUGGESTED READINGS

AAIDD (American Association on Intellectual and Developmental Disabilities). (2010). *Intellectual Disability: Definition, Classification, and Systems of Supports* (11th ed.). Washington, DC: Author.

American Psychiatric Association. (2013). Highlights of Changes from DSM-IV-TR to DSM-5. Available at http://www.dsm5.org/Documents/changes%20 from%20dsm-iv-tr%20to%20dsm-5.pdf

Applicability and definitions. (2011 ed.). *Code of Federal Regulations*, Title 42, Pt. 483, Sec. 102.

Braddock, D., Hemp, R., Rizzolo, M. C., Parish, S., & Pomeranz, A. (2002, June). *The State of the States in Developmental Disabilities: (2002) Study Summary.* Boulder, CO: University of Colorado, Coleman Institute for Cognitive Disabilities and Department of Psychiatry.

Centers for Medicare & Medicaid Services. (n.d.). *Interpretive Guidelines—Intermediate Care Facilities for the Mentally Retarded.* [Online]. http://www .cms.gov/manuals/Downloads/som107ap_j _intermcare.pdf [2011, March 17].

Conditions of Participation for Intermediate Care Facilities for the Mentally Retarded. (2009). *Code of Federal Regulations*, Title 42, Pt. 483, Subpart I, (2009 ed.), § 483.400 through § 483.480.

Council on Quality and Leadership. (2005). Accredited Organizations. [Online]. http://www.thecouncil .org [2010, August 7].

Council on Quality and Leadership. (2005). *Personal Outcome Measures.* Towson, MD: Author. [Online]. http://www.thecouncil.org [2010, August 7].

Goel, N.L, & Keefe, R.H. (2003). Medicaid managed care meets developmental disabilities: Proceed with caution. *Journal of Health & Social Policy, 16*(3), 75–90.

Hewitt, A., & O'Nell, S. (1998, August). Preface. *I Am Who I Am,* Y. Bestgen (Ed.). [Online]. http:// www.acf.hhs.gov/programs/pcpid/docs/help4 .pdf [2010, August 7].

Janicki, M. P. (1992). Lifelong disability and aging. In L.Rowitz (Ed.), *Mental Retardation in the Year 2000.* New York: Springer-Verlag.

Lakin, K.C., Scott, N., Larson, S., & Salmi, P. (2010). Changes in service recipients and expenditures in Medicaid long-term services and supports programs for persons with intellectual and developmental disabilities, 1998–2008. *Intellectual & Developmental Disabilities, 48*(1), 80–83.

National Disability Rights Network. (2009, September 30). *A Decade of "Little Progress" Implementing Olmstead: Evaluating Federal Agency Impact After 10 years.* [Online]. http://www.napas.org/Decade_of_Little _Progress_Implementing_Olmstead.pdf [2010, August 7].

The Joint Commission (TJC). (2009). *2010 Portable Comprehensive Accreditation Manual for Behavioral Health Care.* Oak Brook, IL: Author.

KEY RESOURCES

American Association on Intellectual and Developmental Disabilities
    http://www.aamr.org or http://www. aaidd.org

The Arc of the United States
    http://TheArc.org

Council on Quality and Leadership (formerly Accreditation Council on Services for People with Developmental Disabilities)
    http://www.c-q-l.org

The Joint Commission
    http://www.jointcommission.org

Long-Term Care

Barbara A. Gorenflo, RHIA | Kris King, MS, RHIA, CPHQ

LEARNING OBJECTIVES

Upon successful completion of this chapter, you should be able to:

- Describe the type of care and caregivers typically associated with long-term care facilities.
- Discuss the impact of stringent state and federal regulation on the long-term care industry and its effect on information management and documentation content.
- Identify the significance of state and federal surveys to long-term care facilities.
- Describe the types of reimbursement and payer relationships within a long-term care facility.
- Describe the purpose of the *minimum data set* and its use in the federal survey process and in case-mix payment systems.
- Identify the priorities for health information management in the long-term care setting.

Setting	Description	Synonym/Examples
Freestanding Nursing Facility	A facility or a portion of a facility licensed by the state as a nursing facility or nursing home, where the majority of patients are regarded as permanent residents for long-term nursing care	Nursing facility (NF) Nursing home Long-term care facility (formerly called intermediate care facility)
Freestanding Skilled Nursing Facility	A facility or a portion of a facility licensed by the state as a skilled nursing facility and certified, either wholly or in part, as a Medicare Part A skilled nursing facility provider	Skilled nursing facility (SNF) Skilled nursing unit
Acute Care Hospital	A designated area, attached wing, or a separate structure on the hospital campus that is licensed for skilled nursing care	Distinct part SNF Skilled nursing facility (SNF) Skilled nursing unit SNF unit

INTRODUCTION TO SETTING

Long-term care typically describes the care of frail, institutionalized elderly people and those who are permanent residents of a nursing facility. For purposes of this chapter, long-term care does not include boarding care, assisted living, residential care, long-term care for individuals with mental illness, individuals with intellectual disabilities (ICF/IID), or other types of institutionalized care settings that are not subject to the federal long-term care regulations or the state licensure regulations for a **nursing facility (NF)**, or a **skilled nursing facility (SNF)**.

With the exception of ICF/IID facilities, these other components of the care continuum are less regulated and do not have the broad range of caregivers found in the typical long-term care facility. As stated in federal regulations, the term *nursing facility* is defined as a facility that is qualified for reimbursement under the Medicaid program. A *skilled nursing facility* meets the requirements for reimbursement under Medicare. The definitions can be found at www.cms.gov (CMS, 2009a).

The discussion of the long-term care setting in this chapter relates to nursing facilities and skilled nursing facilities. Although nursing facilities and LTCHs both are considered to be "long-term care," LTCHs and skilled nursing facilities represent two distinctly different levels of care, with different licensing and different payment systems. LTCH facilities are licensed as hospitals and have their own prospective payment system (PPS) under Medicare.

As the percentage of our population age 65 and older continues to grow, there will likely be several different care settings that will fall under the global term of *long-term care*; however, this chapter addresses long-term care as it applies to the settings and care descriptions identified.

Types of Patients

In the long-term care setting the term *patient* is often replaced with *resident*, because the person receiving care is not only a recipient of nursing care but,

nursing facility (NF) an institution or a distinct part of an institution that provides skilled nursing care, rehabilitation services, or health-related care to individuals who, because of their condition, require services above the level of room and board. Either a registered nurse or a licensed practical nurse is on active duty at all times. If properly licensed and certified, a nursing facility may receive reimbursement under the Medicaid program.

skilled nursing facility (SNF) an institution or a distinct part of an institution that provides skilled nursing care or rehabilitation services. Either a registered nurse or a licensed practical nurse is on active duty at all times. If properly licensed and certified, a skilled nursing facility may obtain a Medicare provider agreement and be reimbursed under the Medicare program.

in many cases, also is residing in the facility permanently. The nursing facility becomes the home or place of residence, and, as such, the facility is responsible for providing quality of care, as well as high quality of life under the long-term care regulations.

Within the broad category of *long-term care*, more specific distinctions can be drawn to describe the types of residents and the care they receive. As specialization of services increases within the long-term care industry, facilities find the need to categorize levels of care and often physically separate types of care to distinct units or floors within the same facility. Therefore, residents can be placed in areas with other residents who have similar care needs.

Permanent Residents Receiving Nonskilled Care

These residents are distinguished by their need for general oversight and supervision in performing **activities of daily living (ADL)** (e.g., bathing, eating, dressing); however, their needs generally can be met without the direct care or services of a licensed professional on a 24-hour basis. Although a licensed practical nurse or registered nurse supervises their general care under the direction of the attending physician, their immediate care needs—such as injections, intravenous therapy, parenteral feeding, or skilled wound care—do not involve direct skilled treatment on a daily basis.

From a level-of-care perspective, these residents require more care than those in a residential, boarding, or assisted living environment, either because of cognitive impairment or physical incapacity. For example, these residents, either because of physical or cognitive impairment, could not negotiate their way to safety in an emergency. Their daily care needs, however, do not require continual intervention by a licensed nurse or other skilled health care professional.

Permanent Residents, Special Care

The **special care unit (SCU)** often is a distinct service within a long-term care facility. For example, some of these units are designed to care specifically for Alzheimer's residents who benefit from a physical environment that is quiet, homelike, and adapted to their specific cognitive impairment. The physical separation of this unit assures that the residents are afforded the opportunity to move throughout the area without fear of wandering off the property. In addition, staff members assigned to these units usually receive special training in the care of Alzheimer's residents, because their needs typically are more behavior oriented than medically oriented. Other special care units may be designed for patients using ventilators or those with special needs.

Permanent Residents, Skilled Care

In contrast to the permanent residents who do not receive daily skilled care, permanent residents requiring skilled care receive services from one or more licensed professionals on a frequent, and often daily, basis. Typically, these

activities of daily living (ADL) for purposes of the federal long-term care regulations, activities of daily living include the resident's ability to (1) bathe, dress, and groom; (2) transfer and ambulate; (3) toilet; (4) eat; and (5) use speech, language, or other functional communication systems (CMS, 2011). Federal regulations include ADL as a component part of the quality-of-care requirements, and information concerning individual resident ADL capability is a significant portion of the monitoring information in the minimum data set.

special care unit (SCU) a distinct service within a long-term care facility such as an Alzheimer SCU.

residents have received as much benefit from rehabilitation services as can be reasonably expected, and their improvement or progression has plateaued. As a result, their potential to be discharged is not good. Types of care include the need for continuous tube feeding, long-term ventilator care, complex wound care, and/or an aggregate combination of nursing and restorative professionals to meet the daily care needs of feeding, performing ADLs, and maintaining the highest functional level for as long as possible.

Often, the term *heavy care* is used to describe the care needs of these residents because of the intensity of their dependence on the staff for mobility, toileting, bathing, eating, and performing all ADLs. Their care can be described as more custodial in nature.

Short-Term Patients

A short-term patient in a long-term care facility generally is considered as one whose length of stay is less than 100 days, and in the traditional health care sense would be regarded as a patient, because the intent is to ultimately discharge the patient to a more independent level of care. In some long-term care facilities, the distinct unit in which these patients are found is categorized as a **sub-acute care** unit, where patients are provided with a higher level of care than that associated with the traditional skilled nursing setting. Care in these distinct units consists of skilled care for treatment of a specific condition, and often placement is temporary because the goal of treatment is rehabilitation to discharge the patient home or to a lower level of care. In some situations, discharge from this unit may correlate with an internal transfer to a long-term care bed within the same facility.

sub-acute care   a transitional type of care representing a level of service that is less intensive than traditional acute care but is more goal-oriented and resource-intensive than what generally is regarded as skilled nursing care.

Respite Care

Respite care involves a short stay for the purpose of providing relief or "respite" to the primary caregivers of frail elderly people who cannot live in an independent environment and do not require the intensity of services and supervision required of the traditional long-term care facility. The period of respite care may range anywhere from overnight to several weeks, depending on the caregiver's needs. In respite care admissions, a long-term care facility provides meals and general supervision to assure that the necessary medications are administered and also provides a safe environment for the respite residents, with opportunities for socialization and no need for active care intervention.

Types of Caregivers

Licensed Physicians

Doctors of medicine and osteopathy are responsible for overall medical supervision in the long-term care facility; however, their physical presence in the nursing facility generally is limited. Frequency of visits to a long-term care resident can range from once a month to once a year, depending on the level of care the resident requires. In some instances, the physician does not actually visit the nursing facility but, instead, requires that the resident be transported to his or her office for necessary medical examinations. Therefore, the majority of communication with the physician is done through the nursing staff via telephone rather than face-to-face encounters with the physician.

In the SNF or sub-acute units of long-term care facilities, frequency of physician involvement is generally greater and can range to several visits a week, with monthly visits being the outside range, depending on the level of acuity of the SNF/sub-acute unit. The minimum visit requirement for physician visits in the SNF and sub-acute units is once every 30 days for the first 90 days and then every 60 days thereafter.

Advanced Practice Clinicians

Advanced practice clinicians, such as nurse practitioners, clinical nurse specialists, and physician assistants, work with physicians to care for their patients who reside in long-term care facilities. Particularly in rural settings, the availability of advanced practice clinicians enables more contact with the resident than if only a physician were making visits to the nursing facility.

Registered Nurses

Registered nurses are the primary coordinators of daily care within the long-term care facility. Because physicians ordinarily do not visit residents daily in most long-term care settings, care is nursing-driven. In most regulatory environments, the director of nursing is required to be a licensed, registered nurse. Depending on the number of beds, the facility will employ additional registered nurses for supervisory positions or as charge nurses on specific nursing units.

Licensed Practical Nurses

Licensed practical nurses are the most predominant caregivers among the licensed professionals in the long-term care nursing facility setting. Their responsibilities range from administering medications, tube feedings, and treatments to being in charge of a nursing division and serving in a supervisory capacity within the nursing department.

Nursing Assistants

Nursing assistants comprise the bulk of the nursing department in a long-term care nursing facility. They are nonlicensed staff members who have completed a basic training course for providing daily care needs to geriatric patients, including basic skills in bathing, transfer training, lifting, range of motion, and related supportive services that would be provided under the general supervision of a licensed nurse.

In some facilities, a distinction is made for nursing assistants who strictly provide restorative therapy. They are called restorative aides or rehabilitation aides. With additional training from licensed therapists, the restorative or rehabilitation aides have the responsibility for providing maintenance services to residents after skilled rehabilitation has been discontinued. At this point in the resident's care, a plateau has been reached and no active improvement is expected from continued skilled therapy. The restorative therapy is intended to maintain the level of functioning that has been achieved from skilled therapy and/or to prevent further functional decline.

Certified Medication Technicians

In some states, a certified medication technician (CMT) is a distinct type of caregiver in the long-term care setting, provided for in the state's long-term care regulations. Requirements for this position typically include a minimum of nursing assistant training with an additional course in medication administration. The scope of competency requirements varies with each state's regulations. The purpose of this caregiver category is to recognize a lower-cost health care position with limited responsibilities that can lessen the workload of licensed nursing professionals.

Social Services

Providing medically related social services to residents is assigned to the department that typically is described as "social services" in the long-term care setting. Depending on the size of the facility, this department may or may not be staffed with a credentialed social worker (BSW or MSW). Federal long-term care regulations require that a facility with more than 120 beds employ a fulltime social worker or a person with qualifications outlined in the federal requirements.

These requirements describe a qualified social worker as an individual with a bachelor's degree in social work or a bachelor's degree in a human services field such as sociology, special education, rehabilitation counseling, or psychology and with one year of supervised social work experience in a health care setting working directly with individuals.

In the long-term care setting, the social services staff takes on many responsibilities that affect the care and well-being of the residents, such as making arrangements for adaptive equipment, clothing, and financial assistance; coordinating discharge planning; coordinating and initiating referrals and appointments with outside services; providing counseling to residents, family members, and facility staff as related to the care needs of individual residents; and providing any other services that promote the psychosocial well-being of the residents. Social services staff members are advocates for many residents who no longer are able to protect their rights to decision-making, fair treatment, dignity, respect, and so on, or who cannot realize what their rights are.

Activities/Therapeutic Recreation

Although therapeutic recreation is not a direct care service in the same category as administration of a treatment or a medication, providing stimulating activities or therapeutic recreation services is extremely important in the long-term care setting. In most long-term care facilities, a licensed or credentialed individual does not necessarily direct the activity program. Licensing of activity professionals other than recreational therapists is not universal in each state. Federal regulations provide several alternative options as qualifications for an activity professional, including two years of direct experience in a patient activities program in a health care setting and/or completion of a training program approved by the state agency.

The activities for which the staff is responsible include assessing the therapeutic recreational needs and preferences of each resident and developing an individualized program that responds to those needs. The program includes providing sufficient group and individual activity and recreational programs to respond to the needs of the various levels of care within the facility. The types of activity programs within the scope of the typical long-term care facility include planning and providing for outings such as shopping and recreational activities off the premises of the facility; planning and providing supplies and materials for independent, in-room activities; establishing small-group programs such as reminiscence therapy for residents with cognitive impairments; conducting in-room, one-on-one activities such as music therapy and tactile stimulation for room-bound and unresponsive residents; and planning and conducting facility-wide social events for residents and their families.

If a facility population consists of mostly alert and oriented residents with limited physical impairments, the recreational program is much different than that for a population of semi-comatose residents or residents with severe dementia. As a result, the therapeutic activities program must be responsive to the varying needs of the resident population.

Independent Contractors

In the long-term care facility, most of the ancillary services and many of the professional services are provided through independent contracts with outside resources such as those of laboratory, radiology, pharmacy, and rehabilitation, including physical, occupational, speech, and respiratory therapy services. As independent contractors, these providers are not employees of the facility and usually are not present physically within the facility on a fulltime basis.

Laboratory and Radiology   Laboratory and radiology services may be necessary to further evaluate or treat chronic or acute medical conditions, and these services are performed in accordance with physician orders. Laboratory and radiology services are evaluated in terms of their timeliness of response to stat and routine calls and for the additional services they provide for enhancing the overall quality of health information. For example, laboratory services typically provide the facility with a monthly computerized report outlining the types of tests performed in the previous month, patterns and trends with respect to nosocomial infections, use of antimicrobial agents, and related infection control issues.

Rehabilitation Services   Rehabilitation services such as physical therapy, occupational therapy, and speech therapy usually are provided through independently contracted arrangements, because the volume of rehabilitation cases in the typical long-term care facility does not warrant fulltime employees in any of the respective rehabilitation disciplines. Registered physical and occupational therapists visit the facility based on the volume of skilled therapy services required by the resident population. Often, these services are supplemented by physical therapy and occupational therapy assistants, who provide the daily therapy under the general supervision of the registered therapist. Speech therapists provide daily skilled therapy for dysphagia and dysphasia, primarily in the post-acute care of patients who have had a cerebrovascular accident.

Respiratory Therapists   Respiratory therapists are more prevalent in facilities with long-term ventilator patients and facilities with a high number of residents requiring daily suctioning and respiratory therapy treatments.

Registered Dietitians   Federal regulations and many licensure regulations require the services of a registered dietitian on either a fulltime or consulting basis. In the larger long-term care facilities, those with more than 150 beds, a registered dietitian may be a fulltime employee of the facility, particularly if the resident population predominantly requires skilled care and has more complex nutritional care needs. If a registered dietitian is not employed in the facility fulltime, the day-to-day management of the dietary service is the responsibility of a food services manager, while the dietitian, during regularly scheduled consultation visits, approves menus for therapeutic diets and provides individual clinical assessments for residents with high risk or clinically complex nutritional needs. Diet technicians also may be utilized to assist with nutritional care under the supervision of a registered dietitian.

Registered Pharmacists   With rare exceptions, pharmaceutical services are not available directly within a long-term care facility and instead are provided by a supplier that is not close to the facility. The services of a pharmacist also are required by the long-term care federal regulations, either on a fulltime, part-time, or consulting basis. The consulting pharmacist role may or may not be provided by the same entity that services the facility as the pharmaceutical supplier. The provider of drugs and biologicals or the actual pharmaceutical service is responsible for ensuring that medications are dispensed to the facility in a timely and appropriate manner.

The responsibilities of the facility pharmacy consultant are somewhat different, in that consultation extends to all facets of providing pharmacy services within the facility and includes performing a monthly drug regimen review for each resident in the facility to evaluate potential irregularities in the administration of medications. This includes monitoring for unnecessary drugs, evaluating proper dosages and indications for psychotropic medications, and evaluating internal storage and administration procedures within the facility. This review is required by the federal regulations and can be accessed by long-term care surveyors in the event of a question regarding the medication profile of a specific resident.

SELF REVIEW 10.1

1. True or False? Long-term care typically describes care of the frail, institutionalized elderly or those who are permanent residents of a nursing facility.

2. _____ is a facility that is qualified for reimbursement under Medicare.

3. _____ facilities are licensed as hospitals and have their own prospective payment system under Medicare.

4. In long-term care settings, the patient often is referred to as a(n) _____.

5. A short-term patient in a long-term care facility generally has a length of stay fewer than _____ days.

   a. 50

   b. 100

   c. 75

6. Describe respite care.

7. What type of caregiver is responsible for the overall medical supervision in the long-term care hospital?

8. Matching

   a. Primary coordinators of daily care within the long-term care facility:

   b. They comprise the bulk of the nursing department in a long-term care nursing facility:

   c. Department providing medically related social services to residents:

   d. Predominant caregivers among the licensed professionals in the long-term care nursing facility setting:

      1. __B__ nursing assistant

      2. __A__ registered nurse

      3. __C__ social services

      4. __D__ licensed practical nurse

9. List three types of activities associated with the long-term care facility.

10. True or False? Most ancillary services provided in long-term care facilities are through independent contractors.

REGULATORY ISSUES

The long-term care industry is one of the most— if not the most—highly regulated industries in the United States. In addition to federal regulations for long-term care facilities participating in Medicare and Medicaid, each state has separate licensure laws applying to long-term care facilities. In the case of overlapping or conflicting laws, the facility is obligated to abide by the more stringent of the two laws.

The **standard survey** is unannounced and is conducted at least every 15 months. The two general survey outcomes are *substantial compliance* and *substandard quality of care*. **Substantial compliance** means that any deficiencies the surveyors find are deemed to be of minimal potential for harm to the residents. **Substandard quality of care** means that surveyors find one or more deficiencies that constitute either immediate jeopardy to resident health or safety; a pattern of widespread actual harm that is not immediate jeopardy; or a widespread potential for more than minimal harm but less than immediate jeopardy, with no actual harm (e-CFR, 2015). Results of all surveys are accessible to the public, with federal regulations requiring that the most recent survey be posted in a public area of the facility for easy access by residents, family members, and the general public.

In addition to the certification and the **licensure survey**, long-term care facilities are subject to surveys conducted in response to complaint investigations, which result from calls to the state agency concerning care concerns and potential regulatory violations. These survey findings also are subject to public access and can affect the facility's license in the event of substantial noncompliance. Table 10-1 provides examples of several surveys to which a long-term care facility may be subjected.

In 1995, federal enforcement regulations were implemented by the Health Care Financing Administration (now CMS), outlining remedies, including **civil money penalties** of up to $10,000 per day, for findings of substantial noncompliance and substandard quality of care. In addition to federal enforcement regulations, individual states may pass legislation that also gives the state agency authority for fines and civil money penalties. Therefore, findings of substandard quality during a facility survey can result in civil money penalties from both the federal and the state licensing agency.

Further, federal enforcement regulations provide for mandated temporary management of a facility, termination from the Medicare/Medicaid program, and denial of Medicare/Medicaid payment for new admissions and/or for all current nursing facility residents, in addition to the civil money penalties. As a result, the regulatory environment and impact of state and federal regulation on the long-term care facility is without comparison in other sectors of the health care industry.

State Licensure

If a long-term care facility does not participate in the Medicare or Medicaid program, federal regulations do not apply, and the facility is subject only to

standard survey
a periodic, resident-centered inspection that gathers information about the quality of service provided in a facility to determine compliance with the requirements of participation in the federal Medicare and Medicaid programs (CMS, 2011).

substantial compliance
a level of compliance with the Conditions of Participation, such that any identified deficiencies pose no greater risk to resident health or safety than the potential for causing minimal harm. Substantial compliance constitutes compliance with participation requirements (CMS, 2011).

substandard quality of care one or more deficiencies that constitute either immediate jeopardy to resident health or safety; a pattern of widespread actual harm that is not immediate jeopardy; or a widespread potential for more than minimal harm, but less than immediate jeopardy, with no actual harm (CMS, 2011).

licensure survey a survey conducted by the state agency to determine compliance of long-term care facilities with state licensure laws.

civil money penalties
fines levied by the federal government against providers who are found to be in substantial noncompliance with federal regulations; may be as much as $10,000 per day.

TABLE 10-1	Types of Surveys Unique to a Long-Term Care Facility

Surveying Agency/Entity	Purpose and Frequency	Potential Impact and Outcome
State licensing agency	Annual licensure renewal and interim review, depending on state law (unannounced)	Written deficiencies requiring a plan of correction and revisit Monetary fines Ban on admissions and other penalties and restrictions, depending on state law
State licensing agency	Complaint investigation in response to state hotline calls concerning abuse and/or neglect (unannounced)	Written deficiencies requiring a plan of correction and revisit Monetary fines Ban on admissions and other penalties and restrictions, depending on state law Full survey in response to findings of substantial noncompliance
Centers for Medicare & Medicaid Services (CMS)	Annual certification for participation in Title XVIII or XIX federal programs (unannounced)	Written deficiencies requiring a plan of correction and letter of credible allegation stating date corrections will be implemented Revisit may or may not be conducted to determine facility compliance Federal agency may conduct follow-up survey to validate findings of state agency Civil money penalties, temporary ban on admissions, and denial of payment for Medicare/Medicaid admissions or current residents, depending on scope and severity of noncompliance
The Joint Commission (TJC)	Optional survey for long-term care facilities and special care and sub-acute units within long-term care facilities (unannounced survey between 18–39 months after previous survey)	Accredited Provisional accreditation Conditional accreditation Preliminary denial of accreditation Denial of accreditation Preliminary accreditation

the state licensure requirements. The respective state legislative bodies pass these requirements, and, consequently, the 50 states vary considerably in the scope of issues promulgated in their long-term care requirements (CMS, 2010a).

Joint Commission Accreditation

The number of long-term care facilities seeking accreditation from The Joint Commission (TJC) is relatively insignificant. There is no clear advantage for a long-term care facility in seeking Joint Commission accreditation, unless it is required as part of an overall hospital accreditation for hospital-owned and -operated long-term care facilities. The Joint Commission has sought deemed status from the Centers for Medicare & Medicaid Services that would present long-term care facilities with the option of choosing between the current survey system by state and federal agencies or applying for Joint Commission long-term care accreditation. At this writing, however, the options are limited, and deemed status for long-term care is approved in only some states.

1. Distinguish between substantial compliance and substandard quality of care.
2. True or False? If a long-term care facility does not participate in the Medicare and Medicaid program, federal regulations still apply.
3. True or False? Long-term care facilities are required to seek Joint Commission accreditation.

DOCUMENTATION

quality of care   a broad category of the long-term care federal regulations that requires a facility to provide the necessary care and services to attain or maintain the highest practicable physical, mental, and psychosocial well-being, in accordance with the comprehensive assessment and plan of care.

quality of life   a broad category of the long-term care federal regulations that requires a facility to care for its residents in a manner and in an environment that promotes maintaining or enhancing each resident's quality of life.

federal survey   a survey based on the federal long-term care requirements using the federal long-term care survey procedures; required for facility participation in the Medicare and/or Medicaid programs.

Quality Indicator Survey (QIS)   a long-term care survey process developed by CMS to standardize resident-centered, outcome-oriented quality review processes.

Documentation in the resident's record has tremendous significance for the nursing facility. Documentation is vital in evaluating how a facility has contributed to and/or affected the **quality of care** and **quality of life** of individual residents, strongly linking documentation with regulatory compliance. In addition, accuracy and appropriateness of documentation affects facility reimbursement by Medicare, Medicaid, and commercial insurance. Finally, as litigation involving negligence for poor outcomes of care becomes more pervasive in the long-term care industry, proper documentation can be crucial in defending a provider against a wrongful claim for failure to provide quality care and services.

Although documentation of key information is important when a resident is transferred or discharged, the primary emphasis on routine documentation monitoring should be concurrent for detecting significant omissions in individual records as well as in identifying key training issues for ongoing staff education and quality improvement.

Federal Requirements

The quality of documentation is highly significant in the **federal survey** process known as the **Quality Indicator Survey (QIS)**, in that the resident record is used as a means of validating positive and negative care outcomes both in the annual survey and in complaint investigations. Survey procedures for the federal long-term care survey process include record review under Task 4, stage I Admission Sample Review and Census Sample Review, where the record is used along with observations and interviews to identify resident-centered outcome and process indicators called Quality of Care Indicators (QCIs). When compared to national norms, QCIs focus on the more detailed quality investigation during stage II of the survey (CMS, 2014).

The **comprehensive resident assessment** is the primary vehicle for evaluating care outcomes in the federal long-term care survey process. It includes at least the following information: (1) medically defined conditions and prior medical history; (2) medical status measurement; (3) physical and mental functional status; (4) sensory and physical impairments; (5) nutritional status and requirements; (6) special treatments or procedures; (7) mental and psychosocial status; (8) discharge potential; (9) dental conditions; (10) activities potential; (11) rehabilitation potential; (12) cognitive status; and (13) drug therapy (CMS, 2011). Comprehensive resident assessment refers not only to the actual resident assessment document but also to the federally mandated **resident assessment instrument (RAI)**. The RAI consists of three basic components: the **minimum data set (MDS)**; the **care area assessment (CAA) process**, formerly **resident assessment protocols (RAPs)**; and **utilization guidelines** as specified in the *Resident Assessment Instrument Manual*. As a process, each of the three basic components flows into the next component. The MDS is a core set of screening, clinical, and functional status elements that constitute a standardized means of assessing all residents in Medicare and/or Medicaid certified facilities. (CMS, 2004)

The Omnibus Budget Reconciliation Act (OBRA) regulations have defined a schedule of assessments that will be performed for a nursing facility resident at admission, quarterly, and annually, whenever the resident experiences a significant change in status, and whenever the facility identifies a significant error in a prior assessment. These are known as **OBRA assessments**. CMS (2009b) states that:

> "...MDS assessments also are required for Medicare payment purposes. When the OBRA and Medicare assessment time frames coincide, one assessment may be used to satisfy both requirements. When combining OBRA and Medicare assessments, the most stringent requirement for MDS completion must be met. It is important for facility staff to fully understand the requirements for both types of assessments in order to avoid unnecessary duplication of effort." (CMS, 2009b, p. 2–1)

Components of the CAA process include care area triggers (CATs), CAA resources, and the care area assessment (CAA) summary. The CAA process provides structure for assessing social, medical, and psychological problems by providing a systematic method for reviewing key components of the MDS and directing caregivers to evaluate causes, interrelationships, and particular strengths that affect the development of the **care plan**.

A key element of this process involves care area triggers (CATs), "specific resident responses for one or a combination of MDS elements. The triggers identify residents who have or are at risk for developing specific functional problems and require further assessment" (CMS, 2010b, p. 1–5). As of this writing, there are 20 CATs:

1. Delirium
2. Cognitive loss/dementia

comprehensive resident assessment a key element in the the long-term care federal regulations, this assessment describes the resident's ability to perform daily life functions and significant impairments in functional capacity.

resident assessment instrument (RAI) a requirement for completing the performance of a standardized assessment system, composed of the MDS, CAA process, and utilization guidelines. This assessment system provides a comprehensive, accurate, standardized, and reproducible assessment of each long-term care facility resident's functional capabilities and identifies medical problems (CMS, 2011).

minimum data set (MDS) a core set of screening and assessment elements, including common definitions and coding categories, that forms the foundation of the comprehensive resident assessment for all residents of long-term care facilities certified to participate in Medicare or Medicaid.

care area assessment (CAA) process a component that helps the assessor and clinician interpret and utilize MDS data by focusing on key issues; components include care area triggers (CATs), CAA resources, and the CAA summary.

resident assessment protocols (RAPs) structured, problem-oriented frameworks for organizing MDS information and additional clinically relevant information about an individual that identifies medical problems and forms the basis for individual care planning (CMS, 2011). Although RAP terminology is still in common use, CMS now uses the term *care area assessment (CAA) process* to describe this concept.

3. Visual function

4. Communication

5. ADL functional/rehabilitation potential

6. Urinary incontinence and indwelling catheter

7. Psychosocial well-being

8. Mood state

9. Behavioral symptoms

10. Activities

11. Falls

12. Nutritional status

13. Feeding tubes

14. Dehydration/fluid maintenance

15. Dental care

16. Pressure ulcer

17. Psychotropic drug use

18. Physical restraints

19. Pain

20. Return to Community Referral (an assessment to assist nursing facility residents interested in transitioning back to their communities)

Based on the resident data entered on the MDS, care areas may or may not be triggered. If a care area is triggered, this indicates a potential need to address the issue in the care plan. At this point, the interdisciplinary team can use the utilization guidelines to evaluate the problem and determine whether to continue a care plan for it.

CAA resources offer a list of resources to consult in performing the assessment of a triggered care area. The interdisciplinary team must document the outcome of the assessment process for that specific care area and the decision regarding care planning for a given problem or need. The **care area assessment (CAA) summary** (formerly RAP summary) form is used to document the location within the resident's record where the assessment information may be found. Surveyors then use the CAA summary to locate pertinent assessment information within the record, to evaluate whether nursing facility staff members have properly utilized MDS information to assess and plan care for avoidable negative outcomes and to recognize resident strengths in the development of a comprehensive care plan. (See Figure 10-1 for an example of a Care Area Assessment Summary form.)

According to federal regulations, a comprehensive assessment must be completed, within 14 days of admission or after any significant change in condition, for each resident admitted to a certified bed, and on at least an annual basis thereafter. Between comprehensive assessments, the staff must complete a quarterly review of specific assessment categories of physical, mental, and psychosocial information.

FIGURE 10-1

Care Area Assessment (CAA) Summary.

Resident __TEST1 MDS 1_____ Identifier _____ Date _____

Section V	**Care Area Assessment (CAA) Summary**

V0200. CAAs and Care Planning

1. Check column A if Care Area is triggered.
2. For each triggered Care Area, indicate whether a new care plan, care plan revision, or continuation of current care plan is necessary to address the problem(s) identified in your assessment of the care area. The <u>Addressed in Care Plan</u> column must be completed within 7 days of completing the RAI (MDS and CAA(s)). Check column B if the triggered care area is addressed in the care plan.
3. Indicate in the <u>Location and Date of CAA Information</u> column where information related to the CAA can be found. CAA documentation should include information on the complicating factors, risks, and any referrals for this resident for this care area.

A. CAA Results

Care Area	A. Care Area Triggered	B. Addressed in Care Plan	Location and Date of CAA Information
	↓ Check all that apply ↓		
01. Delirium	☐	☐	
02. Cognitive Loss/Dementia	☐	☐	
03. Visual Function	☒	☒	1/25/20YY CARE PLAN
04. Communication	☒	☒	1/26/20YY CARE PLAN
05. ADL Functional/Rehabilitation Potential	☒	☒	
06. Urinary Incontinence and Indwelling Catheter	☒	☒	1/26/20YY URINARY
07. Psychosocial Well-Being	☐	☐	
08. Mood State	☐	☐	
09. Behavioral Symptoms	☐	☐	
10. Activities	☐	☐	
11. Falls	☒	☒	1/25/20YY ADL
12. Nutritional Status	☒	☒	1/27/20YY DIETARY
13. Feeding Tube	☐	☐	
14. Dehydration/Fluid Maintenance	☒	☒	
15. Dental Care	☐	☐	
16. Pressure Ulcer	☒	☒	1/26/20YY CARE PLAN
17. Psychotropic Drug Use	☐	☐	
18. Physical Restraints	☐	☐	
19. Pain	☐	☐	
20. Return to Community Referral	☐	☐	

B. Signature of RN Coordinator for CAA Process and Date Signed

1. Signature

2. Date | 0 | 1 | – | 2 | 7 | – | 2 | 0 | Y | Y |
                 Month   Day   Year

C. Signature of Person Completing Care Plan and Date Signed

1. Signature

2. Date | 0 | 1 | – | 2 | 7 | – | 2 | 0 | Y | Y |
                 Month   Day   Year

From the Centers for Medicare & Medicaid Services, www.cms.gov

Although the comprehensive assessment (MDS form) and the quarterly reviews are data sets, they are regarded as a permanent part of the long-term care resident record. Therefore, these documents are valuable not only in providing aggregate care information concerning intensity of services and ongoing care outcomes, but also are used to track individual resident care outcomes in the long-term care survey process. As changes occur in assessed categories on the MDS, the resident record should include explicit documentation to explain and individualize these changes in condition, particularly if negative outcomes, such as unplanned significant weight loss or acquired pressure ulcers, are reflected in the course of care.

Data from the MDS have a variety of uses in the long-term care industry. Depending on the state, MDS data may be used as the basis for Medicaid reimbursement for the nursing facility. In many states, MDS data are required to be submitted to the state agency monthly, in either paper or electronic form. The state agency uses the data to evaluate care trends and may use the information as a pre-survey evaluation tool for targeting potential care concerns before a formal survey. For example, MDS data can be used to track the number of residents with facility-acquired pressure sores, urinary tract infections, increased use of indwelling catheters, decline in functional ability, increased use of antipsychotic medications, and increased use of physical restraints, as well as the number of residents receiving rehabilitation and restorative services. Consequently, the data are valuable not only to the state agencies and surveyors but also to the individual provider. As a result, accurate and focused documentation is extremely valuable in its relationship to the comprehensive assessment. Documentation must support the assessment information in the MDS and should explain and describe how this information affects the individual resident.

The record review portion of the long-term care federal survey procedures instructs surveyors to evaluate the care and outcome of care provided to residents as portrayed through direct observation of the staff and assessed through improvement/decline as noted on the MDS. In this phase of the survey, the record is used as a source of information to determine if the assessment process is accurate and consistent with what actually is observed with the residents and to evaluate if the staff members are properly planning and implementing care goals and interventions to avoid decline and/or to facilitate improvement in physical or psychosocial well-being (CMS, 2011). If a given resident has an identified negative care outcome, documentation of the CAA process and other elements of the resident record would be used as a means to validate whether the negative outcome was facility-related compared to clinically unavoidable.

Care Plan

The care plan content and its use are linked to the comprehensive assessment in the federal long-term care survey process. Depending on the individual state licensure regulations, additional emphasis may be placed on care plan documentation; however, this varies from state to state. In some states, care plans are not required specifically for residents who are not in Medicare- or Medicaid-certified beds.

In the federal long-term care regulations, the care plan is a subcategory of the comprehensive assessment regulation (42 CFR §483.20). These requirements specify content as well as timeliness guidelines. The care plan must be completed within 7 days after the comprehensive assessment and should be an interdisciplinary process that involves not only the professional disciplines involved in the resident's care but also the attending physician and the resident or the resident's legal representative.

Specific documentation guidelines for the comprehensive care plan include the following items (CMS, 2011):

- Measurable objectives and timetables to meet medical, nursing, and mental and psychosocial needs that are identified in the comprehensive assessment
- Description of the services that are to be furnished to attain or maintain the resident's highest practicable physical, mental, and psychosocial well-being
- Description of the services that otherwise would be required but are not provided because of the resident's exercise of rights, including the right to refuse treatment

Because the care plan is an inherent part of federal regulatory compliance, it is viewed not only as a tool for direct caregivers but also has far-reaching implications from a legal point of view. If the content of the care plan does not show that appropriate and individualized care was provided to a resident, the facility has increased vulnerability to claims of poor and/or inappropriate care if there are avoidable negative care outcomes (Sullivan, 1996). Care plans have to be individualized to the residents' care needs, strengths, and individual preferences. Standardized care plans that do not list the caregiver's daily care responsibilities for the individual resident are not regarded as resident-centered. Further, if the facility has a survey record of noncompliance with care plan requirements that can be correlated with quality-of-care deficiencies, the legal vulnerability of the facility is heightened.

The care plan is viewed as the focal point for communicating significant care findings, resident preferences, and goals for the individual long-term care resident. For that reason, a well-documented care plan should reflect areas of concern identified from the comprehensive assessment and an individualized view of the resident, such that it introduces the resident to each caregiver on the interdisciplinary team, from the nursing assistant on each tour of duty to the licensed therapists and physicians who care for the resident on a less frequent basis. Consequently, standardized care plans that do not reflect individualization of care routines based on specific resident preferences, strengths, and care priorities are not regarded as individualized or resident-specific. From the perspective of a long-term care survey, individualization of care information is the single most important content characteristic of a care plan in the long-term care setting.

Discharge/Transfer

In the closed record review, documentation is evaluated with reference to the circumstances surrounding the transfer and/or discharge of the resident from the facility. Emphasis is placed on whether federal regulations were followed concerning involuntary transfer or discharge of a resident to another health care facility. Federal regulations outline specific circumstances in which a facility may transfer or discharge a resident involuntarily, and proper documentation is critical in demonstrating compliance with these requirements:

1. The transfer or discharge is necessary for the resident's welfare, and the resident's needs cannot be met in the facility.
2. The transfer or discharge is appropriate because the resident's health has improved sufficiently so the resident no longer needs the services provided by the facility.
3. The safety of individuals in the facility is endangered.
4. The health of individuals in the facility would otherwise be endangered.
5. The resident has failed, after reasonable and appropriate notice, to pay for (or to have paid under Medicare or Medicaid) a stay at the facility. For a resident who becomes eligible for Medicaid after admission to a nursing facility, the nursing facility may bill a resident for only those charges allowable under Medicaid.

    When the facility transfers or discharges a resident under any of the circumstances specified in paragraphs (a) (2) (i) through (v) of this section, the resident's clinical record must be documented. The documentation must be made by:

    (i) The resident's physician when transfer or discharge is necessary under paragraph (a)(2)(i) of this section and

    (ii) A physician when transfer or discharge is necessary under paragraph (a)(2)(iv) of this section (CMS, 2011)

In addition, circumstances leading to the transfer, discharge, or death are evaluated to identify if any specific avoidable negative care outcomes or lapses in care contributed to the resident's final status. Consequently, discharge and transfer documentation is crucial in determining key quality-of-care and quality-of-life compliance issues. At a minimum, discharge documentation should include a discharge summary, a post-discharge plan, and resident status at time of discharge.

Resident Rights

Resident rights represent a major focus in the long-term care setting, and documentation often becomes crucial in the evaluation of potential resident rights issues and whether a facility has acknowledged and recognized the rights of residents properly in the provision of care and services. Documentation affects the evaluation of compliance with resident rights requirements in a variety of ways. In addition to providing each resident or resident's legal representative with a written explanation of his or her basic rights under state and federal law, ongoing documentation of care preferences and explanations for various care outcomes becomes essential in determining compliance with resident rights requirements.

For example, if a resident has a certain diet order (such as an order for a diabetic diet) but the resident is not compliant with that diet and frequently is eating candy and other restricted items on that diet, documentation becomes essential as a resource for determining whether staff members are aware of this dietary compliance concern and how they manage the situation and balance clinical priorities with observing residents' rights. Ideally, documentation would reflect that the staff had advised the resident of the adverse complications associated with dietary noncompliance. If the resident knowingly chooses to continue a behavior that has potentially negative consequences, documentation should reflect ongoing attempts to educate and reverse the behavior, as well as the ongoing assessment of the resident's ability to understand and participate in this decision-making process.

Although the need to recognize the rights of residents to participate in their own care and care planning is significant, there is an equally important need for the facility to demonstrate that the staff acted appropriately and responsibly to supervise the resident's care needs and to inform the appropriate individuals of the consequences of their actions or inactions. Often, these types of situations are portrayed differently depending on the perspective of the resident or caregiver. Therefore, documentation plays a crucial role in the balance between observing resident rights and providing necessary care and services for the resident's well-being.

In addition to ongoing documentation by caregivers, various consents are necessary to document that permission has been obtained for activities specified in the federal regulations, and additional resident rights issues also may be included in state-specific requirements. These include, but are not limited to, permission to open mail, designation of attending physician and pharmacy service, permission to be photographed, handling of funds deposited with the facility, and informed consent for use of physical and chemical restraints.

New resident rights under the Health Insurance Portability and Accountability Act (HIPAA) include the residents' right to know what information is obtained about them and how it is used and disclosed. Residents have the right to review and amend their information and to have an accounting of all disclosures. Residents have the right to be notified of any breach of PHI (Protected Health Information) that might result in a risk to them.

State Licensure Requirements

The scope and intensity of state long-term care licensure requirements vary. In some states, the need for specific documentation above and beyond the content of the federal regulations is extensive, whereas in other states the focus is less stringent. From a health information management standpoint, the long-term care facility must evaluate documentation needs both from the perspectives of state and federal requirements. If a facility is not certified for Medicare or Medicaid, state licensure requirements provide the regulatory structure for documentation standards. If, however, a facility is certified for Medicare or Medicaid, both the federal requirements and the state requirements must be met.

In some cases, the state requirements require more stringent documentation than the federal requirements. For example, in the state of Missouri, the state licensure requirements specify that telephone orders must be signed within 7 days. No federal requirement specifies a timeframe for signature of telephone orders; however, long-term care facilities in Missouri are obligated to understand and comply with this separate licensure requirement during a state licensure survey.

Joint Commission Long-Term Care Accreditation Requirements

The emphasis on comprehensive assessments and care plans is reflected equally in the long-term care accreditation requirements of The Joint Commission. In many respects, Joint Commission long-term care requirements are similar to the federal long-term care requirements. The standards refer to the need for the facility to establish and follow specific care protocols depending on the scope and intensity of services provided in a given facility or unit.

In addition to long-term care accreditation standards, The Joint Commission offers disease-specific care certification programs. For example, a long-term care facility with a special care unit for the care of Alzheimer's-type dementia residents could elect to seek certification for this unit with or without seeking accreditation for the entire facility (The Joint Commission, n.d.). If a facility is seeking both facility accreditation and certification for one of its disease-specific programs, however, both sets of standards must be utilized in determining compliance. From the facility perspective, compliance with multiple Joint Commission standards and federal and state long-term care standards presents a significant challenge to all clinical disciplines.

SELF REVIEW 10.3

1. Documentation is vital in the evaluation of how a facility has contributed to and/or affected the _____ and _____ of individual residents.

2. When the resident record is used as a means of validating positive and negative care outcomes both in the annual survey and in complaint investigations, it is known as _____.

3. _____ is the primary vehicle for evaluating care outcomes in the federal long-term care survey process.

4. List the three basic components of the resident assessment instrument.

5. Defined as a schedule of assessments that will be performed for a nursing facility resident at admission, quarterly, and annually, whenever the resident experiences a significant change in status, and whenever the facility identifies a significant error in a prior assessment.

6. _____ provides structure for assessing social, medical, and psychological problems by providing a systematic method for reviewing key components of the MDS and directing caregivers to evaluate causes, interrelationships, and particular strengths that affect the development of the care plan.

7. True or False? MDS assessments are required for Medicare payment purposes.

8. True or False? If a care area is triggered, there is no need to address the issue in the care plan.

9. _____ is used to document the location within the resident's record where the assessment information may be found.

10. The care plan must be completed within _____ days of the comprehensive assessment.

11. List three of the five requirements that a facility must abide by when transferring or discharging a resident involuntarily.

12. True or False? If a facility if not certified for Medicare and Medicaid, the state licensure requirements provide the regulatory structure for documentation standards.

REIMBURSEMENT AND FUNDING

Reimbursement ranges from simple to the complex in the long-term care setting because of the various sources of payment, type and level of care provided by the facility, and whether a facility participates in Medicare and/or Medicaid. Within the industry as a whole, Medicaid reimbursement methodology varies from state to state. Moreover, depending on the type of long-term care facility, care and services may be billed to Medicare Part A and B, Medicaid, managed care, commercial insurance, and private pay, depending on the licensure and certification of the facility and the type and scope of services provided.

A general overview of the various payment categories that are typically found in a long-term care facility is provided in Table 10-2. Depending on the extent to which a long-term care facility participates in each of these types of payer options, the complexity of documentation and information systems increases proportionately. The most simplistic environment is the strictly private pay facility in which all care and services are billed monthly to the resident or the resident's guarantor. The most complex setting is one in which the facility participates in both Medicare Part A and Medicaid, has managed care contracts for sub-acute care, bills directly for Medicare Part B services, and has residents with commercial insurance policies that pay on a fee-for-service basis for daily care.

TABLE 10-2   Basic Reimbursement Categories and Pay Sources

ITEM	Medicaid	Medicare Part A	Medicare Part B	Managed Care	Commercial Insurance	Private Pay
Daily room and board	If all other financial resources have been exhausted and resident meets state criteria, basic care services are reimbursed at a daily rate.	If resident meets eligibility and level of service criteria, pays up to 100 days per period of illness.	Does not apply to sub-acute patients.	For rehabilitation and policy, daily care individual and/or provider contracts are negotiated for room and board and other services.	May be reimbursed at the skilled level or at a daily cap outlined in the individual policy.	Paid by family funds.
Durable medical equipment	Coverage varies from state to state; most equipment is expected to be provided by the facility as a part of the daily rate. Medicaid will pay as a secondary payer for care/services billed and paid under Medicare Part B.	Daily Medicare Part A rate is all inclusive for the period of certification. Use and cost of supplies and equipment is tracked for cost-reporting purposes.	Ancillary services such as physician visits, use of rehabilitation services outside of a Part A bed, some durable medical equipment, injections.	Reimbursement for durable medical equipment may be a part of the daily negotiated rate or negotiated and reimbursed separately by the managed care payer.	Coverage of durable medical equipment varies with individual policy.	Billing for use of special equipment and services over and above room and board varies from facility to facility.
Drugs	Specific coverage of drugs in the Medicaid program varies from state to state.	Cost of pharmaceuticals during care under Medicare Part A is included in the daily rate.	Coverage of medication is limited to that reimbursed under Part B.	Reimbursement for medications and treatments may be a part of the daily negotiated rate or negotiated and billed separately to the managed care payer.	Coverage for medications varies with individual policy.	Generally, the supplier bills the facility, which in turn bills the resident or guarantor on a monthly basis.

Medicaid Per Diem Based on Overall Facility Costs

The Medicaid program is an indigent health care program that is promulgated by individual state legislation. Therefore, Medicaid reimbursement for nursing facilities varies from state to state, depending on the type of reimbursement methodology adopted by the state agency and the type of Medicaid coverage available in a given state. A common methodology is to calculate an overall facility per diem rate based on basic facility cost reporting. These types of systems have no level-of-care distinction, and all residents are reimbursed at a flat daily rate based on facility-specific cost data using a reimbursement formula developed by the state agency.

Medicare Part a Skilled Nursing Facility (SNF) Benefit

Medicare Part A coverage is limited in that a resident first must be eligible for Medicare Part A coverage and qualify with a 3-day hospital stay within the previous 30 days prior to admission to a Medicare-certified bed and require the services of a skilled professional on a daily basis. If these criteria are met, the duration of the SNF coverage is limited to the need for daily skilled care up to a maximum of 100 days per period of illness. Therefore, not every admission to a nursing facility will qualify for Part A benefits, and not every long-term care facility will choose to participate in the Medicare Part A program. Consequently, if a resident chooses to utilize the Medicare SNF benefit following discharge from an acute care facility, he or she must select a facility/provider that is certified to participate in the Medicare program unless the resident is covered under a Medicare risk contract with a health maintenance organization.

Beginning in 1998, Medicare payments to SNFs changed from a cost-based reimbursement to a prospective payment system (PPS). Medicare Part A payment rates now utilize a case-mix adjusted per diem rate. The per diem payments for each qualified admission are based on **resource utilization groups (RUGs)**, a case-mix methodology driven from the MDS. One of the 66 groups is assigned, and that payment is reimbursed to the facility for a specific period of time or until the next MDS is completed according to the defined schedule.

The SNF PPS also assigns billing responsibility to the SNF for the entire package of care that residents receive during a stay. This concept is called **consolidated billing**. For example, physical therapy services are billed by the SNF (not by the physical therapy provider) as part of the package of care. The physical therapy provider, in turn, receives payment from the SNF. The consolidated billing requirement has some exceptions. For example, Medicare does make separate payments for physicians' professional services, certain dialysis-related services, and other items (CMS, 2013a).

From a health information management perspective, a **case-mix reimbursement** system such as the SNF PPS is affected greatly by documentation and accurate submission of MDS data. Therefore, the quality and accuracy of

resource utilization groups (RUGs) a case-mix methodology based on data submitted on the MDS. RUGs are used to adjust per diem payments to SNFs under the Medicare PPS and to NFs under some state Medicaid programs.

consolidated billing under Medicare, a responsibility of the skilled nursing facility for billing the entire package of care that residents receive during a stay, with certain specified exceptions such as physicians' professional services.

case-mix reimbursement a long-term methodology designed to provide a mechanism for facilities to be paid in a manner reflecting the types of residents served and the types of services provided. The system also is designed to provide greater access to nursing facility beds for heavier care residents and to improve the quality of care for all nursing facility residents. Payment is based on a specific methodology that considers direct-care costs, care-related costs, administrative and operating costs, and property.

documentation has a direct relationship with the financial viability of a facility that is heavily dependent on Medicare reimbursement.

Medicaid Per Diem Based on Level of Care

In some states, a Medicaid per diem or daily rate is established based on a level of care distinction for intermediate or skilled care or on a case-mix methodology developed by the state agency. In some states, the MDS is used as a resource document for calculating the level of care and extent of resources utilized for individual residents and for the facility as a whole. Depending on the state methodology, additional reimbursement may be recognized for intensity of services, such as may be the case with the care of AIDS, or for specific quality of care outcomes, such as would apply for improvement in functional independence as a result of rehabilitation and restorative services.

Resource Utilization Groups in Medicaid Reimbursement

Resource utilization groups (RUGS) reimbursement methodology is a specific case-mix payment system used in a growing number of states for long-term care Medicaid reimbursement. Using the MDS as the foundation for the data collection, states categorize reimbursement for individual residents based on their characteristics and service needs. From a general perspective, the methodology is based on the premise that if a resident has special or heavy care needs, the facility will be reimbursed at a higher rate than that for a resident who is more independent in care and requires less skilled or clinically complex services. Some states calculate the facility overall rate by averaging RUG scores from scheduled MDS assessment submissions. In addition to a direct care rate, the facility also is reimbursed at a rate that includes cost of administrative services, capital costs, and other financial categories that are not directly related to the provision of individual care and services. As with the Medicare SNF PPS, attention to documentation and the accuracy of MDS data is crucial when RUGs form the basis of a large portion of a provider's reimbursement.

Commercial Insurance

Commercial insurance coverage for long-term care services is growing and is projected to increase with the aging of our population. There is great variability, however, in terms of the type and duration of services that are covered, because there is no standard definition of long-term care coverage as there is, to some degree, with *major medical* in relation to acute hospitalizations. In some instances, coverage mirrors the Medicare Part a SNF benefit and will reimburse the beneficiary only for a maximum of 100 days or for the period of time that daily skilled care is needed. In other instances, room and board expenses are reimbursed for a predetermined period of time regardless of level of care. Often, the commercial insurance carrier will request copies of the resident medical record on a monthly basis to verify services rendered and to substantiate the level of care required by the beneficiary. Depending on the specific policy coverage, documentation of the level of care and scope/intensity of services is essential for assuring reimbursement from the third-party payer.

Managed Care Payers

The penetration of managed care into the long-term care industry is increasing over time. The predominant influence at this time is in the Medicare SNF and sub-acute sector of the long-term care industry. Managed care payers have entered into a Medicare **risk contract** (a contract between an HMO and CMS to provide services to Medicare beneficiaries, under which the health plan receives a monthly payment for enrolled Medicare members) and therefore assumes responsibility for the SNF benefit for the enrollees.

> risk contract   also known as a Medicare risk contract, an agreement between an HMO and CMS to provide services to Medicare beneficiaries, under which contract the health plan receives a monthly payment for enrolled Medicare members and then must provide all services on an at-risk basis (Kongstvedt, 1993).

In addition, an increasing number of managed care payers are contracting with long-term care facilities for the care of non-Medicare enrollees who require the intensive post-acute rehabilitation and nursing services provided by SNF and sub-acute units. To control cost of care, managed care payers are seeking affiliations with long-term care facilities that can provide the same or higher-quality outcomes at a lesser cost-per-care episode than can the acute-care setting. Consequently, managed care reimbursement is projected to increase in the long-term care setting for the low-cost, high-quality providers.

Managed care reimbursement can occur as a result of a variety of affiliations with a long-term care facility. For those facilities that are a part of a large, multifacility chain, managed care payers and health maintenance organizations (HMOs) may enter into national agreements on an exclusive basis. Facilities that are a part of an integrated delivery system may be involved in a managed care payment situation for an entire episode of care for enrollees. An example might be a workers' compensation claim in which the global care episode is reimbursed at a designated rate that includes acute care, post-acute care, and related physician or other outpatient services.

On an individual facility basis, negotiation with a managed care payer is done on both an individual or patient-to-patient basis and on a capitated basis, based on predetermined levels of care and reimbursement. These negotiated rates may or may not include separate charges for pharmaceuticals, durable medical equipment, and/or rehabilitation services beyond a designated minimum number of units per day.

The term *negotiation* implies a certain amount of bargaining on both sides, in that the managed care payer is looking for the lowest price and the provider is looking for the highest price for the same outcome. For this reason, information becomes essential to the successful managed care negotiator. If a provider has insufficient or inaccurate information from which to understand where specific care costs can be controlled, profits maximized, and losses minimized, a capitated rate can be financially devastating if care needs exceed reimbursement.

Private Pay

Private pay in the long-term care setting denotes payment by the individual without any third-party payer. In some facilities, a global daily rate is billed to the resident monthly, including all meals, treatments, and supplies, with no additional line item charges other than medications supplied by the pharmacy. In other facilities, a basic daily rate includes only room, board, and a nominal list of supplies/services, with additional services being charged for restorative services, incontinent care, specialized therapeutic activity programs, feeding assistance, and other services that are regarded as nonroutine by the facility. The extent to which additional services are charged over and above routine services varies from provider to provider.

SELF REVIEW 10.4

1. In which type of system is there no level of care distinction; all residents are reimbursed at a flat daily rate based on the facility-specific cost data using a reimbursement formula developed by the state agency?

2. The per diem payments for each qualified admission are based on:
   a. consolidated billing
   b. case mix reimbursement
   c. resource utilization groups

3. Medicare payments to SNF's changed from a _____ to a _____ in 1998.

4. _____ is a specific case-mix payment system used in a growing number of states for long-term case Medicaid reimbursement.

5. Which type of insurance often requests copies of the resident's medical record on a monthly basis to verify services rendered?

6. A contract between an HMO and a CMS to provide services to Medicare beneficiaries, under which the health plan receives a monthly payment for enrolled Medicare members, is known as _____.

7. _____ denotes payment by the individual without any third-party payer.

INFORMATION MANAGEMENT

Management of information is an area of growing significance in the long-term care setting, not only from a reimbursement perspective but also from a regulatory compliance and risk management perspective. This need is seen more dramatically in facilities participating in Medicare and Medicaid because of the information emphasis in the survey process and successful management of information-based reimbursement.

Coding and Classification

Whereas coding has a place in tracking various types of care, reimbursement is less affected by codes in the residential long-term care setting. Certain codes are reimbursement-significant when reported on MDS assessments; however, as a general rule, ICD codes have limited value in describing the level of care or intensity of services required for a long-term, chronically ill institutionalized resident. Consequently, although coding is used for billing of services and tracking clinical information in NFs and SNFs, its role is diminished somewhat when compared to the acute care environment.

ICD

The current clinical modification of the *International Classification of Diseases* diagnosis codes must be used for submitting Medicaid, Medicare Part A SNF, and Medicare Part B claims; however, their role is not significant in dictating the level of reimbursement the facility receives for an individual resident. Although inaccurate or incomplete codes may affect the timely processing of claims or increase the chances of a claim being isolated for medical review, reimbursement decisions are not linked solely to *ICD* codes. The individual facility may use *ICD* codes to track reasons for admission and hospitalization and to monitor clinical care issues such as incidence of acquired pressure ulcers, urinary tract infections, fractures, and other care outcomes that would be relevant to the overall monitoring and surveillance of quality. The use of *ICD* codes for tracking of clinical information beyond basic admission and discharge data varies from provider to provider.

ICD codes also are a part of the diagnosis reporting information included in the minimum data set (Section I). In this section, diagnoses are to be recorded in relation to current ADL status, cognitive status, mood and behavior status, medical treatments, nursing monitoring, or risk of death. A minimum amount of space is provided for recording actual *ICD* codes, because checking the relevant box on the form enters the majority of diagnosis information.

If a diagnosis code provides more specific information relative to intensity of care or level of skilled services, a code should be entered in preference to the checked box. For example, if a resident has insulin-dependent diabetes mellitus or uncontrolled diabetes, greater skilled supervision and monitoring is required than for a resident whose diabetes is diet-controlled. Consequently, an *ICD* code would provide greater information concerning that resident's level of care than would the simple description "diabetes mellitus." Diagnoses and/or diagnosis codes, however, are not adequate to describe the level and intensity of care required by long-term care residents.

Current Procedural Terminology

Current Procedural Terminology (*CPT*) codes are used for billing Medicare Part B services for rehabilitation (PT, OT, speech) and for physician visits to residents in a nursing facility. For the rehabilitation services, *CPT* codes indicate the type of therapy provided. For physician visits, the *CPT* codes describe the level of service provided, which thereby dictates the reimbursement for the visit performed. In a retrospective review of claims by the Medicare carrier, physician documentation must support that the level of service billed was actually performed and was medically justified. Therefore, if a *CPT* code is used that correlates with a more intensive visit, documentation should support that more time was involved than for a routine physician visit.

Often, billing for Part B physician services is not done directly by the nursing facility, because these services are billed through the private practice. Therefore, nursing facility staff members have much less familiarity with *CPT* codes compared to *ICD* codes.

Data and Information Flow

Management of data and use of automation for data management have increased dramatically in the long-term care industry in the twenty-first century. In large part, this has resulted from efforts of the Centers for Medicare & Medicaid Services to mandate automation of the MDS for all facilities participating in the Medicare and/or Medicaid programs. Also, individual state agencies are increasing their own requirements for electronic submission of MDS data on a monthly basis. Consequently, discussion of data and flow of information is relevant not only from the internal facility viewpoint but also from the perspective of reporting information to external agencies. Growth also includes long-term care providers in an electronic health information exchange (HIE) with an objective to foster improved communication in care transitions, promote less duplication of medical services, and in an effort to reduce unnecessary hospital readmissions.

Data and Information Flow within the Facility

MDS Data   In the Medicare- and/or Medicaid-certified facility, data and information flow centers on the MDS, which is not only a vehicle for a clinical assessment process but also is a mandated data set linked to regulatory compliance. Therefore, timeliness and accuracy of assessment information must be coordinated among the various disciplines and is a significant activity within the facility. From a data management perspective, the facility must ensure that systems are in place to monitor timeliness of completion of the MDS and accuracy of reported items (see Table 10-3). Further, a system must be in place to ensure that significant changes in condition are properly identified, assessed, and communicated to the appropriate individuals, as this represents an area of federal regulatory compliance.

After the MDS is completed, information is used to establish which care areas are triggered, either through an automated RAI process or through manual review of the MDS trigger legend. Therefore, coordination of completion among the various disciplines is an ongoing process within the nursing facility. In addition, information regarding changes in resident condition must be monitored continually to determine if specific criteria are met that indicate a possible need for new comprehensive assessment.

TABLE 10.3	Monitoring Assessment Timeliness and Content
Time	**Content of Information**
Within 14 days of admission	MDS information is consistent with interdisciplinary assessment information recorded in the resident record.
Within 14 days of significant change in condition	Care plan content reflects appropriate use of care area triggers for development of goals and interdisciplinary interventions.
At least annually	Documentation explains the clinical reason(s) for not completing a new comprehensive assessment if some significant change criteria are met based on a quarterly review and/or at any time between scheduled assessment or review intervals.
Review of specific data elements quarterly	

The criteria for determining if a resident has experienced a significant change in condition, either improvement or decline, are included in the federal long-term care regulations and, as such, have a significant role in evaluating compliance with the resident assessment regulations. Consequently, concurrent information regarding resident condition must be communicated and evaluated on an ongoing basis.

Federal regulations define a "significant change" as a major change in the resident's status with the following conditions (CMS, 2002):

1. Normally will not resolve itself without intervention by staff or by implementing standard disease-related clinical interventions, is not self-limiting (for declines)
2. Impacts on more than one area of the resident's health status
3. Requires interdisciplinary review and/or revision of the care plans. According to this definition, a significant change reassessment would be indicated if decline or improvement is noted consistently in two or more areas of decline or two or more areas of improvement.

Following are examples that *could* indicate a significant change (CMS, 2011):

- Any decline in ADL functioning for which a resident is newly coded as 3, 4, or 8 (extensive assistance, total dependency, activity did not occur)
- Increase in the number of areas in which behavioral symptoms are coded as "not easily altered"
- Resident's decision making changes from 0 to 1, 2, or 3
- Resident's incontinence pattern changes from 0 or 1 to 2, 3, or 4, or to placement of an indwelling catheter
- Emergence of sad or anxious mood as a problem that is not easily altered
- Emergence of an unplanned weight loss problem (5% in 30 days or 10% in 180 days)

- Begin to use trunk restraint or a chair that prevents rising for a resident when it was not used before
- Emergence of a condition/disease in which a resident is judged to be unstable
- Emergence of a pressure ulcer at Stage II or higher when no ulcers were previously present at Stage II or higher
- Overall deterioration of resident's condition; received more support (e.g., in ADLs or decision making)

In terms of improvement (CMS, 2011):

- Any improvement in ADL physical functioning in which a resident is newly coded as 0, 1, or 2 when previously scored as a 3, 4, or 8
- A decrease in the number of areas in which behavioral symptoms or sad or anxious mood are coded as "not easily altered"
- Resident's decision-making changes from 2, 3, or 4 to 0 or 1
- Overall improvement of resident's condition; resident receives fewer supports

Level of Care Evaluation   Reasons differ for residents who require permanent care in a long-term care facility. Some require a higher level of skilled intervention daily, whereas others may need less intensive care. Depending on their diagnoses and overall condition, residents may decline rapidly and require more intensive services. For this reason, facilities develop methods for defining individual resident acuity and care needs and will attempt to place residents with similar needs in the same physical area or unit of the facility. As residents' conditions change, their care needs change, and relocation to more appropriate areas within the facility may be required. Generally, the type of information that would be utilized for this assessment would depend on the care issues outlined in Figure 10-2.

Utilization of Supplies and Services   Regardless of the resident's pay source, information regarding utilization of central supply items and special services must be

FIGURE 10-2

Information needs for level-of-care evaluation.

Skilled Nursing Requirements	Dependence on staff for Activities of Daily Living
• Enteral feedings	• Supervised feeding or totally fed by staff
• Wound care	• Number of staff required for transfer and/or mobility
• Ostomy care	• Number and extent of staff assistance required for dressing and personal hygiene
• Acute, unstable condition requiring skilled monitoring	

maintained for cost-accounting purposes. Some facilities manage supply information with the use of scanners, a system in which charge information is captured automatically at the point of use. In other instances, supply utilization is managed totally by a manual tracking system. Improper management of this key area of the facility operations can result in tremendous amounts of lost revenue to the long-term care facility.

For facilities that participate in managed care contracts with capitated payments, concurrent monitoring of supply utilization is essential to the successful provider. If the facility is paid a negotiated rate of a certain amount per day, it is important that the facility have a system in place that ensures effective monitoring of actual facility cost versus what the managed care payer will reimburse. This also applies to use of pharmaceuticals and durable medical equipment.

External Data Reporting

Facilities participating in the Medicare and/or Medicaid programs are required to submit MDS data to the state agency. In compliance with the individual state requirements, facilities submit individual resident MDS data to the state agency electronically. The state and federal agencies both utilize individual resident and aggregate facility data to monitor quality by individual provider and to evaluate trends in care throughout various regions of the country. The submitted MDS data are utilized by state surveyors to identify focus areas to review when performing the facility standard survey. In some states, MDS data also are used to establish the facility Medicaid reimbursement.

Electronic Information Systems

With the advent of mandated electronic submission of MDS data, the long-term care industry has seen a growing number of vendors specializing in long-term care software. The extent to which facilities are able to totally computerize clinical and financial data, however, is still dependent on the financial constraints of the average long-term care provider. As a result, there are wide ranges of utilization of electronic information systems within the industry, from stand-alone systems used strictly for processing MDS data to systems that integrate all financial and clinical information successfully within the facility.

Some of the more common electronic software applications are as follows:

- Electronic physician orders, medication, and treatment records either within the facility or provided by the pharmacy service off-site
- Electronic financial information (census, payroll, billing, cost-reporting data)
- Electronic MDS system, care area triggering system, and care plans
- Integration of care plan with nurse aide assignments
- Electronic interdisciplinary progress notes
- Electronic assessment templates
- Electronic tracking of incidents/accidents, infections, and other significant events

Often, these systems are not integrated and/or are not designed such that the facility has full advantage of the data in a repository. As the impact of concurrent information management grows within the long-term care industry, the demand for effective and affordable automated systems will increase.

CMS provides free software, called RAVEN, for entering and transmitting MDS assessment data. The RAVEN software "imports and exports data in standard MDS record format, maintains facility, resident, and employee information, enforces data integrity via rigorous edit checks, and provides comprehensive on-line help" (CMS, 2002, p. 1). Facilities also may choose to submit MDS data using software purchased commercially through a vendor, provided that the software meets the CMS standards.

President Obama's economic stimulus package of 2009 encouraged implementation of electronic health records (EHRs). Although long-term care providers were generally excluded from the initial EHR incentive program, these incentives served to create a demand for electronic information systems in all areas of health care, whether or not the incentives applied directly to a particular group of providers. The increased use of information technology in all settings has been accompanied by increased regulation to protect the privacy and security of health information. Efforts to include long-term care providers in electronic health information exchange can contribute overall to the betterment and continuity of health care.

Data Sets

MDS has become the universal data set for the long-term care industry. Although some states have made additional data submission requirements to accommodate their Medicaid reimbursement systems, the MDS 2.0 became the universal basic reporting instrument for all 50 states effective January 1, 1996, with MDS 3.0 taking effect October 1, 2010. The initial goal of CMS in establishing MDS was to combine the benefits of a standardized clinical assessment tool with a universal data set for monitoring key information within the long-term care industry.

Now that the MDS also supplies information important to reimbursement, CMS is concerned with the potential for fraudulent reporting of MDS data. The MDS form includes a formal statement certifying accuracy of information for all MDS sections. Each staff member completing a portion of the MDS document must certify the accuracy of that portion by signing an attestation statement, which includes verbiage warning of criminal, civil, and/or administrative penalties for submitting false information. Figure 10-3 includes an example of the attestation statement as incorporated into the MDS form.

For the PPS/Medicare covered admission, the MDS is required to be completed on a 5-day, 14-day, 30-day, 60-day, and 90-day schedule to

FIGURE 10-3

MDS attestation and signatures.

Resident __TEST1 MDS 1__   Identifier _____   Date _____

Section Z	Assessment Administration

Z0400. Signature of Persons Completing the Assessment or Entry/Death Reporting

I certify that the accompanying information accurately reflects resident assessment information for this resident and that I collected or coordinated collection of this information on the dates specified. To the best of my knowledge, this information was collected in accordance with applicable Medicare and Medicaid requirements. I understand that this information is used as a basis for ensuring that residents receive appropriate and quality care, and as a basis for payment from federal funds. I further understand that payment of such federal funds and continued participation in the government-funded health care programs is conditioned on the accuracy and truthfulness of this information, and that I may be personally subject to or may subject my organization to substantial criminal, civil, and/or administrative penalties for submitting false information. I also certify that I am authorized to submit this information by this facility on its behalf.

Signature	Title	Sections	Date Section Completed
A.			
B.			
C.			
D.			
E.			
F.			
G.			
H.			
I.			
J.			
K.			
L.			

Z0500. Signature of RN Assessment Coordinator Verifying Assessment Completion

A. Signature:	B. Date RN Assessment Coordinator signed assessment as complete:
	`0` `1` – `2` `7` – `2` `0` `Y` `Y` Month Day Year

acquire Medicare payment. (Refer to item A0310.B in Figure 10-4.) Deviation from this schedule while the resident is covered under Medicare results in the default or lowest payment rate. Additional required PPS MDS assessments include Readmission/Return, SCSA (Significant Change in Status), SCPA (Significant Correction to Prior Assessment), Swing Bed Clinical Change, as well as OMRAs (Other Medicare Required Assessments) for Start of Therapy (SOT), End of Therapy (EOT), Both Start and End of Therapy and Change of Therapy (COT).

FIGURE 10-4

First page of the MDS, including timeframes for assessments.

Resident **TEST1 MDS 1** _____   Identifier _____   Date _____

MINIMUM DATA SET (MDS) - Version 3.0
RESIDENT ASSESSMENT AND CARE SCREENING
Nursing Home Comprehensive (NC) Item Set

Section A	Identification Information

A0100. Facility Provider Numbers

A. National Provider Identifier (NPI):

1	1	2	2	3	3	4	4	5	5

B. CMS Certification Number (CCN):

2	9	5	7	0	1				

C. State Provider Number:

C	M	C	A	I	D						

A0200. Type of Provider

Enter Code [1]

Type of provider
1. **Nursing home (SNF/NF)**
2. **Swing Bed**

A0310. Type of Assessment

Enter Code [0][1]

A. Federal OBRA Reason for Assessment
01. **Admission** assessment (required by day 14)
02. **Quarterly** review assessment
03. **Annual** assessment
04. **Significant change in status** assessment
05. **Significant correction** to **prior comprehensive** assessment
06. **Significant correction** to **prior quarterly** assessment
99. **Not OBRA required** assessment

Enter Code [9][9]

B. PPS Assessment
PPS Scheduled Assessments for a Medicare Part A Stay
01. **5-day** scheduled assessment
02. **14-day** scheduled assessment
03. **30-day** scheduled assessment
04. **60-day** scheduled assessment
05. **90-day** scheduled assessment
06. **Readmission/return** assessment
PPS Unscheduled Assessments for a Medicare Part A Stay
07. **Unscheduled assessment used for PPS** (OMRA, significant or clinical change, or significant correction assessment)
Not PPS Assessment
99. **Not PPS** assessment

Enter Code [0]

C. PPS Other Medicare Required Assessment - OMRA
0. **No**
1. **Start of therapy** assessment
2. **End of therapy** assessment
3. **Both Start and End of therapy** assessment

Enter Code [ ]

D. Is this a Swing Bed clinical change assessment? Complete only if A0200 = 2
0. **No**
1. **Yes**

Enter Code [1]

E. Is this assessment the first assessment (OBRA, PPS, or Discharge) **since the most recent admission?**
0. **No**
1. **Yes**

Enter Code [9][9]

F. Entry/discharge reporting
01. **Entry** record
10. **Discharge** assessment-**return not anticipated**
11. **Discharge** assessment-**return anticipated**
12. **Death in facility** record
99. **Not entry/discharge** record

From the Centers for Medicare & Medicaid Services, www.cms.gov

1. True or False? ICD codes have great value in describing the level of care or intensity of services required for a long-term care, chronically ill institutionalized resident.

2. Briefly distinguish between ICD and CPT code sets with regard to claim submission.

3. Who is responsible for mandating automation of the MDS for all facilities participating in the Medicare and/or Medicaid programs?

4. Define a "significant change" according to federal regulations.

5. List two examples of a "decline" significant change and two examples of an "improvement" significant change.

6. True or False? Facilities participating in the Medicare and/or Medicaid programs are required to submit MDS data to the state agency.

7. List three of the more common electronic software applications.

8. What was the initial goal of CMS in establishing MDS?

QUALITY IMPROVEMENT AND UTILIZATION MANAGEMENT

Quality Improvement

Researchers at the University of Wisconsin developed the first MDS-derived quality indicators. These indicators can be utilized to monitor quality, both in process and outcome, through the automated use of MDS data. Figure 10-5 provides examples of quality indicators based on MDS data. From a facility perspective, many of these indicators also correlate directly with compliance monitoring for key federal quality of care and quality of life regulations (F-tags) as noted in Figure 10-5. (Note: An "F-tag" is an alphanumeric label that identifies a federal regulation and the associated interpretive guidelines used by surveyors. When a survey team cites a facility for a deficiency, it is cited by the appropriate tag number.)

As part of the CMS Nursing Home Quality Initiative, CMS hosts a "Nursing Home Compare" website that provides information about nursing homes in the form of quality measures. This information is posted for nursing homes in all states, with the intent of assisting potential residents and their families in making an informed selection if they have to consider nursing home placement. Quality measures are derived from the MDS, with some being adjusted per facility profile. Providers can utilize the information to compare themselves to similar nursing homes in a QI process.

Ever since 2008, the Nursing Home Compare website (www.medicare.gov /NHC Compare/home.asp) has included a Five-Star Quality Rating System for all Medicare or Medicaid certified nursing homes. CMS intends this system to be a tool to assist consumer decision-making. The rating is updated monthly with any new information. The five-star rating includes three categories of performance measures: health inspections, staffing, and quality measures. The three measures determine a facility's overall composite rating. A rating of one to five stars in each of the three categories, as well as a composite star rating, is assigned. One star indicates much below average and five stars indicate much above average quality. The health inspections category is based on three years of data, including standard health surveys, complaint investigations, and on-site revisits. Data are weighted most heavily toward the most recent survey.

The staffing measure takes currently reported staffing information from nursing homes and case-mix adjusts the information according to the resource utilization group classification system. RN staffing and overall nurse and nurses aide staffing is looked at and converted into a single one- to five-star rating. The staffing measure distributes nursing homes nationally along a quintile distribution.

FIGURE 10-5

MDS-derived quality indicators.

Quality Indicator	Quality of Care and Quality of Life Requirement (F-tags)
Accidents	F323, F324—The facility must ensure that (1) the resident environment remains as free of accident hazards as is possible; and (2) each resident receives adequate supervision and assistance devices to prevent accidents.
Behavioral and emotional patterns	F319, F320—Based on the comprehensive assessment of a resident, the facility must ensure that (1) a resident who displays mental or psychosocial adjustment difficulty receives appropriate treatment and services to correct the assessed problem; and (2) a resident whose assessment did not reveal a mental or psychosocial adjustment difficulty does not display a pattern of decreased social interaction and/or increased withdrawn, angry, or depressive behaviors, unless the resident's clinical condition demonstrates that such a pattern is unavoidable.
Infection control/ prevalence of UTIs	F315—A resident who is incontinent of bladder receives appropriate treatment and services to prevent urinary tract infections and to restore as much normal bladder function as possible.
Prevalence of weight loss	F325—Based on a resident's comprehensive assessment, the facility must ensure that a resident maintains acceptable parameters of nutritional status, such as body weight and protein levels, unless the resident's clinical condition demonstrates that this is not possible.
Prevalence of tube feeding	F321, F322—Based on the comprehensive assessment of a resident, the facility must ensure that (1) a resident who has been able to eat enough alone or with assistance is not fed by nasogastric tube unless the resident's clinical condition demonstrates that use of a nasogastric tube was unavoidable; (2) a resident who is fed by a nasogastric or gastrostomy tube receives the appropriate treatment and services to prevent aspiration, pneumonia, diarrhea, vomiting, dehydration, metabolic abnormalities, and nasal-pharyngeal ulcers and to restore, if possible, normal eating skills.
Prevalence of dehydration	F327—The facility must provide each resident with sufficient fluid intake to maintain proper hydration and health.

FIGURE 10-5 *(continued)*

Quality Indicator	Quality of Care and Quality of Life Requirement (F-tags)
Incidence of decline in late loss ADLs	F310—A resident's abilities in activities of daily living do not diminish unless circumstances of the individual's clinical condition demonstrate that diminution was unavoidable. This includes the resident's ability to (1) bathe, dress, and groom; (2) transfer and ambulate; (3) toilet; (4) eat; and (5) use speech, language, or other functional communication systems.
Incidence of contractures	F317, F318—Based on the comprehensive assessment of a resident, the facility must ensure that (1) a resident who enters the facility without a limited range of motion does not experience reduction in range of motion unless the resident's clinical condition demonstrates that a reduction in range of motion is unavoidable; and (2) a resident with a limited range of motion receives appropriate treatment and services to increase range of motion and/or to prevent further decrease in range of motion.
Psychotropic drug use	F329—Each resident's drug regimen must be free from unnecessary drugs. Based on a comprehensive assessment of a resident, the facility must ensure that residents who have not used antipsychotic drugs are not given these drugs unless antipsychotic drug therapy is necessary to treat a specific condition as diagnosed and documented in the clinical record. Residents who use antipsychotic drugs receive gradual dose reductions, and behavioral interventions, unless clinically contraindicated, in an effort to discontinue these drugs.
Quality of life: prevalence of daily physical restraints	F221—The resident has the right to be free from any physical or chemical restraints imposed for purposes of discipline or convenience and not required to treat the resident's medical symptoms.
Prevalence of stage 1–4 pressure ulcers	F314—Based on the comprehensive assessment of a resident, the facility must ensure that (1) a resident who enters the facility without pressure sores does not develop pressure sores unless the individual's clinical condition demonstrates that they were unavoidable. (2) resident having pressure sores receives necessary treatment and services to promote healing, prevent infection and prevent new sores from developing.

In the initial rating system, the performance measure incorporated 10 quality measures (7 long-stay measures and 3 short-stay measures) that were believed to be the most appropriate and reliable for the purpose of the Five-Star Quality Rating System. Long-stay measures included activities of daily living, mobility, pressure ulcers, restraints, urinary tract infections, pain, and catheterization. The short-stay measures included delirium, high-risk pressure ulcers, and pain. (See end-of-chapter Web Activity to obtain the most current list of quality measures.) The quality measures distribute nursing homes nationally along a quintile distribution. Staffing and quality measures both use a national distribution, but the health inspections measure uses a state-based distribution.

The composite or overall rating begins with the health inspections rating, and this is moved up or down based on whether the staffing and quality measures ratings are extreme (either one star or five stars). The purpose of the system is to separate high-performing nursing homes from low-performing nursing homes.

Utilization Management

In the long-term care setting, utilization management applies to the Medicaid, Medicare Part A, and managed care residents who may be in an SNF or sub-acute unit of a facility. Each state has individual requirements for qualifying for Medicaid nursing home payments, and the manner in which this process is monitored varies from state to state. In some instances, qualification is monitored through the MDS data in conjunction with additional state-specific information submission. In other instances, the state agency adopts a separate review process to determine initial and continuing Medicaid eligibility.

For the Medicare Part A SNF benefit, utilization must be monitored to ensure that the condition of the resident meets ongoing criteria for daily skilled care. In addition, the facility must be aware of SNF days that the resident may have used before being admitted to the SNF unit to ensure that the stay does not exceed the maximum benefit of 100 days per period of illness. If the resident's level of care changes such that the facility believes that care no longer meets Medicare skilled criteria, an internal denial letter must be issued to the beneficiary (or the beneficiary's representative). In addition, the beneficiary must be advised of the right to submit an appeal to the intermediary if the denial decision is questioned or challenged.

Utilization management for managed care residents, typically those in an SNF or sub-acute bed, is a dynamic process that requires frequent monitoring by the facility case manager to ensure that care needs and progress are communicated to the managed care case manager on an ongoing basis. The facility must be in a position to communicate changes in resident status and discharge plans to the managed care payer. If care needs increase such that additional services must be ordered or are recommended by the attending physician, this must be communicated and generally approved through the managed care case manager. Most often, this monitoring and communication process is the responsibility of the facility RN case manager who serves as the primary communicator of care progress to the managed care payer.

SELF REVIEW 10.6

1. Who developed the first MDS derived quality indicators?

2. For the _____ benefit, utilization must be monitored to ensure that the condition of the resident meets ongoing criteria for daily skilled care.
   a. Medicare Part B
   b. Medicare Part A SNF

3. List the three categories included in the Five Star quality rating system for the Nursing Home Compare website.

4. _____ is a dynamic process that requires frequent monitoring by the facility case manager to ensure that care needs and progress are communicated to the managed care case manager on an ongoing basis.

RISK MANAGEMENT AND LEGAL ISSUES

Risk management and legal issues in the long-term care setting are similar to those in other health care settings. Proper tracking and documentation of incidents or potentially compensable events is just as important in the long-term care facility as in other settings. Clinical issues that present risk to the facility include pressure ulcers, falls, fractures, medication errors, infections, and dehydration. Long-term care facilities can use quality management techniques and monitor quality indicators to improve the quality of care and lower the level of legal risk.

SELF REVIEW 10.7

1. What two things can long-term care facilities use to improve the quality of care and lower the level of legal risk?
2. True or False? Proper tracking and documentation of incidents or potentially compensable events is not important in the long-term care facility.

ROLE OF THE HEALTH INFORMATION MANAGEMENT PROFESSIONAL

Credentialed health information managers (i.e., RHIT, RHIA) are not required in the federal long-term care regulations but may be required on either a part-time or a consulting basis in some of the state long-term care licensure laws. The trend toward automation and use of health information in long-term care reimbursement has increased the importance of the credentialed health information manager in the long-term care setting. As a result, independent facilities and long-term care management corporations are expanding their use of full-time registered health information technicians (RHITs) and registered health information administrators (RHIAs). RHITs and RHIAs have received formal education in health information management that can equip them for several roles in long-term care.

Many long-term care facilities employ credentialed health information managers as fulltime directors of health information services. Another role is that of a health information management consultant, who may focus on a specific area of information management such as auditing documentation. Whatever the role, the health information manager must understand, apply, and stay abreast of pertinent regulations and follow professional best practices.

Auditing

One role of the health information manager in long-term care is to design and implement auditing systems. Of significance to the long-term care facility is the content, completion, accuracy, and timeliness of medical record documentation. Documentation affects the quality of care provided. Assessment and ongoing care planning are determined in part by what is written in the medical record. Documentation also is a necessary factor in outcomes for reimbursement systems, survey compliance, and in the event of legal action. The medical record serves as a tool in QI studies and is used in facility planning.

Health information managers and other trained staff can be a valuable asset to the long-term care organization by conducting routine documentation audits against established criteria. Results of such audits can be used to help ensure quality care, survey readiness, and proper reimbursement. In addition, audit outcomes can be utilized as measures in training health care staff and for system evaluation and improvement.

Audits can be quantitative or qualitative in nature. Quantitative audits include review of whether medical record forms are complete, timely, and signed by the authors of the forms. Qualitative audits generally require more training, because they entail a more in-depth look at the actual content of the medical record.

Typical intervals for auditing records in long-term care occur when admission assessments are complete, concurrently at regularly scheduled intervals throughout the resident/patient stay (such as quarterly), and upon discharge. The purpose of regular ongoing monitoring is to identify any problems or trends in documentation while correction is possible or when changes can be made. In many cases, because of the extended length of stay and volume of the record, delaying review of documentation until discharge is not as effective as employing an ongoing review system. Incomplete documentation often cannot legally be completed at a time well after the event and most likely would not be to anyone's benefit. Computerization of medical records in long-term care has made records more accessible for auditing.

Utilizing a defined set of criteria for auditing or a review form promotes consistency and objectivity. Audit forms can be created by giving consideration to regulatory requirements and what the facility defines as useful information to collect. Typical items on a long-term care audit form include the following:

- Timeliness of MDS assessments
- Physician orders signed
- Advance directives addressed
- Allergies identified
- Assessments completed by each discipline
- Medication orders consistent with medication records
- Physician progress notes coinciding with required visit schedule
- Laboratory results in the record for all lab testing ordered

The auditor can review several items in a sample of records or focus on one issue in a larger sample of records. To be effective, any type of auditing has to be done in a timely manner to report the results accurately. Problems or trends should be identified, a plan of correction developed, and further monitoring done to measure improvement.

External Consultant versus Fulltime Employee

As a consultant, the HIM professional conducts periodic visits ranging, for example, from monthly to quarterly to monitor documentation trends within the facility, particularly as this relates to potential regulatory compliance concerns. The HIM professional brings expertise in terms of resident confidentiality and release of confidential information, and also serves as an ongoing resource for development of forms and documentation systems and procedures that facilitate compliance and promote proper reimbursement.

With the increase in automation, the HIM consultant also is a useful resource in selecting electronic information systems that are suited to the needs of the facility while also meeting specific state and federal requirements pertaining to automation of resident information. From that perspective, the HIM professional offers expertise in terms of evaluating the adequacy of existing traditional paper systems and provides valuable insight as to the necessary steps for streamlining and preparing manual systems for the gradual transition to an electronic resident record.

Because of the resident's length of stay and the scrutiny that nursing home documentation receives, the HIM staff must ensure that the medical record, whether automated or paper, is safeguarded throughout the resident's stay and thereafter. HIM staff members must be diligent in protecting privacy and confidentiality by adhering to proper release-of-information standards.

Whether as a fulltime employee or as an independent consultant to the long-term care facility, the HIM professional often is the key resource for monitoring federal regulatory compliance and alerting the facility to potential survey compliance concerns. Key quality-of-care concerns often are detected by monitoring current documentation in residents' records. As a result, the HIM professional can serve as an ongoing compliance monitor for the facility.

In some long-term care facilities, the documentation of assessments and progress notes by social services, activities, and dietary staff is the responsibility of noncredentialed personnel who have limited training for their jobs. As a result, the HIM professional is a valued resource for training these personnel in the proper methods and procedures of charting, and for emphasizing the importance of their documentation as a part of the permanent medical record.

Training and education of long-term care facility staff is ongoing with respect to the various documentation requirements affecting long-term care reimbursement and regulatory compliance. This need is seen in all of the departments of the nursing facility as new graduates in nursing enter the long-term care setting and as more personnel from the acute-care setting are moving into the long-term care and sub-acute care facilities. The HIM professional is a valuable resource for ongoing in-service with all disciplines and for providing initial training as to the role of the MDS and the proper procedures to follow in the RAI and care planning processes.

The expertise of the HIM professional offers numerous opportunities in the long-term care environment, particularly as information management becomes more crucial to monitoring regulatory compliance and ensuring proper reimbursement from Medicare, Medicaid, and managed care payers. Skills in streamlining workflow, management of information for QI initiatives, and data collection and analysis for critical pathways are growing areas in the SNF and sub-acute care settings in which the HIM professional can offer tremendous value.

PROFESSIONAL SPOTLIGHT **FAITH-BASED, NOT-FOR-PROFIT NETWORK**

Who I am: Joshua King, MHA, RHIA, Director of Health Information Management

Where I Work: Lutheran Senior Services (LSS) a faith-based, mission-driven, not-for-profit network that specializes in enhancing life for seniors age 62+. Centralized in St. Louis, Missouri, LSS provides services in Greater St. Louis, Columbia, MO, Jefferson City, MO, Springfield, IL, and Peoria, IL, with 21 total locations in Missouri and Illinois. LSS offers services to seniors as part of its mission, including the following programs:

- LSS Senior Living Communities or Continuing Care Retirement Communities (CCRCs) provide full continuums of care, from independent living homes and apartments to residential care/assisted living to skilled nursing and memory care. Overall, LSS CCRCs provide care

to more than 3,300 individuals per year. In addition, LSS CCRCs provide REACH Short Stay, which is recovery and rehabilitation after a hospital stay. REACH Short Stay includes interdisciplinary expertise from a team that includes licensed nursing, therapy, nutritional management, social services, and spiritual care with a focus on improving activities of daily living to a residents highest potential.

- LSS Home and Community Based Services (HCBS) includes home health, hospice care, living-safe technologies, private duty, outreach social services, and senior connections. These programs provide service to more than 5,100 seniors who live independently at home. Through these service lines, seniors can receive assistance from medical care to help around the house, wherever they call home.

What I do: I am the Director of Health Information Management, responsible for leading and directing health information management staff and systems (both EHR and paper) at all LSS locations and programs. I oversee all ICD Coding, Release of Information (ROI) activities, and auditing procedures related to health information practice. I also oversee HIPAA Privacy, which includes developing policies and procedures and implementing auditing processes to ensure compliance at LSS. In addition, I have responsibilities for organizational projects including: oversight of data and analytics for the LSS Bundle Payment Care Initiative (BPCI) project and development/management of the LSS contract system.

Why HIM knowledge is important in my role: HIM knowledge has been the central most important value to the development and advancement of my professional career. I began as an Assistant Director of HIM in an acute-care setting, and from there advanced to my current role as Director of HIM for LSS. As the first Director of HIM at LSS, my primary initiative was to assess and understand practice in post-acute care, and based on those findings to develop policies and procedures to support a best practice of HIM operations. When creating the policies and procedures, I relied on reference resources obtained during my HIM studies while in school, as well as the AHIMA LTC resources. State and federal regulations for post-acute care are largely different from acute care settings, although my training and education in HIM assisted in understanding how regulations are developed and the importance of health care resources needed to research and obtain post-acute rules and regulations.

HIM knowledge has allowed me to develop and maintain a strong expertise of record management, whether it be information kept in an EHR, Enterprise Content Management (ECM) systems, or paper format. Although there are no Meaningful Use incentives for post-acute health care organizations, my knowledge allows me to provide input into processes that improve communication with other health care organizations and advance development of the Continuing Care Record (CCR). We make this possible through our objective to implement direct messaging and a patient portal to improve the transition of our residents from acute facilities. My knowledge and training from HIM allows me to understand the functionality of health care systems, ensuring that the HIM department can successfully provide an important component of data capture and analytics of organizational and patient care information.

In addition, HIM knowledge has kept me informed with all release of information regulations and allows me to make confident decisions when developing efficient and effective processes to ensure protected health information is accurately and appropriately released.

My HIM background is the foundation of my professional development in health care and continues to allow me to serve at LSS in many ways to ensure the mission of "Older Adults Living Life to the Fullest."

Other duties at LSS:

- BPCI Committee
- Lead of ICD-10 Implementation Committee
- Post-Acute Care (PAC) Collaborative Committee
- EHR Committee

As in other settings, an HIM professional who has gained experience in a certain setting and who has honed his or her management skills is often well-positioned for promotion involving more administrative responsibility.

SELF REVIEW 10.8

1. Distinguish between quantitative and qualitative audits.
2. True or False? The purpose of regular ongoing monitoring is to identify any programs or trends in documentation while correction is possible or when changes can be made.
3. List four items that a long-term care audit form might include.
4. Who is often the key resource for monitoring federal regulatory compliance and alerting the facility to potential survey compliance concerns?

TRENDS

Across the United States, a growing number of nursing homes and other residential care facilities are embracing the philosophy and values of a culture change. The residents, staff, and other stakeholders associated with these facilities are on a journey to transform traditional institutions into places where people are proud to live and work. This effort is a person-directed model called the **culture change movement**.

culture change movement a person-centered philosophy that creates a more homelike environment for residents of a nursing facility. Culture change involves providing individuals with privacy and the ability to make choices similar to what they would experience were they living in their own homes.

This movement challenges the institution-centered culture traditionally found in nursing homes, where control is in the hands of facility leadership and staff. This conventional hospital-type model treats residents as patients who are sick and unable to care for themselves or make decisions. The traditional model emphasizes efficient operation of the facility rather than the physical, social, and spiritual needs of the residents.

The culture change movement, in contrast, emphasizes the social model rather than the medical model in the way that care is rendered to elders. In the words of the culture change movement, it is about "creating home." A person-directed or self-directed model of care is one in which elders make their own decisions about their care and daily activities (Doty et al., 2008). Caregivers still are involved in decisions that are relevant to their jobs and to the individuals to whom they provide care. The elders, their families, and the staff form a community in which relationships are important.

Under the leadership of the Pioneer Network and culture change organizations such as the Eden Alternative, Action Pact, Wellspring, and the Live Oak Institute, the culture change movement has been gaining recognition for its successes in creating a better world for the elders, staff, and leadership of many nursing homes. This movement has regulatory support. The Centers for Medicare & Medicaid Services (CMS) released new interpretive guidance for several quality of life and environmental F-tags in April of 2009. CMS and the Pioneer Network also have cosponsored "Creating Home" national meetings promoting self-directed living and other concepts of the culture change movement.

These meetings have served to identify changes to the interpretive guidelines that CMS has used to enhance instructions to surveyors, with a sharpened focus on elements of quality of life. Some of the areas include F242 Self-Determination and Participation, which addresses resident choices about daily schedules; F172 Access and Visitation Rights; F241 Dignity; and F252 Homelike Environment.

SELF REVIEW 10.9

1. The _____ challenges the institution-centered culture traditionally found in nursing homes, where control is in the hands of the facility leadership and staff.

2. The model of care allowing elders to make their own decision about their care and daily activities is referred to as _____

3. _____ addresses resident choices about daily schedules.
   a. F172 Access and visitation rights
   b. F242 Self-determination and participation
   c. F252 Homelike Environment
   d. F241 Dignity

SUMMARY

As the population continues to age, the demand for long-term care facilities will continue to grow. Often considered to be one of the most regulated industries in the country, long-term care has unique information system needs and documentation requirements. Consequently, health information managers have valuable skills to offer this growing segment of the health care industry.

Prior federal regulations required the services of a credentialed health record practitioner as either an employee or a consultant of long-term care facilities participating in the Medicare or Medicaid programs. Although this regulation was deleted in the early 1990s, there has been a growing trend for long-term care facilities to employ credentialed health information managers as a result of the increasing demand for efficient and effective documentation and information systems. In the culture-changed environment, health information managers will find new challenges and at the same time will likely find pleasant features in their workplace, including interacting with the elderly and the aspects of their everyday living.

REVIEW QUESTIONS

Knowledge-Based Questions

1. Which two primary agencies regulate long-term care facilities?
2. What are the primary reimbursement categories for care of residents in long-term care facilities?
3. Who determines how long-term care facilities are reimbursed under the Medicaid program?
4. What are the three categories for which ratings are provided in the Five-Star Rating System for nursing homes? What are some of the specific long-stay and short-stay quality measures used in this system?
5. What is the single most important content characteristic of a care plan in a long-term care facility that is subject to federal regulations?

6. List common electronic software applications in long-term care.

Critical Thinking Questions

1. How is ICD coding relevant to the long-term care setting? Compare its impact in long-term care to acute care.
2. Why is there greater focus on concurrent documentation monitoring in the long-term care setting compared to evaluating documentation in the closed medical record?
3. Conduct additional research as necessary to discover the principal uses of the MDS in the long-term care industry (a) by the individual provider, (b) by the state agency, and (c) by CMS.

WEB ACTIVITY

Go to the CMS Nursing Home Quality Initiatives website at http://www.cms.gov/NursingHomeQualityInits Explore some of the links at the Nursing Home Quality Initiative website to answer the following questions:

1. What version of the MDS is currently in use?
2. Click on the "Quality Measures" link.

3. What items are included in the current long-stay and short-stay quality measures? How many additional measures have been added since the initial list of 10 measures?

CASE STUDY

You are the consultant for a long-term care facility that recently has undergone a long-term care survey in which the facility received several deficiency notations for noncompliance with federal requirements. The most significant deficiency involved a noted pattern (7 of 10 examples reviewed in the surveyor sample) in which comprehensive assessments (MDSs) were not completed within the required timeframe (within 14 days of admission).

In addition, the surveyors identified that no documentation supported the use of triggered care areas in the assessment and care-planning process. This resulted in related quality-of-care deficiencies for failure to adequately assess and manage urinary incontinence and psychosocial needs.

In three additional examples, the surveyors identified that residents had experienced a significant change

in condition without evidence of a new assessment being done. Within the statement of deficiencies, the surveyors noted that the director of nursing stated that she was unaware that assessments had not been done. And the nursing staff members stated that they did not understand what the care area triggers were, and that they were unaware of the federal criteria for determining when a significant change had occurred. The administrator of this facility has asked you to help develop a plan to correct these deficiencies. Here are the questions:

1. What would be your recommendations for overall system evaluation and revision?
2. What would be your recommendations for staff education?
3. How could the facility medical records designee be utilized to prevent similar problems from occurring in the future?

REFERENCES AND SUGGESTED READINGS

CMS (Centers for Medicare & Medicaid Services). (2002). Chapter 2: The assessment schedule for the RAI. *CMS's RAI Version 2.0 Manual.* [Online]. http://www.cms.gov/Medicare/Quality-Initiatives-Patient-Assessment-Instruments/NursingHome QualityInits/downloads/MDS20rai1202ch2.pdf

CMS (Centers for Medicare & Medicaid Services). (2004). Appendix R: Resident assessment instrument for long term care facilities. *State Operations Manual.* [Online]. http://cms.hhs.gov/manuals/Downloads/som107ap_r.pdf

CMS (Centers for Medicare & Medicaid Services). (2009a). *State Operations Manual, Appendix PP—Guidance to Surveyors for Long Term Care Facilities, Rev. 133, 02-06-15.* [Online]. https://www.cms.gov/Regulations-and-Guidance/Guidance/Manuals/downloads/som107ap_pp_guidelines_ltcf.pdf

CMS (Centers for Medicare & Medicaid Services). (2009b). *RAI User Manual* [Online]. http://www.cms.gov/NursingHomeQualityInits/20_NHQIMDS20.asp

CMS (Centers for Medicare & Medicaid Services. (2010a). Chapter 2: The Certification Process. *State Operations Manual.* [Online]. http://www.cms.hhs.gov/manuals/downloads/som107c02.pdf

CMS (Centers for Medicare & Medicaid Services). (2010b). Chapter 7: Survey and enforcement process for SNFs and NFs. *State Operations Manual.* [Online]. http://www.cms.hhs.gov/manuals/downloads/som107c07.pdf

CMS (Centers for Medicare & Medicaid Services). (2011). Appendix PP: Guidance to surveyors—long term care Facilities. *State Operations Manual.* [Online]. http://cms.hhs.gov/manuals/Downloads/som107ap_pp_guidelines_ltcf.pdf

CMS (Centers for Medicare & Medicaid Services). (2013a). *Overview on SNF Consolidated Billing.* [Online]. https://www.cms.gov/Medicare/Billing/SNFConsolidatedBilling/index.html

CMS (Centers for Medicare & Medicaid Services. (2013b). *CMS's RAI Version 3.0 Manual* [Online]. http://www.cms.gov/NursingHomeQualityInits/45_NHQIMDS30TrainingMaterials.asp

CMS (Centers for Medicare & Medicaid Services). (2014). Appendix P: Survey protocol for long term Care Facilities. *State Operations Manual* [Online]. http://www.cms.gov/NursingHomeQualityInits/45_NHQIMDS30TrainingMaterials.asp

CMS (Centers for Medicare & Medicaid Services). (2015). RAVEN Software. [Online]. http://www.cms.gov/Medicare/Quality-Initiatives-Patient-Assessment-Instruments/NursingHomeQualityInits/index.html?redirect=/NursingHomeQualityInits/45_NHQIMDS30TrainingMaterials.asp

Doty, M. M., Koren, M. J., & Sturla, E. L. (2008, May). Culture change in nursing homes: How far have we come? Findings from the Commonwealth Fund 2007 National Survey of Nursing Homes. *Commonwealth Fund.* [Online]. http://www.commonwealthfund.org/Content/Publications/Fund-Reports/2008/May/Culture-Change-in-Nursing-Homes—How-Far-Have-We-Come--Findings-From-The-Commonwealth-Fund-2007-Nati.aspx

e-CFR (Electronic Code of Federal Regulations). (2015). *Title 42, Public Health, section 488.301.* [Online]. http://www.ecfr.gov/cgi-bin/text-idx?SID=357173cb44afefef19a5da65f91babe8&mc=true&node=se42.5.488_1301&rgn=div8

Sullivan, J. G. (1996, March). Long term care on trial. *Contemporary Long Term Care,* p. 46.

The Joint Commission. (n.d.). *Certification: Disease-Specific Care.* [Online]. http://www.jointcommission.org/NR/rdonlyres/2933D499-84CC-4EC1-83A2-6990DDC7D977/0/Mktg_DSC_Brochure.pdf

KEY RESOURCES

American College of Health Care Administrators
http://www.achca.org

American Health Care Association
http://www.ahca.org

American Health Information Management Association
http://www.ahima.org

American Medical Directors Association
http://www.amda.com

Assisted Living Facilities Federation of America
http://www.alfa.org

Leading Age
http://leadingage.org

National Association for Directors of Nursing Administration in Long Term Care (NADONA/LTC)
http://www.nadona.org

The Joint Commission
http://www.jointcommission.org

CHAPTER 11

Rehabilitation

Ann H. Peden, PhD, RHIA, CCS | Terry Winkler, MD

LEARNING OBJECTIVES

Upon successful completion of this chapter, you should be able to:

- Identify and describe the various levels of rehabilitative care.
- Describe the major accrediting agencies for rehabilitation.
- List the members of an interdisciplinary rehabilitation team.
- Describe key features of the inpatient rehabilitation facility prospective payment system (IRF PPS).
- Explain the classification systems used to grade severity of injury/disability and relate them to outcome measures.
- Define the basic rehabilitation terms and distinguish between the concepts of impairment, disability, and handicap.
- Review sample forms that are used to track a person's progress in rehabilitation.
- Explain current trends in rehabilitation.

Setting	Description	Synonyms/Examples
Acute Care Hospitals	Inpatient facilities that provide acute medical care	Community hospitals Regional or tertiary care centers
Long-Term Acute Care Hospitals	Inpatient rehabilitation services to the patient who has an acute illness superimposed on chronic disability or for medically complicated patients	Long-term acute care
Freestanding Rehabilitation Centers	A center for rehabilitation that stands alone and is not physically part of another health care center	Physical therapy clinics Rehabilitation centers
Skilled Nursing Programs	Inpatient rehabilitation for patients who are progressing too slowly to meet criteria for standard rehabilitation programs	Nursing home rehabilitation Skilled nursing facilities
Outpatient Rehabilitation	Programs where therapy is provided but patient does not stay overnight	Day treatment centers Work hardening programs Occupational rehabilitation Chronic pain treatment centers Therapy clinics
Home Health Rehabilitation	Rehabilitation services provided to patients in their home by a home health care agency	Area agency on aging Various county health department programs Hospital-owned/operated home health National home health agencies

INTRODUCTION TO SETTING

Rehabilitation is the development of a person to the fullest physical, psychological, social, vocational, avocational, and educational potential consistent with his or her physiological or anatomic impairment and environmental limitations. Rehabilitation should begin when the patient enters a hospital with an injury or illness that will result in some limitations in the patient's functional status. The end result of comprehensive rehabilitation should be increased independence, increased overall functional status, and improved quality of life.

Types of Rehabilitation Settings

Rehabilitation is a continuum of care that begins with the patient's stay in the acute care hospital setting, extends throughout the post-acute hospital phase, and, in many cases, continues through outpatient treatment. The types of rehabilitation facilities expanded greatly in the late twentieth century. Rehabilitation now is provided in numerous types of settings.

Acute Rehabilitation

The **acute rehabilitation unit** in hospitals is the most common setting, and these units have more than doubled since around 1990. Rehabilitation wards usually have a set number of beds, ranging from 10 to 30, designated in one

rehabilitation the development of a person to the fullest physical, psychological, social, vocational, avocational, and educational potential consistent with his or her physiological or anatomic impairment and environmental limitations.

acute rehabilitation unit a designated unit in a hospital to which patients can be transferred for rehabilitation after treatment for the original acute illness or injury. Length of stay in these units is typically 2 to 4 weeks.

ward of a hospital where patients are transferred for their acute care rehabilitation. Length of patient stays vary from 2 to 4 weeks. When a patient is medically stable and has reached his or her maximum short-term improvement, the patient is transferred to a different setting based on his or her needs at that point.

Long-Term Acute Care (LTAC)

Long-term acute care (LTAC) facilities provide services to patients who have an acute illness superimposed on a chronic disability or for medically complicated patients. These facilities bridge the gap between acute hospitals and rehabilitation programs. (For more information on long-term acute care, see Chapter 2.)

Freestanding Rehabilitation Hospitals

In the 1990s, several national corporations were created to operate rehabilitation hospitals. These facilities are freestanding, but usually in proximity to larger medical centers to guarantee a referral base. **Freestanding rehabilitation hospitals** include acute rehabilitation centers and post-acute rehabilitation centers.

freestanding rehabilitation hospitals   inpatient rehabilitation facilities that may operate both acute and post-acute rehabilitation units.

Rehabilitation Provided in Skilled Nursing Settings

Skilled nursing rehabilitation centers are usually located in a wing of a nursing home or a hospital and serve a skilled-level patient. These facilities can accommodate a patient with multiple problems or older patients who are progressing more slowly than would be acceptable in an acute rehabilitation setting.

As a result of economic factors, patients are being discharged earlier from the hospital, which has resulted in the discharge of some patients who are not completely recovered yet and are unable to care for themselves. In many instances, because of their age, multiple medical problems, or other factors, patients may not be considered as a good candidates for an acute rehabilitation center. But if patients seem to be able to continue to make some progress given proper rehabilitation, they are ideal candidates for skilled-level rehabilitation. Skilled rehabilitation centers serve the population of patients who would benefit from inpatient rehabilitation but do not meet the criteria for rehabilitation admissions and acute or post-acute centers.

Outpatient Rehabilitation Facilities

Most rehabilitation centers, whether acute or post-acute, have outpatient components. Some freestanding outpatient rehabilitation facilities are independent and not affiliated with acute care hospitals. These facilities provide therapies and rehabilitation strategies for patients who do not require hospitalization or overnight stays. Most commonly, these facilities provide care for workers' compensation or sports injuries and/or services to patients who have progressed through acute and post-acute rehabilitation facilities.

A comprehensive outpatient rehabilitation facility (CORF) is a type of outpatient rehabilitation program certified by Medicare as a Part A provider. According to the Conditions of Participation, a CORF is "established and operated exclusively for the purpose of providing diagnostic, therapeutic, and restorative services to outpatients for the rehabilitation of injured, disabled, or sick persons, at a single fixed location, by or under the supervision of a physician..." (42 C.F.R. 485.51). At a minimum, a CORF must provide physicians' services, physical therapy services, and social or psychological services in a comprehensive and coordinated manner.

Home Health Care Rehabilitation

Home health care agencies provide rehabilitation services to the homebound patient who does not require hospitalization and who is unable to obtain transportation to an outpatient rehabilitation facility. "Homebound" means that that patient has substantial difficulty in being mobile in the community. A person with tetraplegia, for example, who requires a power wheelchair and a handicap van, would have substantial difficulty being mobile in the community. This is interpreted differently from agency to agency and in different regions.

Types of Caregivers

A rehabilitation team can be organized taking a multidisciplinary approach, which means that team members evaluate the patient in their specific discipline, or in an interdisciplinary approach, which means that the team members work together in a synergistic fashion to solve specific problems for the patient. An interdisciplinary approach, used in goal setting, problem solving, and coordination of treatment, provides a more cost-effective and nonfragmented treatment to the patient and is generally considered to be best. The interdisciplinary approach also improves patient learning, because all team members are reinforcing the learned concepts to approach the patient's specific problems. In 2009, CMS changed the wording in its regulations from *multidisciplinary* to *interdisciplinary* to reflect the most common and best practice for rehabilitation teams (CMS, 2009).

> rehabilitation team an interdisciplinary team made up of numerous allied health professions.

Several clinical specialists might be part of a patient's rehabilitation team. These include the physiatrist, occupational therapist, physical therapist, speech pathologist, psychologist, social worker, and rehabilitation nurse, as well as vocational rehabilitation counselors, recreational therapists, kinesiotherapists, music therapists, audiologists, and chaplains.

Physiatrist

A physiatrist, or physical medicine and rehabilitation physician, is generally the head of the rehabilitation team. A physiatrist is a physician who has completed 4 years of approved residency training after medical school in physical medicine and rehabilitation. The American Academy of Physical Medicine and

> physiatrist a physical medicine and rehabilitation physician.

Rehabilitation, the specialty board for physiatry, is recognized by the American Board of Medical Specialties. Physiatry is a small specialty, with some states having as few as a half-dozen physiatrists. The specialty has been in existence for some time, however, with the first specialty boards being given in 1947.

Occupational Therapist

occupational therapist (OT)   a therapist who has completed an educational program accredited by the American Occupational Therapy Association at the bachelor's level or higher. OTs address activities of daily living, upper-extremity movement, higher cognitive processes, and community skills, among other areas of rehabilitation.

An **occupational therapist (OT)** has completed a master's degree in an OT program accredited by the American Occupational Therapy Association (AOTA). Occupational therapists address several areas in their rehabilitation of a patient, including activities of daily living (ADLs) such as dressing, bathing, grooming, toileting, and transfers. OTs are members of the team that focuses on upper-extremity movement and function, including fine-motor control and hand-eye coordination. For example, they may fashion various splints for the upper extremity to preserve range of motion and improve function. OTs also address higher cognitive skills and community skills, such as homemaker chores, driving, and money handling. OTs assist in evaluating future equipment needs such as wheelchairs, cushions, and bathtub benches, and assist in recommendations for home modifications.

Physical Therapist

physical therapist (PT)   a therapist who has completed an educational program accredited by the American Physical Therapy Association at the bachelor's level or higher. PTs help patients improve their strength, range of motion, balance, and mobility, among other things.

The **physical therapist (PT)** is a member of the rehabilitation team who has completed a graduate program in physical therapy from a college or university program accredited by the American Physical Therapy Association's (APTA's) accrediting body, the Commission on Accreditation of Physical Therapy Education (CAPTE). In keeping with APTA's vision, most training programs now lead to a doctoral degree, with some master's-level training still available. Physical therapists are licensed by the state in which they practice. The physical therapist is the member of the team who is primarily responsible for improving the patient's strength, range of motion, balance, and mobility. The physical therapist specializes in appropriate strength and endurance exercises, assisting in controlling pain, providing skin care treatment, and providing modalities (such as ultrasound, diathermy, hot packs, and whirlpool treatments).

When rehabilitating injured workers, the physical therapist teaches proper lifting techniques, offers ergonomic suggestions, and conducts work-hardening programs and functional capacity evaluations. Work-hardening programs are outpatient treatment programs that assist an injured worker in maximizing his or her strength, range of motion, and functional status. They improve a worker's chances of returning to the job and avoiding future injuries. These treatment programs try to simulate activities that the worker would have to do in the workplace. A functional capacity evaluation is a formalized series of tests, usually with some parts computerized, that helps the physician determine safe levels of lifting, pushing, toting, bending, and climbing to which an injured worker would be able to return.

Speech-Language Pathologist

The **speech-language pathologist** has a master's level of education and is certified by the American Speech-Language-Hearing Association (ASHA). Almost all states have a licensure process for speech-language pathologists. The speech pathologist evaluates and treats patients who have aphasia, apraxia, dysarthria, dysphasia, communication disorders, and cognitive deficits. A speech pathologist would be concerned primarily with three broad areas: (1) swallowing problems, (2) communication problems, and (3) cognitive deficits.

Psychologist

A **psychologist** has a PhD level of training from a school accredited by the American Psychological Association (APA) and has completed the necessary requirements for licensure within his or her state. The primary role of the psychologist is to assist the person with recently acquired disabilities and his or her family in adjusting to the disability and developing a relationship of cooperation between the patient and the rehabilitation team. The psychologist has two primary roles in the rehabilitation team: (1) testing to identify problem areas in cognition or behavior on which the rehabilitation team should focus, and (2) counseling for the patient and his or her family members. When the person performing these roles has a master's degree instead of a doctor's degree, the position usually is termed *counselor*, *specialist*, or *clinician* rather than psychologist.

Social Worker

The **rehabilitation social worker** has a master's level of training with specific training and knowledge in the area of social work and may be certified by the National Association of Social Workers. Social workers also are licensed by the state in which they are practicing. The social worker assists the rehabilitation team by providing background information about the patient and his or her family situation, and in coordinating funding resources for the patient. The social worker also assures a smooth transition from the rehabilitation program back to the community.

Rehabilitation Nurse

The **rehabilitation nurse** is an RN who has completed a 2-year or 4-year accredited nursing program, is licensed in the state in which he or she practices, has completed additional training in rehabilitation nursing, and may be certified by the Association of Rehabilitation Nurses. The rehabilitation nurse plays a key role in the patient's rehabilitation by teaching the patient about proper bowel and bladder management programs and skin care. The rehabilitation nurse also is responsible for teaching the patient about medications, their indications, and their side-effects. This member of the rehabilitation team teaches the patient about the most common complications and problems associated with a disability—such as

speech-language pathologist a rehabilitation team member with a bachelor's or master's level of education who is certified by the American Speech, Language, and Hearing Association. The speech pathologist evaluates and treats patients with swallowing problems, communication problems, and cognitive deficits.

psychologist a person trained in psychology at the doctoral level who is certified by the American Psychological Association. In rehabilitation, a psychologist tests patients to identify problems in cognition or behavior and counsels the patient and family. A master's-level counselor also may perform some of these duties.

rehabilitation social worker a member of the rehabilitation team who has specific training and knowledge in the area of social work and who may be certified by the National Association of Social Workers. The social worker provides background information on the patient and family, coordinates funding resources, and helps the patient with the transition back to the community.

rehabilitation nurse a registered nurse who has received training and credentialing as a rehabilitation nurse.

deep vein thrombus, skin breakdown, or heterotopic ossification—and how to monitor them.

Kinesiotherapist

The **kinesiotherapist** has received specialized training in the proper techniques to maximize range of motion, strength, balance, and gait—a role similar to the physical therapist's role within the rehabilitation team. Typically, kinesiotherapists are employed in the VA system or in professional sports and training programs.

Other Health Care Workers

Numerous other health care professionals can contribute to the rehabilitation team. These might include dietitians, vocational rehabilitation counselors, recreational therapists, music therapists, audiologists, and chaplains.

Rehabilitation programs vary in which members of the rehabilitation team are essential, depending on the setting of the rehabilitation, the type of facility, and the types of rehabilitation patients who are accepted. In general, core members of the rehabilitation team for almost any program include, at a minimum, the physiatrist, occupational therapist, physical therapist, and speech pathologist. An inpatient program also requires a rehabilitation nurse and a social worker. The ratio of therapists to patients is critically important. The therapist should not be required to have more than approximately 6 hours of hands-on therapy time per day, to allow the therapist an opportunity for adequate patient record documentation and time for interdisciplinary meetings.

Types of Patients

Numerous diseases and injuries lead to a variety of disabling conditions. These disabilities can be divided into several general categories, including patients who require rehabilitation to treat injuries or disorders in the following areas:

- Orthopedic
- Neurologic
- Medical
- Pediatric
- Involving management of acute or chronic pain
- Sensory impairment

Patients requiring orthopedic rehabilitation have injuries such as fractured hips, total joint replacements, multiple fractures, amputations, or soft-tissue injuries. Pain management patients include those with acute pain and chronic pain such as back pain or cervical pain, cumulative trauma disorders, or reflex sympathetic dystrophy. Patients with neurologic injuries or diseases include those who have conditions such as stroke, traumatic brain injuries, spinal cord injuries, multiple sclerosis, or muscular dystrophy. Sensory-impaired patients have hearing or visual disabilities. Medical disabilities include chronic obstructive pulmonary disease (COPD), myocardial infarction, diabetes mellitus and its complications, and cancer.

Pediatric rehabilitation patients usually are viewed as a separate category because of their special needs. These patients often are considered to be *habilitation* patients rather than *rehabilitation* patients. Conditions that are commonly treated include cerebral palsy, spina bifida, and various genetic disorders. With regard to school-age and adolescent patients, the rehabilitation team also must consider the patient's educational needs, and the facility may be in communication with the patient's school regarding educational programs and progress.

Similarly, the aged population often has different rehabilitation issues and goals. They tend to be treated in a geriatric rehabilitation setting.

Because of the subspecialization required by rehabilitation team members, rehabilitation hospitals and programs tend to be specific to certain types of injuries. For example, some rehabilitation centers treat only brain injuries, spinal cord injuries, or burn survivors.

Spinal cord injury treatment centers have evolved to treat some of the 12,000 to 20,000 new cases of spinal cord injury each year in the United States (Centers for Disease Control, 2010). There are model system treatment centers specializing in treating spinal cord-injured patients, such as Craig Hospital in Englewood, Colorado, the Rehabilitation Institute of Chicago, and the Shepherd Center in Atlanta. These are among the 14 Spinal Cord Injury (SCI) Model System treatment centers funded by grants from the National Institute on Disability and Rehabilitation Research (NIDRR), a branch of the National Institutes of Health (NIH) in the 2011–2016 funding cycle.

The SCI Model System "supports innovative projects and research in the delivery, demonstration, and evaluation of medical, rehabilitation, vocational and other services to meet the needs of individuals with SCI" (see www.msktc.org). Many other hospital and rehabilitation centers across the United States also provide treatment for spinal cord injury (see www.sci-info-pages.com/rehabs.html).

Similarly, some rehabilitation centers focus on traumatic brain injury (TBI), such as the Texas TBI Model System of the Institute for Rehabilitation and Research (TIRR) Memorial Hermann, in Houston, Texas, and the Ohio Regional TBI Model System of the Department of Physical Medicine & Rehabilitation of Wexner Medical Center at the Ohio State University. These are among the 16 organizations that received Model Systems grants for traumatic brain injury treatment from NIDRR in the 2012–2017 funding cycle (see www.msktc.org).

According to the Centers for Disease Control and Prevention (2014), "In 2010, about 2.5 million emergency department (ED) visits, hospitalizations, or deaths were associated with TBI (and) TBI contributed to the deaths of more than 50,000 people."

According to the U.S. Census Bureau, "About 56.7 million people—19 percent of the population—had a disability in 2010, according to a broad definition of

disability, with more than half of them reporting the disability was severe" (www
.census.gov/newsroom/releases/archives/miscellaneous/cb12-134.html).

Understanding the proper terminology regarding this population is essential.
The World Health Organization (WHO) developed an international standard of
definitions for terms that are used to discuss individuals with functional limitations. **Impairment** is any temporary or permanent loss or abnormality of a body
structure or function, whether physiological or psychological. **Disability** is a restriction or inability to perform an activity in the manner or within the range considered normal for a human being, mostly resulting from impairment. **Handicap**
is the result of an impairment or a disability that limits or prevents the fulfillment
of one or several roles that are regarded as normal (depending on age, sex, social,
and cultural factors) for that individual. Stated differently, the impairment might
be the disease or diagnosis. The disability is how the impairment (i.e., the disease
or diagnosis) affects the person.

Finally, the handicap is an interaction between the impairment or disability and the person's socioeconomic environment. How does the problem
affect the person's life? What functional limitations or problems are posed by
the impairment or the disability? For example, amputation of a distal segment
of the index finger and the long finger of a hand would result in an impairment
(i.e., partial amputation of digits) and some disability (decreased range of
motion, decreased grip strength). In most situations, this injury would not result
in a major handicap. Given some rehabilitation and time, the individual would
learn how to adapt quite well to a relatively minor impairment. Now suppose
that the individual is a concert classical pianist. The handicap is overwhelming
in this situation, and the person would be totally disabled from pursuing his or
her occupation.

Consider an example of an individual with a spinal cord injury resulting in
paraplegia. This person then attends college, medical school, and residency training to become a rehabilitation physician. The impairment is spinal cord injury
with paraplegia; the disability is a mobility impairment with an inability to walk.
In this situation, however, the handicap is mild or moderate, because the hospital
is an accessible environment and the individual is able to practice rehabilitation
medicine in the environment of a hospital. Remember that the handicap is defined by the socioeconomic environment and the interaction of the impairment.
The same individual would be severely handicapped in being a tree surgeon or a
mountain climber!

Durable Medical Equipment Commonly Used

Assistive devices fall into many different categories depending on the type of
function the device is intended to supplement or augment. They can be divided
into several broad categories: orthotics, prosthetics, ambulation aids, wheelchairs,
and high-tech assistive devices such as computers. Table 11-1 provides examples
of the various types of durable medical equipment used in rehabilitation.

impairment any
temporary or permanent
loss or abnormality of a
body structure or function,
whether physiological
or psychological.

disability a restriction
or inability to perform an
activity in the manner or
within the range consid-
ered to be normal for a
human being, mostly
resulting from impairment.

handicap the result of an
impairment or a disability
that limits or prevents a
person from fulfilling one
or several roles that are
regarded as normal
(depending on age, sex,
social, and cultural factors)
for that individual.

TABLE 11-1	Examples of Durable Medical Equipment Used in Rehabilitation	
Device	**Definition**	**Examples**
Orthotics	An orthopedic appliance to support, align, prevent, or correct deformity or to improve function	AFO, KAFO, WHO, neck, back, or spine braces*
Ambulation aids	A device to provide stability and support for walking	Straight cane, walker, quad cane, crutches
Prosthetics	A device to replace a missing body part	Mechanical arm or leg, artificial eye, dentures, myoelectric arms
Wheelchairs/ mobility devices	A wheeled chair to provide mobility when ambulation is difficult or not possible	Standard wheelchair, power wheelchair, power scooter
High-technology assistive devices	Computer to control environments and wheelchairs	Kurzweil readers, Peachtree control systems

*AFO (ankle-foot orthosis); KAFO (knee-ankle-foot orthosis); WHO (wrist-hand orthosis)

Orthotics

An **orthotic device** is an external appliance or brace that can supplement an extremity's function or improve stability and positioning. Orthotics have existed for more than 300 years and come in a variety of shapes, sizes, and styles from leather to metal to polyethylene plastics. Spinal braces, either cervical or lumbar, are common. Cervical orthoses often are prescribed after trauma to the cervical spine, such as a motor vehicle accident, or after surgery. Various devices are available, from the Philadelphia collar—which is a soft foam-like collar that provides very little restriction of head movement and serves only as a proprioceptive reminder to the person to limit range of motion—to the halo, which is placed by the surgeon and provides the most stability for an unstable cervical spine. One of the most commonly seen cervical orthoses is a SOMI-type brace, named for the body parts that it contacts and its function (sternal occipital mandibular immobilizer).

Similarly, thoracolumbar orthoses come in a variety of styles and shapes, including the Jewett brace, which provides support in the upper sternal, midthoracic, and lower anterior abdominal area, and a chair-back-type brace that resembles a straight-back chair, with straps to keep it positioned properly on the back. For scoliosis, the Milwaukee brace is used most commonly to limit the progression of scoliotic spine. Interestingly, thoracolumbar orthoses tend to be named for the city in which they were developed.

There are several devices to stabilize or assist the function of an upper extremity that is impaired. These devices can be static or dynamic. A static device assists in positioning; the dynamic orthosis assists in replacing some function. A sling suspension orthosis, or ball-bearing feeder orthosis, assists a person with quadriplegia who has limited strength in the upper extremities, allowing this person to perform functional activities such as feeding himself or herself. A Cock-up

orthotic device an external appliance or brace that can supplement an extremity's function or improve stability and positioning.

splint, or flexor hinge splint, can be used in the C6 quadriplegic to replace the lost pinch grasp between the forefingers and the thumb.

Extremity orthoses are named for the body part with which they interact. For example, an orthosis that crosses the wrist and hand is a WHO (wrist-hand orthosis). One that goes over the back of the leg and around the bottom of the foot is an AFO (ankle-foot orthosis). If that same brace extends up the leg and just above the knee, it is a KAFO (knee-ankle-foot orthosis).

The most common lower-extremity orthotic is an AFO to replace weakened muscles in the leg and prevent the foot from dropping when ambulating. An additional brace that is seen commonly is the Swedish knee cage, which is used for athletes who have suffered injury to the ligaments in their knee.

Ambulation Aids

ambulation aids devices that provide additional stability and support for individuals who have trouble walking.

Ambulation aids provide additional stability and support for individuals who have trouble walking. These aids range from a straight cane to a walker. Wheels may be added to the walker to allow the person to move at a faster pace without having to pick up the walker. A variety of canes exist, from a straight cane to a quad cane, a device that has four feet to broaden the base of support. Crutches, such as wooden axillary crutches, are common. A Lofstrand (forearm) crutch is also used commonly, and sometimes platform crutches are required depending on the person's functional level.

Prosthetic Devices

prosthesis a device designed to replace a missing extremity or partially missing extremity.

Prosthetic devices are divided into upper-extremity and lower-extremity devices. A **prosthesis** is a device designed to replace a missing extremity or partially missing extremity. Prosthetics are divided into several categories: mechanical prostheses (body-powered prostheses), which are the most common; myoelectric prostheses, which are high-tech and use a series of electric motors to replace the missing action; and cosmetic prostheses, which improve appearance for social reasons and usually are less functional than body-powered or myoelectric prostheses. Lower-extremity amputations are much more common than are upper-extremity amputations.

Amputations are further defined by the level of amputation. A major body joint is used to make this distinction. For example, if the person is missing a portion of the hand and wrist, the amputation is said to be a BE (below-the-elbow) amputation. If the amputation is above the elbow, it is an AE amputation. In the lower extremity, if it is below the knee, it is a BKA (below-the-knee amputation). Above the knee, it is an AKA (above-knee amputation).

A variety of prosthetic devices are available depending on the patient's functional status and age. Terminology regarding prosthetics is presented in a standardized form. The prosthetic device is described based on the type of suspension, the type of skeleton, the type of joint, and the type of terminal devices. For example, a below-the-knee prosthesis is a PTB (patellar tendon-bearing) socket endoskeleton. The ankle is specified as a multi-axis or a single-axis ankle, and the type of foot is a SACH foot, Flex foot, or Seattle foot. Upper-extremity prosthetics terminology is presented in the same fashion: a description of the socket that fits over the amputated extremity, the type of skeleton support (endoskeleton or exoskeleton), the type of joint, and the type of terminal device.

Wheelchairs

Many different types and styles of wheelchairs are available. The choice depends on the patient's age, size, and intended use of the device. The two general categories for wheelchairs are manual wheelchairs and power wheelchairs.

Manual wheelchairs are divided into lightweight sports-type wheelchairs and standard wheelchairs. The lightweight sports-type chairs are used by those who pursue an active lifestyle, whereas the standard chairs are seen more commonly in hospitals and nursing homes and often are used by the elderly population.

Power wheelchairs (they should not be referred to as "electric chairs") and mobility devices are available and manufactured by the same companies that make manual wheelchairs. A variety of configurations are available depending on the person's functional status. Chairs are available that bring the person to a standing position, lay the person down, or tilt him or her in space if these functions are required. Chairs that have ventilator support also are available. Extremely advanced power wheelchair control systems now are available, such as the Peachtree system, which has a sensory array behind the chair user's head, and movement of the head controls the chair. Thus, looking to the left will make the chair turn left and looking to the right will make it turn right.

Technology Assistive Devices

There has been an explosion of computer technology designed to assist the disabled person. **Environmental control units (ECUs)** are now available that allow a person with limited mobility to run many everyday functions in the home, at work, or at school—such as turning on lights, using appliances, and opening and closing doors and windows. Recently, many devices on the market allow the disabled person to have greater access to the computer. Previously, computer technology was limited to individuals who had hand dexterity and could type on a keyboard. Now computers can be run with a variety of switching systems such as an eye-blink switch, an infrared beam that is able to catch a reflex from the eye, head control systems such as Head Master by Ultraphonics, and voice recognition systems such as Dragon NaturallySpeaking®.

Computer systems are available to assist visually impaired people. These devices, such as a Kurzweil reader, are able to scan print and convert it to spoken language. Augmentative communication devices are available to replace speech for individuals who are unable to communicate verbally.

environmental control units (ECUs) equipment that allows a person with limited mobility to perform many everyday functions in the home, at work, or at school—such as turning on lights, using appliances, and opening and closing doors and windows.

1. What are the six types of rehabilitation settings?
2. What are the differences regarding education and responsibilities between an occupational therapist and a physical therapist?
3. True or False? Geriatric patients typically are considered as habilitation patients rather than rehabilitation patients.
4. Differentiate the following functional limitations: impairment, disability, handicap.
5. What are some of the broad categories of assistive devices used in rehabilitation?

REGULATORY ISSUES

Medical rehabilitation is both medical and rehabilitative in nature. The dual nature of medical rehabilitation has resulted in two independent accreditation options—The Joint Commission and CARF (Commission for Accreditation of Rehabilitation Facilities)—as nationally recognized voluntary agencies to review care. The Centers for Medicare & Medicaid Services (CMS) regulate rehabilitation for Medicare recipients. The *Code of Federal Regulations* contains Conditions of Participation for hospitals, comprehensive outpatient rehabilitation facilities (CORFs), and clinics and other agencies providing inpatient/outpatient physical therapy and speech-language pathology services.

In addition, because inpatient rehabilitation facilities have their own prospective payment system for Medicare, CMS has outlined criteria that an inpatient facility must meet to be classified as a rehabilitation hospital. State licensure agencies generally use these regulations and criteria as basic components in the process of licensing rehabilitation facilities. Other criteria for state licensure varies from state to state.

The Joint Commission

The Joint Commission (TJC) surveys facilities according to standards that are intended to promote quality and improve outcomes in rehabilitation at all levels of medical care. To receive Medicare reimbursement, a facility must have Joint Commission accreditation or otherwise be deemed to meet the Conditions of Participation. An organization accredited by TJC may choose to pursue additional disease-specific care certifications, if desired. Certifications applicable to rehabilitation programs can be sought by acute-care hospitals, rehabilitation hospitals, long-term care facilities, or home care organizations. These disease-specific certification programs include stroke rehabilitation, brain injury rehabilitation, cardiac rehabilitation, orthopedic rehabilitation, and pulmonary rehabilitation (see www.jointcommission.org).

CARF International

CARF International (formerly Commission on Accreditation of Rehabilitation Facilities) standards and criteria for full accreditation are comprehensive and specific in regard to the rehabilitation care of patients. CARF accreditation is difficult to attain; thus, many rehabilitation centers fail to apply for CARF accreditation. The quality of care in a rehabilitation program, however, is markedly affected by meeting the standards of CARF. In the managed care market, insurance companies seek out CARF-accredited programs to ensure the best patient care.

The standards (Section A) for a comprehensive inpatient rehabilitation program require the medical director to be a physical medicine and rehabilitation physician (physiatrist) or a physician who is qualified by virtue of his or her training and experience in rehabilitation and who is board-certified in his or her area of specialty and has the appropriate experience and training necessary to provide rehabilitation physician services through one of the following:

1. Formal residency in physical medicine and rehabilitation
2. A fellowship in rehabilitation for a minimum of one year or
3. A minimum of two years of experience in providing rehabilitation services for patients

Accrediting agencies and third-party payers strongly advocate that the medical director of a rehabilitation facility be a board-eligible or board-certified physiatrist. If a physiatrist is not available, board-eligible or board-certified neurologists or orthopedists may serve.

The rehabilitation physician has the responsibility for care of the patient who has the potential for continuing, unstable, or complex medical conditions or must make arrangements for the care to be provided through other physicians (consults). In addition, general inpatient standards may be applied to specific programs in brain injury, spinal cord injury, stroke, and amputation.

Centers for Medicare & Medicaid Services (CMS)

The Centers for Medicare & Medicaid Services (CMS) promulgate regulations affecting several types of rehabilitation providers. There are Conditions of Participation for hospitals (inpatient rehabilitation services), as well as for outpatient services (physical and occupational therapists in independent practice, outpatient physical therapy, occupational therapy, and speech pathology services), and comprehensive outpatient rehabilitation facilities (CORFs).

The 60 Percent Rule

One set of CMS regulations provides criteria that determine whether a hospital or unit can be classified as an inpatient rehabilitation facility. A hospital that meets the criteria can receive Medicare reimbursement under the **inpatient rehabilitation facility prospective payment system (IRF PPS)** rather than under the diagnosis related group (DRG) system of reimbursement applied to short stay acute care hospitals. One of the criteria, the **60 percent rule**, defines the types of conditions that should comprise the caseload of a rehabilitation hospital. The original rule, which took effect in 1983, was used to determine whether a hospital or unit was exempt from the DRG-based inpatient prospective payment

inpatient rehabilitation facility prospective payment system (IRF PPS) the prospective payment system by which inpatient rehabilitation facilities are paid for services provided to Medicare beneficiaries. Each patient stay is categorized into a case-mix group (CMG) that determines the payment that will be received by the facility from Medicare.

60 percent rule one of the criteria for defining a hospital as an inpatient rehabilitation facility (IRF); requires that at least 60 percent of the patients treated have at least one of 13 qualifying medical conditions.

system and required that certain conditions comprise 75 percent of the caseload for classification as an IRF.

After implementation of the IRF PPS in 2002, CMS suspended enforcement of the 75 percent rule in order to evaluate whether changes were needed in the regulation. The study commissioned by CMS showed that the majority of IRFs did not meet the criteria specified in the 75 percent rule. The Medicare, Medicaid, and SCHIP Extension Act of 2007 (MMSEA) established the threshold at 60 percent and allowed secondary conditions to be counted as qualifying conditions. The conditions that count toward the 60 percent are as follows:

(A) Stroke.

(B) Spinal cord injury.

(C) Congenital deformity.

(D) Amputation.

(E) Major multiple trauma.

(F) Fracture of femur (hip fracture).

(G) Brain injury.

(H) Neurologic disorders, including multiple sclerosis, motor neuron diseases, polyneuropathy, muscular dystrophy, and Parkinson's disease.

(I) Burns.

(J) Active, polyarticular rheumatoid arthritis, psoriatic arthritis, and seronegative arthropathies resulting in significant functional impairment of ambulation and other activities of daily living that have not improved after an appropriate, aggressive, and sustained course of outpatient therapy services or services in other less-intensive rehabilitation settings immediately preceding the inpatient rehabilitation admission or that result from a systemic disease activation immediately before admission, but have the potential to improve with more intensive rehabilitation.

(K) Systemic vasculitides with joint inflammation, resulting in significant functional impairment of ambulation and other activities of daily living that have not improved after an appropriate, aggressive, and sustained course of outpatient therapy services or services in other less-intensive rehabilitation settings immediately preceding the inpatient rehabilitation admission or that result from a systemic disease activation immediately before admission, but have the potential to improve with more intensive rehabilitation.

(L) Severe or advanced osteoarthritis (osteoarthrosis or degenerative joint disease) involving two or more major weight-bearing joints (elbow, shoulders, hips, or knees, but not counting a joint with a prosthesis) with joint deformity and substantial loss of range of motion, atrophy of muscles surrounding the joint, significant functional impairment of ambulation and other activities of daily living that have not improved after the patient has participated in an appropriate, aggressive, and sustained course of outpatient therapy services or services in other less-intensive rehabilitation settings immediately preceding the inpatient rehabilitation admission but have the potential to improve with more intensive rehabilitation. (A joint replaced by a prosthesis no longer is considered to have osteoarthritis, or other arthritis, even though this condition was the reason for the joint replacement.)

(M) Knee or hip joint replacement, or both, during an acute hospitalization immediately preceding the inpatient rehabilitation stay and also . . . one or more of the following specific criteria:

(1) The patient underwent bilateral knee or bilateral hip joint replacement surgery during the acute hospital admission immediately preceding the IRF admission.

(2) The patient is extremely obese with a Body Mass Index of at least 50 at the time of admission to the IRF.

(3) The patient is age 85 or older at the time of admission to the IRF.
(42 C.F.R. 412.23)

The health information department has an important role to play in ensuring correct coding and data quality so the percentage of patients falling into the various condition categories can be calculated accurately.

Other CMS Requirements

Other CMS requirements include regulations regarding the services that must be provided in an inpatient rehabilitation facility and preadmission screening requirements.

Medical Supervision and Other Services   CMS also requires that patients in an inpatient rehabilitation facility receive "close medical supervision" (Classification criteria for payment under the inpatient rehabilitation facility prospective payment system, 2014). Other services needed in a rehabilitation hospital are rehabilitation nursing, physical therapy, occupational therapy, speech therapy, social or psychological services, and orthotic and prosthetic services. A qualified physician must serve as fulltime director of rehabilitation.

Preadmission Screening   CMS requires that the rehabilitation hospital have a preadmission screening procedure to determine whether a prospective patient is likely to benefit from inpatient rehabilitation. Figure 11-1 provides a quick overview of key points in meeting the CMS requirements for preadmission screening documentation. Pertinent functional information about the patient should be collected during the preadmission screening process to help define areas of functional deficit and thus assist in goal development. Each inpatient selected for admission must have a plan of treatment established, with an interdisciplinary team approach, and the preadmission screening must be validated by the admitting physician.

FIGURE 11-1

An excerpt from the CMS Fact Sheet, "Inpatient Rehabilitation Therapy Services: Complying with Documentation Requirements"

Required Preadmission Screening

A preadmission screening is a detailed and comprehensive evaluation of the patient's condition and need for rehabilitation therapy and medical treatment that must be conducted by a licensed or certified clinician(s) (appropriately trained to assess the patient medically and functionally) within the 48 hours immediately preceding the IRF admission. This screening is the initial determination of whether the patient meets the requirements for IRF admission.

If the preadmission screening is completed more than 48 hours prior to admission, there must be a reassessment. The reassessment may be completed by telephone. Any changes from the previous assessment must be documented.

While a physician extender can complete the preadmission screening, the rehabilitation physician must give concurrence that the patient meets the requirements for IRF admission. A rehabilitation physician must review, sign, and date the screening before the patient is admitted to the IRF. The preadmission screening may be completed in person or by telephone (a preadmission screening conducted entirely by telephone will not be accepted without transmission of the patient's medical records from the referring hospital to the IRF and a review of those records by licensed or certified clinical staff in the IRF).

Preadmission screening documentation must justify that the patient requires, will benefit significantly from, and is able to actively participate in intensive rehabilitation therapy. Check-off lists are not acceptable documentation. The preadmission screening documentation must include:

- The specific reasons that led the IRF clinical staff to conclude the IRF admission would be reasonable and necessary;
- The patient's prior level of function;
- The patient's expected level of improvement;
- The expected length of time necessary to achieve the expected level of improvement;
- An evaluation of the patient's risk for clinical complications;
- Treatments needed (OT, PT, SLP, or prosthetics/orthotics);
- The expected frequency and duration of treatment in the IRF;
- The anticipated discharge destination;
- Any anticipated post-discharge treatments; and
- Other information relevant to the care needs of the patient.

Source: http://www.cms.gov/Outreach-and-Education/Medicare-Learning-Network-MLN/MLNProducts/downloads/Inpatient_Rehab_Fact_Sheet_ICN905643.pdf

---

SELF REVIEW 11.2

1. True or False? The Joint Commission offers disease-specific certifications that are applicable only to inpatient rehabilitation facilities.

2. Why do insurance companies seek out CARF-accredited programs?

3. The CARF standards (Section A) require the medical director to be a _____ or a _____.

4. True or False? The Centers for Medicare & Medicaid Services (CMS) do not promulgate regulations affecting rehabilitation providers.

4. A hospital that meets the CMS criteria to be classified as an inpatient rehabilitation facility is not reimbursed through the MS-DRG system under the acute inpatient prospective payment system, but, instead, under _____.

DOCUMENTATION

As in all health care facilities, specific guidelines indicate the documentation that must be completed in a patient's medical records. This chapter does not cover this topic in its entirety, but basic principles of medical record documentation should be followed, as in other health care settings. This chapter focuses on additional or specific documentation requirements in the rehabilitation facility as applied to specific sections of the records.

The admission history should include a functional history. The functional history should cover the patient's functional status before the onset of the illness or injury. If the person had a preexisting disability and now is returning to rehabilitation because of a change in condition, a discussion of the patient's functional status before the onset of the new illness or change is required. The functional history addresses activities of daily living, required assisted devices, reliance on other caregivers, and a discussion of community mobility.

The history also includes a discussion of equipment that the person has at home. A full description of braces, orthoses, prosthetics, or durable medical equipment is required. Also included is a description of the type of vehicle the individual has, because this will affect in many ways the type of wheelchair that can be prescribed for the patient.

The social history must include a discussion of available family members or caregivers, a description of the home (e.g., multilevel, single level, number of steps at entrance, accessibility of bathroom), educational status, employment status, and previous hobbies, in addition to standard social history information such as alcohol and drug abuse.

The physical examination includes a comprehensive neurologic and musculoskeletal exam, adequate documentation of the condition of the skin, and a description of interventional devices such as a catheter, feeding tube, or tracheostomy. The neurologic exam includes cranial nerves, motor strength, reflexes, and sensory nerves. It also includes mention of the patient's cognitive, speech, and language capabilities. The examination must clearly describe the functional status of the individual both cognitively and physically. The musculoskeletal exam should document the range of motion of all joints and extremities, note contractures, amputations, or missing body parts, and indicate the presence or absence of complications such as deep vein thrombosis or heterotopic ossification.

The section on psychiatric history and physical diagnosis includes standard medical diagnoses as well as functional rehabilitation diagnoses. For example, a spinal cord-injured patient's admission diagnoses may be (1) T9 spinal cord injury, (2) decreased strength and endurance, and (3) dependence for ADL activities. Stating the functional limitations or problems in the diagnostic sections helps to focus the rehabilitation team on the primary issue of concern that has led to the rehabilitation treatment.

The history and physical report also includes a specific discussion of goals as they relate to the interdisciplinary team. For example, a physician notes that occupational therapy is to focus on dressing, bathing, grooming, and equipment needs or that physical therapy is to address decreased strength, transfer skills, balance, and range of motion. The plan section is specific and outlines the goals in quantitative terms for the entire rehabilitation team. The plan concludes with a statement of the estimated length of stay for the hospitalization.

In summary, the history and physical report by the physician should provide identification of presenting problems, goals and expected benefits, initial estimated timeframes for accomplishing goals, and services needed. The individual's pathological diagnosis, impairment, and functional limitations must be discussed thoroughly in the physician history and physical. This serves as basis for the initial plan of care for the interdisciplinary team to follow. With regard to team conferences in general, the physician documents, in each of the areas of concern, the comments of the interdisciplinary team regarding the patient's progress. In addition, the team conference sets goals to be accomplished in the rehabilitation stay.

Federal regulations outlining coverage criteria include requirements for information that must be documented regarding the type and frequency of services that the patient receives, documentation of the preadmission screening, a post-admission physician evaluation, and an individualized overall plan of care, including weekly team meetings, as follows:

42 CFR § 412.622 Basis of payment.

(a) *Method of payment* . . .

(3) *IRF coverage criteria.* In order for an IRF claim to be considered reasonable and necessary under section 1862(a)(1) of the Act, there must be a reasonable expectation that the patient meets all of the following requirements at the time of the patient's admission to the IRF—

   (i) Requires the active and ongoing therapeutic intervention of multiple therapy disciplines (physical therapy, occupational therapy, speech-language pathology, or prosthetics/orthotics therapy), one of which must be physical or occupational therapy.

   (ii) Generally requires and can reasonably be expected to actively participate in, and benefit from, an intensive rehabilitation therapy program. Under current industry standards, this intensive rehabilitation therapy program generally consists of at least 3 hours of therapy (physical therapy, occupational therapy, speech-language pathology, or prosthetics/orthotics therapy) per day at least 5 days per week. In certain well-documented cases, this intensive rehabilitation therapy program might instead consist of at least 15 hours of intensive rehabilitation therapy within a 7 consecutive day period, beginning with the date of admission to the IRF. Benefit from this intensive rehabilitation therapy program is demonstrated by measurable improvement that will be of practical value to the patient in improving the patient's functional capacity or adaptation to impairments. The required therapy treatments must begin within 36 hours from midnight of the day of admission to the IRF. Is sufficiently stable at the time of admission to the IRF to be able to actively participate in the intensive rehabilitation therapy program that is described in paragraph (a)(3)(ii) of this section.

(iii) Requires physician supervision by a rehabilitation physician, defined as a licensed physician with specialized training and experience in inpatient rehabilitation. The requirement for medical supervision means that the rehabilitation physician must conduct face-to-face visits with the patient at least 3 days per week throughout the patient's stay in the IRF to assess the patient both medically and functionally, as well as to modify the course of treatment as needed to maximize the patient's capacity to benefit from the rehabilitation process.

(4) *Documentation.* To document that each patient for whom the IRF seeks payment is reasonably expected to meet all of the requirements in paragraph (a)(3) of this section at the time of admission, the patient's medical record at the IRF must contain the following documentation—

(i) A comprehensive preadmission screening that meets all of the following requirements—

  (A) It is conducted by a licensed or certified clinician(s) designated by a rehabilitation physician described in paragraph (a)(3)(iv) of this section within the 48 hours immediately preceding the IRF admission. A preadmission screening that includes all of the required elements, but that is conducted more than 48 hours immediately preceding the IRF admission, will be accepted as long as an update is conducted in person or by telephone to update the patient's medical and functional status within the 48 hours immediately preceding the IRF admission and is documented in the patient's medical record.

  (B) It includes a detailed and comprehensive review of each patient's condition and medical history.

  (C) It serves as the basis for the initial determination of whether or not the patient meets the requirements for an IRF admission to be considered reasonable and necessary in paragraph (a)(3) of this section.

  (D) It is used to inform a rehabilitation physician who reviews and documents his or her concurrence with the findings and results of the preadmission screening.

  (E) It is retained in the patient's medical record at the IRF.

(ii) A post-admission physician evaluation that meets all of the following requirements—

  (A) It is completed by a rehabilitation physician within 24 hours of the patient's admission to the IRF.

  (B) It documents the patient's status on admission to the IRF, includes a comparison with the information noted in the preadmission screening documentation, and serves as the basis for the development of the overall individualized plan of care.

  (C) It is retained in the patient's medical record at the IRF.

(iii) An individualized overall plan of care for the patient that meets all of the following requirements—

  (A) It is developed by a rehabilitation physician, as defined in paragraph (a)(3)(iv) of this section, with input from the interdisciplinary team within 4 days of the patient's admission to the IRF.

  (B) It is retained in the patient's medical record at the IRF.

(5) *Interdisciplinary team approach to care.* In order for an IRF claim to be considered reasonable and necessary under section 1862(a)(1) of the Act, the patient must require an interdisciplinary team approach to care, as evidenced by documentation in the patient's medical record of weekly interdisciplinary team meetings that meet all of the following requirements—

(A) The team meetings are led by a rehabilitation physician as defined in paragraph (a)(3)(iv) of this section, and further consist of a registered nurse with specialized training or experience in rehabilitation; a social worker or case manager (or both); and a licensed or certified therapist from each therapy discipline involved in treating the patient. All team members must have current knowledge of the patient's medical and functional status.

(B) The team meetings occur at least once per week throughout the duration of the patient's stay to implement appropriate treatment services; review the patient's progress toward stated rehabilitation goals; identify any problems that could impede progress towards those goals; and, where necessary, reassess previously established goals in light of impediments, revise the treatment plan in light of new goals, and monitor continued progress toward those goals.

(C) The results and findings of the team meetings, and the concurrence by the rehabilitation physician with those results and findings, are retained in the patient's medical record.

The physical therapist and occupational therapist, as well as other disciplines, are required to document daily notes regarding their treatment, interactions with the patient, and the results. This documentation should be done in functional terms and be related clearly to the specific goals identified for the hospitalization. The number of minutes or hours that the patient has actually participated in therapy should be clearly indicated in the therapist's documentation.

Nursing documentation includes information about the patient's skin status; bowel and bladder status; knowledge of medications, uses, and side-effects; information regarding the patient's functional status in terms of self-care and skin care; and documentation of the patient's knowledge regarding common complications given the disability.

At the conclusion of hospitalization, the discharge summary includes a discussion, in quantifiable terms, of the patient's functional status at the time of admission and his or her functional status at the time of discharge, and should reflect the patient's progress or lack of progress. Recommendations regarding equipment needs or home support services are addressed specifically in the discharge summary.

The discharge recommendations and a discharge conference should be held with the patient and/or responsible family members. The discharge summary and recommendations should contain specific warnings or limitations for the patient. Safety issues and other concerns—such as driving, preparing meals, and the need for attendant care—should be discussed.

CARF-accredited facilities are required to have a set of policies that clearly address how the rehabilitation patient may gain access to his or her own records. In addition, there must be documentation that the patient has been provided with orientation to the rehabilitation facility, which includes a statement of the organization's mission and philosophy, participation in goal setting, and a list of the patient's rights and responsibilities.

Further, CARF requires that individual program planning be performed and documented. The plans must be individualized, establish the goals and objectives for the admission, and incorporate the unique strengths, needs, abilities, and preferences of the person served. There must be documentation that the patient understands the goals, and this must reflect the person's informed choice.

Functions of the interdisciplinary team that must be documented in the record include: (1) assessment of the person served; (2) determination, modification, and implementation of the individual plan and the discharge plan of the person served; (3) provision of direct services consistent with needs; (4) active participation in care planning of the person served; and (5) promotion of interdisciplinary functions and mutual support among all members of the team. Medical records systems can be established in such a way as to meet these requirements and minimize the number and types of forms required. Examples are provided later in the chapter.

The rehabilitation assessment must document (1) the needs of the person from a rehabilitation perspective; (2) desired outcomes and expectations of the patient; (3) outcomes anticipated by the interdisciplinary team; (4) the use of assistive technology as needed; and (5) the use of assessment findings to direct the development of the individual's plan.

SELF REVIEW 11.3

1. The _____ history should cover the patient's functional status before the onset of the illness or injury.

2. The _____ history must include a discussion of available family members or caregivers, a description of the home (i.e., multilevel, single level, number of steps at entrance, accessibility of bathroom, etc.), educational status, employment status, and previous hobbies, in addition to alcohol and drug abuse.

3. In the notes regarding a patent's treatment, the therapist should clearly indicate the number of _____ the patient has actually participated in therapy.
   a. months or weeks
   b. days or sessions
   c. minutes or hours

4. True or False? The history and physical by the physician should provide identification of presenting problems, goals and expected benefits, initial estimated time frames for accomplishing goals, and services needed.

5. What are the five items that the rehabilitation assessment must document?

REIMBURSEMENT AND FUNDING

Equitable reimbursement for rehabilitation cannot be made on the basis of diagnosis related groups (DRGs), because many factors other than those considered by the DRG system determine the patient's functional level and, thus, recovery of the patient. In other words, two patients with an identical diagnosis can have different functional problems and handicaps based on a host of factors. (Recall the previous discussion of the definitions of *impairment, disability,* and *handicap.*) These factors include age, weight, gender, comorbidities, psychological factors, premorbid personality, educational status, and occupation, to name a few. Implemented in January 2002, the Medicare inpatient rehabilitation facility prospective payment system (IRF PPS) does consider more than the patient's diagnoses and procedures, but it does not take into account every factor that affects the patient's recovery.

Under the IRF PPS, a rehabilitation hospital is reimbursed for each patient admission. Patient stays are classified into **case-mix groups (CMGs),** which determine the payment the facility will receive from Medicare. The factors that influence the assignment of a case into a given CMG include rehabilitation impairment categories (RICs), functional measurements, age, and comorbidities. Diagnosis codes determine the RICs, which group cases that are similar in clinical characteristics and resource use. Functional measures that influence CMG assignment are motor and cognitive scores. Some CMG categories also consider the patient's age. Finally, comorbidities, or secondary diagnoses, affect CMG assignment and are classified into three categories, or tiers, based on whether the costs are considered high, medium, or low.

Most of the CMGs are subject to four relative weights—the three that reflect the comorbidity tiers and one for patients with no comorbidities. Comorbidity tiers do not apply to the CMG for patients discharged before the fourth day (short-stay outliers) or to the CMGs for the relatively unusual cases in which patients expire in a rehabilitation facility. The IRF PPS has increased emphasis on coding with the current clinical modification of the *International Classification of Disease (ICD).* This is because the CMG payment is influenced by RICs, which correspond to certain categories of codes, and also by comorbidities, which are reported directly as diagnosis codes.

In addition, a length of stay is assigned to each CMG under the payment system. Providers know that these lengths of stay are merely averages, and many patients have longer or shorter lengths of stay than the time outlined in the regulations. CMGs, however, have required rehabilitation hospitals to give attention to the length of time necessary to treat patients. See Figure 11-2 for an excerpt from the CMG table demonstrating the assignment of relative weights and average lengths of stay for selected CMGs (CMS, 2014, August).

The CMG assignment is based on information recorded on the patient assessment tool, the **Inpatient Rehabilitation Facility Patient Assessment Instrument (IRF-PAI).** This tool captures all of the information necessary to assign a CMG, including codes for up to 25 comorbidities. The IRF-PAI must be completed upon the patient's admission and again at discharge, with the admission and discharge data transmitted together after the patient has been discharged. The complete IRF-PAI instrument and instructions, including the IRF-PAI Training Manual, are available at the CMS Web site. In addition to codes and other information needed to assign a CMG to the case, the IRF-PAI also includes admission and discharge quality indicators. Figure 11-3 provides

case-mix groups (CMG) any of 100 categories into which an inpatient rehabilitation stay can be classified based on data submitted on the IRF-PAI; determined by factors such as rehabilitation impairment category (RIC), functional measurements, age, and comorbidities.

Inpatient Rehabilitation Facility Patient Assessment Instrument (IRF-PAI) an instrument used to gather data regarding each patient stay that will be used to determine the payment for that stay under the Medicare inpatient rehabilitation facility prospective payment system.

FIGURE 11-2

Examples of relative weights for case-mix groups (CMGs).

CMG	CMG Description	(M=motor, C=cognitive, A=age)	Relative Weight				Average Length of Stay			
			Tier 1	Tier 2	Tier 3	None	Tier 1	Tier 2	Tier 3	None
101	Stroke	M>51.05	0.7853	0.7150	0.6512	0.6248	9	10	8	8
102	Stroke	M>44.45 and M<51.05 and C>18.5	0.9836	0.8955	0.8155	0.7826	11	11	10	10
103	Stroke	M>44.45 and M<51.05 and C<18.5	1.1636	1.0594	0.9648	0.9258	12	14	12	12
104	Stroke	M>38.85 and M<44.45	1.2121	1.1036	1.0050	0.9644	13	13	12	12
105	Stroke	M>34.25 and M<38.85	1.4155	1.2888	1.1737	1.1262	14	14	14	14
106	Stroke	M>30.05 and M<34.25	1.6135	1.4691	1.3379	1.2838	16	16	15	15
107	Stroke	M>26.15 and M<30.05	1.8026	1.6412	1.4946	1.4342	17	19	17	17
108	Stroke	M<26.15 and A>84.5	2.2467	2.0456	1.8629	1.7876	22	24	21	21
109	Stroke	M>22.35 and M<26.15 and A<84.5	2.0570	1.8728	1.7055	1.6366	19	20	19	19
110	Stroke	M<22.35 and A<84.5	2.6928	2.4518	2.2328	2.1425	28	27	24	24
201	Traumatic brain injury	M>53.35 and C>23.5	0.8145	0.6636	0.5954	0.5680	10	9	8	8
202	Traumatic brain injury	M>44.25 and M<53.35 and C>23.5	1.0591	0.8629	0.7741	0.7385	12	10	9	10
203	Traumatic brain injury	M>44.25 and C<23.5	1.2162	0.9909	0.8890	0.8481	13	12	12	11
204	Traumatic brain injury	M>40.65 and M<44.25	1.3397	1.0915	0.9793	0.9342	12	13	12	12
205	Traumatic brain injury	M>28.75 and M<40.65	1.5924	1.2974	1.1640	1.1104	14	15	14	14
206	Traumatic brain injury	M>22.05 and M<28.75	1.9327	1.5747	1.4127	1.3477	19	18	16	16
207	Traumatic brain injury	M<22.05	2.5640	2.0890	1.8741	1.7880	32	25	21	20

Source: CMS. http://www.cms.gov/Medicare/Medicare-Fee-for-Service-Payment/InpatientRehabFacPPS/Data-Files.html.

FIGURE 11-3

Quality Indicators – Discharge – from the proposed 2016 draft of the IRF-PAI.

OMB No. 0938-0842

Patient _____   Identifier _____   Date _____

DISCHARGE

Section GG	**Functional Abilities and Goals**

GG0130. Self-Care (3-day assessment period)

Code the patient's usual performance at discharge for each activity using the 6-point scale. If activity was not attempted at discharge, code the reason.

CODING:
Safety and **Quality of Performance** - If helper assistance is required because patient's performance is unsafe or of poor quality, score according to amount of assistance provided.

Activities may be completed with or without assistive devices.

06. **Independent** - Patient completes the activity by him/herself with no assistance from a helper.

05. **Setup or clean-up assistance** - Helper SETS UP or CLEANS UP; patient completes activity. Helper assists only prior to or following the activity.

04. **Supervision or touching assistance** - Helper provides VERBAL CUES or TOUCHING/STEADYING assistance as patient completes activity. Assistance may be provided throughout the activity or intermittently.

03. **Partial/moderate assistance** - Helper does LESS THAN HALF the effort. Helper lifts, holds or supports trunk or limbs, but provides less than half the effort.

02. **Substantial/maximal assistance** - Helper does MORE THAN HALF the effort. Helper lifts or holds trunk or limbs and provides more than half the effort.

01. **Dependent** - Helper does ALL of the effort. Patient does none of the effort to complete the activity. Or, the assistance of 2 or more helpers is required for the patient to complete the activity.

If activity was not attempted, code the reason:
07. **Patient refused**
09. **Not applicable**
88. Not attempted due to **medical condition or safety concerns**

3. **Discharge** **Performance** Enter Codes in Boxes ↓	
☐☐	**A. Eating:** The ability to use suitable utensils to bring food to the mouth and swallow food once the meal is presented on a table/tray. Includes modified food consistency.
☐☐	**B. Oral hygiene:** The ability to use suitable items to clean teeth. [Dentures (if applicable): The ability to remove and replace dentures from and to the mouth, and manage equipment for soaking and rinsing them.]
☐☐	**C. Toileting hygiene:** The ability to maintain perineal hygiene, adjust clothes before and after using the toilet, commode, bedpan or urinal. If managing an ostomy, include wiping the opening but not managing equipment.
☐☐	**E. Shower/bathe self:** The ability to bathe self in shower or tub, including washing, rinsing, and drying self. Does not include transferring in/out of tub/shower.
☐☐	**F. Upper body dressing:** The ability to put on and remove shirt or pajama top; includes buttoning, if applicable.
☐☐	**G. Lower body dressing:** The ability to dress and undress below the waist, including fasteners; does not include footwear.
☐☐	**H. Putting on/taking off footwear:** The ability to put on and take off socks and shoes or other footwear that is appropriate for safe mobility.

FIGURE 11-3 *(continued)*

OMB No. 0938-0842

Patient		Identifier		Date	

Section GG	**Functional Abilities and Goals**

GG0170. Mobility (3-day assessment period)

Code the patient's usual performance at discharge for each activity using the 6-point scale. If activity was not attempted at discharge, code the reason.

CODING:

Safety and **Quality of Performance** - If helper assistance is required because patient's performance is unsafe or of poor quality, score according to amount of assistance provided.

Activities may be completed with or without assistive devices.

06. **Independent** - Patient completes the activity by him/herself with no assistance from a helper.

05. **Setup or clean-up assistance** - Helper SETS UP or CLEANS UP; patient completes activity. Helper assists only prior to or following the activity.

04. **Supervision or touching assistance** - Helper provides VERBAL CUES or TOUCHING/STEADYING assistance as patient completes activity. Assistance may be provided throughout the activity or intermittently.

03. **Partial/moderate assistance** - Helper does LESS THAN HALF the effort. Helper lifts, holds or supports trunk or limbs, but provides less than half the effort.

02. **Substantial/maximal assistance** - Helper does MORE THAN HALF the effort. Helper lifts or holds trunk or limbs and provides more than half the effort.

01. **Dependent** - Helper does ALL of the effort. Patient does none of the effort to complete the activity. Or, the assistance of 2 or more helpers is required for the patient to complete the activity.

If activity was not attempted, code the reason:

07. **Patient refused**

09. **Not applicable**

88. Not attempted due to **medical condition or safety concerns**

3. Discharge Performance Enter Codes in Boxes ↓	
☐☐	**A. Roll left and right:** The ability to roll from lying on back to left and right side, and return to lying on back.
☐☐	**B. Sit to lying:** The ability to move from sitting on side of bed to lying flat on the bed.
☐☐	**C. Lying to sitting on side of bed:** The ability to safely move from lying on the back to sitting on the side of the bed with feet flat on the floor, and with no back support.
☐☐	**D. Sit to stand:** The ability to safely come to a standing position from sitting in a chair or on the side of the bed.
☐☐	**E. Chair/bed-to-chair transfer:** The ability to safely transfer to and from a bed to a chair (or wheelchair).
☐☐	**F. Toilet transfer:** The ability to safely get on and off a toilet or commode.
☐☐	**G. Car transfer:** The ability to transfer in and out of a car or van on the passenger side. Does not include the ability to open/close door or fasten seat belt.
☐	**H3. Does the patient walk?** 0. **No** → *Skip to GG0170Q3. Does the patient use a wheelchair/scooter?* 2. **Yes** → *Continue to GG0170I. Walk 10 feet*
☐☐	**I. Walk 10 feet:** Once standing, the ability to walk at least 10 feet in a room, corridor or similar space
☐☐	**J. Walk 50 feet with two turns:** Once standing, the ability to walk at least 50 feet and make two turns
☐☐	**K. Walk 150 feet:** Once standing, the ability to walk at least 150 feet in a corridor or similar space

Quality Indicators - Discharge
DRAFT Corrected Version 1.4

(continues)

FIGURE 11-3 *(continued)*

OMB No. 0938-0842

Patient	Identifier	Date

Section GG	**Functional Abilities and Goals**

GG0170. Mobility (3-day assessment period) - Continued

Code the patient's usual performance at discharge for each activity using the 6-point scale. If activity was not attempted at discharge, code the reason.

CODING:

Safety and **Quality of Performance** - If helper assistance is required because patient's performance is unsafe or of poor quality, score according to amount of assistance provided.

Activities may be completed with or without assistive devices.

06. **Independent** - Patient completes the activity by him/herself with no assistance from a helper.

05. **Setup or clean-up assistance** - Helper SETS UP or CLEANS UP; patient completes activity. Helper assists only prior to or following the activity.

04. **Supervision or touching assistance** - Helper provides VERBAL CUES or TOUCHING/STEADYING assistance as patient completes activity. Assistance may be provided throughout the activity or intermittently.

03. **Partial/moderate assistance** - Helper does LESS THAN HALF the effort. Helper lifts, holds or supports trunk or limbs, but provides less than half the effort.

02. **Substantial/maximal assistance** - Helper does MORE THAN HALF the effort. Helper lifts or holds trunk or limbs and provides more than half the effort.

01. **Dependent** - Helper does ALL of the effort. Patient does none of the effort to complete the activity. Or, the assistance of 2 or more helpers is required for the patient to complete the activity.

If activity was not attempted, code the reason:

07. **Patient refused**

09. **Not applicable**

88. Not attempted due to **medical condition or safety concerns**

3. Discharge Performance Enter Codes in Boxes ↓	
☐☐	**L. Walking 10 feet on uneven surfaces:** The ability to walk 10 feet on uneven or sloping surfaces, such as grass or gravel.
☐☐	**M. 1 step (curb):** The ability to step over a curb or up and down one step.
☐☐	**N. 4 steps:** The ability to go up and down four steps with or without a rail.
☐☐	**O. 12 steps:** The ability to go up and down 12 steps with or without a rail.
☐☐	**P. Picking up object:** The ability to bend/stoop from a standing position to pick up a small object, such as a spoon, from the floor.
☐	**Q3. Does the patient use a wheelchair/scooter?** 0. **No** → *Skip to J1800. Any Falls Since Admission* 1. **Yes** → *Continue to GG0170R. Wheel 50 feet with two turns*
☐☐	**R. Wheel 50 feet with two turns:** Once seated in wheelchair/scooter, the ability to wheel at least 50 feet and make two turns.
☐	**RR3. Indicate the type of wheelchair/scooter used.** 1. **Manual** 2. **Motorized**
☐☐	**S. Wheel 150 feet:** Once seated in wheelchair/scooter, the ability to wheel at least 150 feet in a corridor or similar space.
☐	**SS3. Indicate the type of wheelchair/scooter used.** 1. **Manual** 2. **Motorized**

FIGURE 11-3   (continued)

OMB No. 0938-0842

Patient _____   Identifier _____   Date _____

Section J	Health Conditions

J1800. Any Falls Since Admission

Enter Code	Has the patient **had any falls since admission?**
☐	0. **No** ➔ *Skip to M0210. Unhealed Pressure Ulcer(s)* 1. **Yes** ➔ *Continue to J1900. Number of Falls Since Admission*

J1900. Number of Falls Since Admission

CODING: 0. None 1. One 2. Two or more	↓ **Enter Codes in Boxes**	
	☐	**A. No injury:** No evidence of any injury is noted on physical assessment by the nurse or primary care clinician; no complaints of pain or injury by the patient; no change in the patient's behavior is noted after the fall
	☐	**B. Injury (except major):** Skin tears, abrasions, lacerations, superficial bruises, hematomas and sprains; or any fall-related injury that causes the patient to complain of pain
	☐	**C. Major injury:** Bone fractures, joint dislocations, closed head injuries with altered consciousness, subdural hematoma

Section M	Skin Conditions

> Report based on highest stage of existing ulcer(s) at its worst; do not "reverse" stage

M0210. Unhealed Pressure Ulcer(s)

Enter Code	**Does this patient have one or more unhealed pressure ulcer(s) at Stage 1 or higher?**
☐	0. **No** ➔ *Skip to M0900A. Healed Pressure Ulcer(s)* 1. **Yes** ➔ *Continue to M0300. Current Number of Unhealed Pressure Ulcers at Each Stage*

M0300. Current Number of Unhealed Pressure Ulcers at Each Stage

Enter Number	**A. Stage 1:** Intact skin with non-blanchable redness of a localized area usually over a bony prominence. Darkly pigmented skin may not have a visible blanching; in dark skin tones only it may appear with persistent blue or purple hues. **Number of Stage 1 pressure ulcers**
☐	

Enter Number	**B. Stage 2:** Partial thickness loss of dermis presenting as a shallow open ulcer with a red or pink wound bed, without slough. May also present as an intact or open/ruptured blister. **1. Number of Stage 2 pressure ulcers** *If 0* ➔ *Skip to M0300C. Stage 3*
☐	
Enter Number ☐	**2. Number of <u>these</u> Stage 2 pressure ulcers that were present upon admission** - enter how many were noted at the time of admission

Enter Number	**C. Stage 3:** Full thickness tissue loss. Subcutaneous fat may be visible but bone, tendon or muscle is not exposed. Slough may be present but does not obscure the depth of tissue loss. May include undermining and tunneling. **1. Number of Stage 3 pressure ulcers** *If 0* ➔ *Skip to M0300D. Stage 4*
☐	
Enter Number ☐	**2. Number of <u>these</u> Stage 3 pressure ulcers that were present upon admission** - enter how many were noted at the time of admission

FIGURE 11-3   (*continued*)

OMB No. 0938-0842

Patient _____   Identifier _____   Date _____

Section M	Skin Conditions

M0300. Current Number of Unhealed Pressure Ulcers at Each Stage - Continued

Enter Number ☐

Enter Number ☐

D. Stage 4: Full thickness tissue loss with exposed bone, tendon or muscle. Slough or eschar may be present on some parts of the wound bed. Often includes undermining and tunneling.

    1. Number of Stage 4 pressure ulcers
      If 0 → Skip to M0300E. Unstageable - Non-removable dressing
    2. Number of <u>these</u> Stage 4 pressure ulcers that were present upon admission - enter how many were noted at the time of admission

Enter Number ☐

Enter Number ☐

E. Unstageable - Non-removable dressing: Known but not stageable due to non-removable dressing/device

    1. Number of unstageable pressure ulcers due to non-removable dressing/device
      If 0 → Skip to M0300F. Unstageable - Slough and/or eschar

    2. Number of <u>these</u> unstageable pressure ulcers that were present upon admission - enter how many were noted at the time of admission

Enter Number ☐

Enter Number ☐

F. Unstageable - Slough and/or eschar: Known but not stageable due to coverage of wound bed by slough and/or eschar

    1. Number of unstageable pressure ulcers due to coverage of wound bed by slough and/or eschar
      If 0 → Skip to M0300G. Unstageable - Deep tissue injury

    2. Number of <u>these</u> unstageable pressure ulcers that were present upon admission - enter how many were noted at the time of admission

Enter Number ☐

Enter Number ☐

G. Unstageable - Deep tissue injury: Suspected deep tissue injury in evolution

    1. Number of unstageable pressure ulcers with suspected deep tissue injury in evolution
      If 0 → Skip to M0800. Worsening in Pressure Ulcer Status Since Admission

    2. Number of <u>these</u> unstageable pressure ulcers that were present upon admission - enter how many were noted at the time of admission

M0800. Worsening in Pressure Ulcer Status Since Admission

Indicate the number of current pressure ulcers that were **not present or were at a lesser stage** on admission.
If no current pressure ulcer at a given stage, enter 0.

Enter Number	
☐	**A. Stage 2**
☐	**B. Stage 3**
☐	**C. Stage 4**
☐	**D. Unstageable - Non-removable dressing**
☐	**E. Unstageable - Slough and/or eschar**
☐	**F. Unstageable - Deep tissue injury**

FIGURE 11-3 *(continued)*

OMB No. 0938-0842

Patient _____   Identifier _____   Date _____

Section M	**Skin Conditions**

M0900. Healed Pressure Ulcer(s)

Indicate the number of pressure ulcers that were: (a) present on **Admission; and** (b) have completely closed (resurfaced with epithelium) upon **Discharge.** If there are no healed pressure ulcers noted at a given stage, enter 0.

Enter Number
☐   **A. Stage 1**

Enter Number
☐   **B. Stage 2**

Enter Number
☐   **C. Stage 3**

Enter Number
☐   **D. Stage 4**

Section O	**Special Treatments, Procedures, and Programs**

O0250. Influenza Vaccine - Refer to current version of IRF-PAI Training Manual for current influenza vaccination season and reporting period.

Enter Code
☐

A. Did the **patient receive the influenza vaccine *in this facility*** for this year's influenza *vaccination* season?

   0. **No** → *Skip to O0250C. If influenza vaccine not received, state reason*
   1. **Yes** → *Continue to O0250B. Date influenza vaccine received*

B. Date influenza vaccine received → Complete date and skip to Z0400A. Signature of Persons Completing the Assessment

☐☐ ☐☐ ☐☐☐☐
M M   D D   Y Y Y Y

Enter Code
☐

C. If influenza vaccine not received, state reason:

   1. **Patient not in this facility** during this year's influenza vaccination season
   2. **Received outside of this facility**
   3. **Not eligible** - medical contraindication
   4. **Offered and declined**
   5. **Not offered**
   6. **Inability to obtain influenza vaccine** due to a declared shortage
   9. **None of the above**

Source: http://www.cms.gov/Medicare/Medicare-Fee-for-Service-Payment/InpatientRehabFacPPS/IRFPAI.html

an excerpt from the proposed draft of the 2016 IRF-PAI illustrating the types of quality measures that are captured at admission and at discharge. Quality measures at admission and discharge can be compared to assess the extent of improvement or decline in any of the quality indicators. The complete IRF-PAI, including the FIM instrument, admission indicators, and discharge indicators, is available at http://www.cms.gov/Medicare/Medicare-Fee-for-Service-Payment /InpatientRehabFacPPS/IRFPAI.html.

encoded   with regard to the IRF-PAI, encoding refers to using a specified computer program to enter data that subsequently will be transmitted to the Centers for Medicare & Medicaid Services (CMS).

The data from the IRF-PAI must be **encoded** (entered into a specified computer program) before transmission. CMS has published an assessment schedule in the IRF PPS rule that specifies dates by which the admission and discharge assessments must be performed, encoded, and transmitted. A 25% penalty is deducted from the IRF PPS payment for data transmitted 28 calendar days after discharge or later. According to regulations, IRF-PAI data are considered "late" if not transmitted within 17 calendar days of discharge, but an additional grace period of 10 days is allowed before the penalty is applied; therefore, an IRF-PAI transmission 28 days after discharge would result in a penalty (CMS, 2005).

SELF REVIEW 11.4

1. Why would diagnosis related groups (DRGs) fail to provide equitable reimbursement for rehabilitation?

2. What factors influence the assignment of a case into a specific CMG?

3. True or False? Providers are required to discharge patients before the maximum length of stay listed in the regulations for each CMG.

4. The _____ captures all of the information necessary to assign a CMG, including codes for up to 25 comorbidities and must be completed upon the patient's admission and again at discharge, with the admission and discharge data transmitted together after the patient has been discharged.

5. What is the timeframe for application of the 25% penalty deducted from the IRF PPS payment as a result of late transmission of IRF-PAI data?

INFORMATION MANAGEMENT

Information Flow

The medical record is initiated during admission to the rehabilitation care system and is maintained as an interdisciplinary unit. Each member of the interdisciplinary team records observations daily. If the treatment areas are in separate parts of the hospital, the medical record goes with the patient to the treatment areas.

Coding

The system utilized for diagnostic coding is the current clinical modification of the *International Classification of Disease*. The codes reported most frequently include those that classify neurologic conditions, musculoskeletal disorders, and amputations. Diagnoses encountered frequently in rehabilitation include neurogenic bladder, fibromyalgia, decubitus ulcer (or pressure sore), spasticity, urinary tract infection, cerebral palsy, and below-the-knee amputation.

Physicians use *Current Procedural Terminology* (*CPT*) for reporting the services provided. Rehabilitation physicians generally address a host of issues on a follow-up visit, frequently utilizing time spent in counseling and coordination of care or complexity of medical decision making as major criteria for coding evaluation and management services. Other common rehabilitation services that would be coded are trigger point injections, motor point blocks, final reports and ratings, medical management conferences, and physician review of care plan.

For inpatient rehabilitation facilities, the diagnostic coding rules differ for the IRF-PAI and the facility's billing form, the UB-04. Unlike the UB-04, the IRF-PAI does not capture the principal diagnosis but reports the etiologic diagnosis instead. Consider the case, for example, of a patient who previously had suffered an intracerebral hemorrhage treated at an acute care hospital and who subsequently was admitted to the IRF for rehabilitation for the late effects of the hemorrhage. These two diagnoses may be related, but usually are not identical.

The World Health Organization (WHO) publishes the *International Classification of Functioning, Disability and Health* (*ICF*). (An earlier version of this publication was known as the *International Classification of Impairments, Disabilities and Handicaps* [*ICIDH*]). The *ICF* classifies disability concepts by body functions and structure, activities and participation, and environmental factors (World Health Organization, 2001).

Electronic Information Systems

Electronic information systems are used administratively in rehabilitation facilities in much the same manner as in other types of health care facilities. Inpatient rehabilitation facilities, however, have the unique requirement to submit IRF-PAI data to fiscal intermediaries. CMS provides software titled **Inpatient Rehabilitation Validation and Entry (IRVEN)** (or jIRVEN for a java-based version) free of charge to facilities that wish to use it to submit the IRF-PAI data. Vendors and other organizations also license software for submitting IRF-PAI data and often include other capabilities, such as the ability to transmit ORYX data to The Joint Commission or the ability to benchmark performance against peer facilities. Some commonly used systems are E-Rehab or Uniform Data Systems (UDS).

Inpatient Rehabilitation Validation and Entry (IRVEN) software provided by CMS for entering IRF-PAI data.

National Databases

National databases on spinal cord injury and traumatic brain injury are examples of systems that provide efficient, large-scale collections of data that facilitate research in rehabilitation and promote uniform treatment, thereby leading to improved functional outcomes. The world's largest spinal cord injury research database is maintained through the National Spinal Cord Injury Statistical Center (NSCISC) at the University of Alabama at Birmingham. The NSCISC collects its data from the Model Systems for spinal cord injury, maintaining the largest longitudinal data set on spinal cord injury in the world, with data collected since June 1973. Information is collected on hundreds of variables in each spinal cord injury case, capturing approximately 15% of all new spinal cord injury cases in the United States.

The Traumatic Brain Injury Model Systems National Data and Statistical Center (TBINDSC), located at Craig Hospital in Englewood, Colorado, maintains a similar national database on traumatic brain injury, using data collected through the Model Systems. Because of the multiple types of brain injuries, it is much more difficult to compare brain injury data than to compare spinal cord injury data.

Other databases track all admissions to rehabilitation units and therapy clinics. A variety of data is collected related to demographics, diagnosis, and outcomes. Specific information collected and the amount varies by providers.

Classification and Rating Systems Used in Rehabilitation

Numerous classification schemes have been developed for spinal cord-injured individuals and for traumatic brain-injured individuals. It is extremely important that a standardized nomenclature system be utilized to facilitate research on spinal cord injury and brain injury.

American Spinal Injury Association Classification System

The international standards for neurologic and functional classification of spinal cord injury have been developed by the American Spinal Injury Association in cooperation with the International Medical Society of Paraplegia. This system of classification standardizes the neurologic motor and sensory examination. It further requires that the diagnosis be stated giving both a sensory and motor neurologic level and a qualifying statement regarding the completeness of the spinal cord injury. For definitions utilized in the development of classification systems, see Table 11-2.

Besides the classifications of tetraplegia, paraplegia, tetraparesis, and paraparesis, spinal cord injuries must be further classified as to whether they are complete—meaning that there is total absence of sensory and motor functions below the level of the lesion—or incomplete—meaning there is partial preservation of sensory and/or motor functions below the neurologic level of injury.

Of the incomplete spinal cord injury syndromes, several can and do occur with frequency and have been assigned to specific nomenclature. These are defined in Table 11-2. Central cord syndrome is more common in the elderly population. Brown-Sequard syndrome is said to occur when there is a hemisection of the spinal

TABLE 11-2	Standardization Classification System Definitions
Classification	**Definition**
Tetraplegia (or quadriplegia)	Spinal cord injury of the cervical level that leads to neurologic and functional damage of the upper extremities and the lower extremities
Paraplegia	Impairment or loss of motor and/or sensory function in the thoracic, lumbar, or sacral segments of the spinal cord affecting the lower extremities only
Tetraparesis or paraparesis	A relative weakness of the extremities (tetraparesis) or the lower extremities (paraparesis) but not complete paralysis
Central cord syndrome	A lesion occurring in the central region of the spinal cord at the cervical level that produces greater weakness in the upper extremities than in the lower extremities
Brown-Sequard syndrome	A lesion that produces a greater motor and proprioception loss ipsilateral (same side as the lesion) and a contralateral (opposite side) loss of sensitivity to pinprick and temperature
Anterior cord syndrome	A spinal lesion that is vascular in origin and produces a loss of motor function and a deficit in sensitivity to pinprick and temperature while preserving proprioception
Conus medullaris syndrome	This injury occurs when there is damage to the conus of the spinal cord, resulting in an areflexic bladder and bowel and areflexic lower extremities
Cauda equina syndrome	Injury to the lumbosacral nerve roots inside the neurocanal before exiting to the peripheral nerves, resulting in an areflexic bladder and areflexic lower extremities

cord. Others are anterior cord syndrome, conus medullaris syndrome, and cauda equina syndrome. Also, the American Spinal Injury Association publishes a handbook of spinal cord injury classification and nomenclature. The Key Resources at the end of this chapter provides information on how to obtain this document.

It is crucial that accurate spinal cord injury classification be performed by physicians who are caring for a spinal cord-injured person so the physicians who come in contact with the patient later on will be able to accurately determine if the neurologic status of the patient has changed.

Traumatic Brain Injury Classification Systems

Traumatic brain injury classification systems have evolved, and two primary systems are useful in rehabilitation. One is the Glasgow Coma Scale, used soon after the injury in the emergency room (ER) and in the first few days of hospitalization. The other is the Rancho Los Amigos Levels of Cognitive Function Scale, which is useful in communicating the patient's recovery from traumatic brain injury.

The Glasgow Coma Scale measures three areas: eye opening on a scale of 4 to 1, best motor response on a scale of 6 to 1, and verbal response on a scale of 5 to 1. The range for a Glasgow Coma Scale is 3 to 15 (the lowest score possible is 3; a person dead on arrival at an ER would score a 3). The Glasgow Coma Scale scores that are recorded upon arrival at the ER and on the second, third, fourth, and seventh post-injury days are extremely predictive of the patient's outcome. Glasgow Coma Scale scores of 8 or less are associated with poor outcomes (see Figure 11-4).

FIGURE 11-4

The Glasgow Coma Scale

GLASGOW COMA SCALE

Eye Opening Response	• Spontaneous—open with blinking at baseline **4 points** • To verbal stimuli, command, speech **3 points** • To pain only (not applied to face) **2 points** • No response **1 point**
Verbal Response	• Oriented **5 points** • Confused conversation, but able to answer questions **4 points** • Inappropriate words **3 points** • Incomprehensible speech **2 points** • No response **1 point**
Motor Response	• Obeys commands for movement **6 points** • Purposeful movement to painful stimulus **5 points** • Withdraws in response to pain **4 points** • Flexion in response to pain (decorticate posturing) **3 points** • Extension response in response to pain (decerebrate posturing) **2 points** • No response **1 point**
References	Teasdale G, Jennett B. Assessment of coma and impaired consciousness. Lancet 1974; 81–84. Teasdale G, Jennett B. Assessment and prognosis of coma after head injury. Acta Neurochir 1976; 34:45–55.
Categorization:	Coma: No eye opening, no ability to follow commands, no word verbalizations (3–8)
Head Injury Classification:	Severe Head Injury—GCS score of 8 or less Moderate Head Injury—GCS score of 9 to 12 Mild Head Injury—GCS score of 13 to 15 (Adapted from: Advanced Trauma Life Support: Course for Physicians, American College of Surgeons, 1993).

Source: http://www.cdc.gov/masstrauma/resources/gcs.pdf

The Rancho Los Amigos Scale is from 1 to 8. A level of 1 or 2 is consistent with a coma or near-coma state. Level 8 equates to purposeful and appropriate behavior. The Rancho Los Amigos Scale is extremely beneficial in communicating to other members of the rehabilitation team the patient's level of recovery, and thereby infers what level of treatment is appropriate at that point. In general terms, once a patient has reached level 6 or above, he or she is ready for discharge to home, but the patient may continue to require some outpatient services.

FIGURE 11-5

Rancho Los Amigos Levels of Cognitive Function Scale.

I. No response
II. Generalized response to stimulation
III. Localized response to stimuli
IV. Confused and agitated behavior
V. Confused with inappropriate behavior (non-agitated)
VI. Confused but appropriate behavior
VII. Automatic and appropriate behavior
VIII. Purposeful and appropriate behavior

Hagen, C., Malkmus, D., Durham, P. (1979). Levels of cognitive functioning, Rehabilitation of the Head Injured Adult; Comprehensive Physical Management, Downey, CA: Professional Staff Association of Rancho Los Amigos National Rehabilitation Center. Source: http://file.lacounty.gov/dhs/cms1_218118.pdf

A person who has a Rancho Los Amigos Scale of 3 or less is not considered to be an inpatient rehabilitation candidate and would be better served in a coma stimulation program (see Figure 11-5). Rancho Los Amigos National Rehabilitation Center is a rehabilitation hospital operated by the Los Angeles County Department of Health Services. More details regarding the Rancho Los Amigos Levels of Cognitive Functioning is available by searching the website at https://dhs.lacounty.gov/wps/portal/dhs/rancho.

Self-Care Assessment Scales and FIM® Scores

A number and variety of tools have been developed to assist in assessing the functional status of the patient in areas addressing bathing, grooming, toileting, and so forth. Some common scales include the Katz index, the Barthel index, and the FIM® rating scale. Deciding which functional assessment tool is most useful depends on the individual institution and patient population that is served.

The **Functional Independence Measure or FIM®** instrument evolved from a task force of the American Congress of Rehabilitation Medicine and the American Academy of Physical Medicine and Rehabilitation, and has established itself as an extremely reliable and valid tool for documenting the severity of disabilities as well as outcomes in rehabilitation. FIM® is the most commonly used measure of independence, and, because of its reliability and validity, it has been incorporated into the IRF-PAI. FIM® scores are issued in 13 motor areas and 5 cognitive areas. The motor areas include self-care (e.g., eating, grooming, bathing, dressing, and toileting), sphincter control (e.g., bowel and bladder management), mobility transfers, and locomotion. The cognitive areas include comprehension, expression, social interaction, problem solving, and memory.

Functional Independence Measure or FIM® instrument a rating tool for measuring function in motor and cognitive areas; FIM documents the severity of disabilities as well as outcomes in rehabilitation and has been incorporated into the IRF-PAI.

Each area receives a score that ranges from 1 to 7. A score of 1 means that the individual requires total assistance, and 7 means that the individual is totally independent. In any given functional category, a score of 1 to 5 means that the patient requires the assistance of another person for that function.

FIM® is a highly reproducible and reliable measure of the patient's independence. FIM® scoring is repeated on a routine basis to help document the progress or lack of progress of the patient in rehabilitation. If FIM® scores do not show improvement, the treatment plan must be reevaluated and modified to meet current needs, or the patient must be placed at maximum medical improvement and discharged from rehabilitation. All members of the rehabilitation team should receive specific training in the proper way to assess the patient and assign FIM® scores.

FIM® is an excellent technique for almost all rehabilitation problems, including traumatic brain injury, spinal cord injury, stroke, amputations, and medical disability. The reason FIM® works well for the various types of disabilities is that it is a measure of the functional status of the patient, irrespective of the etiology of the disability. For some subsets of patients, FIM® does not work well, including patients who are progressing extremely slowly and pediatric patients. A separate scale called WeeFIM® has been developed for pediatric patients. (FIM® and WeeFIM® are registered trademarks of the Uniform Data System for Medical Rehabilitation, a division of UB Foundation Activities, Inc.)

FIM® scores or some other reliable, reproducible measure of functional outcome is required in rehabilitation. This allows the rehabilitation interdisciplinary team to (1) assess the patient's functional improvement and response to the treatment plan; (2) document functional status and, thereby, needs for discharge planning; (3) establish the beneficial role of the rehabilitation service; (4) justify the treatment and cost incurred; (5) allow rapid communication of a patient's functional status to other interested parties such as third-party payers or other rehabilitation teams that may become involved in the patient's score; and (6) standardize the nomenclature system regarding functional outcome.

SELF REVIEW 11.5

1. The system utilized for diagnostic coding is the current clinical modification of _____.

2. Physicians use _____ for reporting services provided.

3. CMS provides software titled _____ free of charge to facilities that wish to use it to submit the IRF-PAI data.

4. What are two examples of national databases that provide efficient, large-scale collections of data?

5. _____ is the most commonly used measure of independence, and, because of its reliability and validity, it has been incorporated into the IRF-PAI.

QUALITY IMPROVEMENT AND UTILIZATION MANAGEMENT

Quality Improvement and Program Evaluation Systems

The primary product of rehabilitation is improvement in the patient's functional status. The three components of quality care are: appropriateness of care, technical competence with which the care was given, and patient dignity and involvement. Quality assessment may be done on a multidisciplinary basis by monitoring the different departments and outcomes. For example, an increase in ADL skills can be used to measure the quality of services provided by the occupational therapy department; an increase in physical functioning indicates an improved outcome for the physical therapy department; and an increase in cognitive and emotional adaptation by the patient and the family can be used to assess the quality of services from the psychology staff. Quality of outcome also is viewed in terms of the absolute level of independence of the patient, a reduction in the need for caregivers, and the setting to which the patient was discharged.

FIM scores lend themselves readily to quality and outcome measurements. In addition, costs can be analyzed in light of changes in FIM scores. For example, a patient's FIM score could improve from 50 to 75—a gain of 25 points—after several weeks of rehabilitation. If the cost of providing rehabilitation services during that time period was $25,000, the cost per point-change in FIM score would be $1,000 for that patient.

Program evaluation systems are best organized along diagnostic and functional groups, such as general inpatient medical rehabilitation and stroke, spinal cord injury, or traumatic brain injury. Program evaluation and assessments of quality in outcome should continue after discharge. The patient should be seen for a follow-up visit to determine how he or she is functioning at home—the true indicator of effectiveness of the rehabilitation program.

A CMS quality reporting program (QRP) has been in effect for inpatient rehabilitation facilities since October of 2012. Some of the measures can be tracked through the IRF-PAI. (See Figure 11-3). Examples of IRF-QRP measures include catheter-associated urinary tract infections (CAUTI) events on all patients and the percent of Medicare patients with new or worsened pressure ulcers since admission. New measures are announced in advance for each reporting year. As of October 2014, IRFs that fail to report quality data are subject to a 2 percentage point reduction to the applicable market basket increase factor. In addition to the items reported to CMS, quality measure data related to health care-acquired infections are reported to the Centers for Disease Control and Prevention's National Healthcare Safety Network (NHSN) (CMS, 2014, September).

Utilization Management

Elements of utilization management have been discussed throughout this chapter. The discussion of various types of rehabilitation settings (inpatient, outpatient, skilled nursing, etc.), mentioned factors that affect the appropriateness of different types of rehabilitation for different types of patients. In an inpatient rehabilitation facility (IRF), the preadmission screening is necessary to determine whether the patient is a suitable candidate for inpatient rehabilitation. For example, a patient who is too acutely ill would not be able to participate in therapy at a level that would be beneficial.

In addition to determining the appropriateness of admission, the IRF must determine when the patient is ready for discharge. As noted previously, FIM® scores may be calculated at routine intervals to measure the progress of rehabilitation. When the patient appears to have achieved optimum benefit from inpatient rehabilitation and continued inpatient rehabilitation would likely improve the patient's status only slightly, a decision to discharge the patient may be in order. When the patient is ready for discharge, appropriate plans for follow-up or continuing outpatient therapy should be in place.

SELF REVIEW 11.6

1. What are the three components of quality care?

2. True or False? FIM scores lend themselves readily to quality and outcome measurements. In addition, costs can be analyzed in light of changes in FIM scores.

3. True or False? Although quality measures can be used to compare quality at different inpatient rehabilitation facilities, there are no reimbursement implications for QRP data.

4. In an inpatient rehabilitation facility (IRF), _____ is important in determining whether the patient is a suitable candidate for inpatient rehabilitation.

5. What determines the decision to discharge a patient from inpatient rehabilitation?

RISK MANAGEMENT AND LEGAL ISSUES
Avoiding and Managing Risk

In the inpatient rehabilitation setting, avoiding risk of harm to the patient involves many of the same precautions and management strategies as in other inpatient settings. Patient safety in areas such as preventing falls merits attention in the rehabilitation population, and other areas are important, too. For example, the IRF may be at risk for failure to meet medical necessity requirements if the patient is not receiving intensive therapy services at least 3 hours a day, at least 5 days a week, during the patient's IRF stay. Faulty coding and billing also put the IRF at financial and regulatory risk (Moran & Heidell, 2012). Leadership must identify and address potential areas of risk and respond appropriately to incidents when they occur.

Staff safety and accident prevention are important as well. This is especially true in the area of community-based rehabilitation in which therapists may be visiting the patient in his or her residence, because the organization has little ability to manage the home environment. Staff training and appropriate counseling and education for patients and family members are necessary components of risk management for community-based rehabilitation (Mooney, Doig, & Fleming, 2009).

Third-Party Litigation

The rehabilitation team, its records, and physiatrists often are called on to provide information in legal proceedings regarding the disability, functional status, and future needs of an individual with a handicapping condition. This is understandable, because the rehabilitation team is the primary caregiver for individuals who have permanent injuries and disabilities. Some of these people have been injured as a result of a motor vehicle accident, a work-related injury, or malpractice. The rehabilitation professional is responsible for maximizing the quality of life and functional status, and follows the individual over a lifetime to meet his or her needs related to the injury and the disability. As a result, the physiatrist frequently is called upon as an expert witness to render opinions in these areas. The physiatrist is uniquely qualified to provide this service to his or her patient because of the specific training in recovery from injuries, an understanding of the natural history of the disease process, and a working knowledge of the types of equipment and supplies necessary to maximize functional status and preserve health.

The rehabilitation medical records, FIM scores, discharge recommendations, medications, and equipment recommendations are useful to help prepare a **life care plan**. The International Academy of Life Care Planners has defined a life care plan as a "dynamic document based upon published standards of practice, comprehensive assessment, data analysis, and research, which provides an organized concise plan for current and future needs with associated cost, for individuals who have experienced catastrophic injury or have chronic health care needs" (IALCP, n.d., p. 1).

life care plan   a dynamic document that details current and future health care needs based on published standards of practice.

The life care plan is developed on an individualized basis, given that person's unique presentation. It lists the items required over a lifetime for the individual, the cost, and the frequency of replacement. This document serves as a medical legal document that may guide court decisions regarding a settlement. The document also could be used as a guide to provide future medical services for the individual.

Medicare Set-Aside Trust

In 2001, CMS addressed guidelines regarding settlement of claims for individuals with work-related injuries or injuries covered under other general liability insurance plans. The objective was to ensure that third-party payers do not shift the responsibility for payment of medical services to Medicare by negotiating a legal settlement that fails to adequately cover future medical services and rehabilitation (Lump-Sum payments, 2014). CMS guidelines require that a life care plan be used to assess future medical care in cases where a high level of future care is likely to be required.

Setting up a Medicare Set-Aside Trust from the proceeds of a third-party settlement is a multifaceted undertaking that requires preparation and submission of a detailed proposal to CMS along with follow-up to gain CMS approval. A variety of professionals—for example, life care planners, case managers, insurance claims managers, and attorneys—engage in this type of work. The International Association of Rehabilitation Professionals has compiled standards of practice and codes of ethics from various organizations that address some of the issues encountered in this complex arena (IARP, 2012).

SELF REVIEW 11.7	
	1. What are some risk management concerns in the inpatient rehabilitation setting?
	2. What are the important components of risk management for community-based rehabilitation?
	3. What is a life care plan?
	4. True or False? The life care plan lists the items required for one year for the individual, their costs, and frequency of replacement.
	5. What is the objective of CMS regulations regarding a Medicare set-aside trust?

ROLE OF THE HEALTH INFORMATION MANAGER

The health information professional in a rehabilitation setting may manage traditional types of services related to the creation, development, storage, and retrieval of patient record and patient information, and, as in other settings, has a significant part to play in obtaining and maintaining accreditation of the rehabilitation facility. In addition, the health information manager may assist in selecting or developing appropriate forms to track patient outcomes and may work with others to develop and implement quality improvement programs. The health information manager may monitor rates of complications, early discharges, or failures to improve, and present findings that can help target processes for improvement.

In inpatient rehabilitation facilities, the health information manager may play a role in managing coding for the IRF-PAI and the UB-04. This role may extend to other aspects of the revenue cycle of the facility, including timely submission of both of these forms. Some of the trends described next call for the skills of a health information manager. For example, the possibility of implementing a bundled payment for post-acute care could involve the HIM professional in managing related systems.

SELF REVIEW 11.8	
	1. What types of services does the health information professional manage in a rehabilitation setting?
	2. In inpatient rehabilitation facilities, the health information manager may play a role in managing coding for the _____ and the _____.

TRENDS

Acute Rehabilitation, Skilled Nursing, and Other Post-acute Care Providers

Since 1990, a continuum of nonhospital-based post-acute rehabilitation facilities has evolved that has been driven by economic factors in the American health care delivery system. Earlier discharges from the hospital have resulted in the discharge of patients who are unable to care for themselves. Skilled rehabilitation facilities provide a cost-effective economic system that allows patients to develop a functional level of independence that allow their safe return to the home. The level of care offered by rehabilitation units in skilled nursing facilities is generally more cost-effective for older patients who often cannot participate in the intensive rehabilitation programs offered at more acute levels of care.

The resulting trend has been toward increasing the number of skilled rehabilitation beds and decreasing the number of acute inpatient rehabilitation beds. All of the following settings provide various types of post-acute care (PAC): skilled nursing facilities (SNFs), home health agencies (HHAs), long-term care hospitals (LTCHs), and inpatient rehabilitation facilities (IRFs). The Medicare Payment Advisory Commission (MedPAC) has noted the following concerns about post-acute care:

- Payments are not accurately calibrated to costs in each sector.
- Services overlap among settings.
- The PAC (post-acute care) product is not well defined.
- Assessment instruments differ among settings. (MedPAC, 2010, p. 165)

One proposal has been to develop a payment system that would bundle payments for post-acute care for all types of PAC providers with the acute care hospital payment for a given episode of care. The rationale is that such a system would give all providers an incentive to provide the proper mix of services for each patient. Another proposal addressing these concerns has been to develop a uniform assessment instrument for post-acute care to be completed at hospital discharge and integrated into PAC assessments.

In 2014, President Obama signed into law the Improving Medicare Post-Acute Care Transformation (IMPACT) Act. The IMPACT Act requires post-acute care (PAC) providers to report standardized assessment data across post-acute settings for the purposes of patient assessment, quality comparisons, resource use measurement, and payment reform. This standardized assessment data can be used to build payment models that Congress can consider for future PAC payment reforms. Figure 11-6 provides a graphical illustration of the timeline of milestones set forth by the IMPACT Act. Inpatient rehabilitation facilities would be required to begin reporting standardized patient assessment data upon patient admission and discharge after October 1, 2018 (APTA, 2014).

FIGURE 11-6

Timeline of Major Deliverables in the IMPACT Act of 2014.

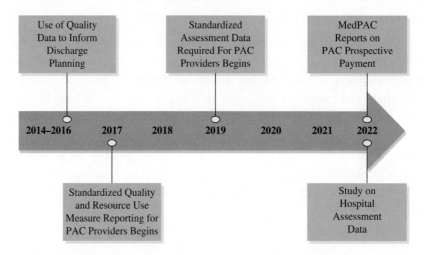

Source: U. S. Senate. http://www.finance.senate.gov/imo/media/doc/IMPACT%20Summary.pdf.

Outpatient Rehabilitation

The cost savings are substantial when rehabilitation services—PT, OT, and speech pathology—can be provided in an outpatient setting. The number of outpatient rehabilitation settings and freestanding rehabilitation clinics has continued to increase in the twenty-first century.

Independent Living

At one time, individuals who had limiting conditions that reduced their functional status had little option other than discharge to nursing homes. The independent living movement advocates for funding to provide support services to an individual with a disability, at the level required to keep the person in his or her home, resulting in decreased morbidity and mortality for the patient and increasing the likelihood that the individual will be employable. The independent living movement will continue to progress because of its cost-effectiveness and, therefore, health care providers are adopting strategies that promote independent living.

Health information management specialists can help to develop systems of documentation that promote good health care in the independent living situation. Along these lines, Title III, Sec. 3024, of the Patient Protection and Affordable Care Act enacted an Independence at Home Demonstration Program that included electronic health records and telehealth methodologies. Initial results of this demonstration program indicated substantial savings for Medicare and improved outcomes for beneficiaries.

Technology

There is a rapid explosion of technology in rehabilitation. Electronic systems are being developed that someday may replace lost vision. Computer-assisted ambulation systems are becoming much more functional and smaller. Robotic devices now are able to supplement the missing function of upper extremities. This technology is in its infancy and will continue to grow. Small pacemaker neurostimulation devices (Neuro-Control) now are commonly implanted in the brachial plexus to replace lost motor function in the upper extremities, and similar devices can be used to cause a neurogenic bladder to function appropriately.

Upper-extremity amputees now can have high-tech I-hands that allow individual finger movement. Persons with above-the-knee amputation now have an option of using the C-leg prosthesis, a computerized prosthesis that increases safety while allowing infinite variability in walking cadences. The modern power wheel chair has infrared and other communication technologies integrated into the chair, allowing the user to interface with home environmental control unit systems (ECUs), home entertainment systems, and telephones via the wheelchair's joystick. Home ECUs can be controlled from anywhere in the world with a smart-phone technology interface.

Care paths once were used to cover the expected course during rehabilitation and to document outcomes. As a result of regulations and pressure from third-party payers, this has given way to uniform data sets such as those required by CMS. The Inpatient Rehabilitation Facility Patient Assessment Instrument (IRF-PAI), previously discussed in the context of payment and the IRF PPS, also is a helpful component in assessing the patient for clinical purposes and developing an individualized overall plan of care.

SELF REVIEW 11.9

1. True or False? The level of care offered by rehabilitation units in skilled nursing facilities tends to be more cost-effective for younger patients.

2. What legislation, signed into law in 2014, requires post-acute care (PAC) providers to report standardized assessment data across post-acute settings for the purposes of patient assessment, quality comparisons, resource use measurement, and payment reform?

3. The cost savings are substantial when rehabilitation services can be provided in a(n) _____ setting.

4. What is the independent living movement?

5. What types of technology are being developed to assist in rehabilitation?

SUMMARY

Rehabilitation is a continuum of care that spans the entire gamut of disabling conditions, involves all age groups, and is provided in numerous types of health care settings. The health care information specialist can play a significant role in developing and maintaining health information systems that improve the quality of care, enhance full-team interdisciplinary communication, and provide the necessary data for accurate reimbursement and quality reporting.

REVIEW QUESTIONS

Knowledge-Based Questions

1. Define the term *rehabilitation*.
2. List and describe various settings in which rehabilitative care may take place.
3. List and describe the two ways of organizing rehabilitation teams. Which method of organization for rehabilitation teams is generally considered best, and why?
4. List the various medical and other specialists that might be part of a rehabilitation team.
5. List the major categories of disabling conditions.
6. List and describe the World Health Organization's definitions of three major terms used to discuss individuals with functional limitations.
7. List, define, and give examples of the five main classes of durable medical equipment used in rehabilitation.
8. List two voluntary accrediting agencies for rehabilitation facilities.
9. What are some of the CMS criteria for inpatient rehabilitation facilities?
10. List the functions of the interdisciplinary team that must be documented in a patient's medical records under CARF guidelines.
11. List the five items that the rehabilitation assessment must document under CARF guidelines.
12. Briefly describe the inpatient rehabilitation prospective payment system (IRF PPS).
13. What are FIM scores, and how are they used?
14. List six advantages that rehabilitation teams reap from using FIM scores.
15. What are the possible roles of the health information manager in rehabilitation facilities?

Critical Thinking Questions

1. Why is accreditation by CARF important to rehabilitative facilities and their patients? What role might the health information manager play in the CARF accreditation process for a rehabilitative facility?
2. How might the practice of health information management in various settings be affected by implementing a bundled payment system for post-acute care?
3. What are some recent changes in the delivery of rehabilitative care?

WEB ACTIVITY

The idea of a bundled payment for post-acute care was proposed as early as the 1990s.

1. Conduct your own Internet search for the latest information on the status of payment bundling for post-acute care or post-acute care payment reform.
2. Write a brief report on what you learn through your search for up-to-date information on these concepts.

CASE STUDY

In monitoring for various complications at XYZ Rehabilitation Hospital, health information manager Mary Moore discovers that, in many instances, patients with deep vein thrombosis or pressure sores are being admitted to the hospital with those conditions. Because rehabilitation cannot proceed until these medical conditions are resolved, these patients may be discharged from rehabilitation to another type of care after a short stay, and later readmitted to rehabilitation. Or these conditions may prolong the patient's length of stay in the rehabilitation facility. Mary plans to report these findings to the quality improvement committee.

1. What recommendations might the committee make regarding these findings?
2. What role can Mary play in improving this situation?

REFERENCES AND SUGGESTED READINGS

APTA (American Physical Therapy Association). (2014, October 7). IMPACT Act standardizing post-acute care data signed into law. *PT in Motion News.* http://www.apta.org/PTinMotion /News/2014/10/7/IMPACTSigned/

Centers for Disease Control and Prevention, National center for injury prevention and control. (2010). http://www.cdc.gov/traumaticbraininjury/scifacts .html

Centers for Disease Control and Prevention, National center for injury prevention and control. (2014). http://www.cdc.gov/traumaticbraininjury/get _the_facts.html

Classification criteria for payment under the inpatient rehabilitation facility prospective payment system. (2014). *Code of Federal Regulations,* Title 42, § 412. 29, 2014 ed.

CMS (Centers for Medicare & Medicaid Services). (2005, July 29). Section 140.3.4: Payment adjustment for late transmission of patient assessment data. *Medicare Claims Processing Manual* [Online] https://www.cms.gov/manuals/downloads /clm104c03.pdf [2010, August 28].

CMS (Centers for Medicare & Medicaid Services). (2014, August 6). 42 C.F.R. pt. 412: Inpatient rehabilitation facility prospective payment system for federal fiscal year 2015; Final rule. *Federal Register, 79*(151), 45872–45936.

CMS (Centers for Medicare & Medicaid Services). (2014, September). Inpatient rehabilitation facility prospective payment system: Payment system fact sheet series. [Online]. http://www.cms.gov/Outreach-and-Education /Medicare-Learning-Network-MLN/MLNProducts /downloads/InpatRehabPaymtfctsht09-508.pdf

IALCP (International Academy of Life Care Planners). (n.d.) Introduction. *Standards of Practice.* [Online]. http://www.rehabpro.org/sections/ialcp/focus /standards/section-i-introduction

IARP (International Association of Rehabilitation Professionals). (2012). IALCP 2012 Summit—code of ethics.[Online] http://www.rehabpro.org /sections/ialcp/events/2012-summit-codes-of -ethics/view

Lump-Sum payments, *Code of Federal Regulations,* Title 42, § 411.46, 2014 ed.

MedPAC (Medicare Payment Advisory Commission). (2010). Report to the Congress: Medicare payment policy. Washington, DC: MedPAC.

Mooney, O., Doig, E. & Fleming, J. (2009). Risk assessment and management for providers of community-based rehabilitation to people with acquired brain injury: Health professionals' perspectives. *Disability and Rehabilitation, 31*(6), 500–507.

Moran, B., & Heidell, C. (2012, April). External risk assessment tool for inpatient rehabilitation facilities. *Compliance Today, 14*(4), 17–19.

World Health Organization. (2001). *International Classification of Functioning, Disability and Health (ICF).* Geneva, Switzerland: WHO.

KEY RESOURCES

American Academy of Physical Medicine and Rehabilitation
  http://www.aapmr.org

American Medical Rehabilitation Providers Association
  http://www.amrpa.org

American Spinal Injury Association (ASIA)
  http://www.asia-spinalinjury.org

CARF International (Commission on Accreditation of Rehabilitation Facilities)
  http://www.carf.org

International Academy of Life Care Planners
  http://www.rehabpro.org/sections/ialcp

International Association of Rehabilitation Professionals
  http://www.rehabpro.org

Model Systems Knowledge Translation Center
  http://www.msktc.org/tbi/model-system-centers

National Institute of Neurological Disorders and Stroke
  http://www.ninds.nih.gov

National Institute on Disability, Independent Living, and Rehabilitation Research (NIDILRR)
  http://www.acl.gov/programs/NIDILRR

The Joint Commission
  http://www.jointcommission.org

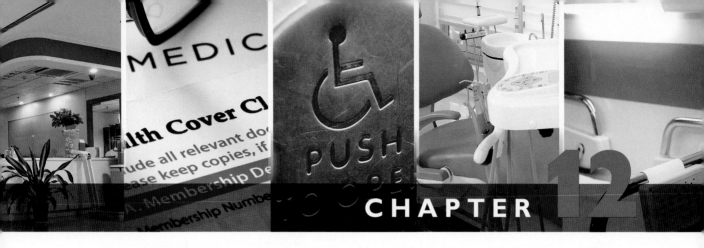

CHAPTER 12

Home Health Care

Pamela R. Dodd, RHIA | Ida Blevins, RHIA | Gwen D. Smith, RHIA | Kim A. Boyles, MS, RHIA

LEARNING OBJECTIVES

Upon successful completion of this chapter, you should be able to:

- Explain the basic operations of a home health care agency, and identify potential future trends of the industry.
- Discuss the importance of data collection, analysis, and reporting to be competitive in the current payment environment.
- Identify the types of services provided by home health care agencies.
- Explain the growth of home health care.
- List the agencies or organizations that develop standards for home health care.
- Explain the purpose of the Outcome and Assessment Information Set-C1 (OASIS-C1).
- Discuss the importance of outcome-based quality improvement (OBQI) and outcome-based quality management (OBQM) in the home care setting.

Setting	Description	Synonyms/Examples
Home Health Care	A service to the recovering, disabled, or chronically ill person, providing for treatment and/or effective functioning in the home environment	Home care, visiting nurses, visiting staff

INTRODUCTION TO SETTING

Home health care encompasses a wide range of health and social services delivered in home to recovering, disabled, and chronically or terminally ill persons in need of medical, nursing, social, or therapeutic treatment and/or assistance with activities of daily living. According to the National Association for Home Care and Hospice:

> "home care is appropriate whenever a person prefers to stay at home but needs ongoing care that cannot easily or effectively be provided solely by family and friends. More and more older people, electing to live independent, non-institutionalized lives, are receiving home care services as their physical capabilities diminish. Younger adults who are disabled or recuperating from acute illness are choosing home care whenever possible. Chronically ill infants and children are receiving sophisticated medical treatment in their loving and secure home environments. Adults and children diagnosed with terminal illness also are being cared for at home, receiving compassionate care and maintaining dignity at the end of life. As hospital stays decrease, increasing numbers of patients need highly skilled services when they return home. Other patients are able to avoid institutionalization altogether, receiving safe and effective care in the comfort of their own homes." (NAHC, 2010, p. 1)

Throughout this chapter and in the real world, the term **home health care** is synonymous with home care, visiting nurses, and visiting staff. Home care may be considered as an alternative to some inpatient and outpatient procedures and treatments that are performed routinely in the traditional hospital or clinic setting. Home care has been around for years, but in earlier days the concept of caring for patients at home was not considered as an industry.

Over the years, the home care industry has grown substantially. The reasons for this growth can be attributed to cost savings, changes in reimbursement, technology, and advances in patients' right to choose. With implementation of the inpatient prospective payment system, government regulations have motivated hospitals to contain their costs, compelling them to consider utilizing other methods to deliver care to their patients. Home care is among the solutions to aid in minimizing hospital expenses while maintaining continuity of care and preventing expensive patient re-hospitalizations.

Advances in technology and medical equipment allow patients to receive treatment in the home versus a visit to the hospital or a stay in a long-term care facility. For example, intravenous (IV) bags and pumps can be used to administer IV treatments such as pain medication, chemotherapy, enteral feedings, and antibiotics at a patient's place of residence.

home health care services and treatment provided in the home environment to individuals who are recovering, have a disability, or are chronically ill, to improve their health or effective functioning.

Many patients choose to receive their treatments at home because it gives them a greater sense of independence and comfort—which are vital in healing many disease processes. If the patient's condition warrants home care, the patient, the physician, the hospital, and the home care provider have to recognize that selection of the home care agency, by regulation, is the patient's choice.

Types of Patients

Home visitation services are provided to individuals who are identified by a physician as having a medical necessity for skilled services. Some payer sources, such as Medicare and many private insurance companies, require the patient to be **homebound** (i.e., confined to the home except for infrequent or relatively brief absences that require considerable and taxing effort) to receive home health services. However, not all payers have this requirement. Patient referrals can be received from a variety of services, such as hospital discharge planners, patients, patients' physicians, insurance companies through their case management programs, preferred provider organizations (PPOs), and health maintenance organizations (HMOs). After the agency receives the referral, it is required to have physician orders to provide services.

Upon referral to a home health agency, a staff person from the home care agency will visit the patient's home to identify needs and to perform a comprehensive assessment. The agency staff works with the patient's physician to begin the patient's plan of care for **home care visits** based upon the results of this assessment. The preliminary work includes identifying the types of services the patient requires, which disciplines are required (e.g., physical therapy, speech therapy, occupational therapy, home health aide, social worker), as well as supplies/medical equipment the patient may need. Further, it is determined how often these disciplines should visit the patient and what special orders are required to ensure continuity of care for the patient.

Types of Caregivers

Many services can be offered to patients in a home care setting. An organization can be selective in determining what services it offers to its patients; however, an agency has a competitive advantage in the home care market if it offers a variety of services. The following discussion explains some of the available home health care options. Most options are paid by Medicare and third-party payers, with a few exceptions.

Skilled Nursing Agencies

Skilled nursing agencies employ health care personnel with a variety of skill levels. Individuals employed by these agencies may include nurses trained in medical-surgical nursing, intravenous therapy, enterostomal therapy, psychiatric or mental health, maternity, or restorative nursing. The level of nursing care used

---

homebound a situation in which individuals with physical or mental limitations are able to leave home only infrequently and with great effort, generally requiring assistance.

home care visits medical and nonmedical care provided to patients within the privacy and comfort of their own homes; often the unit of measure in home health care for evaluating costs, scheduling, and productivity. For some payers, the visit is the unit of payment for services.

skilled nursing agencies agencies that offer nursing services such as trained medical-surgical nursing, intravenous therapy, enterostomal therapy, psychiatric or mental health, maternity, or restorative nursing. Services are provided to patients based on their individual needs.

depends on individual patient need. In the event that a Medicare-certified agency provides psychiatric nursing care, the agency must certify that the psychiatric nurse has met additional qualifying criteria to perform this function. Skilled nursing services must be supervised by a **registered nurse**.

Skilled nursing agencies also employ a **home health aide**, a certified staff person who is able to enhance patient care by assisting with activities of daily living such as checking vital signs, bathing, grooming, and preparing meals. Aides also may provide limited services such as routine wound care (uncomplicated) and prescribed exercise monitoring, depending upon limitations as described by state regulations related to the home health aide's practice.

Specialty Services

Home health care also encompasses a range of specialty services, again depending on the level of care required by the patient. These may include the following **disciplines** and services: physical therapy (PT), occupational therapy (OT), speech-language pathology, medical social services, nutrition (dietitian) services, respiratory therapy, patient transportation, respite care, homemaking services, medical equipment, Meals on Wheels, and so on.

Physical therapists establish a home exercise and maintenance program for the patient, assisting with exercise routines and ambulating devices. Occupational therapists assist the patient to become independent in performing tasks such as dressing, bathing, and other normal activities of daily living. Speech-language pathologists assist patients who suffer from a stroke or adverse effects of feeding tubes or endotracheal tubes. Speech-language pathologists teach proper swallowing techniques, word formation, and word enunciation.

Medical social services help patients and family members cope with a patient's disease process through placement and involvement with community services. They also help to find appropriate resources and make suggestions for long-range planning.

Nutrition (dietitian) services typically are not covered by Medicare, but patients always have the option to pay privately for special assistance with dietary needs. Medicare, however, does pay for skilled nurses who monitor the patient's diet during a home care treatment period, and it also pays for teaching those who need help with special feeding equipment.

For special respiratory conditions, respiratory therapists teach techniques to increase efficiency in the lungs, such as pursed-lip breathing, and safety precautions when using oxygen equipment in the home.

Patient transportation services pick up patients and transport them to their desired destination, such as the physician's office. This service is available for those who are willing to pay the fee.

In-home respite care is a fee-for-service option not paid by Medicare. Those who deliver respite care relieve the primary caregiver of his or her duties for an extended time. During this time, the home respite caregiver monitors the patient

---

registered nurse
a health care professional with an associate's or bachelor's degree in nursing who is licensed by the state as qualified to provide skilled patient care.

home health aide
a certified staff person who is able to enhance the patient's care by assisting with the patient's activities of daily living, such as checking vital signs, bathing, grooming, meal preparation, and other activities.

disciplines   specialty providers offering a variety of treatments or services for patients—for example, physical therapy, maternity services, medical social services.

as the caregiver would. Home respite care simply allows the primary caregiver to have some free time.

Durable medical equipment (DME), such as a wheelchair or a hospital bed, is leased or purchased to aid in the patient's healing within the home setting. The use of durable medical equipment in the home is covered under Medicare Part B. If coinsurance is used, the patient pays a deductible and 20% of the bill. Prior to procuring durable medical equipment, the patient or caregiver should verify if a physician's order is required for insurance or Medicare to cover the expenditure. Meals on Wheels is a charitable organization that provides food services for those who are unable to leave the home. However, Medicare does not cover meals delivered to the home (Medicare.gov).

SELF REVIEW 12.1

1. Home health care can provide patients with care in the home and aid in minimizing hospital expenses by preventing _____.

2. Describe home care according to the National Association for Home Care and Hospice.

3. List three terms that are synonymous with home health care.

4. True or False? Over the years, the need for a home care industry has decreased.

5. True or False? Many patients choose to receive their treatments at home because it gives them a greater sense of independence and comfort.

6. Define *homebound*, and list a major payer source that requires a patient to be homebound to receive reimbursement for home care services.

7. Once a patient is referred to a home health agency, a staff member from the agency will visit the patient's home to identify needs and to perform a(n) _____.

8. Describe individuals who are employed by skilled nursing agencies.

9. The _____ is a certified staff person who assists with activities such as checking vital signs, bathing, grooming, and preparing meals.

10. List three specialty services that home health care may provide.

11. In what different ways do physical therapists and occupational therapists work with home care patients?

12. Describe the role of medical social services personnel.

13. True or False? Nutrition services typically are covered by Medicare.

14. The use of durable medical equipment in the home is covered under _____.

    a. Medicare Part A

    b. Medicare Part B

15. List two reasons for the growth of home care.

REGULATORY ISSUES

Home care agencies may be not-for-profit, or they may be proprietarily owned. They can operate as stand-alone companies, often referred to as freestanding. They also can participate in a partnership or operate as an **affiliate** to another institution, often a hospital. In the latter case, the home care headquarters can be physically separate from its affiliate, or it can be affiliate-based.

Home care organizations have to consider only a few accrediting and certifying agencies:

- Medicare/Medicaid programs (the latter is referred to sometimes as a medical assistance program)
- Individual state licensing agencies
- **The Joint Commission (TJC)**
- **Community Health Accreditation Program (CHAP)**
- **Accreditation Commission for Health Care (ACHC)**

The **National Association for Home Care and Hospice (NAHC)**, though it is not an accrediting or a certifying body, also offers current information at its website (www.nahc.org) on regulatory issues affecting home care providers.

In 1997, the Centers for Medicare & Medicaid Services (CMS, known at the time as the Healthcare Financing Administration, or HCFA), offered **deemed status** to home health agencies that had been accredited by TJC or CHAP. Deemed status means that the voluntary accrediting agency's standards (e.g., TJC's or CHAP's standards) are considered to be equivalent to the standards found in the Medicare and Medicaid programs' **Conditions of Participation (COP)**.

If the agency chooses to accept deemed status, it exempts the accredited home health agency from routine surveys under the COP. In 2006, CMS granted deeming authority for home health care to a third voluntary accrediting organization, the Accreditation Commission for Health Care (ACHC). Historically, there has been little change to the HHCoPs. The published proposed rule that would have made changes to the COPs for HHAs in 1997 was never finalized in its entirety; only pieces of that proposed rule were finalized. Seventeen years later, in 2014, CMS issued a new proposed rule to modernize the Conditions of Participation to better align them with the actualities of home health practice.

Medicare/Medicaid

The **Centers for Medicare & Medicaid Services (CMS)**, a federal agency within the Department of Health and Human Services, was created in 1977 as the Health Care Financing Administration (HCFA) to administer the Medicare and Medicaid programs. CMS maintains its headquarters in Baltimore, Maryland, and has regional offices nationwide. The headquarters administers the national direction of the Medicare and Medicaid programs, and the regional offices provide CMS with the local presence necessary for quality customer service and oversight.

---

affiliate an associate or member of a particular business.

The Joint Commission (TJC) promotes quality in home care by accrediting a variety of organizations that provide home care services. Meeting TJC standards provides a home health agency with deemed status with regard to the Medicare Conditions of Participation.

Community Health Accreditation Program (CHAP) an independent, not-for-profit, accrediting body for community-based health care organizations. Meeting CHAP standards can provide a home health agency with deemed status with regard to the Medicare Conditions of Participation.

Accreditation Commission for Health Care (ACHC) a voluntary accrediting organization with deeming authority for home health, hospice, and suppliers of durable medical equipment, prosthetics, orthotics, and supplies (DMEPOS). Meeting ACHC standards can provide a health agency with deemed status with regard to the Medicare Conditions of Participation.

National Association for Home Care and Hospice (NAHC) an association for organizations and individuals who provide health care and supportive services on an outreach basis to patients in their homes.

CMS acts mainly as a purchaser of health care services for Medicare and Medicaid beneficiaries. Four key principles for Medicare/Medicaid standards are:

1. Assuring that Medicare and Medicaid are administered properly by their contractors and state agencies
2. Establishing policies for the reimbursement of health care providers
3. Conducting research on the effectiveness of various methods of health care management, treatment, and financing
4. Assessing the quality of health care facilities and services

Medicare Conditions of Participation, manuals, interim manual instructions, and Medicare transmittals are distributed to Medicare administrative contractors (intermediaries, carriers), CMS regional offices, federal agencies, state agencies, and congressional offices via the Internet at the CMS website (www.cms.gov).

The Joint Commission

The Joint Commission (TJC) has existed since 1951 and currently is the largest accrediting body in the health care industry. It established its Home Care Accreditation Program in 1988. The scope of accreditation for home care encompasses many types of organizations, such as Medicare-certified home health agencies, hospices, private duty agencies, durable medical equipment companies, and infusion therapy companies.

TJC is a well-known accrediting body for those working in the home care industry. To receive a seal of approval from TJC, an agency must apply for a survey and prepare to be evaluated on performance, functions, and processes aimed at improving patient outcomes, or end results. An evaluation is done by TJC, with qualitative and quantitative standards, or rules. TJC publishes its home care standards in the *Comprehensive Accreditation Manual for Home Care*, which is updated yearly.

Community Health Accreditation Program

The Community Health Accreditation Program (CHAP) was founded in 1965 and is the only accrediting body dedicated exclusively to quality home, community, and public health care. Until 2001, it was a subsidiary of the National League for Nursing and now is an independent, nonprofit corporation focusing on improving community-based health care through voluntary programs.

TJC and CHAP have collaborated in an effort to decrease overlaps within their business operations. TJC now recognizes and accepts the accreditation process, findings, and decisions of CHAP for home care institutions.

Four key principles for all CHAP standards are as follows:

1. The organization's structure and function consistently support its consumer-oriented philosophy and purpose.

2. The organization consistently provides high-quality services and products.

3. The organization has adequate human, financial, and physical resources to accomplish its stated mission and purpose.

4. The organization is positioned for long-term viability.

The CHAP *Standards of Excellence* are composed of *Core Standards* addressing broad concepts that apply to all CHAP-accredited organizations, and *Service-Specific Standards* that address requirements related to the specific services that an organization may offer.

Accreditation Commission for Health Care (ACHC)

The Accreditation Commission for Health Care (ACHC) has deeming authority for Medicare in home health, hospice, and DMEPOS (durable medical equipment, prosthetics, orthotics, and supplies). ACHC was begun by home care providers "endeavoring to create a viable option of accreditation sensitive to the needs of small providers" (ACHC, 2010, para. 1). ACHC is an ISO 9001 certified organization and is integrating ISO concepts into its accreditation processes.

SELF REVIEW 12.2

1. _____ is a federal agency within the Department of Health and Human Services created to administer the Medicare and Medicaid programs.

2. Name two of the key principles set forth in the Medicare/Medicaid standards.

3. _____ is the largest accrediting body in the health care industry, and established its Home Care Accreditation Program in 1988.
   a. Community Health Accreditation Program
   b. The Joint Commission
   c. Accreditation Commission for Health Care

4. _____ was founded in 1965 and is the only accrediting body dedicated exclusively to quality home, community, and public health care.
   a. Accreditation Commission for Health Care
   b. The Joint Commission
   c. Community Health Accreditation Program

5. _____ was begun by home care providers to meet the needs of small providers and is an ISO 9001-certified organization that is integrating ISO concepts into its accreditation processes.
   a. CMS
   b. Accreditation Commission for Health Care
   c. The Joint Commission

DOCUMENTATION

The primary reasons for documentation, whether electronic or hard copy, are to maintain an accurate record of all care and services provided to the patient, so as to provide and maintain high quality patient care, to meet all regulatory requirements, and to support reimbursement.

For Medicare-certified agencies, the Medicare Conditions of Participation for home health agencies specify certain documentation requirements. If an agency is interested in becoming accredited by TJC, CHAP, or ACHC, the agency would have to obtain the appropriate accreditation manuals that outline specific standards regarding content, timeframes, and authorized staff.

The Home Health Certification and Plan of Care, also known as the **485**, certifies the patient's need for home health services (see Figure 12-1). The 485 also outlines the patient's plan of care, which must be established by his or her attending physician. This document includes pertinent diagnoses, types of services, frequency and duration of visits, medication and treatments, safety measures, durable medical equipment (DME), nutritional requirements, functional limitations, allergies, mental status, prognosis, activities of daily living, goals, rehabilitation potential, and discharge plans. (Note: CMS has dropped the requirement for use of this specific form, stating simply that these elements should be included in the patient's plan of care. To make sure that all of these elements are indeed in the patient's plan of care, many agencies have opted to continue using the 485 or a form modeled after it.)

Documentation of physician certification of the need for home care is a requirement for payment under Medicare. Effective January 1, 2011, "As a condition of payment, the Affordable Care Act mandates that prior to certifying a patient's eligibility for the home health benefit, the certifying physician must document that he or she, or an allowed **non-physician practitioner (NPP)** has had a face-to-face encounter with the patient. The face-to-face encounter must occur within the 90 days prior to the start of home health care, or within the 30 days after the start of care" (MLN Matters, 2014, pp. 1–2).

Although the face-to-face encounter is still required, effective for episodes beginning on or after January 1, 2015, CMS eliminated the requirement for physician narrative documentation of the encounter as part of the certification of patient eligibility. The 2015 rule requires that the documentation to support certification of the patient's homebound status must be contained in the certifying physician's medical records and/or the acute/post-acute care facility's medical records (if the patient was directly admitted to home health). The HHA may provide information from the HHA record to the certifying physician and/or the acute/post-acute provider for incorporation into the provider's record to complete a valid face-to-face encounter document.

If the documentation used is not sufficient to demonstrate that the patient is or was eligible to receive services under the Medicare home health benefit, payment will not be rendered for home health services provided. Certifying

485 the document number for a previously required CMS form facilitating a patient's orders for home care. Although the requirement for the form itself has been dropped, the content of the form still is required. Therefore, both the term *485* and the form itself are still in use in many home health agencies. The form provides a plan of care, which must be established and reviewed at least once every 60 days by the patient's attending physician.

non-physician practitioner (NPP) in the context of certifying the necessity of home care services, "a nurse practitioner or clinical nurse specialist…, who is working in collaboration with the physician in accordance with State law, or a certified nurse-midwife…, or a physician assistant…, under the supervision of the physician." (MLN Matters, 2014, p. 2)

FIGURE 12-1

Home Health Certification and Plan of Care.

Department of Health and Human Services Centers for Medicare & Medicaid Services		Form Approved OMS No. 0938-0357

HOME HEALTH CERTIFICATION AND PLAN OF CARE

1. Patient's HI Claim No.	2. Start of Care Date	3. Certification Period From: To:	4. Medica l Record No.	5. Provider No.

6. Patient's Name and Address	7. Provider's Name, Address and Telephone Number

8. Date of Birth	9. Sex ☐ M ☐ F	10. Medications: Dose/Frequency/Route (N)ew (C)hanged

11. ICD-9-CM	Principal Diagnosis	Date
12. ICD-9-CM	Surgical Procedure	Date
13. ICD· 9-CM	Other Pertinent Diagnoses	Date

14. DME and Supplies	15. Safety Measures:
16. Nutritional Req.	17. Allergies

18. A. Functional Limitations

1 ☐ Amputation	5 ☐ Paralysis	9 ☐ Legally Blind
2 ☐ Bowel/Bladder (Incontinence)	6 ☐ Endurance	A ☐ Dyspnea With Minimal Exertion
3 ☐ Contracture	7 ☐ Ambulation	
4 ☐ Hearing	8 ☐ Speech	B ☐ Other (Specify)

18. B. Activities Permitted

1 ☐ Complete Bedrest	6 ☐ Partial Weight Bearing	A ☐ Wheelchair
2 ☐ Bedrest BRP	7 ☐ Independent At Home	B ☐ Walker
3 ☐ Up As Tolerated		C ☐ No Restrictions
4 ☐ Transfer Bed/Chair	8 ☐ Crutches	D ☐ Other (Specify)
5 ☐ Exercises Prescribed	9 ☐ Cane	

19. Mental Status:

1 ☐ Oriented	3 ☐ Forgetful	5 ☐ Disoriented	7 ☐ Agitated
2 ☐ Comatose	4 ☐ Depressed	6 ☐ Lethargic	8 ☐ Other

20. Prognosis: 1 ☐ Poor   2 ☐ Guarded   3 ☐ Fair   4 ☐ Good   5 ☐ Excellent

21. Orders for Discipline and Treatments (Specify Amount/Frequency/Duration)

22. Goals/Rehabilitation Potentia/Discharge Plans

23. Nurse's Signature and Date of Verbal SOC Where Applicable	25. Date HHA Received Signed POT

24. Physician's Name and Address	26. I certify/recertify that this patient is confined to his/her home and needs intermittent Skilled nursing care, physical therapy and/or speech therapy or continues to need cccvcauonattherepy. The patient is under my care, and I have authorized the services on this plan of care and will periodically review the plan.
27. Attending Physician's Signature and Date Signed	28. Anyore who misrepresents, falsifies , or conceals essential information required for payment of Federal funds may be subject to fine. imprisonment, or civil penalty under applicable Federal laws.

Form CMS-485 (C-3) (02-94) (Formerly HCFA-485) (Print Aligned)

From www.cms.gov.

physician records that are noncompliant with this new requirement may result in increased reviews, such as a provider-specific probe review.

Another requirement under the Affordable Care Act is that a physician or other eligible professional has to be enrolled in the Internet-based **Provider Enrollment, Chain and Ownership System (PECOS)** to order or refer home health services. Therefore, the CMS Ordering and Referring Report must be checked to make sure that the certifying physician or NPP is registered prior to establishing a Medicare beneficiary plan of care (MLN Matters, 2013). The patient's physician must review, update, and recertify (if necessary) the plan of care at least every 60 days. This timeframe often is referred to as the patient's **certification period. Recertification** can continue every 60 days as long as the patient meets Medicare coverage guidelines or agrees to pay privately for services until the patient is discharged from services.

Another document required for home care is the **comprehensive assessment,** which is completed on the first visit. The document should include the patient's present illness; significant past history; review of all systems/physical assessment; medications; psychological, social, and economic factors; emergency plans; and skilled nursing performed that day. Based on the initial assessment and the patient's needs, the skilled nurse develops a **care plan** that includes goals, objectives, and those responsible for completing the plan. In addition, CMS expects HHAs to complete the patient's comprehensive assessment *before* assigning the home health diagnoses to the OASIS-C1 instrument (refer to the Key Resources (*OASIS-C1/ICD-9* and *ICD-10 Guidance Manuals*).

An authorized staff person, determined by state law, takes verbal orders from the patient's physician. This staff person must document, date, and sign the order (either on hard copy or electronically). The order also must be signed by the physician and returned to the home care agency within a certain timeframe, determined by state law. Medicare-certified agencies may not bill for services until all orders are signed and returned.

Skilled nursing services must be supervised by a registered nurse and documented at appropriate intervals, determined by state law. Home health aide services require supervisory visits by the registered nurse and documentation at appropriate intervals, also determined by state law. In addition, physical therapy assistant services and certified occupational therapy assistant services require supervisory visits by the physical therapist or occupational therapist and should be documented at intervals required by regulation. Additional documents include the patient database, hospital discharge information, information collected upon referral, patient bill of rights, advance directives, DNR (do not resuscitate) orders, medication profile, all initial baseline assessments and progress notes, problem list, care plans, teaching guides, and discharge summary.

A **source-oriented record** (electronic or hard copy) is the traditional way in which a record is organized in sections according to patient care departments and/or disciplines. Within each section, the forms are arranged according to date. The major advantage to the source-oriented format is that it organizes reports from each source together, thereby making it easy to determine the assessment, treatments, and observations that a particular discipline has provided. One disadvantage of the source-oriented format is that it is not possible to quickly determine all of the patient's problems. It also is difficult to determine all of the treatments being provided for the patient at a given time.

The **problem-oriented record** (electronic or hard copy) provides a systematic method of documentation to reflect logical thinking on the part of the person directing the patient's care. The individual directing the patient's care defines and follows each clinical problem individually and organizes the problems for solution. The record must contain four basic components: database, complete problem list, initial plans, and progress notes.

Advantages of this format are that the individual directing the patient care is required to consider all the patient's problems in total context. The record clearly indicates the goals and methods in treating the patient. Medical education is facilitated by documenting logical thought processes.

A disadvantage of the problem-oriented record is that the format usually requires training of the professional staff. Also, for this chart format to be effective, the professional staff must be convinced of the system's worth.

In an **integrated format** (electronic or hard copy), the information is organized in strict chronological order. The forms from the various sources are intermingled. An advantage of this format is that the information included reads like a book, providing a clear picture of the patient's illness and response to treatment. Still, it is difficult to compare similar information (e.g., fasting blood sugar levels) over a period of time. It also proves difficult for each discipline to quickly determine its treatment regimen and patient outcome.

> **problem-oriented record** a document organized by the patient's problems; follows each clinical problem individually and provides a systematic method of documentation to reflect logical thinking on the part of the one who is directing the patient's care.

> **integrated format** a record in which the information is organized in a strict chronological order.

Outcome and Assessment Information Set-C1 (OASIS-C1)

The **Outcome and Assessment Information Set-C1 (OASIS-C1)** is a group of data items designed to establish a means of systematic measurement of patient home health care outcomes. Outcomes, for the purpose of OASIS-C1, measure changes in a patient's health status between two or more time points.

OASIS-C1 data items address sociodemographic, environmental, support system, health status, functional status, and health service utilization characteristics of the patient. The data are collected at specific time points, including start of care, every 60 days on a follow-up OASIS-C1, post-hospitalization, and at transfer or discharge. Note that the OASIS-C1 data elements alone do not constitute a complete and comprehensive assessment tool and must be incorporated into a comprehensive patient assessment. For example, the OASIS-C1 data elements do not include things such as vital signs, home safety issues, wound measurements, and so on.

> **Outcome and Assessment Information Set-C1 (OASIS-C1)** a data set requirement under Medicare's Conditions of Participation. Medicare-certified home health agencies collect and use OASIS data when evaluating adult, nonmaternity patients. The intent of OASIS is to make the Conditions of Participation more patient-centered and outcome-oriented while providing home care agencies with greater flexibility to operate their programs. It also measures treatment outcomes and provides individual agencies with the ability to compare themselves to the national data set.

Regulatory Overview

Only home health agencies that participate in the Medicare program are required to follow the OASIS-C1 regulations, as stated in the Medicare Conditions of

Participation. An OASIS-C1 assessment should be performed on all patients who are adult (over age 18), nonmaternity, and receiving skilled care. TJC also has requirements and standards that address improving organization performance, which can be met by using OASIS-C1 processes. In addition, state and Medicare surveyors have access to OASIS-generated quality reports, which they may review before an agency's survey. Some reports may be used in the survey process, and surveyors will expect agencies to show how they use OASIS-C1 data reports for quality monitoring. These quality improvement and quality management uses of OASIS-C1 are described later. The OASIS-C1 also is the data collection tool for the Medicare home health prospective payment system.

Reporting of OASIS Information

There are several methods for gathering and reporting the OASIS-C1 information. Some home health agencies gather all of their information electronically in the field and then transmit the data. Others gather the information on paper and manually enter the data into an electronic file—called encoding. Others gather the data on paper and scan the information.

Data also are submitted in a variety of ways. Some agencies have purchased software specifically for the OASIS-C1 data and their transmission. Others have elected to use software available at no charge from CMS. The software available from CMS, termed **Home Assessment Validation and Entry (HAVEN)**, was developed to provide home health agencies with software for data entry, editing, and validation of OASIS-C1 data.

> **Home Assessment Validation and Entry (HAVEN)** software available from CMS, developed to provide home health agencies with an electronic application for data entry, editing, and validation of OASIS-C1 data.

The Medicare Conditions of Participation detail the timeframes for completion and transmission of the OASIS-C1 data. Generally, the data must be encoded and "locked" within 7 days of completion of the assessment. During this 7-day timeframe, the data must be analyzed for accuracy, and edited if needed. Once the data elements have been locked, which prevents subsequent editing and ensures stability of the data, they can be batched in a submission file and transmitted to the state agency.

CMS requires that the data be electronically transmitted at least monthly. Transmissions may occur more frequently at the discretion of the home health agency. Data must be transmitted by the end of the month following the date of collection. For example, an assessment completed in February would have to be transmitted by the end of March. There is no specific date on which the agency must transmit the data, which allows agencies to develop schedules that best meet their needs.

After the data have been transmitted to the state agency, the home health agency must monitor the state reports for initial and final validation of the submission. If any errors or exceptions are found, the home health agency will receive a message in the final validation report, and errors must be corrected and resubmitted.

SELF REVIEW 12.3

1. Identify the primary reasons for documentation in health care.
2. What certifies the patient's need for home health services?
3. True or False? Documentation of physician certification of the need for home care is a requirement for payment under Medicare.
4. Once the patient has gone through the certification period, how often does recertification take place?
5. Distinguish between a source-oriented record and a problem-oriented record.
6. List an advantage and a disadvantage of both source-oriented and problem-oriented records.
7. What is the OASIS-C1?
8. What is the software that has been developed to provide home health agencies with data entry, editing, and validation of OASIS-C1 data?

REIMBURSEMENT AND FUNDING

When a home care agency receives a request to service a patient, it accepts the responsibility to determine the patient's financial eligibility. A patient may be insured by Medicare, Medicaid, private/third-party payer, or is willing to issue payment personally (self-pay). Some organizations also have a charity fund established for those who are uninsured and unable to submit payments.

Upon completion of services and documentation and verification that all physician orders are signed and returned to the agency, a bill is submitted. Payment to the home care organization is provided by one or more of the following:

- Medicare: A home care agency is paid a specific dollar amount for a 60-day period based on the patient's Home Health Resource Group (HHRG), as described in the following discussion of the prospective payment system (PPS).
- Medicaid: A home care agency is paid based on a rate determined by the state legislature; this rate varies with each state.
- Private insurance: A home care agency is paid based on a percentage of charges.
- Self-pay: A patient opts to acknowledge that he or she understands that Medicare/Medicaid or other payers will not pay for the services and determines that he or she will pay for those services out of pocket.

Medicare Prospective Payment System (PPS)

On October 1, 2000, the Home Health Prospective Payment System (HH PPS) became effective and changed the way in which home care agencies were reimbursed for Medicare patients. The HH PPS system was implemented to promote the same efficiencies and cost savings experienced when Medicare payments to hospitals were converted to a prospective payment system.

Under this payment system, home care agencies are paid, based on the OASIS assessment, an episodic payment for 60-days of care, depending on the severity of the patient's illness and the services required. After the assessment of the patient has been performed and the OASIS-C1 completed, the Home Health Resource Group (HHRG)—based on the answers to certain identified OASIS-C1 questions—can be determined. The HHRG is represented by a six-character alphanumeric code indicating severity, which enables the patient to have an assigned episodic rate of payment based on the patient's individual assessment. The challenge to the agency is to ensure that the clinicians adequately assess the patient to demonstrate the patient's severity and provide adequate reimbursement for the patient's care. Implementation of HH PPS forced the home health agencies to look at each patient's plan of care and provide the care needed to meet his or her needs within the constraints of the established reimbursement.

In establishing the reimbursement rate, the patient must be assessed in three areas to determine the HHRG: clinical (C), functional (F), and service utilization (S):

1. *Clinical dimension:* Establishes the scoring based on primary diagnosis and secondary diagnoses for the top six diagnoses on the plan of care, vision, level of pain, presence of ulcers or wounds, dyspnea, urinary and bowel status, need for infusion, and behavior.

2. *Functional dimension:* Assesses the patient's ability to perform activities of daily living (ADLs) such as dressing, bathing, toileting, transferring, and ambulating safely within the home setting. These areas carry more weight depending on the number of therapy visits the patient is projected to receive.

3. *Service utilization:* Determines the level of service that the patient is likely to need based on the number of therapy visits received during the episode of care. Therapy visits are combined for OT, PT, and speech therapy (ST) to get the total number of visits projected for the start of episode. The payment system is set up in a tiered methodology. Therapy reimbursement to the episode is broken down into the following groups: Therapy 0–5 visits, 6–9 visits, 10–13 visits, 14–19, and 20+ visits per episode. The initial assessment is a projection of the possible visits for the episode, and the reimbursement then is adjusted at the final claim for the actual number of therapy visits provided.

There are 157 payment categories relating back to responses from the OASIS-C1. Payments are adjusted to accommodate area wage differences, number of visits, and therapy and supply utilization.

Before submitting the claims to Medicare, the HHRG must be converted to a Health Insurance Prospective Payment System code (HIPPS). HIPPS codes also are alphanumeric but, unlike the HHRG, are made up of five characters, including a character to indicate the level of supply utilization.

Payments for the 60-day episodes are made in two installments—the first when a Request for Anticipated Payment (RAP) is submitted to Medicare, and the second when the final claim is filed. Patients are covered for an unlimited number of episodes as long as they continue to meet the Medicare criteria for skilled care.

Exceptions to the normal 60-day HHRG-based episode payment are as follows:

- *Low Utilization Payment Adjustment (LUPA)*: If a patient receives 4 or fewer visits in a 60-day episode, payment will be made by the visit.
- *Partial Episode Payment (PEP)*: Occasionally, a patient may transfer to another agency for care, in which case the first agency would receive payment only for the part of the episode for which it actually provided care to the patient. When the patient starts receiving care from the new agency, a new episode begins. PEPs also occur if the agency providing care discharges the patient prior to the end of the 60-day episode and then home care is resumed by the same agency before the end of the episode.
- *Outliers*: An outlier occurs when the provision of care to a patient results in unusually high costs to the home care agency. Payment adjustments are made for a portion of the costs above the set threshold.

With implementation of the prospective payment system, home care agencies have had to evaluate how they provide care to their patients and balance quality care with the efficiency and cost-saving measures that this payment method requires.

Payer Mix

Payer mix is a term describing the ratio of various types of third-party payers that provide revenue to a health care organization. For example, an agency may have 70% percent of its patients insured by Medicare, 20% by Medicaid, and 10% by other third-party payers. This ratio is essential to the financial security of the company. The focus of government programs such as Medicare and Medicaid is to pay for care on the basis of agency or industry costs. Other third-party payers generally pay contractually on the basis of charges, which can be higher than costs and are set by the agency.

payer mix the ratio of an agency's various patient insurers and third-party payers.

Financial Stability

Within the federal government, CMS and the Department of Health and Human Services administer the Medicare program. They manage the program through rules and regulations described within the Medicare Conditions of Participation. At the state level, the fiscal intermediaries (Medicare administrative contractors), such as Palmetto GBA, CAHABA, and so on, carry out these rules and regulations.

Each agency must submit a yearly cost report to its fiscal intermediary/ Medicare administrative contractor for review. This report includes such items as operating costs, number of visits, and payer mix. Upon review of this report, a rate is determined for cost reimbursement adjustment.

fixed costs costs that do not change in proportion to changes in volume of services; home health examples are office rent and utilities.

A good business practice is to keep **fixed costs** as low as possible. Fixed costs do not change when the volume of services changes. In a service industry such as home health, examples of fixed costs are rent and utilities. **Variable costs** vary in proportion to the services provided. For example, when visits increase in number, the costs associated with visits, such as labor costs and transportation costs, also increase.

variable costs costs that vary in proportion to the volume of service provided.

Medicare coverage issues also affect the financial stability of the agency. With regard to Medicare, both Part A and Part B apply. The home health care agency is reimbursed for nursing and other patient care through Part A. Durable medical equipment, however, is covered under Part B. What is not covered by Medicare?

- 24-hour care at home (unless it is necessary for only one day)
- Meals delivered to the home
- Homemaker services such as shopping, cleaning, and laundry, except that home health aides may do a minimum amount of these chores at the time they are providing covered services
- Personal care provided by home health aides (such as bathing, toileting, or providing help in getting dressed) *if* this is the only care needed. Medicare classifies this personal care as "custodial" because it could be provided safely and reasonably by people without professional skills and training. When skilled services are needed, however, personal care is covered.

audit a formal way of checking financial and other records.

The financial side of an agency potentially will undergo an **audit**. Possible reasons are a cost report that requires further investigation, a high volume of services, or a history of a high denial rate. However, *if* claims are submitted properly as stated in the guidelines and are delineated further in Medicare Local and National Coverage Determination Policies, and if documentation exists to support the reimbursement (such as the physician review of the plan of care every 60 days), an audit does not pose a serious risk to the agency.

denial lack of payment for home visits/treatments because of failure to meet medical necessity requirements for the services or for some other reason (e.g., provider error, payer error, ineligible patient). A denial sometimes can be appealed successfully.

A **denial** occurs when Medicare notifies the provider that the claim will not be paid and, therefore, the amount billed to Medicare is no longer considered a receivable to an agency. The process begins with Medicare noticing an area in the delivery of care to a patient that does not follow guidelines, such as excessive utilization of a specific service. Medicare then requests documentation. If documentation does not support the utilization, a denial is issued. An agency may appeal by sending written justification and any other data as outlined in Medicare's instructions on responding to denials, additional development requests, and so on. Medicare ultimately remits or denies payment. Most agencies have a low denial rate.

1. Payment to the home care organization is provided by one or more of the following four payers: _____, _____, _____, and _____.

2. What is the purpose of the Home Health Resource Group (HHRG)?

3. List and describe the three areas used to determine the HHRG when establishing the reimbursement rate.

4. True or False? Before submitting the claims to Medicare, the HHRG must be converted to a Health Insurance Prospective Payment System code (HIPPS).

5. Describe the two-installment payment method for the 60-day episode.

6. List two exceptions to the normal 60-day HHRG-based episode payment.

7. _____ is a term that describes the ratio of various types of third-party payers that provide revenue to a health care organization.

8. What is the difference between fixed costs and variable costs?

9. With regard to home care, name three services not covered by Medicare and circumstances under which some of the non-covered services may be provided to a Medicare patient.

10. When does a denial occur?

INFORMATION MANAGEMENT

Coding and Classification

Classification systems include diagnosis, procedural, and—if the primary physician chooses to bill Medicare for certification, recertification, and/or care plan oversight—physician procedural codes. Diagnosis and procedural codes for the home health agency are classified using the current modification of *ICD*, and physician procedural codes are classified using *CPT*.

ICD

Codes from the current clinical modification of the *International Classification of Diseases* are required for home care agencies to receive payment. Codes must be assigned upon completion of the initial assessment and are vital to determination of the HHRG and HIPPS. These may be updated with each certification period, as indicated, to demonstrate changes in the patient's condition. A change in the codes assigned can affect the payment received.

According to CMS's OASIS manual, HHAs are expected to understand the patient's specific clinical status before selecting and assigning the diagnosis. Each patient's overall medical condition and care needs must be comprehensively assessed before the HHA selects and assigns the OASIS diagnoses. CMS expects HHAs to complete the patient's comprehensive assessment before assigning home health diagnoses (*OASIS-C1/ICD-9 Guidance Manual*, 2014).

Home care coding in general follows the traditional inpatient coding conventions, with guidelines that are similar, but not identical, to UHDDS definitions.

Just as the diagnoses coded for the hospital must be relevant to the hospital care provided, diagnoses coded for home care should be relevant to the care provided within the home. Procedural codes are not utilized in home health coding. Additional coding direction for home care coders can be found in the CMS *OASIS-C1/ICD-9 Guidance Manual.*

The items that differentiate home care coding from other coding conventions are as follows:

- Case-mix diagnoses (a diagnosis that determines the Medicare PPS case mix group)
- M1024 (payment diagnoses used when an ICD-9-CM V code or an ICD-10-CM Z code is entered into a case-mix diagnosis field)
- Codes representing "Factors Influencing Health Status and Contact with Health Services" replacing case-mix diagnosis

Figure 12-2 provides an excerpt from the *OASIS-C1/ICD-9 Version Guidance Manual* with instructions regarding assignment of diagnosis codes.

The home care primary diagnosis is the diagnosis that is most related to the plan of care. It may or may not be related to the most recent hospital stay, but it must relate to the skilled services being provided. If more than one diagnosis is treated concurrently, the diagnosis that represents the most acute condition and requires the most intensive services should be assigned as primary. This diagnosis is recorded on the plan of care/485 and should mirror the diagnoses listed on the OASIS-C1 document in item M1020.

If the primary diagnosis has changed by the time of the next recertification (60 days later), the code for the new primary diagnosis is recorded on the recertification plan of care/485 and recertification OASIS-C1.

Secondary diagnoses that affect home care also are coded, because several codes may be required to indicate the seriousness of the patient's condition and to explain the care provided in the home. Secondary diagnoses, or other diagnoses, are defined as all conditions that coexisted with the primary diagnosis at the time the plan of care was established, or that developed subsequently, or that affect the treatment or care of the patient.

Before the autumn of 2003, Codes for factors influencing health status and contact with health services and external cause of injury codes were not accepted on the OASIS forms. With implementation of the transactions and code sets standards of HIPAA, however, OASIS forms were required to accept such codes. For example, when the OASIS reports an ICD-9-CM V code (or Z code in ICD-10-CM) as the primary diagnosis, another code that can be used to determine the applicable HHRG must be submitted as a payment (case mix) diagnosis. (See instructions for Column 3 of Figure 12-2.)

Although home health agencies previously had been required to report procedures performed on inpatient stays within a certain timeframe, procedure reporting on the part of the agency is no longer a requirement. Diagnoses treated on inpatient stays within the past 14 days, however, are still reported. Figure 12-3

FIGURE 12-2

Excerpt from *OASIS-C1 / ICD-9 Version Guidance Manual*, Attachment D: Selection and Assignment of Oasis Diagnosis.

M0230/240/246 Diagnoses, Severity Index, and Payment Diagnoses: List each diagnosis for which the patient is receiving home care (Column 1) and enter its ICD-9-C M code at the level of highest specificity (no surgical/procedure codes) (Column 2).   Rate each condition (Column 2) using the severity index. (Choose one value that represents the most severe rating appropriate for each diagnosis.) V codes (for M0230 or M0240) or E codes (for M0240 only) may be used. ICD-9-C M sequencing requirements must be followed if multiple coding is indicated for any diagnoses. If a V code is reported in place of a case mix diagnosis, then optional item M0246 Payment Diagnoses (Columns 3 and 4) may be completed. A case mix diagnosis is a diagnosis that determines the Medicare PPS case mix group.

Code each row as follows:

Column 1:   Enter the description of the diagnosis.

Column 2:   Enter the ICD-9-C M code for the diagnosis described in Column 1;

   Rate the severity of the condition listed in Column 1 using the following scale:

   0 - Asymptomatic, no treatment needed at this time
   1 - Symptoms well controlled with current therapy
   2 - Symptoms controlled with difficulty, affecting daily functioning; patient needs ongoing monitoring
   3 - Symptoms poorly controlled; patient needs frequent adjustment in treatment and dose monitoring
   4 - Symptoms poorly controlled; history of re-hospitalizations

Column 3: (OPTIONAL) If a V code reported in any row in Column 2 is reported in place of a case mix diagnosis, list the appropriate case mix diagnosis (the description and the ICD-9-C M code) in the same row in Column 3. Otherwise, leave Column 3 blank in that row.

Column 4: (OPTIONAL) If a V code in Column 2 is reported in place of a case mix diagnosis that requires multiple diagnosis codes under ICD-9-C M coding guidelines, enter the diagnosis descriptions and the ICD-9-C M codes in the same row in Columns 3 and 4. For example, if the case mix diagnosis is a manifestation code, record the diagnosis description and ICD-9-C M code for the underlying condition in Column 3 of that row and the diagnosis description and ICD-9-C M code for the manifestation in Column 4 of that row. Otherwise, leave Column 4 blank in that row.

(M0230) Primary Diagnosis & (M0240) Other Diagnoses		(M0246) Case Mix Diagnoses (OPTIONAL)	
(1)	(2)	(3)	(4)
	ICD-9-C M and severity rating for each condition	Complete **only if** a V code in Column 2 is reported in place of a case mix diagnosis.	Complete **only if** the V code in Column 2 is reported in place of a case mix diagnosis that is a multiple coding situation (e.g., a manifestation code).
Description	ICD-9-C M / Severity Rating	Description/ ICD-9-C M	Description/ ICD-9-C M
(M0230) Primary Diagnosis a. **Other physical therapy**	**(V codes are allowed)** a. (_V_ _5_ _7_ . _1_) ☐0 ☐1 ☒2 ☐3 ☐4	**(V or E codes NOT allowed)** a Monoplegia of lower limb affecting dominant side (4̲ 3̲ 8̲ . 4̲ 1̲)	**(V or E codes NOT allowed)** a._____ (_ _ _ . _ _)
(M0240) Other Diagnoses b. **Monoplegia of lower limb affecting dominant side**	**(V or E codes are allowed)** b. (_ 4 3 8 . 41) ☐0 ☐1 ☒2 ☐3 ☐4	**(V or E codes NOT allowed)** b._____ (_ _ _ . _ _)	**(V or E codes NOT allowed)** b._____ (_ _ _ . _ _)
c. **Abnormality of gait**	c. (_ 7 81 . 2) ☐0 ☐1 ☒2 ☐3 ☐4	c._____ (_ _ _ . _ _)	c._____ (_ _ _ . _ _)
d. _____	d. (_ _ _ _ . _ _) ☐0 ☐1 ☐2 ☐3 ☐4	d._____ (_ _ _ . _ _)	d._____ (_ _ _ . _ _)
e. _____	e. (_ _ _ _ . _ _) ☐0 ☐1 ☐2 ☐3 ☐4	e._____ (_ _ _ . _ _)	e._____ (_ _ _ . _ _)

FIGURE 12-3

Excerpt from OASIS-C1, illustrating capture of inpatient codes.

PATIENT HISTORY AND DIAGNOSES

(M1000) From which of the following **Inpatient Facilities** was the patient discharged within the past 14 days? **(Mark all that apply.)**

- ☐ 1 - Long-term nursing facility (NF)
- ☐ 2 - Skilled nursing facility (SNF / TCU)
- ☐ 3 - Short-stay acute hospital (IPP S)
- ☐ 4 - Long-term care hospital (LTCH)
- ☐ 5 - Inpatient rehabilitation hospital or unit (IRF)
- ☐ 6 - Psychiatric hospital or unit
- ☐ 7 - Other (specify) _____
- ☐ NA - Patient was not discharged from an inpatient facility **[*Go to M1016*]**

(M1005) Inpatient Discharge Date (most recent):

_ _ / _ _ / _ _ _ _
month / day / year

- ☐ UK - Unknown

(M1010) List each **Inpatient Diagnosis** and ICD-9-C M code at the level of highest specificity for only those conditions treated during an inpatient stay within the last 14 days (no E-codes, or V-codes):

Inpatient Facility Diagnosis	ICD-9-C M Code
a. _____	_ _ _ _ . _ _
b. _____	_ _ _ _ . _ _
c. _____	_ _ _ _ . _ _
d. _____	_ _ _ _ . _ _
e. _____	_ _ _ _ . _ _
f. _____	_ _ _ _ . _ _

OASIS is the intellectual property of the Center for Health Services Research, Denver, Colorado. Used with permission.

provides an excerpt from the OASIS-C1 document requiring diagnosis codes related to an inpatient stay. With implementation of the PPS in home health, accurate coding has become more important because of the impact of coding on reimbursement and the resulting increased potential for fraud and abuse.

Durable medical equipment (DME) companies also are required to use ICD diagnosis codes for proper payment. The codes must correspond to the type of equipment being billed per patient. For example, a fractured hip would support the use of ambulating devices, and a respiratory condition would support the use of oxygen equipment.

Current Procedural Terminology (CPT)/Healthcare Common Procedure Coding System (HCPCS)

The physicians who do care planning can use *Current Procedural Terminology (CPT)* or *Healthcare Common Procedure Coding System (HCPCS)* to bill for development of the care plan, as well as for oversight of the care plan. These codes allow physicians to bill for their time discussing a patient's care with home health personnel and in developing a care plan. Although a physician may bill for development of the initial certification and/or subsequent recertifications by following some simple steps, the regulations clearly state that the physician (not the home health agency) must keep his or her own records documenting the time spent per patient on care plan oversight. The rationale for this requirement is that the time spent by the physician in this activity provides the basis for payment.

Data and Information Flow

Data collection generally begins upon referral of the patient to home care. During the initial and subsequent home visits, home care staff members collect data using paper-based systems or computer-based systems that utilize laptop or handheld computers. Data are transmitted to the home care agency's office by manual or electronic means. When the patient is discharged from home care, the complete record is maintained in a central location, in either paper or electronic format.

Electronic Information Systems

Most home care agencies manage data through some type of database management system. Some agencies use their own homegrown systems, and others use systems available from various health care information system vendors. Information system vendors specializing in home care systems typically offer the ability to manage information concerning referral, census, OASIS reporting, medication profiles, orders, scheduling, Medicare certification and recertification, progress and visit notes, and other data and documentation.

The use of electronic health record (EHR) systems has been increasing steadily in home health. According to a study published in the *Journal of the American Medical Informatics Association*, about 40% of agencies providing home health services were using an EHR in 2007 (Resnick & Alwan, 2010). This study also showed that more than 20% of home health providers were using some form of telemedicine. Because of the distances involved in rendering services to home health patients, the advantages of electronic systems are obvious.

Data Sets

The previous discussion of the OASIS data set described its documentation and reimbursement features. The OASIS data elements were developed, tested, and refined over a 10-year period through an extensive research and demonstration program funded by CMS. The Center for Health Services Research in Denver, Colorado, developed the OASIS and maintains its copyright but permits the free use of OASIS. This extensive data set is approximately 25 pages when printed.

1. True or False? CMS expects HHAs to complete the patient's comprehensive assessment after assigning home health diagnoses.

2. Diagnosis and procedural codes for the home health agency are classified using the current modification of _____, and physician procedural codes are classified using _____.

3. True or False? Procedural codes are mandatory for home health agencies.

4. What should determine the home care primary diagnosis?

5. Which code sets can be used by physicians who do care planning?

6. According to the *Journal of the American Medical Informatics Association*, what percentage of home health agencies had adopted an EHR?

7. Who developed the OASIS data set?

QUALITY IMPROVEMENT AND UTILIZATION MANAGEMENT

Quality Improvement

Outcome measures are the heart of outcome-based quality improvement (OBQI) and outcome-based quality management (OBQM). These are systematic approaches that home health agencies use to continuously manage and improve the quality of care they provide. Home health agencies are able to access reports on outcomes for their patients through their state agency, and thus compare their results to the national reference. This enables them to identify areas of strength and weakness in their patient outcomes. OBQI/OBQM requires precise, uniform measures, which can be obtained only from standardized data items. The OASIS was designed to provide the necessary standardized data elements to measure outcomes.

In all health care areas including home health, outcomes are of interest and importance to many parties. Payers want to know how the patients they insure are benefiting from the dollars they spend on care. At the federal level, outcomes have been emphasized in changes to the regulations. And, as previously mentioned, accrediting and licensing programs are focusing on outcomes. Consumers and their representatives are requiring outcome information from care providers. For example, data drawn from the OASIS-C1 are compiled and made available to the public at the Home Health Compare website. And last, but not least, home health agencies always have been concerned with measuring their performance relative to other providers.

Although the process of gathering, encoding, and submitting the OASIS-C1 data may seem to be an end in itself, it is merely the means to achieve outcome measurement and only the beginning of the process. OBQI/OBQM is fundamentally a two-stage process. First, the data must be gathered in a uniform manner (OASIS-C1). This results in a report showing the agency's performance in terms of outcomes relative to the national sample. During this first step, risk adjustment occurs through grouping or statistical methods to compensate for the potential influence of case-mix variables that can affect outcomes. Risk adjustment is done by the state agency for some data elements. Reports may be printed with and/or without the risk adjustment. In the second step, the agency selects target outcomes for enhancement, evaluates care for the target outcome, develops a plan of action to change the care, and finally monitors the outcome to see if the desired gains have been accomplished (see Figure 12-4).

CMS has established Quality Improvement Organizations (QIOs) covering various regions of the United States. These organizations are available to assist agencies with understanding the OBQI/OBQM process, selecting a target outcome, and developing action plans.

One added advantage of a fully developed OBQI/OBQM program is that agencies are able to move into the domain of managing resources for the explicit purpose of gaining the best outcome. Agencies can improve outcomes in areas of inadequate performance, reinforce outcomes in areas in which they do well, and maintain outcomes in areas in which performance is acceptable. By managing outcomes in this way, resources naturally are affected. Staffing patterns, as well as frequency of services, can be altered with a clear bottom-line assessment of the impact of such alterations on patients. In the long run, this allows agencies to enhance their quality of care, yet manage their resources to become more cost-effective—a goal of the home health prospective payment system.

FIGURE 12-4

Two-stage OBQI framework.

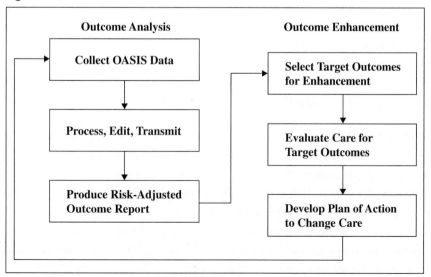

From the Centers for Medicare & Medicaid Services' Outcome-Based Quality Improvement (OBQI) Implementation Manual, pp. 2.4.

Utilization Management

Utilization management focuses on monitoring the increase and decrease in utilization of services provided to patients. Utilization management seeks to assure that services are appropriate to patients' conditions. For example, a patient may be receiving skilled nursing services for a terminal disease. Offering social and mental health services to such a patient is typical for proper utilization.

A home care agency may have separate written plans for quality improvement and utilization management. The plans that seem to produce the best results combine the efforts of all information-based areas: quality improvement, utilization management, risk management, information management/systems, and finance. These areas have a common interest—to improve processes that have an impact on the agency's internal and external customer base and to be competitive in price and quality of service within the market of home care. HIM professionals are increasingly and successfully taking on quality improvement and utilization management duties/roles, using their clinical knowledge and ability to develop tools and reports from the large repositories of clinical data.

SELF REVIEW 12.6

1. _____ are systematic approaches that home health agencies use to manage and improve the quality of care they provide.
2. Briefly describe the OBQI/OBQM process.
3. What organizations are available to assist agencies with understanding the OBQI/OBQM process?
4. _____ focuses on monitoring the increase and decrease in utilization of services provided to patients.
   a. Risk management
   b. Quality improvement
   c. Utilization management

RISK MANAGEMENT AND LEGAL ISSUES

Risk Management

In general terms, risk management is a program that monitors the liability and accountability of home care services delivered to customers. The areas at risk are measured through clinical analysis by way of incident reporting and financial analysis through the agency's insurance policy. Typically, the health information manager manages the incident reporting to minimize the risk of injury to patients, visitors, and employees, and to delineate procedures for reporting and follow-up of incidents.

An **incident/unusual occurrence** is defined as any happening that is not consistent with the routine operations of the agency or the routine care of a

incident or unusual occurrence any happening that is not consistent with the routine operations of the agency or routine care of a given patient.

specific patient. Key elements of the procedure for reporting incidents include the following:

- Establish timeframes for reporting and evaluating the occurrences.
- Establish reporting of occurrences as a positive means of improving the delivery of quality care as opposed to a punitive performance evaluation.
- Record only the facts.
- Write narrative description in the first person, and have the employee who witnessed or experienced the occurrence record it.
- Do not maintain incident reports with the medical record; however, the chart should be documented regarding the occurrence, reflecting the continuation of the treatment provided to the patient.
- Categorize occurrences and utilize reports to identify trends and patterns.
- Share the reports with the appropriate committees, such as the quality improvement committee, to improve processes that are risks and potential risks to the organization.

Satisfaction Committee/Monitoring

Another form of proactive risk management is to utilize a satisfaction committee to monitor customer satisfaction issues. During the initial visit, all patients/caregivers should be informed and presented with the patient bill of rights, which includes the toll-free state department of health hotline number and the agency's contact number if there is a problem. This allows patients/caregivers to express concerns and grievances regarding patient care. The committee should monitor issues for all customers, including patients and their caregivers, physicians, and insurance companies, and try to resolve them in a timely manner while maintaining continuity of care for patients.

Legal Issues

Legal issues are involved in all departments of home care and are handled best if done proactively. The human resource department is legally required to have certain information on file for new employees. Following is a general list of items to complete when hiring new employees:

- Past employment—dates, employer, salary, and work performance
- Education—license in particular profession
- Criminal background check
- State driver's license
- Credit check for finance employees

The most common requirements for licensed professionals in most states are as follows:

- Cardiopulmonary resuscitation (CPR): Each staff person should be certified when hired, and typically is recertified once every 2 years.
- **Occupational Safety and Health Administration (OSHA):** Inservice educational programs are implemented to provide a safe work environment for employees. Safety topics include ergonomics, first-aid, and blood-borne pathogens. OSHA inservice programs typically are presented annually.
- Universal precautions should be practiced at all times.
- Safety in the community should be practiced at all times.
- The Joint Commission requires the original license of all professional staff members to be a part of their personnel file.

Other common in-services required by all home care employees are the following:

- Inservice training pertaining to body mechanics is required and usually completed annually.
- Confidentiality inservice instruction is required at the time of hire and recommended to be done annually.

Occupational Safety and Health Administration (OSHA) a federal agency that develops criteria intended to provide a safe work environment for all employees as part of its mission to enforce occupational safety and health legislation.

Policies and Procedures

The health information manager ordinarily develops, or at least updates, policies related to medical record procedures. Following is a recommended list of certain policies for review and approval by the agency's legal counsel:

- Advance directives
- Release of medical information
- General treatment
- Alcohol and drug treatment
- HIV/AIDS treatment
- Mental health information
- Procedure for responding to subpoena and court orders
- Procedure for do-not-resuscitate orders

SELF REVIEW 12.7

1. List four key elements of the procedure for reporting incidents.
2. Define an incident or unusual occurrence.
3. _____ is a program that monitors the liability and accountability of home care services delivered to customers.

4. _____ monitors issues for all customers and tries to resolve them in a timely manner while maintaining continuity of care for patients.

   a. OSHA

   b. Satisfaction committee

   c. Risk management

5. Which of the following is not a common requirement for licensed professionals in most states:

   a. OSHA training

   b. CPR

   c. Yearly medical jurisprudence certification

   d. Practicing safety in the community at all times

6. True or False? The health information manager develops and updates policies and procedures related to the medical record.

ROLE OF THE HEALTH INFORMATION MANAGEMENT PROFESSIONAL

PROFESSIONAL SPOTLIGHT   CORPORATE HIM MANAGER/PRIVACY OFFICER

Who I am: Pamela Dodd, RHIA

Where I work: Alacare Home Health & Hospice— Corporate Office, Birmingham, AL

What I do: I manage agency-wide HIM functions for 25 offices located throughout the state of Alabama with a patient census of more than 5,000. Management of these functions involves medical record law as applied to preparation and maintenance of patient health information, confidentiality, release of information, computerization of medical records, consents and authorizations. I oversee all ongoing activities related to the development, implementation, maintenance of and adherence to the agency's policies and procedures pertaining to the Health Insurance Portability and Accountability Act (HIPAA) of 1996 and other applicable CMS regulatory requirements. I also monitor hospice coding to ensure that invalid hospice diagnosis codes are not used, per CMS guidelines. In addition, I oversee the validation and monitoring of the physician databases to ensure that the ordering physician are licensed, have a NPI number, are enrolled in PECOS and are not excluded from the OIG or any other federal programs.

Why HIM knowledge is important in my role: Regulatory statutes, guidelines, and practices in the home health environment are constantly changing. Strong knowledge, as well as ongoing education in health information management is essential to the maintenance of electronic records, maintaining patient confidentiality, and training other agency staff. Knowledge of HIM practices and how to maintain a viable electronic health

(continued)

record are key elements when working with health care vendors, agency clinical staff, and upper management to achieve efficient agency operations.

Other information: As an HIM professional in the home health and hospice field, I have had the privilege of working with several schools in mentoring students in health information management. Earlier in my career, I worked four years at a teaching osteopathic hospital as a medical records practitioner.

Due to the small size of the facility, it gave me the opportunity to touch every area of HIM functions required in a hospital environment. This gave me knowledge that assists me today in transitioning HIM guidelines in the home health environment for the past 18 years. In addition to AHIMA, AAHIM and local HIM chapter memberships, I have served for many years and continue to serve as an Advisory Board member for a HIM program at a local community college.

HIM positions within home care are still considered nontraditional; however, this career path is becoming more common for recent graduates. The role can be highly rewarding, because it usually extends beyond medical records. HIM home care positions require knowledge of finance, quality improvement, utilization review, and information systems.

Now, more than ever, to survive and thrive in the data-driven world of home care, agencies must make good use of the information available to them. Health information managers can play a key role in developing, implementing, and maintaining effective information systems for home care. Becoming familiar with the home care market and how to be competitive within that market provides HIM professionals with another arena in which to demonstrate their skills in managing information and making that information useful.

SELF REVIEW 12.8

1. According to the text, HIM home care positions require knowledge of what four things?
2. True or False? Health information managers can play a key role in developing, implementing, and maintaining effective information systems for home care.

TRENDS

Several new types of programs for the delivery of health care in the home have developed in the twenty-first century. Among these innovations are home-based primary care and disease management programs (Turk et al., 2000). Physicians also have shown increased interest in house-call training, education, and practice. In the realm of technology, telemedicine programs for the home likely will expand because of the potential benefits that these provide to patients and providers alike (Leff & Burton, 2001; Resnick & Alwan, 2010). Home care providers should strive to make effective use of technology without losing the personal touch that homebound patients require.

Home health agencies are considered to be a type of post-acute care provider. Home health agencies have to stay abreast of proposed policy changes, such as the possibility of bundling payments for post-acute care. Further, they have to recognize the potential for cost savings and improved outcomes offered by home care, as evidenced by inclusion of the Independence at Home demonstration program in the Patient Protection and Affordable Care Act health reform legislation enacted in 2010. Certainly, the twenty-first century holds promises as well as challenges for the home care industry.

SELF REVIEW 12.9

1. Home health agencies provide what type of care?
2. Name two programs that were developed in the twenty-first century regarding health care in the home.

SUMMARY

The home health care industry continues to evolve to offer quality care at a reasonable level of operating cost. Changing regulations and rapid growth have caused home care providers to be creative in their business planning to make their agency stand out from the rest. HIM professionals can contribute greatly to the future business planning of home care, especially in light of their training and ability to couple the clinical side with the technical side of information management.

REVIEW QUESTIONS

Knowledge-Based Questions

1. Identify a few services that home care agencies deliver.
2. Who are the voluntary accrediting bodies that develop the standards for home care?
3. Define *certification period*.
4. Explain the importance of documentation and coding for proper reimbursement.
5. What is the OASIS-C1, and what is its purpose?
6. Explain how Medicare reimburses home care agencies for the provision of care to patients.

Critical Thinking Questions

1. Compare and contrast home care coding with hospital inpatient coding.
2. As home care agencies implement efficiencies to increase their potential profitability under the Medicare PPS, what are some of the issues and concerns that they face?

WEB ACTIVITY

Visit the Home Health Agency Center at the CMS website at http://www.cms.gov/center/hha.asp

1. Select a link to one of the many topics available on this page.
2. After selecting the link, describe information about home health care that was available through that link.

CASE STUDY

Mary Jones is the health information supervisor at Somewhere Home Care, which is Medicare-certified. As required by Medicare, her agency and staff members have been completing and submitting OASIS-C1 data. The staff has been accessing patient data through the OASIS-C1 reports, as well as monitoring and documenting visit patterns and frequency by the agency. In addition, the personnel have been monitoring the cost of supplies utilized per patient.

In reviewing the financial data, Mary's director has indicated that the agency has performed marginally under the Medicare prospective payment system. The staff would like to improve financial performance, and has met with the leadership team of the agency to discuss a possible plan of action. Although some insurers still pay by the visit, Medicare patients are the largest group in the agency's payer mix, and Medicare pays a set amount of money for providing care over a 60-day period rather than a per-visit fee.

Mary has some statistics available to her to assist the director with formulating a plan. These include:

- The number of patients the agency has had in each HHRG classification over the past 3 years
- The number of visits (by clinician type; i.e., RN, LPN, HHA, PT, OT, SLP) made to each patient for each 60-day episode of care
- The average number of visits to patients in each HHRG classification

- Financial data, including reimbursement amounts for each HHRG and the agency-specific costs per each type of visit
- Primary diagnosis for each patient
- OASIS C1 outcome reports printed for OBQI/OBQM, showing how the agency has performed in outcomes, compared to other agencies in the country
- Payer mix report, showing the percentage of patients the agency has in each payer source (i.e., Medicare, Medicaid, commercial insurance, private pay, etc.). At Somewhere Home Care, 65% of the patients are covered by Medicare.

Investigation into care plans and visit patterns indicate wide fluctuation in visit patterns among clinicians. Patients within the same HHRG category—who basically should be similar—have widely varying visit ranges.

Based on the above information and scenario, answer the following questions:

1. What are some significant factors that Mary and her director should consider about their payment sources as they evaluate their financial performance?
2. What statistical data available to Mary would be most helpful in developing an action plan?
3. Where should Mary focus her clinical and medical record expertise?

REFERENCES AND SUGGESTED READINGS

Abraham, P. R. (2001). *Documentation and Reimbursement for Home Care and Hospice Programs.* Chicago: American Health Information Management Association.

CMS (Centers for Medicare & Medicaid Services). (2015, June 26). *Outcome-Based Quality Improvement (OBQI) Implementation Manual.* [Online] http://www.cms.gov/HomeHealthQualityInits/15_PBQIProcessMeasures.asp [2015, October 19].

Federal Register. (2014, November 6). 42 CFR Part 424.

Leff, B., & Burton, J. R. (2001). The future history of home care and physician house calls in the United States. *Journals of Gerontology Series A—Biological Sciences & Medical Sciences, 56*(10), M603–M608.

MLN Connects. (2014, December 16). *National Provider Call, Certifying Patients for the Medicare Home Health Benefit.* [Online] https://www.cms.gov/Outreach-and-Education/Outreach/NPC/National-Provider-Calls-and-Events-Items/2014-12-16-Home-Health-Benefit.html [2015, October 19].

MLN Matters. (2013, May 1). *Full Implementation of Edits on the Ordering/Referring Providers in Medicare Part B, DME, and Part A Home Health Agency (HHA) Claims.* Number: SE1305. [Online]. https://www.cms.gov/Outreach-and-Education/Medicare-Learning-Network-MLN/MLNMattersArticles/Downloads/se1305.pdf [2015, October 19].

MLN Matters. (2014, April 8). *Home Health Face-to-Face Encounter: A New Home Health Certification Requirement,* Number: SE1038. [Online]. https://www.cms.gov/Outreach-and-Education/Medicare-Learning-Network-MLN/MLNMattersArticles/downloads/SE1038.pdf [2015, October 19]. pp. 1–2. [Online]. http://www.cms.gov/Outreach-and-Education/Medicare-Learning-Network-MLN/MLNMattersArticles/downloads/se1038.pdf [2015, October 19].

NAHC (National Association for Home Care and Hospice). (2010). *How to Choose a Home Care Agency.* Washington, DC: Author.

Resnick, H. E., & Alwan, M. (2010). Use of health information technology in home health and hospice agencies: United States, 2007. *Journal of the American Medical Informatics Association, 17,* 389–395.

The Joint Commission. (2010). *Comprehensive Accreditation Manual for Home Care.* Oakbrook Terrace, IL: Author.

Turk, L., Parmley, J., Ames, A., & Schumacher, K. L. (2000). A New Era in Home Care. *Seminars for Nurse Managers, 8*(3), 143–150.

KEY RESOURCES

Accreditation Commission for Health Care
http://www.achc.org

American Academy of Home Care Medicine
http://www.aahcm.org

CMS *OASIS-C1/ICD-9* and *ICD-10 Guidance Manuals,*
https://www.cms.gov/Medicare/Quality-Initiatives-Patient-Assessment-Instruments/HomeHealthQualityInits/HHQIOASIS
UserManual.html

Community Health Accreditation Program, Inc.
http://www.chapinc.org

Medicare Coverage: Home Health Services
http://www.medicare.gov/coverage/home-health-services.html

National Association for Home Care and Hospice
http://www.nahc.org

The Joint Commission
http://www.jointcommission.org

CHAPTER 13

Hospice

Teresa Sherfy, RHIT | Karen M. Staszel, RHIA

LEARNING OBJECTIVES

Upon successful completion of this chapter, you should be able to:

- Explain the criteria that must be met for a patient to enter hospice care.
- Define the term "hospice."
- Compare and contrast hospice care and traditional acute care.
- Designate the participants and their role in the interdisciplinary group that provides hospice care to patients and their caregivers.
- Recognize the four reimbursement levels of hospice care: routine home care, respite care, general or acute inpatient care, and continuous care.
- Discuss documentation requirements in the hospice clinical record.
- Relate the use of hospice benefit periods to the associated documentation requirements.
- Discuss the capture of clinical visit information to track the cost of hospice care.
- Explain the Conditions of Participation relating to hospice care.
- Discuss Quality Assessment/Performance Improvement in the hospice setting.
- Describe bereavement care and documentation following the death of the hospice patient.

Setting	Description	Synonyms/Examples
Patient's Residence	The majority of hospice programs provide patient care in the patient's place of residence, which may include the patient's home, a relative's or friend's home, a nursing home, or a senior citizen complex.	
Nursing Home or Hospital	Some hospices contract with major hospital complexes and/or nursing homes to establish hospice units or wings. The hospice wing then becomes the patient's place of residence. These units are used primarily when patients have no primary caregiver in their home, for acute pain and symptom management, if the patient is too sick to leave the existing facility and can just be transferred to another wing, or for respite care.	Hospice inpatient unit, IPU (inpatient unit), care center, hospice wing.
Stand-Alone Hospice	Some hospice programs own their own facilities. These facilities are not associated with an existing hospital or nursing home. Similar to nursing home and/or hospital beds, the bed in the stand-alone hospice becomes patients' place of residence. Again, these facilities are used primarily when there is no primary caregiver in the home, for pain and symptom management, or for respite care.	Freestanding hospice, hospice inpatient unit, hospice care center, IPU (inpatient unit). Depending on the state requirements, hospices may license these facilities as nursing homes, adult foster care homes, or freestanding hospice units (if the state has a category for them).

INTRODUCTION TO SETTING

The roots of **hospice** can be traced along the same timeline as the history and development of the hospital. Charitable religious organizations and individuals were caring not only for the sick and diseased throughout history, but also for the dying and those grieving for them. *Hospice* is a French word derived from the Latin *hospitium*, which was a place in which a guest was received. Not until 1967, when Dame Cicely Saunders opened St. Christopher's Hospice in London, was caring for dying patients recognized and developed as a philosophy and practice. The time period, it seems, was especially ripe for the emergence of the hospice discipline:

> A hundred years ago, doctors cured only a few patients because they lacked the powerful medical tools that exist today. With the advent of safer surgery and the enormous advances in therapeutics, doctors have apparently developed the power to remove problems and effect cures. The relentless pursuit of cures for more and more diseases can lead the blinkered into believing that care of those who are incurable is less important. (Corr & Corr, 1983)

Hospice is limited to individuals with a life expectancy of 6 months or less. An interdisciplinary approach is used to address the spiritual, physical, social, and economic needs of terminally ill patients and their families or caregivers. **Palliative care** is provided to relieve the patient's discomfort, symptoms, and stress of serious illness. Hospice care always includes palliative care, in which the goal is to ease the patient's suffering and improve quality of life for the patient experiencing a serious illness.

hospice a facility or a program designed to provide a caring environment to meet the physical and emotional needs of terminally ill patients and their families and significant others.

palliative care clinical measures taken to reduce the intensity of disease symptoms rather than provide a cure for the disease. Hospice attempts to reduce the intensity of symptoms such as pain, nausea, and anxiety with a variety of pharmacological and nonpharmacological methods.

place of residence
wherever the patient is
currently living—his or
her own home, a relative's
home, a senior citizen's
complex, a nursing home,
assisted living.

Hospices provide care in (1) a patient's **place of residence**, defined as the patient's home, a relative's or friend's home, a nursing home, or a senior citizen complex, (2) hospice facilities owned and operated by the hospice, or (3) hospice units or wings contracted with major hospital complexes and/or nursing homes. The hospice facility, hospice unit or wing then becomes the patient's place of residence.

Types of Patients

The Terminally Ill

curative therapy   any
medical therapy for the
purpose of curing disease.

terminally ill   a limited
life expectancy, usually less
than 6 months.

Hospices provide palliative care or symptom management rather than **curative therapy** to patients who are considered to be **terminally ill**, with a life expectancy of 6 months or less based on the physician's clinical judgment regarding the normal course of the individual's illness. Hospice care is not restricted to certain diagnoses, but is available for any patient whose prognosis for the end of life is 6 months or less. Symptom management includes not only methods to relieve chronic pain and other physical results of the disease process but also helps to relieve the emotional and mental stress of the dying process.

Hospices use non-narcotic analgesics and narcotic analgesics (titrated to manage pain and not cause mental confusion). Changes of position, back rubs, massage, oxygen, tranquilizers, antidepressants, music, conversation, and companionship to relieve terminal symptoms are used frequently. Hospices do not routinely use x-rays, transfusions, chemotherapy, radiation therapy, intubations, cardiopulmonary resuscitation (CPR), or any other therapy that would be considered curative.

The Unit of Care

Traditional hospital-based acute care focuses on providing curative treatment that allows the patient to be discharged as soon as feasible. Hospice care focuses on palliative care with the understanding that the patient will receive care through the end of life. Hospice philosophy recognizes that the dying process is difficult not only for the patient but also for the patient's family and significant others. Thus, the needs of the patient, as well as the physical, spiritual, emotional, and mental states of those around the patient are incorporated into hospice care. This concept is such an integral part of a hospice treatment plan that the National Hospice and Palliative Care Organization (NHPCO, 2008) has stated that, "the unit of care in hospice is the patient/family." Treatment plans and options are discussed with the patient and with family members; goals are written for the patient and family members.

interdisciplinary group
(IDG)   a patient care
group consisting of a physician, nurse, social worker,
and pastoral or other
counselor. The group also
may include members
such as a hospice aide,
volunteer, therapist, dietician, or pharmacist.

Types of Caregivers

The Interdisciplinary Group

Hospice is similar to other patient care settings in managing the treatment plan using an **interdisciplinary group (IDG)**. The difference, however, is in the composition of the hospice IDG. The NHPCO requires the interdisciplinary group to include:

1. A doctor of medicine or osteopathy (employed by the hospice or under contract)
2. A registered nurse
3. A social worker and
4. A pastoral or other counselor

As part of the interdisciplinary group, hospices also may include a volunteer or volunteer coordinator, a pharmacist, a bereavement counselor, a dietitian, or a hospice aide.

Each member of the interdisciplinary group plays a specific role, as follows (ASHP, 1993):

- A physician oversees the general health of the patient and assesses patient status.
- A registered nurse acts as the case manager and coordinates changes to the care plan with other members of the group.
- A social worker provides psychosocial assessment and social resources that the patient and family can utilize.
- A pastoral or other counselor offers spiritual support and comfort. The bereavement counselor prepares the patient and family for the impending death and provides grief support to the family after the patient's death.
- A dietitian offer expertise in nutritional support for the patient by addressing swallowing difficulties, loss of appetite, weight loss and other conditions often associated with end-of-life palliative care.
- A pharmacist works with the nurse and attending physician to provide adequate symptom relief. This individual can monitor medications, provide instructions to the family or caregiver on how to take the medicine as well as what side effects could occur.

The **volunteer**, who receives special hospice training, offers companionship, comfort, transportation, light housekeeping, and even direct patient care (depending on his or her professional qualifications). The nurse assigns the hospice aide to provide bathing, personal care, light housekeeping, and other non-skilled treatments such as dressing changes.

Primary Caregivers

Because most hospice care is provided in the patient's home, someone from the patient's immediate family and/or circle of friends acts as a **primary caregiver**. The primary caregiver is an individual or group of individuals who provide ongoing care to the patient when hospice personnel are not present in the residence. Members of the patient's interdisciplinary group visit the patient a few times per

volunteer a person who provides a service, such as clerical, clinical, or companionship, without any monetary or other reimbursement.

primary caregiver the person designated to provide care for the patient when hospice staff is not available—can be any relative, a spouse, a friend, a significant other, a paid caregiver, an adult child, or any other person. The primary caregiver provides a range of care depending on his or her comfort level, from giving medications to changing dressings to emptying catheter bags.

week, possibly more often, depending on the patient's condition. Representatives from the IDG are not with the patient 24 hours per day, which requires primary caregivers to be taught how to give treatments, medications, baths, and to watch for changes in the patient's condition.

Hospice provides two options for patients who cannot live alone and/or do not have anyone who can act as the primary caregiver. There are two options: (1) the hospice has its own facility or contracts with a nursing home or hospital for a hospice unit; the staff members on these units become the primary caregivers, adhering to the treatment plan developed for the patient by the IDG; or (2) the hospice can arrange to have volunteers and/or hospice aides provide additional hours of care in the patient's home.

SELF REVIEW 13.1

1. What prognosis is necessary for a patient to elect hospice care?
2. True or False? Palliative care is the same as curative care.
3. Name four required members of the hospice interdisciplinary group as specified by the NHPCO.
4. What is the primary purpose of a hospice?
5. Explain the term "primary caregiver" as the term pertains to hospice.

REGULATORY ISSUES

Licensure and Accreditation

A hospice program is licensed by the state in which it is located. In many states, licensure regulations closely follow the Conditions of Participation for hospice care. For a hospice to participate in and receive payment from the Medicare/Medicaid program, the hospice must be certified to be in compliance with the Conditions of Participation. The certification survey often is conducted by the state in which the hospice is located, on behalf of the Centers for Medicare & Medicaid Services (CMS).

In June of 2008, major revisions to the hospice Conditions of Participation were finalized by the CMS. This revision marked the first major change in Medicare regulations for hospice since their inception in 1983. The National Hospice and Palliative Care Organization provided a crosswalk comparing the 1983 and the 2008 Medicare Hospice Conditions of Participation. (NHPCO, 2008).

Significant changes were made to requirements for the patient's plan of care, requirements for assessment and reassessment of the patient, and the standards for quality assessment of hospice services. The Joint Commission (TJC) the Community Health Accreditation Program (CHAP), and the Accreditation Commission for Health Care, Inc. (ACHC) have standards that comply with the Conditions of Participation. The Center for Medicare/Medicaid (CMS) can grant a national accrediting organization, such as The Joint Commission, the authority to survey the hospice and "deem" the hospice as meeting the certification requirements for Medicare/Medicaid.

It is noteworthy that CMS is the final authority on Medicare certification for the hospice. Hospice organizations must meet the voluntary accreditation standards plus the Conditions of Participation to participate in "deeming" status (see Conditions of Participation, Section 418.110).). Licensure issues faced by some hospices in the United States relate to regulations for stand-alone facilities, or hospice facilities that are not directly affiliated with a larger hospital system. These stand-alone facilities have inpatient beds that can be used by hospice patients for management of acute symptoms and/or as a residence if there is not someone in their home to help care for them.

Hospices that provide inpatient care have to directly address the standards for the facility to demonstrate compliance. Major areas include: staffing, 24-hour nursing services, physical environment, fire protection, patient areas, patient rooms, toilet and bathing facilities, plumbing facilities, infection control, sanitary environment, linen, meal service and menu planning, restraint or seclusion, plus staff training requirements and death reporting requirements.

The National Hospice and Palliative Care Organization (NHPCO) provides resources that hospices can utilize to validate the quality of care being provided, staffing guidelines, and performance measures, as well as their standards of hospice care. NHPCO does not require hospices to be certified or accredited under its standards to date, and does not have a survey process similar to The Joint Commission (TJC), the Community Health Accreditation Program (CHAP), and the Accreditation Commission for Health Care, Inc. (ACHC).

All three voluntary accrediting agencies offering the option of deemed status—The Joint Commission (TJC), the Community Health Accreditation Program (CHAP), and the Accreditation Commission for Health Care, Inc. (ACHC)—publish accreditation standards for hospice organizations. The number of hospices seeking voluntary accreditation is increasing; however, many hospices still are not accredited. For this reason, this chapter specifically addresses the **Conditions of Participation** that all hospices (regardless of size) must meet to qualify for reimbursement under the Medicare program.

The Conditions of Participation for hospice include regulations pertaining specifically to Medicare patients; however, some third-party payers refer back to the Conditions of Participation when evaluating the acceptability of electing hospice for their clients. In addition, state regulators commonly utilize the Conditions of Participation to assess hospice programs for licensure, making the Conditions of Participation the primary standards that hospices follow.

Conditions of Participation. federal regulations outlining standards that an organization must meet to participate as a provider of services under the Medicare program.

Hospice Medicare Benefit and Regulations

Throughout the Conditions of Participation, using hospice coverage is referred to as "electing the hospice benefit." Medicare pays for hospice care provided that the care received is from a Medicare-approved hospice program. Hospice services are reimbursed under Medicare Part A, otherwise known as "hospital insurance." Once the patient has elected the hospice benefit, Medicare no longer will pay for treatment to cure the terminal illness or care from a hospice provider that is not set up by the patient's hospice group. While in hospice, Medicare will pay for injuries or other health problems that are not related to the terminal illness (CMS, 2013).

Medicare's hospice benefit helps not only the patients but also their families, because coverage includes all hospice services: clinical staff, medications, durable medical equipment such as home oxygen equipment and supplies, hospital beds, commode chairs, ostomy supplies, walkers, and wheelchairs. Laboratory tests, physical or occupational therapy, speech pathology and bereavement support are examples of services that can be reimbursed provided that the physician includes them in the palliative care plan. Once in hospice, out-of-pocket expenses are minimal, and the paperwork burden on the family is minimized.

Certification

To elect hospice coverage under Medicare, the patient must: (1) be eligible for Medicare Part A, (2) be certified as terminally ill by the attending physician and the hospice medical director, and (3) provide a signed statement indicating acceptance of the palliative care and that the patient is choosing hospice care in place of Medicare-covered benefits for the patient's terminal illness. An individual is considered to be terminally ill if he or she has a life expectancy of 6 months or less based on the physician's clinical judgment regarding the normal course of the individual's illness.

Health information management (HIM) department staff members usually are not responsible for obtaining the oral certifications, as these typically are obtained by a clinical staff member (usually a registered nurse), but HIM staff may have significant involvement in obtaining the signed certification statements. The certification must be signed by both the attending physician and the hospice medical director within 3 calendar days after hospice care has been initiated.

Hospices are required to have signed certification before submitting a claim to Medicare. Hospices focus significantly on this process of obtaining the certification statements so as not to affect reimbursement, which, based on the regulations, cannot be paid without both signatures. Medicare administrative contractors have begun to more actively request copies of hospice patient clinical records and have requested the return of payment when the above signatures were not in place.

Election of Hospice Care

Medicare regulations require that the patient or his or her legal representative sign an election statement at the time of admission to hospice care. The election statement must include specific requirements described in the Conditions of

Participation. The statement must identify the hospice and contain a statement acknowledging that the patient understands the palliative rather than curative nature of hospice care, and that the standard coverage for Medicare services related to the patient's terminal diagnosis is waived. The statement must have an effective date and be signed by the patient or legal representative.

The HIM staff must ensure that if the election statement is signed by the patient's legal representative, the clinical record must have documentation (of health care power of attorney, legal guardian, or health care surrogate) reflecting that this person is indeed the legal representative. The HIM staff must provide significant clinical education in this area.

Revocation

A patient may choose to revoke the election of hospice care at any time, at which point standard Medicare coverage for the terminal illness resumes. There must be a revocation form signed by the patient or legal representative and filed with the hospice, stating that the patient loses the remaining days in the current benefit period and the effective date of the revocation. The effective date may not be earlier than the date on which the form is signed by the patient or legal representative. The Hospice Medicare Benefit is structured into benefit periods, the first of which begins on the date of election. Patients have three types of benefit periods: an initial 90-day period, a subsequent 90-day period, followed by an unlimited number of 60-day periods. Patients can **revoke** or leave hospice care and return at a later time with no risk to their Medicare coverage. Patients must continue to be eligible for hospice care at the beginning of each new period. This process is described later in this chapter.

The HIM department has to ensure that the revocation statement is received and filed in the clinical record. Upon revocation of the Medicare hospice benefit, the patient resumes regular Medicare coverage and loses all remaining days within the election period. To elect hospice care again, the patient would be admitted into the subsequent election period. Monitoring the election periods to ensure correct billing practices may be the responsibility of the HIM department or the billing department. Verification of the validity of the signature on this form is also appropriate.

revoke/revocation performed by a hospice patient (or family or legal representative) to give back or annul his or her hospice benefit. Once a patient has revoked the hospice benefit, the patient returns to standard Medicare or other commercial insurance benefits and loses all remaining days in the current benefit period.

Change of Designated Hospice Provider

The patient may change hospices (transfer from one to another) once during each benefit period without having to revoke hospice status. A statement must be filed with the hospice from which care has been received and with the new hospice. The statement must indicate the date the change is effective and must be signed by the patient or legal representative. The statement must be filed in the patient's record. Verification of the signature, again, is appropriate. The actual date of change must be established and coordinated with the other hospice.

Contracting with Other Facilities

When care is provided to hospice patients in hospitals or nursing homes, the hospice must have a written agreement with the facility and must maintain professional management of the patient's plan of care. The HIM department may be responsible for obtaining documentation from these facilities. It is important that the HIM staff is involved in the establishment of any written agreements with a hospital and/or nursing home that will provide acute treatment to hospice patients, so that the issue of obtaining copies of clinical records on hospice patients can be addressed. The sharing of health information for treatment purposes is permitted under HIPAA privacy regulations.

Plan of Care

A plan of care must be established for all hospice patients by the interdisciplinary group, in collaboration with the attending physician, the patient, and the primary caregiver. The plan of care must include the following components per Conditions of Participation:

1. Interventions to manage pain and symptoms.
2. The scope and frequency of services required to meet the needs of the patient and caregivers.
3. Measurable outcomes anticipated from implementing the plan of care.
4. Drugs and treatments necessary to meet the patient's needs.
5. Medical supplies and equipment necessary to meet the patient's needs.
6. Documentation of the patient's involvement, understanding, and agreement with the plan.

If the patient's attending physician is not a hospice employee, it will be necessary to document the physician's participation in development and maintenance of the interdisciplinary plan of care. This can be done through documentation of items such as physician orders, clinical staff conferences with the patient's attending physician, communication with the attending physician regarding the patient's status, and updates to the plan of care. The plan also must specify the interval until the next review.

Hospice is required to obtain an informed consent that specifies the type of care and services that may be provided. The HIM staff must ensure that the signature on the informed consent is valid and that any associated documentation of personal representative status is included in the clinical record.

Volunteers

A unique regulation in the Conditions of Participation is the requirement for volunteers. Hospices must document volunteer hours in both administrative and patient care activities in an amount that equals 5% of the total patient care hours of all paid employees and contract staff. To substantiate that volunteers provide direct patient care, the HIM department staff should participate in volunteer orientation programs to provide basic documentation guidelines.

The volunteer staff may or may not be clinically oriented. The volunteers may never have provided documentation in a patient's record, so basic education on the do's and don'ts of documentation is necessary. Capturing volunteer hours may or may not be an HIM department function. It is made easier with the use of volunteer logs, completed by all volunteers, regardless of the functions being performed. The log documents the name of the volunteer, the patient seen or activity performed, number of hours and minutes, and any miles driven, if applicable. The data then can be captured in a spreadsheet program or hospice software program. The number of hours of volunteer time is then compared to overall paid staff time in direct patient care to determine if the 5% criterion has been met.

Clinical Records

Hospices must establish and maintain a clinical record for every patient receiving hospice care. Services provided by all disciplines should be documented and included in the clinical record. Signatures and dates are required for all entries. The record should include a minimum of the following:

1. Initial and comprehensive assessments
2. Plan of care, including interdisciplinary group updates
3. Signed copies of patient rights, hospice election, and informed consent
4. Responses to medications and treatments, with related physician orders
5. Outcome measure data
6. Physician certification and recertification of terminal illness
7. Copies of advance directives

Records must be evaluated to determine if all progress notes have been signed appropriately. In addition, records should be easily accessible. Paper records could be filed numerically or alphabetically, depending on patient volume.

SELF REVIEW 13.2

1. True or False? A hospice election statement must be signed by the patient's physician.
2. True or False? A patient can choose to change (transfer) hospices.
3. Who is included in establishing the hospice plan of care?
4. Name three parts of the hospice clinical record.
5. Provide an example of "deeming."

DOCUMENTATION

Hospice providers are required to establish and maintain a clinical record for every patient receiving care and services. Accurate, timely and complete descriptive notes facilitate communication among the care providers and document the progression of the terminal illness. Objective, measurable entries should be used to support hospice services such as the change in pain intensity from a 6 to an 8 on a 0–10 scale. (See the website at the end of the chapter).

Clinical staff members (nurses, social workers, hospice aides) visit the patient's home at least once a week, usually more, depending on the patient's condition The length of the visit varies depending on the patient's condition and the family's needs. The patient may or may not be seen by a hospice physician depending how long he or she receives hospice services. If the patient has an attending physician outside of the hospice, the patient may go to the physician's office, if able. The hospice physician may visit in an emergency situation or if the patient does not have an attending physician. The registered nurse acts as the case manager, coordinating care from all disciplines and communicating changes in the patient's condition with the physician.

Certification Requirements

Medicare requires that two physicians certify that the patient is terminally ill, with a life expectancy of 6 months or less based on the physician's clinical judgment regarding the normal course of the individual's illness. One physician must be the patient's attending physician, and the other must be the hospice physician. The certification must include narrative documentation from the hospice physician that serves as an attestation statement of terminal illness. The statement could be incorporated into the initial orders for treatment to reduce the amount of paperwork that requires the signature of an outside physician.

In either case, the hospice medical director (or a designee) and the certifying attending physician must sign the certification statement. The HIM staff should determine the most effective method to obtain the statement promptly and reduce the time needed for the medical staff to sign paperwork. As stated previously in this chapter, no claims can be sent for reimbursement until the certification is signed by both physicians.

Assessment, Interdisciplinary Plan of Care, and Associated Documentation

At the time of admission to the hospice program, a registered nurse visits the patient in the place of residence to perform an initial assessment. During the visit, the nurse completes a history of the patient's illness, performs a physical examination, and evaluates the appropriateness of the patient for hospice care. If the nurse determines that the patient is hospice-appropriate, the interdisciplinary care plan will be started. The nurse will establish the interdisciplinary care plan in collaboration with the interdisciplinary group.

The care plan is updated a minimum of every 15 days, based on comprehensive assessments of the patient by the team. The interdisciplinary group usually meets every 2 weeks, or more frequently, depending on the hospice. During the meeting, care plans for each patient are reviewed, allowing the hospice physician to recommend new orders and addressing specific problems. The interdisciplinary care plan may or may not change depending on the patient's condition.

The hospice aide provides basic, unskilled care for patients. As the case manager, the nurse is responsible for determining the need for a hospice aide, including frequency of visits and the scope (what is to be performed). Once the case manager has determined that an aide is required, a hospice aide care plan is initiated by the registered nurse. The registered nurse provides specific instructions on the hospice aide plan of care regarding the tasks to be performed and the frequency of the tasks, as well as any potential complications (or signs and symptoms) of which the aide should be aware. The hospice aide then must document completion of the individual tasks according to the specified frequency, as documented by the case manager. Electronic documentation is less common for hospice aides than for other members of the interdisciplinary groups.

The registered nurse is responsible for supervision of the services provided by the hospice aide. This supervision must be documented in the clinical record and provide evidence that the hospice aide plan is being carried out as specified. The registered nurse must assess the skills of hospice aides by watching them provide services to the patient and/or family, and also evaluate the patient's and/or family's assessment of the hospice aide's services. The registered nurse documents this supervision in the routine progress notes or a separate supervisory visit note.

The registered nurse also may identify additional services needed by the patient and family that cannot be adequately covered or provided by paid hospice staff, including companionship, shopping, transportation to the doctor, or respite for family members. The nurse may initiate a request for volunteer services. The hospice volunteer coordinator then is responsible for locating active volunteers who are willing to provide the requested services. Although the regulations do not require specific documentation of supervision of volunteer services, the case manager should ensure that the volunteer care plan is being carried out effectively.

Volunteer Documentation

Volunteers are required to document all contact with hospice patients, including telephone calls. To help the volunteer staff complete documentation in a timely manner, most hospices have volunteer offices and/or space available for volunteers to come in and document, or they allow the volunteer to document at home and provide self-addressed envelopes for the volunteer to mail in progress notes. The volunteer coordinator must take an active role to ensure that all visits are documented by the volunteer staff. The HIM staff also can help by open and closed chart review.

Inpatient Documentation

hospice inpatient unit a hospice with a specific set of beds either in its own building or as a wing of a hospital or nursing home, providing round-the-clock clinical staff to care for terminally ill patients. These units provide respite care, pain and symptom management, and/or routine home care for patients who have nobody in their home to help care for them.

A **hospice inpatient unit** can take two forms: In the first form, the hospice contracts with a facility to utilize designated beds or a wing for hospice patients. The patients often are in the facility already and are identified by the staff as hospice-appropriate. The facility staff contacts the hospice to admit the patient. In this method, the facility where the patient is staying continues to maintain a clinical record. The hospice creates and maintains a separate clinical record. The hospice nurses continue to visit the patient on a regular basis, as they do in the patient's home. After the patient dies or is discharged, the hospice may supplement the patient's record by taking copies of portions of the facility's clinical record (just the portion during the time the patient was in hospice).

Critical to this program is negotiation of the contract. Administrators as well as staff must know all aspects of the contract relating to caring for the patient. The HIM staff must be involved in this process to obtain portions of the clinical record after the patient's death and to understand the flow of the documentation.

The second way in which a hospice can be considered an inpatient unit is if it has its own inpatient facility. Patients are admitted directly to the facility, although they may have been referred from a hospital or nursing home. In this facility, all care is given around the clock by hospice employees. The clinical record created here is similar to a hospital or nursing home record, with periodic assessment of the patient's condition.

Documentation at the Close of Care

Upon the death of a hospice patient, all active care plans, as well as the interdisciplinary care plan, are closed. If the death is in the patient's home, a registered nurse visits the home. A death in an institutional setting such as a nursing home or hospital may not require the services of a hospice nurse. Depending on the state, and individual cities and counties, a home death may require opening a medical examiner's case file.

In addition, state laws may specify who can legally pronounce a patient dead. The hospice usually notifies local police departments or the coroner's office of hospice patients residing in their district so, upon a patient's death, ambulances and police cars do not come with sirens blaring. This shows consideration for the family's well-being.

Regardless of the specific legal requirements, the nurse must document all steps clearly in the clinical record, including (but not limited to) notification of the medical examiner (if applicable), notification of local police, the time when the patient was pronounced dead, and contact with a funeral home to pick up the patient's body, as well as the condition of the family and significant others who are present. In addition to documenting the death visit, the nurse completes a discharge summary documenting the circumstances surrounding the death of the patient and the family's coping abilities.

After the patient's death, **bereavement** services are available for the patient's family and any significant others for up to one year following the death. The bereavement counselor may have been working with the family before the patient's death to initiate potential care plans. The bereavement counselor performs an assessment to determine the bereavement services needed by the survivors. The HIM staff should monitor the status of bereavement activities continuously to ensure that all bereavement services are documented.

bereavement the time period immediately following the death of the patient. In hospice, the clinical staff helps the family and significant others through this period for up to one year, and longer if requested by the patient's family and friends.

SELF REVIEW 13.3

1. How often is the Interdisciplinary Plan of Care reviewed and updated?
2. True or False? Volunteer documentation should be included in the clinical record.
3. True or False? Bereavement services are available to the patient's family up to 6 months after the death of the patient.
4. According to CMS, attesting that the patient is terminally ill with 6 months or less to live is the responsibility of _____.
5. What should the nurse or physician document in the patient's record at the time of the death visit?

REIMBURSEMENT AND FUNDING

The Conditions of Participation provide four levels of hospice care, as shown in Figure 13-1. All levels of hospice care must be directed by the interdisciplinary group, and the clinical record must document the need for each required level of care. The most common of these is **routine home care**, in which the patient receives care in the place of residence. The patient's "home" can be a facility such as a nursing home or a facility operated by the hospice if the facility is the patient's designated place of residence.

routine home care a form of care that occurs when a patient is receiving routine (or nonproblematic) care in his or her place of residence.

Respite care provides an interval of rest for the primary caregiver and is provided to hospice patients in an approved (or contracted) facility, such as a nursing home, hospital, or hospice inpatient unit. Respite is provided on an occasional basis, for not more than 5 days at a time. The regulations are not specific as to the definition of "occasional," but they do require hospices to evaluate families that require frequent respite periods to determine if the patient more appropriately belongs in a nursing home or inpatient hospice.

respite care a form of care that provides an interval of rest for the primary caregiver and is provided to hospice patients in an approved (or contracted) facility.

When respite services are not provided by the hospice, but instead are provided in a contracted facility, the hospice maintains a separate record from the facility that provides the services. The nurse, social worker, hospice aide, and hospice physician continue to visit the patient and provide services as if the patient were still at home. When hospice staff members are not there, the contracted

FIGURE 13-1

Levels of hospice care.

MEDICARE CONDITIONS OF PARTICIPATION — LEVELS OF HOSPICE CARE

- **ROUTINE HOME CARE**
  - A patient is at "home" and is not receiving continuous care.
- **GENERAL INPATIENT CARE**
  - A patient receives general inpatient care in an inpatient facility for pain control or acute or chronic symptom management that cannot be managed in other settings.
- **CONTINUOUS CARE**
  - A patient receives hospice care consisting predominantly of nursing care on a continuous basis at "home." Must be at least eight hours to be reimbursed at the continuous care rate.
- **INPATIENT RESPITE**
  - A patient receives care in an approved facility on a short- term basis.

---

general or acute inpatient care a form of care that takes place when a patient receives care in an inpatient facility (a hospice inpatient unit or a facility contracted by the hospice) for pain control or acute or chronic symptom management that cannot be managed in the patient's place of residence.

continuous care a form of care that occurs in the patient's place of residence when a patient requires continuous care for a minimum of 8 hours within a 24-hour period. Continuous care is furnished only during brief periods of crisis and only as necessary to maintain the terminally ill patient at home.

facility staff members act as the primary caregivers. The clinical record must clearly indicate the need for respite services and also when and where the services are being provided. The hospice must obtain copies of the corresponding record from the facility that is providing respite care (if not the hospice itself) and incorporate these records in the current hospice clinical record.

In **general** or **acute inpatient care**, the patient receives care in an inpatient facility (a hospice inpatient unit or a facility contracted by the hospice) for pain control or acute or chronic symptom management that cannot be managed in the patient's place of residence. Again, the hospice interdisciplinary group is in charge of the plan of care, even if the services are provided by a nursing home or an inpatient hospital. As with respite care, the hospice maintains its own patient record, and the clinical record from the facility providing general inpatient care must be obtained and incorporated into the hospice clinical record. Medicare limits the number of days that are reimbursed at an inpatient rate (including general inpatient and inpatient respite) to 20% of the total patient care days.

Continuous care occurs in the patient's place of residence when a patient requires care for a minimum of 8 hours within a 24-hour period. Continuous care must be predominantly nursing care, although hospice aides may participate as well. The clinical record must document at least hourly progress notes confirming the presence of continuous care. Continuous care is provided only during brief periods of crisis and only as necessary to maintain the terminally ill patient at home.

The levels of hospice care are directly related to the way that hospices receive reimbursement. Medicare Part A, Medicaid, and most commercial insurance companies reimburse hospice care on a per diem basis (i.e., for each day the patient is enrolled in a hospice program). This is in contrast to a service-based reimbursement (utilized for some non-hospice home care), in which an agency receives payment based on services provided by clinical staff. Per diem payments are paid regardless of whether any services (visits by clinical staff) are actually given each day. Each level of hospice care is reimbursed at a different per diem rate, which is further adjusted based on the patient's geographic location. These rates are published annually by the Centers for Medicare & Medicaid Services.

The hospice per diem includes not only visits by hospice clinical staff (nurses, social workers, hospice aides, and chaplains; only the hospice physician can bill separately from the per diem), but also medications relating to the hospice diagnosis (e.g., pain medication for bone cancer, but not necessarily insulin for long-term diabetes), durable medical equipment, laboratory work, oxygen, supplies, and bereavement services. When the patient expires, reimbursement stops, even though the family and friends may be receiving bereavement services for up to one year. If the patient is seen by the attending physician during the hospice admission, the physician can continue to bill under Medicare Part B, and separately for other insurers as well.

Upon admission to a hospice program, the patient signs an "election of the hospice benefit" statement. This statement indicates not only that the patient is electing the hospice benefit (through Medicare Part A, Medicaid, and most other commercial insurers), but also states that all other services related to the patient's hospice diagnosis—such as skilled home care, inpatient hospitalization, and nursing home care—are not to be paid by the insurer to any other agency. This is an important aspect of hospice reimbursement, especially when a hospice patient receives respite care or general inpatient care in a nursing home or inpatient hospital setting. If a hospice does not have its own inpatient facility, it must contract with an approved nursing home and/or inpatient hospital to provide respite and acute inpatient care.

The contract stipulates that only the hospice can bill Medicare for hospice care. The hospital or nursing home can charge the patient (or an insurance company or even the hospice) for room and board only, but cannot bill for the hospice services (even if services are provided by its staff), according to the election statement. As described previously, the hospice patient is still managed by the hospice interdisciplinary group, regardless of the setting for care. A financial incentive for a nursing home or hospital to sign such a contract with a hospice would be to fill beds that otherwise might be vacant. Inpatient facilities may also see a need to be able to arrange for hospice care on their premises when a terminally ill patient elects comfort care only and cannot be readily moved to another location.

In addition to the levels of hospice care, the Conditions of Participation describe hospice benefit periods, beginning with one 90-day period, followed by a second 90-day period, then an unlimited number of 60-day periods. The hospice must evaluate the patient at the end of each benefit period to determine if the patient is still considered hospice-appropriate or continues to have a limited life expectancy. At the end of each benefit period, if the patient is still considered hospice-appropriate, the hospice medical director or physician designee must recertify the patient as requiring hospice care.

The Affordable Care Act requires a hospice physician or nurse practitioner to have a face-to-face encounter with a hospice patient prior to the patient's 180th-day recertification, and each subsequent recertification. The encounter must occur no more than 30 calendar days prior to the start of the hospice patient's third benefit period.

Evaluating that the patient still has a limited life expectancy can be difficult in some diagnoses—such as congestive heart failure, chronic obstructive pulmonary disease, or Alzheimer's disease—because not every diagnosis follows the same path. NHPCO as well as Medicare intermediaries have developed guidelines to assist hospices in determining the continued appropriateness of a patient for hospice services.

Hospices also may refer to a severity system at the time of admission and when reevaluating the patient for continued services. For example, many hospices use the Palliative Performance Scale to assess patients' decline in physical, functional, and mental status as they near the end of life.

If, according to available criteria and analysis, the hospice finds that the patient no longer has a limited life expectancy of 6 months or less, the hospice is responsible for discharging the patient from the hospice benefit. The hospice patient also can choose not to continue with hospice services. The patient's terminal condition may improve slightly and/or the patient and family may choose to seek more aggressive treatment, such as chemotherapy. If the patient chooses to stop receiving hospice services, he or she may revoke the hospice benefit. Discharge is initiated by the hospice; revocation is initiated by the patient. In both circumstances, the patient loses the remainder of days within the current benefit period. If the patient chooses to be readmitted to a hospice, he or she will be readmitted in the next consecutive benefit period.

It is critical for HIM staff to monitor the level of care and benefit period status of all admitted patients on a daily basis to ensure that billing is correct. This process can be accomplished through completion of the daily census and cooperative communication with clinical staff. The interdisciplinary group, in collaboration with the patient's physician, is responsible for determining if the patient is appropriate for admission to hospice care, continues to be appropriate at the start of each benefit period, and is receiving services at the proper level of care.

SELF REVIEW 13.4

1. What are the four levels of care in hospice?
2. True or False? Hospice care is reimbursed on a per diem basis for all levels of care.
3. Who is responsible for initiating a hospice discharge?
4. Who is responsible for initiating a hospice revocation?
5. How many days at a time can the primary caregiver receive respite care?

INFORMATION MANAGEMENT

Information management in hospice has much in common with that of other health care settings. Hospices maintain a master patient index, diagnosis index, and physician index. Data contained in clinical records are abstracted and utilized for quality assessment, reimbursement, and statistics. Following is a discussion of some of the differences in information management that make hospice unique.

Data and Information Flow

Any database in hospice begins with the first contact with the hospice by a patient or potential patient—from the patient or family, a physician, a hospital, or a nursing home. The hospice admissions area captures the name of the patient, demographic information, diagnosis, referring physician, and all other elements of a standard minimum data set, on a paper referral form or in a computerized information system. Many patients and families are not ready for hospice initially, so every contact may not result in an admission, but they often return to the hospice for admission after a time, so information from these initial contacts should be retained to make any subsequent contact easier.

Once the hospice determines that a patient is to be admitted, a nurse is assigned to the case. At the initial visit, the nurse obtains patient/legal representative signatures for election of hospice, medical and financial consents, and any other appropriate paperwork. In conjunction with this visit, the nurse obtains information about the patient's primary diagnosis and related diagnoses, determines whether the patient's attending physician wants to continue following the patient or would prefer that the hospice physician act as the attending physician, and obtains any initial physician orders for medication.

The clinical record begins with a referral form or face sheet, the history and physical examination, consents, and initial physician orders. After a time, the HIM staff can begin abstracting information for an electronic database, to include the date of admission, benefit period, and level of care, which can be tracked for a daily census and reimbursement.

The nurse coordinates the assignment of additional hospice personnel, social workers, hospice aides, the hospice physician, and volunteers, and begins the interdisciplinary care plan. The clinical record, now housed at the hospice, will be expanded to include the hospice physician's orders, social work assessment, hospice aide assignment, and certification of terminal illness signed by both the attending physician and the hospice medical director. As various clinical staff members make assigned visits to the patient and the physician orders change, documentation will be added to the clinical record at the hospice. At least every 2 weeks, the interdisciplinary group will meet as a group to discuss the care of the patient and update the plan of care. The record will document these meetings, as appropriate.

Upon the death or discharge of the patient, all open interdisciplinary care plans are closed, the nurse documents a discharge summary of all care plans initiated, actions taken, and results, and the bereavement assessment is documented.

At this point, the HIM staff completes a qualitative analysis of the clinical record and an abstract of additional pertinent information, such as diagnosis codes for symptoms and complications addressed in care plans; date of death or discharge; and location of death, or reason why the patient was discharged—revocation, hospice discharge, or transfer to another program.

Depending on the state and city of death, the HIM department also may be responsible for initiating the death certificate or providing information to a funeral home to complete the death certificate. This is true especially if a hospice-employed physician has been acting as the patient's attending physician. The death certificate may require the signature of the hospice physician.

Coding and Classification

The primary requirement for hospice admission is certification of the patient's attending physician that the patient has a limited life expectancy (6 months or less). The per diem reimbursement is based solely on the care level and the benefit periods, not on the patient's diagnosis (unlike the prospective payment system used in acute care hospitals). This reimbursement perspective makes hospice diagnosis coding different from that for other health care settings. The hospice clinical record does not include significant laboratory findings, radiological reporting, or any other ancillary services that could be used to "diagnose" the patient.

The hospice clinical record may include copies of records from a hospital if the patient is a direct transfer, or from the physician's office if the patient has not been to a hospital recently. The hospice must attempt to obtain copies of as many recent records available for the patient to aid in the identification and coding of the principal diagnosis, but in the end, the assignment of codes must be the reason(s) the patient has a limited life expectancy.

ICD

The coding principles of the current clinical modification of the *International Classification of Disease* should be followed in the assignment of diagnosis codes; however, the specificity of coding may be limited depending on what information is available. Whereas in an acute care setting, resources often are invested in clinical documentation improvement programs and in querying and educating physicians to assign highly specific codes because of their importance in diagnosis-related group (DRG) payments and in risk-adjustment for quality monitoring, this level of coding specificity is not imperative for hospice coding. Regulations require that a valid diagnosis code be included on the claim. This is not to imply that HIM coders should not try to be as specific as possible in the coding assignment; it merely indicates that there is not an incentive to devote resources to assuring that highly specific documentation is available.

The hospice clinical record consists of primarily nursing documentation requiring the hospice coding staff to evaluate nursing documentation to identify complications or symptoms that the nurse is trying to manage. Symptoms such as pain at any body location, constipation (as a direct result of pain medication such as morphine), respiratory distress, and fatigue are all acceptable to code in hospice. In addition, complications such as urinary tract infections, decubitus ulcers, open wounds or hemorrhage of tumor sites, and thrush are all coded. Coding these additional signs and symptoms helps to build a diagnosis database that can be used internally to evaluate the quality of care given (such as how many catheter patients develop urinary tract infections), and also captures the components of various diagnosis groups (such as end-stage respiratory diseases).

CPT

Physicians employed by the hospice can bill for their services. Depending on the residence of the patient, either in the home or in an inpatient facility, the current procedure terminology (CPT) evaluation and management codes can be used to bill for hospice physician services. Hospice coders should discuss the CPT evaluation and management codes with hospice physicians to educate them on their correct use. If a hospice physician performs a procedure, *ICD* and *CPT* can be utilized to assign procedure codes. The HIM staff should coordinate the assignment of procedure codes with the hospice billing staff to ensure that physician services are reimbursed appropriately.

Electronic Information Systems

As a result of advancements in implementation of health information technology, the use of electronic health records in hospice care is increasing. Even small hospices with few staff members are investing in technologies to improve communication and continuity of care for their patients and families. Prior to the electronic health record, clinicians documented patient visits on paper and left copies of the hospice record at the patient's residence. Clinicians now are using laptops, tablets, and other technologies to document visits, assessments, care plans, medication orders, medication administration, and other required information into software systems designed specifically for the hospice setting. Using mobile technology allows care providers to document at the patient's bedside. Information then is readily available to other team members and the hospice staff covering patient care after hours and on weekends.

The investment in software and technology devices has many challenges for hospices, including clinician training, equipment failures, connectivity, security, and initial and ongoing costs. Still, the advantages can far outweigh any challenges, because electronic documentation is more current, more accurate, more comprehensive, and more legible than paper records.

Hospices across the country have implemented electronic health records to varying degrees, and most have a combination of both electronic and paper records for their patients. Forms requiring signatures of patients or signatures from physicians still may be maintained in paper format. Whatever the form of records that each hospice maintains, the HIM staff will play a significant role in both the electronic and paper formats and processes. HIM professionals working in the hospice setting should be familiar with using technology and being involved in the implementation and ongoing maintenance of any electronic systems.

Data Sets

Several data sets should be captured and maintained within the hospice. These include patient data, resource data, and census data. Software systems designed specifically for hospice usually can provide all of these types of data sets within one database. Reports can be generated showing data in whatever manner or summary format that is requested.

Patient Data

Patient information should include, as a minimum, those data elements in a standard minimum data set. In addition, the hospice will want to capture the name of the primary caregiver and any other significant family members (for bereavement tracking), the referral source (useful to aid marketing staff), where the patient is or was employed, religion, directions to the home, funeral home, language spoken, location of death, and reason for discharge. NHPCO requests significant statistical information about the patient population from each hospice on a yearly basis. In addition, many hospices are involved with grant writing to obtain additional funding for programs, which also requires significant descriptions of the patient population to be served. Computerized systems make retrieval of patient data for statistical reporting both faster and easier.

Resource Data

Resources include all the clinical staff members and vendors who provide services to a patient. Because hospice is reimbursed on a per diem basis, the hospice has to monitor its actual cost per patient versus reimbursement per patient. A resource database can help to provide this information. Resource data and resource utilization should capture the name and specialty (such as registered nurse, nurse practitioner, social worker) of all clinical staff members; the names of all vendors (such as those of durable medical equipment, pharmacy, and supplies); all durable medical equipment dispensed to the patient and associated costs to the hospice; all supplies dispensed to the patient and associated costs to the hospice; the date, clinician, mileage, type of visit, and length of visit for every patient seen; other clinician time associated with the patient, including telephone calls, interdisciplinary group conferences, and staff conferences; the cost of clinician time, using salary plus benefits to obtain a cost per hour; cost of mileage reimbursement; and all medications dispensed to the patient and associated costs.

The contents of the resource data set can be utilized in combination with the patient data set to provide total costs per patient, total costs by diagnosis, and total costs by resource. In addition to costs, staff hours by patient, staff hours by diagnosis, and staff hours by resource are examples of other reports that can be created to monitor resource utilization.

Other Data

Census data include the number of admissions, discharges, transfers, and the number of patients under the care of the hospice on a given day. Other statistics that should be captured include patient days, average length of stay, and average daily census not only by patient, but also by insurance, age group, and location (nursing home, inpatient hospital, home care). Many agencies request census information on a yearly basis from each hospice, and the hospice itself monitors census status.

Hospices also may want to create databases or ensure that hospice software contains data elements for the following:

- *Donations*, including type and amount of all monetary and nonmonetary donations, donors, and relationship to any previous patients. (This is useful for fund-raising efforts.)
- *Bereavement*, including names and current addresses of bereaved family members, associated patient and date of patient's death, and status of bereavement efforts (active or inactive).
- *Volunteers*, including names and addresses, training dates, evaluation dates, cost savings attributable to volunteers, special skills (e.g., barber or nurse), availability (days, evenings, weekends), and status (active or inactive).

Ultimately, it is better to collect too much information at least initially than not to collect enough information. After the data entry document is filed, it is time-consuming to retrieve it and go back later to capture the information.

SELF REVIEW 13.5

1. True or False? Coding in hospice is critical for DRG reimbursement.
2. Name the coding systems used by hospice.
3. Name some of the data sets used by hospice.
4. Durable medical equipment and supplies dispensed to the patient would be found in the _____ database.
5. What are the pros and cons of using an electronic documentation system in a hospice?

QUALITY ASSESSMENT/PERFORMANCE IMPROVEMENT AND UTILIZATION MANAGEMENT

Quality Assessment/Performance Improvement (QAPI)

Conditions of Participation require that hospices implement a Quality Assessment/ Performance Improvement (QAPI) program. QAPI must be an ongoing,

FIGURE 13-2

Quality Assessment and Performance Improvement (QAPI) cycle.

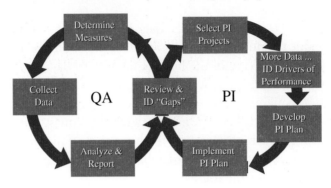

Courtesy of Weatherbee Resources, Inc., Hyannis, MA.

hospice-wide, data-driven program that involves all hospice services, including those provided by contractors. QAPI can be broken down into two parts that are separate but still related (see Figure 13-2). Quality assessment requires the hospice to develop indicators that measure the quality, effectiveness, and safety of its services. An example of a quality indicator for most hospices might be the percentage of patients whose pain is controlled within 48 hours of admission. Hospices must establish benchmarks for each quality indicator and measure them continuously to assess performance.

When benchmarks are not being met, the performance improvement aspect of QAPI begins. Hospices must implement performance improvement projects that address areas of performance that are not meeting standards. These projects must develop and implement strategies to improve performance and ultimately demonstrate the improvement goal. Hospices then continue to monitor the results of performance improvement projects by measurements described in the QA process.

The hospice governing body is responsible for approval and oversight of the QAPI program, and most hospices also have a QAPI committee that meets regularly and a QAPI manager for day-to-day activities. Committee members may contribute to quality measurement as well as participate in performance improvement projects.

Quality Measures

The patient, family, significant others, caregivers, and physician satisfaction surveys are examples of quality measures used by many hospices. Satisfaction surveys are geared toward evaluating responses to the specific services offered to patients/families/physicians by the hospice (Did you find volunteers helpful?) as well as those pertaining to regulatory requirements (Did you receive a copy of the patient's rights?).

Beginning in July of 2014, hospices were required to submit standard quality measures to Medicare on each patient. These measures are called the **Hospice Item Set (HIS)**:

> "The HIS is not a patient assessment and will not be administered to the patient and/or family or caregivers. Typically, assessments are administered at the patient level concurrent with regular patient care, and are intended to capture baseline information for use in developing the plan of care. In contrast, an item set is a standardized mechanism for abstracting data from the medical record."

The Hospice Item Set includes the following seven National Quality Forum Measures:

1. Treatment Preferences
2. Beliefs/Values
3. Pain Screening
4. Pain Assessment
5. Dyspnea Screening
6. Dyspnea Assessment
7. Patients treated with opioids given a bowel regimen

An item set is submitted to Medicare at the time the patient is admitted to hospice and also when the patient is discharged.

hospice item set (HIS) a set of standardized measures that can be abstracted from patient assessments. These items are reported to Medicare on each hospice patient at the time of admission and at the time of discharge.

Quality Monitoring and HIM

Quality monitoring in the hospice HIM department can take the form of two distinct operations. The first is to monitor the contents of the record to ensure compliance with federal, state, and local regulations, as well as standards of accrediting agencies such as The Joint Commission. The second is to ensure the quality and integrity of all data abstracted and captured electronically.

The HIM staff evaluates the contents of each clinical record, ensuring compliance with all appropriate regulations. The review should monitor compliance with the care plans. If the hospice aide's care plan states that the patient should be bathed at each visit, the record should document that this activity was performed. If the nurse's care plan states that the patient is to be educated about the cleaning of a wound, the clinical record should document that this education was performed. Clinical record review by credentialed health information professionals looks at the documentation objectively by comparing documentation in the patient's record to established criteria.

The HIM staff should continuously monitor the documentation of all clinicians caring for the patient to determine who is compliant with the established standards of documentation and who is not. Hospice and home care tend to be high-pressure, high-burnout working environments for the clinical staff, with staff turnover high in some areas. Therefore, ongoing monitoring of the documentation ensures that clinical records reflects care being rendered to the patient and that entries into the patient's record are timely.

Because of the number of outside physicians who continue to follow patients through the hospice, clinical record documentation review also points out many occasions when it is necessary to obtain progress notes and/or signatures from outside physicians—for example, on physician telephone orders, physician certification of terminal illness, and any related physician office documentation to supplement the hospice record.

The physician's office should be contacted or visited (marketing personnel or volunteers are options) to determine the status of any original documents that are not returned. The original clinical record should not be filed as complete without these documents. Computerization has improved the tracking of signatures and authentication within the clinical record by providing reports that point out unsigned documentation or missing dates for signatures.

Utilization Management

Utilization management activities and criteria are built into hospice regulations. For example, the initial certification by the physician and medical director of the patient's terminal illness provides an assessment of the appropriateness of hospice admission.

Another example is that the number of days of inpatient care for which Medicare will pay is limited to not more than 20% of total patient care days. A mechanism to monitor a situation in which the combined general inpatient and inpatient respite care days for a patient were approaching 20% would enable the hospice to avoid exceeding this threshold. Because the Medicare reimbursement system has four different levels of care, the hospice must take steps to assure that care is being rendered at the appropriate level and that documentation in the clinical record supports the level of care billed.

SELF REVIEW 13.6

1. What does the acronym QAPI stand for?
2. Is the percentage of patients whose pain was controlled within 48 hours of admissions an example of a quality measure or an example of a performance improvement project?
3. What are the seven measures in the Hospice Item Set?

RISK MANAGEMENT AND LEGAL ISSUES

To decrease the risk for legal issues, hospice staff need to be educated on the importance of obtaining proper consents for admission and for procedures. Many hospice patients are unable to consent for themselves and have appointed personal representatives.

The clinical staff should verify that the designated person is actually a legal representative, by reviewing proper legal documents. Ideally, a copy of the documents should be filed in the clinical record. If no representative has been assigned, the clinical staff should be educated to help the family obtain legal representative status. The patient, however, should be the first to sign consents; an *X* is appropriate if the signature is witnessed. If the patient is unable to sign, the clinical record should document why the patient was unable to sign (such as patient in a coma, patient has Alzheimer's disease).

Upon the death of the patient, the HIM department may get requests from insurance companies or attorneys to settle a claim or probate the patient's estate. HIM professionals working in hospice should be knowledgeable of, and remain current with, HIPAA regulations regarding disclosure of protected health information. No copies of the clinical record should be released without proper authorization from the legal representative of the estate. State laws should be consulted to determine the legal authority to act on behalf of the deceased.

Documentation verifying legal authority should be requested and kept in the clinical record. Requests for copies of records also may come from family members, sometimes in dispute of a will or an insurance claim. The HIM department staff must verify the legal authority of the requestor or seek proper authorization prior to any disclosure.

SELF REVIEW 13.7

1. True or False? Documentation regarding who has legal authority to act on behalf of an incapacitated or deceased patient should be maintained in the clinical record.

2. True or False? HIPAA regulations regarding the release of protected health information do not apply to hospice patients.

ROLE OF THE HEALTH INFORMATION MANAGEMENT PROFESSIONAL

PROFESSIONAL SPOTLIGHT   HEALTH INFORMATION MANAGER

Who I am: Teresa Sherfy, RHIT

Where I work: Hospice of Southern Illinois

What I do: I am responsible for the staff and all functions of the Health Information Management Department. I am the administrator of the electronic medical record (EMR), and I manage the computer help desk. I also serve as the HIPAA Privacy Officer. Hospice of Southern Illinois serves 27 counties of Southern Illinois and provides services in a 16-bed hospice home. Our clinicians all document into the EMR by taking laptops to the patient's bedside. After closed review, paper records are scanned into the system by HIM staff. Help desk staff ensure the integrity of the EMR by following policies on modifications to electronic documentation. As HIPAA Privacy Officer, I monitor compliance with privacy policies and perform a breach assessment on any HIPAA occurrence.

(continued)

Why HIM knowledge is important in my role:

My HIM education served an important role in the successful implementation of our EMR in 2004. I've been involved in compliance, quality management, privacy and data integrity for my entire 18 years with Hospice of Southern Illinois. Previous inpatient coding experience helps to ensure that our code assignment is accurate. Knowledge of release of information and associated legal requirements has been essential.

Other information: I believe that a successful HIM professional must have strong computer skills. Electronic records are becoming commonplace, making computer skills crucial in the HIM profession.

The HIM professional in hospice must be the expert on all documentation standards from all accrediting and licensing agencies. The HIM professional should continually offer workshops to the clinical staff about basic documentation techniques, including the legal viewpoint on documentation and documentation requirements of accrediting and licensing agencies.

Another role for the HIM professional is that of data manager. Assertiveness in offering to retrieve information at meetings and team conferences is a way to build a reputation as a data manager. The HIM professional can offer to complete statistical reports requested by agencies and compile and distribute a daily census. The HIM professional can graph admissions or discharges or patient days for a period of time. The HIM professional can look at trends and describe them to others. Again, he or she must be assertive in telling people what an HIM professional is able to do. Many hospices are not yet as sophisticated as hospitals in their interpretation and evaluation of data, and they benefit from an expert who can educate them.

The HIM professional also may serve as a member or chairperson of a QAPI committee or as a HIPAA privacy and/or security officer. In small hospices, HIM professionals may find themselves involved in many aspects of hospice operations in addition to traditional HIM responsibilities.

SELF REVIEW 13.8

1. The HIM professional in hospice must be the expert on all documentation standards from all _____ and _____ agencies.
2. What roles do HIM professionals play in hospice?

TRENDS

In the future, hospice will be challenged by issues related to:

- Increased scrutiny of hospice eligibility
- Decreasing lengths of stay
- OIG annual work plan related to hospice care

- Revisions to federal, state, and local regulations
- Expansion of the palliative care specialty and
- Increased use of electronic information systems and electronic health records

Hospice eligibility has come under increased scrutiny by Medicare and other auditors contracted with the federal government to focus on fraud and abuse. Hospices have to show documentation that supports eligibility and makes clear why the patient has a 6-month or less prognosis. Medicare contractors provide criteria to be used to assess eligibility under certain common diagnoses, and records providing historical data on the patient's course of treatment and disease progression are critical.

Hospices across the nation have experienced a sharp decline in the average length of stay for hospice patients to the point that one- and two-day lengths of stay are becoming common. A short stay prevents the patient and family from receiving the optimum comfort care and other benefits available through hospice during the final weeks and months of the patient's life. Short stays also are a problem from a financial standpoint because the per diem reimbursement provided by Medicare does not cover all costs associated with an extremely brief stay. Increasing the average length of stay is a constant challenge facing hospices. Educational outreaches to both the health care community and the lay community about the benefits of hospice help to combat this trend.

The Office of the Inspector General (OIG), which is the arm of the Department of Health and Human Services charged with investigating and monitoring the Medicare and Medicaid programs, publishes a new work plan annually at its website. All types of health care providers, including hospices, should be aware of OIG investigations that could affect their organizations.

Changes to hospice regulations, including the Conditions of Participation, have been frequent in recent years. Changes in billing requirements, documentation of the certifications and recertifications, and changes in HIPAA regulations have all had an effect on hospices. HIM professionals working in hospice must remain current on all regulations related to their field, to assist in keeping their organization in compliance.

Many hospices have expanded their scope of practice to include palliative care services for patients who are not eligible for hospice benefits. Members of the hospice team work together to provide comfort care by control of pain and symptoms for patients who are chronically ill or who have issues with chronic pain and symptoms. Certifications now are available for physicians, nurses, social workers, and hospice aides in the specialty of hospice and palliative care.

There is an expanded need for data management and information management personnel. The use of electronic health records, laptops, handheld devices, telemedicine, and the Internet requires expertise that some health care professionals do not have. HIM professionals will continue to be in high demand in light of their skills in document management, electronic information systems, privacy, and statistical management.

SELF REVIEW 13.9

1. To avoid charges of fraud, hospice documentation must support _____ and make clear why the patient has a prognosis of 6 months or less.
2. True or False? The HIPAA regulations have not changed since their inception.

SUMMARY

Hospice care for terminally ill patients is significantly different from the care provided in other health care settings. It is the only health care setting in which the focus of care is not on curing the patient. With this philosophy in mind, the HIM professional must realize that his or her role also will be unique. What is significant about coding in hospitals, outpatient facilities, skilled home care, and other facilities relying on a prospective payment system for reimbursement does not apply in hospice. Further, other settings may have a high volume of requests from insurance companies, attorneys, and patients for clinical records to the extent that a correspondence service is needed to help process the requests. The volume of requests is much lower in hospice. HIM professionals often play a diversified role when working in hospice, finding themselves involved in quality programs, privacy concerns, and assistance with transitioning to electronic health records and further computerization.

REVIEW QUESTIONS

Knowledge-Based Questions

1. True or False? Hospice takes care of only cancer patients.
2. What are some examples of how hospice tries to relieve terminal symptoms for patients?
3. Who are the members of a hospice interdisciplinary group?
4. What is the role of the primary caregiver?
5. Describe how a Medicare patient elects to receive hospice care.
6. What roles do volunteers play in hospice care?
7. Describe bereavement services provided by hospice.
8. What are the four levels of hospice care found in the Conditions of Participation?
9. Define the QAPI process.

Critical Thinking Questions

1. Provide examples of some of the data that can be collected by hospices.
2. Why are information technology skills necessary for HIM employees working in hospice?

WEB ACTIVITIES

Access the *Code of Federal Regulations* through the Federal Digital System of the U.S. Government Printing Office at http://www.gpo.gov/fdsys

Follow these steps to find the appropriate section of the regulations:

1. At the Federal Digital System main page, select *Code of Federal Regulations.*
2. At the next page, choose the previous (not the current) year from the drop-down menu and click "Go."
3. Scroll down to Title 42, "Public Health" and click "Download."
4. Hospice regulations are found in Part 418 of Title 42, so click on your preferred format (PDF recommended) for the range of "Parts" that includes 418.
5. Search for Section 418.104, which contains the requirements for hospice clinical records.

How might a hospice health information manager use this document?

Visit the Victoria Hospice Society's website at http://palliative.info/resource_material/PPSv2.pdf to view and read about the Palliative Performance Scale.

1. What three purposes might the Palliative Performance Scale serve?

CASE STUDY

A 66-year-old woman and her two daughters present themselves at the hospice. The woman's attending physician suggests that she investigate hospice as a health care alternative. The woman has breast cancer with bilateral mastectomies and recently was found to have metastases to the liver. Her physician stated that she could have additional chemotherapy but that her liver cancer may not respond. At this point, other than mild pain, she is able to get around relatively well. She is not sure she wants to have additional chemotherapy because it made her terribly ill the first time.

Her daughters and their families (both have two children, all under the age of 10) are her only close relatives. She has been divorced since her first mastectomy.

One daughter lives 5 minutes away; the other daughter lives 40 minutes away. Upon further discussion with the daughters, you learn that the first daughter wants only what her mother wants and will support whatever decision she chooses; the second daughter wants her mother to have the additional chemotherapy no matter what and cannot understand why anyone would "just give up." You are the admission representative.

1. What would you tell this woman and her daughters about hospice?
2. What problems do you anticipate for this family?
3. How would you respond to the second daughter's comment that hospice is "just giving up?"
4. Is this patient appropriate for hospice?

REFERENCES AND SUGGESTED READINGS

ASHP (American Society of Hospital Pharmacists). (1993). ASHP statement on pharmaceutical care. *American Journal of Hospital Pharmacists, 50*: 1720–1723.

CMS (Center for Medicare and Medicaid Services). (2013). *Medicare Hospice Benefits.* Baltimore: Author.

Corr, C., & Corr, D. (1983). *Hospice Care Principles and Practice.* New York: Springer Publishing Company.

NHPCO (National Hospice and Palliative Care Organization). (2006). *Standards of Practice for Hospice Programs.* Arlington, VA: Author.

NHPCO (National Hospice and Palliative Care Organization. (2008). *Crosswalk of Current Medicare Hospital Conditions of Participation 1983 to Final Medicare Hospice Conditions of Participation.* Arlington, VA: Author.

KEY RESOURCES

Celerian Group Company (as an example of a Medicare Administrative Contractor for Home Health and Hospice)
http://www.cgsmedicare.com/HHH

Center for Medicare & Medicaid Services
http://www.cms.gov

Hospice Association of America
http://www.nahc.org/haa

National Hospice and Palliative Care Organization
http://www.nhpco.org

National Institute of Nursing Research
http://www.ninr.nih.gov

The Joint Commission
http://www.jointcommission.org

Dental Care Settings

Francis G. Serio, DMD, MS, MBA | Denise D. Krause, PhD |
Cheryl L. Berthelsen, PhD, RHIA

LEARNING OBJECTIVES

Upon successful completion of this chapter, you should be able to:

- Identify the various practitioners associated with dental care, and describe their roles.
- Describe the documentation requirements specific to the practice of dentistry.
- Explain the benefits of electronic dental records.
- Discuss the potential impact of managed care on dental practices.
- Describe utilization management strategies used in dentistry.
- Identify specific risks associated with dentistry and strategies to manage the risks.
- List the information needs of the dental office.
- Identify the components of electronic dental record and practice management systems.
- Describe potential career opportunities in the dental setting for HIM practitioners.

Setting	Description	Synonyms/Examples
Dental Office	A private practice facility where patients receive dental care	
Dental Clinic	A department within a larger health organization where patients receive dental care	Within a community health center Within a VA medical center Within a prison Within a dental school Within a local government health department
Dental School	A school within a university where dentists and dental hygienists are educated and trained	School of Dentistry or Dental Medicine College of Dentistry or Dental Medicine

INTRODUCTION TO CARE SETTINGS

Dental practitioners treat patients in a variety of settings, and whenever a patient receives a dental examination or treatment, a dental record is created or supplemented. Each setting poses unique conditions and challenges in the dental care provided to patients, the type of documentation generated, and the management of dental records. Today, all new dental facilities are likely to use an **electronic dental record (EDR)** and digital imaging, and many older facilities are converting analog to digital record keeping as well.

> **electronic dental record (EDR)** a computer-based dental record that stores the patient's pertinent demographic, diagnostic, treatment, and financial information.

Care Settings

The following discussion describes various settings that are used in dental practices.

Solo Dental Practice

A **solo dental practice** is owned and operated by one dentist. The dentist owns or leases the office building or suite and all the necessary equipment and furnishings to run what in essence is a small business. The solo-practice dentist usually employs several personnel consisting of at least a receptionist and a dental assistant, but also may employ an office manager to oversee the day-to-day business operations of the practice and an insurance specialist to keep up with the filing and adjudication of claims. Dentists may employ a full-time dental hygienist or contract with a hygienist to come to the office one or several days per week to provide either routine preventive care or definitive periodontal treatment. Some dentists elect to perform routine checkups and cleanings themselves.

> **solo dental practice** a dental practice owned and operated by one dentist.

Although the solo-practice dentist is responsible for his or her patients 24 hours a day, in reality a general dentist is not often called for a dental emergency outside of business hours. Occasionally, a patient may need a prescription for an antibiotic or a pain medication, but the instances in which a dentist has to meet a patient at the office during off-hours are rare.

The solo-practice setting had been remarkably stable over the years, despite increasing competition. This is beginning to change as more recent graduates

FIGURE 14-1

Distribution of dentists in initial practice.

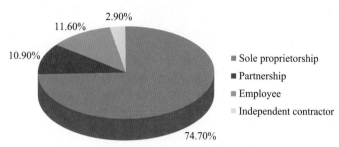

have significant educational debt and cannot enter a solo private practice or they prefer to be an employee and not have to worry about managing a small business.

Dental service organizations (DSOs) are emerging, in which a dentist may have an ownership stake in the practice while the DSO manages the administrative duties of the practice. Data from the American Dental Association (2013) show that 6.4% of dentists report that their practice is part of a larger multi-location entity, up from 5.4% in 2008.

Figure 14-1 contains information about the practice setting of dentists in the United States in 2007. Solo-practice dentists sometimes rent space in their offices to another practicing dentist to supplement their office income or hire a newly licensed dentist to work as an associate. The associate dentist, possibly either an employee or an independent contractor, receives only a portion of the fees collected for the work performed, and the remainder of the fee reimburses the practice for use of office and equipment, with some profit for the owner dentist.

The solo-practice dentist is responsible for maintaining dental records of all his or her patients. Dental records for patients of tenant dentists who rent space on evenings and weekends are the responsibility of the tenant, not the dentist-owner of the practice. When the solo practitioner retires, he or she must store and maintain the dental records of patients as long as state statute dictates—often 7 to 10 years. If a dentist sells the practice, the dental records usually transfer to the dentist who is buying the practice, as these patient records constitute the majority of the value of the practice.

Group Dental Practice

group dental practice
two or more dentists
practicing together.

A **group dental practice** is composed of two or more dentists practicing together. The group of dentists usually is incorporated as a legal entity, and the corporation, rather than the individual dentists, owns and operates the business. Ownership of the corporation may be shared equally among the owner-dentists, or there may be one or two majority owners, with the remaining dentists as minority owners.

The amount of money that each dentist earns from the business usually is based on how well the business does as a whole and the percentage of ownership in the corporation instead of individual productivity. There may be, however, bonuses based on individual productivity. A group practice also may be composed of two or more dentists who share office expenses and equipment but are not incorporated. They practice as a group to benefit from sharing the expenses of running the business but maintain separate financial records and are distinct business entities.

Group dental practices may be composed of dentists practicing in the same specialty (orthodontists) or different specialties (general dentists plus an endodontist–root canal specialist, periodontist–gum treatment specialist, and prosthodontist–trained to replace missing teeth in complex cases). Multiple specialties allow the dentists to refer patients who need specialty care to a dentist within the group rather than to an outside practice. Single-specialty groups use the same type of equipment and instruments and can share them. Multispecialty groups need a wide variety of instruments specific to the specialties involved. Dentists within the group practice usually share on-call service with each other to deal with patient emergencies. Dental records of patients of group practices also are usually shared. The records are available to any dentist in the group who sees a patient during an emergency appointment. The corporation is responsible for storing and maintaining the dental records over time.

Clinics in Academic Institutions

As of this writing, there are 60 dental schools in the United States. Although most are located in major metropolitan areas, several are located in more rural areas. All universities that have a dental school to educate and train dentists have clinics for patients to receive dental treatment. Dental students under close supervision of faculty, who are licensed dentists, provide dental care. The patients pay significantly reduced fees for dental care, but the treatment usually requires more visits to complete than in a private dental office. Schools that educate and train dental hygienists may be associated with a dental school, a four-year college, or a community college. The care provided to patients at a dental hygiene clinic is limited to procedures that a dental hygienist is allowed to perform according to state licensure rules. These rules may vary significantly from state to state.

The dental records generated in academic settings serve purposes beyond the documentation of care provided. They are necessary evidence of the student's progress toward and preparation for graduation and licensure. Most schools require dental students and dental hygiene students to complete a certain number of specific dental treatments and procedures or to successfully pass competency examinations before they are eligible to take state board licensing examinations or graduate.

Dental records in academic settings are also important in research. Faculty members are involved in the discovery of new treatment modalities, diagnostic tests, restorative materials, prostheses and anesthetics; the invention of new devices, instruments, and equipment; and research into the prevalence and incidence of disease, patient pool characteristics, and success of various treatment modalities. New methods of preventing dental decay and periodontal (gum) disease are being studied and proven at major dental schools throughout the world. Dental records within these institutions are necessary to that progress. Dental records in large institutions also may be used for public health research, such as tracking disease trends.

Third-Party Organizations

Dentists and patients may participate in a variety of third-party organizations (primarily insurance plans or managed care organizations) to assist patients in the payment for dental services. Some of these organizations, such as unions, may run their own clinics. These clinics usually have employee dentists or independent contractors to provide patient care. For more detail on these organizations, see the Reimbursement section of this chapter. In most instances of third-party payment, the care is provided in the dentist's private office, although some health plans in certain parts of the country have separate dental clinics.

Acute Care Hospital

Large academic health centers and acute care hospitals may have an associated dental clinic or dental emergency room. Patients served in this setting may be victims of trauma who have sustained an injury to the face or teeth (alone or in addition to other types of injuries), or patients requiring general anesthesia for dental treatment. Patients may receive dental treatment in the emergency room, as an inpatient, or as an outpatient. Dental records of these treatments may be included in hospital records for an inpatient or maintained separately for emergency room patients or outpatients. Storage and maintenance of these dental records are the responsibility of the associated institution.

Many of these hospitals also provide outpatient dental care through general dental residency, pediatric dentistry, or oral maxillofacial surgery programs. Graduate dentists who are receiving advanced training in general dentistry or their chosen specialty from a group of attending dentists provide care. These dental records are maintained by the dental department or may be part of the hospital's general medical record.

Other Settings

Dental treatment may be provided and dental records created and maintained in many other settings. Prisons usually have dental clinics to care for inmates. The Department of Veterans Affairs (VA) hospitals also have dental clinics to serve the dental needs of veterans. Active military bases usually have dental clinics associated with the base hospital or medical clinic. Some colleges and universities have dental clinics to care for the dental needs of students. Community health centers also may provide both routine and emergency dental care for patients. The storage and maintenance of dental records are the responsibility of the entity operating the clinic, not the dentists providing the care, as most dentists are employees in these settings.

Types of Patients

Children and Adolescents

Dentistry has changed for children in the twenty-first century. In some localities, the use of fluoride has made a tremendous impact in preventing dental **caries** in children. The National Institute of Dental and Craniofacial Research (NIDCR) estimated that 58% of children aged 2 to 11 were caries-free in their primary dentition and that 41% of children aged 11 to 17 were caries-free in their permanent dentition (CDC, 2007). The most recent CDC data show that in children ages 2–5, 19.5% of caries are untreated and 22.9% of caries in children age 6–19 are untreated. These are national averages, so there may be significant deviations from these values in areas without fluoridated water, with a high consumption of sugary foods and beverages, or with a shortage of dental personnel (CDC, 2013).

> **caries** the correct technical term for tooth decay.

Early childhood caries (ECC), also known as nursing caries or baby bottle tooth decay (BBTD), is a problem for infants and toddlers. Children who are allowed to go to bed at night with a bottle filled with liquid other than water develop caries in their **primary teeth** (baby teeth). A study of Head Start children found that 42.5% had early childhood caries and 17.3% had severe caries (Kopycka-Kedzierawski, et al. 2008). This rate is significantly higher in rural and minority populations and single-parent families (Plutzer & Keirse, 2011).

> **primary teeth** the baby teeth, also known as the primary dentition; the baby teeth are replaced by adult (permanent teeth).

Unfortunately, the public has not been well educated about this problem. A study of Midwestern college students found that only 39% of respondents had heard of BBTD and 32% of those thought it was a fictional health problem (Logan et al., 1996). A 1991 study on inappropriate infant bottle feeding for Healthy People 2000 found that 95% of children 6 months to 5 years old had used a bottle, and 20% of them were put to bed with a bottle containing contents other than water (Kaste & Gift, 1995). More than 8% of children 2 to 5 years old still used a bottle—highlighting the need for widespread education on the risks of bottle-feeding. Retention of primary teeth is important for function, aesthetics, childhood self-esteem, and to hold proper space for the eruption of permanent teeth.

Chipping, fracturing, and loss of primary and permanent teeth caused by falls and accidents are common. A child typically begins to lose primary teeth between ages 5 and 7. When development is delayed, dental intervention may be needed to ensure the eruption of healthy permanent teeth. The dentist may have to pull stubborn primary teeth that fail to come out on their own. Many U.S. children and adolescents receive orthodontic treatment—braces to straighten teeth. Orthodontic and palatal deformities caused by thumb-sucking or persistent use of pacifiers also are problems requiring corrective orthodontic care and sometimes **orthognathic surgery** (corrective jaw surgery).

orthognathic surgery surgery to bring jaws into proper alignment.

Adults

Adults generally have more dental disease that may require costly treatment than do children. Many children from 1950 to 1970 had their teeth filled with a variety of materials to treat dental caries. Over time as these patients age, dental restorations may gradually fail, requiring replacement by larger and larger fillings, with the possible need for **root canal therapy (RCT)** and a prosthetic **crown**. The National Institute of Dental and Craniofacial Research (NIDCR) has estimated that 57% of the elderly and 21% of the 18- to 64-year-old population have root caries (NIDCR, 2014).

root canal therapy (RCT) removal of the nerve of the tooth from the canal inside the root, and replaced with a filling material.

crown full-coverage restoration of a tooth when it cannot be restored by a filling.

Adults also develop gingivitis and periodontal disease. If periodontal disease is left untreated, the jawbone supporting the teeth is lost, teeth loosen, and teeth eventually fall out. A missing tooth, from trauma, gum disease, or decay, can cause problems. The empty space in the adult's dental arch allows teeth to shift, changing the way the person bites and chews. Bony tissue in the mandible and maxilla can erode, making prosthetic restoration difficult. Adults also suffer chips, fractures, and loss of teeth from falls, accidents, and assaults.

Some adults seek dental treatment for solely cosmetic reasons. Cosmetic dentistry includes dental implants for missing teeth, orthodontics to straighten teeth, veneers to cover badly stained teeth, and tooth whitening, all to improve smile aesthetics.

Pregnant Females

The dentist has to be careful about inadvertently exposing a developing fetus to radiation from a **radiograph** (X-ray film). Female patients of childbearing age are questioned routinely about the possibility of being pregnant before radiological exams are performed. Use of digital radiographs significantly reduces a patient's exposure to radiation. Routine dental cleaning and checkups are particularly important for pregnant women. Although dental treatment can be performed safely on pregnant women into the second trimester, some choose to wait until after delivery to have their teeth repaired. Gingival inflammation (gingivitis) also may occur in some pregnant women because of hormone fluctuations and poor oral hygiene.

radiograph a graphic image produced by the use of radiation.

The Elderly

As more individuals live longer, they are more likely to keep most, if not all, of their teeth. The number of adults over age 65 who had all of their natural teeth extracted dropped from 26.2% in 1999 to 18.5% in 2008 (National Center for Chronic Disease Prevention & Health Promotion, 2009) although this number may approach 40% in certain rural areas. This retention of teeth has changed the approach to treatment for the elderly, with an emphasis on prevention and maintenance of the natural dentition. At one time, the loss of teeth meant having to use removable complete dentures that often were unstable, but significant progress in the use of dental implants has allowed people to have a stable dentition, either of crowns and bridges or of implant-stabilized and implant-retained dentures.

The living situations of the elderly can have a great effect on oral health and disease. Those who live independently are generally in good physical health and also enjoy good oral health. Those with chronic illnesses or in dependent living situations may have many oral health problems. One study of VA patients found that only 6% of healthy, independent-living patients were edentulous (without teeth), and those who had teeth were missing an average of 4.5 teeth. But 49% of the patients living in a VA nursing home or those hospitalized for illness were edentulous, and those who had teeth were missing an average of 12 teeth and had an average of 5 decayed teeth (Loesche et al., 1995).

edentulous   having no teeth; toothless.

The lack of proper dental care and oral hygiene for nursing home residents is well documented. Increasing the percentage of long-term care facility residents receiving dental services was identified as a national goal in Healthy People 2010 and continued as an objective for Healthy People 2020 (DHHS, 2009). Figure 14-2 demonstrates the prevalence of dental health problems among nursing home residents in the state of Washington (Kiyak et al., 1993).

FIGURE 14-2

Dental needs of residents in nursing homes.

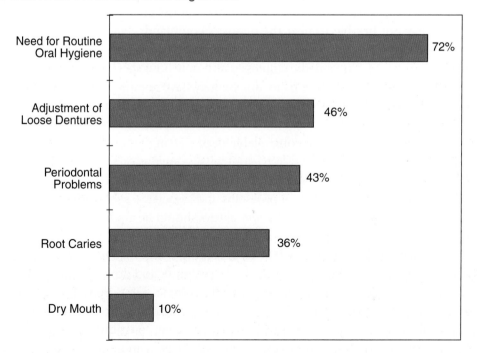

Graphic created by C. Berthelsen, based on data from Kiyak et al., 1993.

Patients with Special Challenges

Patients who are physically or mentally developmentally challenged pose special problems when they need dental care. These patients may not cooperate with the dentist and may be unable to understand simple commands such as, "Open your mouth." More functional individuals may be able to cooperate for a short time but may be unable to sit still long enough for the needed treatment. Nevertheless, they still need preventive and restorative dentistry to maintain optimum health. Major restorative treatment for these patients is usually carried out under deep sedation or general anesthesia, which may preclude treatment at a typical dental office and require admission to an outpatient surgery facility or hospital.

Individuals with mental illness can be difficult for the dentist to treat. Patients who suffer from hallucinations and uncontrolled psychosis may not cooperate with the dentist. They may be treated normally if they are well controlled on proper psychotropic medications. Still, the dentist must be aware of what medications the patient takes—to avoid interaction with anesthetic drugs used in dentistry. Psychotropic medications can cause drowsiness, drooling, extremely dry mouth, excessive salivation, nervousness, uncontrolled movements of the tongue, muscle rigidity, and nasal congestion requiring mouth breathing. These side-effects may cause discomfort to the patient undergoing dental treatment as well as difficulties for the dentist.

Patients who are physically challenged may not be easy to treat. Deformities may make sitting in the dental chair uncomfortable. Paralysis may impair the patient's ability to sit or balance in a normal dentist chair. A hearing-impaired patient may not be able to hear the dentist's commands. These patients should be treated in a setting that can adapt to their disability.

Patients with serious medical illnesses also may pose special problems for the dentist. A patient with severe heart disease may have angina pectoris or elevated blood pressure while at the dentist's office. Patients may be using portable oxygen tanks, feeding tubes, or a central line for intravenous fluids. Neurologic disease (Parkinsonism) may cause uncontrollable head shaking and tongue movements. Stroke survivors may be less able to control swallowing or have a minimal gag reflex. Care must be taken when treating these patients. Thus, a thorough understanding of the patient's medical problems and associated symptoms is essential. The patient's medical and dental history always should be available for the dentist to review when treating the patient.

Another group of patients that is becoming a significant challenge is the drug abusing patient. Methamphetamine, oxycontin, and now the resurgence of heroin use creates particular problems for the dentist. First, these patients tend to have a high carbohydrate diet (think snack foods and Mountain Dew-type soft drinks) and poor to nonexistent home care that contribute to generalized severe tooth decay. Second, these patients may have some psychological issues due to their drug use making them a challenge to manage. Third, these patients may have adverse reactions to local anesthetics and other medications if they are self-medicated when they come to their dental appointments.

Types of Providers

General Dentists

A **dentist** usually completes 4 years of college and 4 years of dental education before becoming licensed to practice. A dentist earns either a DDS or a DMD degree. A general dentistry practice focuses on a wide range of skills, including examination, diagnosis, and treatment of simple and complex conditions in patients from young to old.

    The general dentist is much like a family practice physician, taking care of the dental health of all members of the family, providing periodic checkups and cleanings, and monitoring the condition of teeth and gums. The general dentist is allowed to perform almost all dental procedures for which he or she is appropriately trained to perform according to state license, but many choose to refer patients to specialty dentists for more complex care. Many general dentists focus on prevention, basic restorative care (fillings, crowns, bridges, and dentures), and cosmetic procedures.

dentist a licensed health care professional specializing in the prevention and treatment of disorders of the oral cavity and associated body structures; a dentist has either a DDS or a DMD degree.

Dental Specialties

The following nine dental specialties are recognized by the American Dental Association:

1. Dental public health
2. Endodontics
3. Oral and maxillofacial radiology
4. Oral and maxillofacial surgery
5. Oral pathology
6. Orthodontics
7. Pediatric dentistry
8. Periodontics
9. Prosthodontics

Although several of these specialties are recognizable to most people, public health dentists, oral pathologists, and oral and maxillofacial radiologists usually practice in institutional settings. Specialty training ranges from an additional 2 to 6 years after dental school.

    An **orthodontist** is a dentist who specializes in straightening teeth. Many orthodontists complete 2 years of specialty education following the 4 years of dental school to prepare for their specialty. Orthodontic treatment may be medically necessary or may be cosmetic. A general dentist usually refers patients to an orthodontist for a consultation, and treatment begins when appropriate.

orthodontist a dentist who specializes in straightening teeth.

Orthodontists use radiographs, impressions of the patient's teeth and bite, and a variety of orthodontic appliances (braces, retainers, bands and brackets bonded to teeth, headgear) to accomplish the goal of straightening teeth. Patients undergoing treatment see their orthodontist regularly over a period of several years. The dental record is important to the orthodontist to monitor the progress of treatment and must be available for reference every time the patient is seen.

periodontist a dentist who specializes in the treatment of diseases of the gum or bone (supporting structure).

gingiva the gums.

loss of attachment (LA) the loss of the supporting structure of the teeth that causes the tooth to become loose; may result in loss of the tooth.

A **periodontist** is a dentist who specializes in treating the tissues surrounding and supporting the teeth. Periodontal disease begins as an inflammation of the **gingiva** (gum tissue) and can progress to abscesses around the teeth and infection of the jawbones. As the disease progresses, the victim develops **loss of attachment (LA)**, the loss of supporting structures of the teeth. The teeth become loose and eventually will be lost.

Although periodontal disease is preventable, it is still quite prevalent among Americans. Studies during 1988 to 1991 indicate that more than 90% of Americans over 12 years of age had experienced some clinical LA. The LA increases with age, with 15% of Americans showing moderate or severe LA, although 2007 data (CDC, 2007) showed a decrease in the prevalence and severity of periodontal disease across all adult age groups.

To show how the data may change over time and also by how the data are gathered, a 2012 study using NHANES (National Health and Nutrition Examination Survey) data estimated that more than 47% of the adult sample had some form of periodontitis. Periodontal disease was more prevalent in those over age 65, with 64% having either moderate or severe periodontal disease (Eke et al., 2012).

Periodontal disease is treated by removing the bacterial plaque (the causative agent of the disease) and the calcified calculus deposits on the teeth. Depending on the severity of the disease, surgery or the use of antibiotics may be necessary. The key is to prevent the buildup of plaque and the initiation of disease in the first place. Patients usually are referred to the periodontist by a general dentist, although they may self-refer if they suspect a problem developing. Periodontists also perform surgical procedures to improve smile aesthetics and place implants.

endodontist a dentist who specializes in treating diseases or injuries that affect the root tip or nerve of the tooth, most commonly a root canal.

An **endodontist** is a dentist who specializes in treating the inside of the tooth, the nerve and pulp. An endodontist performs root canal therapy to remove the dying or dead tissue from the root canal system found within the tooth and to eliminate infection in the jawbone. The patient may need a root canal after complaining about a severe toothache or a tooth that is extremely sensitive to anything hot or cold—foods, liquids, or breathing cold air. After the root canal is completed, the patient goes back to the referring dentist or a prosthodontist for restoration of the tooth with a crown.

The endodontist may never see the patient again or may treat the patient for problems with a different tooth in the future. Even though the endodontist may see the patient only once or twice, the same rules for completeness and retention of records applies as if there was a long-term relationship.

A **prosthodontist** is a dentist who specializes in replacing missing teeth with a prosthetic device. Full-mouth dentures are required for an edentulous person. Other **prostheses** include partial **denture**, **bridge** with **pontic**, and dental **implant**. Terms related to prostheses are defined in the accompanying box.

Prosthesis – a fixed or removable appliance to replace missing teeth; examples are bridges, dentures, and partials.
Denture – a removable prosthesis (false teeth) that replaces the teeth in either the upper or lower jaw.
Bridge – a fixed appliance (prosthesis) that replaces missing teeth; a series of crowns (abutments and pontics).
Abutments – the teeth on either end of a bridge on which the bridge sits.
Pontic – the part of a bridge that replaces the missing tooth; the false teeth between the two abutments.
Implant – a post that is implanted in the bone; a crown, bridge, or denture then is attached to the implant.

An **oral maxillofacial surgeon** is a dentist who specializes in surgery to the mouth and facial bones. A patient may be referred for oral surgery by a general dentist for removal of an unusual growth of the mouth or tongue. A patient with **impacted wisdom teeth** (wisdom teeth that will not erupt through the gum) is referred for surgical removal of the **impacted** teeth. An orthodontist not uncommonly refers a patient for extraction of teeth before applying braces. Oral maxillofacial surgeons may work with orthodontists on patients with complex orthodontic and skeletal problems.

General dentists, periodontists, and oral surgeons usually place dental implants in the jaws surgically, although prosthodontists and endodonists now are receiving this training as well. Implant-supported restorations are placed by general dentists or prosthodontists.

Dental Hygienists

A dental hygienist usually completes 2 years of special training at a community college or university before becoming eligible to take state board examinations for licensure. (The student may earn an associate's or a bachelor's degree, depending on the length of the education program and the institution attended.) Dental hygienists are licensed to perform some of the same procedures that dentists perform; however, the majority of states do not allow the dental hygienist to establish an independent practice.

The hygienist must be under the direct or indirect supervision of a licensed dentist when performing treatments. The hygienist typically performs oral and dental exams, cleans teeth by removing **biofilm/plaque** and scraping off hardened **calculus/tartar**, polishes teeth, and applies fluoride and a **sealant** to the teeth. These terms are defined in the accompanying box.

prosthodontist a dentist who specializes in replacing missing teeth with a prosthetic device.

prosthesis a fixed or removable appliance to replace missing teeth; examples are bridges, dentures, and partials, and sometimes single crowns.

denture a removable prosthesis (false teeth) that replaces all of the teeth in either the upper or lower jaw.

bridge a fixed appliance (prosthesis) that replaces missing teeth; a series of crowns (abutments and pontics).

pontic the part of a bridge that replaces the missing tooth.

implant a post that is implanted in the bone; a crown, bridge, or denture then is attached to the implant.

oral maxillofacial surgeon a dentist who specializes in surgery to the mouth and facial bones.

impacted wisdom teeth third molars that will not erupt through the gum.

impacted an unerupted or partially erupted tooth that will not fully erupt because it is obstructed by another tooth, bone, or soft tissue.

biofilm an aggregate of microorganisms organized into a dynamic community that collects on the teeth and under the gums; also known as plaque.

plaque also known as biofilm, the sticky film on teeth made up predominantly of bacteria.

calculus/tartar plaque that has hardened.

sealant clear application
of acrylic placed over the
biting surface of the tooth
to prevent decay.

Plaque – (also known as biofilm) the sticky film on teeth made up predominantly of bacteria
Calculus – plaque/biofilm that has hardened, also known as tartar
Sealants – Formed from a plastic liquid applied to the chewing surfaces of the teeth, sealants
quickly harden and protect teeth from bacteria that cause tooth decay.

Depending on the state, the hygienist may inject anesthetic agents and make and interpret radiographs (X-ray films). The hygienist plays an important role in the prevention of dental disease and usually is responsible for educating the dental patient about hygiene and dietary habits that promote good oral health. Instructions provided to the dental patient include proper brushing and flossing techniques and recommendations for diet and lifestyle changes. In many dental practices, the hygienist is the professional who collects the patient's medical and dental history, records initial vital signs, and documents examination findings in the dental chart.

Mid-Level Providers

Mid-level providers are oral health care providers trained to perform certain clinical procedures, which allow the dentist more time to examine and diagnose patients and perform more complex procedures. These providers, known as dental health aide therapists (DHATs) in Alaska and Minnesota, may be able to address the dentist shortage in various parts of the United States. Although controversy surrounds the use of these providers, at the time of this writing, several other states are considering licensing this type of provider. One major issue to be addressed is the cost of doing business if mid-level providers work independently. They usually will have to work in a sponsored clinic to make it economically viable.

Dental Assistants

A dental assistant may receive formal training at a technical college or may be personally trained by a dentist. Many states do not license dental assistants, although there is a national certifying agency. The dental assistant's primary role is to assist the dentist in treating patients. The assistant anticipates what instruments will be needed, hands the instruments to the dentist, holds instruments in position in the patient's mouth, and prepares dental materials. The hands of the dental assistant act as the dentist's second pair of hands. The dental assistant also may help the dentist in charting dental exam findings and writing treatment notes. Most dental assistants have limited education and training, and most state laws limit the dental assistant to an assistive role rather than a treating role except for limited procedures.

SELF REVIEW 14.1

1. Distinguish between a solo dental practice and a group dental practice.
2. True or False? Today, all new dental facilities are likely to use electronic dental records and digital imaging.

3. Within a dental school, dental care can be provided by dental students under the supervision of faculty members who are _____.

4. Dental records generated in academic settings serve many purposes beyond the documentation of care provided. List two other purposes of the dental record.

5. Patients who are victims of trauma with injuries to the face or teeth or patients requiring general anesthesia for dental treatment may be cared for in what type of setting?

6. Apart from the acute care setting, name three other settings that provide dental care.

7. Children who are allowed to go to bed at night with a bottle filled with anything other than water may develop early childhood caries also knows as _____.

8. Give two examples of cosmetic dentistry.

9. Match the type of provider with the correct service he or she provides.

   a. Takes care of the dental health of all members of the family, providing periodic checkups and cleanings, and monitors condition of teeth and gums

   b. Specializes in treating the inside of the tooth, the nerve and pulp

   c. Specializes in treating the tissues surrounding and supporting the teeth

   d. Specializes in replacing missing teeth with a prosthetic device

   e. Specializes in straightening teeth

   f. Specializes in surgery to the mouth and facial bones

   _____ Periodontist

   _____ Oral maxillofacial surgeon

   _____ General dentist

   _____ Orthodontist

   _____ Endodontist

   _____ Prosthodontist

10. Distinguish between a dental hygienist and a dental assistant.

REGULATORY ISSUES

Professionals who provide dental care in the United States are regulated by the individual states. Each state is responsible for licensing dentists and dental hygienists who will practice in their state. Although there is no national licensure or credentialing for dental care providers, many states recognize the license of a dentist from another state through credentialing or reciprocity procedures. In recent years, testing agencies have been consolidating, and many states have agreed to accept the results of any licensing test as part of the licensing process.

State Licensure

Most states have a board of dentistry that issues licenses to practice. The applicant must provide evidence of adequate training and demonstrate treatment skills through licensing board examinations. In New York and some other states, a dental school graduate must complete a one-year residency *in lieu* of a licensing exam. The applicant's personal integrity, mental health, and moral behavior are all evaluated to determine whether the person can safely practice in the state.

Licensure is the primary means of protecting the public from incompetent dental practitioners. Dentists may have their licenses suspended or revoked for gross negligence, behavior that endangers a patient, sexual abuse of a patient, dispensing narcotics inappropriately, abusing drugs or alcohol themselves, or mental unfitness. Dentists also may be required to carry adequate malpractice insurance, to be current with their CPR certification, and take the requisite amount of continuing dental education to be licensed to practice.

Drug Enforcement Agency (DEA) Regulations

Dentists prescribe a variety of medications during their treatment of patients. They must adhere to federal and state regulations whenever a controlled substance is involved. A dentist may prescribe narcotic pain relievers, and the same laws that physicians must follow regulate dentists, too. A dentist must have a valid Drug Enforcement Agency (DEA, a division of the U.S. Department of Justice) number for patients to fill prescriptions for narcotics and other controlled substances at a pharmacy.

The DEA number may be revoked if a dentist violates DEA regulations in prescribing narcotics. Dentists now must also have a National Provider Identifier (NPI) number from the Federal government to be able to write prescriptions and to be reimbursed by many insurance companies. Many states also require a state prescription number.

Reporting of Adverse Effects of Medications and Dental Materials

Dentists use a variety of substances and materials in their treatment of patients and must report adverse or untoward effects of medications to the manufacturer, just as physicians and hospitals do. Dentists also are supposed to report patients' adverse reactions to dental materials used in restorations, including allergic reactions to metals and composite resin materials.

Other Reporting Requirements

Because many spousal batteries involve blows to the victim's face and teeth, loosened, broken teeth and facial fractures often are diagnosed and treated by dentists. Dentists are legally obligated to report suspected cases of abuse to law enforcement authorities, just as physicians and other health care providers are required to do. Dental records may be used as evidence of repeated trauma indicative of battery or abuse.

In some states, the clinician who first diagnoses a malignant neoplasm is required to report it to a state cancer registry. Dental practitioners routinely screen patients for oral cancer, and when dental professionals diagnose a malignant neoplasm, they may be responsible for reporting it.

SELF REVIEW 14.2

1. True or False? Each state is responsible for licensing dentists and dental hygienists who will practice in their state.
2. Dentists may have their licenses suspended for many reasons. List three.
3. What two things must a dentist have to prescribe medication?
4. True or False? Dentists are not subject to reporting adverse or untoward effects of medications to the manufacturers.

TREATMENT DOCUMENTATION

Over the past decade, many dental practices have shifted from analog/paper records to electronic dental records and digital radiographs. The typical dental record of a patient visiting a general dentist consists of patient demographic information, financial information (especially insurance coverage), medical and dental history, dental examination and charting, periodontal exam, dental radiographs, diagnoses, and treatment notes. Specialists record additional exam information, dental radiographs, and treatment notes. At a minimum, most practices use electronic scheduling, billing, and financial programs. Electronic filing of insurance claims usually speeds the reimbursement process considerably.

Patient Information

The first time that a person visits a dental practice, certain identifying information is collected routinely. It includes name, gender, date of birth, age, marital status, address, home and work phone numbers, and Social Security Number. The patient usually is given a form to complete to provide this information or may use an electronic kiosk with digital forms. The patient also is asked to provide the name and phone number of his or her personal physician, because the dentist may have to contact the patient's physician regarding proposed treatment, medication allergies, or medical conditions that affect the patient's dental care.

The patient information form typically includes a statement that the patient or parent is asked to sign authorizing and consenting to the dental exam and treatment. Additional information, such as employer, insurance carrier, and spouse's name, address, phone, and Social Security Number (SSN), usually is obtained to assist the dentist in collecting fees and insurance benefits to pay for care provided. The form also may include an assignment of benefits that allows the dentist to bill the insurance carrier and authorizes the carrier to send payment

FIGURE 14-3

Patient information screen in an electronic dental record.

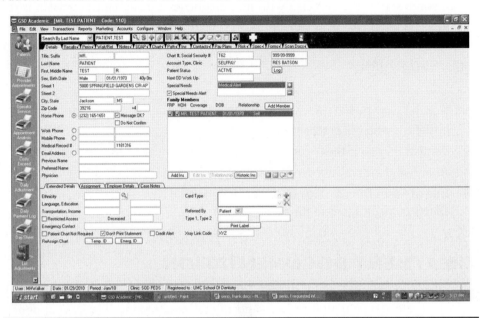

Courtesy of General Systems Design Group, Inc., Cedar Rapids, IA.

directly to the dentist. This information then is entered into the electronic dental record (Figure 14-3). In this day and age of identity theft, it is critical that the office take every possible precaution to safeguard protected health information (PHI), especially the patient's Social Security number.

Health and Dental History

A health history questionnaire usually is given to the patient to complete at the first visit, along with the personal information form. The questions usually are answered with a *yes* or *no* and cover a wide range of medical symptoms and diseases. *Yes* answers may require additional details. Many medical conditions relate to dental disease and treatment, so the dentist has to be provided with complete and accurate information before caring for a patient. Patients are asked to identify prescription and over-the-counter medications that they take regularly and the date of their last visit to a physician. The form also asks the patient about the use of recreational drugs, HIV (human immunodeficiency virus) status, and history of hepatitis. Allergies to drugs and substances must be identified.

Increasing numbers of health care workers and patients have developed a sensitivity to latex, the material used to manufacture disposable gloves. An estimated 12% of dental and health care workers are hypersensitive to latex (Safadi et al., 1996). Dental professionals must identify patients who are hypersensitive to latex so they do no wear latex gloves while treating these patients. Many practices and institutions are now latex-free.

FIGURE 14-4

A medical history in an electronic dental record.

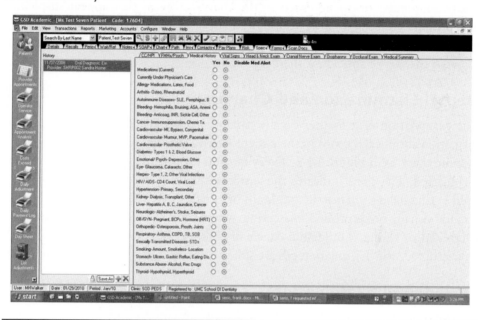

Courtesy of General Systems Design Group, Inc., Cedar Rapids, IA.

Figure 14-4 is an example of an electronic medical history. The medical record may have different formats depending on the needs of the practice and individual preferences.

The patient also completes a dental history, which usually is part of the health history form. The patient is asked about dental symptoms, previous dental treatments, and what prompted the visit to the dentist. The form also may contain questions about patients' dental routines at home, whether they are satisfied with the cosmetic look of their smile, and whether they are nervous or anxious about seeing the dentist.

The dentist or dental hygienist reviews the patient's health and dental histories with the patient. The professional asks further questions about items to which the patient answered *yes* to get a complete picture or clarification. Notes are made on the history form or elsewhere to document additional information provided in the interview.

Head, Neck, and Intraoral Examination

The first part of a routine dental exam consists of an evaluation of the patient's general health. The dental care professional may take and chart an adult's blood pressure and other vital signs and make a note of the patient's general appearance. Next, the head and neck are examined for any abnormal findings such as enlarged lymph nodes, bruises or cuts on the face, or abnormal-looking growths. Positive findings are noted in the chart.

The intraoral exam evaluates the appearance of the patient's mouth, lips, tongue, mucosa inside the cheek, tonsils, palate, and gums. Any abnormal or positive findings are documented in the chart. Growths that appear suspicious may prompt a referral to an oral surgeon. Patients with active cold sores and fever blisters (herpes simplex) should not receive treatment until the sores are healed, to avoid the risk of spreading the herpes infection.

Dental Examination and Charting

The examination next focuses on the patient's teeth. The dentist documents information about each tooth in the patient's chart. This commonly is done using a graphic chart, as in Figure 14-5. Every missing tooth and all existing restorations are charted. The chart indicates the surfaces involved, the size, and the material used in each filling, such as an **amalgam** or a **composite filling**. Each tooth is examined visually and is probed to ascertain whether decay is present or a restoration is cracked or failing. The dental charts of children note which permanent teeth have erupted, which primary teeth are still present, and the condition of the teeth.

amalgam   a silver-colored filling composed of several metals; usually placed on the back (posterior) teeth.

composite filling a tooth-colored filling.

Periodontal Examination

The periodontal exam evaluates the health of the gingiva and supporting tissue of the patient's teeth. The dentist or hygienist gently inserts a probe between the base of the tooth and the gingiva to measure the depth of pockets around

FIGURE 14-5

Example of a dental charting screen.

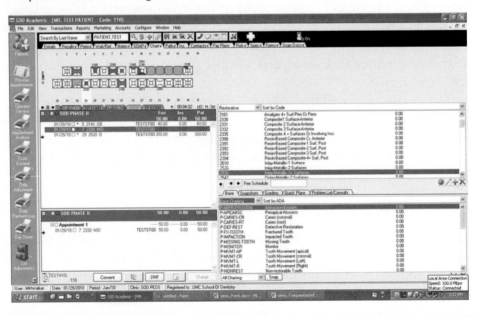

Courtesy of General Systems Design Group, Inc., Cedar Rapids, IA.

the tooth. Periodontal disease is manifested by deepening pockets around the tooth, receding of the gingiva, and loss of attachment of the tooth. Each tooth is probed at six locations—three on the front surface and three on the tongue surface. Adults typically have a probing depth of 2 to 3 millimeters in each area around the teeth, which is considered normal.

If the gums bleed when probed, this may be a sign of early gingivitis. A depth of 4 to 6 millimeters is worrisome, and a depth of 9 millimeters or more all-around means that the tooth has little remaining attachment and likely will be quite loose. Each probe measurement is recorded on a periodontal chart (Figure 14-6). The probing results are discussed with the patient, and the dental caregiver points out specific teeth that should be flossed and brushed more carefully. A general description of the amount of calculus (hardened plaque) present is noted in the chart. Patients who have regular cleanings and checkups at recommended 6-month intervals have a lot less calculus to be scraped off than do patients who have not seen a dentist in years.

Dental Radiography and Intraoral Photography

The dentist usually orders dental radiographs during the patient's first visit and at appropriate intervals thereafter. These may be full-mouth radiographs (multiple radiographs), a **panoramic radiograph** (all teeth shown on one film), or just **bitewing** radiographs (selected upper and lower teeth simultaneously).

panoramic radiograph a radiograph taken outside of the mouth that shows all the teeth on one film; this also may be a digital image.

bitewing a radiograph that shows the upper and lower teeth's biting surfaces on the same film.

FIGURE 14-6

Example of a periodontal chart.

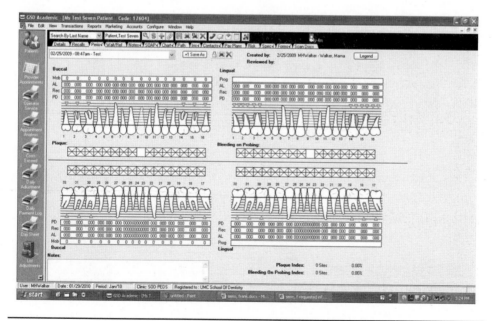

Courtesy of General Systems Design Group, Inc., Cedar Rapids, IA.

The radiographs become part of the patient's chart and usually are stored with the chart or electronically. Subsequent radiographs can be compared with previous radiographs to monitor the progress of decay or periodontal disease or identify when a defect first appeared. Radiographs help the dentist to confirm or discover the presence of dental disease.

Insurance companies may ask the dentist to submit radiographs to verify the necessity of or completion of dental treatment. (Figures 14-7 and 14-8 are examples of dental radiography images.) Abnormal lesions on the tongue or mucosa may be photographed using an intraoral camera. Computer imaging technologies allow dentists to digitize the image of teeth and gums with a tiny video camera on a dental instrument inside the patient's mouth and display the image on a computer screen for the patient to see. When the patient is shown the problem, he or she may be more willing to have the problem fixed.

Treatment Plan

prophylaxis the scaling, cleaning, and removal of calculus; a preventive treatment.

After the dental exam, periodontal exam, and radiographic exam, the dentist summarizes the diagnoses and outlines a properly sequenced treatment plan for the patient. The patient may just need **prophylaxis** (cleaning of teeth) and

FIGURE 14-7

Full mouth series of radiographs.

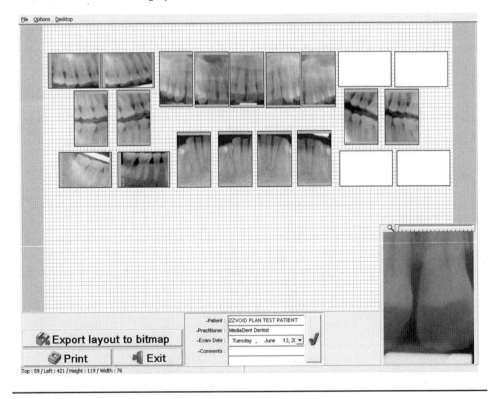

Courtesy of Multi Media Dental Systems, Atlanta, GA.

FIGURE 14-8

X-rays using digital imaging software.

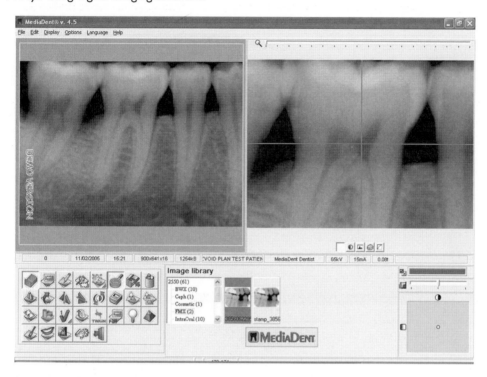

Courtesy of Multi Media Dental Systems, Atlanta, GA.

application of fluoride to prevent decay. Any decay, periodontal disease, or pathology that is found should be treated as soon as possible to minimize damage to the teeth. The dentist tells the patient what should be done, and the patient is encouraged to make a return appointment. Unfortunately, not all patients are willing to have the work done, and some never return to receive the recommended treatment. Others may get minor restorations but refuse to have an expensive root canal or crown until an unbearable toothache develops.

Treatment Notes

All dental treatment is documented in the patient's dental chart. The dentist notes the type of anesthetic agent used, the type of nerve block and injection approach, the diagnosis or location of decay on the tooth, and the type of material used to restore the tooth after removing the decay. This information is needed for future dental care. The dentist may find that certain anesthetic agents do not numb the patient's tooth fast enough, long enough, or sufficiently. If so, the dentist makes a note to choose a different agent for this patient at the next visit. Details about the restorative materials and techniques are essential to track premature failures of restorations.

FIGURE 14-9

An example of treatment or progress notes.

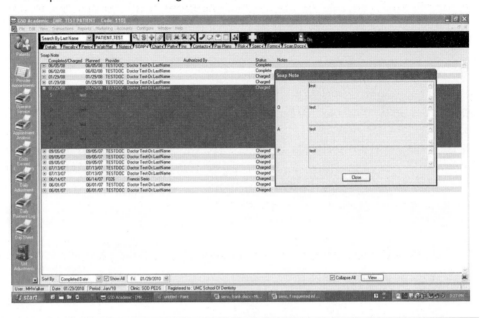

Courtesy of General Systems Design Group, Inc., Cedar Rapids, IA.

Legally, the dentist must keep complete treatment notes. If the dentist is called into any legal proceedings, the information in the chart may be critical to the dentist's defense. In a legal context, if something is not written down, it is assumed not to have happened. The surreptitious alteration of documents after the fact is illegal. Electronic dental records have safeguards against altering records after the fact. Electronic treatment notes are date- and time-stamped and locked once they are saved or the person has logged out of the program. Figure 14-9 provides an example of electronic treatment notes.

Patient Education

Dentistry has made great strides in preventing dental caries and periodontal disease—accomplished through education, the use of fluoride, changes in diet, and an improvement in personal oral hygiene. Most people now know that to maintain healthy teeth, they need to brush and floss their teeth daily to disrupt bacterial deposits (now known as biofilms), cut down on consumption of sugary sweets, and use toothpaste and drinking water that contain fluoride.

Another aspect of patient education emphasizes the importance of periodic dental checkups and prophylaxis. Most dentists send patients a postcard or an electronic message reminding them that it is time to come in for a checkup. These notices are helpful both to the patient and to the financial viability of the dental practice. Electronic and phone messages must be suitably vague so as not to violate HIPAA by leaving PHI on a device that could be accessed by someone other than the patient. Thanks to patient education, the current generation of children has a lower prevalence of tooth decay and a higher probability of keeping their teeth for life. As Americans become more health conscious and take better care of their teeth, dentures may become a thing of the past.

Diet Evaluation

Some dental practices perform an evaluation of the patient's dietary habits because poor nutrition can contribute to dental disease. Adequate calcium is particularly important for the calcification of tooth enamel and maintenance of alveolar bone. Children, teenagers, and pregnant and menopausal women are most at risk for softening of the enamel and tooth decay caused by calcium deficiency. If a dietary evaluation is done, it is documented in the patient's chart along with recommendations provided to the patient.

SELF REVIEW 14.3

1. The typical dental record of a patient visiting a general dentist consists of _____.

2. When would it be necessary for the dentist to contact the patient's primary care physician?

3. What form is given to the patient to complete at the first visit, to include information on medical conditions, prescriptions, recreational drug use, and allergies?

4. The _____ exam evaluates the appearance of the patient's mouth, lips, tongue, mucosa inside the cheek, tonsils, palate, and gums.

5. The _____ exam evaluates the health of the gingiva and supporting tissue of the patient's teeth.

6. Match each term with its correct description:

   a. full-mouth radiographs

   b. bitewing radiographs

   c. panoramic radiographs

   _____ all teeth shown on one film

   _____ multiple radiographs

   _____ selected upper and lower teeth simultaneously

REIMBURSEMENT

In contrast to medical care, dental patients often pay for all or a substantial part of their own dental care, but many have dental benefits through their employers. The most common form of third-party plan is traditional dental insurance. Under this form of reimbursement, the patient is covered for a percentage of the fee, based on the agreement negotiated between the employer and the third-party insurance carrier. The patient is responsible for any deductible and that part of the dentist's fee that is not covered by the insurance plan. Employers, patients, and dentists also may participate in managed care plans, capitation plans, preferred provider organizations (PPOs), and health maintenance organizations (HMOs). Under these arrangements, the dentist agrees to provide certain services for a set rate of reimbursement from the plan. The patient is responsible for the full fee for any necessary or elective services that are not specifically covered by the plan.

Dental Insurance

American employers have become more conscious of the dental needs of their employees, and many now offer dental insurance in their benefit packages. About half of the U.S. population has private dental insurance coverage (U.S. Government Accountability Office, 2013). Sometimes dental insurance is optional and the employee must pay a small premium for coverage. Sometimes it is totally free for the employee, with a small premium for the employee's spouse and family.

A typical indemnity-type dental insurance policy covers checkups and preventive dentistry at 100%; filling-type restorations and extractions at 80%; and crowns, bridges, and other prosthetics at 50% of the plan's fee schedule for these services. Orthodontic treatment may be covered at 50% to a lifetime maximum of $1,000. Some policies require the patient to pay a deductible on non-preventive treatment each year before any treatment is covered, and most have a $1,000 to $2,000 limit of benefits per year.

Dentists typically appreciate treating patients who have dental insurance. Collection of fees is simpler and easier for the patient, and many times the dentist can confirm insurance coverage and get the treatment plan approved before initiation of treatment. Dental insurance policies pay the percentages listed based on usual and customary fees for the geographic area or zip code. Often, the amount the insurance company says it will pay for a given treatment is lower than what the dentist charges. Either the patient must pay the difference or the dentist forgives it. Dental insurance payments are processed promptly if they are submitted correctly with all of the supporting documentation, such as charting, radiographs, and treatment notes.

Dentists participating in a PPO agree to charge the patient only the amount allowed by the insurance company. Dentists agree to the reduced reimbursement because the plan also provides benefits for the dental practice. For example, the number of patients may increase because insured patients have incentives to receive care from a participating dentist. There may be discounts for PPO members on the cost of making crowns, bridges, and dentures from a central dental lab. Government plans such as Medicaid and CHIP (Children's Health Insurance Plan) cover dental care at a set reimbursement rate for children. Children's coverage under these programs includes restoration of teeth and maintenance of dental health.

Medicaid coverage for dental care for adults tends to be minimal and varies from state to state. One thing to remember is that fee discounts usually affect the practice profitability because fixed costs cannot be changed and variable costs usually cannot be reduced by the same percentage as the fee discount.

Self-Pay Patients

A significant number of patients still must pay cash directly for their dental check-ups and treatments. Dental insurance rarely is available to retired people, and Medicare does not cover dental care for elderly people. Working poor, unemployed, disabled, and elderly people have a difficult time paying for dental care. Most self-pay dental patients are those who recognize the importance of good dental health and can afford it or are willing to sacrifice to receive it.

HMO Plans

HMO dental plans vary in what is covered, amount of the patient copayment, and availability. Typically, dental HMO plans are a less expensive form of coverage, but, as a general rule, only dental services from providers in the HMO network are covered. The dentist/patient ratio of the HMO plan can affect the patient's ease of access to services.

Centers for Medicare & Medicaid Services

Medicare does not include benefits for dental care for elderly people. This segment of the population, with years of wear on the teeth or with no teeth left, is in great need of dental care to improve the quality of life. The cost to taxpayers of adding dental coverage for the elderly, however, likely would be prohibitive.

Medicaid and the Children's Health Insurance Program (CHIP) offer some dental benefits for children. Medicaid covers preventive checkups and necessary restorations for children, but the number of dentists accepting Medicaid patients is limited. Medicaid coverage for adult recipients is an optional benefit by federal regulations, so many state Medicaid programs do not provide more than emergency coverage for adult dental care because of the expense.

Even though Medicaid is a federal program, it is administered by each state independently with some state contribution to the coverage. Therefore, Medicaid coverage for adults varies widely from state to state. Medicaid and SCHIP coverage for children is generally more uniform. The Affordable Care Act (ACA) has made pediatric dental insurance mandatory in many health plans. The issue is that for the lesser (bronze level) plans, the deductible is so high that unless there is a medical catastrophe, the plan effectively will not pay any pediatric dental benefit because the high deductible has not been met.

TRICARE Dental Program

The TRICARE Dental Program (TDP) provides dental benefits for families of active-duty military personnel (Department of Defense, 2014). TDP coverage is generally good and is as acceptable to dentists as dental insurance. TRICARE replaced the Civilian Health and Medical Program of the Uniformed Services (CHAMPUS), which used to be the source of dental coverage for families of military personnel.

Veterans Affairs

Dental care is available to qualifying veterans at Department of Veterans Affairs medical centers. The patients pay little or no fees for treatment if it is obtained at the VA facility. There is no billing involved, but the facility must keep track of utilization in order to staff and budget adequately for the VA dental clinic. More recently, productivity goals have been established for individual clinics. Veterans with private dental insurance policies usually obtain dental care through private dental practices rather than at a VA dental clinic.

SELF REVIEW 14.4

1. Distinguish between traditional dental insurance and PPOs and HMOs.
2. About _____ percent of the U.S. population has private dental insurance coverage.
3. True or False? Dentists participating in a PPO agree to charge the patient only the amount allowed by the insurance company.
4. What government plans cover dental care at a set reimbursement rate for children?
5. Patients who pay cash directly for their dental checkups and treatments are termed _____ patients.
6. True or False? Medicare includes benefits for dental care for the elderly.
7. What program provides dental benefits for families of active-duty military personnel?

INFORMATION MANAGEMENT

Information is crucial to the practice of dentistry, including information about individual patients, dental equipment and supplies, vendors, dental coverages of each insurance company, new medications and anesthetic agents, new treatment modalities, the epidemiology of dental disease, financial information about the practice, withholding and employment taxes, and more.

Treatment Coding and Classification

Three main coding systems are used in dentistry, listing descriptive terms and numeric codes for reporting services and procedures:

> The Current Procedural Terminology (*CPT*)
>
> The Health Care Common Procedural Coding System (*HCPCS*) and
>
> The Current Dental Terminology (*CDT*)

CDT codes are revised and published each year by the American Dental Association (ADA, 2015). The *CDT* coding system typically is used to file dental insurance claims for patients. It also is used by dental schools and dental hygiene training clinics to collect statistical information. Table 14-1 provides a list of sample ADA codes.

TABLE 14-1	Common ADA Codes
Code	**Description**
D0140	Limited oral evaluation
D0150	Comprehensive oral evaluation
D0210	Intraoral full mouth X-rays
D1110	Prophylaxis—adult, age 14 and over
D1208	Topical application of fluoride

Source: Excerpted from *Delta Dental Utilization Review Guidelines* 2014 online at https://www.deltadentalrionline .com/Public/PDF/URGuidelines.pdf

Hospitals occasionally bill a third-party payer for dental procedures. For example, although Medicare does not provide dental coverage, it will pay for dental services that are an integral part of a covered procedure (e.g., reconstruction of the jaw following accidental injury). Medicare also will pay for extractions done in preparation for radiation treatment of neoplastic jaw lesions. Diagnosis codes from the current clinical modification of the *International Classification of Diseases* are used by hospitals and medical centers for dental patients who are treated as inpatients, hospital outpatients, or emergency department patients. *ICD* dental procedure codes are used for inpatients.

Codes from the Health Care Common Procedural Coding System are used by the hospital to code dental procedures for hospital outpatients and emergency department patients or by dentists for procedures for which dental codes do not exist. Although most hospitals do not bill dental insurance on a regular basis, they follow the reporting and coding requirements of the dental insurance company when this occurs.

A dentist in private practice performing a procedure covered under a dental plan in a hospital setting would submit his or her claim to the dental insurance company using *CDT* or other codes as appropriate and required by the payer. Again, dental coding and medical coding techniques are not compatible with each other, and requirements of the third-party payer for the given type of provider and setting must be followed.

Electronic Information Systems in Dentistry

Computers originally were used in dentistry primarily for practice management applications, which typically include accounting, patient billing, insurance claim tracking, appointment scheduling, payroll, and patient recall notices. In recent years, computers have been used increasingly for clinical applications as well. The American Dental Association (ADA) has done a side-by-side comparison of 40 practice management software packages, although there are many more on the market. The ADA website is a good resource for comparing dental software.

Practice Management Software

A computer software package to manage a dental practice may include the following modules.

Patient Registration   One of the primary functions of the software is to collect patients' demographic information, including address, contact numbers, e-mail address, date of birth, insurance information, and possibly a digital photograph for the dental record.

Appointment Scheduling   The scheduling software should be flexible and fit the way the dental practice operates. It should provide for multiple dentists, multiple chairs, and double booking of patients if implemented in a group practice. The time slots must be variable according to individual practice patterns. One dentist may want to routinely allow an hour for a crown preparation, and another may want an hour and a half. Despite the routine time allowed for a procedure, special patients or more complicated procedures may require more than the normal amount of time. The software must allow a standard allotment of time or a custom allotment of time for scheduling appointments. (See Figure 14-10.)

FIGURE 14-10

Individual provider or multiple schedules displayed simultaneously.

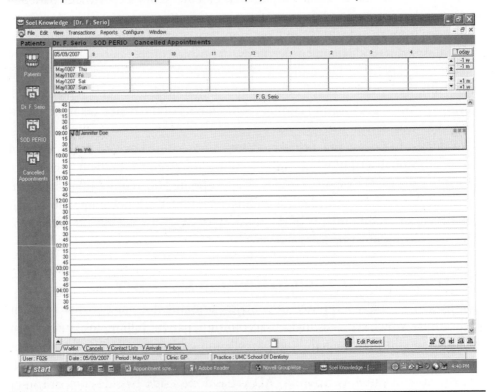

Courtesy of General Systems Design Group, Inc., Cedar Rapids, IA.

The software must provide easy and flexible query capabilities. The receptionist may have to answer questions such as: What day is Jane Doe scheduled to come in? What is the next available one-hour slot for Dr. Brown? Which patient can be called to reschedule a later appointment so another patient with an emergency can be seen? Who is next to be scheduled on the waiting list?

Insurance Billing and Claims Tracking   Insurance patients sometimes comprise a large portion of a dentist's practice. The cash flow of the practice will suffer severely if the process of billing and tracking claims is inefficient. The insurance claims module should be integrated with the patient accounts module and may be set up for electronic claims submission to third-party payers, thereby reducing paperwork, providing for greater accuracy, and permitting more rapid settlement of electronic claims. The software should be able to identify patients who have received treatment but for whom claims have not yet been submitted, patients who have preauthorization for treatment, claims that have not been paid 30 days after submission, and accounts that have received only partial payment from the insurance company.

Another essential function for dental practices serving large numbers of insurance patients is the ability to confirm benefit amounts and patient copayment amounts or deductibles. Most dentists prefer to collect copayment and deductible amounts at the time of service rather than to bill the patient after receiving partial payment from the insurance company. If the software identifies this amount at the time of checkout, the patient can be asked to pay the amount at that time.

Patient Accounting Information   Although dentists would like to have all patients pay when treatment is rendered, it is not realistic to believe that this always will happen. Patient accounts software should keep track of total charges for the day, total charges for the family, amount paid and when, remaining balance, remaining deductible, and age of balance, as well as the financially responsible party. The software should be able to print regular monthly billing statements for accounts with outstanding balances, as well as an individual statement on demand, and allow insertion of a special message to some or all recipients.

Software should follow accepted accounting principles and provide for closing the month, quarter, and fiscal year. Many dentists contract with an accountant to prepare tax returns and provide financial statements for the business. Accounting software must provide acceptable output and verification of financial matters for the dentist's accountant. Some dentists charge interest on outstanding balances but may request that a special account be exempt from interest charges. The software should be able to charge a specified interest rate on some accounts and none on others.

Preferably, patient accounts are integrated with scheduling and patient recall. The system then can alert the receptionist when an appointment is being scheduled for a patient who has an unpaid balance from a previous visit. The system also can send a recall notice to a patient with an outstanding balance, with a message that the account has to be brought up to date before scheduling another appointment.

Patient Recall Reminders   Periodic checkups and teeth cleanings are necessary for dental health. Dentists recognize that it is their professional responsibility to encourage patients to have this routine care and send reminders when it is time to be seen again. It also is essential to the financial viability of the dental practice to see patients regularly. Practice management software should be able to identify patients who should receive a recall notice and patients who failed to respond to a previous recall notice. The software should be able to print envelopes and perform a mail merge to personalize the recall notices that the patients receive. The system should keep track of when patient recalls are due and when they are sent. Some software programs can send recall notices as e-mail or text messages.

Patient Referral   Dentists, particularly specialists, like to know who is referring patients to their practice for care. Software should keep track of who referred each patient, prepare statistical reports based on the referring source and payment source, and compile a list of all patients referred by a specific dentist. The dentist may foster a social relationship with professionals who frequently refer patients. Referral letters also can be generated to send to the general dentist.

Practice Reporting   Reporting is an integral function of practice management software for monitoring and effectively managing the business. Administrative and clinical reports providing data about patient account status, provider productivity, appointment utilization, and treatment plan procedures (completed or in progress) can be invaluable tools for running a successful dental practice.

Inventory Management   Some software includes the functionality to monitor inventory items, including supplies and equipment. This can make reordering more timely and efficient. The software application may even provide an interface for online ordering.

Electronic Dental Record

The electronic dental record is now commonly used in dental practices. Some software packages for the dental practice store the complete dental record, including digital radiographs and clinical images, and others are more limited in functionality. The comprehensive electronic dental record stores health and dental histories and the results of dental and periodontal examinations; diagnoses, treatment plans, lab and medication prescriptions; provides alerts about medical conditions, allergies, and the need for antibiotic premedication; facilitates comparison between previous exams and current exams to aid in monitoring progression of disease; and manages treatment notes. The electronic record should interface seamlessly with digital radiography and imaging software, which provides compact and safe storage of dental radiographs and allows the dentist to share radiographs with a specialist or an insurance company via the Internet.

Computers in dental practice can be enhanced through alternate methods of input such as voice recognition, as well as touch-screen and pen-based computing. These features may facilitate ease of use by the dentist, hygienist, or dental assistant. Voice recognition is a particularly promising feature, because it allows hands-free data entry. This type of input also could be useful in controlling the spread of infection in the dental office by removing the pen and paper, display, or keyboard as potential vectors for bacteria and viruses. If these methods are not used, screens and keyboards may be covered with plastic wrap to minimize cross-contamination and allow for easier disinfection.

Computer Hardware and Networking

Most dental offices now have multiple computers. There may be a computer at each patient chair, in the radiology area, in private offices, as well as in the reception and business areas. Determining the layout and specifications of computers depends heavily on the practice management software being used and its specific requirements. Networking the computers allows them to communicate with one another, to share practice management and clinical software, to store and back up data in a single central location, and to share hardware resources such as printers, intraoral cameras, or digital signature pads.

Other Technological Devices

Digital cameras are extremely popular in the dental practice for making photographs for the dental record to help identify the patient or to show before-and-after treatment photos. Intraoral cameras capture images that can be helpful to educate the patient about treatment needs or to show progression of ongoing treatment. **Digital imaging** devices provide an alternative to traditional film X-rays. Digital radiographs can be integrated directly into the patient record and decrease the amount of radiation to which patients are exposed.

digital imaging the use of computer-based technologies to make radiographic (X-ray) and other clinical images to diagnose dental diseases and conditions.

Application Service Providers (ASPs)

For dental professionals who do not wish to maintain an office network, or to handle hardware and software upgrades, or to be responsible for daily backups of data, an alternative may be to enlist the services of an application service provider (ASP). The dentist can contract with an ASP who, through an Internet connection, provides the practice management software in a hosted environment. The ASP can store data for the practice, maintain network server equipment, upgrade software applications, and perform daily data backups. An unreliable or slow internet connection, however, could be extremely detrimental to the well-being of the dental practice.

1. List the three main coding systems used in dentistry for reporting services and procedures.
2. Which coding system is used to file dental insurance claims for patients?
3. Which disease classification system is used by hospitals and medical centers for dental patients who are treated as inpatients, hospital outpatients, or emergency room patients?
4. A computer software package to manage a dental practice is known as _____.
5. List and briefly describe the modules included in practice management software.
6. Dental professionals who do not wish to maintain an office network may contract with a(an) _____, to provide the practice management software via an Internet connection.

QUALITY IMPROVEMENT AND UTILIZATION MANAGEMENT

In small dental practices, a formal quality improvement program or plan is not the focus. A wise dentist, however, will continuously try to improve the quality of the service provided. The Dental Society of the State of New York developed a peer-review program for quality assurance that stands as a model for other dental societies across the country (Benton & Shub, 1995). The American Dental Association (ADA, 2009) also promotes and supports peer-review programs for state dental associations.

Clinical dental practice guidelines are well developed. For example, one model clinical guideline for general dentists for managing patients with adult periodontitis provides recommendations on the content of the medical, dental, social, and habit history; exam, diagnosis, and treatment documentation; and treatment guidelines (Workshop, 1994). Organizations that have published practice guidelines and/or parameters of care for dentistry are as follows:

- American Academy of Pediatric Dentistry
- American Academy of Periodontology
- American Association of Endodontists
- American Association of Oral and Maxillofacial Surgeons
- American Association of Orthodontists
- American College of Prosthodontists
- American Dental Association

To assist dental professionals with clinical decision making, the American Dental Association also provides a database of studies on dental topics, clinical recommendations, and resources at its Center for Evidence-Based Dentistry website: http://ebd.ada.org.

Large dental practices, particularly those associated with managed dental care, HMOs, institutional care such as the VA, and dental service organizations are more interested in formally measuring quality and using quality indicators. Some suggested quality indicators for managed dental care are as follows:

- How long does it take to get an appointment for a routine checkup and cleaning?
- How long does it take to get an appointment for a new dental symptom?
- How many child and adolescent patients have sealants applied?
- How many third molar extractions are performed?
- How many enrollees received prophylaxis and checkups during the year?
- How many referrals were made to dental specialists?

Utilization of dental services is generally managed by dental insurance plans and HMOs providing dental benefits. The approaches to limiting expenses include the exclusion of benefits for preexisting dental conditions, requiring pretreatment authorization, and actively evaluating the necessity for treatment. Dentists may be required to submit copies of dental records and radiographs to justify the need for treatment. Patients' self-manage utilization if large copayments and deductibles are instituted. Most dental plans, however, recognize the importance of preventive care in controlling costs, so they cover semiannual checkups and cleanings.

Some plans impose an annual limit to benefits, exclude coverage for cosmetic dental procedures, and require the dentist to use the least expensive restorative method—for example, limiting the use of expensive gold crowns to molars only. Many dental plans do not cover treatment for temporomandibular joint (TMJ) syndrome, cosmetic orthodontics, and dental implants.

Recently, some large insurers have started looking at systemic health outcomes and dental care. There is an inverse relationship between the cost of caring for diabetic patients and their frequency of dental visits. Some plans now have enhanced benefits for periodontal care for diabetic patients, paying for more frequent recalls and deep cleanings (scaling and root planing) than in the past. Savings on medical costs may range in the thousands of dollars for patients with better oral health.

SELF REVIEW 14.6

1. _____ developed a peer review program for quality assurance that stands as a model for other dental societies across the United States.
2. List three organizations that have published practice guidelines and/or parameters of care for dentistry.

3. _____ provides a database of studies on dental topics, clinical recommendations, and resources at its Center for Evidence-Based Dentistry website.

4. List three treatments not covered by many dental plans.

RISK MANAGEMENT AND LEGAL ISSUES

Injuries to Caregivers and Patients

An important area of risk management involves injury to patients and practitioners. Potential for injury includes instrument traumas from needles, drills, and probes. Proper use of a "rubber dam," which isolates the operative field to the tooth undergoing treatment, can help prevent injury to the mouth and tongue. Other area of risk are burns from sterilization equipment and skin injuries from grinders. Proper training of personnel and consistent use of safety measures are essential to prevent injuries.

There is the potential for the patient or practitioner to incur a foreign body or debris in the eye, which can be prevented if the patient and dental practitioner both wear safety goggles during dental treatment. Another potential risk is for the dental patient to accidentally swallow a foreign body during treatment. Because of the natural gag reflex, a patient can easily swallow a cotton roll, bite block, or small object that the dentist drops accidentally. A rubber dam can be helpful in preventing this accident.

Occupational hazards in dentistry include musculoskeletal injuries to the neck and back from long hours of leaning over dental chairs. Repetitive motion injuries such as carpal tunnel syndrome and ulnar nerve compression also are common. To control risk, educating personnel about these issues is vital. All dental personnel also should protect themselves from contaminants by using standard barrier precautions, including safety glasses, a mask, disposable gloves, and possibly a full-length gown.

Malpractice and Negligence

It is universal practice for practitioners to routinely use disposable gloves and face masks while treating all patients. Practitioners should be particularly careful when they have open lesions on their fingers and hands, as cuts and abrasions can be a source of bacteria transfer from patients to providers. Patients are at low risk for acquiring hepatitis, HIV, and other infections at the dental office, but infections acquired through dental treatment can be the result of negligent and improper procedures in the office.

Another source of potential problems is an inappropriate or inadequate diagnosis or treatment of a patient's dental disease. For example, failure to treat early pulpitis can progress to dental abscess. Or a patient can lose a permanent tooth because the dentist failed to diagnose or adequately treat a tooth early enough to save the tooth.

As in the medical field, adequate documentation is the best defense against malpractice and negligence suits. Dentists must document post-treatment instructions provided to patients, the procedures performed, reactions to medications, and complaints of tooth pain and sensitivity. Dentists also must know the limits of their expertise. Failing to refer a patient to a specialist for complicated conditions can result in malpractice.

Adverse Reactions to Medications and Dental Materials

Dentists should report dangerous and unusual medication reactions to the pharmaceutical company just as physicians do. It is particularly important to document any reactions in the patient's dental record, to avoid using the same agent again with that patient in the future. The various materials used in dentistry become a permanent part of a person's mouth. Therefore, adverse reactions to metal and other substances have to be carefully evaluated and reported.

Dental Records for Identification of Individuals

Dental records are useful in the identification of an individual, either dead or alive. Coroners and medical examiners typically use dental records to identify decedents. In mass disasters, such as airplane crashes and fires, dental records may be the only way to confirm the identity of a body. Occasionally, dental records are useful in discovering the identity of a living patient who is unable to identify himself or herself because of some impairment.

SELF REVIEW 14.7

1. Name the precautions that all dental personnel should take to protect themselves, as well as their patients, by using standard barrier precautions.
2. What is the best defense against malpractice and negligence lawsuits?
3. True or False? Coroner and medical examiners typically use dental records to identify decedents.

ROLE OF THE HEALTH INFORMATION MANAGEMENT PROFESSIONAL

Health information management (HIM) professionals have a unique set of skills that can greatly benefit dental practitioners. Principles of documentation, confidentiality, and good information management are all relevant to the practice of dentistry. The growth of managed care and capitation requires education and planning for the financial survival of dental practitioners. HIM professionals have many opportunities to share their skills with the dental profession.

With the continual advancement of technology, many dental practices are assessing their needs as they relate to information technology (IT) and IT infrastructures. What dental software package is the most appropriate for the practice? What other applications might be useful? How do the systems integrate for best business practices? What are the hardware requirements? Is a computer network necessary? If so, how should it be set up? How is electronic insurance filing done? How secure are the data? Many other questions may arise as technology is integrated into the dental practice. The HIM professional can be an invaluable consultant in these areas.

As more Americans receive dental care through managed care plans and insurance, there is a need for individuals with expertise in electronic billing, revenue cycle, and utilization review. The HIM professional who can manipulate and analyze electronic data may be invaluable in helping dental practices with business decisions such as estimating a capitation amount for a managed care plan or determining whether it would be advantageous to join a preferred provider organization. Expertise in quality improvement may be valuable for the compilation of quality indicators and the evaluation of patient satisfaction.

Opportunities for HIM careers also present themselves at dental clinics associated with academic institutions. The information management tasks are much like those of a large ambulatory care clinic. Statistics must be collected and reported on patients seen in the clinic and the procedures that each dental student has performed.

HIM professionals also can be involved in the design, selection, and implementation of dental information systems, particularly as health care becomes more integrated. The goal of an electronic patient record with a comprehensive, lifetime history of each patient is a relatively new idea for dentistry, and the dental profession may need help in understanding the technologies and approaches to integrating data.

As dental records and systems become integrated with existing medical records and systems, the development of data dictionaries and combined master patient indexes are becoming major issues. Also, as development of the national health information network moves forward, health information managers' knowledge of health information exchange and privacy and security regulations can be an asset to dental care providers who desire to participate in this endeavor.

Irrespective of the practice location or type, the HIM professional can play a key role in regulatory compliance. As part of the Affordable Care Act, the rules governing the security of PHI under the Health Insurance Portability and Accountability Act (HIPAA) have been tightened. The rules are complicated, especially when PHI must be shared by various parties: practices, insurance companies, regulators, referring offices, and others. Penalties may be significant for privacy breaches. The HIM professional possesses knowledge of privacy and security regulations and can help dental providers maintain compliant practices in this area.

SELF REVIEW 14.8

1. Principles of _____, _____, and _____ are all relevant to the practice of dentistry.

2. True or False? With the advancement of technology, many dental practices are assessing their needs as related to information technology (IT) and IT infrastructure.

3. Name two areas within the dental setting where the HIM professional can be an invaluable consultant.

TRENDS

Dental Services

The face of dentistry is changing in the twenty-first century. The dentist-to-population ratio is declining after having peaked in 1998. Because there are fewer dentists in an increasing general population, and as older individuals continue to keep more of their natural teeth, the demand for dental services likely will remain strong for the foreseeable future. Many of these services will be elective in nature as more people ask for aesthetic dental procedures to improve their appearance. The demand for implant dentistry also will continue to increase as people want stability for their prostheses and are in a position to afford this type of care.

Dentists considered a contract with a third-party payer, should weigh the financial benefits and risks. For example, in a preferred provider organization (PPO), dentists provide services at a discount to members of the PPO. Because a PPO is a fee-for-service arrangement, the dentist is paid for each covered service rendered, but at a reduced rate. In contracting with dental health plans, the dentist must determine whether the payments provided by the contract will be sufficient. Regardless of the type of arrangement, health plans should be carefully scrutinized as to the financial viability of the dental benefits offered before dental practitioners join.

Dental Treatment

Dentistry is among the few health professions that have successfully discovered how to prevent disease and decrease its financial impact on society. The public has been well educated about the value of fluoridated water and toothpaste, the need to brush and floss regularly, and the value of frequent teeth cleaning and removing calculus. The number of children and teens with dental caries has decreased greatly, and the number of elderly people who still have their own teeth is increasing. The need for dentures is on the decline.

New restorative materials, medications, and treatment procedures are being used. New methods of treating periodontal disease—the major cause of tooth loss—are being discovered. The use of dental implants to support restorations replacing missing teeth is continuing to increase. Until individuals take greater responsibility for maintaining their oral health, however, the need for dental services will not diminish.

As the American lifestyle becomes more active, dental injuries are increasing. Most dental emergencies are the result of trauma, frequently involving the maxillary anterior teeth. Sports dentistry is a relatively new practice specialty, and the treatment of dental traumas continues to show great progress. As examples, teeth that have been knocked out can be reimplanted; and fractured teeth can be splinted and restored rather than extracted.

Dental implants have found their rightful place in mainstream dentistry. Cosmetic dentistry is popular, although the demand fluctuates with the health of the overall economy. Methods of treating discoloration of teeth from smoking and coffee are popular. In addition, the number of adults undergoing orthodontic treatment has increased.

Alternative methods to reduce anxiety in dental patients include biofeedback, hypnosis, acupuncture, and other techniques. Painless dentistry enhances the willingness to go to the dentist, and thus increases the dental health of Americans.

Another more recent development in the practice of dentistry is the sale of oral devices. An antisnore device can be obtained from a dentist, which may be the solution to sleepless nights because of a loud, snoring partner. A splint called a nightguard, worn in the mouth at night to prevent bruxing or grinding of teeth, offers relief to many who have temporomandibular joint (TMJ) syndrome. Dentists even have become involved in making mouthguards for sports. Although outside the realm of traditional dentistry, devices for the mouth available through dentists can improve the quality of life.

Technology in Dentistry

As noted above, a significant trend is the increase in electronic information systems in dental practices. Virtually all new practices have electronic dental records, digital financial packages, and digital imaging. Electronic billing and benefit confirmation can contribute to a healthy cash flow. Efficient and convenient handling of appointment scheduling and recall notices provides great financial benefits. Technologies such as digital radiography, intraoral imaging, computer modeling of prostheses, and displaying after-treatment appearance further stimulate the interest in integrating new technologies into dental practice.

Dental Informatics

Dental informatics refers to the application of computer and information sciences to improve dental practice, research, education, and management. The field of dental informatics is growing as dentists are beginning to realize the value of expert systems, automated clinical alerts and warnings, and digital information for clinical practice. Systems have been developed for digital imaging, digital radiology, digital charting, computer-assisted design and manufacture of dental restorations, and diagnostic aids. Dentists must keep up with these emerging technologies to be able to make informed decisions in their clinical practice.

Bioinformatics is another emerging interdisciplinary field of science, incorporating the principles of biology and computer science. Bioinformatics involves collecting, storing, retrieving, and analyzing large amounts of biological data from a variety of data sources. Oral pathology is one dental field that has benefitted significantly from the evolution of bioinformatics with advancements in diagnosis and treatment of diseases.

1. _____ is the application of computer and information sciences to improve dental practice, research, education, and management.

2. _____ involves collecting, storing, retrieving, and analyzing large amounts of biological data from a variety of data sources.

3. In a/n _____, dentists provide services at a discount to members. This is a fee-for-service arrangement.

4. List the technologies that are stimulating interest in integrating new technologies into dental practice.

SUMMARY

Although dental care is not a traditional setting of practice for health information management, increasing opportunities exist and future careers are possible in this area. The knowledge and skills of a health information manager can be applied to the management of dental records. The electronic health record is comprehensive and includes dental records. HIM professionals have the knowledge and skills to help dentists make the transition from paper to electronic records. As progress continues, information managers will need to understand both medical and dental records to manage integrated health information systems.

Growth in managed dental care plans, dental service organizations, and other large practice management configurations will demand better information systems for dentists to manage their dental practices, as well as knowledgeable individuals to manage the revenue cycle of the practice, thereby providing opportunities for consulting and careers in managing dental information. Treatment and technological advances make dentistry an exciting and interesting field. The dental health care setting has great career potential.

REVIEW QUESTIONS

Knowledge-Based Questions

1. What are the roles of the dentist, the dental hygienist, and the dental assistant?
2. What are the typical percentages covered by dental insurance for various types of services?
3. What are the potential risks of injury to dentists or their employees?
4. List several important functional components of a dental practice management system.
5. Define the following terms: plaque, calculus, sealants.

Critical Thinking Questions

1. Why does the dentist need to have a complete and accurate medical history for a patient?

2. Compare the frequency and purpose of patient visits to an orthodontist with those for an endodontist. What effect do these differences have on the management and content of dental records?
3. Computerization of which functions of a dental practice will have the most impact on the dentist's finances?
4. How could a dentist evaluate the quality of care that he or she provides?
5. In general, how can the use of electronic systems in dentistry improve the quality of dental care?

WEB ACTIVITY

Visit the American Dental Association's (ADA) website at http://www.ada.org.

1. Select "Public Programs."
2. Then select "MouthHealthy."

3. Choose a topic, and write a brief report on the topic you selected and how this information might help the public or promote understanding of the profession of dentistry.

CASE STUDY

Valley Dental Group is composed of three general practice dentists in the suburb of a large city. The group has a receptionist and an office manager. Most of the group's patients are from families with dental insurance. The benefits and coverages of the insurance policies are different. Some require preauthorization of all restorations, and others require only preauthorization for crowns, bridges, and dentures. Some policies have a family deductible for all dental care, whereas others have individual deductibles for non-preventive care only. The usual and customary prices that the insurance companies allow for procedures are different, so the amount the patient must pay depends on the insurance policy.

The practice has to organize the way the office handles the information flow to process insurance billing and track payments. Some of the tasks to be performed are as follows:

- Verify the patient's insurance company and policy number.
- Keep track of deductible paid so far for family and/or family members.
- Submit insurance claim for services rendered.
- Determine the amount the patient's insurance policy will pay for the procedure.

- Collect the patient's copayment and deductible before the patient leaves the office.
- Follow up on insurance claims submitted that have not been paid.
- Handle claim rejections and bill the patient for the amount not covered.
- Collect statistics on the number of procedures done, the number of self-payments and insurance payments, the amount paid by insurance, and the number of claims rejected.
- Collect statistics that measure the productivity of each dentist in the group.

Design a system to accomplish these tasks. Each student could be assigned a function to design a solution as a class project, or students could be assigned one or more parts to do individually. Avoid duplication of effort and the storing of redundant data in your design. Write a report detailing a design that includes the following:

1. What information must be collected?
2. What procedures are to be used to accomplish the tasks?

REFERENCES AND SUGGESTED READINGS

ADA (American Dental Association). (2009). *Peer Review & Quality Assessment*. [Online]. http://www.ada .org/prof/prac/tools/peer_review.asp [2010, February 21].

ADA (American Dental Association). (2013). *A Profession in Transition: Key Forces reshaping the Dental Landscape*. [Online] http://www.ada.org/~/media /ADA/Member%20Center/FIles/Escan2013 _ADA_Full.ashx [2014, May 12].

ADA (American Dental Association). (2015). *CDT: Code on Dental Procedures and Nomenclature*. [Online]. http://www.ada.org/en/publications/cdt/ [2015, October 19].

Benton, R. M., & Shub, J. L. (1995). Peer review. It's good for dentists and patients [CD-ROM]. *New York State Dental Journal, 61*(6), 28–29. [Abstract from SilverPlatter File: MedLine Item 95349891].

CDC (Centers for Disease Control and Prevention). (2007, April). *Trends in Oral Health Status: 1988–1994 and 1999–2004*. Washington, DC: U.S. Department of Health and Human Services. [DHHS Publication Number (PHS) 2007-1698].

CDC (Centers for Disease Control and Prevention). (2013). *Untreated Dental Caries (cavities) in Children Ages 2–19, United States*. [Online]. http://www.cdc

.gov/Features/dsUntreatedCavitiesKids [2014, May 13].

Department of Defense. (2014, June 16). *TRICARE Handbook.* [Online]. http://www.tricare.osd.mil /TricareHandbook/default.cfm [2003, July 25].

DHHS (Department of Health and Human Services). (2009). *Developing Healthy People 2020.* [Online]. http://www.healthypeople.gov/ [2010, February 12].

Eke, P. I., Dye, B.A., Wei, L., Thornton-Evans, G.O, Genco R.J. Beck, J., Douglass, G, & Page, R. (2012). Prevalence of periodontitis in adults in the United States: 2009 and 2010. *J Dent Res., Oct., 91*(10):914-920 [Epub 2012 Aug. 30].

Kaste, L. M., & Gift, H. C. (1995). Inappropriate infant bottle feeding. Status of the healthy people 2000 objective [CD-ROM]. *Archives of Pediatric and Adolescent Medicine, 149*(7), 786–791. [Abstract from SilverPlatter File: MedLine Item 95316126].

Kiyak, H. A., Grayston, M. N., & Crinean, C. L. (1993). Oral health problems and needs of nursing home residents [CD-ROM]. *Community Dentistry and Oral Epidemiology, 21*(1), 49–52. [Abstract from SilverPlatter File: MedLine Item 93161712].

Kopycka-Kedzierawski, D.T., Bell, C.H., & Billings, R.J. (2008). Prevalence of dental caries in early Head Start children as diagnosed using teledentistry. *Pediatr Dent.; 30*:329–333.

Loesche, W. J., Abrams, J., Terpenning, M. S., & Bretz, W. A. (1995). Dental findings of geriatric populations with diverse medical backgrounds [CD-ROM]. *Oral Surgery, Oral Medicine, Oral Pathology, Oral Radiology, and Endodontics, 80*(1), 43–54. [Abstract from SilverPlatter File: MedLine Item 96012668].

Logan, H. L., Baron, R. S., Kanellis, M., Brennan, M., & Brunsman, B. A. (1996). Knowledge of male and female midwestern college students about baby bottle tooth decay [CD-ROM]. *Pediatric Dentistry, 18*(3), 219–223. [Abstract from SilverPlatter File: MedLine Item 96379379].

National Center for Chronic Disease Prevention & Health Promotion. (2009). Behavioral Risk Factor Surveillance System (BRFSS). [Online] http:// apps.nccd.cdc.gov/BRFSS/ [2010, September 5].

NIDCR (National Institute of Dental and Craniofacial Research). (2014). *Dental Caries Tooth Decay in Adults (age 20–64).* [Online]. http://www.nidcr.nih.gov /DataStatistics/FindDataByTopic/DentalCaries /DentalCariesAdults20to64.htm [2015, May 13].

Plutzer, K., & Keirse, M.J.N.C. (2011). Incidence and prevention of early childhood caries in one- and two-parent families. *Child: Care, Health and Development, 37*:5–10.

Safadi, G. S., Safadi, T. J., Terezhalmy, G. T., & Taylor, J. S. (1996). Latex hypersensitivity: Its prevalence among dental professionals [CD-ROM]. *Journal of the American Dental Association, 127*(1), 83–88. [Abstract from SilverPlatter File: MedLine Item 96166172].

U.S. Government Accountability Office. (2013, September 6). *Dental Services: Information on Coverage, Payments, and Fee Variation,* GAO-13-754: Publicly Released: September 12, 2013. [Online]. http://www.gao.gov/products/GAO-13-754 [2015, October 19].

Workshop on Quality Assurance in Dentistry. (1994). Model clinical guidelines for primary dental health care providers for managing patients with adult periodontitis. *Journal of Dental Education, 58*(8), 659–662.

KEY RESOURCES

American Dental Association
http://www.ada.org

American Dental Hygienists Association
http://www.adha.org

Academy of General Dentistry
http://www.agd.org

Center for Evidence-Based Dentistry
http://ebd.ada.org

CHAPTER 15

Veterinary Settings

Valerie Ball, RHIA, CHIT-IS | Margaret L. Neterer, MM, RHIA

LEARNING OBJECTIVES

Upon successful completion of this chapter, you should be able to:

- Name the types of veterinary patients and health care providers for this profession.
- List at least five similarities between veterinary and human health records.
- Explain why SNOMED CT® is preferred over *SNVDO* as a veterinary nomenclature, and describe its importance to human and animal welfare in the twenty-first century.
- Explain the necessity of maintaining records for groups of animals rather than individual animals in specific veterinary care settings.
- Illustrate the similarities between veterinary medicine and human medicine professionals.
- Describe the client's rights in information ownership, and be able to identify the client in a given situation.
- Identify key organizations that provide the most current information relating to the practice of veterinary health information management.

Setting	Description	Synonyms/ Examples
Veterinary Medical Center	A facility in which consultative, clinical, and hospital services are rendered and in which a large staff of basic and applied veterinary scientists perform significant research and conduct advanced professional educational programs.	Veterinary Teaching Hospital Animal Medical Center Animal Hospital
Veterinary Hospital	A facility in which the practice conducted includes the confinement as well as the treatment of patients.	
Veterinary Clinic	A facility in which the practice conducted is essentially on an outpatient basis.	
Veterinary Office	A facility where a limited or consultative practice is conducted that provides no facilities for the housing of patients.	
Veterinary Mobile Facility	A practice conducted from a vehicle with special medical or surgical facilities or from a vehicle suitable only for making house or farm calls. Regardless of mode of transportation, such practice has a permanent base of operations with a published address and telephone facilities for making appointments or responding to emergency situations.	
Veterinary Emergency Facility	A veterinary medical service whose primary function is the receiving, treatment, and monitoring of emergency patients during its specified hours of operation. A doctor is in attendance at all hours of operation, and sufficient staff is always available to provide timely and appropriate care. Doctors, support staff, instrumentation, medications, and supplies must be sufficient to provide an appropriate level of emergency care. This service may be an independent after-hours service, an independent 24-hour service, or part of a full-service hospital or large teaching institution.	
Veterinary On-Call Emergency Service	A veterinary medical service whose doctors and staff are not on premises during all hours of operation or whose doctors leave after a patient is treated.	

INTRODUCTION TO SETTING

The **veterinary** profession is practiced in a variety of care settings. The information presented in this chapter centers on the veterinary teaching hospital within a college or university of veterinary medicine, in which health information technology offers the most probable employment setting.

> **veterinary** of, relating to, or being the science and art of prevention, cure, or alleviation of disease and injury in animals, especially domestic animals.

Types of Patients

The term "patient" in this chapter refers to an **animal**. The animal's owner is the hospital's client. According to James F. Wilson, DVM, JD, "Animals are usually classified according to species and distinguished as either domestic or wild. Problems occur with this simple classification because certain species or individual animals do not fall neatly into either category. Others fit into both categories based on their use" (Wilson et al., 1988). For our purposes, this discussion distinguishes between domestic animals, including pets, and wild animals.

> **animal** any animal other than humans, including fowl, birds, fish, and reptiles, wild or domestic, living or dead.

The domestic animals most commonly treated in a veterinary teaching hospital include small animals such as **canine** (dog), **feline** (cat), and other small animals such as birds, parrots, snakes, lizards, hamsters, and ferrets. Small exotic animals also are referred to as "pocket pets." "Large" animals or "food" animals

> **canine** dog.
>
> **feline** cat.

typically are seen in the veterinary teaching hospital, or on a farm visit. These animals include: **bovine** (cow), **ovine** (sheep), **porcine** (swine), and **caprine** (goat). **Equine** (horse) patients are considered to be "large animals," whereas llamas, bears, big carnivore cats (e.g., tigers, lions) and ratites (e.g., ostriches, emus, and rheas) are considered to be large exotic animals.

Other wild animals that sometimes are cared for in the veterinary teaching hospital setting include owls, eagles, hawks, songbirds such as sparrows and cardinals, deer, moose, and bears. These animals usually are cared for under the direction of the staff zoological veterinarian. Wolves or wolf-hybrid dogs generally are not treated in the veterinary teaching hospital, because they are unpredictable and could seriously injure a health care provider, the client, or other patients in the health care facility.

Types of Caregivers and Staff

Veterinary health care providers in the twenty-first century not only provide diagnostic, therapeutic, and rehabilitative services for animals of various species and uses, but also are engaged in protecting human health through their roles in environmental protection, food safety, and public health (AVMA, 2011).

The **veterinarian** has a professional degree (DVM/VMD-4yr) from a college of veterinary medicine. Women now comprise nearly 68% of veterinarians in the 30-to-39 age group. In the group under age 30, more than 75% are female (Towner, 2009).

The **American Veterinary Medical Association (AVMA)** has accredited 33 veterinary schools in the United States and Canada and 9 in foreign countries. A list of schools, along with each school's contact information, accreditation status, and website link is available through the AVMA at www.avma.org.

Similar to medical doctors (MDs) and doctors of osteopathic medicine (DOs), doctors of veterinary medicine (DVMs)—or veterinary medical doctors (VMDs)—may choose to pursue advanced training and take examinations in specialty boards. These include anesthesiology, critical care, dentistry, epidemiology, oncology, toxicology, laboratory animal medicine, **theriogenology** (animal reproduction), and many more. The most up-to-date information on the recognized veterinary specialty organizations is available through the AVMA (Veterinary Specialty Organizations, 2010).

"A **veterinary technician** (or **animal health technician**) is a graduate of a two- or three-year AVMA-accredited program in veterinary technology. In most cases the graduate is granted an associate degree or certificate" (AVMA, n.d.). A graduate of an AVMA-accredited four-year baccalaureate program in veterinary technology is known as a **veterinary technologist**. The veterinary technician or technologist performs under the direction, supervision, and responsibility of the veterinarian and is not allowed to diagnose, prescribe, or perform surgery unless permitted by state regulations. Information about individual programs is available through the American Veterinary Medical Association website at www.avma.org.

---

bovine   cow or ox.

ovine   sheep.

porcine   swine.

caprine   goat.

equine   horse.

veterinarian   a professional who is qualified and authorized to treat disease and injuries of animals.

American Veterinary Medical Association (AVMA)   has an objective to advance the science and art of veterinary medicine, including its relationship to public health, biological science, and agriculture; provides a forum for discussing issues of importance to the veterinary profession and for developing official positions. The association is the authorized voice for the profession in presenting its views to government, academia, agriculture, pet owners, the media, and other concerned publics (AVMA Constitution, Article II).

theriogenology   the study of animal reproduction.

veterinary technician   a member of the veterinary health care team who is knowledgeable in the care and handling of animals, in the basic principles of normal and abnormal life processes, and in routine laboratory and clinical procedures. The technician is primarily an assistant to veterinarians, biological research workers, and other scientists. A veterinary technician is a graduate of a 2- or 3-year AVMA-accredited program in veterinary science that generally awards an associate degree or certificate.

animal health technician   See **veterinary technician.**

The veterinary practice manager is responsible for the veterinary facility's business management, including human resource and financial management, marketing, legal aspects insurance, and compliance with ethical standards. Formal education in areas such as psychology, accounting, marketing, and business management is recommended. The practice manager is eligible for certification as a **certified veterinary practice manager (CVPM)** through the **Veterinary Hospital Managers Association (VHMA)**.

veterinary technologist a graduate of a 4-year AVMA-accredited program in veterinary technology or a person so recognized by the board in rules and regulations promulgated to regulate veterinary technologists.

SELF REVIEW 15.1

1. What types of animals are treated most commonly in a veterinary teaching hospital?
2. What is the difference between equine patients and large exotic animals?
3. Under what conditions are wild animals cared for in the veterinary teaching hospital, and what risks may be involved?
4. What is the difference between a veterinary technician and a veterinary technologist?
5. What are the responsibilities of the veterinary practice manager?

REGULATORY ISSUES

In many ways, the practice of health information management in the veterinary setting is less stressful than in human medicine settings, which have to address multiple layers of government and third-party regulations. The obvious lack of detailed regulations often makes it easier to practice health information management because the HIM professional is freer to apply creative trends from human medicine that will work best for health care delivery for patients and procedures in the veterinary practice. Stricter rules, however, have the advantage of forcing compliance with good veterinary practice in situations in which a few veterinarians may be reluctant to relearn procedures or to expend money to make necessary advancements.

The practice of veterinary medicine is governed by individual state veterinary practice acts. The AVMA has established a model veterinary practice act, found at www.avma.org.

The purpose of a **model act** is to serve as a recommended pattern for state laws. This AVMA model act provides definitions related to the practice of veterinary medicine (e.g., "animal," "licensed veterinarian"). It also outlines licensing requirements and exceptions; establishes state boards of veterinary medicine; and outlines the processes of license application for the practice of veterinary medicine, license renewal, discipline of licensees, and appeal.

The veterinary practice act may fall under one of a variety of state codes (examples: Public Health Code [Michigan], Business and Professions Code [California], and Education Laws [New York]). A link to each state's veterinary medical association, practice act, board of veterinary medicine, and various rules affecting the veterinarian and his or her practice can be found at

certified veterinary practice manager (CVPM) an individual who, with at least 3 years of experience as a practice manager within the past 7 years, at least 18 acceptable college or university credit hours pertinent to management, evidence of 48 hours of continuing education specifically devoted to management, and appropriate references, who may apply to the Veterinary Hospital Manager's Association (VHMA) to take the written and oral examinations which, if successfully passed, designate the individual as a CVPM.

Veterinary Hospital Managers Association (VHMA) provides individuals who are actively involved in veterinary practice management with a means of education, certification, and networking; membership is composed of animal hospital administrators, practice managers, office managers, veterinarians, and consultants.

model act recommended legislation drafted by a national organization with the intent of promoting uniformity among state laws; state legislatures may or may not approve a model act in its entirety, or at all.

http://www.avma.org along with the name, address, and phone number of the state's board of veterinary medicine or executive officer of the board.

The AVMA establishes guidelines and policy statements for the practice of veterinary medicine through its executive board or House of Delegates. These guidelines are printed annually in the *AVMA Membership Directory and Resource Manual* and are available at http://www.avma.org.

The AVMA's **Council on Education (COE)** is the accrediting body for programs of study in veterinary medicine. An accreditation review is conducted every 7 years for colleges of veterinary medicine. More frequent review is required should a college be placed on probationary accreditation.

Purpose of Accreditation

The objective of the AVMA, through the Council on Education, is to ensure that each veterinary medical college meets the minimum standards, and that each graduate of an accredited college of veterinary medicine will be prepared for entry-level positions in the practice of veterinary medicine, and a variety of career activities including clinical patient care, research, and other nonclinical options relevant to animal and human health. These fundamentals should be the basis for a lifetime of learning and professional development (AVMA, March 2014).

Reference to the importance of medical record keeping is found in Standard 9.4, Clinical Resource: "Medical records must be comprehensive and maintained in an effective retrieval system to efficiently support the teaching, research, and service programs of the college" (AVMA, 2009).

The HIM Service/Department may provide the statistics necessary to document the number of patients available to the students in a typical year; to show that there are enough patients to provide quality clinical instruction. The survey forms request data on the **number of accessions** (the total number of times all patients were treated by the facility in a given time period), which include statistics on patient visits, hospitalizations, and field services. The required survey forms can be accessed at www.avma.org.

The data collected in these surveys correspond with data collected by the Association of American Veterinary Medical Colleges (AAVMC) that are used, along with other statistical data, in describing all aspects of academic veterinary medicine. The AAVMC also manages the Veterinary Medical College Application Service (VMCAS), which collects, processes, and distributes applications for admission to veterinary medical colleges.

Voluntary accreditation for companion animal hospitals is offered through the **American Animal Hospital Association (AAHA)**. The AAHA, established in 1933, develops and circulates standards for traditional, general accreditation, as well as for referral facility accreditation.

AAHA is the only organization that accredits veterinary practices throughout North America. Practices that accept the challenge of accreditation are evaluated on stringent quality standards that encompass all aspects of pet care—ranging from patient care and pain management to team training and medical record keeping.

Council on Education (COE) the American Veterinary Medical Association's accrediting body for programs of study in veterinary medicine.

number of accessions the total number of times that all patients were treated by the facility in a given time period; one patient may have multiple accessions.

American Animal Hospital Association (AAHA) promulgates standards for companion animal hospitals.

The AAHA Standards of Accreditation are updated continuously to keep accredited practices at the forefront of veterinary medicine and advanced business practices.

Approximately 15% of veterinary practices in North America hold the "AAHA-accredited" designation. Accreditation through AAHA helps veterinary practices operate at a high level and enhances their ability to provide excellent patient care.

SELF REVIEW 15.2

1. What are some advantages to a lack of detailed regulation within the veterinary setting?

2. The _____ provides definitions related to the practice of veterinary medicine (e.g., "animal," "licensed veterinarian"); also outlines licensing requirements and exceptions; establishes state boards of veterinary medicine; and outlines the processes of license application for the practice of veterinary medicine, license renewal, discipline of licensees, and appeal.

3. True or False? The Veterinary Practice Act falls under federal government regulation codes.

4. True or False? According to the AVMA Council on Education (COE), the fundamentals with which each graduate of an accredited college of veterinary medicine are expected to achieve provide only a basis for a variety of career activities, including clinical patient care, research, and other nonclinical options relevant to animal health.

5. What department is responsible for providing the statistics necessary to document the number of patients available to the students in a typical year, to show that there are enough patients to provide quality clinical instruction?

DOCUMENTATION

The current elements of documentation will seem familiar to the traditional HIM professional. These include the following:

1. Owner (client) identification: name, address, telephone numbers for home and office at a minimum; additional information may include names, addresses, and telephone numbers for alternative or co-owners of the animal.

2. Animal (patient) identification: name, identification number if applicable (i.e., tattoo or identification chip), species, breed, date of birth, sex, color, and/or markings.

3. Vaccination history of the patient.

4. Chief complaint: observations reported by the client.

5. Medical history.

6. Physical examination, including the current weight of the animal.

7. Problem list.

8. Diagnostic reports (e.g., laboratory, diagnostic imaging, etc.).

9. Patient-identifiable source data, including photographs, video recordings, audio recordings, diagnostic films, and electrocardiogram tracings.

10. Consultation reports, including those of telephone consultations.

11. Prognosis.

12. Progress notes recording medical and surgical events, in chronological order; and documentation of communications with the client, including waiver or deferral of recommended care.

13. Surgical and dental records, including the consent form signed by the client.

14. Written discharge summary and instructions.

15. Necropsy reports, when applicable. (A **necropsy** is a postmortem examination that may be conducted to determine the cause of death or the character and extent of changes produced by the disease.)

16. Financial records.

necropsy   a postmortem examination for determining the cause of death or the character and extent of changes produced by disease.

Standards

The American Animal Hospital Association (AAHA) medical record service standards have much in common with accreditation standards for health information in human health care. For example, they address:

- Legibility
- Use of standard abbreviations
- Authentication of entries
- Documentation of communications between the health care providers and the client
- Security and confidentiality of paper and electronic records
- Use of standardized medical nomenclature for diagnosis and problem lists
- A recognized mechanism for standardized transmission and analysis of data

During the evaluation visit, the surveyor will ask for random medical records to be pulled, as well as targeted specialty case records for review. At the conclusion of the evaluation visit, the consultant will determine whether the practice has successfully passed each section of the accreditation standards, including the mandatory standards. The recommendation is sent to the Membership Audit and Control Committee of AAHA for approval. The initial approval is for 2 years, with subsequent evaluations every 3 years.

Revisions to the standards from August 2013 have resulted in an increase in the passing point percentage of the medical records section from 68% to 78%. Standards for the Electronic Medical Record were incorporated in August 2011.

The AVMA has produced several policy statements and guidelines that support the maintenance of veterinary health records. Those referenced below can be found in the current issue of the *AVMA Membership Directory and Resource Manual,* as well as in the "Guidelines for Veterinary Prescription Drugs," initially approved in 1998 by the AVMA House of Delegates and updated regularly. These guidelines are as follows (AMVA, 2010):

Adequate treatment records must be maintained by the veterinarian for at least two years (or as otherwise mandated by law), for all animals treated, to show that the drugs were supplied to clients with whom a VCPR [veterinarian-client-patient relationship] has existed....

Basic Information for Records (R) Prescriptions (P), and Labels (L)

- Name, address, and telephone number of veterinarians (RPL)
- Name (L), address, and telephone number of clients (RP)
- Identification of animal(s) treated, species and numbers of animals treated, when possible (RPL)
- Date of treatment, prescribing, or dispensing of drug (RPL)
- Name, active ingredient, and quantity of the drug (or drug preparation) to be prescribed or dispensed (RPL)
- Drug strength (if more than one strength available) (RPL)
- Dosage and duration
- Route of administration (RPL)
- Number of refills (RPL)
- Cautionary statements, as needed (RPL)
- Expiration date if applicable
- Slaughter withdrawal and/or milk withholding times, if applicable (RPL)
- Signature or equivalent (P)

Format

The **problem-oriented medical record (POMR)** format or a combination of POMR and source-oriented format (SOMR) is most commonly used in the veterinary teaching hospital. The source-oriented health record is more common in nonteaching hospitals.

A variation of the family-oriented format is also quite common for **herd health** (sometimes referred to as **production medicine** or ambulatory/field service care) programs in teaching and nonteaching facilities. For instance, rather than generate a separate record on each of the one hundred cows examined or treated at Mr. MacDonald's farm on a given day, the "MacDonald Farm" record would be maintained through the use of specialized forms or electronic formats that enable the health care provider to document treatments on a large number of animals at one time. Figure 15-1 displays a sample format for this "family" record for production medicine (PM) and equine (EQ) patients.

Forms of Documentation

The sophistication of record-keeping formats varies from paperless to handwritten 5-by-7-inch cards.

problem-oriented medical record (POMR) a structured approach to patient care developed by Dr. Lawrence Weed in the late 1950s, which has four major parts: database, problem list, initial plan, and progress notes/discharge summary.

herd health veterinary care provided to a group of animals at their residence rather than in a hospital setting.

production medicine the study and care of food animals that produce milk, meat, eggs, and so forth.

SELF REVIEW 15.3

1. True or False? The current documentation elements contain both the owner and the animal identification.

2. True or False? A necropsy report is not mandatory upon the death of the patient (animal).

3. What are seven documentation issues addressed by the American Animal Hospital Association (AAHA) accreditation standards?

4. After approval by the Membership Audit and Control Committee, what is the length of AAHA accreditation?

5. True or False? Adequate treatment records must be maintained by the veterinarian for at least 2 years (or as otherwise mandated by law), for all animals treated, to show that the drugs were supplied to clients with whom a VCPR (veterinarian-client-patient relationship) has existed.

6. What is the family-oriented format commonly used for herd health?

FIGURE 15-1

Sample format for equine and production medicine records.

MICHIGAN STATE
U N I V E R S I T Y
MSU Veterinary Teaching Hospital
Production Medicine
East Lansing, Michigan 48824-1314
Appointments: (517) 355-3500   Billing: (517) 353-4957

№   05287

WHITE-CLIENT
YELLOW-MED. REC.
PINK-BUS. OFF.

CLIENT _____

_____

CLINICIAN _____
DATE _____
REGFERRING _____
VETERINARIAN _____

TRIP FEE
___ 32011 CHUTE FEE   ___
___ 32110 REFERRAL   ___
___ 32109 REGULAR   ___

EMERGENCY FEE
___ 32211 6 A.M.-8P.M.   ___
___ 32212 8P.M.-6 A.M.   ___

EXAMINATION
___ 35219 A
___ 35220 B   ___
___ 32020 PROF. SERV.   ___
___ _____   ___
___ _____   ___
___ _____   ___

TECHNIQUES

___ 32002 EPIDURAL   ___

___ 32107 TREATMENT   ___
___ _____   ___
___ _____   ___
___ _____   ___

REGULATORY
___ 32317 ANAPLASMOSIS   ___
___ 32319 BOVINE BTV
___ 32321 BRUC. TEST-BOV ___
___ 32044 CALFHOOD VAC   ___
___ 32047 HEALTH PAPERS   ___
___ 35065 PRV   ___
___ 35064 PRV + BRUC.   ___
___ 32048 SEROLOGY FORMS ___
___ 32049 TB INJ.   ___
___ 32050 TB READ   ___
___ _____   ___

SURGERY
___ 32058 CASLICKS
___ 32331 CASTRATE BOV (A)
___ 32332 CASTRATE BOV (B)
___ 32064 CASTRATE PROCINE
___ 32329 DEHORN BOVINE A
___ 32330 DEHORN BOVINE B
___ 35501 DEHORN ELEC C
___ 32031 LAMENESS-BOV. FOOT
___ 32035 LAME-WOOD BLOCK
___ 32075 LDA ROLL
___ 32074 LDA SURGERY
___ 32076 LDA TOGGLE
___ 32082 PROCINE HERNIA
___ 32307 TEAT
___ _____
___ _____
___ _____
___ _____

REPRODUCTION/OBSTETRICS
___ 32087 BSE-BULL
___ 35252 BSE-BULL PROGRAM
___ 32302 OB 15 MIN.
___ 32303 OB 30 MIN.
___ 32304 OB 45 MIN.
___ 32305 OB 60 MIN.
___ 35502 PELVIC MEASURE
___ 35214 RP
___ 32097 RECTALS-BOVINE
___ 32101 ULTRASOUND-BOV.
___ 32300 UTERINE INF.
___ 32105 VAGINAL EXAM-FA
___ _____
___ _____

CONSULTATION
___ 32310   0.5 HRS   ___
___ 32311   1.0 HRS   ___
___ 32311   1.5 HRS   ___
___ 32318 FIELD INVESTIGATION
___ 32320 EQUIPMENT   ___

PHARMACY/SUPPLIES
___ 24083 BANAMINE/ML   ___
___ 24063 ASPIRIN 240GM   ___
___ 25303 BROWN GAUZE   ___
___ 24149 CAL GLUCONATE   ___
___ 24145 CAL MPK   ___
___ 25001 CATTLEMASTER-4-L5(5)
___ 24220 CYSTORELIN   ___
___ 24262 DEXYTROSE 50%   ___
___ 24469 LA-200 ML   ___
___ 24518 LUTALYSE 10ML/ML ___
___ 24519 LUTALYSE 30ML/ML ___
___ 24571 NAXCEL 1GM   ___
___ 24572 NAXCEL 4GM   ___
___ 24509 OTC 100MG/ML/ML   ___
___ 24620 OXYTOCIN 20U/ML/ML ___
___ 24629 PANMYCIN BOLUS/E ___
___ 24638 PEN G 100ML/ML   ___
___ 25047 SOMUBAC 10 DS/VL ___
___ 26666 TRIANGLE 9   ___
___ 35070 SIMPLEX   ___
___ 35221 MAGNET   ___
___ 24943 VENOSET IV SET   ___
___ 25163 VETRAP ROLL   ___
___ 35300 MISC. SUPPLIES   ___
___ _____   ___
___ _____   ___
___ _____   ___

OTHER SERVICES
___ 32010 BANDAGING   ___
___ 32030 LABS.-NON. CLINIC ___
___ 32051 SAMPLES HANDLING ___
___ 32052 SAMPLES SHIPPING ___
___ _____   ___
___ _____   ___

SUBTOTAL   ___
TEACHING DISCOUNT ___

TOTAL   ___
NUMBER OF STUDENTS ___
SPECIES_____ NO_____ TREATED
_____ CONSULTED

COMMENTS _____
_____
_____
_____
_____

O-21781

FIGURE 15-1 *(continued)*

EQ 05080

MSU Veterinary Teaching Hospital
Equine Field Service
East Lansing, Michigan 48824-1314
Appointments: (517) 355-3500   Billing: (517) 353-4957

WHITE-CLIENT
YELLOW-MED. REC.
PINK-BUS. OFF.

CLIENT _____
CLINICIAN _____
DATE _____

TRIP FEE
__ 32208 EMERG. FEE 8AM-5PM   ____
__ 32210 EMERG. FEE 5PM-8AM   ____
__ 32109 REGULAR   ____
__ 32111 STABLE   ____

ANESTHESIA
__ 24004 ACEPROMZINE ML   ____
__ 32006 ADMIN. LOCAL   ____
__ 32007 ADMIN. NERVE BLOCK   ____
__ 34160 CARBOCAINE HCL/ML   ____
__ 25571 DORMOSEDAN ML   ____
__ 24735 ROMPUN 100MG/ML   ____
__ 24814 STADOL 2MG/ML   ____
__ 24913 TORBUGESIC ML   ____
__ 24944 VETALAR ML   ____
__ _____   ____

PHARMACY/SUPPLIES
__ 25305 ADAPTIC DRESSING   ____
__ 25441 AKTROL OPTH.   ____
__ 24048 ANTHELCIDE   ____
__ 24071 ATROPINE OINT   ____
__ 24074 AZIUM ML   ____
__ 24081 BANAMINE PASTE   ____
__ 24080 BANAMINE PK.   ____
__ 24083 BANAMINE INJ./ML   ____
__ 24094 BENZA-PEN INJ./ML   ____
__ 24097 BET. SCRUB OZ   ____
__ 25303 BROWN GAUZE   ____
__ 24141 BUTE 1GM. TAB   ____
__ 24138 BUTE INJ ML   ____
__ 25476 BUTE 4GM PASTE   ____
__ 24184 CHLORO OPTH   ____
__ 25174 COTTON SHEET   ____
__ 25667 DMSO SWEAT   ____
__ 24312 ELASTIKON 3" ROLL   ____
__ 24326 EQVALAN   ____
__ 24322 EQUIMATE VL   ____
__ 24383 GENT 100MG/ML   ____
__ 24379 GENT. OPTH.   ____

SURGERY
__ 32014 DENT. FLOAT   ____
__ 32016 DENT. WOLF TOOTH   ____
__ 32059 CASLICKS   ____
__ 32342 CASTRATION (B)   ____
__ 32077 LACERATION (A)   ____
__ 32202 LACERATION (B)   ____
__ 32203 LACERATION (C)   ____
__ 32204 LACERATION (D)   ____
__ _____   ____
__ _____   ____
__ _____   ____

REPRODUCTION
__ 32086 AI-EQUINE   ____
__ 32024 DIAG. UTER. CULTURE   ____
__ 32098 RECTALS   ____
__ 32100 ULTRASOUND   ____
__ 32091 UTERINE BIOPSY   ____
__ 32337 UTERINE INF W/O MED   ____
__ _____   ____
__ _____   ____

PHARMACY/SUPPLIES
__ 24190 HCG VIAL   ____
__ 24519 LUTALYSE ML   ____
__ 24530 MAXITROL OPTH.   ____
__ 24549 MINERAL OIL OZ.   ____
__ 24591 NOL. OINT OZ.   ____
__ 24608 OPTHOCORT TUBE   ____
__ 24626 PANACUR PASTE   ____
__ 24638 PENICILLIN G ML   ____
__ 25216 PRD FLESH OINT OZ   ____
__ 25379 SMZ 480/TAB   ____
__ 25380 SMZ 960/TAB   ____
__ 24816 STATROL OPTH   ____
__ 24826 STRONGID PASTE   ____
__ 25163 VETRAP ROLL   ____
__ 24950 VETROPOLYCIN   ____
__ 25434 VETROPOLYCIN/HC   ____
__ 35300 MISC. SUPPLIES   ____
__ _____   ____
__ _____   ____
__ _____   ____

EXAMINATIONS
__ 32314 EXAM-/RECHECK   ____
__ 32315 EXAMINATION B   ____
__ 32316 EXAMINATION C   ____
__ 35210 EXAM-INSURANCE   ____
__ 32033 LAMENESS(UNITS)   ____
__ 32339 PREPURCHASE (B)   ____
__ 32045 REG.-HEALTH EXAM   ____
__ 32047 REG.-HEALTH PAPER   ____
__ _____   ____

VACCINATIONS
__ 32344 EQUINE FIVE WAY   ____
__ 32346 PNEUMABORT K   ____
__ 32347 POT. HORSE FEVER   ____
__ 32349 RHINOMUNE   ____
__ 32350 STRANGLES   ____
__ 32352 TETANUS TOXOID   ____
__ _____   ____
__ _____   ____

LAB
__ 32020 DIAG.-FOAL CITE TEST   ____
__ 32030 NON CLINIC LAB   ____
__ 32354 REG. COGGINS   ____
__ _____   ____

PROFESSIONAL
__ 32004 ADMINISTRATION   ____
__ 32010 BANDAGING   ____
__ 32040 PROFESSIONAL SVC.   ____
__ 32066 RADIOGRAPHS BASIC   ____
__ 32205 RADIOGRAPHS ADD.   ____
__ 32053 STOMACH TUBE   ____
__ _____   ____
__ _____   ____

SUBTOTAL _____
CASH DISCOUNT _____
_____
TOTAL _____

NUMBER OF STUDENTS _____
SPECIES ____ NO __ TREATED
_____ (GROUP)

COMMENTS _____
_____
_____
_____
_____

O-20181

REIMBURSEMENT

Out of Pocket

Many companion pet owners now have health insurance for their animals; therefore, they often make treatment decisions based on how much they can afford to pay out-of-pocket for an animal's care. For this reason, detailed and accurate written cost estimates, together with a signed informed consent, are essential elements in establishing the contractual relationship between the owner and the veterinarian, and they become an essential part of the veterinary health record. When generated through an electronic record-keeping system, the account can be flagged when the cost of care is reaching the estimated total agreed to by the owner. At that time, the health care provider attempts to reach the owner for authorization to continue beyond the original estimate. If the owner cannot be reached, the health care provider must make the decision of whether to continue testing and/or treating or surgical intervention, and must document that decision in the patient's medical record.

Veterinary teaching hospital health records and computer applications have the ability to produce detailed invoices including the patient's final bill from each episode of care. Along with an understanding of the patient's current medical condition, a review of expenditures incurred will help the owners make the correct decision for themselves and the animal.

Mortality Insurance

The economic value of some animals (e.g., performance horses) and valuable breeding show animals (e.g., cattle) necessitates that the owner or owners secure mortality insurance on the animal. The insurance company's authorization to euthanize the animal may be more critical than the owner's when the insured animal is ill or injured and euthanasia is a strong option (Wilson et al., 1988). Euthanasia without the insurance company's authorization may lead to the company's refusal to pay the death benefit. Therefore, documentation of the name of the person(s) authorizing the euthanasia, along with the telephone number, the date, and the time of verbal authorization(s) in the health record, becomes vital for payment of the death benefit (Wilson et al., 1988).

Pet Health Insurance

As the availability of pet health insurance and veterinary medical and surgical insurance increases, so does the importance of complete, accurate veterinary health records. If the insurance company finds the health record inadequate to justify the claim and refuses to pay for services rendered, the client may choose to take legal action against the veterinarian for the amount of the claim or seek assistance from the state's insurance commissioner in resolving the issue (Wilson et al., 1988).

1. What are two essential elements of the veterinary health record in establishing the contractual relationship between the owner and the veterinarian?

2. True or False? Veterinary teaching hospital health records and computer applications do not have the ability to produce detailed invoices.

3. Regarding mortality insurance, what documentation is vital for payment of the death benefit?

4. For what insurance-related reason may a client choose to take legal action against the veterinarian?

5. For what type of animals do owners secure mortality insurance?

INFORMATION MANAGEMENT

Coding and Classification

The ability to easily retrieve information based on diagnoses or procedures is essential in veterinary research, as well as to track and study emerging or re-emerging vector-borne or zoonotic infections. A **zoonotic infection** is one that can be transmitted from animals to humans. Several systems are used for this purpose in the veterinary setting. Coding and classification systems can meet this need, as can other methods such as the use of a controlled vocabulary, which also is described in this section.

> zoonotic infection
> an infection that can be transmitted from animals to humans. Zoonoses are of concern to both veterinary and human medicine.

SNVDO

The *SNVDO (Standard Nomenclature of Veterinary Diseases and Operations)* is based on the *Standard Nomenclature of Diseases and Operations*. The second abridged edition of *SNVDO* was published in 1976 by the Public Health Service. The nomenclature has been maintained only intermittently since that time but is still being used in a few North American veterinary teaching hospitals.

> SNVDO (Standard Nomenclature of Veterinary Diseases and Operation) coding system created in 1963 to standardize the collection of veterinary data in a national database; has been updated only intermittently since the 1970s.

The diagnosis code in *SNVDO* consists of three parts: topography (four characters), etiology (four characters), and the structural or function code (one character). Unlike human medicine coding procedures, the *SNVDO* does not emphasize differentiating principal and secondary diagnoses. The procedure code in *SNVDO* consists of two parts: The first three characters are an abbreviated topography code, and the last two characters depict the procedure performed in that topography.

Through the efforts of several members of the AVMA Committee on Standard Nomenclature and Coding, who also were board members of the Veterinary Medical Database, it was decided in the early 1980s that the *Systematized Nomenclature of Medicine (SNOMED)*, with the addition of unique veterinary terms, would best meet the veterinary profession's information needs.

SNOMED CT®

The **SNOMED CT®** (Systematized Nomenclature of Medicine Clinical Terms) originally was developed by the College of American Pathologists by combining SNOMED RT and the United Kingdom's Clinical Terms Version 3, or Read Codes Version 3, as it formerly was called. In April 2007, SNOMED CT® was acquired by the International Health Terminology Standards Development Organisation (IHTSDO). IHTSDO is a not-for-profit association that is owned and governed by its National Members. In April 2014, 27 countries were members of IHTSDO, with more countries joining every year. SNOMED CT is a clinical health care terminology with comprehensive, scientifically validated content, essential for electronic health records (EHRs). SNOMED-CT can cross-map to other international standards and already is used in more than 50 countries. The terminology is available in U.S. English, UK English, Spanish, and Danish. Work continues on translations into French, Swedish, Lithuanian, and other languages. The following quote from the IHTSDO website (see Key Resources) explains the components of SNOMED CT®:

> From abscess to zygote, SNOMED CT includes more than 311,000 unique concepts. The concepts are organized in hierarchies, from the general to the specific. This allows very detailed ("granular") clinical data to be recorded and later accessed or aggregated at a more general level. "Concept descriptions" are the terms or names assigned to a SNOMED CT concept. There are almost 800,000 descriptions in SNOMED CT, including synonyms that can be used to refer to a concept.
>
> In addition, there are approximately 1,360,000 links or semantic relationships between the SNOMED CT concepts. These relationships provide formal definitions and other characteristics of the concept. One type of link is the "IS_A" relationship. This is used to define a concept's position within a hierarchy, e.g. Diabetes Mellitus IS_A disorder of glucose regulation (IHTSDO, n.d., para. 1–2).

SNOMED CT® is an electronic application that is accessed through a compatible browser. Exploration of SNOMED CT is beneficial to see the hierarchical structure that makes this system extremely powerful, rich, and intricate. SNOMED CT allows the user to enter and/or retrieve data as broadly or with as much granularity as necessary. Exploring SNOMED CT can be accomplished by using one of the online browsers listed on the website at www.snomed.org.

SNOMED Clinical Terms (SNOMED CT) is the most comprehensive, multilingual clinical health care terminology in the world according to the International Health Terminology Standards Development Organisation (IHTSDO). Whether used for human or veterinary applications, SNOMED CT contributes to the improvement of patient care by "underpinning" the development of electronic health records that record clinical information in ways that enable meaning-based retrieval. This provides effective access to information required for decision support and consistent reporting and analysis. Patients benefit from the use of SNOMED CT because it improves the recording of the EHR information and facilitates better communication, leading to improvements in the quality of care.

Kathleen Ellis, RHIT, RN, BS, and Roberta Schmidt, RHIA, CHIT-IS, health information management professionals for the colleges of veterinary medicine at the University of Illinois and Ohio State University, respectively, along with Jeff R. Wilcke, DVM, MS, DACVCP, Director of the AVMA's Secretariat to SNOMED International at the Virginia-Maryland Regional College of Veterinary Medicine, have been the leaders in adapting SNOMED CT® for use in the veterinary profession. The Secretariat has created a website, snomed.vetmed.vt.edu, offering user discussion forums for the purpose of developing standardized usage of the nomenclature in daily practice in the veterinary setting. For the most current information on SNOMED CT®, refer to Internet link www.ihtsdo.org

Recognizing that "using standardized nomenclature improves communication from veterinarian to veterinarian and really improves patient care" (Sommars, 2009), the American Animal Hospital Association's Electronic Health Records Task Force chose SNOMED CT® as the platform for its list of standardized diagnostic terms that could be used by practitioners in small animal hospitals.

Free Text

The Veterinary Medical Teaching Hospital of the University of California at Davis developed its own in-house system, which requires no coding of diagnoses or procedures. Health care providers enter their findings and recommendations into the information system in English and then are able to retrieve records the same way. A controlled vocabulary has evolved that standardizes the entries, but authors are able to bypass this vocabulary and enter their unique concept in their preferred terminology.

Data Sets

Veterinary Medical Database (VMDB)

The Veterinary Medical Database (VMDB) began in 1963 when a group of scientists from the National Cancer Institute (NCI) recognized a common interest in the prevalence of various forms of cancer in animals and met at Michigan State University in East Lansing to discuss how to best collect the data for study. They hypothesized that if data were collected on animal cancer, the study of that data would reveal information relevant to the study of cancer in humans. They recognized the necessity of abstracting data from the medical records of veterinary teaching hospitals and decided to modify the Standard Nomenclature of Diseases and Operations (SNDO) used for coding human medical records at that time. The resultant nomenclature, *SNVDO*, has been described previously. These data were gathered into a database at Michigan State University, supported by NCI until 1975, when the principal scientists were planning to retire.

Veterinary Medical Database (VMDB) a national collection system for data from veterinary teaching hospital patient records from the United States and Canada.

NCI representatives wanted to continue to purchase the data, and the participating veterinary schools wished to continue to participate because of the increased interest by the faculty to also use the data in teaching and research. Therefore, the American Association of Veterinary Medical Data Program Participants, Inc. (AAVMDPP) was created.

At that time, the database was referred to as *VMDP*, the *Veterinary Medical Data Program*. The database was moved to Cornell University in 1975 because of the university's advances in computing capabilities. It remained at Cornell until 1987, when it was relocated to Purdue University and its name was officially changed to *Veterinary Medical Database (VMDB)* and became an umbrella organization to manage other veterinary databases such as the Canine Eye Registry Foundation (CERF), the Equine Eye Registration Foundation (EERF), and a DNA registry for progressive retinal atrophy (PRA).

After moving to the University of Illinois at Urbana-Champaign and more recently relocating to the University of Missouri, the VMDB is used mainly by clinicians in veterinary teaching hospitals as a starting point for retrospective studies, teaching, and in scholarly publications. The database does not accommodate herd health or production medicine settings. Clinicians from participating university hospitals may search through their individual school's data or perform a nationwide or regional search for cases relevant to their topic, at no cost to the user. Outside agencies such as drug companies, pet food producers, and nonparticipating universities are charged for the searches they order.

Data Flow   Data elements are abstracted from the patient's health record by the veterinary HIM professional in the teaching hospital. The abstract then is submitted electronically via VVDEA Veterinary Data Entry Application to the Veterinary Medical Database (VMDB), where it is stored for future retrieval by university faculty or administration, representatives of drug companies, breed clubs, pet food producers, and so on. The data may be useful in the process of making an application for a grant proposal, decision-making about services to be offered by the health care facility, or marketing of a new product.

Maintenance of the Database   Once the patient health record has been completed by the clinician, the diagnoses and procedures are coded by an HIM professional or, in some facilities, by the clinician. Additional data abstracted from the patient's record for submission include: medical record number, zip code of the animal's residence, attending clinician code, species, breed, date of birth, sex (including spayed or neutered), weight, color, admission date, discharge date, and discharge status (alive, died, euthanized, or discharged and referred). Data are submitted electronically.

The VMDB database administrator then runs the data through two edit programs. The *pre-edit* checks the internal consistency of the current abstract. Examples: Are the species and breed codes consistent? If the animal was spayed, does the abstract record the sex as "female-spay?" If the abstract fails the pre-edit checks, it is rejected and returned to the submitting institution for error correction and resubmission.

When an abstract passes the pre-edit, it moves into the next editing stage, the *edit-update*, which now compares the current abstract with the existing database, looking for a match in patient identification numbers for that institution. If there is a match with the identification number, several data elements are checked for consistency. For example, are the species, breed, and sex codes consistent with past submissions? If not, the record is rejected. Is the discharge status logical? If the identification number was abstracted as dead or euthanized in the past but now is alive with a subsequent discharge date, the record is rejected.

Rejected abstracts are reported to the participating institution for correction and resubmission. After it is accepted by the VMDB for inclusion in the database, the record is available for reference by users.

Orthopedic Foundation for Animals

The **Orthopedic Foundation for Animals (OFA)** was established in 1966 to provide registries for standardized evaluation for canine hip and elbow dysplasia. The organization's core objective of establishing control programs to lower the incidence of inherited disease has expanded to also include the following databases: patellar luxation, autoimmune thyroiditis, congenital heart disease, Legg-Calve-Perthes disease, sebaceous adenitis, congenital deafness, shoulder osteochondritis dessicans, and several DNA-based databases such as von Willebrand's Disease and progressive retinal atrophy (Orthopedic Foundation for Animals, n.d.).

Orthopedic Foundation for Animals (OFA) a collection of voluntary orthopedic and genetic disease databases of animals.

Electronic Information Systems

The listing of vendors of veterinary hospital information systems changes frequently. Refer to Figure 15-2 for a listing of some current vendors. AVMA members continue to represent veterinary interests and concerns regarding standardized collection, storage, maintenance, and transmission of data by maintaining active membership in organizations such as **Health Level 7 (HL7)**, which is a standard for data exchange in health care, and **Logical Observations, Identifiers, Names, and Codes (LOINC®)**, a code system for laboratory and clinical observations.

Health Level 7 (HL7) the application level, which is the highest level of the International Standards Organization's (ISO) communications model for Open Systems Interconnection (OSI); a standard for data exchange in health care.

Logical Observations, Identifiers, Names and Codes (LOINC®) facilitates the exchange and pooling of results or vital signs for clinical care, outcomes management, and research; a code system for laboratory and clinical observations.

International Species Information System (ISIS)

The **International Species Information System (ISIS)** is an electronic, global zoological animal information system that began in 1973 and now is used by at least 825 zoos and aquariums in 76 countries on 6 continents. ISIS collects the age, sex, parentage, place of birth, circumstance of death, etc., on the specimen. It now has data on more than 2 million animals. The ISIS organization created

International Species Information System (ISIS) a computer-based information system for wild animal species in captivity.

FIGURE 15-2

Examples of veterinary practice information systems.

Company Name	Location	Product Name
Advanced Technology Corp.	www.vetstar.com	VetStar
American Data Systems, Inc.	www.pawsnet.com	PAWS Veterinary Practice Management™
Animal Hospital Management System	www.bwci.com	Animal Hospital Management System
Animal Intelligence Software, Inc.	www.animalintelligence.com	
AVImark	www.avimark.net	AVImark
CCS, Inc.	www.completeclinic.com	Complete Clinic Software
ClienTrax	www.clientraxtechnology.com/	ClienTrax
Doty Software	www.dotysoftware.com	VetMaster
IDEXX	www.idexx.com/cornerstone	Cornerstone Practice Management System
ImproMed, LLC	www.impromed.com	ImproMed Infinity and DVM Manager
Informavet, Inc.	www.alisvet.com/	AlisVet
IntraVet	www.intravet.com	IntraVet
NuSoft Technologies	www.nusofttech.com	Preferred Veterinary System
Ross Group	www.rossgroupinc.com	UVIS: Universal Veterinary Information System
VIA Information Systems	www.viainfosys.com/	VIA® Practice Management Software

Note: This list is not exhaustive and is not meant to be an endorsement by the author.

the MedARKS (Medical Animal Records Keeping System) software package for each facility to assemble and report its own data. MedARKS includes anesthesia records; parasitology examination records; prescription records; diagnostic test and sample storage records; clinical notes; pathology records; inventory, history reports; and problem lists.

SELF REVIEW 15.5

1. According to the *Standard Nomenclature of Veterinary Diseases and Operations* (*SNVDO*), what are the parts of the diagnosis code and the procedure code?

2. How are the concepts in SNOMED CT organized, and why?

3. What hypothesized research led to creation of the American Association of Veterinary Medical Data Program Participants, Inc. (AAVMDPP)?

4. True or False? The *Veterinary Medical Database (VMDB)* does not accommodate herd health or production medicine settings.

5. Through what two edit programs does the VMDB database administrator run the data, and for what purpose is each edit program designed?

QUALITY IMPROVEMENT AND UTILIZATION MANAGEMENT

Veterinary health care has no formal requirements for quality assurance or utilization management processes. Informally, however, quality of care is studied each time a veterinary teaching hospital health care provider uses health records for retrospective study in preparing for a lecture, writing a research grant proposal, or writing an article for a scholarly publication. The outcome of such a review is often discussed during faculty conferences, in meetings, or through publication. Changes to implement improvement are undertaken as appropriate.

SELF REVIEW 15.6

1. True or False? There are no formal requirements for quality assurance or utilization management processes in veterinary health care.

RISK MANAGEMENT AND LEGAL ISSUES

Risk Management

With increasing public awareness of the value of animals in people's lives, litigation, attorney awareness of veterinary issues, the rising expectations of animal owners, and the increasing economic value of some animals, risk management is becoming more important in veterinary health care settings. An incident report form specifically for use in the veterinary teaching hospital should be completed when an incident has occurred involving one of the animals. The form is initiated by the faculty or staff as soon as they become aware of the incident. Date and time of the incident, along with the animal's information and client information, are recorded on the incident report. A detailed description of the incident and injury is required. Other information, such as witness name(s) and contact information, is documented, along with the name of the individual completing the form. After completion, the incident report is forwarded to hospital administration, and then to the university's risk management office. It is not kept in the patient's health record.

One area of tremendous risk in the veterinary health care setting is patient restraint. The AVMA's Professional Liability Insurance Trust quarterly report, *Professional Liability*, routinely provides synopses of claims received in the Trust office. Reports of human or patient injury sustained when owners attempt to restrain their ill or injured pets are numerous. When the owner is injured while attempting to restrain his or her own animal, the owner's insurance company often sues the veterinarian for recovery of medical costs associated with the incident.

Legal Issues

Determining Who the Client Is

Sometimes it is difficult to determine who the client is. The legal system generally considers an animal to be a form of personal property. When someone calls to arrange an appointment for an animal or simply presents an animal for examination or treatment, ownership is implied, unless information is given to the contrary. In the large animal setting, the person who actually presents the animal for examination or treatment may be the owner, an agent for the owner, or simply a transporter. The owner(s) may not live in the same state where the animal resides or where the animal is being presented for examination or care.

It is necessary, then, to carefully question the person who presents the animal, to accurately document the name(s) of the owner or owners, address, and phone number on the health record. If the presenter claims to be the agent, does this person have authorization from the owner to seek medical care for the patient and sign consents for treatment?

The above reference to *owners* is another complicated issue. Some animals are owned by multiple people who are classified as co-owners. Some animals, especially horses, may be owned by a syndicate, which is an official association of persons. In these situations, it is wise to have one person identified as spokesperson for the group of owners, who is contacted for consent to treatment. The information system must be able to document these various parties and their relationship to the patient.

Another consideration for the Health Information Manager, is the unique relationship between the breeder of the animal and the person who now has possession of the animal. The person with possession may be the "adopted" owner or simply a trainer. Again, careful questioning will produce records that are more accurate.

Dogs used in police canine units sometimes are registered incorrectly if the admissions staff fails to ask enough clarifying questions to validate and/or verify "ownership." The animal actually may live with its handler but is the property of the police department (i.e., local, state, or federal government agencies). The police department must be named as owner of the animal, with the officer listed as an alternate owner/handler/representative.

Litigation for Debt Collection

Debt collection accounts for most of the litigation encountered in the veterinary teaching hospital setting today. As discussed earlier, a signed estimate of charges and a signed informed consent are instrumental in collection of practice debts.

Prepurchase Examinations

Prepurchase exams are a common practice and present unique challenges for record creation, management, and documentation standards. These exams are typical in large animal hospitals, for performance use, economic, food production animals of the following species: equine (horses), bovine (cattle), ovine (sheep), caprine (goats), porcine (pigs). These exams still are referred to occasionally as "breeding soundness examinations." The relationship between the examiner, the buyer, the seller, and agents for either the buyer or the seller can be complicated. Therefore, the relationships must be established correctly at the time the appointment is set up and/or when the animal presents to the facility during the admission process.

An incorrect relationship and record can have an adverse impact if the owner/agent/representative requests information. State veterinary boards may address this issue in their regulations. This topic is addressed thoroughly in *Law and Ethics of the Veterinary Profession* (Wilson et al., 1988). In the best interests of the animal, the owner is responsible for authorizations and consents until the sale is final.

Wildlife Management

This venture is a cooperative one between the federal government and individual states. This is a broad topic ranging from international law and international agreements to the issuance of permits for importation, exportation, transportation, inspection, and the use of animals in scientific research. Federal regulations also address wildlife rehabilitation facilities, pet stores, and wildlife auctions. For more information in a given state, the agency to contact is the Department of Fish and Game or the Department of Natural Resources.

Animal Cruelty

"Studies have shown a correlation between the incidence of animal abuse on the one hand, and child abuse, spousal abuse or mass murder on the other.... Animal abusers have a greater propensity of committing acts of violence against humans than those with no history of animal cruelty" (Lacroix, 1998).

With these startling facts in mind, veterinarians and animal health records are becoming vital resources in identifying, documenting, and reporting suspected abuse, to prevent further injury to the animal, other animals, and humans.

Stray Animals

Stray animals may be presented to a veterinary teaching hospital for treatment before being sent to the local humane society or animal control facility, where they also have the potential for adoption and continued care and treatment. It is essential to accurately document the date and time of arrival and departure or euthanasia of these animals, in addition to the treatment rendered while hospitalized, so there is no question or doubt about what transpired during the animal's stay.

Euthanasia

The owner has to consider the euthanasia option when the quality of the animal's life is determined to be minimal and/or when the financial obligation outweighs the potential outcome of continued care. Documentation of the consent for euthanasia is best made in writing to verify the relationship of the signer to the animal. It also is necessary at the time of consent for euthanasia to determine whether the animal has bitten another animal or a human being, because of the potential for rabies exposure.

During the discussion between the veterinary health care provider and the owner and subsequent signing of the consent for euthanasia, arrangements can be made for payment of the final bill. The actual procedure of euthanasia then should be documented with the time, date, product used, and signature of the veterinary health care provider performing the procedure. This documentation fully verifies that the owner's wishes were carried out and that the animal was not transferred to a new owner or a research project.

Change of Ownership

Ownership of animals changes frequently in the veterinary field. Therefore, the animal's health record must be documented thoroughly, having the original owner sign a form verifying no further responsibility for the patient, transferring ownership to a new party, and identifying the new owner on the form. The new owner then receives access to past health records of the patient for continued care.

Blood Donors

Animal blood donors are available to give blood for a transfusion to a patient. They sometimes reside at the hospital to be available on short notice and often are long-term residents whose health records become quite bulky. Detailed blood donation records are maintained, along with health and vaccination updates.

Donation of Animals

If their animal has a unique condition that, in their opinion, is not worth the financial commitment to treat, owners sometimes request to donate their animal as a teaching model rather than selecting euthanasia. The client is asked to sign a form transferring ownership of the animal to a specific clinical or research program and include the dollar value of the animal. This donation often can be used as a tax deduction.

1. What is one area of tremendous risk in the veterinary health care setting?

2. Regarding legal issues, how is an owner generally determined?

3. What may be some complications regarding the ownership of animals?

4. True or False? Wildlife management is a venture regulated solely by the individual states governments.

5. Veterinarians and animal health records are becoming vital resources in identifying, documenting, and reporting suspected _____, to prevent further injury to the animal, other animals, and humans.

6. True or False? Documentation of the consent for euthanasia is best made by verbal authorization to verify the relationship of the signer to the animal.

ROLE OF THE HEALTH INFORMATION MANAGEMENT PROFESSIONAL

The veterinary HIM professional is responsible for establishing and maintaining information collection and retention systems that ensure accurate, complete, timely, and confidential health information for use in continued patient care, legal defense, education, and management decision-making. These records also must support the final bill.

Statistics are compiled and maintained for use by veterinary and human medicine professionals. For instance, each year the veterinary school is asked to submit statistics to the American Association of Veterinary Medical Colleges, which then develops a comparative data summary. Data elements collected include number of clients, number of patients, number of accessions, number hospitalized, and number of hospital days. Ambulatory care statistics also are collected on herd health or production medicine services. These statistics include number of farm calls made, number of animals involved, number of animals treated, and number of animals at risk.

Active participation in the **American Veterinary Health Information Management Association (AVHIMA)** helps the HIM professional develop a network for seeking new ideas and support. Unlike the human health care delivery setting, in which another professional may be practicing just down the road, the AVHIMA membership is spread across the United States and Canada, usually with only one member in a given state. The use of a listserv keeps members connected and helps them to work-through issues on a timely basis. It is difficult to maintain continuity and momentum within AVHIMA, considering such long distances between members. Active membership in the component state association of the American Health Information Management Association (AHIMA) is still relevant. Athough there are major differences between human and animal patients, the use of technology and basic roles and functions are not changed, and those liaisons should be maintained for professional support and continuing education.

American Veterinary Health Information Management Association (AVHIMA) promotes quality patient care through the management of health information; is the nation's authoritative body on the management of veterinary health information; advances the competency of those working with veterinary health information; and advocates for the profession on government, education, social, and business issues that affect the management of veterinary health information.

SELF REVIEW 15.8

1. For what is the veterinary HIM professional responsible?
2. Provide examples of data elements that are collected for the compilation of statistics for the American Association of Veterinary Medical Colleges.

PROFESSIONAL SPOTLIGHT: HEALTH INFORMATION MANAGEMENT

Who I am: Valerie E. Ball, RHIA, CHIT-IS

Where I work: North Carolina State University, College of Veterinary Medicine

What I do: I serve as the department manager for a tertiary care North Carolina State Government academic and teaching hospital.

Why HIM knowledge is important in my role: The department functions like a human major medical teaching facility. Our patients just happen to have fur, feathers, fins, or feet! Standard departmental processes include: Chart Assembly, Analysis, Coding (SNOMED-CT), Release of Information, and more. I also serve on the University's

National Coalition Building Institute (NCBI) Affiliate Chapter as an Associate Director, facilitating workshops on leadership development, prejudice reduction, and conflict resolution with faculty, staff, and students campus-wide.

Also, our facility serves as a nontraditional HIT role preceptor site for Edgecombe Community College and Pitt Community College students. We are able to demonstrate another application of our unique and diverse skills as we embrace advances for both the human and animal bond. Indeed, it is a unique and wonderful experience to get out of the department to see our patients and their owners and celebrate their recovery on a daily basis!

TRENDS

The electronic health record (EHR) is the major focus in many veterinary teaching hospital settings today. The integration of SNOMED CT® into the veterinary teaching hospital setting, as well as those of private practices, runs parallel to development of the EHR. The increased use of telemedicine influences the veterinary field and the EHR.

Lawsuits are increasing as public and attorney awareness of the practice and expectation of veterinary medicine increase. In addition, demands are placed on the veterinary profession to answer to animal welfare advocates who wish to ensure the safety and wellness of all animals.

The increasing interest in and expanding use of animal health statistics as sentinels in human health necessitate common data elements that can be easily matched between the two areas of practice. Fewer family farms and more agribusiness ventures have necessitated more involved record keeping to meet state and federal government regulations.

Veterinary record systems also are used in detecting, tracking, and controlling potential bioterrorism agents, many of which have been identified as zoonotic agents. Diseases that threaten human welfare and/or the safety of our food supply, such as the bovine spongiform encephalopathy (BSE) or "mad cow disease," anthrax, the West Nile virus, avian flu (H5N1), swine flu (H1N1), and bovine tuberculosis, also are under the purview of the veterinary health information system.

Animals (such as canine, equine, and marine mammals) are used by the Department of Defense and by local public safety departments in various capacities. They are trained at great expense in search-and-rescue and drug or explosives detection, for instance, to serve and safeguard the public, which makes efficient, accurate documentation of their health maintenance as essential as maintaining the health record of their handlers.

SELF REVIEW 15.9

1. True or False? The electronic health record (EHR) is not a major focus in many veterinary teaching hospital settings today.

2. True or False? Lawsuits are increasing as public and attorney awareness of the practice and expectation of veterinary medicine increase.

3. True or False? Diseases that threaten human welfare and/or the safety of our food supply are under the purview of the veterinary health information system.

4. How are animals used by the Department of Defense and by local public safety departments?

SUMMARY

Many of the current roles and functions defined for the HIM professional in the traditional human health care delivery setting can be directly applied to the veterinary hospital. The additional information provided in this chapter can help a health information manager with an interest in animal health decide to apply to a veterinary teaching hospital, local veterinary hospital, nearby zoo, veterinary information management software vendor, or research facility with an offer of expertise in establishing or maintaining an information system that also will protect the legal and financial interests of the veterinary professionals and the client.

The HIM professional can benefit by moving into this setting. Fewer government regulations related to maintenance of health records can be attractive. Also, opportunities are available to contribute to the field of veterinary science. The last, more subtle benefit is the contact with animals—which is often a stress reliever.

REVIEW QUESTIONS

Knowledge-Based Questions

1. Which organization's accreditation program provides minimum standards for maintenance of veterinary health records in both general and referral facilities?
2. Why is a written cost estimate so important in veterinary practice?
3. Where would you find the most current advice on how to use SNOMED CT® properly in a veterinary setting?
4. Who authorizes release of information in a prepurchase situation?
5. Briefly explain the operation and uses of the VMDB.

Critical Thinking Questions

1. Provide an example of an instance in which a record would be maintained for a group of animals rather than an individual patient.

2. In the absence of a specific law or state regulation, what source should be consulted for advice in an uncomfortable legal situation related to a veterinary teaching hospital where you are employed?
3. Networking and continuing education activities are a necessary part of keeping up-to-date in a profession. The component state associations of the American Health Information Management Association, however, do not offer programs specific to veterinary medicine. How would one keep current in veterinary health information management and still be able to maintain the credential as a registered health information technician or registered health information administrator?

WEB ACTIVITIES

1. Visit the website of the International Health Terminology Standards Development Organisation at http://www.ihtsdo.org and click on the link to SNOMED-CT. Explore the SNOMED-CT resources available at this website and write a brief summary.

2. Search the internet for information on pet insurance, visiting the websites of various pet insurance companies and reviews of different pet insurance products. Write a brief report on your findings.

CASE STUDY

Melanie Maloney has just taken a position as director of health information services at the Any State University College of Veterinary Medicine. The associate dean to whom she reports has informed her that the college is beginning work on the self-study report in preparation for an upcoming accreditation survey from the AVMA Council on Education (COE). To prepare for a discussion of the AVMA COE survey with the associate dean, Melanie decided to "do some homework" by visiting the AVMA website to obtain insights into how she might participate in the accreditation process. She finds the COE manual at the AVMA website and locates information on the self-study report and a typical site visit schedule.

After reviewing the information from the COE manual at the AVMA website, answer the following questions:

1. Discuss the COE standards with which Melanie will have to be most familiar.
2. With which sections of the self-study might she assist?
3. How might she interact with the site visit team?
4. What issues might Melanie want to discuss with the associate dean to fully understand her role in the process?

REFERENCES AND SUGGESTED READINGS

AVMA (American Veterinary Medical Association). (2004, April). AVMA policy on veterinary technology. [Online]. http://www.avma.org/issues/policy/veterinary_technology.asp [2009, October 11].

AVMA (American Veterinary Medical Association). (2009, April). Accreditation policies and procedures of the AVMA Council on Education (COE). [Online]. http://www.avma.org/education/cvea/coe_standard.asp [2011, April 14].

AVMA (American Veterinary Medical Association). (2010, November). Guidelines for veterinary prescription drugs. [Online]. http://www.avma.org/issues/policy/prescription_drugs.asp [2011, April 13].

AVMA (American Veterinary Medical Association). (2011, September). Veterinarians: Protecting the health of animals and people. [Online]. https://ebusiness.avma.org/files/productdownloads/Veterinarians%20_Eng.pdf [2015, October 19].

AVMA (American Veterinary Medical Association). (2014, March). COE accreditation policies and procedures: AVMA. [Online]. https://www.avma.org/ProfessionalDevelopment/Education/Accreditation/Colleges/Pages/coe-pp-the-AVMA-and-accreditation.asp [2015, August 8].

AVMA (American Veterinary Medical Association). (n.d.). AVMA Policy on Veterinary Technology. [Online]. https://www.avma.org/KB/Policies/Pages/AVMA-Policy-on-Veterinary-Technology.aspx [2015, October 19].

IHTSDO (International Health Terminology Standards Development Organisation). (n.d.). *SNOMED CT Components.* [Online]. http://www.ihtsdo.org/snomed-ct/snomed-ct0/snomed-ct-components [2009, October 11].

Lacroix, C. A. (1998). December. Animal cruelty and the role of veterinarians. *AVMLA Newsletter, IV*(1).

Orthopedic Foundation for Animals. (n.d.). [Online]. http://www.offa.org/history.html [2009, October 11].

Sommars, J. (2009). Cracking the codes. *Trends Magazine, 25*(6), 59–63.

Towner, W. (2009, September 13). Women in veterinary medicine growing. NewsandSentinel.com. [Online]. http://newsandsentinel.com/page/content.detail/id/521626.html?nav=5054 [2009, October 11].

Veterinarians. (2009, February). [Online]. http://www.avma.org/animal_health/brochures/veterinarian/veterinarian_brochure.asp [2009, October 11].

Veterinary Specialty Organizations. (2010). [Online]. http://www.avma.org/press/profession/specialties.asp [2010, September 5].

Wilson, J. F., Garbe, J. L., & Rollin, B. E. (1988). *Law and Ethics of the Veterinary Profession.* Yardley, PA: Yardley Press, Ltd.

KEY RESOURCES

American Animal Hospital Association (AAHA)
http://www.aahanet.org

American Veterinary Health Information Management Association (AVHIMA)
http://www.avhima.org

American Veterinary Medical Association (AVMA)
http://www.avma.org

American Veterinary Medical Association Professional Liability Insurance Trust
http://www.avmaplit.com

Animal Legal & Historical Web Center Michigan State University College of Law
http://www.animallaw.info

IHTSDO (International Health Terminology Standards Development Organisation)
http://www.ihtsdo.org

International Species Information System (ISIS)
http://www.isis.org

Orthopedic Foundation for Animals
http://www.offa.org

The One Health Initiative
http://www.onehealthinitiative.com

Veterinary Hospital Managers Association, Inc. (VHMA)
http://www.vhma.org

Veterinary Medical Database
http://vmdb.org

Consulting

Karen Wright, MHA, RHIA, RHIT | Scott Wright, MBA

LEARNING OBJECTIVES

Upon successful completion of this chapter, you should be able to:

- Identify the advantages and disadvantages of consulting.
- Assess personal strengths and weaknesses.
- Recognize the importance of positive leadership.
- Develop a business plan.
- Develop action plans.
- Evaluate government regulations, accreditation and information technology (IT) standards, and industry best practices.
- Develop compliance audits.

Examples of Settings	Examples of Possible Consultant Roles
Acute Care Hospital	Consults 8 to 40 hours per week until a project is complete; serves as project coordinator to help health care facilities understand information flow and reduce legal and regulatory risk and e-discovery review costs; serves as project coordinator of ICD-10-CM/PCS transition; researches Recovery Audit Contractor's (RAC) websites; reviews documentation necessary for determining medical necessity, present-on-admission indicators, and severity of illness; performs compliance audits (coding and security); serves as member of the charge master team; provides coding support; reviews bill holds and claims denied; provides education to administrators, the medical staff, and department supervisors and staff, in addition to health information department coders and staff
Veterinary Teaching Hospital	Consults 20 hours per month providing expertise regarding data collection for research purposes; storage and retrieval of records; and computerized databases utilized to collect health information of animals
Nursing Facility	Consults 8 to 16 hours per month; evaluates accreditation standards, government regulations, and industry best practices; serves as project coordinator for ICD-10-CM/PCS transition; researches RAC Web sites regarding audits; develops and conducts audits to ensure documentation compliance by various health care providers; substantiates health care services provided to Medicare and Medicaid residents; and prepares for state surveys and RAC audits
Home Health and Hospice	Consults 16 hours per month to review government regulations; develops and performs compliance audits to ensure information technology (IT) security and documentation to substantiate services provided in the patient's home via the supervision of a physician utilizing nurses, various therapies, and home health aides
Dialysis Center	Consults 8 to 16 hours per month; serves as project coordinator for the ICD-10-CM/PCS transition; provides support for compliance with government regulation, accreditation, IT transmission standards, and industry best practices; provides support and education of staff regarding privacy, security, and documentation compliance
Behavioral Medicine	Consults 25 hours per month; provides support for compliance with government and accreditation documentation regulations; provides education for staff regarding HIPAA, the American Recovery and Reinvestment Act (ARRA), and maintaining the security of protected health information; prepares and analyzes statistical reports related to documentation compliance, performance assessment, medical necessity, utilization review, and risk management; serves as project coordinator for the ICD-10-CM/PCS transition
Managed Care and Insurance Companies	Consults 8 to 40 hours per month to educate staff regarding compliance with HIPAA and ARRA, the maintenance and security of protected health information (PHI); provides support for the ICD-10-CM/PCS transition; develops and conducts compliance audits
Physician's Office or Group Practice	Consults 8 to 16 hours per month; oversees electronic health record (EHR) implementation and maintenance, educates and trains staff regarding HIPAA/ARRA and coding compliance; develops, writes, and revises policies; reviews denied claims, appeals, accounts receivable management, and review of remittance advice against charges listed on the patients' accounts; serves as project coordinator for the ICD-10-CM/PCS transition
Legal Practice	Consults 20 hours per month; evaluates government and Joint Commission documentation requirements; develops and performs audits to review health information documentation compliance or lack thereof
Health Information System Vendor	Consults 40 hours per month; provides expertise regarding information flow within health care facilities, e-discovery, HIPAA and ARRA privacy and security issues; develops information technology (IT) solutions that prevent breaches; as well as facilitates the accurate data capture, accessibility, and interoperability for health care facilities that meet all government, accreditation, certification, and electronic data transaction standards

INTRODUCTION TO SETTING

Health information management (HIM) consultants work in any setting where health care is provided or for organizations that reimburse or bill for health services. Examples of organizations that potentially can benefit from the services of a HIM consultant include acute care hospitals, ambulatory surgery centers, veterinary teaching hospitals, nursing facility corporate offices, and/or multiple facilities, hospice, dialysis centers, home health, behavioral medicine (mental health and substance abuse), rehabilitation facilities, third-party billing companies, large and small physician group practices, governmental agencies, and technology vendors. Although this chapter is geared toward the independent consultant, many job opportunities are available for HIM professionals in consulting firms as well.

Working as a Team Member

The HIM professional usually is hired to provide expertise related to documentation improvement, billing, reimbursement and compliance issues. These areas each cover many diverse tasks that require extensive HIM experience and knowledge prior to becoming a consultant. The most challenging and rewarding part of a consultant's job is to work as a team member with key decision makers such as health care executives; administrators, physicians, nurses, and clinical researchers; quality, utilization review, and risk management professionals; accountants, attorneys, and therapists (physical, occupational, and speech); as well as psychiatrists, psychologists, dietitians, social workers, and information technology professionals, to name just a few.

Understanding the scope and expectations of a potential consulting role is essential. Conducting interviews with managers at the facility provides an opportunity for the consultant to gain firsthand knowledge of the organization's perception of its needs. This two-way interview process helps to clarify the tasks or projects for which the consultant will be hired.

Following the investigative interviews with the various managers, the consultant prepares a summary statement reflecting the scope of the project for which he or she is being considered, the project timeline, and deliverables. Consultants should thank potential clients for considering them for the project (Wildi, 2014). The organization or the consultant then may decide whether or not to proceed. Moving forward requires negotiation and acceptance of a contract, which normally calls for a legal opinion prior to signing the document.

Examples of Consulting Projects

The HIM consultant's knowledge of biomedical science; the legal and regulatory environment; classification systems; the revenue cycle, reimbursement; electronic health records; data capture and computerized databases; privacy, security, and coding compliance issues; as well as retrieval, security, storage, and retention of health information in any medium makes him or her an asset to any health care facility.

A consultant may be hired by an acute care hospital to provide training related to the revision of policies and procedures as a result of strengthening of the: (a) Health Insurance Portability and Accountability Act (HIPAA) of 1996, (b) Health Information Technology for Economic and Clinical Health (HITECH), enacted as part of the American Recovery and Reinvestment Act of 2009, (c) Genetic Information Nondiscrimination Act of 2008 (GINA), which strengthened patient's rights to privacy and accessibility to their health information as well as breach notification, and (d) Medicare and Medicaid incentives for meaningful use of EHRs.

Moreover, a consultant may review workflow processes; revise policies and procedures; design a compliance plan, offer coding and classification system education; assess physician documentation to ensure that it supports medical necessity, present on admission (POA), and the severity of illness, as well as the accuracy of the diagnosis and procedure codes assigned. In this setting, the consultant also could serve as a member of the revenue cycle team that includes representatives from information technology (IT), clinical documentation improvement, patient financial services, utilization review, the HIM department, and individuals reporting on clinical quality measures.

In nursing, behavioral medicine, and rehabilitation facilities, the consultant's focus may be quality improvement efforts designed to improve clinical documentation and the collection of statistics. For example, the consultant may work in the corporate office for a nursing facility chain reviewing Recovery Audit Contractor (RAC) websites regarding audit information, reviewing minimum data set (MDS) statistics reported to the state for each facility, or performing quality improvement activities.

Specific reviews could include review of physicians' orders on admission to ensure that the follow-up care ordered by the physician who discharged the resident from the hospital is carried out; to ensure appropriate documentation of wound care and percentages related to significant changes such as percentage of residents who have decreased independence in their ability to perform two activities of daily living, percentage of residents with a new infection, percentage of residents with a moderate level of pain occurring every day, percentage of residents with one or more pressure sores, or percentage of residents whose lab values demonstrate inappropriate levels of anticoagulants.

The consultant may be a member of a team that designs care paths aimed at improving treatment outcomes or an educator who provides inservice education regarding how to improve documentation, confidentiality, security, or how to assure that only the HIM department releases personal health information (PHI). The consultant also may provide recommendations related to the retention of health information, as well as develop, write, and revise polices.

A large or small physicians' group practice or individual physician who wishes to reduce medical claim denials and improve efficiency may seek a HIM consultant to provide coding and billing expertise as well as to select, implement, and manage an electronic health record (EHR) that is certified and meets HITECH and ARRA meaningful use requirements that, in addition, also streamlines the appointment, clinical data collection, and billing processes.

Another consulting opportunity is in veterinary medicine facilities. Some veterinary teaching hospitals utilize the Systematized Nomenclature of Medicine-Clinical Terms (SNOMED CT®) medical nomenclature standards. For research purposes electronic information systems for animal medical data are similar to those maintained by acute care hospitals for humans. An HIM consultant can provide expertise in several areas, including data collection for research purposes, storage and retrieval of records, EHR record implementation, and design of electronic documents for the collection of animal health information.

As the elderly population increases and health care facilities move toward an EHR, the demand for health care services and health information technologists and administrators also will increase. Today's fragmented health care system, the ICD-10-CM/PCS transition, the federal government's prospective inpatient and outpatient payment methodologies, the complexity of third-party payers' billing requirements, and the Centers for Medicare & Medicaid Services (CMS) Recovery Audit Contractor (RAC) program are providing numerous challenging employment and consulting opportunities for HIM professionals.

SELF REVIEW 16.1

1. What are three types of health care facilities where a consultant may work?
2. What are the most challenging yet rewarding aspects of being a consultant?
3. What are five tasks that a consultant may be asked to perform?

REGULATORY ISSUES

Federal health care regulations continue to increase in number and complexity. Incentives and penalties authorized by HIPAA, ARRA, and HITECH means that many providers need assistance in converting to an EHR, updating policies and procedures, complying with complex meaningful use standards, interacting with multiple vendors, and managing e-discovery. Regulations implementing ICD-10-CM/ PCS provide opportunities for consultants to assist with the transition. The Recovery Audit Contract (RAC) program is another federal initiative that can result in health care institutions looking to HIM professionals for expertise, in addition to the need to comply with CMS's Prospective Payment

System regulations, as well as a multitude of different insurance companies' requirements.

These are just a few of the challenges that health care facilities face. Thus, there is a high demand for the skills of HIM professionals. Consultants must stay abreast of the changes in the health care environment by networking with other consultants; reading professional trade journals; researching the *Federal Register,* as well as licensing, accrediting, certification, and IT transaction standards; and pursuing additional education to keep up with technological changes.

To help the client organization accomplish its goals with regard to regulatory requirements, the consultant may have to facilitate the development of an action plan that includes establishing the overarching goals of the project, developing measurable objectives to achieve the goals and, assigning tasks and deadlines for completing the assigned tasks. Having an action plan keeps the project focused, thereby preventing "scope creep," which occurs when the project for which the consultant has been hired expands beyond the contractually agreed upon project or service.

SELF REVIEW 16.2

1. How do CMS government regulations impact the consulting profession?
2. When is it necessary to research the Federal Register?

DOCUMENTATION

If the client organization has contracted with the consultant to evaluate compliance with documentation standards, the consultant will have to research all appropriate regulations, accreditation guidelines, and best practices, as well as develop and perform a clinical documentation and compliance **audit**. The key documentation points can be incorporated into an audit sheet, which the consultant can use to review a random sample of the client organization's records. The consultant then computes, analyzes, and presents a statistical summary of the audit results to the appropriate executives. Completion of the audit cycle may involve educating those who document in the records and then conducting routine follow-up surveillance to determine improvement. Figure 16-1 illustrates documentation of the audit cycle.

audit a retrospective review of selected health care records or data documents to evaluate the quality of care, services provided, documentation, or coding compared to predetermined standards.

SELF REVIEW 16.3

1. True or False? When conducting a documentation compliance audit, consultants typically review every record of every patient treated during the previous month.
2. True or False? According to Figure 16.1, the audit worksheet should be developed based on documentation requirements found in regulations and standards.

FIGURE 16-1

Documentation of the audit cycle.

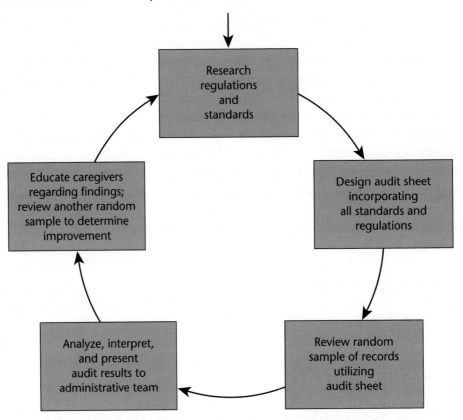

REIMBURSEMENT AND COMPLIANCE

The HIM professional has many consulting opportunities in the area of reimbursement and compliance, including issues of documentation, coding, the revenue cycle, and reimbursement. If the client organization believes that its code-based reimbursement is not what it should be, the organization may contact a coding consultant for assistance. Sometimes the consultant finds that the organization's coders are coding properly but that inadequate clinical documentation is the true cause of missed revenue. At other times the consultant finds that both coding and clinical documentation are in need of improvement.

Whatever the finding, the consultant must be careful to be as objective as possible when auditing for reimbursement purposes. To guard against bias in findings, the consultant should not enter into a "contingency" contract with a client in which the consultant's fees are based on increasing reimbursement (e.g., the client pays the consultant a percentage of the increased revenue).

The initial CMS Recovery Audit Contractor (RAC) program identified incorrect coding and a failure to document medical necessity as major issues (Wilson, 2009). RAC audits identify improper payments for Medicare claims and recover funds for the Medicare program. When a pattern of improper payments indicates possible fraud, the RAC auditors are required to notify CMS, and the **Office of the Inspector General (OIG)**, the agency charged with protecting the integrity of the Medicare and Medicaid programs, may investigate the providers involved.

In some cases, a provider may enter into a **corporate integrity agreement (CIA)** as part of a settlement with the OIG, to avoid defending itself against fraud or abuse charges. In this circumstance, the provider may contract with the consultant as an independent reviewer to meet the OIG's requirements for ongoing monitoring and training in appropriate coding.

Finally, all health care providers who receive payments under Medicare or Medicaid are expected to have compliance programs to guard against fraud and abuse. Guidance documents for developing compliance programs for various types of providers have been available from the OIG since 1998 (see https://oig.hhs.gov).

Compliance programs were voluntary until mandated by the Patient Protection and Affordable Care Act in 2010. Although the details of the OIG's guidance vary somewhat for each type of provider, typical components of compliance programs include internal monitoring and auditing, development of compliance standards or policies, designation of a compliance officer or contact, appropriate training and education of the workforce, an appropriate response or investigation when offenses are detected, as well as other elements (OIG, n.d.). A small provider may not have the resources to fully implement its own compliance program and, therefore, may contract with a consultant for services to meet some of the requirements.

Office of the Inspector General (OIG) a subdivision of the U.S. Department of Health and Human Services. "The mission of the Office of Inspector General is to protect the integrity of Department of Health and Human Services (HHS) programs, as well as the health and welfare of the beneficiaries of those programs." (OIG, n.d.).

corporate integrity agreement (CIA) an agreement that a health care provider or health plan reaches with the Department of Health and Human Services' Office of the Inspector General (OIG) as part of a settlement agreement when allegations of improper reimbursement have been made.

SELF REVIEW 16.4

1. Explain the relationship between clinical documentation and revenue.
2. Name a website where a HIM consultant can locate information related to compliance guidelines for the health care industry.

PROFESSIONAL SPOTLIGHT **CERTIFIED CODING SPECIALIST-PHYSICIAN**

Who I am: My name is Rebecca Haines, CCS-P. I received my certification from the American Health Information Management Association (AHIMA) in 2001.

Where I work: Muskingum Valley Health Centers (MVHC), Coshocton, Zanesville, Malta, Ohio.

What I do: As the Manager of Patient Financial Accounts, I manage the staff at three locations of MVHC and occasionally consult in the HIM field. MVHC is a Federally Qualified Health Center. Approximately 8% of our revenue comes from grants. The remainder of our revenue is generated through patient visits. An accurate, efficient revenue cycle is essential for our center to keep serving our population of patients. This consists of supplying the registration and billing staffs with the tools of education and training to submit claims correctly. I educate the staff on submitting insurance carrier claims, how to collect demographics from patients properly.

A billing/registration supervisor reports directly to me and works at all three locations as well. Each service line has a lead staff that oversees the day-to-day operations and schedules. I work closely with our software vender,

(continued)

reviewing accounts receivable reports, looking for trends related to carriers and specific providers. I monitor our clearinghouse reports for trends in submission of claims and remittance processing. We use an electronic medical record in which the CPT code is calculated according to the documentation; the diagnosis code is assigned according to the provider definition. We currently have two coders who review claims for accuracy of coding, compliance, and carrier-specific needs before submitting them. We use a sliding fee scale for our patients who qualify for a discount based on income. I review our fee schedule annually and calculate the tiers of the slide for the discount according to the Federal Poverty guidelines. This is approved by our board of directors annually as well.

Consulting with the staff on current CMS guidelines is a key role that I provide for MVHC; this includes provider education as well as staff education. I internally audit medical documentation for accuracy and provide feedback to each provider concerning any coding issues. I research carrier-specific coding and educate the staff about documentation from the research.

Why HIM knowledge is important in my role: For our centers to stay in compliance with changes in health care, with our federal government, with the office of inspector general, and to receive proper timely reimbursement, I must have the essential research tools and information. Therefore, I study AHIMA, AMA, CMS, Medicaid, and carrier-specific education updates. I keep up on my certification with an annual self-review test that is mandatory for AHIMA certification; this requires several hours of study and research. I also am required to report 20 hours of continuing education every 2 years, and I attend seminars provided by various health care organizations such as Ohio State Medical Association (OSMA).

Other: I have worked in health care for 28 years in Southeastern Ohio. At the start of my career, I worked in private medical offices, and in the last 16 years I have worked with nonprofit organizations through private contributions and various grants to open and facilitate offices. I also have had the past opportunity to be an instructor for Washington State Community College in Marietta, for the evening Medical Coding classes. Finally, I have enjoyed working with the underserved populations in the rural areas, bringing them quality affordable health care.

ROLE OF THE HEALTH INFORMATION MANAGEMENT PROFESSIONAL

Choosing to be an independent consultant is synonymous with starting a new business and being self-employed. A successful health information consulting practice requires a credential as a Certified Coding Specialist (CCS), Certified Coding Specialist-Physician-based (CCS-P), Registered Health Information Technologist (RHIT), or Registered Health Information Administrator (RHIA), along with relevant work experience and careful research and planning. This process should begin by performing a rigorous self-assessment of interpersonal communication skills. Individuals who possess these skills often have a strong network of professional contacts in place already, making it easier to market themselves.

Research indicates that organizations use their contact networks more than any other method to select consultants. Many independent consultants start by consulting on a part-time basis. Health care facilities often seek consultants who can provide certain services for a few hours each month or for a specific project. Satisfied clients often provide referrals. It may take some time to build a client base that provides an income that will permit giving up the benefits associated with a fulltime job.

Having expertise in a specific profession or skill is important, as well as learning how to run a business. Although a health information consulting business may be launched with a minimum of capital expense, it is critical to formalize the business by developing key documents. The consultant should formally document a mission statement, a marketing plan, and a list of services to be offered. It also is helpful to compile a list of strengths and weaknesses, and measurable personal and business objectives that can serve as an annual plan.

Additional documentation should include an objective statement of the percentage by which the client base will increase yearly, a list of clients who need these services, the demographics of potential clients, a list of competitors, equipment and office space requirements, and the number of employees now and projected for the future. Finally, the consultant should develop both monthly and yearly revenue and expense budgets.

Later, if the consultant needs to develop a **business plan** (a formal document summarizing the operational and financial objectives of a business), the basics are in place already. A business plan includes the details of how the objectives are to be attained, including budgets and other financial forecasts. Lenders and investors usually require a business plan as one of the documents they study when deciding whether to lend to or invest in a business.

Formulating a business plan as well as an annual plan is a good idea. As the consulting business grows, more capital may be needed, and a business plan is necessary if the consultant seeks capital (e.g., a loan from a bank). A typical business plan format includes the following:

- Executive Summary
- Description of Business
- Industry Analysis
- Customer Analysis
- Competitor Analysis
- Marketing Strategies
- Operational Plan
- Financial Projections

Some consultants have found it helpful to utilize business plan software in developing their business plans. A quick search of the Internet yields numerous business planning programs to evaluate. Examples of business planning are available on the following websites:

- http://www.bplans.com
- http://www.planware.org
- http://www.sba.gov
- http://www.entrepreneur.com/howto

business plan a formal written document summarizing the operational and financial objectives of a business. The business plan also includes details of how the objectives are to be attained, including budgets and other financial forecasts. Lenders and investors generally require a business plan as one of the documents they study when making a decision whether to lend to or invest in a business.

Leadership Ability

A consultant should possess credentials and experience that provide credibility, be an excellent communicator, possess leadership skills, and, above all, have a good reputation. Being of good repute means that others believe an individual is trustworthy, hardworking, and honest. Leadership has been defined as an influence process (Maxwell, 2007). Any time an individual motivates others to accomplish a goal, he or she is practicing leadership.

A key role of the consultant is to work with others to ensure organizational and departmental compliance with laws, regulations, standards, policies, and procedures. In addition, consultants must be able to write proposals, develop process maps, manage a project, solve problems, train staff, perform research (qualitative and quantitative), deal well with complexity and chaos, and be self-confident, self-reliant, disciplined, resilient, and financially astute. A consultant must be able to read between the lines to assess potential clients' needs and to negotiate mutual expectations about the consultant's role in that process. He or she must be able to see the big picture and to communicate it clearly to others.

Leaders have high standards. When leaders lack character, they also lack integrity. Good leaders show no discrepancy between what they appear to be and who they are. They take responsibility and are credible, transparent, honest communicators with nothing to hide. Good leaders follow through to the final detail.

An astute businessperson has interpersonal intelligence—the ability to understand other people, what motivates them, how they work, and how to work cooperatively with them (Koch, 1996). The consultant has to take the time to focus, give undivided attention to clients, and really listen as they communicate their needs.

Thus, consultants must continuously seek to strengthen their interpersonal as well as their technical skills. HIM professionals have to pursue additional education and training to stay current with the vast changes occurring in the field and to meet the continuing education requirements necessary to maintain their own professional credentials.

Just as essential as current knowledge of the rapidly changing health care environment is to gauge the attitude and ability of self, as well as others, to accept the changes. Consultants have to be prepared to listen and allow the individuals who are most affected by a change to provide ample input regarding decisions that affect them.

For example, it can take physicians and nurses as long as 3 months to fully learn and adapt to using a computer to document clinical information, but a well-implemented system is worth the transition (Wager et al., 1999). One of the keys to successful EHR implementation is to involve the clinician users in the transition.

A leadership challenge that a consultant faces is that the consultant's power often is based on influence and expertise, not on organizationally mandated authority. The consultant makes recommendations to the client, and the client can choose to follow or not follow those recommendations. The consultant may have challenges with clients—such as working with people who lack technical expertise and need clear goals and direction, training, and development. On occasion, a consultant meets with resistance, conflict, intense competition, or rejection and criticism and, as a result, the client discards the consultant's ideas or terminates the consultant's contract.

Learning to nurture, mentor, and encourage oneself can help the consultant handle failures and continue to be willing to take risks. Also, developing a supportive personal and professional network assists consultants in maintaining a positive attitude when difficulties arise.

Being responsible for influencing others requires consultants to act ethically. Consulting involves a personal struggle based on acting on self-interest versus acting for the benefit of others. The consultant may encounter individuals who are self-serving and arrogant, those who withhold information, those who seek power and recognition, those who are poor listeners, those who spend a great deal of time protecting their own status, and those who are unable to accept criticism. In these circumstances, consultants must demonstrate leadership and not be discouraged. They must serve as a constant positive force to each facility they serve.

In the past few years, newspapers have reported numerous incidences of financial failures of businesses as a result of the illegal and unscrupulous acts of individuals in high-level management positions. In these situations, unbridled greed, the improper use of power, and a sense of entitlement have replaced integrity. Consultants, therefore, must guard against conflicts of interest and maintain high ethical standards.

SELF REVIEW 16.5

1. One desired trait for a consultant is to have a good reputation. What does this mean to you?

2. In addition to a mission statement, a marketing plan, and services to be offered, what are two elements that could be included in a business plan?

3. How can a consultant mentor himself or herself in the face of failure and adversity?

4. True or False? Effective consultants avoid communication with individuals who will be most affected by the proposed change.

HIM Consulting Fees

Consultants must carefully assess their future needs along with their current financial needs. When determining what to charge, consultants should consider the following questions.

First, what will it cost the consultant to provide services? The consultant must invest in clothes and office accoutrements that exemplify professionalism. For example, the consultant should purchase software that can be utilized to produce invoices, contracts, and other deliverables. The most common software utilized is Microsoft Office. An office where professional phone calls can be made and received is a necessity after employees are hired. If desiring to work from home, it is not acceptable to talk to a client with a dog barking, children talking, or a video playing in the background. Whether travel is involved also affects the costs of operating a consulting practice. Success depends upon generating enough revenue to cover all expenses. Often, the most financially successful consultants are those who can minimize their expenses.

Another question to consider: What will the market bear? In a market where there many self-employed consultants there may be fierce competition. In setting fees, the consultant will have to consider what others charge for similar services.

A third question: What is the consultant's reputation based on the testimony and referrals of others? What an independent consultant charges is determined in part by the individual's abilities, prior experience, and previous success.

Managing any business requires meticulous record keeping and careful analysis of current as well as future expenses. Preparing a personal income statement that includes all current revenue and expenses is helpful. An individual who is considering self-employment should have adequate cash reserves to cover expenses for a 3-month period, given that consultants may have to wait for payment for periods longer than 90 days.

When an employer pays a salary, it often includes holidays, personal or vacation leave, medical leave, health insurance plans, and the employer portion of FICA tax. Benefits that an employer provides are estimated at between 20% and 30% of the employee's gross salary. In addition, the employer provides office space, furniture, computer equipment, telephone, travel, and training. A person who is in the process of making a decision to give up the benefits of working for someone else in order to establish his or her own business has to realize that business revenue must be high enough to cover more than just the consultant's salary.

As a case study, consider a consultant who desires to earn a salary of $75,000 per year. The consultant adds 30% to this gross salary figure for fringe benefits and $20,000 for operating expenses.

$$\$75,000 \times 1.30 + \$20,000 = \$117,500$$

$$\$117,500/220 \text{ workdays per year} = \$534 \text{ per day}$$

$$\$534/8 \text{ hours per day} = \$67 \text{ per hour}$$

Because an independent consultant commonly experiences gaps in workload, it isn't realistic to expect to be engaged in billable consulting work 220 days per year. Therefore, to be able to pay oneself a salary of $75,000 may require charging a higher daily or hourly fee to allow time for seeking new clients and other activities for which no revenue is earned directly. If travel is involved, the consultant must cover those expenses as well and might charge a flat fee (for example, $1,000 per day) or may negotiate a contract in which the client agrees to pay travel expenses.

Failing to plan and count the cost of being self-employed can lead to business collapse. Individuals who are interested in consulting should seek wise counsel and learn from others how they made the transition from being employees to being self-employed. Networking at professional meetings and conferences as well as in online forums can help consultants who seek advice. Many have been deceived and have failed because of the assumption that high hourly charges by consultants mean that self-employment will be financially lucrative and provide more personal freedom. In addition, not considering the importance of a balanced lifestyle that provides adequate time with spouse, children, extended family, and friends can lead to great personal loss as well as financial failure. In establishing an independent consulting practice, it is advisable to proceed cautiously and conservatively.

Seeking Clients

The best sources of referrals are individuals whom the consultant knows professionally and personally. The consultant should keep in regular contact with these individuals. Membership in professional organizations, such as AHIMA, also is valuable. To build credibility, the consultant should consider the following:

* Volunteer to speak at professional meetings.
* Write blogs and articles for professional publications.
* Send e-mails and a quarterly newsletter to clients and potential new clients.
* Join a business-oriented social networking site.
* Stay in touch with satisfied clients—excellent sources of referrals.
* Create a Web page to market services on the Internet, and perhaps hire an expert to achieve the desired result. Ask past satisfied clients if you can include a quote from them on your Web page.
* Develop a logo and color scheme and use it consistently on stationery, business cards, and the Web page. Develop a professional one-page résumé, as well as an academic résumé that lists publications and work experience.
* Provide free seminars.
* Possibly advertise in a trade journal, after assessing how previous or current clients were obtained.

Working at Home

Consulting requires the ability to develop a *container* for oneself, stay focused, work unsupervised, and have healthy boundaries. A *container* refers to the place in which focused work is done both physically and mentally. For consultants who work from home, a physical workspace container has to be planned—a place recognized and respected as the office space of the new business. This space can be a guest room planned in such a way that a sofa or futon in the room provides an extra bedroom when necessary, yet serves most of the time as an attractive, efficient office. Explore the tax laws with an accountant if you plan to use this office space as a tax deduction. Plan a space that meets your work needs. Finding furniture at a reasonable price that utilizes all current physical space may require creativity. A countertop around the periphery of a room, with shelves above it and file cabinets under it, can provide a lot of inexpensive desktop and storage space.

ergonomics workspaces and equipment designed to fit the human body to maximize comfort, convenience, and efficiency at work.

The consultant should utilize **ergonomic** principles that facilitate comfort and convenience. For example, an adjustable computer monitor should be purchased so the top of the screen can be positioned at or slightly below eye level (OSHA, n.d.). An adjustable keyboard tray is needed for the keyboard so the fingers, wrists, and elbows remain in a straight line to reduce the risk of cumulative trauma disorder. The chair should have adjustable arms, back, and seat. The seat should be capable of being lowered or raised so the knee and hipbone are in a straight line, with the feet placed firmly on the floor or on a footrest.

As part of the office plan, the computer should be placed to allow work materials to be placed on both sides so everything needed for work is within arm's reach. The workspace and desktop should be free of glare and shiny objects. A window as a backdrop for a computer is not advised because of the glare; however, miniblinds to regulate outside light can be utilized. Paint, furnishings, and countertops that have a matte finish and are of soft colors create a space that facilitates calm, clarity, and simplicity. Fabric and carpet can be utilized to reduce noise and create an ambiance of comfort and softness.

Computer software can be used to accomplish many tasks. Examples include word processing, résumé and form design, and data analysis and computation, as well as producing professional presentations.

Being focused mentally requires setting boundaries. Work at home is conducted in the same way as one would act as a HIM department director in a health care facility. The integrity of the home office must be respected. An answering machine can be used to handle personal calls and unwanted telephone marketing calls. To minimize interruptions, friends and family should be educated about work hours.

A parent working at home does not mean that a babysitter is no longer necessary. Being focused and productive means devoting full attention to the task at hand, with minimal interruptions. If young children are at home, hire a babysitter and set clear boundaries. Develop instructions that will minimize telephone and television use and noise levels; where, what, and with whom activities and children are permitted; how to handle minor emergencies; any medications that a child routinely takes; if and which neighborhood children are permitted in the house or yard; and caring for household pets. Train pets to be willingly and quietly confined in areas other than your workspace.

Family members sometimes have difficulty accepting and respecting an individual's professional role at home. Generally, they do not know what an individual really does at work, and might not recognize activities conducted in a home office as work. Relatives can present multiple disruptions and expect work to cease so their personal needs are met. Therefore, a consultant must set firm boundaries and limits with family members, as well as babysitters and friends.

In some instances, a consultant may find that a working environment away from home is indeed the best solution. A thriving practice may warrant employing an administrative assistant for networking, marketing, and seeking additional contracts.

Office Equipment

Consultants must have certain equipment to conduct business efficiently. Following is a checklist of suggested items:

- Computer with high-speed Internet access
- Dedicated and reliable phone service (usually a cell phone and a landline)
- Answering system or voice mail
- Fax machine
- Copier, scanner, and printer

Computers and Tablets

Computers and tablets are an integral part of day-to-day business for consultants. To determine what type of computer setup is best for an individual's needs, a few questions have to be answered:

- Is access to the computer needed when traveling to clients?
- Are heavy graphics involved?
- What type of software will be used (e.g., word processing, database, spreadsheet, graphics, presentations, reporting, data mining, video conferencing)?
- What computing equipment are clients using?

Thinking-through these questions will help in determining the type of computer that will best fit one's needs. In most cases, it is not necessary to purchase the latest model with the fastest speed available. Current models available in any large electronics store can easily handle most consultant applications. Generally, it is not necessary or prudent to procure the most advanced system in the store. Buying a model that has been on the market for 6 months will cost considerably less and be more than adequate.

Regardless of the type of computer selected, the consultant must have a means of backing up critical data to protect important business assets in the event of a system failure. Software is available to schedule automatic backups to an external hard drive. Online backup services also are available and offer the advantage of storing backup data securely offsite. The most economical way to store files is to use a cloud system such as Dropbox.com, Box.com or Google Drive. These systems offer free online storage and often keep up to five of the most recent versions of each file.

The consultant will have to decide whether to invest in a laptop, a desktop computer, a tablet or all three. The advantage with laptops and tablets is their portability. While in a hotel room, at a restaurant, or flying to an appointment, work can be accessed readily. Many laptop models are just as capable as their desktop counterparts. As useful as a laptop can be, however, some features of the smaller version are inferior to a desktop model. For one thing, the smaller keyboard can be awkward and mouse control usually is relegated to a touchpad on which the user maneuvers his or her fingers to direct the cursor. The variety of portable computing devices continues to grow, with new options appearing regularly.

Tablets usually are more difficult than a laptop to type on and enter data unless an external keyboard is utilized. Much of the software being developed today, however, takes advantage of the tablet platform. Tablets, such as the iPad, are being used to streamline operations for firms transitioning to electronic health records. Again, the consultant should consider the type of device needed for his or her specific situation and weigh the costs and benefits before purchasing a mobile computing solution.

Internet access is a necessity in the consulting arena today. E-mail is a way of life in business. E-mail accounts can be set up at no cost on sites such as Yahoo.com and Gmail.com. For a fee, one also can obtain an e-mail domain name using the name of the consultant's business. Consultants should consider having their own Web page that describes their expertise and services and usually a simple one can be built for a nominal fee. A consultant who uses the Internet extensively will need high-speed Internet access, such as cable, DSL, or satellite. Video conferencing is another wise use of the Internet. Communicating with clients via the Internet utilizing software such as Adobe Connect or Skype can save wasteful travel time.

Telephone and Wireless Services

Consultants definitely need a cell phone and possibly a landline if they need to fax documents. The landline typically connects to the internet with DSL service. Although faxing is being used less and less, it is still advantageous in some situations. Consultants who visit clients in various locations need a cell phone to be reached easily. Many consultants find that a smart phone offers numerous advantages, including the ability to send and receive e-mail messages and to keep track of contacts and appointments while away from the office. Some cell phone applications can easily convert pictures of documents to PDF format. Once saved as a PDF file, they can be signed on the phone with a finger and then e-mailed.

Answering System or Voice Mail

Consultants have to be able to receive voice messages at any time. An answering system or voice mail is critical. Answering devices must have very good sound quality. Remember—consultants always have to maintain a professional image, and a voice greeting that presents a garbled or muffled message does not make a good impression. Also, if the consultant will need to check messages while away from the office, an answering system that provides this feature should be selected. Voice mail is simply an automated answering service provided by the phone company or wireless communications provider. Voice mail messages generally can be checked from any telephone. Most providers charge a small monthly fee for voice mail services.

Fax Machines, Copiers, Scanners, and Multipurpose Devices

Documents often have to be sent back and forth between a consultant and a client. Fax machines allow for rapid transmission of printed documents that cannot or should not be e-mailed. Fax machines are affordable and easy to use. The consultant also may have to scan documents to e-mail to clients, so a scanner may be a desirable piece of equipment. The consultant should be aware, however, that unencrypted e-mail does not always meet HIPAA security requirements; therefore, the consultant should not transmit documents containing protected health information to a client across different networks by regular e-mail. Some companies offer HIPAA-compliant e-mail systems.

If copies have to be made on a regular basis, a copy machine should be purchased or leased. Copiers range in price from hundreds to tens of thousands of dollars. If purchasing or leasing a copier, also consider the cost of toner and other supplies, which can add quite a bit to the operating costs of some machines. If copies are not made that often, using a local copying service may be more feasible.

An alternative to buying several different pieces of office equipment would be to purchase a multipurpose machine that acts as a printer, fax machine, scanner, and copier. Prices for these devices are reasonable, and they can save substantial office space.

Negotiating Contracts

The HIM consultant should take an active role in designing a work contract, seeking the help of an attorney in producing a contract that clearly spells out the consultant's needs regarding pay, authority, responsibility, and so forth. A written contract may outline the number of hours to be worked in a specific health care facility and the fee charged per hour by the consultant. Some contracts include reimbursement for mileage and other travel expenses. The contract outlines responsibilities on the part of both participants. It often states that the contract employee (consultant) is responsible for all payroll deductions such as taxes, health insurance, and retirement. If the consultant is going to charge for information provided to the facility via phone consultation or if some projects are going to be completed in the consultant's home office (such as preparing a policy and procedure manual or designing forms), clarify how this time will be billed.

Most consulting contracts are for a one-year period, and a new contract is signed annually or is self-renewing. Most health care facilities want the contract to state that it can be voided at any time with 30 days' advance notice. Usually it is not possible to negotiate a termination clause. Clients often require the consultant to maintain professional liability insurance coverage. Figure 16-2 provides only an outline of possible contract elements and should not be considered as a model for contract development. The consultant should seek legal advice and ensure that any contract is HIPAA-compliant and appropriate to the legal and business environment of the state and community.

The privacy standards of HIPAA and Title XIII of ARRA and the Health Information Technology for Economic and Clinical Health (HITECH) Act, have specific requirements regarding the business associates of a covered entity. (Recall from Chapter 1 that a covered entity may be a health plan, a health care clearinghouse, or a health care provider. In this discussion, we will use a health care provider as an example of a covered entity.)

FIGURE 16-2

A sample contract (not to be used as a model).

CONSULTING AGREEMENT

This Agreement is made effective as of July 1, 20XX, by and between **Agency** and **Consultant**.

Consultant has a background in Health Information Systems Management and is willing to provide services to **Agency** based on this background.

Agency desires to have services provided by **Consultant**.

Therefore, the parties agree as follows:

1. DESCRIPTION OF SERVICES. Beginning on July 12, 20XX, **Consultant** will provide the following services (collectively the "Services"):
   - Provide education for personnel regarding appropriate documentation for medical records.
   - Provide information and other technical assistance for compliance with XXXX Department of Mental Health regulations.
   - Provide technical assistance with quality assurance plans, activities, and reviews.
   - Provide technical assistance to ensure compliance of Medical Records with XXXX Department of Mental Health regulations.
   - Other duties within the scope of Health Information Systems Management expertise as requested by the Executive Director.

FIGURE 16-2   (*continued*)

2. PERFORMANCE OF SERVICES. The manner in which the Services are to be performed and the specific hours to be worked shall be determined by **Consultant**. **Agency** will rely on **Consultant** to work as many hours as may be reasonably necessary to fulfill **Consultant's** obligations under this Agreement, not to exceed six and one-half hours per month unless approved in advance by the board of directors of **Agency**.

3. PAYMENT. **Agency** will pay a fee to **Consultant** of $XX.00 per hour for the Services. This fee shall not be payable until receipt of third-party revenues.

4. LICENSURE/CERTIFICATION. **Consultant** shall at all times maintain all licensure and certifications required of a medical records technician and shall be responsible for any costs associated with such licensure and certification.

5. TERM/TERMINATION. Either party may terminate this Agreement upon giving 30 days, written notice to the other party. This Agreement shall terminate automatically on June 30, 20XX.

6. RELATIONSHIP OF PARTIES. It is understood by the parties that **Consultant** is an independent contractor with respect to **Agency** and not an employee of **Agency**. **Agency** is not responsible for withholding and shall not withhold FICA or taxes of any kind from payments made to **Consultant**. **Consultant** shall not be entitled to receive any benefits that employees of **Agency** may be entitled to receive, and shall not be entitled to workers' compensation, unemployment compensation, medical insurance, life insurance, paid vacations, paid holidays, pension or social security on account of her work under this Agreement.

7. EMPLOYEES. **Consultant's** employees, if any, who perform services for **Agency** under this Agreement shall also be bound by the provisions of this Agreement. At the request of **Agency**, **Consultant** shall provide adequate evidence that such persons are **Consultant's** employees.

8. INJURIES. **Consultant** acknowledges **Consultant's** obligation to obtain appropriate insurance coverage for the benefit of **Consultant** (and **Consultant's** employees, if any). **Consultant** waives any rights to recovery from **Agency** for any injuries that **Consultant** (and/or **Consultant's** employees) may sustain while performing services under this Agreement.

9. INDEMNIFICATION. **Consultant** agrees to indemnify and hold **Agency** harmless from all claims, losses, expenses, fees including attorney fees, costs and judgments that may be asserted against **Agency** that result from the acts or omission of **Consultant**, **Consultant's** employees, if any, and **Consultant's** agents. If professional liability insurance is available to cover her acts or failure to act as a health information manager, **Consultant** shall obtain such insurance, at her own expense.

10. CONFIDENTIALITY. **Consultant** recognizes that **Agency** has and will have the following information:

   — client information and other proprietary information (collectively, "Information") that are valuable, special and unique assets of **Agency**. **Consultant** agrees that **Consultant** will not at any time or in any manner, either directly or indirectly, use any Information for **Consultant's** own benefit, or divulge, disclose, or communicate in any manner any Information to any third party without the prior written consent of

(*continues*)

FIGURE 16-2 *(continued)*

Agency. **Consultant** will protect the Information and treat it as strictly confidential. A violation of this paragraph shall be a material violation of this Agreement.

11. CONFIDENTIALITY AFTER TERMINATION. The confidentiality provisions of this Agreement shall remain in full force and effect after the termination of this Agreement.

12. RECORDS AND RETURN OF RECORDS. Upon termination of this Agreement, **Consultant** shall deliver all records, notes, data, memorandum, models and equipment of any nature that are in **Consultant's** possession or under **Consultant's** control and that are **Agency's** property or relate to **Agency's** business.

13. NOTICES. All notices required or permitted under this Agreement shall be in writing and shall be deemed delivered when delivered in person or deposited in the United States mail, postage prepaid, addressed as follows:

Company: name/address

Consultant: name/address

Such address may be changed from time to time by either party by providing written notice to the other in the manner set forth above.

14. ENTIRE AGREEMENT. This Agreement contains the entire agreement of the parties and there are no other promises or conditions in any other agreement whether oral or written. This Agreement supersedes any prior written or oral agreements between the parties.

15. AMENDMENT. This Agreement may be modified or amended if the amendment is made in writing and is signed by both parties.

16. SEVERABILITY. If any provision of this Agreement shall be held to be invalid or unenforceable for any reason, the remaining provisions shall continue to be valid and enforceable. If a court finds that any provision of this Agreement is invalid or unenforceable, but that by limiting such provision it would become valid or enforceable, then such provision shall be deemed to be written, construed, and enforced as so limited.

17. WAIVER OF CONTRACTUAL RIGHT. The failure of either party to enforce any provision of this Agreement shall not be construed as a waiver or limitation of that party's right to subsequently enforce and compel strict compliance with every provision of this Agreement.

18. APPLICABLE LAW. This Agreement shall be governed by the laws of the State of (name of state).

Consultant

By:

Agency

By:

A **business associate** is a person who is not a member of the health care provider's workforce but performs work on behalf of the provider that involves the use or disclosure of protected health information (USDHHS, 2003). Because a consultant is not considered to be a member of the health care provider's workforce, the HIPAA privacy rule dictates that the consultant have a written business associate agreement or contract with the facility. One example of the types of issues covered by the business associate agreement is a provision for safeguards to prevent inappropriate use or disclosure of protected health information on the part of the consultant. The U.S. Department of Health and Human Services' Office for Civil Rights provides simple business associate provisions that the HIM consultant may want to review, on its website, www.hhs.gov.

The HITECH Act has placed additional obligations for privacy and security on business associates and also extends the threat of civil and criminal penalties for violations of privacy and security standards to business associates.

business associate under HIPAA, a person who is not a member of the covered entity's (e.g., the health care provider's) workforce but performs work on behalf of the covered entity that involves the use or disclosure of protected health information.

SELF REVIEW 16.6

1. What should a consultant charge per hour if he or she desires an annual salary of $80,000, has operating expenses of $10,000 and has fringe benefits of 20%? (Assume that he or she works 200 days at 8 hours a day.)

2. Dropbox.com is an example of a(n)
    a. flash drive
    b. external hard drive
    c. moving company
    d. online storage system

3. The best sources of referrals for consultants are:
    a. individuals whom the consultant knows professionally and personally
    b. trade journals
    c. AHIMA
    d. online blogs

4. Which technology is becoming less utilized?
    a. Cell phones
    b. Computers
    c. Tablets
    d. Fax machines

TRENDS

Because of changing regulations, the adoption of ICD-10 CM/PCS, and health care reform, the demand for HIM services and health care consultants probably will remain strong. Other factors contributing to the need for consultants are an increased emphasis on compliance activities, the complexity of regulations and managed care and their effect on various health care settings, and health care providers' need to operate effectively and efficiently in an ever-changing environment.

SELF REVIEW 16.7

1. Name two trends occurring in the United States that may increase the demand for HIM consultants.

2. True or False? Compliance issues and government regulations are decreasing in complexity.

SUMMARY

Starting a new business as a consultant is challenging and requires careful research and planning. Once consulting contracts are obtained, success depends on the ability to gain administrative support and rapport and on the delivery of excellent service. Therefore, consultants must develop long-range goals and money management skills. Obtaining the help of an attorney and an accountant can help to avoid legal difficulties and to ensure compliance with the tax code.

To promote personal marketability, the consultant should seek and gain employment in various health care settings, volunteer, read professional journals, attend workshops and seminars, take college courses, and pursue additional credentials. The ability to set healthy boundaries and provide a container where focused work can be performed both mentally and physically is necessary. The consultant may design a home office space that incorporates ergonomic techniques to facilitate comfort and convenience or rent office space away from home.

The HIM consultant should take an active role in negotiating a contract. The contract should meet the needs of both client and consultant and clearly spell out the fee charged, what is covered, what is not covered, and when payment is expected.

The first item on the consultant's agenda is to seek a clear understanding of the client's needs. The initial interview with the client should be considered as a two-way interview to find out the client's needs and whether he or she clearly understands and can meet these needs. The consultant then prepares a written summary of the interview and writes a thank-you letter.

After obtaining a new contract for a health care facility, the consultant considers the client's needs and develops a plan to address them. For example, if the contract calls for assessment of facility documentation, the consultant reviews all of the relevant regulations regarding documentation requirements, develops an assessment tool, conducts random audits, prepares reports that apprise the client of the findings, and seeks the client's feedback. Copies of all audits and reports submitted to the client should be kept and maintained for future reference.

REVIEW QUESTIONS

Knowledge-Based Questions

1. Explain the concept of a corporate integrity agreement (CIA) and the role that a consultant might play when such an agreement is in effect.
2. Explain what a documentation audit is and the documentation audit cycle.
3. Describe desirable characteristics of a consultant.
4. Explain the basis for the consultant's power in a consulting situation.
5. Explain the factors that a consultant should consider in setting fees.
6. Describe the equipment that an independent consultant may need.
7. Explain the concept of a business associate under HITECH/HIPAA.
8. Define leadership and its role.
9. Describe why a consultant should not enter into a "contingency" contract with a client.
10. Provide examples of the privacy standards of HIPAA and ARRA/HITECH regarding business associates.
11. Describe the key elements of a business plan for an independent consultant.

Critical Thinking Questions

1. Explain the difference between cognitive intelligence and interpersonal intelligence.
2. A health information consultant charges $100 per hour and works the equivalent of 200 billable 8-hour days per year. Taxes, insurance, travel, and other expenses consume about 70% of the consultant's gross revenue.
   a. What is the consultant's gross annual revenue (i.e., the total amount he or she receives from his or her clients before taxes and other expenses)?
   b. What is the consultant's net annual income (i.e., take-home pay after taxes and other expenses)?

WEB ACTIVITY

Find the Conditions of Participation or Conditions for Coverage for one of the settings discussed in any previous chapter. (One Web source for locating these documents is http://www.cms.gov at the Centers for Medicare & Medicaid Services.) Search for Conditions of Participation.

1. Within the Conditions, locate the medical or clinical record standards for the selected setting.
2. Develop an audit form that a consultant could use to audit the documentation in the selected setting, based on the record standards found in the Conditions.

CASE STUDY

Identify the problem areas for the facility described below, and prepare a written recommendation addressing a plan of correction for each site.

You have been hired as a consultant for a behavioral health care facility comprising 11 client service sites. They are Joint Commission accredited and are anticipating a survey soon. After initial visits to each site, your analysis of deficiencies includes:

Site 1—Residential Chemical Dependency Program for Adolescents

The medical records are well organized and in good order, but after closer inspection you find that the physician responsible for completing physical exams does not assess clients' motor skills, which is a requirement for adolescent admissions. You also find that although the history and physical is performed and dictated by the physician within 24 hours, the typed report does not appear in the chart for weeks.

Site 2—Residential Chemical Dependency Program for Adult Women

The Joint Commission and state standards require that a master treatment plan be completed within 14 days of admission. A representative sample review of the facilities' charts reveals no treatment plans. Upon closer scrutiny, you learn that none of the clients admitted in the past 3 months has a treatment plan in the charts either.

Site 3—Outpatient Mental Health Clinic with 600 Active Clients

After conducting a study to determine the record retrievability rate, it is learned that 75% of the records are inaccessible. The day the study was completed, only 40 clients had been scheduled for appointments. This location has only two health information clerks, and one has been pulled frequently to answer the phone at the intake desk.

Site 4—Outpatient Chemical Dependency Site with 125 Active Clients

A quantitative analysis process has been set up and the record clerk trained, but no quantitative analysis has occurred. Upon a return visit to analyze the situation, it is found that the records clerk is also the office manager with responsibilities to answer the phone, schedule appointments, conduct financial intakes, maintain time sheets for clinicians, and complete general correspondence.

Site 5—Outpatient Chemical Dependency Site with 40 Active Clients

Upon receiving a subpoena *duces tecum* and a court order, a clinical supervisor fails to notify the organization's clinical director, health information manager, or an administrator. Instead, she takes the records home and asks her husband, who is an attorney, for advice.

REFERENCES AND SUGGESTED READINGS

Koch, Charles G. (2007). The Science of Success. Hoboken, NJ: John Wiley & Sons, Inc.

Levin, D. I., & Gilbert, A. (1998). Knowledge transfer. managerial practices underlying one piece of the learning organization. [Online]. www.irle.berkeley.edu/cohre/knowledge.html [2015, October 1].

Maxwell, J. C. (2007). The 21 Irrefutable Laws of Leadership. Nashville, TN: Thomas Nelson, Inc.

OIG. Office of the Inspector General. (n.d.). Compliance guidance. [Online]. http://oig.hhs.gov/fraud/complianceguidance.asp [2011, April 19].

OSHA (Occupational Safety & Health Administration). (n.d.). Computer workstations. [Online]. http://www.osha.gov/SLTC/etools/computerworkstations/components_monitors.html [2011, April 19].

Pyle, L. S. (2008, December 03). Home based business reality check. Entrepreneur. [Online]. http://www.entrepreneur.com/homebasedbiz/homebasedbizcolumnistlestleyspencerpyle/article [2010, March 9].

USDHHS (U.S. Department of Health and Human Services Office of Civil Rights, HIPAA Privacy). (2003, April). Business associated. [Online]. http://www.hhs.gov/ocr/privacy/hipaa/understanding/coveredentities/businessassociates.pdf [2015, August 9].

USDHHS (U.S. Department of Health and Human Services Office of Inspector General). (2010, February). Recovery audit contractors' fraud referrals. [Online]. http://oig.hhs.gov/oei/reports/oei-03-09-00130.pdf [2010, March 30].

Wager, K. A., Lee, F. W., Glorioso, R., & Bergstrom, L. (1999). Working smarter, not harder, in a family practice. Journal of the American Health Information Management Association, 70(6), 44–46.

Wildi, R. (2014, February 20). Consultant [personal communication]

Wilson, D. D. (2009, May). Five RAC coding targets: Demonstration program identified key areas of improper payment. Journal of AHIMA 80(5), 64–66.

KEY RESOURCES

American Health Information Management Association
http://www.ahima.org

Association of Management Consulting Firms
http://www.amcf.org

Bureau of Labor Statistics, U.S. Department of Labor
http://www.bls.gov

Centers for Medicare and Medicaid Services
http://www.cms.gov

Electronic Discovery Reference Model
http://edrm.net

Federal Register
https://www.federalregister.gov

Institute of Management Consultants USA
http://www.imcusa.org

Internal Revenue Service
http://www.irs.ustreas.gov

National Center for Health Statistics. ICD-9-CM
Official Coding Guidelines for Coding and Reporting
http://www.cdc.gov/nchs/icd/icd9cm_addenda
_guidelines.htm

National Center for Health Statistics. ICD-10-CM
Official Coding Guidelines for Coding and Reporting
http://www.cdc.gov/nchs/icd/icd10cm.htm

Office for Civil Rights. Sample Business Associate
Contract Provisions
http://www.hhs.gov/ocr/privacy/hipaa
/understanding/coveredentities/contractprov.html

Unixwiz.net Tech Tips—So You Want to Be a Consultant?
(Steve Friedl)
http://unixwiz.net

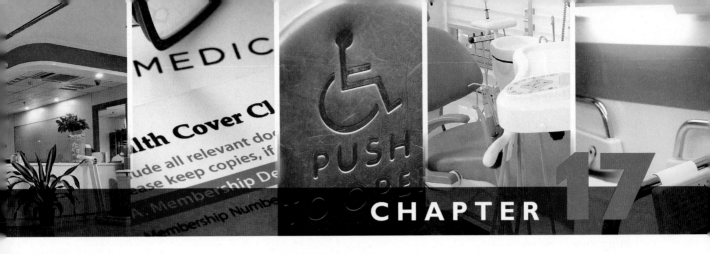

CHAPTER **17**

Cancer Registry

Deirdre B. Rogers, MS, CTR

LEARNING OBJECTIVES

Upon successful completion of this chapter, you should be able to:

- Explain the purpose and typical functions of a cancer registry.
- Distinguish among population-based, hospital-based, and specialty cancer registries.
- Describe key standards for cancer registries and cancer registry data.
- Explain the role of key organizations, associations, and programs in cancer registry, including the Commission on Cancer (CoC), the National Cancer Registrars Association (NCRA), the National Program of Cancer Registries (NPCR), the North American Association of Central Cancer Registries (NAACCR) and the Surveillance, Epidemiology, and End Result (SEER) program.
- Describe issues in coding for cancer registry, as well as other specific issues related to cancer registry data, such as cancer staging.
- Explain certifications available for cancer registry professionals.
- Explain the nature of quality improvement processes with regard to cancer registry.

Type of Cancer Registry	Description
Population-Based Cancer Registries	Collect all newly diagnosed cancers in a defined geographic area
Hospital-Based Cancer Registries	Collect all newly diagnosed cancer cases in a hospital or group of hospitals
Specialty Cancer Registries	Collect cancer data for the following: • Specific facilities • Particular Type of Cancer • Familial Cancers

INTRODUCTION TO THE SETTING

The term **cancer** is applied to more than 100 diseases that are characterized by uncontrolled growth of cells. The American Cancer Society (2015) estimated that approximately 1,658,370 new cases of cancer would be diagnosed and there would be 589,430 deaths from cancer in that year. Cancer is a public health concern because of its impact on people and on the health care system.

The **cancer registry** is a surveillance system that systematically collects newly diagnosed cancer cases for the purpose of monitoring the disease burden, the quality of care of cancer patients, cancer survival, and disparities. The earliest known example of such surveillance was the "General Census of Cancer" in London in 1728. The first hospital-based cancer registry in the United States was established at Yale-New Haven Hospital in 1926. In 1935, the first population-based cancer registry was established in Connecticut. Today, all U.S. states and territories have cancer registries to monitor the burden of cancer (see Key Resources: National Cancer Institute, SEER Training Modules).

cancer a general term for more than 100 diseases characterized by uncontrolled growth of cells.

cancer registry a surveillance system that systematically collects newly diagnosed cancer cases for the purpose of monitoring the disease burden, the quality of care of cancer patients, cancer survival, and disparities.

Types of Cancer Registries

Population-Based Cancer Registries

Population-based cancer registries collect data on all newly diagnosed cancer cases in the population of a defined geographic area, such as a state, region, or country. Sources of data for the population-based registry include treatment facilities including hospitals, ambulatory surgery centers, radiation facilities, physician offices, pathology laboratories, radiology facilities, other population-based cancer registries, and death certificates.

The focus of a population-based cancer registry is on public health and epidemiology. The registry is useful for monitoring cancer trends and patterns of cancer in populations. The data collected assist in prioritizing the use of health resources, planning and evaluation of cancer control efforts in the population, and clinical, epidemiological, and public health research.

Currently, every state in the United States has a statewide cancer registry. Beyond monitoring trends in cancer diagnoses, these registries provide valuable information on the distribution of cancer in sub-populations such as

population-based cancer registries registries that collect data on all newly diagnosed cancer cases in the population of a defined geographic area such as a state, region, or country.

racial/ethnic groups and sub-state geographies. They also can assist in monitoring cancer screening efforts by examining the stage distribution of cancers using effective screening methods. Population-based cancer registries are a helpful tool in examining health disparities related to cancer (see www.cancer.org).

Hospital-Based Cancer Registries

hospital-based cancer registry a registry that collects data for individual hospitals or networks of hospitals on new cancer cases diagnosed and/or treated in that hospital or group of hospitals.

A hospital-based cancer registry collects data for individual hospitals or networks of hospitals on new cancer cases diagnosed and/or treated in that hospital or group of hospitals. The focus is on administration and clinical care. The registries are useful in evaluating whether or not patients are receiving "standard of care" treatment based on type of cancer and for monitoring cancer outcomes such as survival or recurrence of disease (Commission on Cancer, 2012). The data in the cancer registry can be used for health care provider education, facility utilization studies, and research.

The data collected in hospital cancer registries include the information required for the population-based registry, covering the geographic area where that hospital is located. The same coding standards are used for both types of registries. Thus, the hospital registry transmits the necessary data to the population-based registry at regular intervals as required by the population-based registry and state or regional cancer reporting regulations (see www.cancer.org /cancer).

Specialty Cancer Registries

specialty cancer registries registries established for the purpose of collecting data from specific facilities, for a specific cancer site, or for familial cancers.

Specialty cancer registries are registries established for the purpose of collecting data from specific facilities, for a particular cancer site, or for familial cancers. These specialized registries also may serve as an educational resource, an advocacy group, or a support system for those suffering from a specific type of cancer.

National Cancer Database (NCDB) an outcomes database with data collected from more than 1,400 cancer programs in the United States and Puerto Rico, used to examine cancer treatment trends and survival and for quality improvement in cancer care.

American College of Surgeons Commission on Cancer's National Cancer Database The National Cancer Database (NCDB) is an outcomes database that can be used to examine cancer treatment trends and survival and for quality improvement in cancer care. It began in 1989 and contains data from more than 1,400 Commission on Cancer-approved cancer programs in the United States and Puerto Rico. The database includes approximately 70% of all newly diagnosed cancer cases in the country. The data collected for the NCDB include patient characteristics, tumor site and histologic characteristics, staging, first course of treatment, and patient follow-up information for survival (Commission on Cancer, 2015).

Familial and Site-Specific Cancer Registries These registries serve as research tools and potential sources of education and advocacy for cancer patients. Many times, patient enrollment is voluntary. There are many of these registries, of which the following are examples:

- Central Brain Tumor Registry of the United States (CBTRUS): CBTRUS began in 1992 to collect data on benign, borderline, and malignant brain tumors. The purpose of the registry is to increase awareness of these tumors, describe the incidence and survival of brain tumors, evaluate the diagnosis and treatment, and facilitate research on etiology.

- The Breast Cancer Family Registry (B-CFR): The NCI began this registry in 1995 as an international coalition of academic and research institutes from countries including Australia, Canada, and the United States together with their medical affiliates. The registry is used to conduct clinical and population-based studies of the molecular and genetic epidemiology of breast cancer.

- Gilda Radner Familial Ovarian Cancer Registry: This international registry contains information on families that have two or more relatives with ovarian cancer. Besides research, this registry offers ovarian cancer educational resources.

- National Familial Lung Cancer Registry: This registry collects information on families with two or more members diagnosed with lung cancer who refer themselves to the registry. The registry seeks to determine causes beyond smoking for lung cancer and to provide educational resources.

The remainder of this chapter focuses primarily on the population-based and hospital-based cancer registries, though further discussion of the NCDB also is included.

Types of Professionals Working in the Cancer Registry

An array of professionals work in the cancer registry. Many have health information backgrounds. Others have backgrounds in epidemiology, statistical methods, or information technology. Still others represent various nontraditional backgrounds but have found roles in the cancer registry.

For many of the jobs in a cancer registry, a certified tumor registrar (CTR) credential from the National Cancer Registrars Association (NCRA) is required. Those with health information backgrounds are well-suited for obtaining this credential and working with the data collected in the cancer registry. The CTR credential will be described in more detail later in the chapter.

SELF REVIEW 17.1

1. Cancer is a title applied to more than 100 diseases that are characterized by
   _____.

2. Describe the earliest known cancer surveillance in the world.

3. _____ are registries that are established for the purpose of collecting data from specific types of facilities, for a specific cancer site, or for familial cancers.
   a. Hospital-based cancer registries
   b. Specialty cancer registries
   c. Population-based cancer registries

4. _____ collect data on all newly diagnosed cancer cases in the population of a defined geographic area, such as a state, region, or country, for the purposes of public health and epidemiology.
   a. Hospital-based cancer registries
   b. Specialty cancer registries
   c. Population-based cancer registries

5. With a focus on administration and clinical care, _____ collect data for individual hospitals or networks of hospitals on new cancer cases diagnosed and/or treated in that specific hospital or group of hospitals.
   a. hospital-based cancer registries
   b. specialty cancer registries
   c. population-based cancer registries

6. Where was the first U.S. cancer registry established?

7. List three data sources used by the population-based registry.

8. True or False? Population-based cancer registries are useful for monitoring cancer trends.

9. True or False? Some states have never had a statewide cancer registry.

10. Explain the purpose of familial and site-specific cancer registries, and give two examples.

11. What credential is required for most jobs in a cancer registry?

REGULATORY ISSUES

In the United States, cancer registration is considered to be a high-quality public health surveillance system. One of the reasons for this designation is data standardization. In the late 1980s, when a push to aggregate data across cancer registries occurred, there was a dearth of data standardization across cancer registries of different types. This limited the utility and comparability of the data collected and resulted in a considerable amount of time and money spent just to make data from hospital cancer registries integrate into central cancer registry systems. Cancer registries also were subject to inconsistent standards from national organizations to which they submitted data for aggregate surveillance. This desire to aggregate data finally led to the development of standards.

Today, standards of data collection allow for comparison of data across cancer registries and for compilation of data on regional and national levels. Requirements for data elements and timeliness of data collection, however, vary across different types of registries based on state laws and reporting regulations and to what national organization the registry submits data. In addition, the purpose of the registry dictates the data elements necessary for collection. Hospital-based cancer registries usually collect a larger set of data elements than a population-based cancer registry.

Several standard-setting organizations and professional organizations work under the umbrella organization of the North American Association of Central Cancer Registries (NAACCR). This organization establishes and maintains uniform data standards for hospital-based and population-based cancer registries.

Commission on Cancer

The American College of Surgeons (ACoS) established the Commission on Cancer (CoC) in 1922. The CoC developed the first standards of quality multidisciplinary and comprehensive cancer care delivery in the health care setting. The first minimum standards for cancer clinics were published in 1931. In 1956, the CoC included the requirement of a cancer registry for hospitals to be CoC-approved, and in 1962 published the first manual on tumor registration. There are more than 1,500 CoC cancer programs in the United States (American College of Surgeons Commission on Cancer, 2015).

The CoC continues to provide hospital-based cancer registries with data standards and coding instructions that are updated regularly to meet the needs of cancer surveillance in the form of the *Facility Oncology Registry Data Standards (FORDS)* manual. The CoC also requires hospital registry data to pass a prescribed set of data quality edits for fitness of use at the hospital level and in the NCDB (Commission on Cancer, 2013b).

The Surveillance, Epidemiology, and End Result Program (SEER)

The National Cancer Institute's Surveillance, Epidemiology, and End Result (SEER) program is a population-based cancer registry that funds specified states, metropolitan areas, and native populations for data collection. SEER began collecting data in 1973 from a limited number of registries and continued to expand the number of registries to cover a greater percentage of different demographics (see Key Resources, National Cancer Institute, SEER). As of 2014, the SEER program included 20 population-based registries and covered approximately 28% of the U.S. population. SEER data are comparable to the U.S. population in poverty status and education, but contain more foreign-born people than the general

Commission on Cancer (CoC) the organization that developed the first standards of quality, multidisciplinary, and comprehensive cancer care delivery in the health care setting and continues to provide hospital-based cancer registries with data standards and coding instructions.

Facility Oncology Registry Data Standards (FORDS) a manual published by the Commission on Cancer that provides data standards and coding instructions for facility-based cancer surveillance for the purposes of quality patient care.

Surveillance, Epidemiology, and End Result (SEER) a program of the National Cancer Institute that includes a population-based cancer registry funded for specified states, metropolitan areas, and native populations. Because of its follow-up program, the SEER registry is as the only population-based cancer registry in the United States with longitudinal data on stage of disease at both diagnosis and survival.

U.S. population. SEER registries, like other population-based registries, collect data on patient demographics, tumor site and morphology, and treatment. The SEER-funded registries, unlike other population-based cancer registries, collect active follow-up on patients for survival. SEER serves as the only population-based cancer registry with both longitudinal data on stage of disease at diagnosis and survival.

SEER published the first coding manual for its registries in 1976 and continues to update the *SEER Program Coding and Staging Manual* annually with required data elements, coding standards, and standards of data quality. Standards of data coding and collection have not always been consistent between SEER and the CoC because of their differing purposes. SEER serves the needs of epidemiology and research, whereas the CoC is focused on quality patient care. SEER, however, depends on hospital-based cancer registries as sources of data, so in 1980, the CoC and SEER collaborated to develop surgery-specific codes that both could use. Over time, many SEER standards also have been incorporated into the CoC cancer registry standards. Still, minor differences between data coding rules exist. Like the CoC, SEER requires registry data to pass rigorous edits and standards for quality (Adamo et al., 2013).

National Cancer Registrars Association

The **National Cancer Registrars Association (NCRA)** began as the National Tumor Registrars Association (NTRA) in 1974. The association began a certification process in 1983 for cancer registrars and other cancer registry professionals. The Certified Tumor Registrar (CTR®) credential establishes the standards of knowledge for cancer registry professionals. Passing an exam is required to receive the credential, which assures that a cancer registry professional possesses the required knowledge and experience to hold the certification. Every 2 years, a CTR must submit 20 continuing education hours to NCRA to maintain the certification.

North American Association of Central Cancer Registries

The **North American Association of Central Cancer Registries (NAACCR)**, established in 1987, serves as the umbrella organization for central cancer registries, government agencies, professional organizations, and other cancer-related organizations to come together to improve quality and utility of cancer data. The membership of NAACCR includes groups from the United States and Canada. NAACCR establishes and promotes uniform data standards, certifies population-based registries in the United States and Canada on data quality, timeliness and completeness, and provides education to members of the cancer registry

SEER Program Coding and Staging Manual a document that includes required data elements, coding standards and standards of data quality to serve the needs of epidemiology and research.

National Cancer Registrars Association (NCRA) an association for individuals working in cancer registries; the NCRA certifies cancer registry professionals who meet its standards through its Certified Tumor Registrar (CTR®) credential.

North American Association of Central Cancer Registries (NAACCR) the umbrella organization for central cancer registries, government agencies, professional organizations, and other cancer-related organizations to come together to improve quality and utility of cancer data; the NAACCR serves groups from the United States and Canada and publishes a five-volume set of standards for population-based cancer registries.

community. NAACCR also promotes the use of the cancer registry in public health, research and patient care.

NAACCR published the first sets of standards for population-based cancer registries in 1994. *Standards for Cancer Registries, Data Exchange Standards and Record Description, Volume I,* provides the standard record layout for cancer registry records for electronic data exchange. This allows for ease of integration of data from reporting sources into the population-based cancer registries. *Standards for Cancer Registries: Data Standards & Data Dictionary, Volume II,* provides information on reporting requirements of the various standard-setters and a dictionary of every data element available for collection in the cancer registry (Havener, 2013).

The *Standards for Completeness, Quality, Analysis, Management, Security, and Confidentiality of Data, Volume III* provides information on data collection, data management, data quality, and data use (Hofferkamp, 2008). *Standards for Cancer Registries (Vol. IV) NAACCR Standard Edits* gives a comprehensive list of data edits with their definitions, the standard-setting organization that created the edit, and by which standard-setter each edit is required. *Pathology Electronic Reporting (Vol. V)* provides population-based cancer registries with standards on collection of electronic pathology laboratory data (Klein & Havener, 2011). These volumes are updated as needed. NAACCR has a formal approval process for standard-setting organizations to make changes to the standards included in these volumes. (North American Association of Central Cancer Registries (2013a, 2013b).

National Program of Cancer Registries

In 1992, Congress passed the Cancer Registries Amendment Act, authorizing the Centers for Disease Control and Prevention (CDC) to provide funding to states and territories for collection of cancer data and to establish standards for this data collection process. The CDC established the National Program of Cancer Registries (NPCR) and began providing funds to statewide population-based cancer registries in 1994. NPCR also established program standards and standards of data quality, timeliness and completeness. These standards are updated to address changes in the landscape of cancer registration. NPCR also adopted NAACCR standards and established a minimum data set required to be collected by funded cancer registries. In 2001, NPCR began receiving annual data submissions from funded cancer registries.

NPCR currently supports population-based cancer registries in 45 states, the District of Columbia, Puerto Rico, and the U.S. Pacific Island Jurisdiction covering 96% of the U.S. population. NPCR partners with the SEER program to achieve coverage of the entire U.S. population. This partnership allows for monitoring the U.S. burden of cancer incidence, shown in Figure 17-1 (CDC, National Program of Cancer Registries, 2013b).

National Program of Cancer Registries (NPCR) a program established by the Centers for Disease Control that provides funds to statewide population-based cancer registries. NPCR provides program standards and standards of data quality, timeliness, and completeness and also has adopted NAACCR standards and established a minimum data set. NPCR receives annual data submissions from funded cancer registries.

FIGURE 17-1

Incidence of cancer across the United States in 2011 recorded by the Interactive Cancer Atlas.

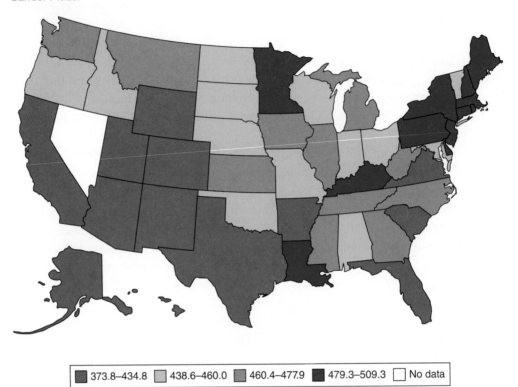

| ■ 373.8–434.8 | ▢ 438.6–460.0 | ▨ 460.4–477.9 | ■ 479.3–509.3 | ▢ No data |

Source: Centers for Disease Control (CDC), https://nccd.cdc.gov/DCPC_INCA.aspx.

SELF REVIEW 17.2

1. True or False? There are more than 1,500 CoC cancer programs in the United States.

2. _____ established program standards and standards of data quality, timeliness, and completeness and established a minimum data set required to be collected by funded cancer registries.
   a. NAACCR (North American Association of Central Cancer Registries)
   b. NPCR (National Program of Cancer Registries)

3. _____ serves as the umbrella organization for central cancer registries, government agencies, professional organizations, and other cancer-related organizations to come together to improve the quality and utility of cancer data.
   a. NAACCR (North American Association of Central Cancer Registries)
   b. NPCR (National Program of Cancer Registries)

4. _____ developed the first standards of quality, multidisciplinary and comprehensive cancer care delivery in the health care setting.

5. _____ began a certification process for cancer registrars and other cancer registry professionals.

   a. NCDB

   b. NCRA

   c. SEER

   d. NPCR

6. _____, developed by the National Cancer Institute, this program includes a population-based cancer registry funded in specified states, metropolitan areas, and native populations; it is the only population-based cancer registry in the United States that collects follow-up data, allowing it to provide longitudinal data on stage of disease at both diagnosis and survival.

7. Match the organization with the type of standards it provides:

   North American Association of Central Cancer Registries (NAACCR)

   _____

   Surveillance, Epidemiology, and End Result (SEER) program _____

   Commission on Cancer (CoC) _____

   National Program of Cancer Registries _____

   a. Standards serve the needs of epidemiology and research

   b. Standards focus on quality patient care

   c. Five-volume set of standards are used in both the U. S. and Canada

   d. Standards developed for statewide population-based cancer registries

DOCUMENTATION

One purpose of a cancer registry is to maintain a complete, accurate record of the cancer experience of all newly diagnosed cancer patients diagnosed and/or treated in the hospital or in the population they serve. An **abstract** is a summary record that allows for this systematic collection of information on a cancer patient's experience in a standardized format. Thus, abstracts are the most important documents maintained by the cancer registry, and they form the basis for all of the registry operations. These abstracts are maintained electronically in the cancer registry database.

A cancer abstract contains several categories of information on the cancer patient and diagnosis. These categories are described next.

abstract   a summary record in a standardized format that allows for systematic collection of information on a cancer patient's experience.

Patient Information

Each patient is assigned a nine-digit unique number in the hospital cancer registry system, usually computer-generated and commonly called the

accession number   a
nine-digit unique number
in the hospital cancer
registry system that identifies the patient.

accession number. Typically, the first four digits of the accession number specify the year and the last five digits specify the order in which the patient was entered into the registry. Using this pattern, the first patient entered in 2016 would be assigned accession number 201600001. The patient also is given a sequence number indicating the order of the cancer diagnoses that the patient had in his or her lifetime. Other information in the patient information section includes the patient's medical record number, name, social security number, birth date, address at the time of the cancer diagnosis, place of birth, race, Spanish/Hispanic origin, primary payer at the time of diagnosis, any co-morbid conditions the patient may have, and the physicians involved in the cancer care. This information assists in linking the patient to additional primary cancers, follow-up information and death records (Menck, et al., 2011).

Cancer Information

The cancer identification section describes the disease. Data items included are the class of case, which describes the relationship the patient had with the facility reporting the cancer. In addition, the facility that referred the patient to the reporting facility and any facility to which the reporting facility referred the patient are included. Dates included in this section are the date the facility first had contact with the patient for cancer and the date the patient initially was diagnosed with cancer. Cancer-specific information includes the primary site, histology, behavior (benign, borderline, in situ, or malignant), laterality, and grade or differentiation of the cells. Also included are diagnostic confirmation details about whether the cancer was confirmed by histology or cytology or if the case was confirmed by clinical means without a tissue diagnosis (See Key Resources—National Cancer Institute, *SEER Training Modules*, *Biographical Information*).

Stage of Disease at Diagnosis

The stage of disease at diagnosis consists of fields that describe the size and local extension of the primary tumor, whether or not regional lymph nodes are involved with cancer and whether or not distant metastasis was present when the cancer was diagnosed. Stage can be assessed clinically to assist the clinician in planning treatment, and then pathologically to assess the effect of neoadjuvant therapy or the need for adjuvant therapy. Both stages would be recorded in a hospital cancer registry. Staging data also is useful in population-based cancer registries for assessing screening patterns for cancers with effective screening (National Cancer Institute, Cancer Staging, 2015).

Understanding the terms in the accompanying box is helpful in understanding some of the data recorded in a cancer registry abstract

Adjuvant therapy – Additional cancer treatment given after the primary treatment to lower the risk that the cancer will return. Adjuvant therapy may include chemotherapy, radiation therapy, hormone therapy, targeted therapy, or biological therapy.

Grade or *Tumor Grade* – Description of a tumor based on how abnormal the tumor cells and the tumor tissue appear under a microscope. This is an indicator of how quickly a tumor is likely to grow and spread. If the cells of the tumor and the organization of the tumor's tissue are close to those of normal cells and tissue, the tumor is called "well-differentiated." These tumors tend to grow and spread at a slower rate than tumors that are "undifferentiated" or "poorly differentiated," which have abnormal-looking cells and may lack normal tissue structures.

Neoadjuvant therapy – Treatment as a first step to shrink a tumor before the main treatment, which usually is surgery. Examples of neoadjuvant therapy include chemotherapy, radiation therapy, and hormone therapy. It is a type of induction therapy.

Primary cancer – The term used to describe the original, or first, tumor in the body. Cancer cells from a primary cancer may spread to other parts of the body and form new, or secondary, tumors. This is called metastasis. Secondary tumors are categorized as the same type of cancer as the primary cancer. The location of the primary cancer or primary tumor is called the primary site.

Staging – the severity of a person's cancer based on the size and/or extent (reach) of the original (primary) tumor and whether or not cancer has spread in the body.

Source: National Cancer Institute, *NCI Dictionary of Cancer Terms*, available at http://www.cancer.gov/dictionary and NCI Fact Sheets, available at http://www.cancer.gov/cancertopics/factsheet/ [2015, October 3]

Treatment

Hospital-based cancer registries and population-based cancer registries both collect information at the first course of treatment. Hospital cancer registries at CoC-approved hospitals also collect information on subsequent treatment and palliative care. Surgical procedures, radiation, chemotherapy, hormone therapy, and immunotherapy are recorded with dates and type of treatment administered. In addition, transplants and endocrine procedures are documented in the treatment section. If the patient receives only palliative care as the first course of treatment, this is recorded both as first course of treatment and as palliative care in a hospital cancer registry at a CoC-approved hospital. If the patient does not receive treatment for the cancer, this also is recorded in the treatment section, as is whether the patient undergoes active surveillance (CDC, 2004).

Outcomes

All cancer registries collect information on the last date of contact with the patient, whether or not they are alive on that date, and if the patient has died, the place of death, cause of death, and whether an autopsy was performed. Hospital cancer registries in CoC-approved facilities also record information on the patient's current address and phone number and the contact information of a person who would know about the patient over time. This information is used to conduct active follow-up. In addition, hospital cancer registries collect and update information annually on the status of the patient's cancer and information on cancer recurrence, if applicable (Menck, et al., 2011).

Case Administration

Case administration includes information on the abstractor and reporting institution, as well as information on the versions of coding manuals and coding systems used in abstracting the case. This section also includes over-ride flags that can be set to clear up data edits where the edit indicates coding combinations that are unusual. The over-ride flags indicate that the unusual combination is actually correct.

Text Documentation

The text fields are included in the abstract for the abstractor to justify the codes that are assigned in the abstract. These text fields provide information necessary for quality control at the reporting facility, as well as the population-based cancer registry. The text should provide a concise summary of the patient's cancer experience that matches the coded summary in the abstract.

Suspense Cases

The electronic abstract has defined fields and codes that meet the standards set forth by NAACCR and can be exported from the cancer registry system in a format that can be transmitted to standard-setters and population-based cancer registries, as required. Before preparing an abstract, the hospital registry must identify the cases to be abstracted. This is done in a suspense system within the registry software. Pathology reports and disease indices are used to identify potential cancer cases for abstracting. These documents are used to create an abbreviated abstract called a suspense case. The registrar examines suspense cases to determine if they are reportable and should be abstracted (See Key Terms: National Cancer Institute, *SEER Training Modules: Suspense File*).

suspense case an abbreviated abstract developed from pathology reports and disease indices used to identify potential cancer cases for abstracting; the cancer registrar examines suspense cases to determine if they are reportable and should be abstracted.

Additional Documentation

Hospital-based cancer registries at CoC-approved facilities must maintain a current policy and procedure manual as defined in the Commission on Cancer program standards. Population-based cancer registries also must have a policy and procedure manual for internal activities and a reporting manual for reporting sources that details reporting requirements and methods of reporting. In addition, many hospital-based cancer registries in CoC-approved facilities maintain documentation necessary for meeting the CoC cancer program standards unrelated to the cancer registry, such as minutes for Cancer Committee meetings and attendance at cancer conferences.

All cancer registries maintain documentation on data provided for research studies. To ensure the confidentiality of patient data, the Commission on Cancer (CoC) requires an agreement to exchange data between population-based cancer registries and hospital-based registries in CoC-approved cancer programs. In addition, the CoC requires a Business Associate Agreement to submit data to the National Cancer Database (Commission on Cancer, *Data Use Agreement,* 2013a).

SELF REVIEW 17.3

1. _____ are documents maintained by the cancer registry and form the basis for all of the registry operations.
   a. Records
   b. Abstracts
   c. Cases

2. Identify three pieces of patient information contained in the hospital cancer registry system.

3. True or False? Cancer-specific information includes the primary site, histology, behavior, laterality, and grade of the cells.

4. A(n) _____ is an abbreviated abstract developed from pathology reports and disease indices used to identify potential cancer cases for abstracting.

5. How often do hospital cancer registries collect and update information on the status of patient's cancer?

6. Explain the usefulness of cancer staging (i.e., describing the size and/or extent of the primary tumor and whether or not cancer has spread in the body).

7. Who set forth the standards that are used in electronic abstracting?

REVENUE GENERATION

Funding for a hospital-based cancer registry comes from the hospital budget. Cancer registries are not revenue-generating. The data contained in the registry, however, can be used by the hospital administration for marketing and improvement of patient care. This can impact the bottom line of the hospital's budget.

The NCI SEER program began providing funding to 20 population-based cancer registries. Beginning in 1973, SEER funded registries in Connecticut, Iowa, New Mexico, Utah, Hawaii, metropolitan areas of Detroit, and San Francisco-Oakland. In 1974 and 1975, metropolitan Atlanta and the 13 counties of the Seattle-Puget Sound area were added. Ten predominantly Black counties in rural Georgia were added to the SEER program in 1978. In 1980, American Indians in Arizona were added to the SEER program. In 1992, the SEER program expanded to include Los Angeles County and four counties in the San Jose-Monterey area of California. In 200, Kentucky and the remaining counties of California (Greater California) were added to the SEER program. New Jersey also rejoined SEER in 2001 after having been funded by SEER previously in 1979–89. Louisiana rejoined the SEER registry in 2001 after New Orleans, Louisiana, was funded by SEER in 1974–77. In 2010, SEER expanded to include the remaining counties of Georgia. Puerto Rico was once funded by SEER in 1973–89. The NCI funds a registry for Alaska Native populations in Alaska, which receives technical assistance from the SEER program. (See Key Resources, National Cancer Institute.)

CDC's NPCR, which was established in 1992, provides grant funding to population-based cancer registries in 45 states, Puerto Rico, and the U.S. Pacific Island Jurisdiction. Additional funds are provided by entities within the states, such as the health department, a university, or other cancer partners. In addition, some population-based cancer registries generate funds through payments made for research files requested for local, regional, and national research.

SELF REVIEW 17.4

1. True or False? Cancer registries are revenue-generating.
2. Hospital-based cancer registries are funded by _____.
3. Which two agencies provide funding for population-based cancer registries?

INFORMATION MANAGEMENT

Coding and Classification

For each item collected in a cancer registry, a set of standard codes is established. These codes are maintained in several different manuals used by the abstractor in the process of completing the abstract. One of these manuals is the *International Classification of Diseases for Oncology* (ICD-O). The first edition of this manual was published in 1976 after physicians expressed a desire for a cancer supplement to the *International Classification of Diseases, Ninth Revision* (ICD-9) that would include morphology.

The topography codes in ICD-O were patterned after the neoplasm chapter of ICD-9, and the morphology codes were based on the American Cancer Society's *Manual of Tumor Nomenclature and Coding* (MOTNAC) published in 1951. ICD-O provides a 10-digit code with four digits for topography, four digits for histology, a slash, one digit for behavior (malignant, benign, *in situ* or otherwise classified) and one digit for tumor grade (which describes how closely the tumor tissue resembles normal tissue). The histology, behavior, and grade codes comprise the six-digit morphology code.

The second edition of ICD-O was published in the 1990s. The topography codes were changed, to be based on ICD-10 instead of ICD-9. Widespread use of the second edition in the United States began in 1993. In addition, new morphology terms were added to the second edition and the lymphoma section was expanded.

The third edition of ICD-O was published in late 2000 and implemented in U.S. registries on January 1, 2003. This edition incorporated the WHO classification of hematopoietic and lymphoid neoplasms. Morphology terms were defined further with new synonyms included in the manual based on terminology used by pathologists. Several neoplasms changed behavior codes from borderline to malignant. The third edition of ICD-O was still in use in 2014.

The ICD-O is used to code the topography and morphology codes in an abstract. Detailed coding instructions are included in the front of the manual and should be studied before using the manual. In addition, the ICD-O uses a "matrix principle" which allows the abstractor the flexibility to change the behavior code listed in the manual if another behavior code reflects the diagnosis provided by the pathologist more accurately (Fritz et al., 2000).

SEER Multiple Primary and Histology Coding Rules

In 2007, the SEER *Multiple Primary and Histology Coding Rules* (MP/H), developed by a Task Force of cancer registry professionals and standard-setting organizations, were implemented to guide cancer registries in determining the number of abstracts to prepare for solid tumors and how to assign the appropriate histology code for each primary tumor abstracted. These rules replaced all previous rules that had been used to determine the number of abstracts to be completed for solid tumors. Physicians and pathologists provided input, and the Task Force sought to ensure that the histology coding rules would overlay properly with the morphology codes in the ICD-O manual (Johnson et al., 2007).

In 2010, a supplement to the MP/H rules was implemented, titled the *Hematopoietic and Lymphoid Neoplasm Case Reportability and Coding Rules* (Heme MP/H Rules). The Heme MP/H Rules provide rules on the number of abstracts to complete for malignant lymphomas, leukemias, and myeloproliferative and myelodysplastic syndromes. In addition, this manual provides information on disease reportability, and assigning topography and grade codes. The manual helps to clear up confusion about the coding of hematopoietic diseases that had existed with the ICD-O manual (Ruhl, et al., 2014).

Cancer Staging

The stage of the cancer refers to the extent of the disease. Assessing the stage of the disease can assist the physician in determining the appropriate treatment and in determining the patient's prognosis. The stage of disease includes the local spread of the tumor, involvement of regional lymph nodes, involvement of distant lymph nodes or tissues, and prognostic factors. The stage of disease can be determined through information from the physical exam, radiological procedures, endoscopy, surgical procedures, pathology reports, prognostic factors, progress reports, and discharge summary.

Several different systems exist for assessing the stage of disease. They include the American Joint Committee on Cancer (AJCC) Staging System, SEER Summary Stage, and the Collaborative Staging Data Collection System. These systems have different purposes and are selected for use by standard-setters based on how they align with the mission of that group.

AJCC Staging System   The AJCC Staging System is based on examination of the size and invasiveness of the primary tumor (T), the presence of metastasis in the regional lymph nodes (N), and the presence of metastatic disease in distant tissues and lymph nodes (M). The AJCC Staging System is helpful in clinical care to assist in determining appropriate treatment and prognosis. It is required for collection by hospital-based cancer registries that are approved by the CoC (Edge et al., 2009).

The first edition of the *AJCC Cancer Staging Manual* was published in 1977. In 2010, the seventh edition of the manual was implemented and currently is used with the eighth edition in the planning stages. The manual consists of chapters based on cancer sites/types that describe how to classify the T, N, and M categories and assign a stage group based on the T, N, M, and prognostic factors.

There are multiple types of AJCC staging. First, the clinical stage is based in information acquired during the work-up prior to start of definitive treatment. This stage is used in determining the course of treatment for the patient. The pathological stage is based on information prior to definitive treatment, together with information from surgery and pathological examination of the resected tissue. The pathological stage is used to assess prognosis and survival. The post-therapy, or post-neoadjuvant therapy, stage is assigned after radiation or systemic therapy, or both, have been administered. This stage can be clinical or pathological, depending on whether a surgical resection follows the radiation and/or systemic therapy. This stage assesses the effectiveness of the neoadjuvant therapy. In addition, AJCC staging can be assigned when a cancer recurs or when a cancer is diagnosed at autopsy.

SEER Summary Stage   The SEER Summary Stage is a single-digit code for staging that is not as detailed as other staging systems. It is used primarily by population-based cancer registries for epidemiology. The codes are relatively stable and, thus, can be used for longitudinal studies.

SEER Summary Stage 1977 was the first version of this staging system. The second version, SEER Summary Stage 2000, was implemented with cases diagnosed January 1, 2001, and later. This version of SEER Summary Stage was still in use in 2014. SEER Summary Stage describes the tumor as *in situ* (non-invasive), localized when the primary tumor is confined to the organ of origin, regional when the tumor has spread locally beyond the organ of origin or to regional lymph nodes, distant if there are metastases in distant organs or distant lymph nodes, benign if the tumor is not malignant, or unknown if the stage cannot be determined (Young, et al. 2001).

Collaborative Staging Data Collection System (CS) The standard-setting organizations in the United States and Canada, together with the AJCC, developed the Collaborative Staging Data Collection System (CS) for cancer cases diagnosed January 1, 2004, and later. The purpose of CS was to standardize data collection across hospital-based registries and population-based registries. The CS System derived the AJCC Clinical and Pathological Stages, as well as the SEER Summary Stage. In addition, CS combined the clinical and pathological stages from AJCC to determine a "best stage" for the patient and resolved issues that previously had existed between the different staging systems.

The main part of CS contains nine data elements, including tumor size, tumor extension, involvement of regional lymph nodes and presence of distant metastases. In addition, there are codes to determine the basis (pathological or clinical) for the tumor size and extension, regional lymph node involvement, and presence of distant metastasis.

The first version of CS, which was used for cases diagnosed from January 1, 2004, to December 31, 2009, had an additional six site-specific factors or tumor markers that potentially were important in prognosis or treatment of the specific cancer diagnosed. The second version of CS, implemented for cases diagnosed January 1, 2010 and later, expanded the number of potential site-specific factors to 25 from the original 6.

CS includes an algorithm that takes the individual data elements coded and derives the AJCC 6th and 7th Edition Clinical and Pathological Stages, SEER Summary Stage 1977, and SEER Summary Stage 2000. As CS is updated, all data coded in the previous versions are converted to the newest version. Although this provides a common staging system across registries, it is a complex and expensive system to maintain. This system was scheduled to cease for newly diagnosed cancers beginning in 2016. Current information on CS can be found at www.seer.cancer.gov.

Cancer Treatment

Cancer treatment is dependent on the type and stage of cancer diagnosed. Treatments for cancer include surgery, radiation, chemotherapy, hormonal therapy, immunotherapy, and transplant or endocrine procedures. Many patients receive multiple forms of treatment. Treatment can be curative or can be palliative.

Dates are coded when treatment is initiated and the start date of each treatment modality is used. There are surgery codes for cancer-directed procedures done to the primary site, regional lymph nodes, and distant sites. Radiation codes exists for type of radiation, radiation volume, and radiation doses, as well as the date the treatment ended. Codes for other treatment modalities are not as extensive as those for surgery and radiation.

Coding Rules and Data Elements

Specific codes can be found in several manuals, including the *Facility Oncology Registry Data Standards* (FORDS) developed by the CoC and the *SEER Program Coding and Staging Manual* developed by the SEER program. The FORDS manual contains coding rules for the data elements required by the CoC for its approvals program. The SEER manual contains coding rules for the elements required for collection by SEER population-based registries. Even though the two manuals exist, the coding is the same for common data elements collected by both types of registries, with the exception of the date of first course of treatment. The CoC and SEER have separate data elements for that date because their rules differ slightly on how to assign the date. Other population-based cancer registries not funded by SEER may choose which of the dates of first course of treatment to use in their registry. In addition to these two manuals, the NAACCR *Standards for Cancer Registries: Data Standards & Data Dictionary, Volume II* contains coding instructions for every historical and current cancer registry data field collected by any of the standard-setting organizations.

The data elements required by the CoC are more extensive than those required by population-based registries. This is because clinical care is the primary focus of data collection in these hospital registries. CoC-approved cancer registries collect data on first course of treatment, subsequent treatment, and palliative care. CoC also collects more extensive surgery and radiation codes than do population-based cancer registries. Hospital-based cancer registries may transmit all of their treatment data or just the required fields to the population-based cancer registry in whose jurisdiction they fall.

Details for coding of patient demographics, primary payer at diagnosis, occupation and industry of the patient for the majority of his or her life, vital status (i.e., whether or not the patient is still living), and administrative data items can be found in the FORDS, SEER, and NAACCR manuals. Information on coding follow-up, cancer recurrence, and co-morbid conditions can be found in the FORDS and the NAACCR manuals because the CoC is the only entity that requires this information.

Data Information and Flow

The hospital-based cancer registry uses several sources of data and information for casefinding. The primary source for casefinding is the documentation found in pathology reports. Other casefinding sources for registries include disease indices and discharges, medical and radiation oncology logs, outpatient records, and diagnostic radiology reports. Potential cases identified then are put in the suspense system until a final decision on reportability is made and an abstract is begun.

Some hospitals abstract cases concurrently as data become available on the case. Others wait two or more months before abstracting the case. The CoC has a Rapid Quality Reporting System for breast and colorectal cases to monitor whether or not patients receive timely treatment according to national treatment guidelines. This system requires concurrent abstracting of breast and colorectal cases for participating hospitals.

As cases are completed, edits and quality control procedures are carried out and the cases then are ready for use. At this point, they also are ready for reporting to the central cancer registry and to the National Cancer Database (NCDB) when applicable.

Information and flow of data are more complex in the population-based cancer registry. Sources of data for the population-based registry include hospitals, both those with and those without cancer registries, independent pathology laboratories, private clinics, ambulatory surgery centers, freestanding radiation centers, oncology clinics, death certificates, nursing homes, hospices, out-of-state cancer registries, and out-of-state facilities. Population-based cancer registries make as many of these sources electronic as possible.

After the information comes into the registry from all of the reporting sources, quality control is done on the data. Additional information may have to be sought to complete cases from more limited data sources such as pathology reports. Linkage and data item consolidation then must be done on multiple reports for the same patient and the same cancers. Automation of this process improves the efficiency of the cancer registry. Methods of quality control, however, must be built into the process. The cases then are ready for use and for reporting to the NPCR, SEER, and NAACCR when applicable.

Electronic Systems

Cancer registry data are stored in a database that allows data retrieval and manipulation. Commercial databases used in cancer registries include Microsoft SQL, Oracle, and Sybase. Some open-source databases used in registries include MySQL and Postgres. No matter what database application is used, an element necessary in a registry database is a key that ties the patient information to each individual cancer case belonging to that patient. Thus, cancer registry databases are relational databases.

Cancer registries must acquire a Data Management System (DMS) to manage the database. Many of the functions of the DMS are similar for both the hospital cancer registry and the population-based cancer registry. The hospital DMS, however, is used to manage data for the hospital entered by its registrar(s). The population-based cancer registry DMS is used to import data from external sources and consolidate multiple reports on the same patient and same cancers. The DMS for both the hospital and population-based registries must include mechanisms for security, quality control, analysis and reporting, data exchange, and record management.

The central registry DMS can be obtained commercially, produced in-house, or acquired from the SEER or NPCR programs. Several software vendors offer systems that are available to utilize in hospital-based cancer registries. In addition, some central registries provide their software to hospitals because hospitals are the primary source of cancer registry data. The provided software may be web-based on stand-alone.

Hospital registries also utilize the electronic hospital systems for casefinding and follow-up and may be able to automatically populate some data items, such as demographics, in the abstract. Hospital-based registries also may use linkage software, either built into their DMS or stand-alone, to link state death certificate data to their incident cases.

Population-based registries use a variety of electronic systems in addition to the DMS. Probabilistic record linkage software may be used to link to external databases such as death certificates for vital status information, voter registration and driver's license records for follow-up, and hospital discharge data sets for data quality, treatment, and follow-up. The linkage software also is used for linking research cohorts to the cancer registry data. Hospital-based cancer registries also may use probabilistic record-linking software to conduct follow-ups.

Many population-based registries have implemented infrastructure and systems for real-time reporting and processing of electronic pathology reports. In addition, cancer reporting to public health was incorporated as a "menu" (i.e., optional) measure for Meaningful Use Stage 2 for eligible professionals. Population-based registries are implementing the infrastructure and systems for this data stream as well.

Geographic Information Systems (GIS) can be used in the cancer registry for mapping data and applying information on socioeconomic status, distance from health care facilities, and environmental factors to the cancer data for cancer control and research. Proprietary and free GIS is available for use in the cancer registry for this type of data enhancement. In addition, proprietary and free software systems are used for the statistical analysis of registry data and web query systems for aggregate statistics.

Data Sets

A variety of data sets may be used in a cancer registry. Data sets produced by cancer registries are constructed based on how the data within the set will be used. Confidential data sets based on standards developed by NAACCR are produced by hospital cancer registries and other electronic reporting sources for reporting to the population-based cancer registry. A data exchange layout developed by NAACCR exists for producing the data sets for exchange of data between population-based cancer registries. Specified data sets without individual identifiers are produced for reporting to NCDB, NPCR, SEER, and NAACCR based on the data elements required by each standard-setter.

Some population-based cancer registries also will produce de-identified public use data sets and restricted access data sets that can be used for research and epidemiology.

Match the following:

1. Incorporated the WHO classification of hematopoietic and lymphoid neoplasms : _____

2. Published in 1976 after physicians expressed a desire for morphology codes : _____

3. Based topography codes on ICD-10 :_____

   a. ICD-O first edition

   b. ICD-O second edition

   c. ICD-O third edition

4. _____ were implemented to guide cancer registries in determining the number of abstracts to prepare for solid tumors and how to assign the appropriate histology code for each primary tumor abstracted.

   a. Hematopoietic and Lymphoid Neoplasm Case Reportability and Coding Rules (Heme MP/H Rules)

   b. AJCC Cancer Staging Manual

   c. Multiple Primary and Histology Coding Rules (MP/H)

5. True or False? The stage of the cancer is the extent of the disease.

6. List three systems for assessing the stage of disease.

7. True or False? The AJCC Staging System is based on type of cancer (T), the number of tumors (N), and the method of treatment (M).

8. Which staging system is used primarily by population-based cancer registries for epidemiology?

9. Which staging system has provided a common staging system across registries but has been a complex and expensive system to maintain, and has been scheduled to be discontinued?

10. List four types of cancer treatments.

11. The primary source of casefinding in a hospital-based cancer registry is

    _____.

12. Describe how Geographic Information Systems (GIS) can be used in the cancer registry.

QUALITY IMPROVEMENT AND UTILIZATION MANAGEMENT

Cancer registries utilize several methods to monitor and improve the data collected to increase the utility for evaluating patient care and outcomes, as well as for epidemiology and population-based research. The CoC, SEER, and NPCR all require edits that must be run on data to ensure that the codes are valid and that the code combinations make sense. The CoC requires cancer programs to have a quality control plan for the cancer registry data. Population-based cancer registries conduct visual review of data and casefinding and re-abstracting audits to ensure complete, high-quality data from reporting sources including hospital-based cancer registries. In addition, population-based registries compare cancer deaths from vital records to cancer incident records to identify potential missed cases from reporting facilities.

Because patients may seek diagnosis and treatment in multiple facilities, population-based cancer registries frequently receive multiple reports on the same primary cancer. These registries must combine the multiple reports on the same cancer into one concise and accurate record. Record consolidation is key in producing quality data for the population served.

Collecting complete, high quality data by cancer registries is essential for utilization of the data for improvements in cancer care and cancer control. Hospital-based cancer registries at CoC-approved hospitals submit data to the National Cancer Database (NCDB). This is a national oncology outcomes data registry developed in 1989 by a partnership between the CoC, the American College of Surgeons (ACoS), and the American Cancer Society (ACS). More than 1,500 hospital cancer registries submit data to the NCDB, covering more than 70% of newly diagnosed cancer cases. The NCDB provides CoC-approved cancer programs with access to national data to be able to compare their treatment and patient outcomes on a local, regional and national basis. Administrators also use data from their hospital cancer registry and from these comparison data to determine how to allocate resources to equipment, staff, research, and facilities (American College of Surgeons: *National Cancer Data Base*, 2015).

The CoC sets quality measures for patient care. The cancer registry data provide the basis for determining how the hospital is measuring up to the quality measures. This information is used by administrators and physicians for quality improvement programs to ensure delivery of quality cancer care.

Population-based cancer registries provide frequencies, incidence rates, and, in some cases, prevalence rates for cancer in the population they serve. This information is used to develop cancer control programs, monitor the disease burden and how it differs for different groups in the population, map the disease burden, and generate hypotheses for studies to determine causes of cancer and cancer disparities. Through the use of stage data, areas of high stage can be identified for screening programs so more cancers can be identified at an earlier stage when they are more amenable to treatment.

Also, population-based cancer data can be used to study perceived and potential cancer hot spots in a community and the relationship between cancer incidence and ecological factors, such as dietary fat or chemical exposures. Population-based cancer registries also can be a source of cases for case-control studies and cohort studies. Some population-based registries are able to provide data for patterns of care studies on a population level and to monitor survival of the population.

Population-based cancer registries funded by the SEER program and/or NPCR submit data annually to those programs for the purpose of national cancer statistics. National surveillance data can be used to compare across geographic areas and populations and also allow for examination of rare cancers and small populations.

Most state cancer registries submit data to NAACCR annually. NAACCR certifies registries based on criteria for data completeness, timeliness, and quality. Canadian provinces also submit data to NAACCR, allowing comparisons between the United States and Canada. NAACCR makes restricted access data available for researchers associated with NAACCR-member registries for studies.

SELF REVIEW 17.6

1. How do the CoC standards and NCDB help CoC-approved hospitals monitor and improve their care and outcomes?
2. What are some of the methods that cancer registries use to monitor and improve the quality of the data collected?
3. Describe several uses of population-based cancer data.

LEGAL AND ETHICAL ISSUES

The data collected and maintained by the cancer registry are confidential and subject to numerous laws and ethical considerations. Collection of cancer data by state cancer registries is mandated by state law. Thus, cancer patients do not consent to collection of their cancer information or, in many cases, do not even know that it is collected. Confidentiality for the patient and for the reporting facility is essential.

Several federal laws have had an impact on the collection, maintenance, and use of cancer data. The first is the National Cancer Act of 1971. This Act mandated collection, analysis and dissemination of data regarding the prevention, diagnosis, and treatment of cancer. From this act, the NCI SEER program was developed. Then, in 1992, Congress signed the Cancer Registries Amendment Act, which gave the CDC the authority to fund and set standards for population-based registries in states and territories. In 2002, Congress enacted the Benign Brain Tumor Cancer Registries Amendment Act, requiring cancer registries to collect benign and borderline brain tumors in addition to the malignant cancers already collected. In 2008, the Caroline Pryce Walker Conquer Childhood Cancer Act was signed, for the collection of childhood cancer cases, even though population-based cancer registries always have collected these cases.

Federal laws surrounding data confidentiality have an impact on cancer registries. The first is the Privacy Act of 1974, and the second is HIPAA. Part 164 of HIPAA, which governs the protection of PHI is pertinent to the cancer registry.

Cancer registry functions generally are carried out under the "Operations" section of HIPAA. Under this section, PHI can be exchanged between hospitals and physicians, including treatment and follow-up, as long as both entities have a relationship with the patient. This allows for hospital-based cancer registries to obtain complete information when patients go to multiple facilities. Of course, if stronger confidentiality laws exist within a state, the cancer registry staff must follow those regulations.

In addition to HIPAA, the cancer registry staff must be aware of the American Recovery and Reinvestment of 2009 (ARRA). ARRA requires that records be kept of disclosures of information, such as treatment, that is exempt by HIPAA. In addition, the individual staff can be penalized for violations of ARRA.

All states have cancer-reporting laws to which hospital-based cancer registries are subject. Health care facilities without cancer registries also are subject to reporting laws within the state. The laws and penalties for failure to comply differ by state. Many state laws have provisions allowing for exchange of information between cancer registries in other states to ensure collection of information for all residents of the population served.

Ethical conduct is essential for the cancer registry staff. NCRA has established guidelines called the *Professional Practice Code of Ethics* for ethical conduct of certified tumor registrars (CTR). One of the major issues covered in this document is the duty to produce complete, accurate, and timely information in accordance with standards, to meet the needs of cancer patients. Falsifying information to appear to meet the standards set by the standard-setting and funding organizations is unacceptable. Other issues covered in the code concern data confidentiality and security, as well as professional conduct.

SELF REVIEW 17.7

1. Name three federal laws that impact the collection, maintenance, and use of cancer data.
2. Collection of cancer data by state cancer registries is mandated by _____ law.
3. What guidelines were established by the NCRA relating to ethical conduct of certified tumor registrars?

ROLE OF THE HEALTH INFORMATION MANAGEMENT PROFESSIONAL

HIM professionals may play a key role in cancer registries. Most of the positions in a cancer registry require the CTR credential from NCRA. Graduates of HIM programs hired by a cancer registry must have earned a C or better in two semesters of Human Anatomy and Physiology and obtain one year of experience prior to being eligible for the exam, which is offered in March, June, and September of each year. Alternately, HIM graduates could earn a certificate in Cancer Registry Management (CRM) or Cancer Information Management

PROFESSIONAL SPOTLIGHT MANAGER OF THE MISSISSIPPI CANCER REGISTRY

Who I am: My name is Kristy Brister. I received a bachelor's degree in Health Information Management and hold a RHIA and a CTR certification.

Where I work: The Mississippi Cancer Registry in Jackson, Mississippi

What I do: I am manager of the Mississippi Cancer Registry, overseeing the daily operations of the cancer registry. The MS Cancer Registry began in 1996 in response to a state law (Mississippi Code 41-91). It is funded by a grant from the CDC's National Program of Cancer Registries, the Health Department, and The University of Mississippi Medical Center. The MCR is a population-based incidence registry, and we collect timely, complete, and high-quality incidence data. The data that are collected are used for program planning, for monitoring rates in the population, and for research. Aggregated data also are posted on our website for the public. To have accurate data, all staff members are trained extensively in coding and staging. I perform quality reviews on staff members to ensure that they are knowledgeable and up-to-date on all the latest coding rules. I also help to prepare new employees for the Certified Tumor Registrar (CTR) exam.

Why HIM knowledge is important in my role: Having a background in HIM has helped tremendously in my current role as Manager. The knowledge I obtained about the patient record, medical terminology, human anatomy and physiology, and management all helped to shape me into the professional I am today. Also, the training and education I received in ICD-9-CM helped me to transition to coding cancer cases using the ICD-O manual.

Other Information: I started out in the cancer registry as a Cancer Registrar. I worked in that position for a year before I sat for the Certified Tumor Registrar (CTR) exam. I worked in the Cancer Registrar position for 3 years before I transitioned into the Manager role. During my time as a Cancer Registrar, I really focused on learning all I could about cancer registration, coding, and staging. The knowledge and skills I learned in school and as a Cancer Registrar prepared me for my role as Manager.

(CIM) from an NCRA-accredited certificate program and complete a 160-hour practicum in a CTR-staffed cancer registry to be eligible for the exam. Although not necessary for someone who possesses an HIM degree already, there are also NCRA-accredited associate degree programs that include the required practicum that can lead to eligibility for the CTR.

Many job functions available in the cancer registry can be filled by HIM professionals, especially those with a CTR credential. These include the following:

- Casefinding
- Abstracting and coding cancer incident records
- Follow-up on patients in the cancer database
- Quality control of cancer records

- Record linkage
- Management
- Supervision
- Maintenance of software and other databases
- Software and database design
- Development of edit sets
- Technical support for cancer registries
- Training
- Auditing
- Consolidation of duplicate records at the population-based registry
- Maintaining documentation for the hospital's CoC approval
- Data analysis
- Liaison with researchers who are interested in using cancer registry data
- Development of cancer registry standards
- Geocoding

Cancer registry professionals are the experts on the utility and limitations of the cancer data contained in their registry. They serve as a valuable resource to the hospital's administration in interpreting the information to ensure that decisions are made based on the cancer data that are most beneficial for the patient and the hospital. The staff at the population-based registry is valuable in assisting the general public and policymakers in understanding the data, and also plays a key role in ensuring that cancer data drive the cancer control agenda. The cancer registry staff bears the responsibility of ensuring that the data collected are not only accurate, timely, and complete, but also secure.

SELF REVIEW 17.8

1. What credential is required for most positions within a cancer registry?
2. List four job functions that can be filled by a HIM position within a cancer registry.
3. True or False? An individual may take the CTR exam without ever working or completing a practicum in a cancer registry.

TRENDS

The cancer registry community is striving to obtain usable data more quickly. One movement in this direction consists of concurrent abstracting at the hospital level. Some population-based cancer registries utilize rapid case reporting to capture limited information about cancers of particular interest for research in their state soon after diagnosis. Currently, funds are being awarded to states to try rapid case ascertainment of pediatric cancers.

The electronic medical record and the inclusion of cancer reporting as a menu option for Meaningful Use Stage 2 for eligible professionals, as well as real-time electronic pathology reporting, provide opportunities for obtaining cancer incidence reports sooner. The availability of these electronic data sources, however, is not uniform across all population-based registries or across reporting sources within each state. This immense flow of information into the registry presents challenges in consolidating reports for the same patients and cancers rapidly to be able to use the more timely data.

SUMMARY

Cancer is the second leading cause of death in the United States (CDC, 2013a) and, therefore, has been a focus of public policy and research. State and federal government policies have supported the creation and maintenance of population-based cancer registries, which play a vital role in epidemiological studies that help to identify environmental and other factors that may play a role in the development of cancer. Cancer registries also provide valuable data on treatment outcomes and survival rates. A hospital-based cancer registry provides data that can be used to enhance the quality of care provided to cancer patients.

Qualified professionals who work in cancer registry settings are essential to their successful operation. The Certified Tumor Registrar (CTR®) credential offered by the National Cancer Registrars Association (NCRA) recognizes individuals who have the knowledge and skills necessary to carry out the information management functions of the cancer registry.

REVIEW QUESTIONS

Knowledge-Based Questions

1. What is the relationship between the hospital-based cancer registry and the population-based cancer registry?
2. Explain the importance of abstracts within the cancer registry.
3. Identify the sponsoring organizations or agencies for the following:
   Commission on Cancer (CoC)
   Surveillance, Epidemiology, and End Result Program (SEER)
4. Why are data elements required by the CoC more extensive than those required by population-based registries?
5. How often are data submitted to NAACCR from most state cancer registries?

6. Describe (a) the National Cancer Act of 1971 and (b) the Cancer Registries Amendment Act.
7. Name a process that some hospitals have undertaken to get usable cancer data more quickly.

Critical Thinking Questions

1. Describe the disease staging process and the key reason for disease staging.
2. What is the purpose of a cancer registry? How is it important?
3. What mechanisms must be included in the Data Management System (DMS) for both the hospital and the population-based registries? Compare and contrast the uses of the DMS between hospital registries and population-based registries.

WEB ACTIVITIES

The following activity provides the learner with the opportunity to use an interactive virtual registry system to develop skills needed by cancer registry personnel. The NPCR's Cyber Cancer Registry offers users the opportunity to learn by reviewing excerpts from de-identified medical records and other documents in various exercises and quizzes. Experienced cancer registry personnel also can utilize these tools to assess their skills.

1. Visit the National Program of Cancer Registries (NPCR) Cyber Cancer Registry page at the Centers for Disease Control website http://www.cdc.gov/cancer/npcr/training/ccr.htm
2. Select the link to the Cyber Cancer Registry.
3. At the login page, as a new user, select the "Register" link to create your login.
4. After answering the questions at the New User Registration page, select "Submit" to return to the login page.

5. After submission, you should receive a temporary password by e-mail that you can use to log in. If not, you can enter your e-mail address and select "Forgot Your Password" to receive a new temporary password.
6. Use the temporary password for your first login. You will be prompted to create a new password.
7. After your successful login to the Cyber Cancer Registry, download the screening list of codes and reportable diagnoses to use when answering questions in the Casefinding exercises and quiz.
8. Select the Casefinding Practice exercises, and try your hand at determining whether or not the examples provided are reportable with regard to the cancer registry or require further investigation. If desired, continue the process with the Casefinding Quiz.

CASE STUDY

An organization that raises funds for cancer research has used mortality data from death certificates to identify a county near you that has an extraordinarily high rate of cancer deaths. The findings do not seem to match the cancer incidence findings from the statewide cancer registry that captures data based on the location where the cancer was diagnosed. Further investigation shows that the only inpatient hospice in the state is located in that county.

1. What most likely accounts for the discrepancy between the cancer rates that the fundraising organization found and the cancer rates indicated by the statewide cancer registry for that county?
2. What recommendations might be made to the fundraising organization by the statewide cancer registry?
3. How can statewide cancer registries interact with private, non-profit groups seeking to locate areas for intervention?

REFERENCES AND SUGGESTED READINGS

Adamo, M. B., Johnson, C. H., Ruhl, J. L., & Dickie, L. A. (Eds.). (2013). *SEER Program Coding and Staging Manual.* Bethesda, MD: National Cancer Institute (NIH Publication number 13-5581).

American Cancer Society. (2015). *Cancer Facts and Figures.* [Online]. http://www.cancer.org/acs/groups//content/@editorial/documents/document/acspc-044552.pdf [2015, October 3].

American College of Surgeons. (2015). *National Cancer Data Base.* [Online]. https://www.facs.org/quality%20programs/cancer/ncdb [2015, October 3].

American College of Surgeons Commission on Cancer. (2015). *About the American College of Surgeons Commission on Cancer.* [Online]. https://www.facs.org/quality-programs/cancer/coc/about [2015, October 3].

CDC (Centers for Disease Control). (2004). *First Course of Treatment.* [Online]. http://www.cdc.gov/cancer/npcr/pdf/abstracting/treatment_codes.pdf [2015, October 3].

CDC (Centers for Disease Control). (2013a). *Leading Causes of Death.* [Online]. http://www.cdc.gov/nchs/fastats/leading-causes-of-death.htm [2015, October 3].

CDC (Centers for Disease Control). (2013b). *National Program of Cancer Registries (NPCR).* [Online]. http://www.cdc.gov/cancer/npcr/about.htm [2015, October 3].

Commission on Cancer (2012). *Cancer Program Standards 2012, Version 1.2.1: Ensuring Patient-Centered Care* [Online]. http://www.facs.org/cancer/coc/programstandards2012.pdf [2014, May 15].

Commission on Cancer. (2013a). *Data Use Agreement.* [Online]. https://www.facs.org/~/media/files/quality%20programs/cancer/ncdb/puf%20data%20use%20agreement.ashx [2015, October 3].

Commission on Cancer. (2013b). *Facility Oncology Registry Data Standards, Revised for 2013* [Online]. http://www.facs.org/cancer/coc/fords/fords-manual-2013.pdf [2014, May 15].

Commission on Cancer. (2015). *National Cancer Data Base* [Online]. https://www.facs.org/quality-programs/cancer/ncdb [2015, October 3].

Edge, S., Byrd, D.R., Compton, C.C, Fritz, A.G., Green, F.L., & Trotti, A. (Eds.). (2009). *AJCC Cancer Staging Manual, Seventh Edition.* New York: Springer.

Fritz, A., Percy, C., Jack, A., Shanmugaratnam, K., Sobin, L., Parkin, D. M., & Whelan, S. (Eds.) (2000). *International Classification of Diseases for Oncology, Third Edition.* Geneva, Switzerland: World Health Organization.

Havener, L.A. (Ed.) (2013). *Standards for Cancer Registries, Volume I: Data Exchange Standards and Record Descriptions.* [Online]. http://www.naaccr.org/LinkClick.aspx?fileticket=61dpE0SeE8Q%3d&tabid=132&mid=472 [2014, May 20].

Hofferkamp, J. (Ed.). (2008, August). *Standards for Cancer Registries, Volume III: Standards for Completeness, Quality, Analysis, Management, Security and Confidentiality of Data.* [Online]. http://www.naaccr.org/LinkClick.aspx?fileticket=hvFzJKUcRM8%3d&tabid=134&mid=474 [2014, May 20].

Johnson, C. H., Peace, S., Adamo, P., Fritz, A., Percy-Laurry, A., & Edwards, B. K. (2007). *The 2007 Multiple Primary and Histology Coding Rules.* Bethesda, MD: National Cancer Institute, Surveillance, Epidemiology and End Results Program.

Klein, W. T., & Havener, L. A. (2011, April). *Standards for Cancer Registries, Volume V: Pathology Laboratory Electronic Reporting, Version 4.0.* [Online]. http://www.naaccr.org [2015, October 3].

Menck, H. R., Gress, D. M., Griffin, A., Mulvihill, L., Hofferkamp, J., Johnson, C. H., & Pearson, M (Eds.). (2011). *Cancer Registry Management Principles and Practice, Third Edition.* Dubuque, IA: Kendall Hunt Publishing Company.

North American Association of Central Cancer Registries. (2013a, November). *Standards for Cancer Registries, Volume II: Data Standards and Data Dictionary, Version 14.* [Online]. http://www.naaccr.org/StandardsandRegistryOperations/VolumeII.aspx# [2014, May 20].

North American Association of Central Cancer Registries. (2013b, November). *Standards for Cancer Registries, Volume IV: NAACCR Standard Edits.* [Online]. http://www.naaccr.org/StandardsandRegistryOperations/VolumeIV.aspx [2014, May 20].

Ruhl, J., Adamo, M., Dickie, L., Sun, L., & Johnson, C. H. (2014, January). *Hematopoietic and Lymphoid Neoplasm Coding Manual.* Bethesda, MD: National Cancer Institute, Surveillance, Epidemiology and End Results Program.

Young, J.L., Roffers, S.D., Ries, L.A.G., Fritz, A.G., & Hurlbutt, A.A. (Eds). (2001). *SEER Summary Staging Manual-2000: Codes and Coding Instructions.* Bethesda, MD: National Cancer Institute. (NIH Pub. No. 01-4969)

KEY RESOURCES

American Cancer Society
http:// www.cancer.org

American College of Surgeons, Commission on Cancer
http://www.facs.org/cancer

American Joint Committee on Cancer
https://cancerstaging.org

Centers for Disease Control and Prevention, National Program of Cancer Registries
http://www.cdc.gov/cancer/npcr

Collaborative Staging Data Collection System
https://cancerstaging.org/cstage

National Cancer Database
http://www.facs.org/cancer/ncdb

National Cancer Institute *SEER Training Modules*
http://training.seer.cancer.gov

National Cancer Institute, Surveillance, Epidemiology and End Result Program
http://seer.cancer.gov

North American Association of Central Cancer Registries
http://www.naaccr.org

National Cancer Registrars Association
http://www.ncra-usa.org

GLOSSARY

A

abstract a summary record in a standardized format that allows for systematic collection of information on a cancer patient's experience.

accession number a nine-digit unique number in the hospital cancer registry system that identifies the patient.

Accountable Care Organization (ACO) a local entity and a related set of providers, including at least primary care physicians, specialists, and hospitals, that can be held accountable for the cost and quality of care delivered to a defined subset of traditional Medicare program beneficiaries or other defined populations, such as commercial health plan subscribers. The primary ways the entity would be held accountable for its performance are through changes in traditional Medicare provider payment featuring financial rewards for good performance based on comprehensive quality and spending measurement and monitoring" (Devers & Berenson, 2009, pp. 1–2).

accreditation a voluntary process in which facilities agree to follow a set of standards and receive recognition for having met those standards.

Accreditation Commission for Health Care (ACHC) a voluntary accrediting organization with deeming authority for home health, hospice, and suppliers of durable medical equipment, prosthetics, orthotics, and supplies (DMEPOS).

active treatment a continuous program for each recipient, which includes aggressive, consistent implementation of specialized and generic training, treatment, health services, and related services.

activities of daily living (ADL) for purposes of the federal long-term care regulations, activities of daily living include the resident's ability to (1) bathe, dress, and groom; (2) transfer and ambulate; (3) toilet; (4) eat; and (5) use speech, language, or other functional communication systems (CMS, 2011). Federal regulations include ADL as a component part of the quality-of-care requirements, and information

concerning individual resident ADL capability is a significant portion of the monitoring information in the minimum data set.

acute rehabilitation unit a designated unit in a hospital to which patients can be transferred for rehabilitation after treatment for the original acute illness or injury. Length of stay in these units is typically 2 to 4 weeks.

Addiction Severity Index (ASI) a rating scale developed for clinicians to measure the severity of a client's substance abuse problems. The ASI measures seven substance abuse–related problem areas: medical condition, drug use, alcohol use, employment, illegal activity, social relations, and psychological findings.

adequacy of dialysis a determination of whether the patient's dialysis treatment is removing sufficient waste and excess fluid from the body. To be adequate, the patient must dialyze long enough and often enough to achieve the goals of treatment. Adequate dialysis is essential to patient survival.

advanced practice clinician also called a mid-level provider; a health care professional whose license permits a degree of independent judgment in treating patients, generally under the supervision of a physician. Examples of advanced practice clinicians include nurse practitioners, physician assistants, and certified nurse midwives. Scope of practice and requirements for supervision vary by type of provider and by state.

affiliate an associate or member of a particular business.

Affordable Care Act of 2010 (ACA) *see* **Patient Protection and Affordable Care Act**.

Alcoholics Anonymous (AA) a worldwide organization of self-help recovery groups that support individuals in maintaining sobriety. AA is based on a 12-step recovery process; other programs that follow the 12-step recovery process sometimes are referred to as 12-step programs.

amalgam a silver-colored filling composed of several metals; usually placed on the back (posterior) teeth.

ambulation aids devices that provide additional stability and support for individuals who have trouble walking.

ambulatory payment classifications (APCs) groupings of outpatient services (based on the HCPCS code assigned) that determine the payment the hospital receives under the Hospital Outpatient Prospective Payment System (HOPPS).

ambulatory surgery (also called "same-day" surgery) surgery in which it is planned that the patient will arrive at the facility, have surgery, recover from any anesthesia, and be ready for discharge in a single day, thus avoiding an overnight stay in the health care facility.

ambulatory surgery center (ASC) a setting provided for surgery on an ambulatory basis. Centers usually have at least one fulltime operating room and provide surgical privileges to physicians in the community.

American Animal Hospital Association (AAHA) promulgates standards for companion animal hospitals.

American College of Surgeons (ACS) a professional organization founded in 1913 to "improve the quality of care for the surgical patient by setting high standards for surgical education and practice" (ACS, n.d.). In the early twentieth century, the ACS established a hospital standardization program that was the forerunner of today's accreditation organizations.

American Correctional Association a professional association of correctional administrators, wardens, superintendents, and other individuals and institutions, promoting improved correctional standards and studying causes of crime and juvenile delinquency as well as methods of crime control and prevention, offering voluntary accreditation for all components of adult and juvenile corrections.

American Correctional Health Services Association (ACHSA) a professional group of health care providers, individuals, and organizations interested in improving the quality of correctional health services.

American Public Health Association (APHA) a professional group of health care workers, administrators, epidemiologists, planners, community and mental health specialists, and interested individuals who seek to protect and promote personal, mental, and environmental health by promulgating standards, establishing uniform practices and procedures, and conducting research.

American Recovery and Reinvestment Act (ARRA) a federal law (Public Law 111-5), also known as the "Stimulus Act" or the "Recovery Act," enacted in 2009, that created an incentive program for health care providers to utilize EHRs for improved patient care.

American Veterinary Health Information Management Association (AVHIMA) promotes quality patient care through the management of health information; is the nation's authoritative body on the management of veterinary health information; advances the competency of those working with veterinary health information; and advocates for the profession on government, education, social, and business issues that affect the management of veterinary health information.

American Veterinary Medical Association (AVMA) has an objective to advance the science and art of veterinary medicine, including its relationship to public health, biological science, and agriculture; provides a forum for discussing issues of importance to the veterinary profession and for developing official positions. The association is the authorized voice for the profession in presenting its views to government, academia, agriculture, pet owners, the media, and other concerned publics (AVMA Constitution, Article II).

animal any animal other than humans, including fowl, birds, fish, and reptiles, wild or domestic, living or dead.

animal health technician *see* **veterinary technician**.

annual staffing an informal term for the annual meeting of the interdisciplinary team during which the individual program plan is reviewed and revised for the coming year; not to exceed 365 days from the previous annual or initial staffing.

appointment scheduled time when a patient is to arrive at the health care facility.

appointment system a plan by which appointments are scheduled for patients.

ASC reimbursement system a Medicare plan for ambulatory surgery in which the HCPCS codes are listed (ASC list) and reimbursed according to a percentage of the outpatient prospective payment system rates.

assessment the process of identifying an individual's functional level, strengths, needs, causes of disabilities, and conditions that hinder development.

audit a formal way of checking financial and other records.

B

bed day an inpatient service received by one member for one 24-hour period.

bereavement the time period immediately following the death of the patient. In hospice, the clinical staff helps the family and significant others through this period for up to one year, and longer if requested by the patient's family and friends.

biofilm an aggregate of microorganisms organized into a dynamic community that collects on the teeth and under the gums; also known as *plaque*.

bipolar disorder a form of serious mental illness in which a person alternates between states of ecstatic mania and severe depression. Also known as *manic depression*.

birth center an ambulatory setting that provides labor and delivery services in uncomplicated deliveries.

bitewing a radiograph that shows the upper and lower teeth's biting surfaces on the same film.

block appointment method an appointment scheduling method that assigns all patients in a large block for the same appointment time (e.g., 9:00 a.m. for all morning appointments), then patients are seen on a first-come, first-served basis.

bovine cow or ox.

bridge a fixed appliance (prosthesis) that replaces missing teeth; a series of crowns (abutments and pontics).

business associate (BA) a partner or contractor performing a job or service on behalf of a covered entity. To perform the contracted work, the original HIPAA legislation required covered entities to have a business associate agreement with any organization that handled or encountered its PHI. BAs also are accountable for complying with certain provisions in the privacy and security regulations, as required by ARRA.

C

CAA resources a component of the care area assessment process that provides "a list of resources that may be helpful in performing the assessment of a triggered care area" (CMS, 2010(b), p. 1–5).

calculus/tartar plaque that has hardened.

cancer a general term for more than 100 diseases characterized by uncontrolled growth of cells.

cancer registry a surveillance system that systematically collects newly diagnosed cancer cases for the purpose of monitoring the disease burden, the quality of care of cancer patients, cancer survival, and disparities.

canine dog.

capitation a method of payment for health care in which the health care provider receives a monthly payment based on the number of persons the provider has agreed to treat, regardless of the number of persons actually treated or the amount of service rendered.

caprine goat.

care area assessment (CAA) process a component that helps the assessor and clinician interpret and utilize MDS data by focusing on key issues; components include care area triggers (CATs), CAA resources, and the CAA summary.

care area assessment (CAA) summary "(Section V of the MDS 3.0) provides a location for documentation of the care area(s) that have triggered from the MDS and the decisions made during the CAA process regarding whether or not to proceed to care planning" (CMS, 2010(b), pp. 1–5).

care area triggers (CATs) "specific resident responses for one or a combination of MDS elements. The triggers identify residents who have or are at risk for developing specific functional problems and require further assessment" (CMS, 2010(b), pp. 1–5).

care plan documentation developed by an interdisciplinary team that includes measurable objectives and timetables to meet a resident's medical, nursing, and mental and psychosocial needs as identified in the comprehensive assessment. According to CMS, a care plan must describe (1) the services that are to be furnished to attain or maintain the resident's highest practicable physical, mental, and psychosocial well-being; and (2) any services that otherwise would be required but are not provided because of the resident's exercise of rights including the right to refuse treatment.

CARF International (Commission on Accreditation of Rehabilitation Facilities) a voluntary accreditation agency that sets standards that promote "the delivery of quality services to people with disabilities" (CARF, 1994). CARF standards include a section devoted to alcohol and other drug treatment programs.

caries the correct technical term for tooth decay.

case-mix group (CMG) any of 100 categories into which an inpatient rehabilitation stay can be classified based on data submitted on the IRF-PAI; determined by factors such as rehabilitation impairment category (RIC), functional measurements, age, and comorbidities.

case-mix reimbursement in the context of long-term care, a methodology designed to provide a mechanism for facilities to be paid in a manner reflecting the types of residents served and the types of services provided. The system also is designed to provide greater access to nursing facility beds for heavier care residents and to improve the quality of care for all nursing facility residents. Payment is based on a specific methodology that considers direct-care costs, care-related costs, administrative and operating costs, and property.

Center for Mental Health Services (CMHS) the federal agency that oversees administration of demonstration and research grants and other initiatives at the federal level related to mental health issues. This entity and its parent organization, the Substance Abuse and Mental Health Services Administration (SAMHSA), were created within the U.S. Department of Health and Human Services after reorganization of the National Institute of Mental Health (NIMH), which formerly had these responsibilities.

Center for Substance Abuse Prevention (CSAP) an agency of SAMHSA that provides national leadership for community-based substance abuse prevention programs. Among other activities, CSAP administers a number of grant programs aimed at reducing the incidence of substance abuse.

Center for Substance Abuse Treatment (CSAT) an agency of SAMHSA that "promotes the quality and availability of community-based substance abuse treatment services for individuals and families...[working] with States and community-based groups to improve and expand existing substance abuse treatment services under the Substance Abuse Prevention and Treatment Block Grant Program" (CSAT, n.d., para. 1).

Centers for Medicare & Medicaid Services (CMS) a federal agency within the Department of Health and Human Services with its main focus to administer the Medicare and Medicaid programs. It formerly was known as the Health Care Financing Administration (HCFA).

certification period the billing timeframe for which a physician's home care order is valid for patient treatment—60 days—during which a patient's physician must review, update, and recertify (if necessary) a patient's plan of care.

Certified Correctional Health Professional Program (CCHP) a certification program for health care professionals working in corrections; administered by the National Commission on Correctional Health Care.

Certified Nurse Midwife (CNM) a nurse practitioner who handles pregnancy, labor, and delivery.

Certified Veterinary Practice Manager (CVPM) an individual who, with at least 3 years of experience as a practice manager within the past 7 years, at least 18 acceptable college or university credit hours pertinent to management, evidence of 48 hours of continuing education specifically devoted to management, and appropriate references, who may apply to the Veterinary Hospital Manager's Association (VHMA) to take the written and oral examinations which, if successfully passed, designate the individual as a CVPM.

chargemaster or charge description master (CDM) a computer file that contains a list of the Healthcare Common Procedural Coding System codes and associated charges for services provided to hospital patients.

chemical restraint the use of a drug or medication that is not part of a person's usual medical regimen that is administered to control behavior or restrict freedom of movement.

Child and Adolescent Service System Program (CASSP) an initiative begun by the National Institute of Mental Health to create a comprehensive network of services for children and adolescents with emotional disturbance through a series of demonstration grants; the program now is overseen by the Substance Abuse and Mental Health Services Administration (SAMHSA) within the U.S. Department of Health and Human Services.

Children's Health Insurance Program (CHIP) also known as Title XXI of the Balanced Budget Act of 1997, it allows states to offer health insurance plans for children to age 19 who are not insured already; CHIP affords families who earn too much to qualify for Medicaid an opportunity to obtain health insurance for their children.

chronic kidney disease (CKD) a gradual loss of kidney function classified into five stages, ranging from mild loss of kidney function in the early stages to severe or total loss in the later stages; in the final Stage 5, the individual's kidneys are no longer able to perform the task of excreting the body's wastes or promoting homeostasis, and the patient requires dialysis or kidney transplant to survive.

civil money penalties fines levied by the federal government against providers who are found to be in substantial noncompliance with federal regulations; may be as much as $10,000 per day.

clinical assessment a procedure conducted by a clinician for every client who enters a substance abuse treatment program; used as a basis for the client's diagnosis and individualized treatment plan.

clinical depression a serious mental illness appearing as a deep feeling of melancholy and futility that is not situational in nature.

clinical documentation improvement (CDI) program a locally implemented program focused upon improving the quality of clinical documentation to "facilitate an accurate representation of health care services through complete and accurate reporting of diagnoses and procedures" (AHIMA, 2010a, 4). Accurate clinical documentation can positively affect reimbursement, severity of illness and mortality risk assessment, and reporting of quality and pay-for-performance measures.

Clinical Laboratory Improvement Amendments of 1988 (CLIA) federal legislation that provides for regulation of all clinical laboratories, including those operated by HMOs and physician practices within managed care networks.

Clinical Performance Measures (CPM) Project an ongoing project of CMS, implemented through the ESRD networks, to measure and report the quality of renal dialysis services provided under the Medicare program.

clinic outpatient an outpatient treated in an organized clinic of the hospital, in which hospital staff evaluate the patient and manage the patient's care.

coinsurance the amount of expense that is the responsibility of the insured under an indemnity insurance policy, often 20% of the charges billed.

color coding a system that helps to prevent the misfiling of records, by assigning colors to numbers or letters and displaying those colors on the record folder so misfiled records are spotted easily by their mismatched color patterns.

Community Health Accreditation Program (CHAP) an independent, not-for-profit, accrediting body for community-based health care organizations. Meeting CHAP standards can provide a home health agency with deemed status with regard to the Medicare Conditions of Participation.

community health center an ambulatory setting developed in the 1960s to provide ambulatory care to indigent people in a specified neighborhood. Subsequent legislation expanded the scope of these health centers to any medically underserved area or population.

community mental health centers (CMHC) a network of publicly funded mental health organizations established in communities throughout the United States by the Mental Health Act of 1965.

compliance plan a method for ensuring that a facility/practice is complying with all laws and regulations, including those pertaining to reimbursement under Medicare and Medicaid.

composite filling a tooth-colored filling.

comprehensive assessment a document that is completed on the first visit to the patient's home. The document should include the patient's present illness; significant past history; review of all systems/physical assessment; medications; psychological, social, and economic factors; emergency plans; and skilled nursing performed that day; and also incorporate the required OASIS data elements.

comprehensive resident assessment as defined by the long-term care federal regulations, describes the resident's ability to perform daily life functions and significant impairments in functional capacity. Specifically, it includes at least the following information: (1) medically defined conditions and prior medical history; (2) medical status measurement; (3) physical and mental functional status; (4) sensory and physical impairments; (5) nutritional status and requirements; (6) special treatments or procedures; (7) mental and psychosocial status; (8) discharge potential; (9) dental condition; (10) activities potential; (11) rehabilitation potential; (12) cognitive status; and (13) drug therapy.

concurrent review verification of the medical necessity of tests and procedures ordered during an inpatient hospitalization.

Conditions of Participation (COP) federal regulations with which health care organizations must comply for participation in the Medicare program. In addition to other regulations, the COP outlines documentation requirements for Medicare-certified home health agencies.

Confidentiality of Drug and Alcohol Abuse Records, 42 C.F.R. Part 2 federal regulations that mandate strict confidentiality of drug and alcohol patient information in federally assisted substance abuse treatment programs.

consolidated billing under Medicare, a responsibility of the skilled nursing facility for billing the entire package of care that residents receive during a stay, with certain specified exceptions such as physicians' professional services.

Consolidated Renal Operations in a Web-enabled Network (CROWNWeb) CMS Internet-based software application, the required method by which dialysis facilities submit data about patients and facility operations.

continuity of care a concept that refers to creation of a comprehensive system of care for persons with serious mental illness, with particular emphasis on a smooth transition from inpatient services to outpatient services.

continuous ambulatory peritoneal dialysis (CAPD) a form of peritoneal dialysis in which the patient is able to dialyze himself or herself three or four times a day without special assistance and with a minimum amount of equipment.

continuous care a form of hospice care that occurs in the patient's place of residence when a patient requires continuous care for a minimum of 8 hours within a 24-hour period. Continuous care is furnished only during brief periods of crisis and only as necessary to maintain the terminally ill patient at home.

continuous cycling peritoneal dialysis (CCPD) a form of peritoneal dialysis in which the patient uses a cycler machine to dialyze once a day for 9 or 10 hours, usually while sleeping.

continuous quality improvement (CQI) a management concept that focuses on customer involvement in planning services and obtaining feedback about satisfaction with service delivery. Also known as total quality management (TQM).

coordination of benefits (COB) determining which insurance is the primary payer and ensuring that no more than 100% of the charges are paid to a provider and/or reimbursed to a patient.

copayment a flat-rate payment, such as $10 per visit, made by the covered individual for a specific service, paid at the time of the service.

Correctional Certification Program (CCP) a program offered by the American Correctional Association to certify correctional officers, correctional staff, staff nurses, and nurse managers working in corrections.

covered entities (CEs) under HIPAA, health plans, health care clearinghouses, or any health care providers that transmit health information in an electronic form.

credentialing a process of review to approve a provider who applies to participate in a health plan.

credentials verification organization (CVO) a third party organization that contracts with a managed care organization or other health care organization to provide credential verification services for health care providers seeking clinical privileges or inclusion in an insurance network.

crown full-coverage restoration of a tooth when it cannot be restored by a filling.

culture change movement a person-centered philosophy that creates a more homelike environment for residents of a nursing facility. Culture change involves providing individuals with privacy and the ability to make choices similar to what they would experience were they living in their own homes.

curative therapy any medical therapy for the purpose of curing disease.

Current Procedural Terminology (CPT) a coding system for procedures that is used extensively in ambulatory care and that forms a part of HCPCS.

D

Data Standards for Mental Health Decision Support Systems ("FN-10") an early reference source for creation of a national mental health services database.

decision-support system a computerized method that assists physicians in deciding on a diagnosis or treatment.

deductible the amount of expense that the insureds must pay each year from their own pockets before the plan will reimburse them.

deemed status the recognition of a health care provider that is said to meet federal Conditions of Participation by virtue of accreditation by a federally approved voluntary accrediting organization. With deemed status, the health care provider's accreditation satisfies the Conditions of Participation.

delusions a form of disordered thinking characterized by unrealistic beliefs (e.g., that someone with this condition is receiving communications from aliens in outer space or that food is being poisoned).

denial lack of payment for home visits/treatments because of failure to meet medical necessity requirements for the services or for some other reason (e.g., provider error, payer error, ineligible patient). A denial sometimes can be appealed successfully.

dentist a licensed health care professional specializing in the prevention and treatment of disorders of the oral cavity and associated body structures; a dentist has either a DDS or a DMD degree.

denture a removable prosthesis (false teeth) that replaces all of the teeth in either the upper or lower jaw.

department of corrections (DOC) a division of state government responsible for the operation of prisons.

dependent the spouse or child of the primary insurance recipient.

detainee a person held in custody awaiting trial or disposition.

developmental disability a disability "attributable to a mental or physical impairment that begins before age 18 and is likely to continue indefinitely, and that results in substantial functional limitation in three or more areas of major life activity" (AAI, 2010).

diagnosis related group (DRG) groupings of inpatient services (based on the diagnosis, expected resource consumption, and other characteristics) that determine the payment the hospital receives under the Hospital Inpatient Prospective Payment System (HIPPS).

Diagnostic and Statistical Manual of Mental Disorders, fifth edition (DSM-5) a classification system and nomenclature of mental disorders developed by the American Psychiatric Association (APA) with the stated purpose of providing "clear descriptions of diagnostic categories in order to enable clinicians and investigators to diagnose, communicate about, study, and treat people with various mental disorders." It also is used as a coding system for mental disorders.

dialysate a solution used to filter products across a semipermeable membrane by the process of diffusion. Waste products filter into the dialysate from the blood, whereas certain other products, such as bicarbonates, filter into the blood from the dialysate.

dialysis "the process of artificially removing metabolic end products and water across a semipermeable membrane by diffusion" (McAfee, 1987). The two most common types of dialysis are hemodialysis and peritoneal dialysis.

dialysis facility "an entity that provides (1) outpatient maintenance dialysis services; or (2) home dialysis training and support services; or (3) both. A dialysis facility may be an independent or hospital-based unit...or a self-care dialysis unit that furnishes only self-dialysis services" (*Conditions for Coverage*, 2008, p. 20476).

digital imaging the use of computer-based technologies to make radiographic (X-ray) and other clinical images to diagnose dental diseases and conditions.

direct care staff personnel whose daily responsibility is to manage, supervise, and provide direct care to individuals in their residential living unit.

disability a restriction or inability to perform an activity in the manner or within the range considered to be normal for a human being, mostly resulting from impairment.

discharge planning arranging post-discharge services for patients prior to discharge to provide continuity of care, to aid in recuperation, and to reduce unnecessary readmissions or emergency department visits.

disciplines specialty providers offering a variety of treatments or services for patients—for example, physical therapy, maternity services, medical social services.

discounted reduced payment for additional procedures or ambulatory patient groups. When discounted, these other items are not paid at the full rate, as they would be if they had been the only services performed in a given encounter.

Drug and Alcohol Services Information System (DASIS) a data system managed by SAMHSA that provides national and state-level data on substance abuse clients and on the facilities that receive federal grants or contracts to provide substance abuse treatment. The three components are: Treatment Episode Data Set (TEDS), National Survey of Substance Abuse Treatment Services (N-SSATS), and Inventory of Substance Abuse Treatment Services (I-SATS).

dual diagnoses two concurrent diagnoses. Most commonly refers to diagnoses in persons with mental illness and chemical or alcohol addiction, but may also refer to persons who are diagnosed as having a developmental disability and are seriously mentally ill.

dually diagnosed refers to clients who have both a substance abuse disorder and a chronic mental illness; these clients typically have special treatment needs.

durable medical equipment (DME) medical equipment provided to patients within the home environment.

"duty to warn" a legal concept holding that mental health professionals have an obligation to issue a forewarning about a person whom a client with mental illness has threatened to harm, despite the usual protections of confidentiality in the client–professional relationship.

E

Early and Periodic Screening, Diagnostic, and Treatment (EPSDT) Service a Medicaid program for children younger than age 21 that ensures that these services (screening, diagnostic, and treatment) are provided and paid for whether or not they normally are included under the state's Medicaid program.

edentulous having no teeth; toothless.

electronic dental record (EDR) a computer-based dental record that stores the patient's pertinent demographic, diagnostic, treatment, and financial information.

electronic health record (EHR) a system in which a health care provider maintains individual patient health records electronically. Fully developed EHRs include capabilities such as generating clinical alerts and reminders and providing readily available decision support.

eligibility determination of whether a person is able to receive benefits under an insurance policy.

Emergency Medical Treatment and Active Labor Act (EMTALA) a federal law that imposes a legal duty on hospitals to screen and stabilize, if necessary, any patient who arrives in the emergency department. The purpose of EMTALA is to prevent the "dumping" of patients who may not be able to pay for emergency department services.

emergency outpatient an outpatient evaluated and treated in the emergency department of the hospital.

employee assistance programs (EAPs) substance abuse assessment and treatment programs established through a contractual arrangement between an organization and a substance abuse treatment facility to serve the employees within the organization.

encoded With regard to the IRF-PAI, encoding refers to using a specified computer program to enter data that subsequently will be transmitted to the Centers for Medicare & Medicaid Services (CMS).

encounter (a) face-to-face contact between the patient and the provider (Uniform Ambulatory Care Data Set); (b) contact between a patient and a health care provider who is responsible for the assessment and evaluation of the patient at a specific contact, exercising independent judgment.

encounter form a document used for billing purposes that includes the services the patient received, the charges, and the diagnosis and procedure codes.

endodontist a dentist who specializes in treating diseases or injuries that affect the root tip or nerve of the tooth, most commonly a root canal.

end-stage renal disease (ESRD) Stage 5 of chronic kidney disease, the extreme at which the patient has irreversible renal failure with little or no kidney function. When a patient is in end-stage renal disease, he or she requires either dialysis or a kidney transplant to maintain life.

environmental control units (ECUs) equipment that allows a person with limited mobility to perform many everyday functions in the home, at work, or at school—such as turning on lights, using appliances, and opening and closing doors and windows.

episode of care a period during which a variety of services (inpatient and/or outpatient) are provided to an individual for a given episode of illness.

e-prescribing a method of entering prescriptions into an electronic system that also transmits the prescription to the pharmacy to be filled.

equine horse.

erythropoiesis stimulating agents (ESAs) agents that stimulate the bone marrow to make red blood cells and are used to treat and prevent anemia, a common complication of chronic kidney disease in patients on dialysis.

ESRD networks organizations that have contracted with the Centers for Medicare & Medicaid Services (CMS) to assess the quality of care rendered to ESRD patients and to collect and analyze ESRD data.

F

Facility Oncology Registry Data Standards (FORDS) a manual published by the Commission on Cancer that provides data standards and coding instructions for facility-based cancer surveillance for the purposes of quality patient care.

family numbering system a method in which the family is given a number and each individual receives that number with a suffix indicating his or her position within the family.

family planning center an ambulatory setting that provides family planning services.

Federal Bureau of Prisons (FBP) a division of the U.S. Department of Justice, responsible for the administration and operation of federal correctional facilities, including penitentiaries, prison camps, and metropolitan correctional centers.

federally qualified health center (FQHC) a nonprofit or public organization that provides or arranges for comprehensive health care services to a medically underserved area or population.

federal survey based on the federal long-term care requirements and using the federal long-term care survey procedures required for long-term care facility participation in the Medicare and/or Medicaid programs.

fee-for-service a method of payment for health care in which the health care provider charges and is paid for each item of service provided.

feline cat.

financial system a computer system that maintains information on services billed, insurance determination, payment received, and collection efforts.

fiscal intermediary (FI) before the implementation of MACs, an organization with a contract with CMS to process and pay Part A Medicare claims.

fixed costs costs that do not change in proportion to changes in volume of services; home health examples are office rent and utilities.

Flexible Spending Account (FSA) pre-tax income that an employee sets aside from his or her salary to use during a specified period for health care expenses; funds left in the account at the end of the benefit year are forfeited by the employee.

Flexner Report a document published in 1910 examining the state of medical education in the United States and Canada. The Flexner Report resulted in sweeping changes in the way North American physicians were educated.

freestanding ambulatory care care provided to patients who do not stay overnight in a hospital setting.

freestanding rehabilitation hospitals inpatient rehabilitation facilities that may operate both acute and post-acute rehabilitation units.

Functional Independence Measure or FIM®️ instrument a rating tool for measuring function in motor and cognitive areas; FIM documents the severity of disabilities as well as outcomes in rehabilitation and has been incorporated into the IRF-PAI.

485 the document number for a previously required CMS form facilitating a patient's orders for home care. Although the requirement for the form itself has been dropped, the content of the form still is required. Therefore, both the term 485 and the form itself are still in use in many home health agencies. The form provides a plan of care, which must be established and reviewed at least once every 60 days by the patient's attending physician.

G

gatekeeper the primary care provider who coordinates all of the patient's health care and decides what, if any, additional care is required.

general or **acute inpatient care** a form of care that takes place when a patient receives care in an inpatient facility (a hospice inpatient unit or a facility contracted by the hospice) for pain control or acute or chronic symptom management that cannot be managed in the patient's place of residence.

gingiva the gums in the mouth.

grievance process a formal administrative process whereby inmates may file complaints against a correctional facility for review by a panel. Institutional policies, and sometimes state statutes, determine timeframes for the review process, decisions, and appeals.

group dental practice two or more dentists practicing together.

group model HMO a model in which the HMO has an exclusive contract with a multispecialty medical group that provides all physician services and contracts with other facilities as necessary to provide comprehensive services.

growth and development chart a graphic recording of a child's height and weight over time.

H

habilitation the process by which a person is assisted to acquire and maintain life skills that enable the person to cope more effectively with personal and environmental demands and to raise the level of his or her physical, mental, and social efficiency; includes, but is not limited to, programs of structured education and training.

hallucination a form of disordered thinking in which a person reports sensory experience that is not valid, such as seeing, hearing, smelling, or feeling things that are not real.

handicap the result of an impairment or a disability that limits or prevents a person from fulfilling one or several roles that are regarded as normal (depending on age, sex, social, and cultural factors) for that individual.

Healthcare Common Procedural Coding System (HCPCS) (a) a method used by ambulatory care facilities to code procedures and services; (b) the system required by CMS for coding services provided to Medicare patients.

Healthcare Effectiveness Data and Information Set (HEDIS) a core set of standard performance measures for managed care in the areas of effectiveness of care, access/availability of care, satisfaction with the experience of care, use of services, cost of care, health plan descriptive information, health plan stability, and informed health care choices.

health information exchange (HIE) a process defined as "the electronic movement of health-related information among organizations according to nationally recognized standards" (NAHIT, 2008, p. 6).

health information management (HIM) "the practice of acquiring, analyzing, and protecting digital and traditional medical information vital to providing quality patient care" (AHIMA, n.d.).

Health Insurance Portability and Accountability Act of 1996 (HIPAA) also known as the Kassebaum-Kennedy Act. Provisions include the portability of health care benefits (for example, upon an individual change of employment), prevention of fraud and abuse in health care, and simplification of the electronic interchange of health care data, while improving the privacy and security of health information.

health information technology (HIT) electronic health records and related information systems to manage health care processes; the major focus of the HITECH Act of 2009 is to promote adoption of HIT in an effort to improve the quality, efficiency, and safety of health care delivery while reducing costs and minimizing medical errors.

Health Information Technology for Economic and Clinical Health Act (HITECH) enacted as part of the American Recovery and Reinvestment Act of 2009 to promote the adoption and meaningful use of health information technology. Subpart D amends the HIPAA privacy and security rules by introducing additional privacy regulations, breach notification rules, and stiffer civil and criminal penalties for security violations.

Health Level 7 (HL7) the application level, which is the highest level of the International Standards Organization's (ISO) communications model for Open Systems Interconnection (OSI); a standard for data exchange in health care.

health maintenance organization (HMO) a business entity that either provides or arranges for health services for a covered population after prepayment of a fixed premium.

Health Reimbursement Arrangement (HRA) a mechanism by which an employer funds an account for its employees to pay for otherwise unreimbursed health care expenses.

Health Savings Account (HSA) an account set up by an employee with pretax income that also is not taxed when the employee withdraws from the account for medical expenses. Amounts left in the account at the end of the benefit year roll over to the next year. Withdrawals for nonmedical expenses are subject to income tax and a 10% penalty.

health services director (HSD) an individual responsible for the administration and operation of health services within a prison system or DOC.

hemodialysis (HD) cleansing of the blood as it circulates through an artificial kidney machine outside of the patient's body.

herd health veterinary care provided to a group of animals at their residence rather than in a hospital setting.

HIE organization an entity that "oversees and governs the exchange of health-related information among organizations according to nationally recognized standards" (NAHIT, 2008, p. 6). Health information exchange, or HIE, can refer to either the process of exchanging information or the organization that oversees the process.

Hierarchical Condition Categories (HCCs) disease groupings based on *ICD* codes from both inpatient admissions and outpatient visits in Medicare Advantage organizations. HCCs are used to risk-adjust Medicare payments to MCOs.

Hill-Burton Act the "Hospital Survey and Construction Act" enacted by Congress in 1946; provided federal money to determine the need for more hospitals and to pay for their construction. (Note: Facilities receiving Hill-Burton funds agreed to provide a reasonable volume of service to patients who are unable to pay, an obligation that is still monitored by the federal government today.)

HIPAA *see* **Health Insurance Portability and Accountability Act**.

Home and Community Based Services (HCBS) Waiver a federal program that allows states to use Medicaid funding to serve persons in their own homes and communities, not just in institutional settings.

Home Assessment Validation and Entry (HAVEN) software available from CMS, developed to provide home health agencies with an electronic application for data entry, editing, and validation of OASIS-C1 data.

homebound a situation in which individuals with physical or mental limitations are able to leave home only infrequently and with great effort, generally requiring assistance.

home care visits medical and nonmedical care provided to patients within the privacy and comfort of their own homes; often the unit of measure in home health care for evaluating costs, scheduling, and productivity. For some payers, the visit is the unit of payment for services.

home health aide a certified staff person who is able to enhance the patient's care by assisting with the patient's activities of daily living, such as checking vital signs, bathing, grooming, meal preparation, and other activities.

home health care services and treatment provided in the home environment to individuals who are recovering, have a disability, or are chronically ill, to improve their health or effective functioning.

hospice a facility or a program designed to provide a caring environment to meet the physical and emotional needs of terminally ill patients and their families and significant others.

hospice inpatient unit a hospice with a specific set of beds either in its own building or as a wing of a hospital or nursing home, providing round-the-clock clinical staff to care for terminally ill patients; these units provide respite care, pain and symptom management, and/or routine home care for patients who have nobody in their home to help care for them.

hospice item set (HIS) a set of standardized measures that can be abstracted from patient assessments;

these items are reported to Medicare on each hospice patient at the time of admission and at the time of discharge.

hospital-based cancer registry a registry that collects data for individual hospitals or networks of hospitals on new cancer cases diagnosed and/or treated in that hospital or group of hospitals.

hospital inpatient an individual receiving health care services as well as room and board and continuous nursing care in a hospital unit where patients generally stay overnight.

Hospital Inpatient Prospective Payment System (HIPPS or IPPS) Medicare's payment system for hospital inpatient services. The basic unit of payment in the IPPS is the Medicare Severity Diagnosis Related Group (MS-DRG).

Hospital Inpatient Quality Reporting (IQR) a national quality initiative implemented by CMS as required by the Medicare Prescription Drug, Improvement, and Modernization Act (MMA) of 2003. IQR requires hospitals to submit data for certain quality measures, which are made publically available to consumers via the Hospital Compare website. Although program participation is voluntary, hospitals that do not participate receive a reduced Medicare Annual Payment Update.

hospitalist "a physician who specializes in inpatient medicine" (Slee, Slee, & Schmidt, 2008, 275).

hospital outpatient a hospital patient who receives care at the hospital but who is not admitted as an inpatient.

Hospital Outpatient Prospective Payment System (HOPPS or OPPS) Medicare's payment system for hospital outpatient services. The basic unit of payment in the OPPS is the ambulatory payment classification (APC) of each service provided.

Hospital Outpatient Quality Data Reporting Program (HOP QDRP) a national quality program implemented by CMS that is modeled after the Hospital Inpatient Quality Reporting (IQR) initiative. Hospitals must report data for standardized quality measures for outpatient hospital services, which are made publically available to consumers via the Hospital Compare website. Participation is required to receive the full annual update to the Outpatient Prospective Payment System (OPPS) payment rate.

Hospital Value-based Purchasing Program (HVBP) established by the ACA to improve quality of care for inpatients by reimbursing acute-care hospitals based upon clinical best practices. These value-based incentive payments are tied to data reported through the Hospital Inpatient Quality Reporting (IQR) Program and are made through Medicare's Inpatient Prospective Payment System (IPPS).

hybrid covered entity an organization whose activities include both covered and noncovered functions under HIPAA.

I

ICD-10-CM the United States' clinical modification of the World Health Organization's diagnostic disease classification (International Classification of Diseases, 10th Revision, Clinical Modification).

ICD-10-PCS the United States' procedural coding system for inpatient, acute care settings (International Classification of Diseases, 10th Revision, Procedural Coding System). ICD-10-PCS is the replacement for ICD-9-CM, volume 3, one of the original code sets required by HIPAA.

immunization record a listing of immunizations that a child has received; often indicates when additional immunizations will be required.

incident report internal documentation of an unusual event such as a fall, incorrect medications given or taken, or some other untoward occurrence.

integrated format a record format in which the information is entered in chronological order.

impacted an unerupted or partially erupted tooth that will not fully erupt because it is obstructed by another tooth, bone, or soft tissue.

impacted wisdom teeth wisdom teeth that will not erupt through the gum.

impairment any temporary or permanent loss or abnormality of a body structure or function, whether physiological or psychological.

implant a post that is implanted in the bone; a crown, bridge, or denture then is attached to the implant.

incident or unusual occurrence any happening that is not consistent with the routine operations of the agency or routine care of a given patient.

incident to services provided to patients by mid-level providers or advanced practice clinicians, such as nurse practitioners or physician assistants, when the physician is onsite.

indemnity insurance traditional health insurance in which the insured is reimbursed for expenses after care is provided.

independent practice association (IPA) model an HMO model that was developed primarily as a way for the solo health practitioners to participate in the managed care market.

individualized treatment plan (ITP) a written plan developed by the client's treatment team to identify the type and frequency of services the client needs; includes measurable goals and objectives that address the problems identified in the clinical assessment and should be updated periodically (usually every 6 months) as the client's treatment needs change.

individual program plan (IPP) a comprehensive written document that states the specific objectives necessary to meet the individual's needs, as identified by a comprehensive individualized assessment. The IPP is the major tool in planning and implementing the care and services rendered to the individual.

industrial or **occupational health center** an ambulatory setting where care is provided to employees at their place of work.

inmate a person who is confined to a correctional institution such as a prison.

inmate self-pay or **copayment** the practice of requiring inmates to pay a (small) fee for predetermined, nonemergency medical treatments.

inpatient psychiatric facility prospective payment system (IPF PPS) Medicare's method of payment both for freestanding psychiatric hospitals and for psychiatric units in acute care hospitals. Under the IPF PPS rule, inpatient psychiatric facilities (IPFs) receive per diem payments that are adjusted up or down by patient-level factors such as age, the MS-DRG, and certain comorbidities, with earlier days of the stay paid at higher rates than later days.

Inpatient Rehabilitation Facility Patient Assessment Instrument (IRF-PAI) an instrument used to gather data regarding each patient stay that will be used to determine the payment for that stay under the Medicare inpatient rehabilitation facility prospective payment system.

Inpatient Rehabilitation Facility Prospective Payment system (IRF PPS) the prospective payment system by which inpatient rehabilitation facilities are paid for services provided to Medicare beneficiaries. Each patient stay is categorized into a case-mix group (CMG) that determines the payment that will be received by the facility from Medicare.

Inpatient Rehabilitation Validation and Entry (IRVEN) software provided by CMS for entering IRF-PAI data.

Institute of Medicine health division of the National Academy of Sciences. It is an independent, nonprofit organization that serves as a national advisor on matters related to health improvement.

integrated delivery systems/network (IDS/N) a group of facilities contracted together to provide the comprehensive set of services that any patient may need. These are owned, leased, or grouped together by long-term contracts and are recognized by the public as a combined operating entity.

integrated format a record in which the information is organized in a strict chronological order.

intellectual disability significant limitations in both intellectual functioning and adaptive behavior expressed in conceptual, social, and practical adaptive skills, and having an onset before the age of 18.

intensive outpatient or partial hospitalization treatment a required minimum of 9 hours of weekly attendance, usually in increments of 3 to 8 hours a day for 5 to 7 days a week; often recommended for patients in the early stages of treatment or those transitioning from residential or hospital settings.

interdisciplinary group (IDG) a patient care group consisting of a physician, nurse, social worker, and pastoral or other counselor. The group also may include members such as a hospice aide, volunteer, therapist, dietician, or pharmacist.

interdisciplinary (ID) team a group that develops an integrated habilitation or program plan that provides individualized services to the individual.

intermediate care facility for individuals with intellectual disabilities (ICF/IID) a facility that provides care and training for persons with intellectual disabilities, to increase their adaptive skills—self-care skills, language skills, social skills, vocational skills, and so on.

International Classification of Diseases (ICD), a classification system used by ambulatory care facilities for coding diagnoses

International Classification of Primary Care (ICPC) a coding system developed by the World Organization of National Colleges, Academies, and Academic Associations of General Practitioners/Family Physicians (WONCA);includes chapters arranged by body systems, with components that describe the reason why the patient is being seen for care at the primary care level.

International Species Information System (ISIS) a computer-based information system for wild animal species in captivity.

Inventory for Client and Agency Planning (ICAP) a standardized assessment instrument that can be used for program planning and also is used in several states as a data collection tool for case-mix reimbursement to ICF/IID organizations.

Inventory of Substance Abuse Treatment Services (I-SATS) a listing of all known public and private substance abuse treatment facilities in the United States and its territories.

involuntary commitment a legal process by which individuals who are deemed to be a danger to themselves or to others may be admitted to a substance abuse (or mental health) treatment program even though they refuse or cannot consent to the treatment.

J

jails institutions administered by local units of government (i.e., cities or counties) with the authority to detain adults for a period of 48 hours or longer and to confine adults convicted of misdemeanors whose sentence does not exceed one year.

juvenile detention facility a facility operated by a unit of government for the confinement of individuals under 18 years of age.

K

kinesiotherapist a person with specialized training in the proper techniques to maximize a person's range of motion, strength, balance, and gait.

Kt/V a means of measuring the adequacy of dialysis (i.e., a way to determine whether the patient is dialyzing long enough or often enough to remove sufficient waste and excess fluid from the body). Target Kt/V values in the *Conditions for Coverage* are 1.2 for hemodialysis and a weekly Kt/V of at least 1.7 for peritoneal dialysis.

L

licensure a governmental process in which a facility must meet certain regulations, set by the State, to provide care.

licensure survey conducted by the state agency to determine compliance of long-term care facilities with state licensure laws.

life care plan a dynamic document that details current and future health care needs based on published standards of practice.

Local Coverage Determinations (LCDs) guidance documents published by Medicare Administrative Contractors (MACs) that include information on codes that indicate medical necessity of services. These policies apply to services covered under Medicare in the region served by the contractor. Local Coverage Determinations formerly were known as Local Medical Review Policies (LMRPs).

locum tenens an arrangement by which one physician temporarily works in place of another physician.

Logical Observations, Identifiers, Names and Codes (LOINC®) facilitates the exchange and pooling of results or vital signs for clinical care, outcomes management, and research; a code system for laboratory and clinical observations.

longitudinal patient record documentation of a patient's health status, conditions, and treatments throughout his or her life and across multiple facilities, providers, and health care encounters.

loss of attachment (LA) the loss of the supporting structure of the teeth that causes the tooth to become loose; may result in loss of the tooth.

M

managed care organizations (MCOs) entities that provide comprehensive health services in a coordinated manner in an effort to improve patient outcomes and reduce costs through efficient health care delivery.

managed indemnity plans indemnity insurance options that do not limit the insured's choice of health care providers but do include cost-control measures such as preauthorization of expensive tests, surgical procedures, and inpatient hospitalization.

meaningful use a concept called for by ARRA. For health care providers to become eligible for reimbursement incentives and avoid financial penalties through Medicare and Medicaid, they must demonstrate meaningful use of certified electronic health record (EHR) technology. The concept refers to a set of criteria and measures, rather than a single definition, and is being implemented in phases though a series of published rules.

Medicaid Title XIX of the 1965 Amendments to the Social Security Act. Medicaid is jointly funded by federal and state governments and provides medical assistance to lower-income individuals and families.

Medicaid Integrity Program (MIP) a national strategy created as a result of the Deficit Reduction Act of 2005 (Section 1936 of the Social Security Act) to detect and prevent Medicaid fraud, waste, and abuse. It uses contracted reviewers to audit the accuracy of Medicaid payments made to health care providers.

medical home a method of providing care in which the primary care provider works with a team of health care professionals to provide care to patients using a whole-person concept.

Medicare Title XVIII of the 1965 Amendments to the Social Security Act, providing health benefits for Social Security recipients and other qualified individuals.

Medicare Administrative Contractor (MAC) a group of organizations or businesses that contract with Medicare to enroll providers, process claims and appeals, and educate providers and beneficiaries. MACs are organized into jurisdictions based upon provider type and geographical location.

Medicare Advantage a program by which eligible Medicare beneficiaries may choose to receive their health care through a qualified managed care plan, which in turn receives capitation payments from Medicare for each enrollee.

Medicare carrier before the implementation of MACs, an organization having a contract with the CMS to process and pay Part B Medicare claims.

Medicare certification a process in which a state agency determines that a health care organization meets the standards set forth in the relevant *Conditions of Participation* or *Conditions of Coverage* and therefore is eligible for participation in the Medicare program.

Medicare Physician Fee Schedule (MPFS or PFS) a list of Medicare-covered services and their payment rates.

Medicare Prescription Drug, Improvement, and Modernization Act of 2003 (MMA) also known as the Medicare Modernization Act. MMA made significant revisions to the Medicare program by calling for the creation of Part D, e-prescribing for prescription drug plans, revision of claims processing, and a Medicare payment recovery demonstration project that ultimately resulted in the Recovery Audit Contractor (RAC) initiative.

Medicare-Severity Diagnosis Related Groups (MS-DRGs) groupings of inpatient services (based on the diagnosis, expected resource consumption, and other characteristics) that determine the payment the hospital receives under the Hospital Inpatient Prospective Payment System (HIPPS) The Medicare severity system adjusts the original DRG algorithm for severity by classifying some complications and comorbidities as major complications and comorbidities (MCCs), indicating the potential for higher resource consumption when an MCC is present.

members individuals who are enrolled in a managed care organization.

mental disorder a syndrome characterized by clinically significant disturbance in an individual's cognition, emotion regulation, or behavior that reflects a dysfunction in the psychological, biological, or developmental processes underlying mental functioning.

Mental Health Statistics Improvement Program (MHSIP) an early initiative begun by the National Institute of Mental Health and continued by the Substance Abuse and Mental Health Services Administration to create a uniform data system nationwide for reporting mental health statistics.

MICA (mental illness with chemical addiction) a program for persons who are dually diagnosed with mental illness and chemical/alcohol addiction. Sometimes written as MIDA or MICAA. This terminology is not considered correct to refer to individuals or to indicate a population.

mid-level provider (MLP) also called an advanced practice clinician; a health care professional whose license permits a degree of independent judgment in treating patients, generally under the supervision of a physician. Examples of mid-level providers include nurse practitioners, physician assistants, and certified nurse midwives. Scope of practice and requirements for supervision vary by type of provider and by state.

minimum data set (MDS) a core set of screening and assessment elements, including common definitions and coding categories, that forms the foundation of the comprehensive resident assessment for all residents of long-term care facilities certified to participate in Medicare or Medicaid. Items in the MDS standardize communication about resident problems and conditions within facilities, between facilities, and between facilities and outside agencies. MDS data also serve as the basis for RUG assignment in the long-term care prospective payment system.

mixed model HMO a HMO that operates within two or more different types of organizational structures to provide flexibility to members.

model act recommended legislation drafted by a national organization with the intent of promoting uniformity among state laws; state legislatures may or may not approve a model act in its entirety, or at all.

N

National Association for Home Care and Hospice (NAHC) an association for organizations and individuals who provide health care and supportive services on an outreach basis to patients in their homes.

National Cancer Database (NCDB) an outcomes database with data collected from more than 1,400 cancer programs in the United States and Puerto Rico, used to examine cancer treatment trends and survival and for quality improvement in cancer care.

National Cancer Registrars Association (NCRA) an association for individuals working in cancer registries; the NCRA certifies cancer registry professionals who meet its standards through its Certified Tumor Registrar (CTR®) credential.

National Commission on Correctional Health Care (NCCHC) a national association that offers voluntary accreditation of the health services in correctional facilities.

National Committee for Quality Assurance (NCQA) an accreditation association that accredits managed care organizations and related services. Its accreditation programs include health plan accreditation, wellness and health promotion, managed behavioral health care organizations, new health plans, and disease management.

National Coverage Determinations (NCDs) guidance documents published by Medicare that include information about codes that indicate medical necessity of services. These policies apply to services covered under Medicare throughout the nation.

National Outcome Measures (NOMS) a reporting system developed by SAMHSA to collect and distribute outcome measures from substance abuse and mental health services.

National Patient Safety Goals (NPSG) a program created by The Joint Commission in 2002 to help accredited health care institutions focus on specific patient safety concerns. In an effort to focus on the most critical patient safety issues, NPSGs are updated annually based upon review of literature and available databases.

National Program of Cancer Registries (NPCR) a program established by the Centers for Disease Control that provides funds to statewide population-based cancer registries. NPCR provides program standards and standards of data quality, timeliness, and completeness and also has adopted NAACCR standards and established a minimum data set. NPCR receives annual data submissions from funded cancer registries.

National Quality Forum (NQF) a private, non-profit, membership organization focused on improving the quality of care through national goal setting, development and endorsement of performance measurement standards, and educational initiatives. NQF collaborated with CMS to develop measures for the Physician Quality Reporting Initiative (PQRI). Through a contract with the U.S. Department of Health and Human Services, NQF continues to provide support for improved quality of health care services.

National Registry of Evidence-based Programs and Practices (NREPP) sponsored by SAMHSA, an online searchable database of treatments and interventions that have been demonstrated to be effective for substance abuse and mental health treatment and prevention programs.

National Survey of Substance Abuse Treatment Services (N-SSATS) an annual survey of all substance abuse treatment facilities known to SAMHSA; collects facility-specific information on location, characteristics, services offered, and utilization.

Nationwide Health Information Network (NwHIN) "is broadly defined as the set of standards, specifications and policies that enable the secure exchange of health information over the Internet. This program provides a foundation for the exchange of health information across diverse entities, within communities and across the country, helping to achieve the goals of the HITECH Act." (HealthIT.gov)

necropsy a postmortem examination for determining the cause of death or the character and extent of changes produced by disease.

network model HMO an HMO that contracts with multiple physician groups, hospitals, and other facilities to provide a comprehensive health care package.

non-physician practitioner (NPP) in the context of certifying the necessity of home care services, "a nurse practitioner or clinical nurse specialist…, who is working in collaboration with the physician in accordance with State law, or a certified nurse-midwife…, or a physician assistant…, under the supervision of the physician." (MLN Matters, 2014, p. 2)

North American Association of Central Cancer Registries (NAACCR) the umbrella organization for central cancer registries, government agencies, professional organizations, and other cancer-related organizations to come together to improve quality and utility of cancer data; the NAACCR serves groups from the United States and Canada and publishes a five-volume set of standards for population-based cancer registries.

number of accessions in the context of veterinary medicine, the total number of times that all patients were treated by the facility in a given time period; one patient may have multiple accessions.

nurse practitioner (NP) a registered nurse who has additional training and credentials that allow for limited independent practice.

nursing facility (NF) an institution or a distinct part of an institution that provides skilled nursing care, rehabilitation services, or health-related care to individuals who, because of their condition, require services above the level of room and board.

O

OBRA assessments performed for a nursing facility resident at admission, quarterly, annually, whenever the resident experiences a significant change in status, whenever the facility identifies a significant error in a prior assessment, and when discharged.

observation services "services furnished by a hospital on the hospital's premises, including use of a bed and periodic monitoring by a hospital's nursing or other staff, which are reasonable and necessary to evaluate an outpatient's condition or determine the need for a possible admission to the hospital as an inpatient" (CMS, 2003a, §230.6A).

Occupational Safety and Health Administration (OSHA) a federal agency that develops criteria intended to provide a safe work environment for all employees as part of its mission to enforce occupational safety and health legislation.

occupational therapist (OT) a therapist who has completed an educational program accredited by the American Occupational Therapy Association at the bachelor's level or higher. OTs address activities of daily living, upper-extremity movement, higher cognitive processes, and community skills, among other areas of rehabilitation.

occurrence report internal documentation of an unusual event such as a fall, incorrect medications given or taken, or some other untoward occurrence; also called *incident report.*

Office of the Inspector General (OIG) the office in the Department of Health and Human Services responsible for monitoring compliance with reimbursement laws and regulations.

Office of the National Coordinator for Health Information Technology (ONC) "the principal Federal entity charged with coordination of nationwide efforts to implement and use the most advanced health information technology and the electronic exchange of health information. The position of National Coordinator was created in 2004, through an Executive Order, and legislatively mandated in the Health Information Technology for Economic and Clinical Health Act (HITECH Act) of 2009" (HealthIT.gov)

oral maxillofacial surgeon a dentist who specializes in surgery to the mouth and facial bones.

orthodontist a dentist who specializes in straightening teeth.

Orthopedic Foundation for Animals (OFA) a collection of voluntary orthopedic and genetic disease databases of animals.

orthotic device an external appliance or brace that can supplement an extremity's function or improve stability and positioning.

outcomes end results or consequences; the patient's health and functional status after a period of treatment.

Outcome and Assessment Information Set-C1 (OASIS-C1) a data set requirement under Medicare's Conditions of Participation. Medicare-certified home health agencies collect and use OASIS data when evaluating adult, nonmaternity patients. The intent of OASIS is to make the Conditions of Participation more patient-centered and outcome-oriented while providing home care agencies with greater flexibility to operate their programs. It also measures treatment outcomes and provides individual agencies with the ability to compare themselves to the national data set.

outpatient commitment judicial diversion, from inpatient to outpatient care, of a person who has been certified as in need of psychiatric care, with stipulations regarding behaviors such as taking medications, remaining sober, and maintaining residence in a designated place. Failure to abide by the stipulations may result in involuntary commitment to an inpatient facility.

outpatient treatment regularly scheduled sessions with a mental health professional; can include individual therapy, group therapy or family therapy. The sessions address current issues and also educate the clients about relapse prevention.

ovine sheep.

P

palliative care non-curative therapy; clinical measures are taken to reduce the intensity of disease symptoms rather than provide a cure for the disease. Hospice attempts to reduce the intensity of symptoms such as pain, nausea, and anxiety with a variety of pharmacological and nonpharmacological methods.

panel the group of patients who have chosen a specific provider as their primary care provider.

panoramic radiograph a radiograph taken outside of the mouth that shows all the teeth on one film; this also may be a digital image.

partial hospitalization program (PHP) an intensive treatment program in which patients receive services for part of each day. These patients would otherwise require inpatient psychiatric care.

patient-centered medical home model a care model in which the primary care physician acts as a "gatekeeper" to coordinate the patient's care across providers. It addresses preventive, acute, and chronic care needs and also provides patients with access to electronic tools such as provider-patient e-mail, online appointment scheduling applications, and electronic health record data. The Patient Protection and Affordable Care Act (PPACA or Health Reform) calls for use of the medical home model to improve health outcomes.

patient identifier an item of data that identifies the patient in the health information management system, such as the patient's name or medical record number.

patient portal a secure method of patient access to his or her own information through a facility's electronic information system.

Patient Protection and Affordable Care Act (PPACA) landmark federal legislation enacted in 2010 that changed coverage requirements for all insurers and employers, established health insurance exchanges, and impacted eligibility for Medicaid and claims and benefit processing for all insurers.

patient registration system a computer system that contains demographic and financial information for every patient.

patient safety organizations (PSOs) "organizations that can work with clinicians and health care organizations to identify, analyze, and reduce the risks and hazards associated with patient care" (AHRQ, online). The Patient Safety and Quality Improvement Act of 2005 called for development of PSOs to help determine the root causes, risks, and harms of health care safety issues.

payer mix the ratio of an agency's various patient insurers and third-party payers.

pay-for-performance (P4P) emerging incentive-based reimbursement programs that reward or penalize providers based upon their ability to meet preestablished quality and performance targets for delivery of health care services. Also known as value-based purchasing.

per diem a reimbursement methodology in which a set payment is reimbursed to a health care provider or facility based on the number of days of care provided to a patient.

periodontist a dentist who specializes in the treatment of diseases of the gum or bone (supporting structure).

peritoneal dialysis (PD) filling the patient's abdominal cavity with a solution (dialysate). The semipermeable membrane across which the products diffuse is the patient's own peritoneal membrane. The fluid containing the wastes is withdrawn later from the peritoneal cavity.

personal health record (PHR) "an Internet-based set of tools that allows people to access and coordinate their lifelong health information and make appropriate parts of it available to those who need it" (Markle Foundation, 2003, p. 2).

person-centered planning a process that focuses on the preferences of the individual who is receiving services in planning the type of future life the individual wishes to live.

person-centered thinking a set of values, skills, and tools used in person-centered planning.

physical restraint "mechanical or personal restriction that immobilizes or reduces the ability of an individual to move his or her arms, legs, or head freely, not including devices ...for the purpose of conducting routine physical examinations or tests or to protect the resident from falling out of bed or to permit the resident to participate in activities without the risk of physical harm to the resident... (P. L. 106-310, 2000, pp. 1195–1196).

physiatrist a physical medicine and rehabilitation physician.

physical therapist (PT) a therapist who has completed an educational program accredited by the American Physical Therapy Association at the bachelor's level or higher. PTs help patients improve their strength, range of motion, balance, and mobility, among other things.

physician assistant a professional who is not a nurse but has received training to use independent judgment in treating patients.

physician private practice a setting in which physicians practice in their own business rather than working for an organization such as a clinic or urgent care center owned or operated by others.

Physician Quality Reporting System (PQRS) a voluntary, incentive-based quality reporting system for eligible professionals who report data on quality measures for covered professional services provided to Medicare beneficiaries; established as a requirement by the 2006 Tax Relief and Health Care Act (TRHCA) (P.L. 109-432) and implemented yearly by CMS through an annual rule-making process; therefore, program requirements and measures may vary from year to year.

place of residence wherever the patient is currently living—his or her own home, a relative's home, a senior citizen's complex, a nursing home, assisted living.

plaque also known as biofilm, the sticky film on teeth made up predominantly of bacteria.

point of service plan (POS) a type of managed care health plan that permits members who are willing to pay larger coinsurance costs to seek treatment at non-network providers. Specialty care referrals may still be coordinated through a primary care physician.

pontic the part of a bridge that replaces the missing tooth.

population-based cancer registries registries that collect data on all newly diagnosed cancer cases in the population of a defined geographic area such as a state, region, or country.

porcine swine.

potentially compensable events (PCEs) occurrences that may result in litigation against the health care provider or that may require the health care provider to financially compensate an injured party.

preadmission certification review and approval of the medical necessity of inpatient care prior to the patient's admission.

preauthorization review and prior approval for payment of a health care service.

preferred provider organization (PPO) an insurance entity that contracts with providers to create a preferred network. The insured population is allowed to use any provider, but using network providers results in lesser cost to the patient.

primary caregiver the person designated to provide care for the patient when hospice staff is not available—can be any relative, a spouse, a friend, a significant other, a paid caregiver, an adult child, or any other person. The primary caregiver provides a range of care depending on his or her comfort level, from giving medications to changing dressings to emptying catheter bags.

primary teeth the baby teeth, also known as the primary dentition; the baby teeth are replaced by adult (permanent) teeth)

Principal In-Patient Diagnostic Cost Group (PIP-DCG) the first risk adjustment model that Medicare used to adjust capitation payments made to Part C plans, based largely on the principal diagnoses of hospitalized enrollees. PIP-DCGs were replaced by HCCs in 2004.

prisons facilities operated by a unit of the state or federal government for the confinement of adults convicted of a felony whose sentence exceeds one year.

problem list a numbered listing of the patient's issues over time that serves as a table of contents for the problem-oriented medical record.

problem-oriented medical record (POMR) a structured approach to patient care developed by Dr. Lawrence Weed in the late 1950s, which has four major parts: database, problem list, initial plan, and progress notes/discharge summary.

problem-oriented record a document organized by the patient's problems; follows each clinical problem individually and provides a systematic method of documentation to reflect logical thinking on the part of the one who is directing the patient's care.

production medicine the study and care of food animals that produce milk, meat, eggs, and so forth.

program manuals for Medicare and Medicaid basic instructions for the two programs, developed by the Centers for Medicare & Medicaid Services.

program transmittals revisions issued periodically by CMS for a specific program manual.

prophylaxis the scaling, cleaning, and removal of calculus; a preventive treatment.

prospective payment system (PPS) a method in which payment levels for health care services are determined before the services are rendered. In a prospective payment system, the unit of payment is not based solely on the individual services provided but, rather, on payment units that represent general groupings of patient encounters, hospital stays, or episodes of care.

prospective review/precertification one of two basic approaches to utilization management, prospective review determines whether services are needed before they are provided.

prosthesis (a) a device designed to replace a missing extremity or partially missing extremity; (b) a fixed or removable appliance to replace missing teeth; examples are bridges, dentures, and partials, and sometimes single crowns.

prosthodontist a dentist who specializes in replacing missing teeth with a prosthetic device.

protected health information (PHI) individually identifiable health information.

Provider Enrollment, Chain and Ownership System (PECOS) Medicare's Internet-based electronic enrollment system for health care providers and suppliers who treat or provide services or equipment to Medicare beneficiaries.

psychologist a person trained in psychology at the doctoral level who is certified by the American Psychological Association. In rehabilitation, a psychologist tests patients to identify problems in cognition or behavior and counsels the patient and family. A master's-level counselor also may perform some of these duties.

psychosis a state of extreme disordered thinking in which the person demonstrates symptoms of serious mental illness as such hallucinations and delusions.

psychosocial rehabilitation a mode of treatment for serious mental illness that focuses on providing an array of community support services (e.g., development of job skills, if needed) for persons with mental illness, sufficient to allow them to live in the least restrictive environment possible outside of an institution.

psychotropic medications a variety of medications designed to reduce psychotic symptoms by altering the chemical processes within the brain. Also sometimes referred to as "neuroleptics."

public health department an organization that provides services to promote the health of the community as a whole, such as immunizations and disease screenings; usually an agency of state or local government.

Q

qualified developmental disability professional (QDDP) a person assigned to monitor and coordinate all activities related to the development and implementation of the individual program plan.

qualified service organization agreement (QSOA) an exception to the 42 C.F.R. Part 2 *Confidentiality of Alcohol and Drug Abuse Patient Records,* which permits disclosure of patient record information to an organization providing services to the substance abuse program, such as laboratory, data processing, bill collecting, dosage preparation, legal, medical, or accounting services. The qualified service organization (QSO) has a written agreement to provide professional services to the substance abuse program, and that agreement requires the QSO to follow the 42 C.F.R. regulations.

quality assessment and performance improvement (QAPI) The *Conditions for Coverage* require each dialysis facility to adopt a data-driven performance improvement program that utilizes indicators or performance measures associated with improved health outcomes and with the identification and reduction of medical errors.

quality improvement organizations (QIOs) "group of health quality experts, clinicians, and consumers organized to improve the care delivered to people with Medicare. QIOs work under the direction of the Centers for Medicare & Medicaid Services to assist Medicare providers with quality improvement and to review quality concerns for the protection of beneficiaries and the Medicare Trust Fund" (CMS, 2014c). In 2014, the contract period for QIOs was extended from three to five years, case review and quality improvement activities were assigned to different types of QIOs, and QIO activity was no longer restricted to a single entity in each state.

Quality Indicator Survey (QIS) a long-term care survey process developed by CMS to standardize resident-centered, outcome-oriented quality review processes.

quality of care a broad category of the long-term care federal regulations that requires a facility to provide the necessary care and services to attain or maintain the highest practicable physical, mental, and psychosocial well-being, in accordance with the comprehensive assessment and plan of care. Substantial noncompliance with quality of care requirements subjects a facility to potential civil money penalties and other punitive measures in the federal enforcement regulations.

quality of life a broad category of the long-term care federal regulations that requires a facility to care for its residents in a manner and in an environment that promotes maintaining or enhancing each resident's quality of life. Substantial noncompliance with quality-of-life requirements subjects a facility to potential civil money penalties and other punitive measures in the federal enforcement regulations.

R

radiograph a graphic image produced by the use of radiation.

reason for visit the patient's reason for requesting care.

recertification additional physician orders that continue home health services after the initial 60-day certification period.

Recovery Audit Contractor (RAC) a third-party entity working under the direction of CMS to detect improper Medicare payments by reviewing providers' medical records and Medicare claims data.

referral an authorization to receive a specific health service from a specialized provider that will be paid for by the HMO.

referred hospital outpatient an outpatient who is referred to the hospital for specific services, such as laboratory or radiology examinations. The hospital is responsible only for providing the diagnostic or therapeutic services requested, while the referring physician is responsible for evaluating and managing the patient's care.

Regional Extension Centers (RECs) Nonprofit organizations called for by ARRA and initially funded by federal grants to provide health information technology support to providers. RECs offer technical assistance, guidance, and support to help providers become meaningful users of certified electronic health record technology.

Regional Health Information Organization (RHIO) a "health information organization that brings together health care stakeholders within a defined geographic area and governs health information exchange among them for the purpose of improving health and care in that community" (NAHIT, 2008, p. 6).

registered nurse a health care professional with an associate's or bachelor's degree in nursing who is licensed by the state as qualified to provide skilled patient care.

registration the process by which basic demographic and financial information is obtained from the patient and entered into the health information system.

rehabilitation the development of a person to the fullest physical, psychological, social, vocational, avocational, and educational potential consistent with his or her physiological or anatomic impairment and environmental limitations.

rehabilitation nurse a registered nurse who has received training and credentialing as a rehabilitation nurse.

rehabilitation social worker a member of the rehabilitation team who has specific training and knowledge in the area of social work and who may be certified by the National Association of Social Workers. The social worker provides background information on the patient and family, coordinates funding resources, and helps the patient with the transition back to the community.

rehabilitation team an interdisciplinary team made up of numerous allied health professions.

renal bone disease also known as renal osteodystrophy, a disorder that results from an imbalance in calcium, parathyroid hormone (PTH), phosphorus, and activated vitamin D, which can occur in chronic kidney disease. It can result in weakened bones that break easily, and also hardening of soft tissues of the body including the heart. Disorders of mineral metabolism are associated with a higher death rate in people with end-stage renal disease (ESRD).

Renal Management Information System (REMIS) a protocol that determines Medicare coverage periods for ESRD patients and serves as the primary mechanism to store and access information in the ESRD Program Management and Medical Information System (PMMIS) Database. REMIS tracks the ESRD patient population for both Medicare and non-Medicare patients.

renal replacement therapy (RRT) a treatment that replaces kidney function. For chronic renal failure,

the treatment typically is some type of dialysis, or it may be kidney transplantation.

resident assessment instrument (RAI) a requirement for completing the performance of a standardized assessment system, composed of the MDS, CAA process, and utilization guidelines. This assessment system provides a comprehensive, accurate, standardized, and reproducible assessment of each long-term care facility resident's functional capabilities and identifies medical problems (CMS, 2011).

resident assessment protocols (RAPs) structured, problem-oriented frameworks for organizing MDS information and additional clinically relevant information about an individual that identifies medical problems and forms the basis for individual care planning (CMS, 2011). Although RAP terminology is still in common use, CMS now uses the term *care area assessment (CAA) process* to describe this concept.

residential/inpatient treatment a program directed at clients with sub-acute medical, behavioral, or emotional problems; provides a live-in facility with 24-hour supervision.

residents in the context of medical education, primarily licensed physicians, dentists, or podiatrists who participate in an approved graduate medical education (GME) program. The term *resident* also may be applied to physicians with temporary or restricted licenses, or to unlicensed graduates of foreign medical schools who are authorized to practice only in a hospital.

resource-based relative value scale (RBRVS) a reimbursement system used by Medicare Part B to reimburse physicians; based on the relative value of the services provided.

resource utilization groups (RUGs) a case-mix methodology based on data submitted on the MDS. RUGs are used to adjust per diem payments to SNFs under the Medicare PPS and to NFs under some state Medicaid programs.

respite care a form of care that provides an interval of rest for the primary caregiver and is provided to hospice patients in an approved (or contracted) facility.

revoke/revocation performed by a hospice patient (or family or legal representative) to give back or annul his or her hospice benefit. Once a patient has revoked the hospice benefit, the patient returns to standard Medicare or other commercial insurance benefits and loses all remaining days in the current benefit period.

risk contract also known as a Medicare risk contract, an agreement between an HMO and CMS to provide services to Medicare beneficiaries, under which contract the health plan receives a monthly payment for enrolled Medicare members and then must provide all services on an at-risk basis.

risk of mortality the likelihood that the patient will die while in the hospital. Ranked on a scale of 1 to 4, indicating mild (1), moderate (2), major (3), or extreme (4) risk of mortality.

root canal therapy (RCT) removal of the nerve of the tooth from the canal inside the root, and replaced with a filling material.

routine home care a form of care that occurs when a patient is receiving routine (or nonproblematic) care in his or her place of residence.

rural health clinic (RHC) a health care setting that, in addition to physician services, utilizes advanced practice clinicians such as physician assistants and nurse practitioners, and is located in an underserved rural area.

S

sealant clear application of acrylic placed over the biting surface of the tooth to prevent decay.

serious mental illness (SMI) a condition in which a person has a diagnosable mental, behavioral, or emotional disorder resulting in functional impairment that substantially interferes with or limits one or more major life activities.

severity of illness the extent of physical illness or ss of organ function of the patient. Ranked on a scale of 1 to 4, indicating mild (1), moderate (2), major (3), or extreme (4) severity.

60 percent rule one of the criteria for defining a hospital as an inpatient rehabilitation facility (IRF); requires that at least 60 percent of the patients treated have at least one of 13 qualifying medical conditions.

skilled nursing agencies agencies that offer nursing services such as trained medical-surgical nursing, intravenous therapy, enterostomal therapy, psychiatric or mental health, maternity, or restorative nursing. Services are provided to patients based on their individual needs.

skilled nursing facility (SNF) an institution or a distinct part of an institution that provides skilled nursing care or rehabilitation services. Either a registered nurse or a licensed practical nurse is on active duty at all times. If properly licensed and certified, a skilled nursing facility may obtain a Medicare provider agreement and be reimbursed under the Medicare program.

Social Security Disability Income (SSDI) federal benefits paid to persons with disability who have worked a sufficient length of time to qualify to receive Social Security benefits; a frequent source of income for persons with serious mental illness who are not able to work.

solo dental practice a dental practice owned and operated by one dentist.

source-oriented format a record format in which the information is organized according to the source of the information, such as laboratory, nursing, etc.

source-oriented record a document organized in sections according to patient care departments and/ or disciplines.

special care unit (SCU) a distinct service within a long-term care facility such as an Alzheimer SCU.

speech-language pathologist a rehabilitation team member with a bachelor's or master's level of education who is certified by the American Speech, Language, and Hearing Association. The speech pathologist evaluates and treats patients with swallowing problems, communication problems, and cognitive deficits.

staff model HMO the most tightly organized HMO structure. The HMO entity owns the facilities and arranges for health care through employed physicians, who are allowed to see only the specified HMO's patients.

Standard Nomenclature of Veterinary Diseases and Operations (SNVDO) coding system created in 1963 to standardize the collection of veterinary data in a national database; has been updated only intermittently since the 1970s.

standards rules used as a basis of comparison for measuring quantitative or qualitative value.

standard scheduling a method in which appointments are scheduled continuously throughout the day, with appointment times at specific intervals (e.g., every 15 minutes).

standard survey a periodic, resident-centered inspection that gathers information about the quality of service provided in a facility to determine compliance with the requirements of participation in the federal Medicare and Medicaid programs.

state agency the agency of the state government responsible for administering the federal requirements for participation in Medicare and Medicaid programs. The state agency is ordinarily charged also with administering applicable licensure requirements for the state.

status indicator an alphabetic character that indicates the type of each APC and whether or how that APC is paid under the Hospital Outpatient Prospective Payment System (OPPS).

sub-acute care a transitional type of care representing a level of service that is less intensive than traditional acute care but is more goal-oriented and resource-intensive than what generally is regarded as skilled nursing care.

subscribers primary recipients of the insurance benefit.

Substance Abuse and Mental Health Services Administration (SAMHSA) an agency created in 1992 under the umbrella of the U.S. Department of Health and Human Services with the purpose of reducing the impact of substance abuse and mental illness on America's communities.

substandard quality of care one or more deficiencies related to participation requirements under 42 C.F.R. 483.13, resident behavior and facility practices; 42 C.F.R. 483.15, quality of life; or 42 C.F.R. 483.25, quality of care. These constitute either immediate jeopardy to resident health or safety; a pattern of widespread actual harm that is not immediate jeopardy; or a widespread potential for more than minimal harm, but less than immediate jeopardy, with no actual harm.

substantial compliance a level of compliance with the Conditions of Participation, such that any identified deficiencies pose no greater risk to resident health or safety than the potential for causing minimal harm; constitutes compliance with participation requirements.

superbill a form used for billing purposes that includes the services the patient received, the charges, and diagnosis and procedure codes.

Supplemental Security Income (SSI) federal benefits paid to persons with disability who have not worked a sufficient length of time to qualify for Social Security benefits. A common, and often only, source of income for persons with serious mental illness who are unable to work.

Systematized Nomenclature of Medicine-Clinical Terms (SNOMED CT®) multilingual health care clinical reference terminology providing a uniform nomenclature facilitating international sharing and analysis of both human and veterinary health data.

system of care "an organizational philosophy and framework that involves collaboration across agencies, families, and youth for the purpose of improving access and expanding the array of coordinated community-based, culturally and linguistically competent services and supports for children and youth with a serious emotional disturbance and their families" (CMHS, 2009, para 2).

T

telemedicine or **telehealth** the practice of medicine in which a patient is generally in a remote location and receives medical care in real-time via an audio-visual connection with a provider located off-site and directly by a provider at that location. Store-and-forward telemedicine is a term used to describe services in which medical information is captured electronically and transmitted to a remote site for a health care provider to review, analyze, or report at a later time, rather than in real-time. Telehealth also "includes such technologies as telephones, facsimile machines, electronic mail systems, and remote patient monitoring devices, which are used to collect and transmit patient data for monitoring and interpretation" (Telemedicine, n.d.). Remote physiological monitoring and medication adherence monitoring are other examples of telehealth services.

telesurgery the use of robotic technology to assist with or perform procedures remotely.

terminal digit a filing system in which records are filed first by the last two digits of their numbers, allowing files to expand evenly.

terminally ill a limited life expectancy, usually less than 6 months.

The Joint Commission (TJC) a voluntary accrediting organization that promotes quality in health care by accrediting a variety of organizations, including ambulatory, behavioral health, hospital, and home care providers, among others.

theriogenology the study of animal reproduction.

training objective a single outcome expected to be achieved by the individual within one year as a result of training; measurable outcome, criteria for measuring progress, and projected completion date should be specified relative to strengths, needs, and established goals.

Treatment Episode Data Set (TEDS) one of the components of DASIS; collects from states uniform data that are client-specific but not client identifiable, including demographic and substance abuse characteristics.

U

Uniform Ambulatory Care Data Set (UACDS) a 16-item data set approved by the National Committee on Vital and Health Statistics (NCVHS); one of the first attempts to standardize ambulatory data collection efforts.

Uniform Hospital Discharge Data Set (UHDDS) standard data elements to be collected from individual inpatient records. The UHDDS data definitions are essential for correct reporting of inpatient data, for example on the UB-04.

Uniform Reporting System (URS) an organized method by which each State Mental Health Authority (SMHA) reports aggregate data to SAMHSA.

university health center an ambulatory setting in which care is provided to the university staff and students.

URAC an independent, nonprofit organization offering accreditation, education, and measurement programs. URAC's Health Plan standards are appropriate for HMOs and other integrated health plans. Its Health Network accreditation does not include utilization management and is better suited for PPO accreditation.

urea reduction ration (URR) a percentage that indicates the amount of urea removed during dialysis. For example, a URR of 60% means that 60% of the pre-dialysis urea was removed through the dialysis process. As a means of measuring the adequacy

of dialysis, the recommended minimum URR is 65%.

urgent care center an ambulatory care setting in which patients are seen on a walk-in basis without appointments. These centers provide service for longer hours than most private physician practices.

utilization guidelines CMS guidelines that provide instructions for when and how to use the RAI. These include instructions for completion of the RAI, as well as structured frameworks for synthesizing MDS and other clinical information. The utilization guidelines can be used to evaluate a care area that has been triggered and to determine whether to continue to care plan for it.

V

validation survey a survey conducted by a regional office of the CMS to determine whether the surveys being conducted by state agencies (or other groups) are assessing the facility's operations appropriately.

value-based purchasing (VBP) a "pay-for-performance" program that can either increase the payment to a health care provider based on whether the provider meets or doesn't meet specified performance standards. The VBP program for ESRD facilities is called the ESRD Quality Incentive Program (QIP), which can reduce the payment to a facility when the facility doesn't meet certain clinical performance and reporting standards.

variable costs costs that vary in proportion to the volume of service provided.

vascular access monitoring physical examination of the dialysis access site to detect possible access complications. Types of monitoring include visual examination of the access site to detect changes, palpation (examination by touching), and auscultation (listening with a stethoscope).

veterinarian a person who is qualified and authorized to treat disease and injuries of animals.

veterinary of, relating to, or being the science and art of prevention, cure, or alleviation of disease and injury in animals, especially domestic animals.

Veterinary Hospital Managers Association (VHMA) provides individuals who are actively involved in veterinary practice management with a means of education, certification, and networking; membership is composed of animal hospital administrators, practice managers, office managers, veterinarians, and consultants.

Veterinary Medical Database (VMDB) a national collection system for data from veterinary teaching hospital patient records from the United States and Canada.

veterinary technician a member of the veterinary health care team who is knowledgeable in the care and handling of animals, in the basic principles of normal and abnormal life processes, and in routine laboratory and clinical procedures. The technician is primarily an assistant to veterinarians, biological research workers, and other scientists. A veterinary technician is a graduate of a 2- or 3-year AVMA-accredited program in veterinary science that generally awards an associate degree or certificate.

veterinary technologist a graduate of a 4-year AVMA-accredited program in veterinary technology or a person so recognized by the board in rules and regulations promulgated to regulate veterinary technologists.

volunteer in the context of hospice care, a person who provides a service, such as clerical, clinical, or companionship, without any monetary or other reimbursement.

W

walk-ins patients who arrive without an appointment or who receive an appointment at the last minute.

wisdom teeth the third molars; each of the four wisdom teeth is the eighth tooth from the center of the mouth to the back of the mouth. Wisdom teeth often are impacted (obstructed from erupting) and have to be extracted.

wrap-around services the predominant method of mental health service delivery to children and adolescents with emotional disturbance and their families, consisting of a comprehensive array of professional services that may include home and/or school settings tailored to meet the specific needs of the child and his or her family.

Z

Zone Program Integrity Contractor (ZPIC) program a program implemented by CMS to identify and investigate malicious fraudulent claims activity within Medicare's seven geographic regions (zones).

zoonotic infection an infection that can be transmitted from animals to humans. Zoonoses are of concern to both veterinary and human medicine.

INDEX

T